Capri II Owners Workshop Manual

by J H Haynes
Member of the Guild of Motoring Writers

and A J Jones BSc Eng, CEng

Models covered
UK: Capri II 3.0 litre GT, S & Ghia 2994 cc. Covers models introduced in
March 1978, sometimes known as Series III
USA: Lincoln-Mercury Capri II, 2800, 171 cu in (2792 cc)

ISBN 0 85696 810 2

Printed in England   (375-1H2)

HAYNES PUBLISHING GROUP
SPARKFORD YEOVIL SOMERSET BA22 7JJ ENGLAND
distributed in the USA by
HAYNES PUBLICATIONS INC
861 LAWRENCE DRIVE
NEWBURY PARK
CALIFORNIA 91320
USA

Acknowledgements

Special thanks are due to the Ford Motor Company in the UK and USA for the supply of technical information and certain illustrations. Castrol Limited provided lubrication data and the Champion Sparking Plug Company provided the spark plug illustrations. The bodywork repair photographs used in this manual were provided by Lloyds Industries Limited, who supply 'Turtle Wax', 'Dupli-color Holts', and other Holts range products.

The Section of Chapter 10 dealing with the suppression of radio interference, was originated by Mr I. P. Davey, and was first published in *Motor* magazine.

Thanks are expressed to the Wimborne Branch of F. English Ltd, for help in the preparation of this manual, and to other Haynes authors whose work has been incorporated.

Lastly, thanks are due to all of those people at Sparkford who helped in the production of this manual; particularly Brian Horsfall and Les Brazier who carried out the mechanical work and took the photographs respectively, Stanley Randolph who planned the layout of each page, and David Neilson who edited the text.

About this manual

Its aims

The aim of this book is to help you get the best value from your car. It can do so in two ways. First, it can help you decide the work to be done, even should you choose to get it done by a garage, the routine maintenance and the diagnosis and course of action when random faults occur. But it is hoped that you will also use the second and fuller purpose by tackling the work yourself. This can give you the satisfaction of knowing that the task has been completed correctly. On the simpler jobs it may even be quicker than booking the car into a garage and going there twice, to leave and collect it. Perhaps more important, much money can be saved by avoiding the costs a garage must charge to cover labour and overheads.

The book has drawings and descriptions to show the functions of the various components so that their layout can be understood. Then the tasks are described and photographed in a step-by-step sequence so that even a novice can cope with complicated work. Such a person is the very one to buy a car needing repair yet be unable to afford garage costs.

The jobs are described assuming only normal spanners are available, and not special tools unless absolutely necessary. But a reasonable outfit of tools will be a worthwhile investment. Many special workshop tools produced by the makers merely speed the work, and in these cases guidance is given as to how to do the job without them. On a very few occasions a special tool is essential to prevent damage to components; then its use is described. Though it might be possible to borrow the tool, such work may have to be entrusted to the offical agent.

To avoid labour costs a garage will often give a cheaper repair by fitting a reconditioned assembly. The home mechanic can be helped by this book to diagnose the fault and make a repair using only a minor spare part.

The manufacturer's official workshop manuals are written for their trained staff, and so assume special knowledge; therefore detail is left out. This book is written for the owner, and so goes into detail.

Using the manual

The manual is divided into thirteen Chapters. Each Chapter is divided into numbered Sections which are headed in **bold** type between horizontal lines. Each Section consists of serially numbered paragraphs.

There are two types of illustrations: (1) Figures which are numbered according to Chapter and sequence of occurrence in that Chapter. (2) Photographs which have a reference number in their caption. All photographs apply to the Chapter in which they occur, so that the reference figure pinpoints the pertinent Section and paragraph number.

Procedures, once described in the text, are not normally repeated. If it is necessary to refer to another Chapter the reference will be given in Chapter number and Section number thus: Chapter 1, Section 16. Cross-references given without use of the word 'Chapter' apply to Section and/or paragraphs in the same Chapter, eg, 'see Section 8' means also 'in this Chapter'.

When the left or right side of the car is mentioned it is as if one is seated in the driver's seat looking forward.

For convenience of presentation, references have been used in the manual as follows:
Capri II. This denotes a car manufactured by Ford of Britain (FOB) or Ford of Germany (FOG) using a 3.0 litre V6 engine.
Mercury Capri II. This denotes a car marketed by the Lincoln Mercury division of the Ford Motor Company in the USA using a 2.8 litre V6 engine.

Unless otherwise stated, nuts and bolts are removed by turning anti-clockwise, and tightened by turning clockwise.

Vehicle manufacturers continually make changes to specifications and recommendations, and these when notified are incorporated into our manuals at the earliest opportunity.

Whilst every care is taken to ensure that the information in this manual is correct, no liability can be accepted by the authors or publishers for loss, damage or injury caused by any errors in, or omissions from, the information given.

Introduction to the Capri II models

The Capri II models were first introduced in the United Kingdom in February 1974 using a wide range of engines previously used on other Ford vehicles. The models covered in this manual use the V6 3.0 litre engine developed by Ford of Germany. In 1975 a similarly styled Capri II was introduced in the United States using an existing V6 2.8 litre engine already used in the Mustang.

The car is conventional in mechanical layout, drive from the engine being transmitted to the rear axle via a 4-speed manual or 3-speed automatic gearbox and a one or two-piece propeller shaft according to the particular model.

Although the UK version is only 1 inch longer and $2\frac{1}{4}$ inches wider than the previous Ford Capri, the appearance of a larger car is obtained by the sleeker lines which evolved with the re-styling. This is even more apparent from the inside due to the increased load-space and opening tailgate.

A wide variety of optional extras is available but the basic equipment including emission control items, is governed by the particular model and intended market.

Contents

Ford Capri II 3.0 Ghia

Lincoln-Mercury Capri II 2.8

Buying spare parts and vehicle identification numbers

Buying spare parts

Spare parts are available from many sources, for example: Ford garages, other garages and accessory shops, and motor factors. Our advice regarding spare part sources is as follows:

Officially appointed Ford garages – This is the best source of parts which are peculiar to your car and are otherwise not generally available (eg complete cylinder heads, internal gearbox components, badges, interior trim etc). It is also the only place at which you should buy parts if your car is still under warranty – non-Ford components may invalidate the warranty. To be sure of obtaining the correct parts it will always be necessary to give the storeman your car's vehicle identification number, and if possible, to take the 'old' part along for positive identification. Remember that many parts are available on a factory exchange scheme – any parts returned should always be clean! It obviously makes good sense to go straight to the specialists on your car for this type of part as they are best equipped to supply you.

Other garages and accessory shops – These are often very good places to buy materials and components needed for the maintenance of your car (eg oil filters, spark plugs, bulbs, fan belts, oils and greases, touch-up paint, filler paste etc). They also sell general accessories, usually have convenient opening hours, charge lower prices and can often be found not far from home.

Motor factors – Good factors will stock all the more important components which wear out relatively quickly (eg clutch components, pistons, valves, exhaust systems, brake cylinders/pipes/hoses/seals/shoes and pads etc). Motor factors will often provide new or reconditioned components on a part exchange basis - this can save a considerable amount of money!

Vehicle identification numbers

Although many individual parts, and in some cases sub-assemblies, fit a number of different models it is dangerous to assume that just because they look the same, they are the same. Differences are not always easy to detect except by serial numbers. Make sure therefore, that the appropriate identity number for the model or sub-assembly is known and quoted when a spare part is obtained.

The vehicle identification plate is mounted on the right-hand front wing apron, and may be seen once the bonnet is open. Record the numbers from your car on the blank spaces of the accompanying illustration. You can then take the manual with you when buying parts; also the exploded drawings throughout the manual can be used to point out and identify the components required.

Emission control decal (Mercury Capri II)

All Mercury Capri II models have an emission control decal in the engine compartment. This gives information such as spark plug type and gap setting, ignition initial advance setting, idle speeds, maintenance schedule code letter and basic details of engine tune-up procedures. A typical decal is shown in the illustration.

Vehicle identification plate

Emission Control Decal (Mercury Capri II)

Tools and working facilities

Introduction

A selection of good tools is a fundamental requirement for anyone contemplating the maintenance and repair of a motor vehicle. For the owner who does not possess any, their purchase will prove a considerable expense, offsetting some of the savings made by doing-it-yourself. However, provided that the tools purchased are of good quality, they will last for many years and prove an extremely worthwhile investment.

To help the average owner to decide which tools are needed to carry out the various tasks detailed in this manual, we have compiled three lists of tools under the following headings: *Maintenance and minor repair, Repair and overhaul,* and *Special.* The newcomer to practical mechanics should start off with the *Maintenance and minor repair* tool kit and confine himself to the simpler jobs around the vehicle. Then, as his confidence and experience grows, he can undertake more difficult tasks, buying extra tools as, and when, they are needed. In this way, a *Maintenance and minor repair* tool kit can be built-up into a *Repair and overhaul* tool kit over a considerable period of time without any major cash outlays. The experienced do-it-yourselfer will have a tool kit good enough for most repair and overhaul procedures and will add tools from the *Special* category when he feels the expense is justified by the amount of use to which these tools will be put.

It is obviously not possible to cover the subject of tools fully here. For those who wish to learn more about tools and their use there is a book entitled *How to Choose and Use Car Tools* available from the publishers of this manual.

Maintenance and minor repair tool kit

The tools given in this list should be considered as a minimum requirement if routine maintenance, servicing and minor repair operations are to be undertaken. We recommend the purchase of combination spanners (ring one end, open-ended the other); although more expensive than open-ended ones, they do give the advantages of both types of spanner.

Combination spanners - 6, 7, 8, 9, 10, 11, & 12 mm
Adjustable spanner - 9 inch
Engine sump/gearbox/rear axle drain plug key (where applicable)
Spark plug spanner (with rubber insert)
Spark plug gap adjustment tool
Set of feeler gauges
Brake bleed nipple spanner
Screwdriver - 4 in long x $\frac{1}{4}$ in dia (flat blade)
Screwdriver - 4 in long x $\frac{1}{4}$ in dia (cross blade)
Combination pliers - 6 inch
Hacksaw, junior
Tyre pump
Tyre pressure gauge
Grease gun (where applicable)
Oil can
Fine emery cloth (1 sheet)
Wire brush (small)
Funnel (medium size)

Repair and overhaul tool kit

These tools are virtually essential for anyone undertaking any major repairs to a motor vehicle, and are additional to those given in the *Maintenance and minor repair* list. Included in this list is a comprehensive set of sockets. Although these are expensive they will be found invaluable as they are so versatile - particularly if various drives are included in the set. We recommend the $\frac{1}{2}$ in square-drive type, as this can be used with most proprietary torque wrenches. If you cannot afford a socket set, even bought piecemeal, then inexpensive tubular box spanners are a useful alternative.

The tools in this list will occasionally need to be supplemented by tools from the *Special* list.

Sockets (or box spanners) to cover range in previous list
Reversible ratchet drive (for use with sockets)
Extension piece, 10 inch (for use with sockets)
Universal joint (for use with sockets)
Torque wrench (for use with sockets)
'Mole' wrench - 8 inch
Ball pein hammer
Soft-faced hammer, plastic or rubber
Screwdriver - 6 in long x $\frac{5}{16}$ in dia (flat blade)
Screwdriver - 2 in long x $\frac{5}{16}$ in square (flat blade)
Screwdriver - 1$\frac{1}{2}$ in long x $\frac{1}{4}$ in dia (cross blade)
Screwdriver - 3 in long x $\frac{1}{8}$ in dia (electricians)
Pliers - electricians side cutters
Pliers - needle nosed
Pliers - circlip (internal and external)
Cold chisel - $\frac{1}{2}$ inch
Scriber (this can be made by grinding the end of a broken hacksaw blade)
Scraper (this can be made by flattening and sharpening one end of a piece of copper pipe)
Centre punch
Pin punch
Hacksaw
Valve grinding tool
Steel rule/straight edge
Allen keys
Selection of files
Wire brush (large)
Axle-stands
Jack (strong scissor or hydraulic type)

Special tools

The tools in this list are those which are not used regularly, are expensive to buy, or which need to be used in accordance with their manufacturers' instructions. Unless relatively difficult mechanical jobs are undertaken frequently, it will not be economic to buy many of these tools. Where this is the case, you could consider clubbing together with friends (or a motorists' club) to make a joint purchase, or borrowing the tools against a deposit from a local garage or tool hire specialist.

The following list contains only those tools and instruments freely available to the public, and not those special tools produced by the vehicle manufacturer specifically for its dealer network. You will find occasional references to these manufacturers' special tools in the text of this manual. Generally, an alternative method of doing the job without the vehicle manufacturer's special tool is given. However, sometimes, there is no alternative to using them. Where this is the case and the relevant tool cannot be bought or borrowed you will have to entrust the work to a franchised garage

Valve spring compressor
Piston ring compressor
Balljoint separator
Universal hub/bearing puller
Impact screwdriver
Micrometer and/or vernier gauge
Carburettor flow balancing device (where applicable)

Dial gauge
Stroboscopic timing light
Dwell angle meter/tachometer
Universal electrical multi-meter
Cylinder compression gauge
Lifting tackle
Trolley jack
Light with extension lead

Buying tools

For practically all tools, a tool factor is the best source since he will have a very comprehensive range compared with the average garage or accessory shop. Having said that, accessory shops often offer excellent quality tools at discount prices, so it pays to shop around.

Remember, you don't have to buy the most expensive items on the shelf, but it is always advisable to steer clear of the very cheap tools. There are plenty of good tools around at reasonable prices, so ask the proprietor or manager of the shop for advice before making a purchase.

Care and maintenance of tools

Having purchased a reasonable tool kit, it is necessary to keep the tools in a clean serviceable condition. After use, always wipe off any dirt, grease and metal particles using a clean, dry cloth, before putting the tools away. Never leave them lying around after they have been used. A simple tool rack on the garage or workshop wall, for items such as screwdrivers and pliers is a good idea. Store all normal spanners and sockets in a metal box. Any measuring instruments, gauges, meters, etc, must be carefully stored where they cannot be damaged or become rusty.

Take a little care when tools are used. Hammer heads inevitably become marked and screwdrivers lose the keen edge on their blades from time-to-time. A little timely attention with emery cloth or a file will soon restore items like this to a good serviceable finish.

Working facilities

Not to be forgotten when discussing tools, is the workshop itself. If anything more than routine maintenance is to be carried out, some form of suitable working area becomes essential.

It is appreciated that many an owner mechanic is forced by circumstances to remove an engine or similar item, without the benefit of a garage or workshop. Having done this, any repairs should always be done under the cover of a roof.

Wherever possible, any dismantling should be done on a clean flat workbench or table at a suitable working height.

Any workbench needs a vice: one with a jaw opening of 4 in (100 mm) is suitable for most jobs. As mentioned previously, some clean dry storage space is also required for tools, as well as the lubricants, cleaning fluids, touch-up paints and so on which become necessary.

Another item which may be required, and which has a much more general usage, is an electric drill with a chuck capacity of at least $\frac{5}{16}$ in (8 mm). This, together with a good range of twist drills, is virtually essential for fitting accessories such as wing mirrors and reversing lights.

Last, but not least, always keep a supply of old newspapers and clean, lint-free rags available, and try to keep any working area as clean as possible.

Spanner jaw gap comparison table

Jaw gap (in)	Spanner size
0·250	$\frac{1}{4}$ in AF
0·275	7 mm AF
0·312	$\frac{5}{16}$ in AF
0·315	8 mm AF
0·340	11/32 in AF; $\frac{1}{8}$ in Whitworth
0·354	9 mm AF
0·375	$\frac{3}{8}$ in AF
0·393	10 mm AF
0·433	11 mm AF
0·437	$\frac{7}{16}$ in AF
0·445	$\frac{3}{16}$ in Whitworth; $\frac{1}{4}$ in BSF
0·472	12 mm AF
0·500	$\frac{1}{2}$ in AF
0·512	13 mm AF
0·525	$\frac{1}{4}$ in Whitworth; $\frac{5}{16}$ in BSF
0·551	14 mm AF
0·562	$\frac{9}{16}$ in AF
0·590	15 mm AF
0·600	$\frac{5}{16}$ in Whitworth; $\frac{3}{8}$ in BSF
0·625	$\frac{5}{8}$ in AF
0·629	16 mm AF
0·669	17 mm AF
0·687	$\frac{11}{16}$ in AF
0·708	18 mm AF
0·710	$\frac{3}{8}$ in Whitworth; $\frac{7}{16}$ in BSF
0·748	19 mm AF
0·750	$\frac{3}{4}$ in AF
0·812	$\frac{13}{16}$ in AF
0·820	$\frac{7}{16}$ in Whitworth; $\frac{1}{2}$ in BSF
0·866	22 mm AF
0·875	$\frac{7}{8}$ in AF
0·920	$\frac{1}{2}$ in Whitworth; $\frac{9}{16}$ in BSF
0·937	$\frac{15}{16}$ in AF
0·944	24 mm AF
1·000	1 in AF
1·010	$\frac{9}{16}$ in Whitworth; $\frac{5}{8}$ in BSF
1·023	26 mm AF
1·062	$1\frac{1}{16}$ in AF; 27 mm AF
1·100	$\frac{5}{8}$ in Whitworth; $\frac{11}{16}$ in BSF
1·125	$1\frac{1}{8}$ in AF
1·181	30 mm AF
1·200	$\frac{11}{16}$ in Whitworth; $\frac{3}{4}$ in BSF
1·250	$1\frac{1}{4}$ in AF
1·259	32 mm AF
1·300	$\frac{3}{4}$ in Whitworth; $\frac{7}{8}$ in BSF
1·312	$1\frac{5}{16}$ in AF
1·390	$\frac{13}{16}$ in Whitworth; $\frac{15}{16}$ in BSF
1·417	36 mm AF
1·437	$1\frac{7}{16}$ in AF
1·480	$\frac{7}{8}$ in Whitworth; 1 in BSF
1·500	$1\frac{1}{2}$ in AF
1·574	40 mm AF; $\frac{15}{16}$ in Whitworth
1·614	41 mm AF
1·625	$1\frac{5}{8}$ in AF
1·670	1 in Whitworth; $1\frac{1}{8}$ in BSF
1·687	$1\frac{11}{16}$ in AF
1·811	46 mm AF
1·812	$1\frac{13}{16}$ in AF
1·860	$1\frac{1}{8}$ in Whitworth; $1\frac{1}{4}$ in BSF
1·875	$1\frac{7}{8}$ in AF
1·968	50 mm AF
2·000	2 in AF
2·050	$1\frac{1}{4}$ in Whitworth; $1\frac{3}{8}$ in BSF
2·165	55 mm AF
2·362	60 mm AF

A Haltrac hoist and gantry in use during a typical engine removal sequence

Jacking and towing

Jacking points

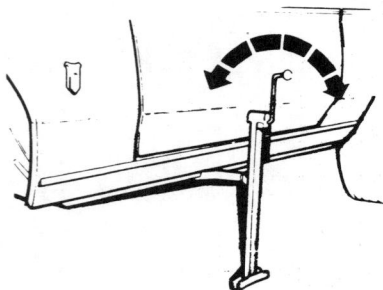

To change a wheel in an emergency, use the jack supplied with the vehicle. Ensure that the roadwheel nuts are released before jacking up the car and make sure that the arm of the jack is fully engaged with the body bracket and that the base of the jack is standing on a firm surface.

The jack supplied with the vehicle is not suitable for use when raising the vehicle for maintenance or repair operations. For this work, use a trolley, hydraulic or screw-type jack located under the front crossmember, bodyframe side-members or rear axle casing, as illustrated. Always supplement the jack with axle-stands or blocks before crawling beneath the car.

Towing points

If your vehicle is being towed, make sure that the tow rope is attached to the front crossmember. If the vehicle is equipped with automatic transmission, the distance towed must not exceed 15 miles (24 km), nor the speed 30 mph (48 km/h), otherwise serious damage to the transmission may result. If these limits are likely to be exceeded, disconnect and remove the propeller shaft.

If you are towing another vehicle, attach a tow rope to the lower shock absorber mounting bracket at the axle tube.

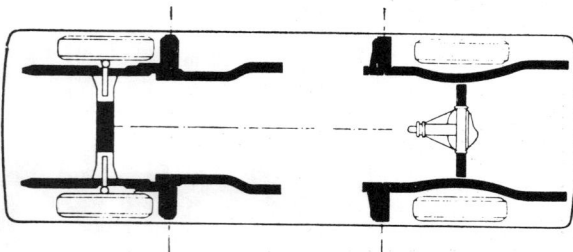

Jacking points

Front towing point

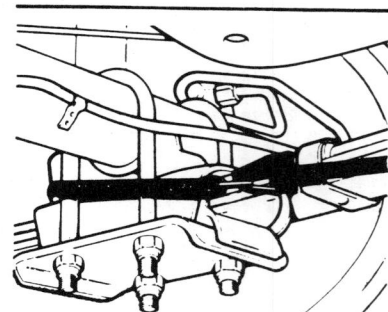

Using the lifting jack

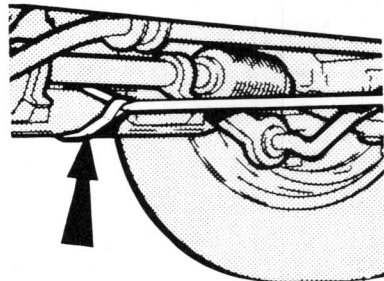

Rear towing point

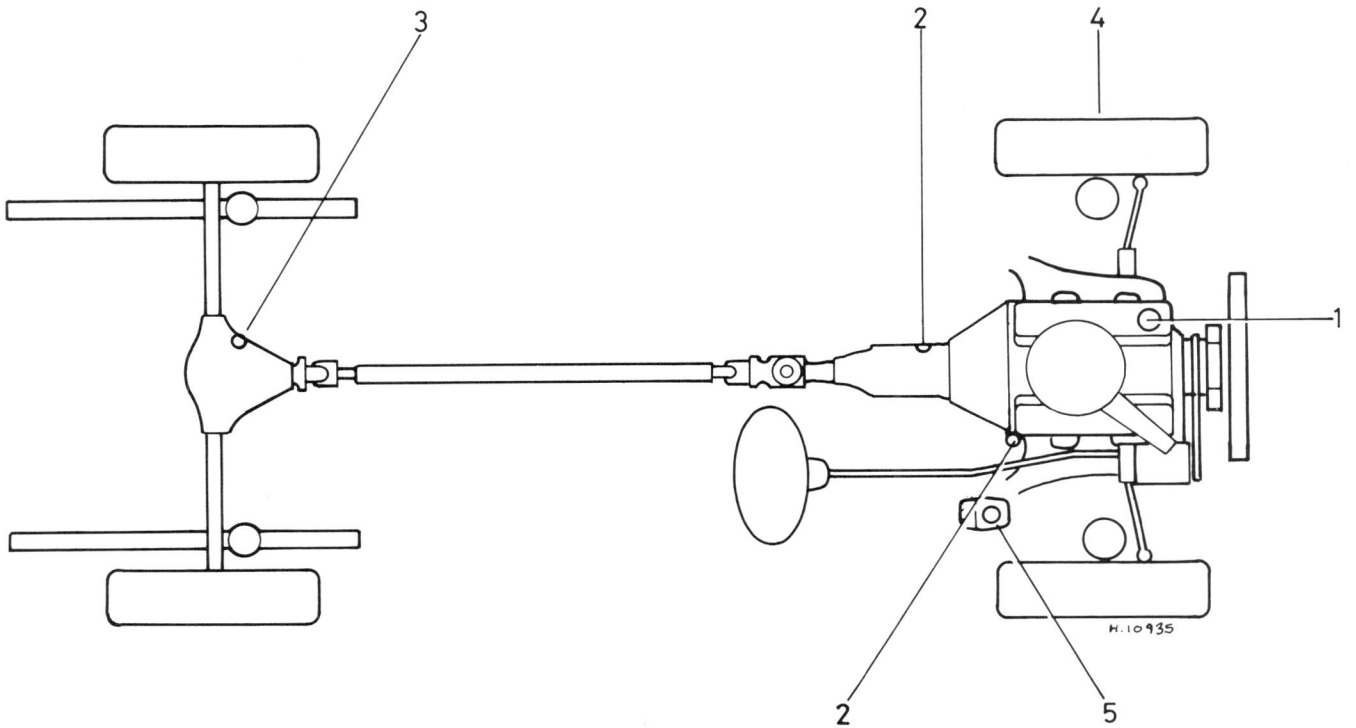

H.10935

Recommended lubricants and fluids

Component	Castrol product
Engine (1)	Castrol GTX
Manual gearbox (2)	Castrol Hypoy Light (80 EP)
Automatic transmission (2)	Castrol TQF
Rear axle (3)	Castrol Hypoy B (90 EP)
Front wheel bearings (4)	Castrol LM Grease
Brake master cylinder (5)	Castrol Girling Universal Brake and Clutch Fluid
Steering gear	Castrol Hypoy B (90 EP)
Oil can	Castrol GTX

Note: *The above are general recommendations. Lubrication requirements vary from territory-to-territory and depend on the usage to which the vehicle is put. Consult the operators handbook supplied with your car.*

Safety First!

Professional motor mechanics are trained in safe working procedures. However enthusiastic you may be about getting on with the job in hand, do take the time to ensure that your safety is not put at risk. A moment's lack of attention can result in an accident, as can failure to observe certain elementary precautions.

There will always be new ways of having accidents, and the following points do not pretend to be a comprehensive list of all dangers; they are intended rather to make you aware of the risks and to encourage a safety-conscious approach to all work you carry out on your vehicle.

Essential DOs and DON'Ts

DON'T rely on a single jack when working underneath the vehicle. Always use reliable additional means of support, such as axle stands, securely placed under a part of the vehicle that you know will not give way.

DON'T attempt to loosen or tighten high-torque nuts (e.g. wheel hub nuts) while the vehicle is on a jack; it may be pulled off.

DON'T start the engine without first ascertaining that the transmission is in neutral (or 'Park' where applicable) and the parking brake applied.

DON'T suddenly remove the filler cap from a hot cooling system — cover it with a cloth and release the pressure gradually first, or you may get scalded by escaping coolant.

DON'T attempt to drain oil until you are sure it has cooled sufficiently to avoid scalding you.

DON'T grasp any part of the engine, exhaust or catalytic converter without first ascertaining that it is sufficiently cool to avoid burning you.

DON'T syphon toxic liquids such as fuel, brake fluid or antifreeze by mouth, or allow them to remain on your skin.

DON'T inhale brake lining dust — it is injurious to health.

DON'T allow any spilt oil or grease to remain on the floor — wipe it up straight away, before someone slips on it.

DON'T use ill-fitting spanners or other tools which may slip and cause injury.

DON'T attempt to lift a heavy component which may be beyond your capability — get assistance.

DON'T rush to finish a job, or take unverified short cuts.

DON'T allow children or animals in or around an unattended vehicle.

DO wear eye protection when using power tools such as drill, sander, bench grinder etc, and when working under the vehicle.

DO use a barrier cream on your hands prior to undertaking dirty jobs — it will protect your skin from infection as well as making the dirt easier to remove afterwards; but make sure your hands aren't left slippery.

DO keep loose clothing (cuffs, tie etc) and long hair well out of the way of moving mechanical parts.

DO remove rings, wristwatch etc, before working on the vehicle — especially the electrical system.

DO ensure that any lifting tackle used has a safe working load rating adequate for the job.

DO keep your work area tidy — it is only too easy to fall over articles left lying around.

DO get someone to check periodically that all is well, when working alone on the vehicle.

DO carry out work in a logical sequence and check that everything is correctly assembled and tightened afterwards.

DO remember that your vehicle's safety affects that of yourself and others. If in doubt on any point, get specialist advice.

IF, in spite of following these precautions, you are unfortunate enough to injure yourself, seek medical attention as soon as possible.

Fire

Remember at all times that petrol (gasoline) is highly flammable. Never smoke, or have any kind of naked flame around, when working on the vehicle. But the risk does not end there — a spark caused by an electrical short-circuit, by two metal surfaces contacting each other, or even by static electricity built up in your body under certain conditions, can ignite petrol vapour, which in a confined space is highly explosive.

Always disconnect the battery earth (ground) terminal before working on any part of the fuel system, and never risk spilling fuel on to a hot engine or exhaust.

It is recommended that a fire extinguisher of a type suitable for fuel and electrical fires is kept handy in the garage or workplace at all times. Never try to extinguish a fuel or electrical fire with water.

Fumes

Certain fumes are highly toxic and can quickly cause unconsciousness and even death if inhaled to any extent. Petrol (gasoline) vapour comes into this category, as do the vapours from certain solvents such as trichloroethylene. Any draining or pouring of such volatile fluids should be done in a well ventilated area.

When using cleaning fluids and solvents, read the instructions carefully. Never use materials from unmarked containers — they may give off poisonous vapours.

Never run the engine of a motor vehicle in an enclosed space such as a garage. Exhaust fumes contain carbon monoxide which is extremely poisonous; if you need to run the engine, always do so in the open air or at least have the rear of the vehicle outside the workplace.

If you are fortunate enough to have the use of an inspection pit, never drain or pour petrol, and never run the engine, while the vehicle is standing over it; the fumes, being heavier than air, will concentrate in the pit with possibly lethal results.

The battery

Never cause a spark, or allow a naked light, near the vehicle's battery. It will normally be giving off a certain amount of hydrogen gas, which is highly explosive.

Always disconnect the battery earth (ground) terminal before working on the fuel or electrical systems.

If possible, loosen the filler plugs or cover when charging the battery from an external source. Do not charge at an excessive rate or the battery may burst.

Take care when topping up and when carrying the battery. The acid electrolyte, even when diluted, is very corrosive and should not be allowed to contact the eyes or skin.

If you ever need to prepare electrolyte yourself, always add the acid slowly to the water, and never the other way round. Protect against splashes by wearing rubber gloves and goggles.

Mains electricity

When using an electric power tool, inspection light etc which works from the mains, always ensure that the appliance is correctly connected to its plug and that, where necessary, it is properly earthed (grounded). Do not use such appliances in damp conditions and, again, beware of creating a spark or applying excessive heat in the vicinity of fuel or fuel vapour.

Ignition HT voltage

A severe electric shock can result from touching certain parts of the ignition system, such as the HT leads, when the engine is running or being cranked, particularly if components are damp or the insulation is defective. Where an electronic ignition system is fitted, the HT voltage is much higher and could prove fatal.

Routine maintenance

Maintenance is essential for ensuring safety, and desirable for the purpose of getting the best in terms of performance and economy from your car. Over the years the need for periodic lubrication — oiling, greasing and so on — has been drastically reduced, if not totally eliminated. This has unfortunately tended to lead some owners to think that because no such action is required, components either no longer exist, or will last forever. This is a serious delusion. It follows therefore that the largest initial element of maintenance is visual examination and a general sense of awareness. This may lead to repairs or renewals, but should help to avoid roadside breakdowns.

In compiling this routine maintenance schedule, the author was confronted with a slight dilemma. For example, why should the maintenance interval for checking the brake fluid reservoir be recommended as 6000 miles (10 000 km) for a Capri II when it is 30 000 miles for a Mercury Capri II? The author therefore has made slight alterations to the manufacturer's schedule for some maintenance tasks, since it is felt that it is better to check and rectify a noticeable drop in fluid level rather than wait for a warning light to tell the driver that something is wrong. Also, an item such as the brake fluid check already mentioned takes so little time compared with its importance that a much more frequent check is recommended.

For vehicles used in the USA two different maintenance schedules are given, according to the maintenance schedule code letter to be found on the engine compartment emission control decal or glovebox door.

It must be appreciated that not all maintenance tasks are applicable to all vehicles; therefore the owner must select those applicable to his particular car.

All models

Every 250 miles (400 km), weekly or before a long journey

Engine
> Check the engine oil level; top up if necessary (photo)
> Check the radiator coolant level (photo)
> Check the battery electrolyte level (photo)

Steering
> Check tyre pressures (when cold)
> Examine tyres for wear or damage
> Check steering for smooth and accurate operation

Brakes
> Check reservoir fluid level (photo). If this has fallen noticeably, check for fluid leakage
> Check for satisfactory brake operation

Lights, wipers, horns, instruments
> Check operation of all lights
> Check operation of windscreen wipers and washers

Check engine oil level

Check radiator coolant level

Check and top-up if necessary the battery electrolyte level

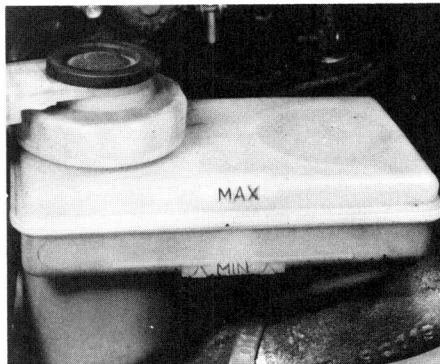
Check the brake fluid reservoir

Renew the engine oil filter

Check drivebelt(s) tension

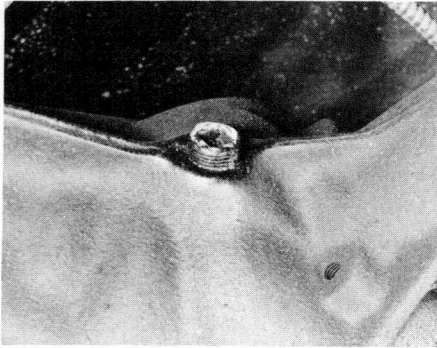
Rear axle oil level/filler plug

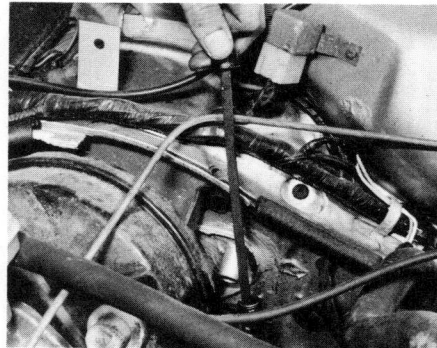
Check the automatic transmission fluid level

Lubricate the front wheel bearings

Mercury Capri II: Schedules A and B

Every 5000 miles (8000 km) or 5 months, whichever occurs first

Renew the engine oil
Check the ignition timing
Adjust engine idle speeds and mixture

Capri II and Mercury Capri II: Schedule C

Every 6000 miles (10 000 km) or 6 months, whichever occurs first

Renew engine oil and oil filter (photo)
Clean distributor points and reset gap (Capri II only)
Lubricate distributor (Capri II only)
Clean spark plugs and reset gaps
Clean all HT leads and top of ignition coil
Check ignition timing (Capri II only)
Check valve clearances (Capri II only)
Check tightness of inlet and exhaust manifold bolts
Check condition of exhaust system
Check condition and tension of all drivebelts (photo)
Renew fuel filter (Mercury Capri II)
Check condition of pipes and hoses in emission control system
Lubricate accelerator linkage
Adjust engine idle speeds and mixture (Capri II only)
Examine cooling system hoses and check for leaks
Clean/tighten battery terminals
Check the automatic transmission fluid level (where applicable), referring to Chapter 13, Section 5 (photo)
Check gearbox oil level (manual transmission)
Check rear axle oil level (photo)
Check clutch adjustment
Check front brake pads for wear
Check rear brake linings for wear
Examine brake hoses for leaks and chafing
Check handbrake adjustment
Check the power steering fluid level (where applicable), referring to Chapter 13, Section 8
Check steering linkage for wear and damage and condition of ball joint covers
Check front suspension linkage for wear and damage
Check front wheel toe-in
Check operation of all doors, catches and hinges. Lubricate as necessary
Check condition of seatbelts and operation of buckles and inertia reels
Check that the horn operates
Check that all instruments and gauges are operating

Capri II and Mercury Capri II: Schedules A, B and C

At first 3000 miles (5000 km), and for vehicles which operate under continual stop/start conditions every subsequent 3000 miles (5000 km)

Renew engine oil

Renew engine oil filter at first 3000 miles (5000 km)
Check automatic transmission fluid level referring to Chapter 6, Section 22.

Mercury Capri II: Schedules A and B

Every 15 000 miles (24 000 km) or 15 months, whichever occurs first

Carry out the maintenance tasks listed at intervals of 12 000 miles for schedule C vehicles.

All models

Every 18 000 miles (30 000 km) or 18 months, whichever occurs first

Check tightness of rear spring mountings

All models

Every 24 000 miles (40 000 km) or 2 years, whichever occurs first

Dismantle, lubricate and adjust front wheel bearings (photo)
Drain engine coolant. Renew antifreeze or inhibitor coolant mixture

Every 36 000 miles (60 000 km) or 3 years, whichever occurs first

Renew all rubber seals and hoses in braking system. Renew brake fluid

Mercury Capri II: Schedules A and B

Every 10 000 miles (16 000 km) or 10 months, whichever occurs first

Carry out the maintenance tasks listed at intervals of 6000 miles (10 000 km) for schedule C vehicles, except where this is a duplication of the items checked every 5000 miles.

Capri II and Mercury Capri II: Schedule C

Every 12 000 miles (20 000 km) or 12 months, whichever occurs first

Renew the contact breaker points (Capri II only)
Renew spark plugs
Check condition of distributor cap and rotor
Clean the positive crankcase ventilation (PCV) system
Arrange for your Ford dealer to check the emission control system operation (Mercury Capri II)
Drain and refill automatic transmission
Arrange for your Ford dealer to adjust the automatic transmission bands

Chapter 1 Part A   2800 V6 engine (Mercury Capri)

Contents

Specifications

Engine (general)

Engine type	6 cylinder 60° 'V' pushrod operated OHV
Compression ratio	8·2 : 1
Bore	3·66 in (92·96 mm)
Stroke	2·70 in (68·58 mm)
Capacity	170·8 cu in (2792 cc)
Oil pressure (hot)	40 – 55 lbf/in² (2·82 – 3·87 kgf/cm²)
Firing order	1 – 4 – 2 – 5 – 3 – 6

Cylinder block

Bore diameter* (standard):

Class 1	3·6616 in (93·005 mm)
Class 2	3·6620 in (93·015 mm)
Class 3	3·6624 in (93·025 mm)
Class 4	3·6630 in (93·040 mm)

*All dimensions ± 0·0002 in (0·005 mm)

Bore diameter* (oversize):

0·020 service	3·6821 in (93·525 mm)
0·040 service	3·7018 in (94·026 mm)

*All dimensions ± 0·0002 in (0·005 mm)

Main bearing bore diameter:

Red	2·386 in (60·604 mm)
Blue	2·387 in (60·630 mm)
Thrust bearing width	0·890 – 0·892 in (22·606 – 22·657 mm)

Vertical inside diameter of fitted main bearing shells standard:

Red	2·2454 – 2·2548 in (56·990 – 57·0 mm)
Blue	2·2450 – 2·2454 in (56·980 – 56·99 mm)

Undersize:

0·010	2·235 in (56·769 mm)
0·020	2·225 in (56·515 mm)
0·030	2·215 in (56·261 mm)
0·040	2·205 in (56·007 mm)

Bores in cylinder block for camshaft bearings:

Front	1·773 in (45·720 mm)
No. 2	1·758 in (44·653 mm)
No. 3	1·743 in (44·272 mm)
Rear	1·728 in (43·891 mm)

Crankshaft

Main bearing journal diameter: Standard

Red	2·244 in (56·998 mm)
Blue	2·243 in (56·972 mm)

Undersize:

0·010	2·234 in (56·748 mm)
0·020	2·224 in (56·490 mm)
0·030	2·214 in (56·237 mm)
0·040	2·204 in (55·982 mm)

Main journal to bearing shell clearance:

Standard	0·0005 – 0·002 in (0·0127 – 0·508 mm)
Undersize	0·0005 – 0·002 in (0·0127 – 0·508 mm)

Thrust bearing width:

Bearing journal	1·039 in (26·391 mm)
Bearing insert	1·034 in (26·264 mm)
Crankshaft end play	0·004 – 0·008 in (0·102 – 0·203 mm)

Connecting rod bearing journal diameter standard:

Red	2·126 in (54·0004 mm)
Blue	2·125 in (53·975 mm)

Undersize:

0·010	2·116 in (53·746 mm)
0·020	2·106 in (53·492 mm)
0·030	2·096 in (53·238 mm)
0·040	2·086 in (52·984 mm)

Connecting rod

Connecting rod bearing shell vertical diameter standard:

Red	2·127 in (54·026 mm)
Blue	2·126 in (53·772 mm)

Undersize:

0·010	2·117 in (53·772 mm)
0·020	2·107 in (53·518 mm)
0·030	2·097 in (53·264 mm)
0·040	2·087 in (53·010 mm)

Journal bearing insert clearance:

Standard	0·0005 – 0·002 in (0·013 – 0·051 mm)
Undersize	0·0005 – 0·0025 in (0·013 – 0·064 mm)

Pistons

Piston clearance	0·001 – 0·0025 in (0·025 – 0·038 mm)

Piston diameter:

Standard	3·6605 – 3·6614 in (92·974 – 93·00 mm)
Oversize (0·020 in)	3·6802 – 3·6812 in (93·477 – 93·503 mm)
Oversize (0·040 in)	3·6999 – 3·7009 in (93·978 – 94·003 mm)

Piston rings

Ring gap (fitted):

Upper compression	0·015 – 0·023 in (0·381 – 0·584 mm)
Lower compression	0·015 – 0·023 in (0·381 – 0·584 mm)
Oil control	0·015 – 0·055 in (0·381 – 1·397 mm)

Camshaft

Number of bearings	4

Bearing diameter:

Front	1·650 in (42·291 mm)
No. 2	1·635 in (41·783 mm)
No. 3	1·620 in (41·275 mm)
Rear	1·605 in (40·767 mm)

Bush inside diameter:
    Front . . . . 1·652 in (41·961 mm)
    No. 2 . . . . 1·637 in (41·580 mm)
    No. 3 . . . . 1·622 in (41·199 mm)
    Rear . . . . 1·607 in (40·818 mm)
End play . . . . 0·001 – 0·004 in (0·025 – 0·102 mm)
Thrust plate thickness standard:
    Red . . . . 0·156 in (3·962 mm)
    Blue . . . . 0·157 in (3·987 mm)
Oversize:
    Red . . . . 0·161 in (4·089 mm)
    Blue . . . . 0·162 in (4·115 mm)
Cam lift . . . . 0·255 in (6·477 mm)
Cam heel to toe dimension . . . . 1·338 – 1·346 in (33·9852 – 34·188 mm)
Camshaft bearings:
    Distance from front face of cylinder block to rear side of assembled bearing
    Tolerance . . . . ± 0·010 in (0·254 mm)
    Front . . . . 0·831 in (21·107 mm)
    No. 2 . . . . 6·559 in (166·599 mm)
    No. 3 . . . . 11·319 in (287·503 mm)
    Rear . . . . 17·091 in (434·111 mm)

Cylinder head

Valve seat angle . . . . 45°
Valve stem diameter (inlet):
    Standard . . . . 0·316 in (8·026 mm)
    Oversize:
        0·008 . . . . 0·325 in (8·230 mm)
        0·016 . . . . 0·332 in (8·433 mm)
        0·024 . . . . 0·340 in (8·636 mm)
        0·032 . . . . 0·348 in (8·840 mm)
Valve stem diameter (exhaust):
    Standard . . . . 0·315 in (8·001 mm)
    Oversize:
        0·008 . . . . 0·323 in (8·204 mm)
        0·016 . . . . 0·331 in (8·407 mm)
        0·024 . . . . 0·339 in (8·611 mm)
        0·032 . . . . 0·347 in (8·814 mm)
Valve stem bore diameter:
    Standard . . . . 0·318 in (8·078 mm)
    Oversize:
        0·008 . . . . 0·326 in (8·280 mm)
        0·016 . . . . 0·334 in (8·484 mm)
Valve lift . . . . 0·373 in (8·474 mm)
Valve clearance (hot):
    Inlet . . . . 0·014 in (0·36 mm)
    Exhaust . . . . 0·016 in (0·4 mm)
Inlet valve timing:
    Opens . . . . 20° BTDC
    Closes . . . . 56° ABDC
Exhaust valve timing:
    Opens . . . . 62° BBDC
    Closes . . . . 74° ATDC
Valve tappet diameter . . . . 0·874 in (22·200 mm)

Engine lubrication

Oil viscosity:
    −40°F to +32°F 5W/20, 5W/30
    −10°F to +70°F 10W/30
    −10°F to +90°F 10W/40
    −10°F to +120°F 10W/50
    +25°F to +90°F 20W/40
    +32°F to +120°F 20W/50
    +25°F to +120°F . . . . 20W/50 'All-season'
Oil change, excluding filter renewal . . . . 3·8 Imp qt (7·5 litres)
Oil change, including filter renewal . . . . 4·3 Imp qt (6·6 litres)
Oil pump:
    Driveshaft to bearing clearance . . . . 0·0015 – 0·003 in (0·038 – 0·076 mm)
    Rotor assembly end clearance . . . . 0·0011 – 0·0041 in (0·028 – 0·104 mm)
    Outer race to housing radial clearance . . . . 0·006 – 0·012 in (0·152 – 0·305 mm)

Torque wrench settings

	lbf ft	kgf m
Camshaft gear	30 – 36	4·2 – 5·0
Camshaft thrust plate	12 – 15	1·7 – 2·1
Carburettor-to-spacer stud	3 – 5	0·4 – 0·7
Carburettor adapter-to-manifold	3 – 5	0·4 – 0·7

Torque wrench settings

	lbf ft	kgf m
Carburettor-to-spacer nut	4 – 18	0·6 – 2·5
Connecting rod	21 – 25	2·9 – 3·5
Crankshaft damper	92 – 103	12·9 – 14·4
Crankcase vent valve	11 – 14	1·5 – 2·0
Cylinder head bolt	65 – 80	9·1 – 11·2
Distributor clamp	12 – 15	1·7 – 2·1
EGR tube fittings	15 – 20	2·1 – 2·8
EGR valve-to-spacer bolt	12 – 15	1·7 – 2·1
Exhaust manifold-to-EGR tube	25 – 35	3·5 – 4·9
Exhaust manifold-to-cylinder head	16 – 23	2·2 – 3·2
Flywheel to crankshaft	47 – 51	6·6 – 7·1
Front cover to cylinder block	12 – 15	1·7 – 2·1
Front plate to cylinder block	12 – 15	1·7 – 2·1
Fuel pump to cylinder block	12 – 15	1·7 – 2·1
Intake manifold to cylinder block	15 – 18	2·1 – 2·5
Main bearing cap	65 – 75	9·1 – 10·5
Monolithic timing pointer to front cover	5 – 7	0·7 – 1·0
Oil pump tube to pump	7 – 9	1·0 – 1·2
Oil pump tube to main bearing cap	12 – 15	1·7 – 2·1
Oil pump cover	7 – 9	1·0 – 1·2
Oil pan drain plug	15 – 20	2·1 – 2·8
Oil pan to cylinder block	5 – 7	0·7 – 1·0
Oil filter to cylinder block insert	10 – 15	1·4 – 2·1
Rocker arm cover	3 – 5	0·4 – 0·7
Rocker arm shaft support	43 – 49	6·0 – 6·9
Water jacket drain plug	14 – 18	2·0 – 2·5
Water outlet connection	12 – 15	1·7 – 2·1
Water pump to cylinder block	7 – 9	1·0 – 1·2
Water temperature sender	7 – 11	1·0 – 1·5
Spark plug	15 – 20	2·1 – 2·8
Fuel filter to carburettor	7 – 9	1·0 – 1·2
Alternator mounting bolt to cylinder head	18 – 25	2·5 – 3·5
Alternator pivot bolt	45 – 60	6·3 – 8·4
Alternator adjustment arm to front cover	50 – 71	7·0 – 10·0
Alternator adjustment arm to alternator	24 – 40	3·4 – 5·6
Crankshaft pulley to damper	18 – 25	2·5 – 3·5
Fan to water pump hub	14 – 20	2·0 – 2·8
Thermactor pump bracket to cylinder block	28 – 40	3·9 – 5·6
Thermactor pump mounting bracket to cylinder head	18 – 25	2·5 – 3·5
Thermactor pump adjustment arm to pump	22 – 32	3·1 – 4·5
Thermactor pump pivot bolt	30 – 45	4·2 – 6·3

1 General description

The 2800 cc engine is petrol driven, with six cylinders arranged in two banks of three in a 60° 'V' formation. The engine is made of light iron, with the cylinder bores machined directly into the cylinder block, into which full length water jackets are incorporated. The cylinder block is cast integrally with the crankcase, which has four large diameter main bearings with removable caps.

The cast iron crankshaft runs in 4 main bearings, which are fitted with renewable copper alloy shells. Crankshaft endfloat is controlled by thrust washers fitted to both sides of the rear intermediate bearing. Oil seals are fitted to both ends of the crankshaft. The camshaft, which is driven by a gear which is in direct mesh with a gear on the crankshaft, has four renewable bearings. Adjacent to the camshaft rear journal, is a skew gear which drives the oil pump and the distributor; and the camshaft also drives a fuel pump which is mounted on the left-hand side of the cylinder block.

The camshaft is mounted between the two banks of cylinders and operates the valves of both banks through a system of tappets, pushrods and rockers, the rockers being mounted on a shaft located on the top of each cylinder head.

The valves are mounted overhead and to improve engine breathing, the inlet valves are of a larger diameter than the exhaust valves. The valve springs are of unusual form in that the pitch of the coils is not uniform and the coil pitch at the cylinder head end is less than at the rocker end.

The connecting rods are of forged steel and the bearing caps are secured by bolts and nuts. The bearings are renewable and are of similar construction to the main bearings. The gudgeon pin is an interference fit in the small-end of the connecting rod.

The pistons have solid skirts and flat crowns, each piston being fitted with two compression rings and a three piece oil control ring.

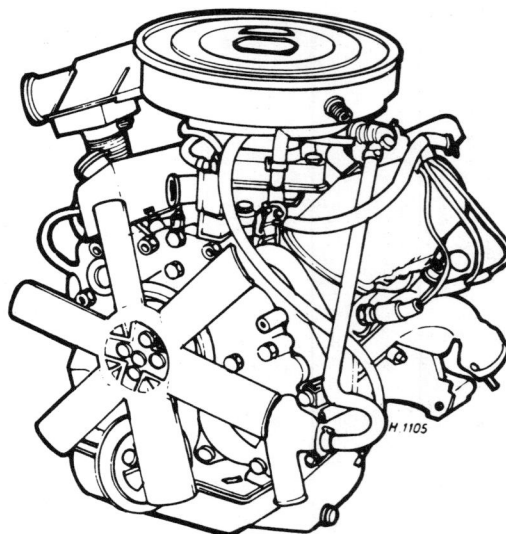

Fig. 1.1 Front LH view of V6 engine

On models with manual transmission a flywheel machined to fit a clutch is attached to the rear end of the crankshaft and the periphery of the flywheel has a shrunk-on ring gear which the pinion of the starter motor engages during starting. On models with automatic transmission a ring gear is shrunk onto an inertia ring attached to the torque converter.

The lower end of the distributor driveshaft engages a double rotor oil pump, which supplies oil under pressure via a full flow filter to the main, connecting rod and camshaft bearings. Oil holes in the rocker arms are fed from the rocker shaft and supply oil to the push rods and valves. The cylinder bores are lubricated by oil sprayed from holes drilled in the connecting rods and a drilling in the front face of the cylinder block lubricates the timing gears.

Incorporated in the top of the left-hand rocker cover is an oil filler with a filter gauze for the positive crankcase ventilation system. Crankcase fumes are discharged into the inlet manifold from an emission control valve in the left-hand rocker cover.

2 Major operations with engine in place

The following major operations may be carried out without removing the engine.

1   *Removing and refitting the cylinder heads*
2   *Removing and refitting the timing gear*
3   *Removing and refitting the engine front mountings*
4   *Removing and refitting the engine/gearbox rear mounting*
5   *Removing and refitting the camshaft*

3 Major operations with engine removed

Although it may be possible to carry out some of the following operations with the engine in place, especially if the transmission has been removed, it is considered preferable to remove the engine in all cases.

1   *Removing and refitting the flywheel*
2   *Removing and refitting the rear main bearing oil seal*
3   *Removing and refitting the crankcase sump*
4   *Removing and refitting the connecting rod bearing*
5   *Removing and refitting the pistons and connecting rods*
6   *Removing and refitting the oil pump*
7   *Removing and refitting the crankshaft and main bearings*
8   *Removing and refitting the camshaft bushes*

4 Methods of engine removal

The engine may be lifted out with the gearbox attached, or it may be separated from the gearbox and the engine only removed. If the gearbox is attached, removal is more difficult because of the added weight and because the assembly has to be removed at a very steep angle. An engine with automatic transmission should never be removed as a unit, because damage to the transmission is likely to result.

5 Engine removal

If air-conditioning is fitted the system must be depressurized by a specialist
1   Open and prop up the bonnet, then cover the wings with cloths, or cardboard, to protect them from scratches during the subsequent operations.
2   Disconnect the battery leads, remove the battery clamp nuts and lift the battery out.
3   To ensure correct refitment of the air cleaner, make a sketch showing the positions of the hoses and the components which are to be removed and then remove the air cleaner.
4   Mark the outline of the bonnet hinges and then with the help of an assistant, remove the bolts, release the bonnet stay and carefully lift the bonnet clear.
5   With the car positioned over a pit, or with the rear wheels chocked, and the front jacked and supported on firm stands, remove the bottom hose of the radiator and drain the coolant into a container having a capacity of three gallons.
6   Release the clip and remove the radiator top hose.
7   Remove the radiator upper splash shield, remove the shroud attachment screws and remove the radiator shroud in two pieces.
8   Disconnect the automatic transmission oil cooler lines if fitted, after positioning a container of two gallons capacity to catch the oil.

Plug the cooler connections and pipe ends, to prevent the entry of dirt.
9   Remove the radiator attachment screws and lift the radiator clear.
10 Remove the cables from the starter solenoid switch, remove thre starter motor attachment bolts and remove the starter assembly.

Automatic transmission
11 Remove the converter bolt access plug.
12 Remove the three converter-to-flywheel bolts.
13 Remove the lower four bolts, attaching the converter housing to the engine.
14 Remove the two upper converter housing bolts, attaching the converter housing to the cylinder block.
15 Disconnect the downshift linkage.

Manual transmission
16 Pull back the clutch release arm rubber boot, if fitted. Pull the clutch lever and detach the cable ball end from the lever fork.

All models
17 Disconnect the oil pressure line.
18 Place a suitable two gallon container under the crankcase sump, remove the drain plug, allow the oil to drain out, then refit and tighten the drain plug.
19 Lower the car to the ground.
20 On models with power steering, loosen the power steering pump idler. Remove the power steering pump-to-bracket bolts and remove the power steering pump from its bracket.
21 Disconnect the fuel lines from the fuel pump and plug the ends of the fuel pipes.
22 Disconnect the heater hoses from the engine. Remove the hose retainer at the rocker cover and secure the hoses out of the way.
23 Remove the distributor low voltage connection, the wire to the ignition coil and the vacuum pipe.
24 Disconnect the transmission vacuum pipe from the inlet manifold, if fitted.
25 Disconnect the vacuum hose to the brake servo.
26 Remove the cable from the temperature gauge sender unit.
27 Disconnect the emission control pipes and electrical connections from the carburettor and inlet manifold, when fitted.
28 Disconnect the accelerator cable retaining clip at the ball stud. Pull on the cable and depress the tangs on the bracket clip one at a time, to remove the throttle cable.
29 Remove the two hoses and the electrical connector from the choke thermostat housing.
30 Remove the engine earth cable securing bolt from the engine and move the earth cable to one side.
31 Remove the electrical connections to the alternator.
32 Remove the two nuts securing each exhaust pipe flange to the exhaust manifold. Disconnect the rubber insulator from the front exhaust system mounting and tie the exhaust pipes clear of the engine.
33 Remove the rear engine mounting crossmember and support the transmission on a jack, or blocks of wood.
34 Attach lifting slings to the engine, with the front slings slightly shorter than the rear ones.
35 Connect the slings to a hoist and lift, to take the weight of the engine.
36 Remove the nuts from the engine front insulators, then raise the engine sufficiently to remove the insulators.
37 Check that all cables and controls have been detached and have been secured out of the way.
38 Draw the engine forward to separate the engine from the transmission. When automatic transmission is fitted, make sure that the torque converter remains attached to the transmission unit. On manual transmissions, take care not to damage the gearbox input shaft.
39 Lift slowly, checking frequently to see that the engine is clear of the transmission and that the engine is clear of the bodywork.
40 When the engine is clear of the body, lower it to the ground, or transfer it to the work bench.

6 Engine dismantling – general

1   Before starting any dismantling, the exterior of the engine should be cleaned thoroughly, either using paraffin and a stiff brush, or by the use of proprietary solvent which can be brushed on and washed off

with water.

2   If a sufficiently strong workbench is not available for dismantling, it is safer to dismantle the engine on the ground. It is essential however that the engine is supported on timber and that precautions are taken to stop the engine from falling over.

3   As the engine is stripped down, clean each part as it comes off. Do not wash parts with oilways in paraffin. To clean these parts wipe down carefully with a petrol dampened rag.

4   Where possible, avoid damaging gaskets on removal, especially if new ones have not been obtained. It is preferable to use all new gaskets, but the old ones may be required as patterns.

5   Wherever possible, nuts and bolts should be refitted after they have been cleaned. This saves a lot of time on reassembly and ensures that the correct length of bolt and the appropriate washers are used.

6   Take great care to ensure that every component is fitted to exactly the same place and exactly the same way round as before it was removed. Parts from each component should all be kept together, preferably in a container and components such as pistons, valves and valve gear should be laid out in the order in which they are fitted to the engine.

7   Whenever anything has been cleaned, cover it over, or place it in a polythene bag, so that it stays clean and dry.

7   Engine ancillaries – removal

1   Before beginning a complete overhaul, or if the engine is being exchanged for a works reconditioned unit, the following items should be removed.

Fuel system components:
  Carburettor
  Inlet and exhaust manifolds
  Fuel pump
  Fuel lines

Ignition system components:
  Spark plugs
  Distributor
  Coil

Electrical system components (if not removed already):
  Alternator and mounting brackets
  Starter motor

Cooling system components:
  Fan and fan pulley
  Water pump, thermostat housing and thermostat
  Water temperature sender unit

Engine:
  Crankcase ventilation tube
  Oil filter element
  Oil pressure sender unit (if fitted)
  Oil level dipstick
  Oil filler cap
  Engine mounting brackets

Clutch:
  Clutch pressure plate assembly
  Clutch friction plate assembly

Optional equipment:
  Air-conditioning compressor
  Power steering pump
  Thermactor pump

8   Cylinder heads – removal with engine in car

1   Open the bonnet and disconnect the battery leads.
2   Remove the air cleaner assembly, as described in Chapter 3.
3   Drain the cooling system as described in Chapter 2, then remove the outlet hose and the hose from the water pump.

4   Disconnect and remove the accelerator linkage from the carburettor.

5   Disconnect the distributor vacuum line, the low voltage connection to the contact breaker and the lead from the distributor to the ignition coil.

6   Remove the two nuts securing each exhaust pipe flange to the exhaust manifold. Disconnect the rubber insulators from the front exhaust system mounting and separate the exhaust pipes from the manifolds.

7   Remove the fuel filter and associated fuel pipes.

8   Remove the rocker cover by undoing and removing the securing screws and lifting off the cover. Remove the gasket if this is not removed with the cover.

9   Progressively loosen the three bolts securing the rocker arm assembly to the cylinder head. When the bolts are free, lift away the rocker assembly and oil baffles (Fig. 1.2). If both rocker shafts are being removed, note which cylinder head each shaft was removed from.

10 Remove the push rods (Fig. 1.3) and either lay them out in order, or push them through a piece of card on which the valve numbers are marked.

11 Remove the carburettor and the inlet manifold.

12 Progressively slacken the eight cylinder head bolts in the reverse order of the sequence shown in Fig. 1.4. Remove the bolts and lay them out in order.

13 If the cylinder head is stuck, pull on the exhaust manifold, or tap the cylinder head with a soft-faced hammer. Do not attempt to prise the head off, because this is likely to damage the face of the cylinder head, or block.

14 Remove the cylinder head and place it with its associated valve gear.

15 Remove the exhaust manifold from the cylinder head.

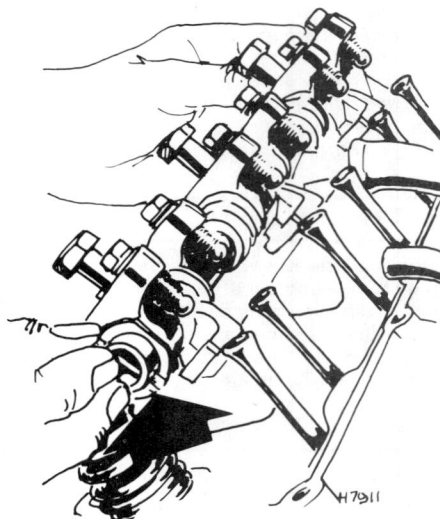

Fig. 1.2 Removing and refitting the rocker gear

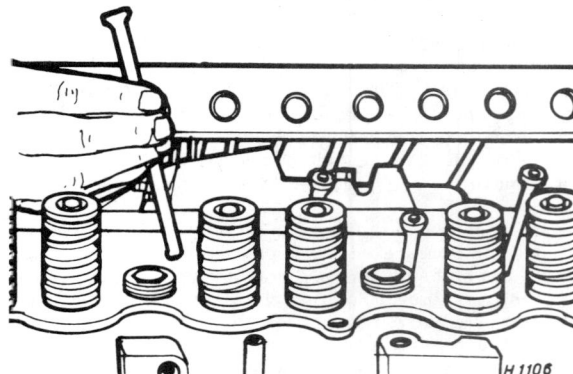

Fig. 1.3 Removing the push rods

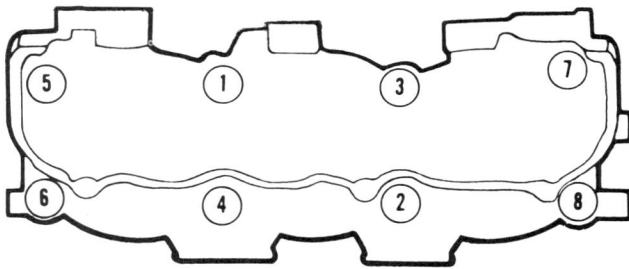

Fig. 1.4 Cylinder head bolt torque sequence

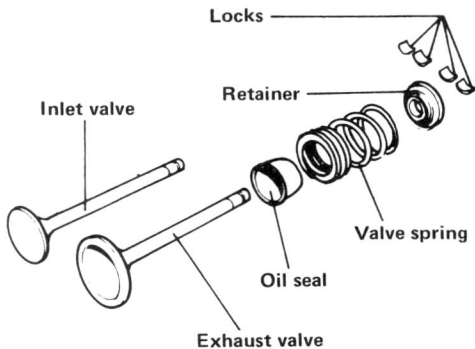

Fig. 1.5 Inlet and exhaust valve components

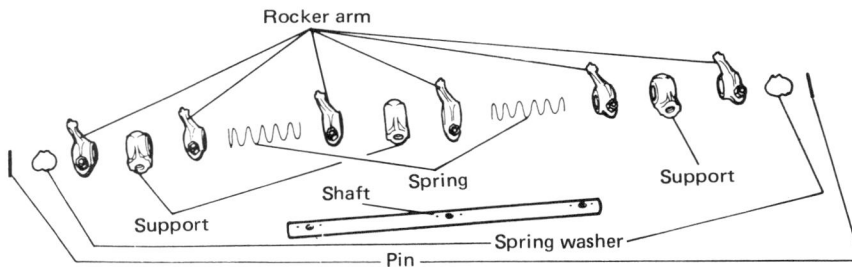

Fig. 1.6 Rocker assembly components

16 Remove the cylinder head gasket. New cylinder head gaskets are required on reassembly. The left and right-hand cylinder gaskets are different and non-interchangeable.

9 Cylinder heads – removal with engine out

Follow the sequence given in Section 8, starting at paragraph 8, disregarding information on parts which have been removed already.

10 Valves – removal

1   Remove the deposits from the combustion chambers and valve heads by scraping and wire brushing. Take care not to scratch the cylinder head gasket faces.
2   Lay the cylinder head on its side and fit the forked end of a valve spring compressor over the spring retainer and the head of the compressor screw in the centre of the valve head.
3   Compress the spring about a quarter of an inch to free the split collet from the top of the valve stem. If the spring retainer and collet sticks, do not screw the compressor down further, because this may damage the valve stem, but tap the spring retainer sharply with a light hammer.
4   When the two halves of the collet have been removed, unscrew the spring compressor until the spring is no longer compressed and remove the compressor.
5   Remove the spring retainer, the spring and the oil seal from the valve stem, then withdraw the valve from the cylinder head (Fig. 1.5). Note that the closed coiled end of the valve spring is towards the cylinder head.
6   Discard the valve stem oil seals and place the other components together, identifying them so that they are refitted in the correct place in the cylinder head.
7   Remove the spark plugs from the cylinder head, if not already removed.

11 Rocker assembly – dismantling

1   Remove the spring washer and pin from each end of the rocker arm shaft.
2   Slide the rocker arms, springs and rocker arm shaft supports off the shaft and lay them out in the order in which they are removed, so that they will be refitted in their original positions (Fig. 1.6).

12 Tappets – removal

1   Remove the tappets from their bores with a magnet and place them in a rack in sequence (Fig. 1.7).
2   If any are difficult to remove, rotate the crankshaft, which will cause the camshaft to turn and rotate the tappets to release them from any gum in their bores.

13 Crankshaft pulley – removal

1   Prevent the crankshaft from rotating, by jamming the flywheel if the engine is out of the car, or by locking the transmission if the engine is still in the car.

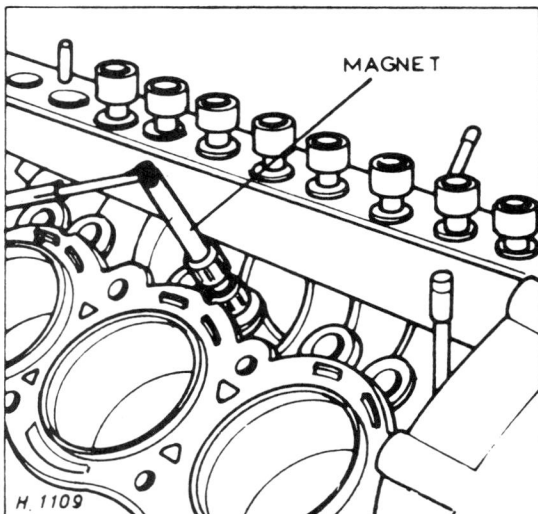

Fig. 1.7 Removing the tappets

2   Release the pulley bolt by fitting a ring spanner and tapping the spanner sharply, then remove the bolt and washer.
3   Use a sprocket puller to draw the pulley off the crankshaft. Do not attempt to lever it off, because the engine front cover is fragile and levering against it may distort, or even break it.
4   Withdraw the Woodruff key from the end of the crankshaft and place it with the pulley, the bolt and its washer.
5   The crankshaft pulley may be removed with the engine in the car, but it is first necessary to remove the radiator and the drive belts.

14 Flywheel – removal

1   Prevent the flywheel from rotating by jamming the ring gear against an improvised stop.
2   On models with manual transmission, remove the clutch pressure plate and disc as described in Chapter 5.
3   Release the six bolts securing the flywheel to the crankshaft and remove five of them.
4   While supporting the flywheel in place, remove the sixth bolt and lift the flywheel off carefully, so that the mating surfaces of flywheel and crankshaft are not damaged.

15 Crankcase sump – removal

1   With the engine out of the car and having ensured that the sump has been drained, first turn the engine over so that the sump is uppermost and fit wooden blocks to support the engine in this position.
2   Remove the 24 bolts securing the oil sump to the crankcase and remove the sump. If the sump is stuck to the crankcase, it may be levered off carefully.
3   To remove the sump with the engine in the car, first remove the oil dipstick.
4   Remove the bolts securing the fan shroud to the radiator and place the shroud over the fan.
5   Disconnect the battery leads.
6   Slacken the alternator mounting bolts and remove the fan belt.
7   Chock the rear wheels.
8   Place a container of at least 12 US pints (5.7 litres) under the sump. Remove the drain plug, allow the oil to drain, then refit the plug.
9   Remove the cables from the starter motor terminals, having noted the terminals to which they are attached. Remove the three fixing bolts from the starter motor and lift the motor away.
10   Undo and remove the bolts and spring washers securing the splash shield.
11   Remove the engine front support nuts.
12   Raise the engine and place wood blocks between the engine front supports and the chassis brackets.
13   Remove the clutch or converter housing cover.
14   Remove the attachment bolts and if necessary prise the sump off.

16 Front cover – removal

1   Remove the crankcase sump as described in Section 15.
2   Drain the cooling system, remove the radiator and cooling fan.

3   Remove the alternator and drive belts.
4   Remove the water pump and the water hoses.
5   Remove the crankshaft pulley as described in Section 13.
6   Remove the guide sleeves from the cylinder block (Fig. 1.8).
7   Remove the bolts securing the front cover and if necessary tap the cover gently with a plastic hammer to break the gasket seal.
8   If the gasket is damaged and needs renewing, it will be necessary to remove the two front coverplate retaining bolts and then remove the front cover plate and the old gasket (Fig. 1.9).

17 Timing gears – removal

1   Remove the front cover to expose the timing gears.
2   Remove the bolt and washer securing the large gear to the camshaft, then pull the gear off and remove the Woodruff key.
3   Draw the gear from the crankshaft (Fig. 1.10) and remove the Woodruff key.

18 Camshaft – removal

1   The camshaft may be removed with the engine in the car, if the following preparatory work is carried out.
2   Drain the cooling system and remove the radiator.
3   Remove the spark plug leads from the spark plugs. Remove the distributor cap and lay it to one side.
4   Detach the distributor vacuum pipe and low tension connections and remove the distributor as described in Chapter 4.
5   Disconnect the leads from the alternator, remove the alternator and drive belt.
6   Undo and remove the screws securing the rocker covers and lift off the rocker covers and their gaskets.
7   Progressively loosen the three bolts securing each rocker shaft. Remove the bolts and washers and lift off the rocker assemblies noting which cylinder bank each was removed from.
8   Remove the push rods, laying them out in order and with the set of rocker gear which they operate, so that each rod is refitted in the position from which it was removed, then remove the cylinder heads as described in Section 9.
9   Use a magnet to lift out the tappets and place every tappet with the push rod which it operates.
10   Remove the crankcase sump, the front cover and the camshaft gear as already described.
11   Remove the two screws securing the camshaft thrust plate and remove the plate and spacer.
12   Pull the camshaft forward to withdraw it, taking care to keep the shaft in line, so that the edges of the cams do not damage the camshaft bearings (Fig. 1.11).

19 Oil pump – removal

1   Remove the crankcase sump as already described.
2   Remove the bolt attaching the oil screen to the main bearing cap.
3   Remove the two bolts securing the oil pump to the crankcase and withdraw the pump assembly and its drive shaft (Fig. 1.12).

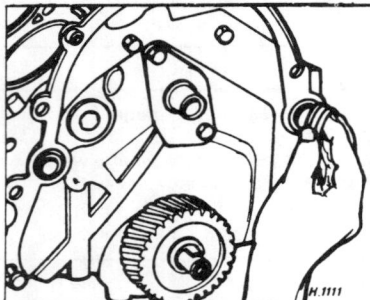

Fig. 1.8 Removing the guide sleeves

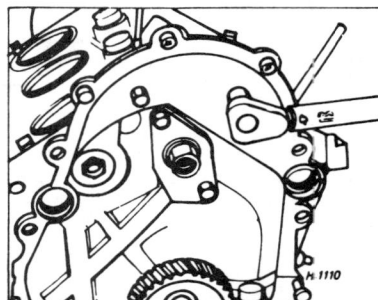

Fig. 1.9 Removing the front cover retaining bolts

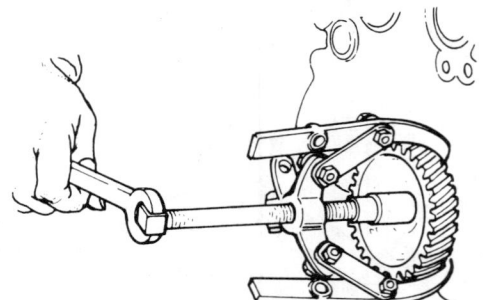

Fig. 1.10 Removing the crankshaft timing gear

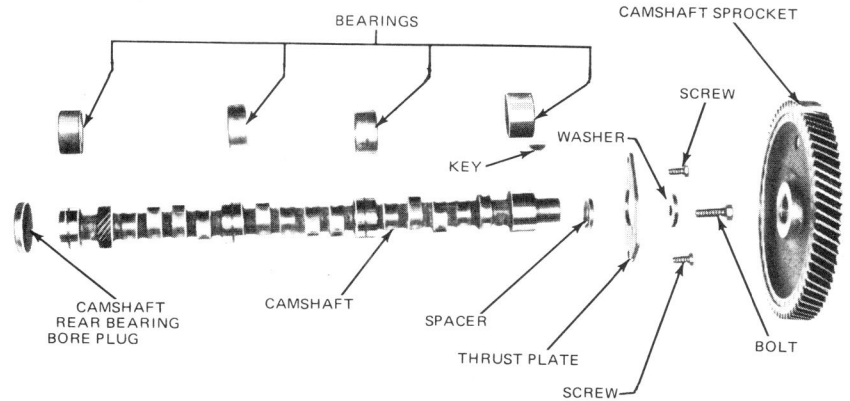

Fig. 1.11 Camshaft components and
drive sprocket

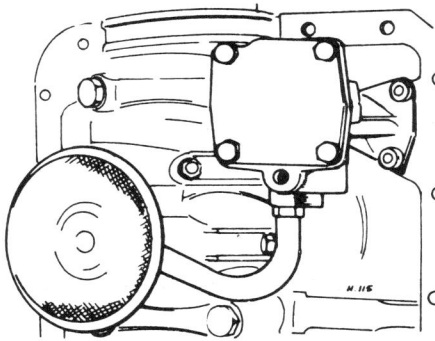

Fig. 1.12 Oil pump and inlet pipe

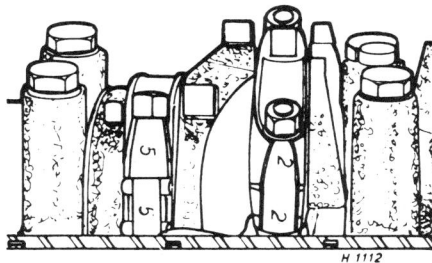

Fig. 1.13 Connecting rod bearing identification

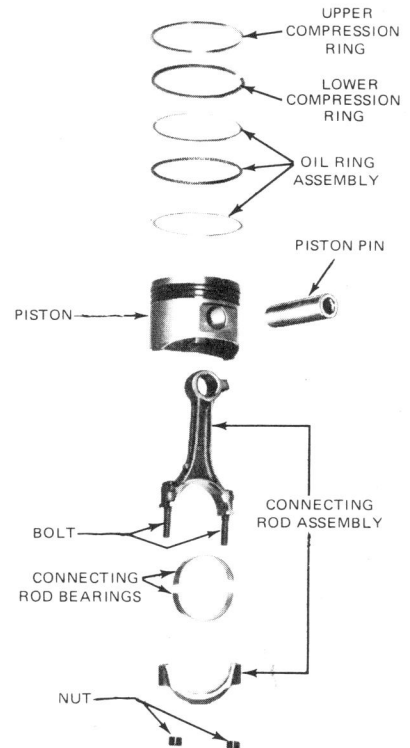

Fig. 1.14 Piston and connecting rod assembly

20 Pistons, connecting rods and bearings – removal

1   If the crankcase sump and the cylinder heads are removed, the pistons and connecting rods can be removed with the engine in the car. The bearing shells can be removed without removing the cylinder heads.

2   Before removing any connecting rod cap, make sure that the cylinder number is marked on both parts (Fig. 1.13). If no marking is visible, put mating marks on the joint before removing the bolts.

3   Turn the crankshaft until the connecting rod being removed is at its lowest position.

4   Remove the connecting rod nuts and pull off the bearing cap.

5   Rotate the crankshaft until the connecting rod being removed is in its highest position then use the handle of a hammer to push the assembly out of the top of the cylinder (Fig. 1.14).

6   Withdraw the assembly from the cylinder and place the bearing cap back on the connecting rod.

7   If the bearings are being renewed, remove the old bearings by sliding them round until the notch in the bearing shell is disengaged from the recess in the bearing seating and then lift the bearing out. If the bearings are removed and the same ones are being used again, it is vital that they are refitted in the same seating as the one from which they were removed.

21 Piston rings – removal

1   Piston rings are very brittle and are easily broken, so it is better not to remove the piston rings unless new ones are being fitted.

2   Insert an old feeler gauge between the piston ring and the piston and slide it round the piston until the feeler gauge is diametrically opposite the piston ring joint.

3   Lift the two ends of the piston ring out of the groove and rest them on the surface of the piston immediately above the ring groove.

4   Carefully slide the piston ring upwards, taking care to keep it parallel with the piston crown, and finally lift it off the top of the piston. If the rings are being put back onto the pistons, make sure that each

ring is refitted the same way up as it was before removal and is fitted to the groove from which it was removed.

5   The oil ring assembly comprises three pieces, two oil control rings and an expander. Remove the upper oil control ring first, then the expander and finally the lower oil control ring.

22 Gudgeon pin – removal

The gudgeon pin is of the semi-floating type, – that is, it is a tight fit in the connecting rod and a sliding fit in the piston. The gudgeon pins should not be removed unless a mandrel press is available, because damage to the pistons will be caused. If neither the piston nor the connecting rod is being renewed, it is better not to separate them. If one or the other is being changed, it is better to have the job done by a garage with the necessary equipment.

23 Crankshaft rear oil seal – removal

1   To remove the oil seal with the engine in the car, first remove the gearbox, or automatic transmission, as detailed in Chapter 6. On manual transmission models, it is then necessary to remove the clutch assembly as described in Chapter 5.
2   Remove the flywheel, flywheel housing and rear plate and the oil seal will then be exposed.
3   Punch two small holes in the seal, on opposite sides of the crankshaft and just above the bearing cap to cylinder block joint line. Screw a long self-tapping screw into each hole (Fig. 1.15) then using a large screwdriver under the head of each screw and a piece of wood against the cylinder block as a fulcrum, carefully lever the seal out. Take great care not to scratch, or damage, the surface of the oil seal seating.

Fig. 1.15 Removing the crankshaft rear oil seal

24 Crankshaft and main bearings – removal

1   Remove the engine from the car.
2   Remove the clutch assembly on manual transmission models.
3   Remove the flywheel, flywheel housing and rear plate.
4   Make sure that the crankcase sump has been drained, then turn the engine upside down, chock it securely and remove the crankcase sump.
5   Remove the crankshaft pulley and the engine front cover.
6   Remove the oil pump and strainer, leaving the oil pump drive shaft in position.
7   Check that all the main and connecting rod bearing caps have their identifying numbers stamped on, so that they can be refitted in their original positions.
8   If the crankshaft is to be reground, or if a different crankshaft is being fitted, remove the crankshaft gear.
9   Remove the two nuts and the bearing cap of each connecting rod in turn and lay out the bearing caps in order.
10   Remove the two bolts from each of the main bearing caps, lift the caps off and lay them out in order.
11   Slide the rear oil seal off the crankshaft and discard it.
12   Carefully lift the crankshaft out of the upper bearings, taking care to keep it parallel with the crankcase, so that the thrust bearing surfaces are not damaged.
13   Remove the bearing inserts from the cylinder block and place each one with its bearing cap to identify its position if they are to be refitted (Fig. 1.16).

25 Engine components – examination for wear

When the engine has been stripped down and all the parts have been cleaned, they should be examined for wear. In cases where no definite wear limit is given, it must be a matter of judgment on whether or not a part is to be renewed or refitted, taking into consideration the further life expected from the engine, the degree of reliability required, the cost of the new part and the amount of dismantling which will be necessary to renew the part later.

26 Crankshaft – examination and renovation

1   Examine the four main bearing journals and the six crankpins, which should all be smooth and highly polished. If there are any deep grooves, or deep scratches and there is a similar deterioration in the corresponding bearing shells, the crankshaft should be reground.
2   If the journals are in good condition and it is suspected that the crankshaft may be sufficiently worn to require regrinding, it is worth seeking the advice of a main Ford agent, or crankshaft regrinding service.
3   If the crankshaft is reground, the works will also supply the new bearings which will be required to match the journal diameters.

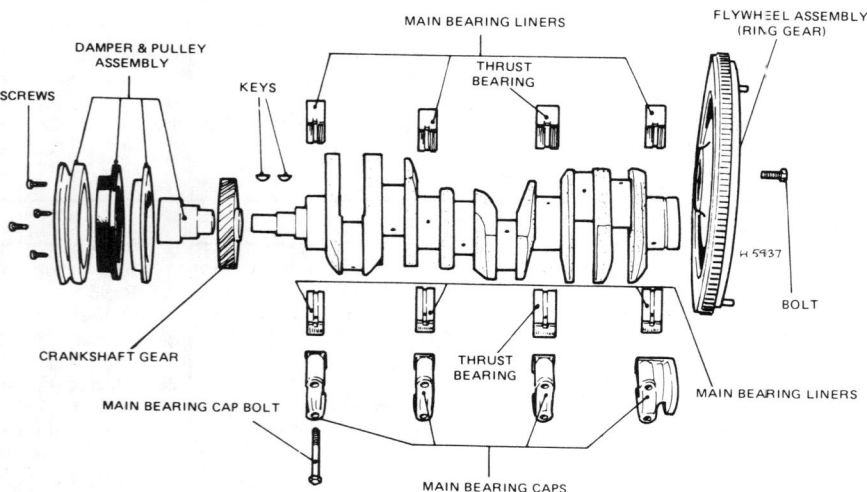

Fig. 1.16 Crankshaft and flywheel assembly

27 Clutch pilot bearing – removal and renewal

1   If the crankshaft has been removed, the clutch pilot bearing should be renewed on manual transmission cars.

2   Remove the bearing from the end of the crankshaft by improvising an impact extractor with a hooked end to pass through the bore of the bearing. Alternatively, select a bolt with a head just large enough to pass through the bore of the bearing. Hook the bolt head onto the rear face of the bearing, place a suitable sized socket over the bolt, so that the bore of the socket is of larger diameter than the bearing and screw a nut on to the bolt to draw the bearing out.

3   Coat the pilot bearing bore of the crankshaft with a small quantity of wheel bearing lubricant.

4   Tap the new bearing into place with the bearing seal facing the transmission.

28 Cylinder bores – examination and renovation

1   A new cylinder is perfectly round and the walls parallel throughout its length. The action of the pistons tends to wear the walls at right angles to the gudgeon pin due to side thrust. This wear takes place principally on that section of the cylinder swept by the piston rings.

2   It is possible to get an indication of bore wear by removing the cylinder heads with the engine still in the car. With the piston down in the bore, first signs of wear can be seen and felt just below the top of the bore where the top piston ring reaches and there will be a noticeable lip. If there is no lip it is reasonable to expect that bore wear is low and any lack of compression or excessive oil consumption is due to worn or broken piston rings or pistons (See next Section).

3   If it is possible to obtain a bore measuring micrometer, measure the bore in the thrust plane below the lip and again at the bottom of the cylinder in the same plane. If the difference is more than 0.003 inch (0.0762 mm) then rebore is necessary. Similarly, a difference of 0.003 inch (0.0762 mm) or more across the bore diameter is a sign of ovality calling for a rebore.

4   Any bore which is significantly scratched or scored, will need reboring. This symptom usually indicates that the piston or rings are damaged in that cylinder. In the event of only one cylinder being in need of reboring it will still be necessary for all six to be bored and fitted with new oversize pistons and rings. Your Ford dealer or local engineering specialist will be able to rebore and obtain the necessary matched pistons.

29 Pistons and piston rings – examination

1   Worn pistons and rings result in low compression and an increased oil consumption, indicated by the smoky appearance of the exhaust. A compression tester, which fits into a spark plug hole will indicate whether the compression is normal, or poor, without the need for any engine dismantling.

2   Another indication of piston wear is 'piston slap', a knocking noise which can be heard when the engine is ticking over, but which is not so pronounced when engine speed is increased.

3   Piston ring wear can be checked by first removing the rings from the pistons, as described in Section 21. Place the rings in the cylinder bores from the top, pushing them down about 1.5 inches (38.1 mm) with the head of a piston (from which the rings have been removed) so that they rest square in the cylinder (Fig. 1.17). Measure the gap at the ends of the ring with a feeler gauge. If it exceeds 0.023 in (0.584 mm) for the two top compression rings, or 0.055 in (1.397 mm) for the oil control ring, new rings should be fitted.

4   The groove in which the rings locate in the piston can also become enlarged in use. The clearance between ring and piston, in the groove, should not exceed 0.004 inch (0.1016 mm) for the top two compression rings and 0.003 inch (0.0762 mm) for the lower oil control ring (Fig. 1.18).

5   When new pistons are fitted, their weight must be checked to make certain that the weights of all six pistons with their connecting rod assemblies are all within 8 grms of each other, to maintain engine balance.

30 Connecting rods and gudgeon pins – inspection

1   The gudgeon pins are an interference fit in the connecting rods and should not be separated unless new pistons are being fitted.

2   New pistons will be supplied with new gudgeon pins and should be fitted by a garage having the correct equipment for pressing the pins.

3   Connecting rods are not subject to wear, but in extreme circumstances, such as engine seizure, they can be distorted.

4   Check the connecting rods for obvious signs of distortion and if any are suspect, have them checked by a Ford dealer.

5   Check that no attempt has been made to file the bearing caps to adjust bearing clearance. Any connecting rods which show signs of filing, should be scrapped.

31 Camshaft and camshaft bearings – inspection and renewal

1   The maximum permissible clearance for the camshaft bearings is 0.006 in (0.015 mm). If the clearance is greater than this, the camshaft journals should be reground and new undersized camshaft bushes fitted.

2   The removal and refitting of camshaft bushes requires special tools and should be entrusted to a Ford dealer, or a workshop which undertakes camshaft renovation.

3   Any small burrs on the camshaft may be removed with a very fine oil stone, but no attempt should be made to remove ridges resulting from wear. If the cam lobes are excessively worn, or if the skew gear is excessively worn, or damaged, a new camshaft must be fitted.

4   Check the lift of the camshaft lobes either with the camshaft mounted between centres, or with the camshaft in the engine with the tappets and push rods fitted (Fig. 1.19). The camshaft should not be renewed unless the lobe lift is 0.005 in (0.013 mm) less than the value given in the Specification.

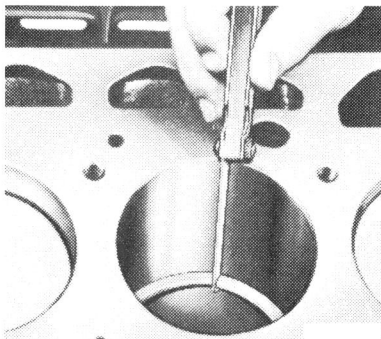

Fig. 1.17 Measuring piston ring gap   Fig. 1.18 Measuring piston ring groove clearance   Fig. 1.19 Checking camshaft lobe lift

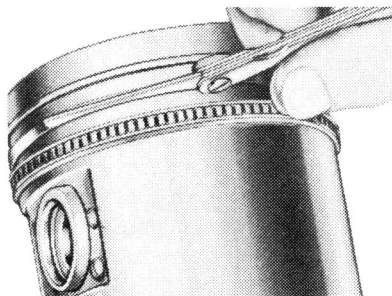

32 Tappets – inspection

1   Clean the tappets thoroughly, to remove all traces of gummy deposits and wipe them with a lint free cloth.
2   Check that the tappets are not scored, or have grooves worn in them and renew any tappet which is badly worn.
3   Check to see whether the bottom of the tappets is convex. If the bottom surface has worn smooth, but is not scored, it may be re-used but with the original camshaft only.

33 Valves and valve seats – inspection and reconditioning

1   Examine the valves for pits and grooves and the valve stems for excessive wear or distortion.
2   Examine the valve head for signs of burning of the valve seats and check the fit of the valves in the valve guides, to see if the valve guides are worn.
3   Worn valve guides can be reamed out and valves with oversize stems fitted. Valves are available with stems which are 0.008 in, 0.016 in and 0.032 in oversize. If a valve guide has been reamed out, the corresponding valve seat must be refaced.
4   Valves and valve seats which show little sign of wear, can be lapped in.
5   To lap the valves, fit a suction type grinding tool to the valve head, smear a little coarse carborundum grinding paste on to the seating face of the valve and insert the valve into the cylinder head. Rub the stem of the valve grinding tool between the palms of the hands, so that the valve is rotated backwards and forwards. When it is felt that cutting has ceased, lift the valve, rotate it through 90°, lower it and repeat the grinding operation, redistributing the grinding paste on the seat if necessary. Continue the process until a matt grey band is produced around the complete periphery of both the valve and the valve seat.
6   Repeat the operation using fine grinding paste, to obtain a finer finish, then clean both the valves and the valve seats to remove all traces of grinding paste.
7   If it is convenient to take the cylinder head and the valves to a workshop with the necessary equipment, it is far better to have all the valves and their seats refaced, so that all the valves and seats are at the correct angle and have the correct width of contact.

34 Timing gears – inspection

1   Inspect the gear teeth for damage, or signs of excessive wear, which will cause noisy operation.
2   Check for signs of excessive run-out of the gears, which will show up as an uneven contact area on the teeth.
3   Check the run-out (Fig. 1.20), which should not exceed 0.007 in (0.018 mm) and if in excess of this, remove the gear and check for burrs, or dirt, between the gear and the camshaft flange. If the run-out still exceeds the specifications, a new gear must be fitted.
4   The backlash between the camshaft gear and the crankshaft gear must not exceed 0.010 in (0.254 mm).

35 Flywheel and ring gear – inspection and renewal

1   Inspect the flywheel for damage and check that the ring gear does not have any broken or badly worn teeth.

Manual transmission

2   If the ring gear is damaged, remove it from the flywheel by cutting a notch between two teeth, using a hacksaw, then splitting the gear with a cold chisel. Polish four equally spaced sections of the new gear, place it on a heat resistant surface, such as firebricks and heat the gear with a blow torch until the polished spots are a light straw yellow colour (400°F 204°C). Take care not to heat the gear higher than this, because its wear resistance will be lowered. Place the hot gear over the flywheel rim, with the chamfered edge of the gear towards the shoulder on the flywheel. Quickly tap the gear onto the flywheel as far as it will go and allow it to cool naturally. Do not attempt to accelerate cooling by quenching.
3   If the friction surface of the flywheel is scored, it can be machined and up to 0.045 in (0.114 mm) may be removed from the original thickness of the flywheel. Beyond this limit of machining, a damaged flywheel must be discarded.

Automatic transmission

4   If the flywheel, or the teeth of the ring gear are worn, or damaged, a new flywheel and ring gear assembly must be fitted.

36 Oil pump – dismantling, inspection and reassembly

1   Remove the two bolts and take the pick-up tube and screen assembly off the pump housing.
2   Remove the two screws from the oil pump cover, lift the cover off and remove the two-piece rotor assembly.
3   Drill a small hole in the centre of the pressure relief valve plug, screw an appropriate size of self-tapping screw into the hole and pull the plug from the housing. Remove the pressure relief valve spring and valve (Fig. 1.21).
4   Wash all the parts, use a brush to clean the inside of the pump housing and the pressure relief valve chamber and make sure that all particles of dirt and metal are removed. Allow the parts to dry naturally, or blow them dry.
5   Check the inside of the pump housing, the outer race and the rotor for damage and excessive wear.
6   Examine the mating surface of the pump cover for wear. If the cover is scored, grooved, or shows any sign of wear a new cover must be fitted.
7   Measure the outer race to housing clearance (Fig. 1.22) which must not exceed 0.012 in (0.3 mm).
8   With the rotor assembly fitted in the housing, place a straight edge over the end of the housing and measure the rotor end play. If this exceeds 0.004 in (0.012 mm), the outer race, shaft and rotor must be renewed as an assembly (Fig. 1.23).
9   Check the drive shaft to housing bearing clearance, by measuring the outside diameter of the shaft and the inside diameter of the housing bearing, which must not exceed 0.003 in (0.075 mm).

Fig. 1.20 Checking timing gear run out

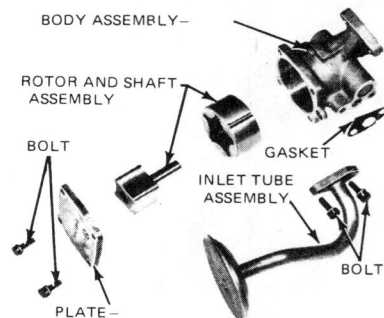

Fig. 1.21 Oil pump components

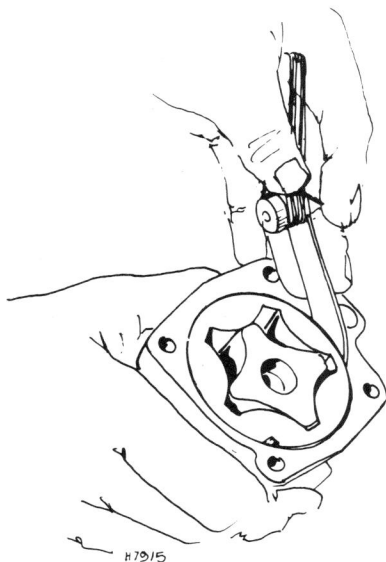

Fig. 1.22 Measuring oil pump rotor clearance

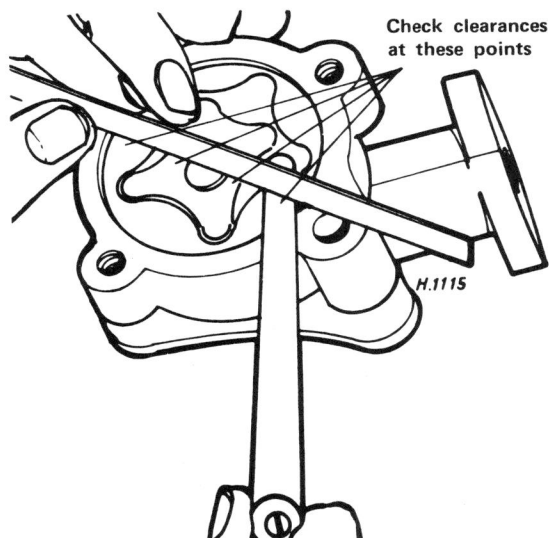

Check clearances at these points

Fig. 1.23 Measuring oil pump rotor end clearance

10 Check that the relief valve spring has not collapsed or been damaged, and that the spring tension is 14 lb (6.4 kg) when its length is 1.4 in (35.6 mm).
11 Check that the relief valve piston is not damaged and that the clearance between the piston and its bore does not exceed 0.003 in (0.075 mm).
12 Apply engine oil to the relief valve plunger and spring and insert them into the housing.
13 Fit a new relief valve retaining plug, push the plug into the housing until it bottoms, ensuring that the flat end of the plug is on the outside. Use a 0.5 in (12.3 mm) diameter drift and a hammer to spread the end of the plug, so that it does not come out accidentally.
14 Fit the inner and outer rotors and shaft assembly so that the dot marks on them are uppermost, then lubricate both rotors with engine oil.
15 Fit the cover and tighten the attachment screws. Check that the rotor moves freely after the cover screws have been tightened.
16 Refit the pick-up tube and strainer assembly to the pump body, using a new gasket and refit and tighten the fixing screws.

37 Decarbonising – cylinder head and piston crowns

1 When the cylinder heads are removed, either in the course of an overhaul or for inspection of bores or valve condition when the engine is in the car, it is normal to remove all carbon deposits from the piston crowns and head.
2 This is best done with a cup shaped wire brush and an electric drill and is fairly straightforward when the engine is dismantled and the pistons removed. Sometimes hard spots of carbon are not easily removed except by a scraper. When cleaning the pistons with a scraper, take care not to damage the surface of the piston in any way.
3 When the engine is in the car, certain precautions must be taken when decarbonising the pistons' crowns in order to prevent dislodged pieces of carbon falling into the interior of the engine which could cause damage to cylinder bores, piston and rings – or, if allowed into the water passages, damage to the water pump. Turn the engine so that the piston being worked on is at the top of its stroke and then mask off the adjacent cylinder bores and all surrounding water jacket orifices with paper and adhesive tape. Press grease into the gap all round the piston to keep carbon particles out and then scrape all carbon away by hand. Do not use a power drill and wire brush when the engine is in the car as it will virtually be impossible to keep all the carbon dust clear of the engine. When completed, carefully clear out the grease around the rim of the piston with a matchstick or something similar – bringing any carbon particles with it. Repeat the process on the other piston crown. It is not recommended that a ring of carbon is left round the edge of the piston on the theory that it will aid oil consumption. This was valid in the earlier days of long stroke low revving engines but modern engines, fuels and lubricants cause less carbon deposits anyway and any left behind tend merely to cause hot spots.

38 Rocker gear – inspection

1 Check the clearance between each rocker arm and its shaft, by checking the inside diameter of the rocker arm bore and the outside diameter of the shaft. If the clearance between any rocker arm and its shaft exceeds 0.030 in (0.75 mm), renew the shaft and/or the rocker arm.
2 Inspect the rocker shaft for straightness, scoring and scuffing.
3 Examine the pad at the valve end of the rocker arm for indications of excessive wear and scuffing. If the pad is grooved, do not attempt to grind out the marks, but fit a new rocker arm.

39 Engine reassembly – general

1 All the components of the engine must be clean and all traces of old gaskets and jointing compound must be removed. Ensure that the working area is clean and that in addition to having a set of socket spanners and the usual range of hand tools, the following are also available:

(a) *Complete set of new gaskets*
(b) *Supply of clean cotton rags*
(c) *An oil can filled with clean engine oil*
(d) *Torque spanner*
(e) *Any necessary new parts*

40 Engine reassembly – camshaft

1 Oil the camshaft journals with engine oil and apply Lubriplate, or an equivalent lubricant to the cam lobes.
2 Insert the camshaft into the block, taking care not to damage the bearing surfaces of the shaft, or the shaft bearings.
3 Fit the spacer ring with its chamfered side inwards and insert the camshaft key.
4 Fit the camshaft thrust plate so that it covers the main oil gallery (Fig. 1.24) then insert the two fixing screws and tighten them to a torque of 12 to 15 lbf ft (1.7 to 2.1 kgf m).
5 Fit the camshaft gear, with the face having the timing mark towards the front. Refit the fixing bolt and washer and tighten the bolt to a torque of 30 to 36 lbf ft (4.2 to 5.0 kgf m).

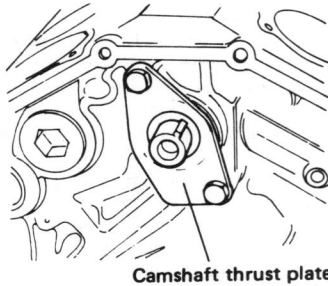

Camshaft thrust plate

Fig. 1.24 Fitting the camshaft thrust plate

6   Measure the endfloat of the camshaft between the rear face of the gear and the front of the cylinder block. If this exceeds 0.009 in (0.023 mm), correct it by fitting another thrust plate, or spacer. Thrust plates and spacers are both available in two different thicknesses.

41 Engine reassembly – crankshaft

1   With the engine upside down, lay each of the upper bearing halves on to the appropriate crankcase web, making sure that the locking tang on the bearing is properly engaged in the corresponding slot in the crankcase web. If the old bearings are being refitted, make certain that each bearing unit is refitted in the place from which it was removed. Fit the thrust washers to each side of No 3 bearing and retain them in place with grease.
2   Fit the four bearing halves to the appropriate bearing caps and secure the thrust washers in place with grease on either side of the No 3 bearing cap.
3   Lubricate the crankcase bearing halves with engine oil and carefully lower the crankshaft onto them.
4   Take each bearing cap in turn, lubricate its bearing half with engine oil. Apply engine oil to the crankshaft journal and fit the bearing cap. The bearing cap must be refitted in the position from which it was removed and the arrow on it must point towards the front of the engine (Fig. 1.25).
5   Insert the two retaining bolts and tighten them to the torque wrench setting given in the Specifications. Turn the crankshaft to ensure that it rotates freely before fitting another bearing cap. If the crankshaft does not rotate freely, remove the bearing cap and check that the bearing shells have seated properly and that the bearing cap is the correct one for that position.
6   When fitting the rear bearing cap, first coat its cylinder block joint face with jointing compound (Fig. 1.27). After fitting fit the wedge seals (Fig. 1.26).

42 Engine reassembly – oil pump refitting

1   Prime the pump by filling either the inlet, or the outlet port, with engine oil and then rotating the pump shaft to distribute the oil within the pump body.
2   Insert the pointed end of the pump drive shaft into the cylinder block. The pointed end is the one closest to the pressed-on flange.
3   Fit a new gasket, place the pump in position, engage the drive shaft and then insert and tighten the retaining bolts.
4   Refit the bolt securing the oil pick-up tube to the main bearing cap and tighten it to the torque wrench setting given in the Specifications.

43 Crankshaft rear oil seal and flywheel – fitting

1   Smear engine oil onto the surface of the oil seal which contacts the cylinder block. Lubricate the crankshaft surface in contact with the seal and also the lip of the seal.
2   Offer the seal up so that the open face of the seal is towards the engine and carefully slide the seal over the end of the crankshaft.
3   Carefully enter the seal into its housing, ensuring that it is square, then tap the seal fully home using a hammer and a block of wood.
4   Fit the flywheel, or starter ring on automatic transmission models. Insert the six bolts and tighten them to the torque wrench setting given in the Specifications.

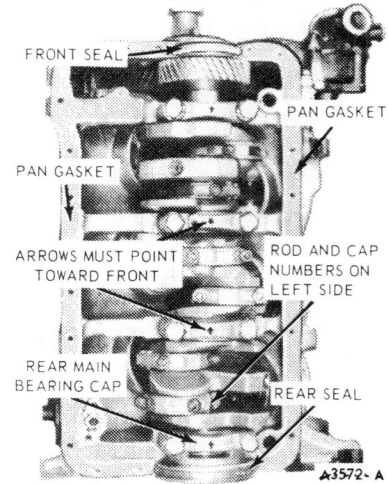

FRONT SEAL

PAN GASKET

PAN GASKET

ARROWS MUST POINT TOWARD FRONT

ROD AND CAP NUMBERS ON LEFT SIDE

REAR MAIN BEARING CAP

REAR SEAL

A3572-A

Fig. 1.25 Underside view of engine

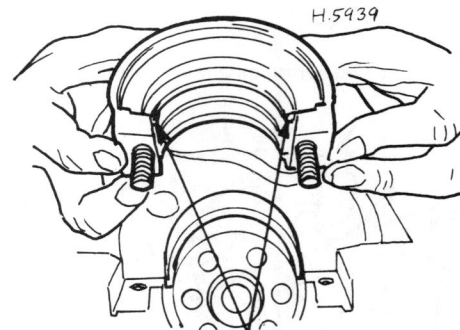

H.5939

APPLY SEALER TO THESE SURFACES

Fig 1.26 Rear crankshaft bearing sealing faces

WEDGE SEALS

A3578-A

Fig. 1.27 Fitting the rear bearing wedge seals

44 Pistons and connecting rods – refitting

1   If new piston rings are being fitted and the cylinders have not been rebored, the glaze on the cylinder bores should be removed by scuffing them with very fine abrasive paper. The piston rings should be fitted in accordance with the manufacturer's instructions, but before being fitted to the piston, they must be inserted into the cylinder about half way down the bore to check that the ring gap is at least 0.015 in (0.38 mm).

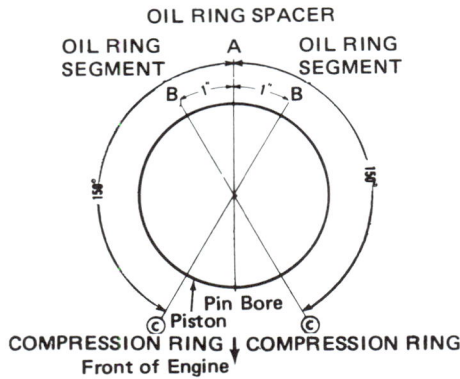

Fig. 1.28 Piston ring gap positions

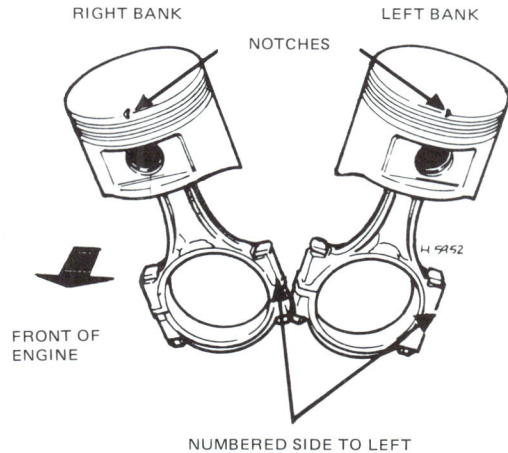

Fig. 1.29 Correct positions for pistons and connecting rods

2   The connecting rods and bearing caps are numbered from 1 to 3 in the right bank and from 4 to 6 in the left bank. Refit the bearing halves which were removed from each connecting rod, or fit new bearings, taking care that the tang on the bearing is properly fitted into the slot in the connecting rod end.

3   Arrange the gaps in the piston rings as shown in Fig. 1.28. Oil the piston ring grooves generously and fit a piston ring compressor to the piston, ensuring that all the rings are compressed.

4   Lubricate the bearing surface and the cylinder bore and insert the piston into the bore, ensuring that the piston is returned to its correct bore and that the arrow on the piston crown is pointing towards the front of the engine (Fig. 1.29). The engine should be resting on its side.

5   Guide the connecting rod towards the crankshaft journal to avoid damage and if necessary tap the piston crown lightly with the wooden handle of a hammer to assist entering the piston rings into the bore (Fig. 1.30). This operation must be done with caution, to avoid breaking any piston rings.

6   Refit the bearing which was removed, or fit a new bearing to the connecting rod cap which bears the same number as the connecting rod and lubricate the bearing.

7   Fit the bearing cap so that its number mates with the number on the connecting rod. Press the piston down so that the connecting rod bearing seats on the crankshaft journal. Fit the connecting rod nuts and tighten to the torque wrench setting given in the Specifications.

8   Rotate the crankshaft to ensure that each bearing is free before proceeding further, then check that the side clearance between the connecting rod and the crankshaft journal is between 0.004 and 0.011 in (0.10 and 0.28 mm).

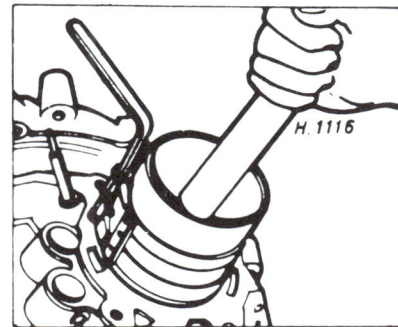

Fig. 1.30 Fitting the pistons

2   Insert the wedge seals between the rear main bearing cap and the rim of the crankcase (Fig. 1.27).

3   Apply jointing compound to the rim of the sump and fit the two pieces of the sump gasket.

4   Apply jointing compound to the curved surfaces of the front and rear end seals (Fig. 1.25). Place the seals so that they are in line with the mounting flange of the sump, making sure that the tabs on the seals are over the sump gasket.

5   Position the sump on the crankcase and fit the four bolts shown in Fig. 1.31. Fit the remaining bolts and tighten them progressively in the sequence shown to the torque wrench setting given in the Specifications.

45 Crankcase sump – refitting

1   Ensure that the gasket surfaces of both the sump and the crankcase are clean and that the sealing surface of the sump is not distorted.

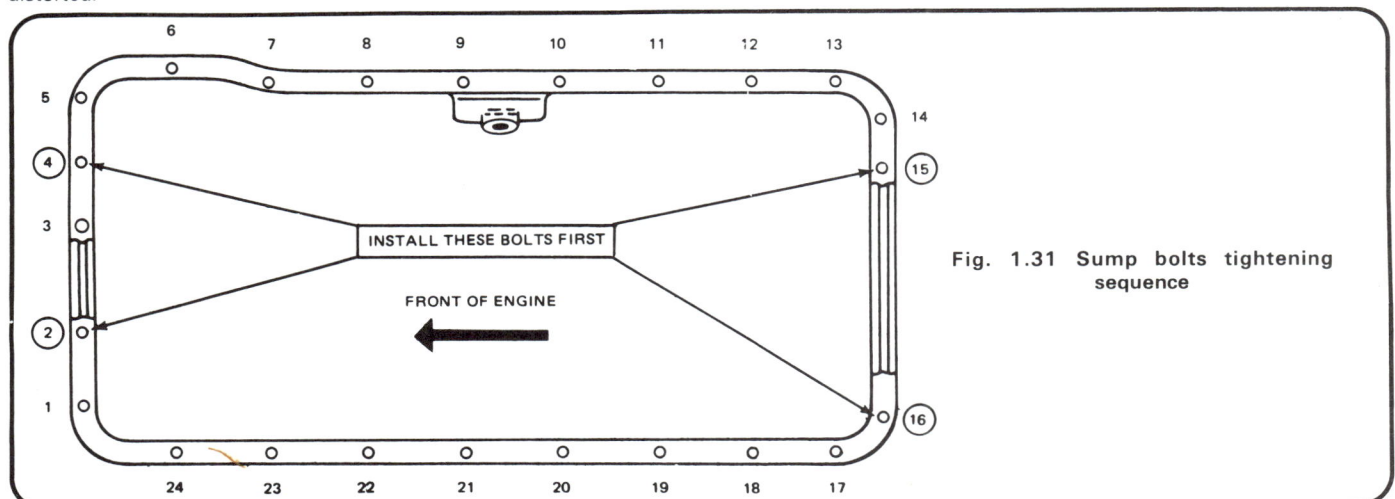

Fig. 1.31 Sump bolts tightening sequence

46 Cylinder head – reassembly

1   Lay the cylinder head on its side, lubricate every valve guide with engine oil and insert the valves into the guide from which they were removed.
2   To avoid damaging the lip of the valve stem oil seal, wrap a piece of adhesive tape, or foil, round the groove of every valve stem. Slide the seals over the valve stems and push them over the tops of the valve guides.
3   Remove the adhesive tape, or foil, from the valve stems.
4   Fit the valve spring over the valve, with the close coiled end towards the cylinder head, then fit the spring retainer on top of the spring.
5   Using a valve spring compressor, compress the spring just enough to insert the two split collets. If the valve spring is compressed too far, there is a danger of the spring retainer damaging the valve stem oil seal.
6   After inserting the split collets, release the spring compressor and remove it.
7   Check that the split collets have seated properly and tap the top of the valve stem lightly with a plastic headed hammer to ensure this.
8   When all the valves have been fitted, measure the length of each valve spring from the surface of the cylinder head spring pad to the underside of the spring retainer using dividers (Fig. 1.32).
9   Check the dividers against a scale and if the assembled height is greater than $1\frac{39}{64}$ in (40.878 mm), remove the spring and fit the necessary spacer(s) between the cylinder head spring pad and the valve spring, to bring the assembled height to within $1\frac{37}{64}$ in (40.084 mm) and $1\frac{39}{64}$ in (40.878 mm). Do not fit spacers unless necessary. Compression of the valve springs below the minimum dimension will result in overstressing the valve springs and the risk of spring breakage, as well as excessive wear on the camshaft lobes.

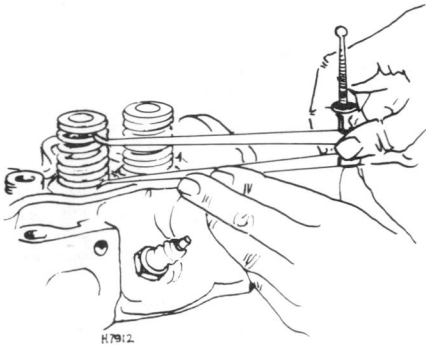

Fig. 1.32 Checking the valve spring installed height

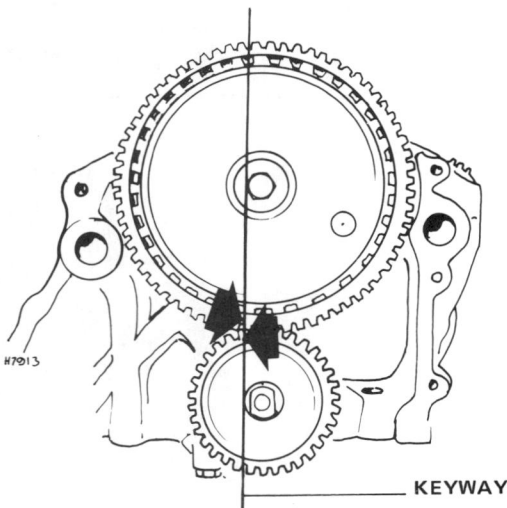

Fig. 1.33 Aligning the timing marks

47 Engine reassembly – crankshaft gear, front cover and water pump

1   Insert the crankshaft key and turn the crankshaft until the keyway is in the position shown in Fig. 1.33.
2   Turn the camshaft gear until the timing mark is as shown, then fit the crankshaft gear so that the timing marks are in line with the common tangent to the two shafts.
3   Use a plastic headed hammer to tap the crankshaft gear fully into mesh with the camshaft gear.
4   Support the front cover on blocks of wood placed or either side of the front oil seal mounting. Smear the outside rim of the seal with engine oil and enter it into its mounting, ensuring that the open face of the seal is inwards.
5   Ensure that the seal is square with the face of the front cover, then place a block of wood over the seal and tap it, to drive the seal fully home.
6   Apply jointing compound to the gasket surfaces of the cylinder block and rear face of the front cover plate. Position the gasket and front cover plate. Temporarily fit four front cover screws to hold the gasket in place, then fit the two front cover attachment bolts and tighten them to the torque wrench setting given in the Specifications.
7   If the guide sleeves were removed, fit new ring seals and refit the sleeves without using jointing compound (Fig. 1.8).
8   Apply jointing compound to the front cover gasket surface and place the gasket in position on the front cover.
9   Place the front cover on the engine and insert all the retaining screws, entering them two or three turns.
10 Centralise the cover with the crankshaft pulley, then tighten the front cover retaining bolts to the torque wrench setting given in the Specifications.
11 Apply jointing compound to both sides of a new water pump gasket and place the gasket on the water pump.
12 Position the water pump assembly on to the front cover and retain it with two bolts, finger tight. Remove any jointing compound from the water inlet sealing surfaces.
13 Apply jointing compound to both sides of a new water inlet gasket and fit the gasket to the water inlet housing.
14 Fit the thermostat and its rubber gasket. Position the water inlet housing and by-pass flange to the water pump and fit the attachment bolts. Tighten the bolts to the torque wrench setting given in the Specifications. When fitting the water pump bolts, note that there are different length bolts and fit the correct length.

48 Cylinder heads – refitting

1   If the tappets were removed, lubricate the tappets and their bores with engine oil and insert the tappets with their dished ends uppermost. Ensure that every tappet is refitted into the bore from which it was taken.
2   Place the cylinder head gaskets in position on the cylinder block. The gaskets are marked with the words FRONT and TOP to ensure correct positioning. The left and right-hand head gaskets are different and non-interchangeable.
3   Lower the cylinder heads over their positioning studs (Fig. 1.34). Although the two cylinder heads are identical, they should have been marked when removed and should be refitted in their original positions.
4   Insert the cylinder head bolts finger-tight then tighten them progressively in the order shown in Fig. 1.4 until they are all at a torque of 29 to 40 lbf ft (4.1 to 5 kgf m).
5   Tighten all the bolts to 40 to 51 lbf ft (5.6 to 7.1 kgf m) then tighten them all to a final torque of 65 to 80 lbf ft (9.1 to 11.2 kgf m).

49 Rocker gear – refitting

1   Ensure that all the push rods are inserted into their proper places and that their lower ends are engaged in the cups of the tappets.
2   Slacken off all the valve adjusting screws on the rocker arms.
3   Lubricate all the moving surfaces of the push rods and rocker assembly with engine oil then refit the oil baffle and rocker shaft assembly onto the cylinder head, ensuring that the head of each adjusting screw engages in the cup of the appropriate push rod.

Fig. 1.34 Cylinder head guide studs

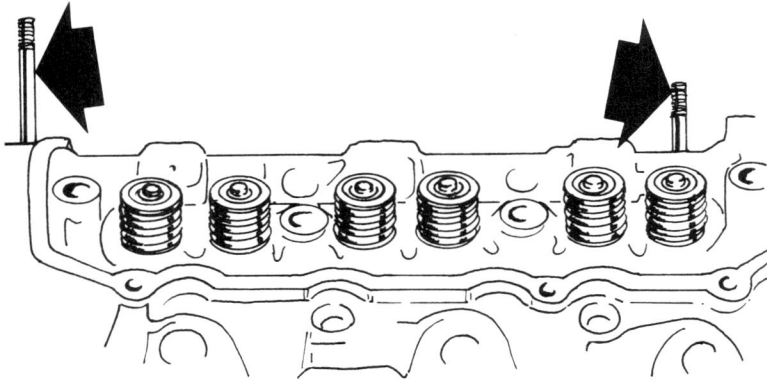

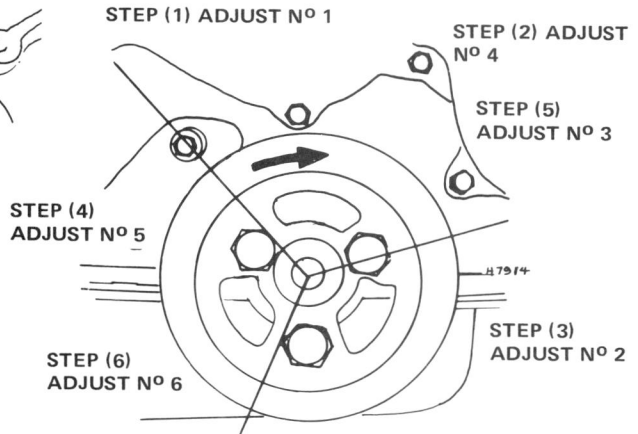

Fig. 1.35 Position of crankshaft for adjustment of valve clearances

4   Ensure that the notch in the end of the rocker shaft is downwards (Fig. 1.2).
5   Fit the rocker pedestal attachment bolts and tighten them two turns at a time until the torque wrench setting given in the Specifications is achieved.
6   Adjust the valve clearances as described in the following Section.
7   Fit the rocker covers, using new gaskets and ensuring that the gaskets are seated evenly all round the cylinder head. Fit the cover attachment bolts and tighten them to the torque wrench setting given in the Specifications.

50 Valve clearances – adjustment

1   The correct clearance between each valve rocker and its valve stem is important. Excessive clearance will result in unnecessary noise, and an incorrect setting, whether it is too great or too small, will have an adverse effect upon engine performance.
2   After renewing any component in the valve train and after an engine overhaul, it will be necessary to set the valve clearances with the engine cold, but as soon as possible afterwards they should be readjusted with the engine at normal operating temperature.
3   Remove the rocker arm covers and check that the rocker pedestal bolts are tightened to the torque wrench setting given in the Specifications.
4   Turn the engine until No 1 piston is at TDC on its compression stroke. This may be checked by making sure that the notch on the crankshaft pulley is opposite the TDC mark on the timing scale and the distributor rotor is pointing towards the ignition lead for No 1 cylinder.
5   Make three radial chalk marks on the crankshaft pulley at 120° intervals (Fig. 1.35).
6   If the crankshaft pulley is now turned to-and-fro a little, using a suitable spanner, it will be seen that the valves of cylinder No 1 or No 5 overlap, ie the rocker arms or pushrods on one cylinder move in opposite directions. If the valves of cylinder No 1 overlap adjust the valve clearances on cylinder No 5 or vice versa. If the procedure described in paragraph 4 has been followed, the valves on cylinder No 5 should be rocking and the valve clearances on cylinder No 1 should be checked. Adjust the valve clearances if necessary. Now crank the engine in its normal direction of rotation until the first chalk mark aligns with the TDC mark and check the next pair of cylinders according to the following table.

Valves rocking	Valves to adjust
No 5 cylinder	No 1 cylinder
No 3 cylinder	No 4 cylinder
No 6 cylinder	No 2 cylinder
No 1 cylinder	No 5 cylinder
No 4 cylinder	No 3 cylinder
No 2 cylinder	No 6 cylinder

7   Continue with this procedure until all valve clearances have been checked and, if necessary, adjusted. The clearances between the valves and the rockers with the engine hot are as given in the Specifications (Fig. 1.36).
8   The valve adjusting screws are self locking and will remain in the set position.

51 Inlet manifold – refitting

1   Apply jointing compound to the jointing surfaces and fit the intake manifold gasket into position. Make sure that the tab on the right bank

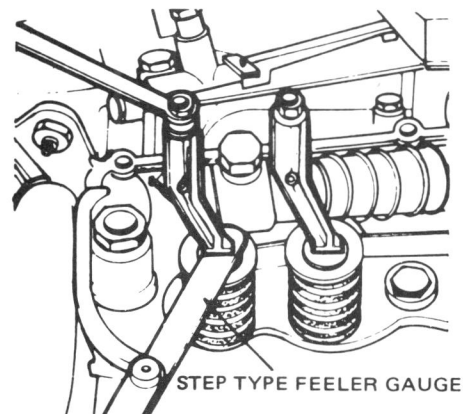

Fig. 1.36 Adjusting the valve clearances

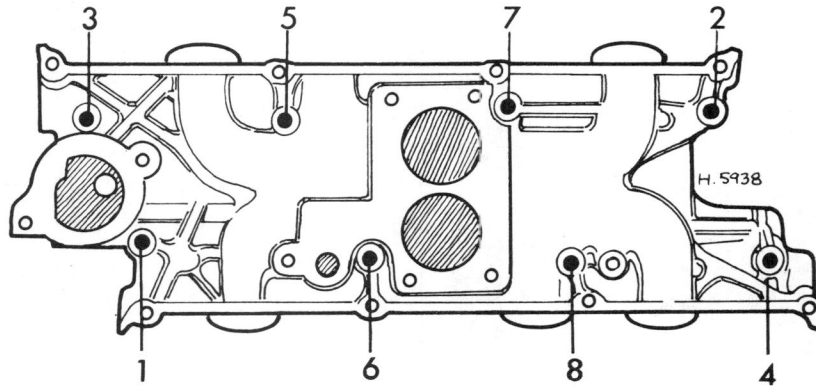

Fig. 1.37 Inlet manifold bolts tightening sequence

cylinder head gasket fits into the cutout on the manifold gasket.

2   Apply jointing compound under the heads of the retaining bolts, screw them home and tighten them in four steps in the sequence shown in Fig. 1.37. Firstly tighten all bolts to 3 to 6 lbf ft (0.42 to 0.84 kgf m) then increase the torque to 6 to 11 lbf ft (0.84 to 1.52 kgf m). The third stage of tightening should be 11 to 16 lbf ft (1.52 to 2.25 kgf m) before finally tightening to 15 to 18 lbf ft (2.1 to 2.5 kgf m) when the engine is hot.

52 Exhaust manifold – refitting

1   Apply a thin film of graphite grease to the exhaust manifold mating surfaces. No gasket is used for the exhaust manifold joint.
2   Position the manifold on the studs and screw on the attachment nuts.
3   Tighten the exhaust manifold nuts to the torque wrench setting given in the Specifications.

53 Oil filter – renewal

1   Place a drip tray under the filter.
2   Unscrew the filter from the adapter fitting using a strap wrench or a large pipe wrench.
3   Clean the filter adapter recess.
4   Coat the gasket of the new filter with engine oil and screw the filter in until the gasket is felt to contact the adapter face. Tighten the filter by hand a further half turn. Do not use any spanner or wrench to tighten the oil filter.
5   Add one quart of the correct grade of engine oil to the crankcase unless the filter is being renewed as part of an oil change.
6   Run the engine at fast idle speed and check for leaks. If leaks are experienced, check that the filter is the correct one and that the adapter flange is clean and undamaged.
7   Check the oil level and top up if necessary.

54 Engine – refitting

1   On manual transmission models, refit the clutch assembly as described in Chapter 5.
2   Sling the engine so that the rear is slightly lower than the front.
3   Protect the front and wings of the car with covers to prevent the paintwork from being scratched and then position the engine on a hoist over the engine compartment.
4   Lower the engine carefully, making certain that the exhaust manifolds are aligned with the exhaust pipe.

Manual transmission

5   Enter the primary drive shaft into the clutch assembly, taking care not to put any strain on the input shaft. To get the shaft to enter the clutch disc, it will probably be necessary to adjust the relative positions of the engine and gearbox to make sure that they are perfectly aligned. If the engine hangs up after the shaft enters the clutch assembly, lock the transmission by selecting a gear and then turn the crankshaft a

small amount to line up the splines of the clutch plate and gearbox shaft.

Automatic transmission

6   Ensure that the torque converter pilot enters the crankshaft.
7   Fit the converter, or bellhousing upper bolts, making sure that the dowels in the cylinder block are engaged in the housing.
8   Refit the engine front mountings, remove the lifting slings and remove the jack from beneath the transmission.
9   Refit the remaining engine to housing bolts and tighten them to a torque of 28 to 38 lbf ft (3.9 to 5.3 kgf m).
10   Refit the rear engine mounting crossmember and the nuts of the engine front mountings.
11   Reconnect the rubber insulator on the exhaust system front mounting. Reconnect the exhaust pipes to the exhaust manifold. Fit the nuts and tighten to a torque of 15 to 20 lbf ft (2.1 to 2.8 kgf m).
12   Clean the termination of the engine earth cable and its attachment point on the engine and reconnect the cable.
13   Refit the electrical connector on the choke thermostat housing. Refit the two hose connections and secure them with their clamps.
14   Fit the throttle linkage cable to the throttle bracket, ensuring that the tangs of the cable clip locate in the bracket. Fit the cable to the ball-stud and fit the cable-to-ball-stud retaining clip.
15   On cars with emission control systems, fit the emission control pipes and electrical connections to the carburettor and inlet manifold.
16   Refit the cable to the temperature gauge sender unit.
17   Refit and clamp the vacuum hose to the brake servo.
18   On models fitted with automatic transmission, refit the transmission vacuum pipe to the inlet manifold.
19   Reconnect the low and high voltage wires to the distributor and refit the vacuum connection.
20   Refit the heater hoses to the engine and clamp them. Refit the heater hose retainer to the rocker cover.
21   Remove the plugs from the ends of the fuel lines and reconnect them to the fuel pump.
22   On power steering models, refit the power steering pump bracket and the pump.
23   Refit the oil pressure gauge connection.
24   On models fitted with manual transmission, reconnect the clutch cable to the fork end of the operating lever and refit the rubber boot.
25   On models fitted with automatic transmission, reconnect the downshift linkage.
26   Refit the starter motor and reconnect the cables to the solenoid switch.
27   Refit the radiator, engine cooling fan and fan shroud. Connect and secure the radiator hoses and the transmission oil cooler pipes, if fitted.
28   Refit the alternator to the engine. Refit the electrical connections, then fit and tension the drive belt.
29   Fill the cooling system and check it for leaks.
30   Check that the sump drain plug is in place and tightened, then fill the sump to the correct level with engine oil.
31   Check that the transmission drain plug is in place and tightened, then fill the transmission to the correct level.
32   Position the bonnet hinge arms against the marks made before

removal and fit the retaining bolts.

33 Refit the air cleaner and intake duct.

34 Refit the battery and reconnect the battery leads.

55 Engine – initial start-up after major overhaul

1 Make sure that the battery is fully charged and that the coolant and all lubricants are at the correct level.

2 Ensure that the car has fuel. If the fuel system has been dismantled, it will take several revolutions of the engine by the starter motor to pump petrol through to the carburettor.

3 When the engine fires and runs, leave it running at a fast tick-over until it achieves normal working temperature. Do not run the engine at a speed greater than a fast tick-over.

4 As the engine warms up, look for oil and coolant leaks. Also check whether the exhaust connections are gas tight. Although there may be unusual smells and some smoke during this period, check to ensure that these are only due to normal causes such as excess oil burning off and parts achieving normal working temperature.

5 When the engine has reached its normal running temperature, adjust the idling speed as described in Chapter 3.

6 Stop the engine, look for signs of oil or coolant dripping from beneath the car. If there are exhaust leaks, re-make the defective joints.

7 Readjust the valve clearances while the engine is hot.

8 Road test the car to check the timing and general performance, but do not race the engine. If new bearings and/or piston rings have been fitted, the engine should be treated as new and be restricted to low speeds and light loading for the first 500 miles (800 km).

56 Fault diagnosis – engine

Symptom	Reason(s)
Engine fails to turn over when starter is operated	Discharged or defective battery Dirty or loose battery leads Defective starter solenoid, or switch Defective starter motor Dirty or broken engine earthing strap
Engine turns at normal speed, but does not start	Ignition components wet or damp Defective low tension lead Defective or incorrectly set contact breaker Defective condenser Distributor cap defective, or central brush in distributor cap not making contact with the rotor arm Insufficient petrol in tank Vapour lock in fuel line (in hot conditions) Carburettor fault (see Chapter 3) Fuel pump failure Excessive choke, causing spark plugs to become wet
Engine stops and will not restart	Ignition failure resulting from breakdown, or presence of water under wet conditions Lack of fuel, or fuel blockage
Engine misfires, or runs unevenly	Loose ignition leads Faulty spark plug Tracking on distributor cap insulation Incorrect mixture Ignition too retarded Dirty contact breaker points, or loose connection in distributor Faulty or loose condenser Leaking carburettor, or manifold joint Defective, or badly adjusted valves
Lack of power and poor compression	Defective valves Blown cylinder head gasket Worn bores or damaged piston
Excessive oil consumption	Worn cylinder bores Defective valve stem seals Leaks

Chapter 1 Part B   3000 V6 engine (Capri II)

Contents

Specifications

Engine (general)

Engine identification	HYF
Position of camshaft	Central between cylinder
Valve control	Push rods and rocker levers
Firing order	1–4–2–5–3–6
Bore	3.688 in (93.67 mm)
Stroke	2.851 in (72.42 mm)
Effective cubic capacity	2993 cc (182.6 in³)
Compression ratio	8.9 : 1
Idling speed	800 ± 25 rpm
Maximum continuous speed	5700 rpm
Power output	138 HP at 5000 rpm
Torque	173 lbf ft (24.0 kgf m) at 3000 rpm

Cylinder block

Identification cast on to block	722 F – 6015 – BA
Cylinder bore diameter	
Standard – Grade A	3.6868 to 3.6873 in (93.647 to 93.658 mm)
Grade B	3.6873 to 3.6878 in (93.658 to 93.668 mm)
Grade C	3.6878 to 3.6883 in (93.668 to 93.678 mm)
Grade D	3.6883 to 3.6888 in (93.678 to 93.688 mm)
Oversize – 0.015	3.7C22 to 3.7044 in (94.036 to 94.091 mm)
0.030	3.7132 to 3.7184 in (94.315 to 94.447 mm)
0.045	3.7318 to 3.7334 in (94.787 to 94.828 mm)
0.075	3.7472 to 3.7484 in (95.178 to 95.209 mm)

Main bearings and crankshaft

Number of main bearings . . . .

Centre main bearing width . . . . 0.868 to 0.870 in (22.047 to 22.098 mm)
Main bearing diameter
    Standard . . . . 2.5016 to 2.5031 in (63.5408 to 63.5789 mm)
    Undersize – 0.010 . . . . 2.4196 to 2.4931 in (63.2868 to 63.3249 mm)
        0.020 . . . . 2.4816 to 2.4831 in (63.0328 to 63.0709 mm)
        0.030 . . . . 2.4716 to 2.4731 in (62.7788 to 62.8169 mm)
Crankshaft
    Endfloat . . . . 0.003 to 0.011 in (0.08 to 0.28 mm)
    Backlash . . . . 0.002 to 0.004 in (0.05 to 0.1 mm)
Journal diameter
    Standard . . . . 2.5006 to 2.5014 in (63.5152 to 63.5366 mm)
    Undersize – 0.010 . . . . 2.4906 to 2.4914 in (63.2612 to 63.2820 mm)
        0.020 . . . . 2.4806 to 2.4814 in (63.0072 to 63.0280 mm)
        0.030 . . . . 2.4706 to 2.4714 in (62.7140 to 62.7532 mm)
        0.040 . . . . 2.4606 to 2.4614 in (62.4992 to 62.5200 mm)
Thickness of half thrust washer
    Standard . . . . 0.091 to 0.093 in (2.311 to 2.362 mm)
    Oversize – 0.0025 . . . . 0.0935 to 0.0955 in (2.375 to 2.426 mm)
        0.005 . . . . 0.096 to 0.098 in (2.438 to 2.489 mm)
        0.0075 . . . . 0.0985 to 0.1005 in (2.502 to 2.553 mm)
        0.010 . . . . 0.1010 to 0.1030 in (2.565 to 2.616 mm)
Main bearing clearance . . . . 0.0002 to 0.0025 in (0.006 to 0.064 mm)
Big end journal diameter
    Standard . . . . 2.376 to 2.377 in (60.366 to 60.376 mm)
    Undersize – 0.010 . . . . 2.366 to 2.367 in (60.099 to 60.119 mm)
        0.020 . . . . 2.356 to 2.357 in (59.845 to 59.865 mm)
        0.030 . . . . 2.346 to 2.347 in (59.591 to 59.611 mm)
        0.040 . . . . 2.336 to 2.337 in (59.337 to 59.357 mm)

Camshaft

Drive . . . . Gear
Thickness of thrust plate . . . . 0.210 to 0.212 in (5.334 to 5.384 mm)
Backlash . . . . 0.0087 to 0.0013 in (0.22 to 0.32 mm)
Spacer thickness . . . . 0.218 to 0.220 in (5.537 to 5.588 mm)
Lift of cams – Endfloat . . . . 0.006 to 0.01 in (0.153 to 0.254 mm)
    Inlet . . . . 0.2837 in (7.205 mm)
    Exhaust . . . . 0.2691 in (6.836 mm)
Camshaft journal diameter
    Front . . . . 1.874 to 1.8745 in (47.592 to 47.616 mm)
    Centre 1 . . . . 1.811 to 1.814 in (46.008 to 46.068 mm)
    Centre 2 . . . . 1.754 to 1.7545 in (44.544 to 44.564 mm
    Rear . . . . 1.7387 to 1.7395 in (44.163 to 44.183 mm)
Internal diameter of bush
    Front . . . . 1.875 to 1.876 in (47.633 to 47.658 mm)
    Centre 1 . . . . 1.815 to 1.816 in (46.109 to 46.134 mm)
    Centre 2 . . . . 1.755 to 1.756 in (44.585 to 44.610 mm)
    Rear . . . . 1.740 to 1.741 in (44.204 to 44.229 mm)

Pistons

Piston diameter
    Standard A . . . . 3.6850 to 3.6854 in (93.600 to 93.610 mm)
        B . . . . 3.6854 to 3.6858 in (93.610 to 93.620 mm)
        C . . . . 3.6858 to 3.6862 in (93.620 to 93.630 mm)
        D . . . . 3.6862 to 3.6866 in (93.630 to 93.640 mm)
    Oversize 0.0025 . . . . 3.6885 to 3.6895 in (93.690 to 93.713 mm)
        0.015 . . . . 3.7011 to 3.7020 in (94.008 to 94.031 mm)
        0.030 . . . . 3.716 to 3.717 in (94.389 to 94.412 mm)
        0.045 . . . . 3.731 to 3.732 in (94.770 to 94.793 mm)
        0.060 . . . . 3.746 to 3.747 in (95.151 to 95.174 mm)
Clearance of piston in cylinder bore . . . . 0.0014 to 0.002 in (0.036 to 0.051 mm)
Piston ring gap (fitted)
    Top . . . . 0.01 to 0.02 in (0.254 to 0.508 mm)
    Centre . . . . 0.01 to 0.02 in (0.254 to 0.508 mm)
    Bottom . . . . 0.01 to 0.015 in (0.254 to 0.15 mm)

Gudgeon pin

Diameter –
    red . . . . 0.9369 to 0.9370 in (23.799 to 23.802 mm)
    yellow . . . . 0.9370 to 0.9371 in (23.802 to 23.805 mm)
    blue . . . . 0.9371 to 0.9372 in (23.805 to 23.807 mm)
Clearance in piston . . . . 0.003 to 0.005 in (0.076 to 0.127 mm)
Interference fit in connecting rod . . . . 0.008 to 0.015 in (0.203 to 0.381 mm)

Connecting rods

Bore diameter
    Big end . . . . 2.521 to 2.522 in (64.033 to 64.054 mm)

Small end	0.9358 to 0.9362 in (23.769 to 23.780 mm)
Bearing shell ID	
Standard	2.377 to 2.379 in (60.3818 to 60.4200 mm)
Undersize 0.010	2.367 to 2.369 in (60.1278 to 60.1660 mm)
0.020	2.357 to 2.359 in (59.8738 to 59.9120 mm)
0.030	2.347 to 2.349 in (59.6198 to 59.6580 mm)
0.040	2.337 to 2.339 in (59.3658 to 59.4040 mm)
Big end bearing clearance	0.00023 to 0.0025 in (0.006 to 0.064 mm)

Cylinder head

Marking cast on cylinder head	722 M-6090-FA
Valve seat angle in head	44°3′ to 45°
Stem bore inlet and exhaust valves	
Standard	0.3115 to 0.3121 in (7.912 to 7.938 mm)
Undersize 0.003	0.3145 to 0.3151 in (7.988 to 8.014 mm)
0.015	0.3175 to 0.3181 in (8.293 to 8.319 mm)
0.030	0.3205 to 0.3211 in (8.674 to 8.700 mm)

Tappets

Tappet diameter	0.8739 to 0.8745 in (22.199 to 22.212 mm)
Tappet clearance in housing	0.002 to 0.0005 in (0.05 to 0.013 mm)

Valves

Length	
Inlet	4.493 to 4.525 in (114.123 to 114.935 mm)
Exhaust	4.495 to 4.524 in (114.17 to 114.92 mm)
Valve head diameter	
Inlet	1.612 to 1.622 in (40.945 to 41.200 mm)
Exhaust	1.448 to 1.458 in (36.78 to 37.03 mm)
Valve stem diameter	
Standard inlet	0.31 to 0.3105 in (7.869 to 7.887 mm)
Exhaust	0.309 to 0.310 in (7.846 to 7.864 mm)
Oversize 0.003 Inlet	0.3128 to 0.3135 in (7.945 to 7.963 mm)
Exhaust	0.312 to 0.313 in (7.922 to 7.940 mm)
Oversize 0.015 Inlet	0.3158 to 0.3165 in (8.250 to 8.266 mm)
Exhaust	0.315 to 0.316 in (8.227 to 8.245 mm)
Valve stem clearance in guide	
Inlet	0.0008 to 0.0025 in (0.02 to 0.63 mm)
Exhaust	0.0019 to 0.002 in (0.048 to 0.05 mm)
Valve lift	
Inlet	0.368 in (9.347 mm)
Exhaust	0.339 in (8.611 mm)
Valve clearances:	
Inlet	0.013 in (0.33 mm)
Exhaust	0.022 in (0.55 mm)
Valve springs	
Free length	1.888 in (47.955 mm)
Height of spring, compressed	1.098 in (27.885 mm)

Engine lubrication

Oil grade	HD oil
Viscosity	
Below -12°C	SAE 5W/20
Below 0°C	SAE 5W/30
-23°C to +32°C	SAE 10W/30, SAE 10W/40 or SAE 10W/50
Above -12°C	SAE 20W/40 or SAE 20W/50
Ford specification	SS-M2C-9001-AA
Sump capacity, including filter	10 pints (5.65 litres)
Oil change, excluding filter renewal	7.5 pints (4.25 litres)
Oil change, including filter renewal	8.8 pints (5.00 litres)
Minimum oil pressure	
at 750 rpm	14 lbs/in² (1.0 kg/cm²)
at 2000 rpm	40 lbs/in² (2.8 kg/cm²)
Relief valve opens at	62.5 to 72.5 lbs/in² (4.4 to 5.1 kg/cm²)
Oil pressure switch operates at	4.2 to 8.4 lbs/in² (0.3 to 0.6 kg/cm²)
Oil pump	
Rotor to housing clearance	0.012 in (0.304 mm) max
Inner to outer rotor gap	0.008 in (0.2 mm) max
Endfloat, rotor sealing face	0.004 in (0.104 mm) max

Torque wrench settings

	lbf ft	kgf m
Main bearing caps	49 to 55	6.8 to 7.6
Big end bearing bolts	38 to 43	5.3 to 5.9
Crankshaft pulley	40 to 45	5.5 to 6.2
Camshaft gear	40 to 44	5.5 to 6.1
Flywheel	50 to 55	6.9 to 7.6

Torque wrench setting

	lbf ft	kgf m
Timing cover	11 to 13	1.5 to 1.8
Oil pump	12 to 15	1.7 to 2.1
Oil pump cover	6 to 9	0.8 to 1.2
Oil sump	6 to 8	0.8 to 1.1
Cylinder head bolts		
Initial	7	1.0
Second stage	22 to 36	3.0 to 5.0
Third stage (after 10 to 20 minutes wait)	59 to 66	8.2 to 9.2
Final (after running engine for 15 minutes at 1000 rpm)	78 to 85	11.0 to 11.7
Rocker cover	2 to 3.6	0.3 to 0.5
Inlet manifold		
Initial	2.9 to 5.8	0.4 to 0.8
Second stage	5.8 to 11	0.8 to 1.5
Final	13 to 16	1.8 to 2.2
Sump drain plug	20 to 25	2.7 to 3.4
Oil pressure switch	9 to 11	1.2 to 1.5
Spark plugs	22 to 29	3.0 to 4.0
Rear oil seal carrier	12 to 14	1.6 to 2.0
Fuel pump	12 to 14	1.6 to 2.0

57 General description

The 3000 cc engine is an overhead valve, six cylinder V formation (Fig.1.38). The overhead valves are operated via tappets, push rods and rocker arms, from the camshaft located centrally in the engine block. The general configuration is the same as the 2800 cc engine fitted to the Mercury Capri, but there are differences of detail in that the 3000 cc engine has flat cylinder heads with the combustion chambers machined in the piston. It also has individually mounted rocker arms, instead of a rocker shaft mounted on pedestals and there are differences in the type and location of the fuel and water pumps.

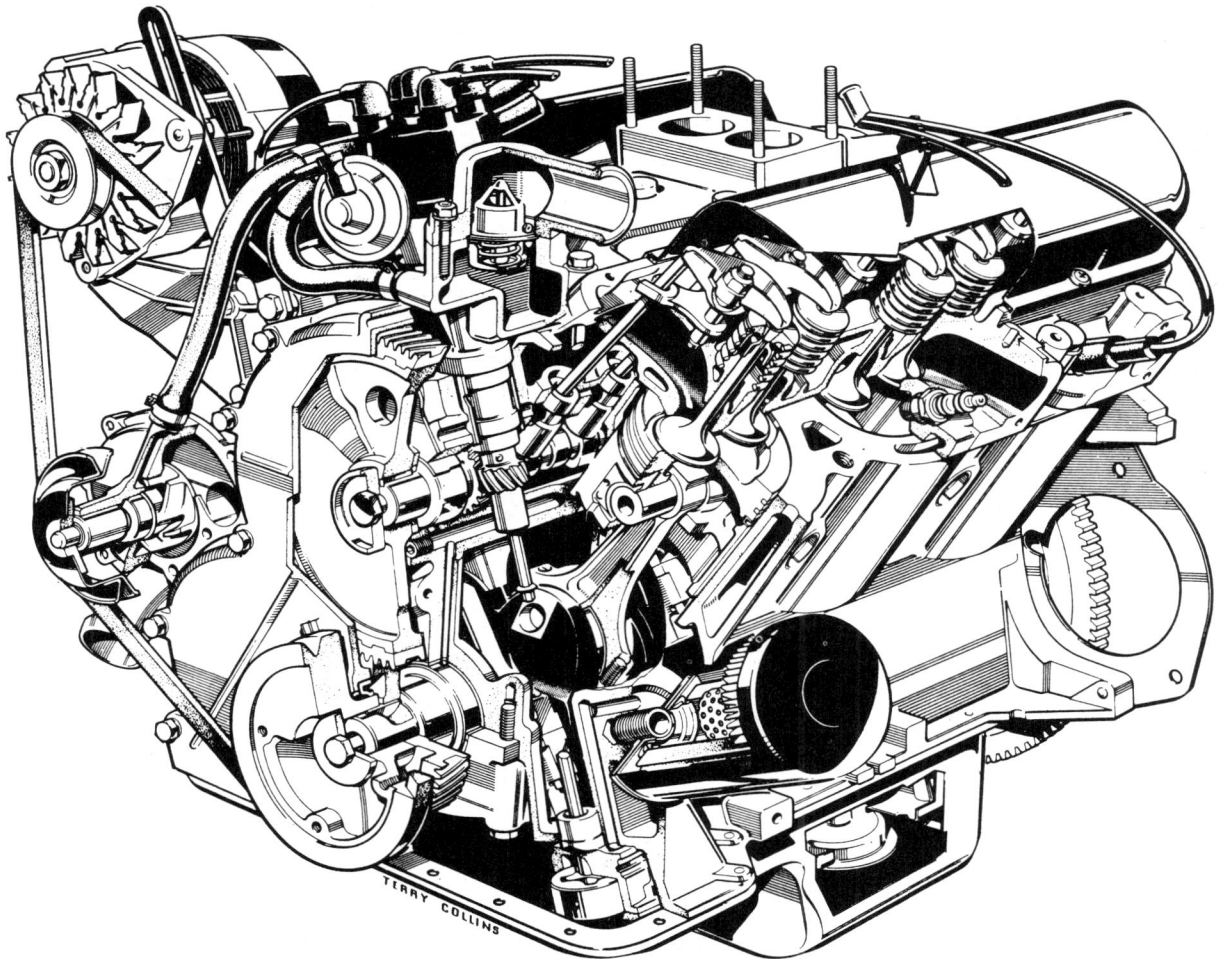

Fig. 1.38 3000cc V6 engine – sectional view

58 Major operations with engine in place

Refer to Section 2 of this Chapter.

59 Major operations with engine removed

Although it is possible to remove the sump with the engine in the car, it is recommended that for any operations which require the removal of the sump, such as the removal of the crankshaft and big end bearings, the engine is removed. A list of the major operations requiring the removal of the engine is given in Section 3 of this Chapter.

60 Methods of engine removal

The engine may be lifted out with the gearbox attached, or it may be separated from the gearbox and the engine only removed. If the gearbox is attached, removal is more difficult, because of the added weight and because the assembly has to be removed at a very steep angle. An engine with an automatic transmission should never be removed as a unit, because damage to the transmission is likely to result.

61 Engine – removal

If air-conditioning is fitted the system must be depressurized by a specialist.
1   Open and prop up the bonnet, then cover the wings with cloths, or cardboard, to protect them from scratches during the subsequent operations.
2   Mark the outline of the bonnet hinges and then with the help of an assistant, remove the four bonnet screws, release the bonnet stay and carefully lift the bonnet clear.
3   Disconnect the battery leads, remove the battery clamp bolt and lift the battery out.
4   Remove the air cleaner.
5   Remove the splash shield by removing the bolts and clips.
6   Place a container of three gallons capacity underneath the radiator, remove the radiator bottom hose and drain the coolant.
7   Remove the upper hose from the water pump. Remove the bolts from the air deflector panel and from the radiator shroud and remove them.
8   Remove the four bolts securing the radiator to the front panel and lift the radiator out.
9   Disconnect the hot water hose from the water pump and automatic choke.
10 Remove the starter motor heat shield and then disconnect the leads from the alternator, temperature sender unit, ignition and starter motor.
11 Remove the two bolts securing the throttle linkage bracket assembly to the inlet manifold and remove it.
12 Remove the fuel lines from the fuel pump, the servo vacuum hose from the inlet manifold and the oil pressure line from the connector and/or lead from the oil pressure switch (Fig. 1.39 and Fig. 1.40).
13 Remove the two bolts securing the starter motor and remove it.
14 Remove the two nuts to disconnect the rubber insulators from the engine mountings.
15 Remove the two nuts from each exhaust flange (Fig. 1.41) and disconnect the exhaust pipes from the exhaust manifold.
16 On manual transmission models, remove four clips and remove the clutch housing cover.
17 Remove the six bolts and disconnect the bellhousing, or transmission housing flange.
18 Place blocks, or a jack under the transmission. Sling the engine so that the front is slightly higher than the rear. Take the weight of the engine on the hoist and then pull the engine forward, to separate it from the transmission.
19 When the engine has been separated from the transmission, lift the engine slowly, checking frequently to see that the engine does not foul any part of the bodywrok.
20 When the engine is clear of the body, lower it to the ground, or transfer it to a work bench.

62 Engine ancillaries – removal

1   Before beginning a complete overhaul, or if the engine is being exchanged for a works reconditioned unit, the following items should be removed.

Fuel system components:
  Carburettor
  Inlet and exhaust manifolds
  Fuel pump (Fig. 1.42)
  Fuel lines

Fig. 1.39 Oil pressure switch

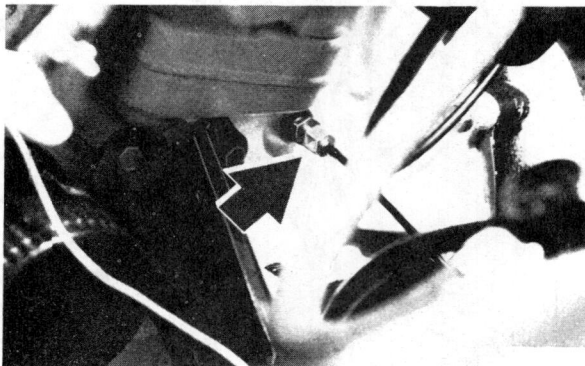

Fig. 1.40 Oil pressure line connection

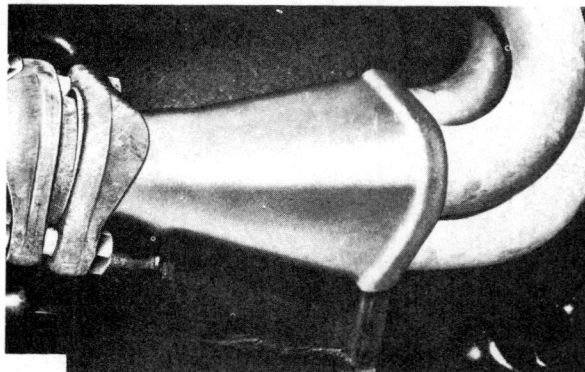

Fig. 1.41 Exhaust pipe to manifold connection

Ignition system components:
    Spark plugs
    Distributor
    Coil
Electrical system components (if not removed already):
    Alternator and mounting brackets
    Starter motor
Cooling system components:
    Fan and fan pulley (Fig. 1.43)
    Water pump, thermostat housing and thermostat
    Water temperature sender unit
Engine:
    Crankcase ventilation tube
    Oil filter element (Fig. 1.44)
    Oil pressure sender unit (if fitted)
    Oil level dipstick
    Oil filler cap
    Engine mounting brackets
Clutch:
    Clutch pressure plate and assembly
    Clutch friction plate assembly
Optional equipment:
    Air-conditioning compressor
    Thermactor pump
    Power steering pump

63 Cylinder heads – removal with engine in car

1   Disconnect the battery leads.
2   Remove the splash shield, by removing four bolts and four clips.
3   Place a container of three gallons capacity underneath the radiator, remove the radiator bottom hose and drain the system.
4   Remove the radiator top hose.
5   Remove the air cleaner, disconnect the fuel pipe from the carburettor and the breather hose from the rocker cover.
6   Remove the servo vacuum hose from the inlet manifold.
7   Remove the three bolts and remove the throttle linkage bracket complete with linkage.
8   Disconnect the radiator hose from the automatic choke. Disconnect the vacuum line from carburettor.
9   Disconnect the lead from the temperature sender unit.
10   Disconnect the HT leads from the spark plugs and from the ignition coil and remove the LT lead to the distributor. Remove one fixing bolt and lift off the distributor assembly.
11   Disconnect the alternator cables. Slacken the alternator mounting bolts and remove the fan belt, then remove the alternator fixing bolts and remove the alternator and its fixing bracket.
12   Remove the spark plugs. Remove the nuts securing the rocker covers and lift off the covers.
13   Remove the five bolts securing the inlet manifold and take off the inlet manifold complete with carburettor (Fig. 1.45).
14   Loosen the rocker arm adjusting nuts until the rocker arms can be turned aside (Fig. 1.46) then remove the push rods and lay them out in line, or push their ends through a sheet of paper on which their position in the engine can be noted. It is very important that the push rods are refitted to the same valve as that from which they were removed.
15   Remove twelve bolts and detach the exhaust manifolds from the cylinder heads.
16   Slacken the cylinder head bolts progressively in the sequence shown in Fig. 1.67. Remove the bolts and lift off the cylinder head. If the gasket has stuck and the cylinder head cannot be lifted off, tap the cylinder head with a hide-faced, or plastic-headed hammer. Do not try to prise them off with a screwdriver or damage will result.

Fig. 1.42 Removing the fuel pump

Fig. 1.43 Fan and clutch assembly

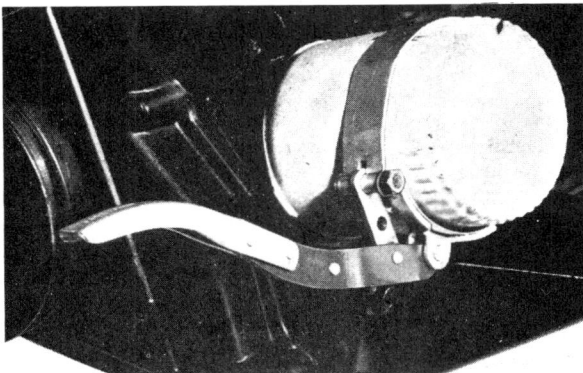

Fig. 1.44 Removing the oil filter

Fig. 1.45 Inlet manifold and carburettor

Fig. 1.46 Rocker arms turned aside

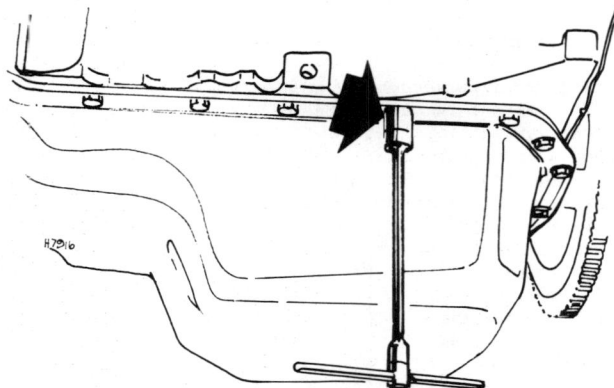

Fig. 1.47 Removing the sump

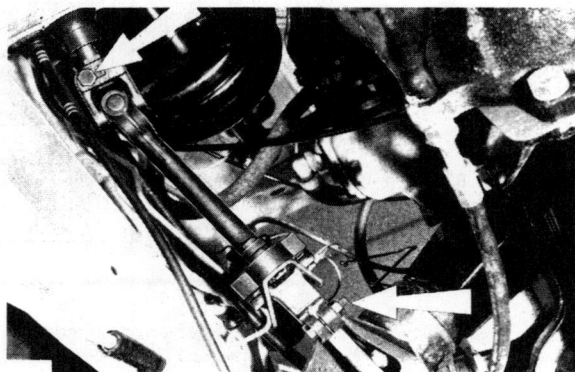

Fig. 1.48 Steering shaft connections

Fig. 1.49 Front stabilizer fixings (arrowed)

64 Cylinder heads – removal with engine out

Follow the sequence given in Section 63, starting at paragraph 10, disregarding references to parts which have already been removed.

65 Valves – removal

The procedure is identical with that described in Section 10. On the 3000cc engine the pitch of the valve springs is the same throughout their length and they can be fitted either way up, but it is good practice to ensure that every component is refitted so that it is exactly the same way up as before removal.

66 Rocker assembly – dismantling

1   Remove the stiff nut from the rocker arm mounting stud.
2   Lift off the rocker arm ball seating and the rocker arm and lay the three parts together. It is important that the rocker arm, its ball seating and nut are refitted to the same stud as the one from which they were removed.

67 Tappets – removal

Refer to the information given in Section 12.

68 Crankshaft pulley – removal

Refer to the information given in Section 13.

69 Flywheel – removal

Refer to the information given in Section 14.

70 Crankcase sump – removal

1   With the engine out of the car, ensure that the sump has been drained and then turn the engine over so that the sump is uppermost. Fit wooden blocks to support the engine in this position.
2   Remove the bolts securing the oil sump to the crankcase (Fig. 1.47) and remove the sump. If the sump is stuck to the crankcase, it should be released by prising one side with a screwdriver.
3   To remove the sump with the engine in the car, first remove the dipstick and disconnect the battery.
4   Remove the four bolts and four clips and detach the oil splash shield.
5   Place a container of at least twelve pints capacity beneath the sump, remove the drain plug and drain the sump. Refit the drain plug and tighten it to the torque wrench setting given in the Specifications.
6   Detach the engine rubber mountings, by removing their nuts and washers.
7   Remove the clamping bolt from the top and bottom ends of the connecting shaft on the steering spindle (Fig. 1.48). Push the top end of the connecting shaft upwards until the lower end can be disengaged.
8   Place a jack under the transmission and use it to raise the engine slightly.
9   Remove the four bolts securing the front anti-roll bar to the sidemember and the four bolts securing each engine mounting bracket to the sidemember (Fig. 1.49).
10   Remove the oil sump bolts and if the sump has stuck to the crankcase, release the sump by pressing it sideways with a screwdriver.

71 Front cover – removal

1   If the engine is in the car, it will first be necessary to disconnect the battery, drain the cooling system and remove the radiator.
2   Loosen the alternator mounting bolts, swing the alternator downwards towards the cylinder block and remove the fan belt.
3   Remove the bolt from the centre of the cooling fan and pull off the fan and clutch assembly.
4   Remove the bolt and washer from the centre of the crankshaft pulley and then use a claw puller to draw the pulley off the shaft. Do not attempt to lever the pulley off, because this may result in damage to the front cover.
5   Remove the six bolts securing the sump to the front cover and then the eleven bolts securing the front cover to the cylinder block.
6   Lift the cover off and remove the gasket.

72 Timing gears – removal

Refer to the information given in Section 17.

73 Camshaft – removal

1   The camshaft may be removed with the engine in the car, if the following preparatory work is carried out.
2   Drain the cooling system and remove the radiator.
3   Disconnect the battery.
4   Remove the spark plug leads from the spark plugs.
5   Disconnect the leads from the alternator, remove the alternator and its drive belt.
6   Undo and remove the screws securing the rocker covers and lift off the rocker covers and their gaskets.
7   Slacken the nuts securing the rocker arms until the rocker arms can be swung aside.
8   Remove the push rods, identifying each one as it is removed, so that it can be refitted in the same position.
9   Remove the cylinder heads, as described in Section 9, then use a magnet to lift out the tappets. Place each tappet with a push rod which it operates, so that they also will be refitted in their original positions.
10 Remove the front cover as described in Section 71.
11 The camshaft plate is secured with two Pozidriv countersunk screws. These cannot be removed with an ordinary screwdriver and any attempt to do so will result in the screws being damaged. If an impact screwdriver is not available, the screws may be removed with a Pozidriv socket and the brace of a socket set.
12 Remove the camshaft thrust plate and the spacer behind it.
13 Pull the camshaft forward to withdraw it, taking care to keep the shaft in line, so that the edges of the cams do not damage the camshaft bearings.

74 Oil pump – removal

Refer to the information given in Section 19.

75 Pistons, connecting rods and bearings – removal

Refer to the information given in Section 20.

76 Piston rings – removal

Refer to the information given in Section 21.

77 Gudgeon pin – removal

Refer to the information given in Section 22.

78 Crankshaft rear oil seal – removal

1   To remove the oil seal with the engine in the car, first remove the gearbox, or automatic transmission as detailed in Chapter 6. On manual transmission models, it is then necessary to remove the clutch assembly as described in Chapter 5.
2   Release the six bolts securing the flywheel and remove five of them. While holding the flywheel, remove the sixth bolt and lift away the flywheel.
3   Remove the four bolts securing the oil seal carrier (Fig. 1.50) and lift off the carrier and seal assembly.
4   Drive the seal out of the carrier (Fig. 1.51) taking care not to damage the bore of the carrier.

79 Crankshaft and main bearings – removal

1   Remove the engine from the car.
2   Remove the clutch assembly on manual transmission models.
3   Remove the flywheel and the rear oil seal carrier.
4   Make sure that the crankcase sump has been drained, then turn the engine upside down, chock it securely and remove the sump.
5   Remove the crankshaft pulley and the engine front cover.
6   Remove the oil pump and strainer (Fig. 1.52).
7   Check that all the main and connecting rod bearing caps have their identifying numbers stamped on, so that they can be refitted in their original positions (Fig. 1.53).
8   Remove the crankshaft gear.
9   Remove the two nuts and the bearing cap of each connecting rod in turn and lay out the bearing caps in order.
10 Remove the two bolts from each of the main bearing caps, lift the caps off and lay them out in order. Note that the centre main bearing cap has thrust washers. Mark their positions before removing them, to ensure that they are refitted exactly as removed.
11 Carefully lift the crankshaft out, taking care to keep it parallel with the crankcase, so that the thrust bearing surfaces of the upper bearing halves are not damaged.
12 Remove the bearing inserts from the cylinder block, being careful to note the position from which each of the four bearings and each of the two thrust washers were removed.

Fig. 1.50 Crankshaft rear oil seal carrier

Fig. 1.51 Removing the crankshaft rear oil seal

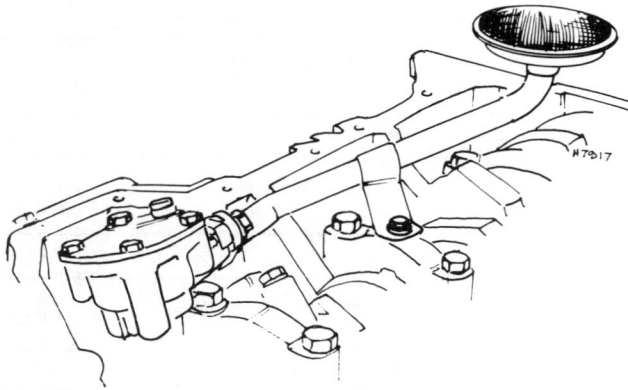

Fig. 1.52 Oil pump and strainer

Fig. 1.53 Main bearing cap identification

80 Engine components – examination for wear

Refer to the information given in Section 25

81 Crankshaft – examination and renovation

Refer to the information given in Section 26.

82 Clutch pilot bearing – removal and renewal

Refer to the information given in Section 27.

83 Cylinder bores – examination and renovation

Refer to the information given in Section 28.

84 Pistons and piston rings – examination

1   Worn pistons and piston rings result in low compression and an increased oil consumption, indicated by the smoky appearance of the exhaust. A compression tester, which fits into a spark plug hole, will indicate whether the compression is normal, or poor, without the need for any engine dismantling. It is also possible to deduce whether low compression results from defective pistons or defective valves.
2   Another indication of piston wear is 'piston slap', a knocking noise which can be heard when the engine is ticking over, but which is not so pronounced when the engine speed is increased.
3   Piston ring wear can be checked by first removing the rings from the pistons as described in Section 21. Take each ring in turn and push it in the top of the bore, then use a piston from which the rings have been removed to push the ring about 1.5 in (40 mm) down the bore. Measure the gap between the ends of the piston ring when it is in this position. If it exceeds 0.02 in (0.51 mm) for the top and middle rings and 0.015 in (0.38 mm) for the bottom ring, new rings should be fitted.
4   The grooves in which the rings fit in the piston can also become enlarged in use. The clearance between the ring and the side of the groove should not exceed 0.006 in (0.15 mm) for the top compression rings and 0.003 in (0.76 mm) for the oil control ring.
5   When new pistons are fitted, their weight must be checked to make certain that the weights of all six pistons with their connecting rod assemblies are all within 8 gms (0.28 oz) of each other, to maintain engine balance. For this reason, if any cylinder has to be bored out by more than 0.004 in (1.0 mm) it is necessary to bore all the cylinders out by the same amount, because a weight deviation of up to 10 gms (0.35 oz) is possible with a 0.004 in oversize piston.

85 Connecting rods and gudgeon pins – inspection

Refer to the information given in Section 30.

86 Camshaft and camshaft bearings – inspection and renewal

1   Undersize camshaft bearings are available 0.020 in undersize, so it is possible to salvage a worn camshaft by regrinding the journals. If the cams, or skew gear, are worn significantly, or are damaged, a new camshaft must be fitted and the bearings should then also be renewed.
2   Worn or damaged camshaft bearings can be replaced by new ones, but this requires special tools and should be entrusted to a Ford dealer, or to a workshop which undertakes camshaft reclaiming.

87 Tappets – inspection

Refer to the information given in Section 32.

88 Valves and valve seats – inspection and reconditioning

Refer to the information given in Section 33, except that oversize valves are only available with stem diameters of 0.003 in and 0.015 in oversize.

89 Timing gears – inspection

1   Inspect the gear teeth for damage, or signs of excessive wear which will cause noisy operation.
2   Check for signs of excessive run out of the gears, which will show up as an uneven contact area on the teeth. If it appears that the gear is skewed on the shaft, remove the gear and check for burrs, or dirt between the gear and the camshaft flange.
3   The backlash between the camshaft gear and the crankshaft gear must not exceed 0.009 in (0.23 mm) and the backlash should be checked at four different points around the periphery of the gear.

90 Flywheel ring gear – inspection

1   Inspect the flywheel for damage and check that the ring gear does not have any broken or badly worn teeth.

Manual transmission
2   If the ring gear is damaged, remove it from the flywheel by cutting a notch between two teeth, using a hacksaw, then splitting the gear with a cold chisel. Polish four equally spaced sections of the new gear, place it on a heat resistant surface, such as fire bricks, and heat the gear with a blow torch until the polished spots are a light straw yellow

colour (400°F) (204°C). Take care not to heat the gear to a temperature higher than this, because its wear resistance will be lowered. Place the hot gear over the flywheel rim, with the chamfered edge of the gear towards the shoulder of the flywheel. Quickly tap the gear on to the flywheel as far as it will go and allow it to cool naturally. Do not attempt to accelerate cooling by quenching.
3   If the friction surface of the flywheel is scored, it can be machined and up to 0.045 in (0.114 mm) may be removed from the original thickness. Beyond this limit of machining, a damaged flywheel must be discarded.

Automatic transmission

4   On cars fitted with C3 automatic transmissions, it is not possible to renew the ring gear and in the event of damage to the flywheel or the gear, a new assembly must be fitted. With C4 and Borg Warner automatic transmission a new ring gear can be fitted in the same way as that on the manual transmission models.

91 Oil pump – dismantling, inspection and reassembly

1   The oil pump maintains a pressure of about 45 lbf/in² (3.16 kgf/cm²) and unless there is a significant drop in oil pressure which is proved to be due to the pump, rather than to worn bearings, it is better to leave the oil pump undisturbed.
2   To dismantle the pump, first remove it from the engine as described in Section 19.
3   Remove the two bolts securing the endcover to the body and remove the cover and the relief valve assembly, then the two piece rotor assembly.
4   Remove the two bolts and take the pick up tube and screen assembly off the pump housing.
5   Wash all the parts in petrol, use a brush to clean the inside of the pump housing and the pressure relief valve chamber and make sure that all particles of dirt and metal are removed. Allow the parts to dry naturally or blow them dry.
6   Check the inside of the pump housing, the outer race and the rotor for damage and excessive wear.
7   Examine the mating surface of the pump cover for wear. If the cover is scored, grooved, or shows any signs of wear, a new cover must be fitted.
8   With the rotor assembly fitted in the housing, place a straight edge over the end of the housing and measure the rotor end play. If this exceeds 0.004 in (0.104 mm), the outer race, shaft and rotor must be renewed as an assembly.
9   Measure the rotor to housing clearance, which should not exceed 0.012 in (0.304 mm) and the inner to outer rotor gap, which should be less than 0.008 in (0.2 mm). If outside these dimensions, a new pump should be fitted.
10   Check that the relief valve and its seating are free of damage and that the relief valve spring has not collapsed, or is damaged, and fit new parts if necessary.
11   Reassemble the pump by first fitting the inner and outer rotors, then lubricating them with engine oil.
12   Apply engine oil to the relief valve plunger and spring and insert them into their housing. Refit the spring cap and the pump cover.

13   Refit the cover attachment screws and tighten them to the torque wrench setting given in the Specifications. After tightening the screws, check that the rotor moves freely.
14   Refit the pick-up tube and strainer assembly to the pump body, using a new gasket and then insert and tighten the two fixing screws.

92 Decarbonisation – cylinder heads and piston crowns

Refer to the information given in Section 37.

93 Rocker gear – inspection

1   The studs on which the rocker arms pivot are a press fit into the cylinder head, and if a straight edge is laid across all six, it can be seen whether any have begun to pull out. If this is the case, the stud will have to be removed, the hole reamed out and an oversize stud fitted.
2   Check that the threads on the studs are in good condition and that a torque of at least 4.3 lbf ft (0.6 kgf m) is required to turn each adjuster on oiled threads. If this figure is not achieved, fit a new adjuster and if still deficient, fit a lock nut to the adjuster.
3   Examine the rocker arms and fulcrum seats for signs of ridging, or excess wear on the bearing surfaces. If either part shows excessive wear, both the rocker arm and the fulcrum seat must be renewed.
4   When checking the rocker arms, remove them one at a time to eliminate any possibility of arms and seats becoming interchanged, or being refitted to the wrong stud.

94 Engine reassembly – general

Refer to the information given in Section 39.

95 Engine reassembly – camshaft

1   Slide the spacer with its chamfered end first onto the camshaft and fit the key.
2   Lubricate the camshaft journals with engine oil and slide the camshaft in from the front, taking care to keep it straight, so as not to damage the camshaft bearings.
3   Fit the camshaft thrust plate without a gasket. Fit the two countersunk head retaining screws and tighten them (Fig. 1.54).

96 Engine reassembly – crankshaft

1   With the engine upside down, lay each of the upper bearing halves onto the appropriate crankcase web, making sure that the locking tang on the bearing is properly engaged in the corresponding slot in the crankcase web. If the old bearings are being refitted, make certain that each bearing half is fitted on the place from which it was removed. Fit the thrust washers to each side of the centre bearing, the grooved faces of the washers being outwards (Fig. 1.55). Retain the thrust

Fig. 1.54 Refitting the camshaft

Fig. 1.55 Fitting the crankshaft thrust washers

washers in place with grease.

2   Fit the four bearing halves to the appropriate bearing caps. Fit the thrust washers on either side of the centre bearing cap, with the tab of the washer fitted into the slot in the bearing cap. Retain the thrust washers in place with grease.

3   Lubricate the crankcase bearing halves with engine oil and carefully lower the crankshaft onto them.

4   Take each bearing cap in turn, lubricate its bearing half with engine oil. Apply engine oil to the crankshaft journal and fit the bearing cap with the arrow pointing towards the front of the engine. Each bearing cap must be refitted in the position from which it was removed.

5   Insert the two retaining bolts and tighten them to the torque wrench setting given in the Specifications (Fig. 1.56). Turn the crankshaft to ensure that it rotates freely, before fitting the next bearing cap. If the crankshaft does not rotate freely, remove the bearing cap and check that the bearing shells have seated properly and that the bearing cap is the correct one for that position.

6   Fit the crankshaft key. Place the crankshaft gear on the end of the crankshaft and position it by temporarily fitting the crankshaft pulley and the original washer and bolt. Tighten the bolt, then remove the bolt, washer and crankshaft pulley.

7   Measure the crankshaft endfloat (Fig. 1.57) which should be between 0.003 and 0.011 in (0.08 to 0.28 mm). If necessary, bring it between these limits by inserting thrust washers of the appropriate thickness.

97 Pistons and connecting rods – refitting

1   If new piston rings are being fitted and the cylinders have not been rebored, the glaze on the cylinder bores should be removed by scuffing them with very fine abrasive paper. The piston rings should be fitted in accordance with the manufacturer's instructions, but before being fitted to the piston, they must be inserted in the piston about half way down the bore, to check the gap between the ends of each ring. For the top and centre ring the gap should be 0.01 to 0.02 in (0.254 to 0.508 mm) and 0.01 to 0.015 in (0.254 to 0.381 mm) for the bottom ring. If the gap is inadequate, it should be increased by gripping the ring close to one end and then carefully filing the end.

2   The connecting rods and bearing caps are numbered from 1 to 3 in the right bank and from 4 to 6 in the left bank. Refit the bearing halves which were removed from each connecting rod, or fit new bearings, taking care that the tang on the bearing is properly fitted into the slot in the connecting rod end.

3   Arrange the piston ring gaps as follows:

Ring gap position – Top	150° offset from oil control ring gap
– Centre	150° offset from oil control ring gap (in the opposite direction from the top ring)
Oil control ring, in 3 parts:	
Intermediate ring, top	Opposite the marked side of the piston
Support spring	Staggered by 1 in (25 mm)
Intermediate ring, bottom	Reverse of top intermediate ring

Oil the piston ring grooves generously and fit a piston ring compressor to the piston, ensuring that all the rings are compressed (Fig. 1.58).

4   Lubricate the bearing surface and the cylinder bore and insert the piston into the bore from the top of the cylinder. Ensure that the piston is returned to its correct bore and that the arrow or notch on the piston crown is pointing towards the front of the engine (Fig. 1.59).

5   Guide the connecting rod towards the crankshaft journal to avoid damage and if necessary tap the piston crown lightly with the wooden handle of a hammer, to assist entering the piston rings into the bore. This operation must be done with caution, to avoid breaking any piston rings.

6   Fit the bearing which was removed, or a new bearing, to the connecting rod cap which bears the same number as the connecting rod and lubricate the bearing. Fit the bearing cap so that its number mates with the number on the connecting rod. Press the piston down so that

the connecting rod bearing seats on the crankshaft journal. Fit the connecting rod nuts and tighten to a torque of 38 to 43 lbf ft (5.3 to 5.9 kgf m).

7   Rotate the crankshaft to ensure that each bearing is free, before proceeding further.

98 Oil pump – refitting

1   Prime the oil pump by filling the inlet port with engine oil and then rotating the drive shaft to distribute the oil within the pump body.

Fig. 1.56 Tightening the main bearing caps

Fig. 1.57 Measuring crankshaft endfloat with a dial gauge

Fig. 1.58 Inserting a piston, using a piston ring compressor

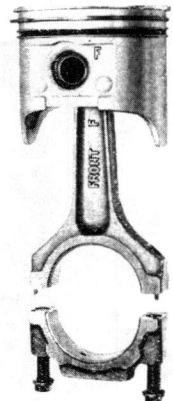

Fig. 1.59 "Front" marking of piston and connecting rod

2   Insert the pointed end of the drive shaft into the pump body and fit the clip to retain it.
3   Place the pump in position, engage the drive shaft and then insert the two retaining bolts. Tighten the bolts to the torque wrench setting given in the Specifications.
4   Refit the bolt securing the oil pick-up tube to the main bearing cap and tighten it to a torque of 12 to 15 lbf ft (1.7 to 2.1 kgf m).

99 Engine reassembly – timing gears and front plate

1   Apply jointing compound to the outer edge of the front end of the cylinder block and to the rear face of the front adapter plate.
2   Position the gasket and adapter plate, securing them with two bolts inserted finger tight.
3   Fit the adapter plate reinforcement (Fig. 1.60); insert its three bolts and tighten them, then remove the two previously inserted locating bolts.
4   Refit the camshaft gear, so that the keyways of both the crankshaft and the camshaft are in line and the marks on the gears are on the same line. The crankshaft gear has two marks on it and it is important that they are positioned as in Fig. 1.61.
5   Measure the endfloat of the camshaft after inserting the camshaft securing bolt and tightening it to the torque wrench setting given in the Specifications. The camshaft endfloat should be 0.006 to 0.01 in (0.153 to 0.254 mm) and can be adjusted by fitting a different length spacer.
6   Measure the backlash of the camshaft gear at four equally spaced points around its periphery. This should be 0.0087 to 0.0013 in (0.22 to 0.32 mm).
7   Apply jointing compound to the circumference of the timing cover joint face and to the front of the adapter plate and offer up the timing cover.
8   Refit the crankshaft pulley to position the timing cover (Fig. 1.62)

then insert the timing cover bolts and tighten them to the torque wrench setting given in the Specifications.
9   Apply jointing compound to one face of the crankshaft pulley washer, place this side towards the pulley, insert the pulley securing bolt and tighten it to a torque of 40 to 43 lbf ft (5.5 to 6.0 kgf m).

100 Crankshaft rear oil seal and flywheel – refitting

1   Fit the engine rear adapter plate and secure it with its five bolts.
2   Smear engine oil onto the crankshaft rim. Smear oil on the lip of the seal and position the seal on the crankshaft.
3   Align the seal carrier holes with those in the cylinder block, insert the four bolts and tighten them to a torque of 12 to 14 lbf ft (1.6 to 2.0 kgf m) (Fig. 1.63).
4   Fit the flywheel, or starter ring on automatic transmission models. Insert the six bolts and tighten them to the torque wrench setting given in the Specifications.

101 Crankcase sump – refitting

1   Ensure that the mating surfaces of both the sump and the crankcase are clean and that the sealing surface of the sump is not distorted.
2   Apply jointing compound to the points where the timing cover abuts the cylinder block and where the rear oil seal carrier adjoins it.
3   Place the oil sump gasket in position, fit the sump and insert the retaining bolts finger tight.
4   Progressively tighten the sump bolts in opposite pairs until all of them are at a torque of 6 to 8 lbf ft (0.8 to 1.1 kgf m).
5   Fit a new washer to the sump drain plug, insert the drain plug and tighten it to a torque of 20 to 25 lbf ft (2.7 to 3.4 kgf m).

Fig. 1.60 Front adapter plate reinforcement with bolts (arrowed)

Fig. 1.61 Camshaft and crankshaft timing marks

Fig. 1.62 Using the crankshaft pulley to centre the timing cover

Fig. 1.63 Tightening the flywheel bolts

102 Cylinder heads – reassembly

1   Lay the cylinder head on its side, lubricate every valve guide with engine oil, and insert the valves into the guide from which they were removed.
2   To avoid damaging the lip of the stem oil seal, with consequent increased oil consumption, wrap a piece of adhesive tape, or foil, round the groove of every valve stem. Slide the seals over the valve stems and push them over the tops of the valve guides.
3   Remove the adhesive tape, or foil, from the valve stems.
4   Fit the valve spring over the valve, with the close coiled end towards the cylinder head, then fit the spring retainer on top of the spring.
5   Using a valve spring compressor, compress the spring just enough to insert the two split collets (Fig. 1.64). If the valve spring is compressed too far, there is a danger of the spring retainer damaging the valve stem oil seal.
6   After inserting the split collets, release the spring compressor and remove it (Fig. 1.64).
7   Check that the split collets have seated properly and tap the top of the valve stem lightly with a plastic headed hammer to ensure this.
8   When the valve springs are fitted, their compressed length should be 1.098 in (27. 889 mm). If it is less than this, the valve spring should be removed and the valve lapped in until the compressed length of the spring is correct. If the compressed length is greater than the dimension specified, it should be corrected by fitting spacers under the spring. Do not fit spacers unless necessary. Compression of the valve springs in excess of the recommended dimension will result in overstressing the valve springs and the risk of spring breakage, as well as excessive wear on the camshaft lobes.

103 Cylinder heads – refitting

1   If the tappets were removed, lubricate the tappets and their bores with engine oil and insert them with their dished ends uppermost (Fig. 1.65). Ensure that every tappet is refitted into the bore from which it was taken.
2   Make sure that the mating surfaces of the cylinder block, cylinder heads and inlet manifold (Fig. 1.66) are clean, then place new cylinder head gaskets over the guides on the cylinder block. The cylinder head gaskets bear the marking 'TOP FRONT' and need to be positioned correctly.
3   Lower the cylinder heads over their positioning studs. Although the cylinder heads are identical, they should have been marked when removed and should be refitted in their original positions.
4   Insert the cylinder head bolts finger tight then tighten them progressively in the order shown in Fig. 1.67 until they are all at a torque of 78 to 85 lbf ft (11.0 to 11.7 kgf m). Back off each bolt individually a half turn prior to applying its specified torque setting (but don't back off all bolts at once).
5   This final torque should be achieved in stages as given in the Specifications.

104 Rocker gear – refitting

1   Ensure that all the push rods are inserted into their proper places and that their lower ends are engaged in the cups of the tappets.
2   Place the rocker arms over the push rods, fit the fulcrum seats and adjuster nuts (Fig. 1.68) and tighten the adjusting nuts finger tight.
3   Set No 1 cylinder at TDC and refit the distributor (see Chapter 4).
4   Adjust the valve clearances as described in the following Section.
5   Fit the rocker covers, using new gaskets, ensuring that the gaskets are seated evenly all round the cylinder head. Fit the cover attachment bolts and tighten them to a torque of 2 to 3.6 lbf ft (0.3 to 0.5 kgf m).

105 Valve clearances – adjustment

1   It is necessary for the HT leads to be removed from the spark plugs and for the rocker covers and air cleaner to be removed.
2   During the adjustment of valve clearances, turn the engine in the

Fig. 1.64 Compressing the valve spring and inserting the split collets

Fig. 1.65 Tappets with dished end uppermost

Fig. 1.66 Mating surfaces of cylinder heads and cylinder block

Fig. 1.67 Cylinder head tightening sequence

Fig. 1.68 Rocker arm, fulcrum seat and adjuster nut

Fig. 1.69 Inlet manifold bolt tightening sequence

normal direction of rotation only.

3   Turn the engine until No 1 piston is at TDC on its compression stroke. This may be checked by making sure that the notch on the crankshaft pulley is opposite the TDC mark on the timing scale and the distributor rotor is pointing towards the ignition lead for No 1 cylinder. Make three radial chalk marks on the crankshaft pulley at 120° intervals (Fig. 1.35).

4   If the crankshaft pulley is moved to and fro a little, the valves of cylinder No 5 will overlap, that is, the two rocker arms move in opposite directions. When this condition is achieved, adjust the clearances of the valves on cylinder No 1.

5   Place a 0.013 in (0.32 mm) feeler gauge between the top of the inlet valve stem and the rocker arm pad until the feeler gauge can only just be moved in and out. Adjust the exhaust valve in similar manner with a 0.022 in (0.55 mm) feeler gauge.

6   Turn the crankshaft pulley 120° in the direction of normal engine rotation so that the first chalk mark made aligns with the TDC mark on the timing scale. It will then be seen that the valves of No 3 cylinder overlap. The valves of No 4 cylinder can then be adjusted.

7   By turning the crankshaft pulley two complete revolutions in 120° increments, all the valves can be adjusted in the following sequence.

Cylinder No 5 overlaps – Adjust cylinder No 1
Cylinder No 3 overlaps – Adjust cylinder No 4
Cylinder No 6 overlaps – Adjust cylinder No 2
Cylinder No 1 overlaps – Adjust cylinder No 5
Cylinder No 4 overlaps – Adjust cylinder No 3
Cylinder No 2 overlaps – Adjust cylinder No 6

8   After adjusting the valve clearances, refit the rocker covers and tighten their securing bolts.

9   Refit the spark plug leads and the air cleaner.

106 Inlet manifold – refitting

1   Apply jointing compound to the mating surfaces at the outer edge of the cylinder heads and the inlet manifold.

2   Fit a new inlet manifold gasket.

3   Position the inlet manifold complete with carburettor and insert the retaining bolts finger tight.

4   Tighten the bolts in the order shown in Fig. 1.69 to a torque of 2.9 to 5.8 lbf ft (0.4 to 0.8 kgf m) as the first stage.

5   Repeat the operation to a second stage torque of 5.8 to 11 lbf ft (0.8 to 1.5 kgf m) then proceed to a final torque of 13 to 16 lbf ft (1.8 to 2.2 kgf m).

107 Exhaust manifold – refitting

1   Fit the bolts to each of the exhaust manifold ports and position a new gasket on each pair of screws.

2   Offer the manifold up to the cylinder head and start the screws in their holes.

3   Tighten the exhaust manifold bolts to a torque of 15 to 18 lbf ft (2.1 to 2.5 kgf m).

108 Oil filter – removal and renewal

Refer to information given in Section 53.

109 Engine – refitting

1   If necessary remove the dowel bushes from the clutch, or transmission housing.

2   Fit new seals to the bushes and fit them without jointing compound. The chamfered end of the bushes should be towards the front of the engine.

3   Before refitting the engine, grease the transmission input shaft and splines.

4   Refit the engine insulator support brackets and the rubber insulators.

5   Jack the transmission, so that its front end is slightly higher than normal.

6   Sling the engine, so that the front is slightly higher than the rear, hoist the engine over the engine compartment and lower slowly, taking care that it is free of all obstruction.

7   Carefully position the engine and transmission so that they are aligned, then push the engine rearwards so that the input shaft engages the clutch, taking great care not to put any strain on the input shaft. If the engine hangs up after the shaft enters the clutch assembly, lock the transmission by selecting a gear and then turn the crankshaft a small amount, to line up the splines of the clutch plate and the gearbox shaft.

8   Fit the converter housing, or bellhousing upper bolts, making sure that the dowels in the cylinder block are engaged in the housing. Tighten the bolts to a torque of 28 to 38 lbf ft (3.9 to 5.3 kgf m).

9   Refit the engine rubber insulators, then remove the jack from beneath the transmission, lower the engine and remove the slings and hoist.

10 Reconnect the exhaust pipes to the exhaust manifolds. Fit the nuts and tighten them to a torque of 15 to 20 lbf ft (2.1 to 2.8 kgf m).

11 On manual transmission models, refit the clutch housing cover and retain it with its four clips.

12 Clean the termination of the engine earth cable and its attachment point to the engine and reconnect it.

13 Refit the starter motor, insert its two fixing bolts and tighten them. Refit the starter motor heat shield and the starter motor electrical connections.

14 Refit the fuel lines to the fuel pump (photo). Reconnect the servo vacuum hose to the inlet manifold and refit the oil pressure connection and/or lead from the oil pressure switch.

15 Refit the throttle linkage bracket assembly to the inlet manifold. Insert and tighten the two bolts (photo).

16 Reconnect the leads to the alternator, the temperature gauge sender unit and the ignition coil.

17 Reconnect the water hoses to the water pump and to the automatic choke and thermostat (photo).

18 Refit the radiator and radiator shroud.

19 Refit the air deflector panel (Fig. 1.70) and splash shield (Fig. 1.71).

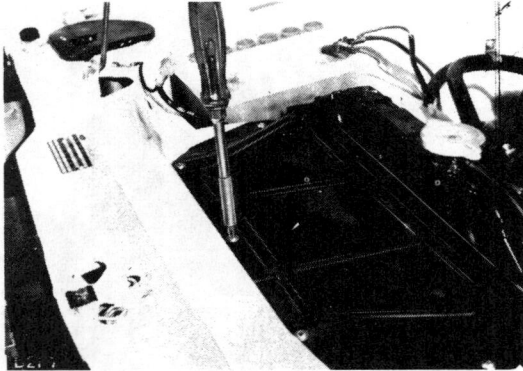

Fig. 1.70 Air deflector panel

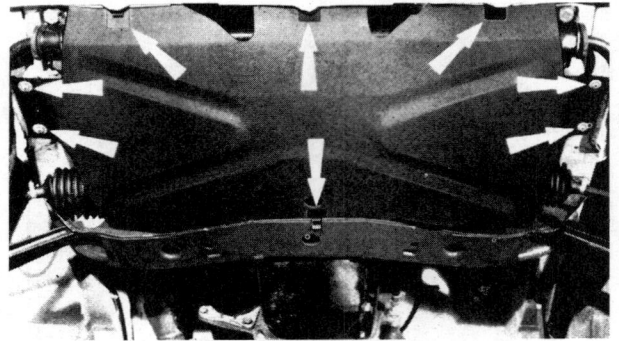

Fig. 1.71 Splash shield fixings

109.14 Reconnect the fuel lines to the pump

109.15 Refit the throttle linkage

109.17 Reconnect the thermostat hoses

109.21 Top-up engine oil level

20 Fill the cooling system and check it for leaks.
21 Check that the sump drain plug is in place and tightened, then fill the sump to the correct level with engine oil (photo).
22 Check that the transmission drain plug is in place and tightened, then fill the transmission to the correct level.
23 Position the bonnet hinge arms against the marks made before removal and fit the retaining bolts.
24 Refit the air cleaner and air intake duct.
25 Refit the battery and reconnect the battery leads.

110 Engine – initial start up after major overhaul

Refer to the information given in Section 55.

111 Fault diagnosis – engine

Refer to the information given in Section 56.

Chapter 2 Cooling system

For modifications, and information applicable to later models, see Supplement at end of manual

Contents

Specifications

System type .... Pressurised, assisted by pump and fan

Thermostat
Type .... Wax

	2800 cc	3000 cc
Location	Bottom LH side of front cover	Front end of manifold casting
Starts to open (new)	185°F to 192°F (85°C to 89°C)	
(used)	178°F to 199°F (81°C to 93°C)	180°F to 197°F (82°C to 92°C)
Fully open (new)	210°F to 216°F (99°C to 102°C)	210°F to 216°F (99°C to 102°C)
(used)	208°F to 223°F (98°C to 106°C)	205°F to 221°F (96°C to 105°C)

Radiator
Type .... Corrugated fin
Pressure cap setting .... 13 lbf/in² (0·91 kgf/cm²)

Water pump
Type .... Centrifugal

Fan belt
	2800 cc	3000 cc
Tension	75 lbf ± 5 lbf	Free play 0·5 in (13 mm) at mid-point of longest span

Cooling system capacity, including heater
2800 Mercury Capri .... 8·5 US qts (8·25 litres)
3000 Capri II .... 8·2 Imp qts (9·32 litres)

Torque wrench settings
Fan blades	lbf ft	kgf m
Mercury Capri 2800 cc	7 to 9	0·97 to 1·2
Capri II 3000 cc	5 to 7	0·69 to 0·97
Water pump	5 to 7	0·69 to 0·97
Thermostat housing	12 to 15	1·66 to 2·09
Alternator mounting and adjustment bolt ...	15 to 18	2·07 to 3·5

---

1 General description

The engine coolant is circulated by a thermo-syphon water pump assisted system, and the whole system is pressurized so that the boiling point of the coolant is much higher than at normal atmospheric pressure. It is important to ensure that the radiator cap is of the correct pressure setting and that its spring and sealing washer are in good condition, so that premature boiling and loss of coolant are avoided.

The cooling system consists of the radiator, water pump, thermostat and fan, the fan being separate from the pump. On the 2800 cc engine, there is a viscous clutch between the fan pulley and the fan blades. A drive disc, integral with the clutch body, transmits torque through a silicone fluid to the clutch body. At higher engine speeds, the fluid permits the drive disc to turn relative to the clutch body, so that the fan rotates at a speed lower than that of the pulley. A schematic

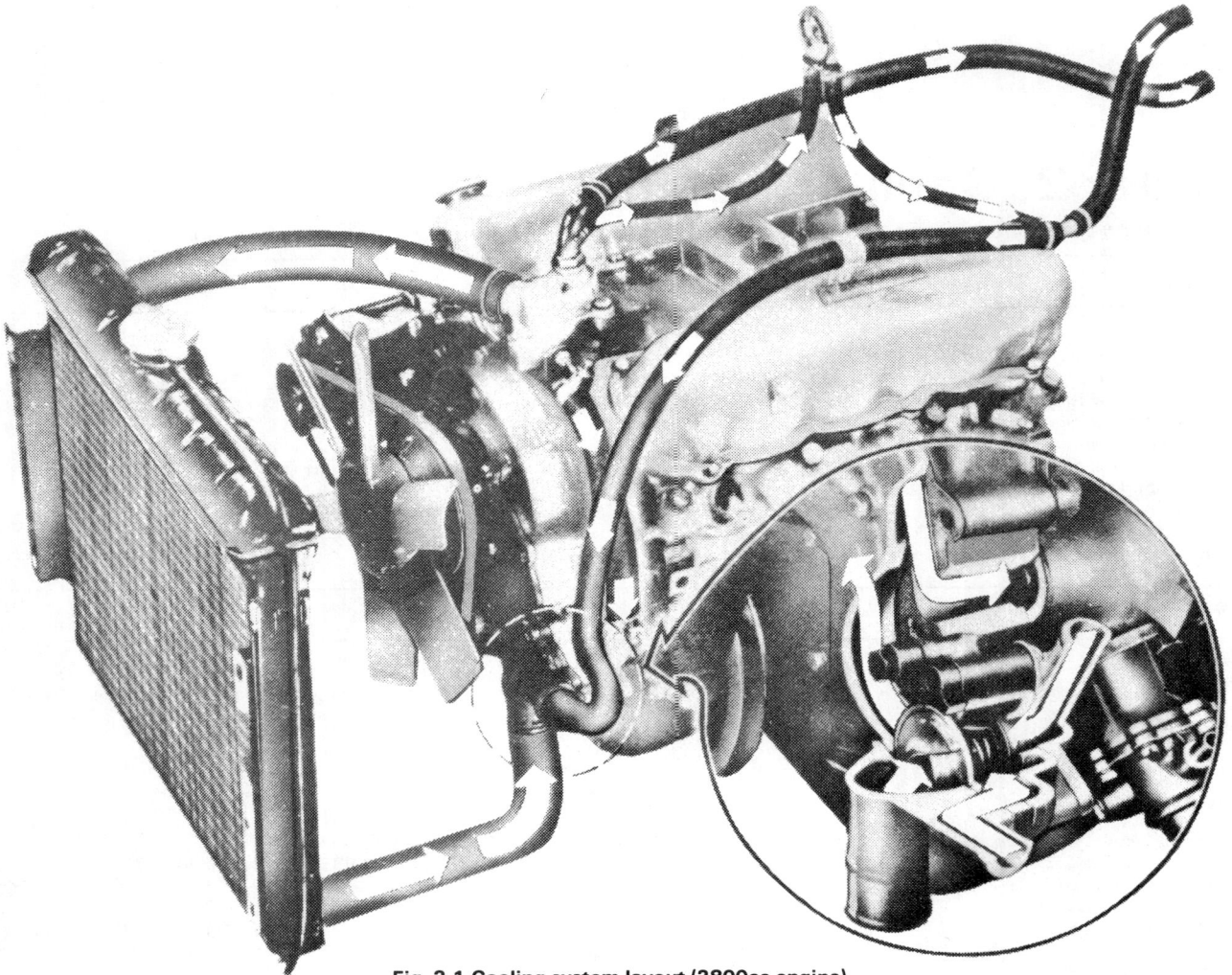

Fig. 2.1 Cooling system layout (2800cc engine)

diagram of the 2800 cc engine cooling system is shown in Fig. 2:2. During engine warm up it passes through three distinct stages, as follows:-

The thermostat front valve is closed and the thermostat rear valve is open. No coolant passes from the pump to the radiator, but the remaining circuits are open. When the engine reaches its normal operating temperature and the coolant is at 185°F (85°C), the thermostat front valve opens and coolant is circulated through the radiator. If the engine begins to overheat, the thermostat rear valve closes, the thermostat front valve remains open and with the by-pass circuits

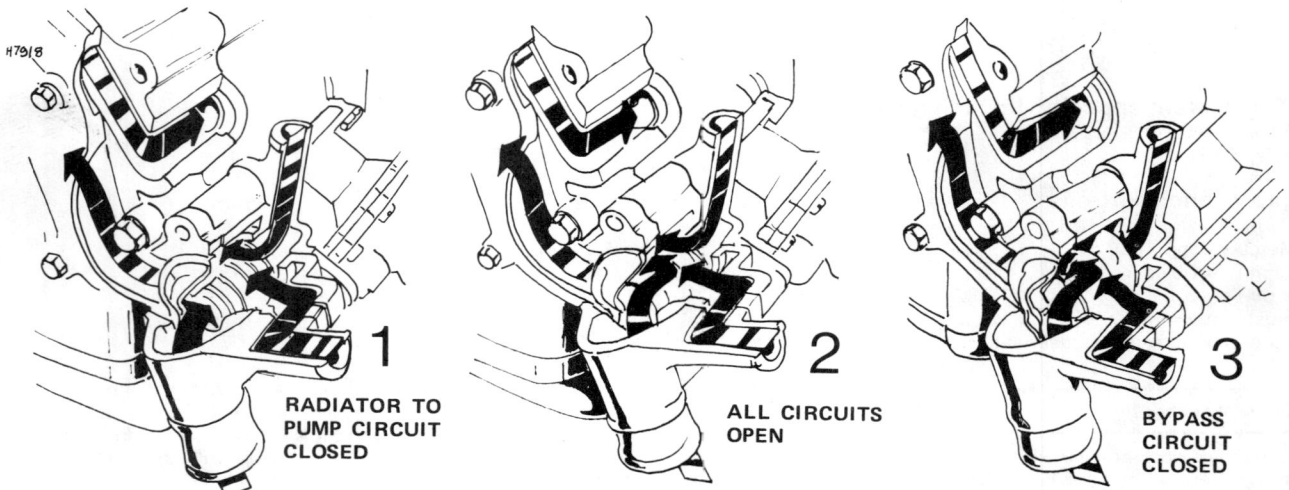

H7918

1 RADIATOR TO PUMP CIRCUIT CLOSED

2 ALL CIRCUITS OPEN

3 BYPASS CIRCUIT CLOSED

Fig. 2.2 Cooling system operation

closed, all coolant is circulated through the radiator.

A schematic diagram of the 3000 cc engine cooling system is shown in Fig. 2.3. At normal operating temperature, or above, coolant is circulated from the base of the radiator, up through the pump and into the right-hand bank of the cylinder block. The holes in both the cylinder head gaskets are graduated in size, so that the coolant flows at an even rate into the cylinder heads from each bank of the cylinder block. Coolant leaves the manifold through the thermostat at the front end of the manifold to the header tank and from there through the radiator core, for cooling before being recirculated.

The cooling system is designed to operate with a 50% concentration of antifreeze, regardless of climate.

The coolant should be drained and fresh antifreeze should be put into the cooling system every two years. If water only is used in the system, there is likely to be severe corrosion.

2 Routine Maintenance

1 Check the level of coolant weekly, or more frequently if the engine has a tendency to overheat. Under normal conditions, coolant loss is negligible and any need for frequent topping up should be investigated.
2 Top up with a mixture of 50% approved antifreeze and 50% water, using soft water if available.
3 Keep the radiator core free from debris, such as dead insects and leaves.
4 Check the fan belt tension at least every 5000 miles and also examine all the hoses for signs of deterioration and leakage.
5 To ensure reliable operation, renew all the hoses every 30 000 miles.

3 Cooling system – draining

1 If possible, ensure that the engine is cold before draining the coolant, to avoid the risk of scalding.
2 Remove the radiator filler cap. If the engine is hot, this must be done very cautiously, because a sudden release of pressure can result in the coolant boiling and blowing out. On a hot engine, place a cloth over the cap and turn it very gently, to release the pressure slowly.
3 Remove the splash shield from beneath the radiator.
4 Unless the coolant is being discarded and the car is over a suitable drain, place a clean two gallon container underneath the radiator.
5 Remove the radiator bottom hose and allow the coolant to drain.

4 Radiator – flushing

1 In time, the cooling system will lose its efficiency because of a build-up of rust and sediment in the radiator. To clean the radiator, remove the filler cap and the bottom hose and flush the radiator, by inserting a hose in the filler cap neck and running water through for about ten minutes.
2 If there is a heavy accumulation of sediment, it is better to reverse flush the radiator, by connecting the water supply to the bottom of the radiator and allowing it to flow out of the top. Special hose adapters are available to enable this to be done with the radiator in position, but it is preferable to remove the radiator and turn it upside down.

5 Cooling system – filling

1 Ensure that the cylinder block drain plugs are screwed in firmly and that all the cooling system hoses are in position and secured with hose clips.
2 Using a mixture of 50% antifreeze and 50% water, fill the cooling system slowly, to minimise the risk of air locks. Ensure that the heater control is turned to the 'HOT' position otherwise an air lock may form in the heater.
3 Do not fill the system higher than $\frac{1}{2}$ inch (13 mm) from the bottom of the filler neck, because the coolant expands when heated and over-filling will result in coolant overflowing and being wasted.
4 To ensure that there is no air lock in the heater, remove the hose from the outlet connection of the heater and hold the hose at the same height as the connection from which it has been removed. Pour coolant into the filler neck until a constant stream flows out of the heater and then refit the heater hose and secure it with a hose clip. If venting is not carried out, it is possible for the engine to overheat. On some models, a bleed nipple is fitted to the hose which is at the rear of the engine (photo).
5 After bleeding the system, pour in sufficient coolant to bring the level to within $\frac{1}{2}$ inch (13 mm) of the bottom of the filler neck, then fit the filler cap and turn it clockwise as far as possible.

6 Radiator – removal and refitting

1 Drain the cooling system as described in Section 3.
2 Remove the splash shield after removing its four bolts and four clips.
3 On automatic transmission models, place a tray beneath the oil cooler unions, wipe the unions clean and undo them. Quickly plug the pipe ends and the cooler unions, to prevent the loss of fluid.
4 Remove the radiator top hose and the bottom hose also if not already removed as part of the radiator draining operation.
5 Remove the four bolts, spring and flat washers which secure the radiator to the front panel and lift the radiator out carefully, so as not to damage the radiator core, or the fan.

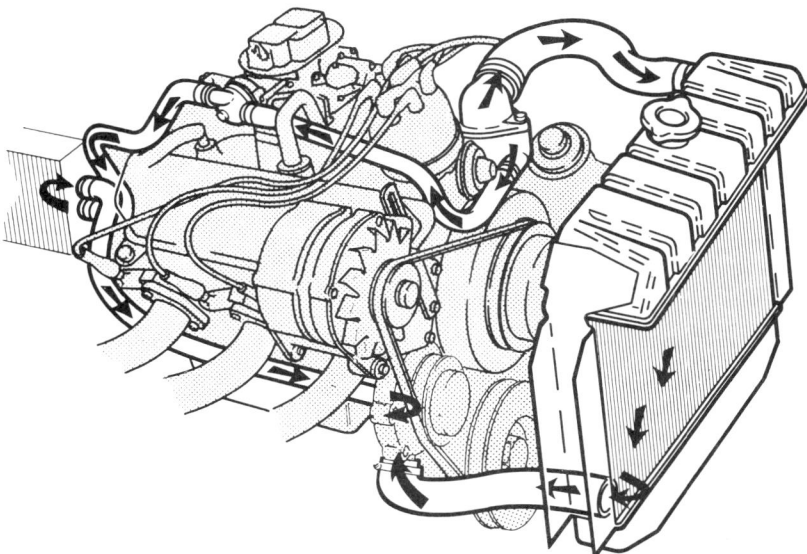

Fig. 2.3 Coolant system layout (3000cc engine)

5.4 Cooling system bleed nipple

6   With the radiator out of the car, reverse flush it to remove the sludge from it and clean the exterior with a jet of compressed air, or water, to remove any dirt or insects.
7   If the radiator requires repair, it is better to fit an exchange radiator, or have the repair done by a radiator specialist.
8   Inspect the radiator hoses for cracks and damage resulting from overtightening the clips and fit new hoses if the old ones have deteriorated. Fit new hose clips if the old ones are damaged, or corroded.
9   When refitting the radiator, fit the bottom hose before bolting the radiator in place. If any new hoses have been fitted, it will be found easier to fit them on to the radiator if their bores are first smeared with soap, or with rubber grease.
10 After refitting the radiator and hoses, tighten the hose clips and refill the cooling system.
11 On automatic transmission models, reconnect the oil cooler pipes and top up the transmission with transmission fluid.

7   Thermostat – removal and refitting (2800 cc engine)

1   Drain the cooling system as described in Section 3.
2   Slacken the clips securing the radiator bottom hose and the heater hose to the thermostat and carefully remove the hoses from the thermostat housing.
3   Undo and remove the three bolts and spring washers securing the thermostat housing.
4   Tap the thermostat housing with a soft-headed hammer to unstick it and lift the cover away. Recover the front cover gasket if it is undamaged, otherwise scrape it off.
5   Carefully ease the thermostat out of its housing, being careful to note which way round it is fitted.
6   Before refitting the thermostat, clean the thermostat sealing face and clean the recess into which the thermostat fits. Use a new joint washer in the recess and fit the thermostat the same way round as when it was removed.
7   Clean the thermostat housing mating surfaces and refit the housing. If the old gasket is re-used, make sure that it is fitted the same way round as it was originally.
8   Refit the hoses and tighten the hose clips, then refill the cooling system.

8   Thermostat – removal and refitting (3000 cc engine)

1   Drain some of the coolant from the system, so that the level is below the thermostat housing.
2   Slacken the clip of the top hose to the radiator and remove the hose.
3   Undo and remove the two bolts and spring washers securing the thermostat housing to the cylinder head.
4   Tap the housing gently with a plastic headed hammer, to break the gasket seal, then carefully lift the housing off. Remove the gasket in one piece if possible, otherwise scrape both joint faces to clean off the remains of the gasket.
5   Mark the thermostat to show which way round and which way up it is fitted, then use a screwdriver to remove its retaining clip.
6   Lift the thermostat out of its housing.
7   Before refitting the thermostat, clean its sealing face and clean the recess into which the thermostat fits. Use a new joint washer in the recess and fit the thermostat the same way round and the same way up as when it was removed.
8   Clean the thermostat housing mating surfaces and refit the housing. If the old gasket is re-used make sure that it is fitted the same way round as it was originally.
9   Refit the radiator top hose and tighten its clip, then top up the cooling system.

9   Thermostat – testing

1   Remove the thermostat as described in the previous Section.
2   Place the thermostat the right way up in a pan of water, with a thermometer to measure the water temperature.
3   Heat the water and note the temperature at which the thermostat begins to open and is fully open. If these are not within the Specifications, fit a new thermostat. A defective thermostat will either fail to open, or will not open fully.
4   Allow the water to cool and note the temperatures at which the thermostat begins to close and is fully closed. If the valve does not seat properly in the closed position, fit a new thermostat.

10   Water pump – removal and refitting (2800 cc engine)

1   Drain the cooling system, as described in Section 3.
2   Remove the radiator and shroud, as described in Section 5.
3   Loosen the alternator adjusting bolts and remove the drive belt. If an air conditioning pump is fitted, the alternator and mounting bracket will have to be removed completely.
4   Remove the fan and pulley from the pump.
5   Unscrew and remove the bolts and washers that secure the water pump assembly, noting the positions of each bolt, because they are of various lengths.
6   Lift away the pump assembly and recover the gasket, if it is not stuck to the pump assembly.
7   Before refitting the water pump assembly, remove all traces of gasket and jointing compound from the front cover and water pump assembly.
8   Apply jointing compound to both sides of a new gasket and position it accurately on the water pump.
9   Position the water pump assembly on the front cover and secure it with two bolts, finger tight.
10 Refit the remaining securing bolts and washers, making sure that they are returned to their original positions and tighten all the bolts progressively and in a diagonal sequence to a torque of 6 to 12 lbf ft (1.0 to 1.6 kgf m).
11 Refit the fan, drive belt and radiator, then refill the cooling system.

11   Water pump – removal and refitting (3000 cc engine)

1   Drain the cooling system as described in Section 3.
2   Slacken the three alternator mounting bolts, push the alternator towards the engine, lift the fan belt from the water pump pulley and remove it.
3   Slacken the lower radiator hose clip at the inlet connection to the pump. Carefully ease the hose from the water pump elbow.
4   Slacken the hose clip at the rear of the pump and carefully ease the hose from the top of the pump.
5   Slacken the third hose clip situated at the top of the pump and carefully ease the hose from the top of the pump.
6   Undo the three bolts securing the water pump to the cylinder block. Note that each bolt is fitted with a spring washer and that as the bolt is trapped by the fan pulley, it will be necessary to progressively slacken the bolts and pull the water pump away from the cylinder

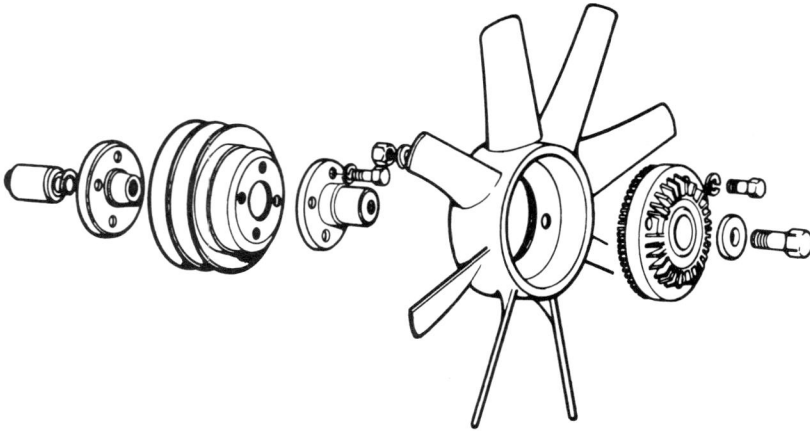

Fig. 2.4 Viscous drive fan assembly (2800cc engine)

block. The location of the bolts should be noted, so that they are refitted in their original positions.

7 Once all three bolts have been unscrewed from the cylinder block the water pump may be removed.

8 Refitting is the reverse sequence to removal. Always ensure the water pump and cylinder block mating faces are clean and free from dirt.

9 The fan belt tension must be correctly adjusted as described in Section 15. If the belt is too tight undue strain will be placed on the water pump bearings and if it is too loose it will slip, which could cause the engine to overheat.

12 Water pump – overhaul

1 Water pump failure is indicated by leaks, noisy operation and/or excessive slackness of the pump spindle.

2 Although new parts are obtainable, the dismantling of the pump and fitting of the seals and bearings requires a press and correctly sized mandrels. In the event of pump failure, it is recommended that a new pump is fitted, rather than trying to repair the old one.

13 Fan – removal and refitting (2800 cc engine)

1 Disconnect the lower radiator hose and drain the coolant from the system. Save the coolant for refilling the system.

2 Disconnect the radiator upper hose.

3 Remove the four screws and washers attaching the fan shroud to the radiator and pull the shroud back over the fan.

4 Remove the four screws and washers attaching the radiator to the front panel and remove the radiator.

5 Unscrew and remove the centre bolt attaching the fan assembly to the extension shaft and remove the fan assembly (Fig. 2.4).

6 Remove the four nuts and bolts attaching the viscous clutch to the fan and separate the clutch and the fan.

7 Refitting is a reversal of the removal procedure.

8 Refill the cooling system with the coolant which was removed, or with fresh antifreeze of 50% concentration. Start the engine and run it for a few minutes with the radiator cap removed, to purge air from the system.

9 Stop the engine, top up with coolant if necessary and refit the radiator cap. Check for leaks.

14 Fan – removal and refitting (3000 cc engine)

1 Remove the fan belt.

2 Remove the four bolts and washers securing the fan blade assembly and remove the blade assembly from the hub.

3 Remove the engine front cover (see Chapter 1, Section 16).

4 Remove the circlip which retains the bearing in the housing, then press the bearing, expansion plug and hub out of the front cover.

5 Press the shaft out of the hub.

6 Press a new shaft and bearing assembly into the housing, so that the circlip grooves are in alignment and refit the circlip.

7 Press on the hub until its front face is $3\frac{3}{8}$ in (85.8 mm) from the rear face of the front cover.

8 Fit a new expansion plug to the shaft bore in the rear face of the bearing housing.

9 Refit the front cover, pulley and fan blades.

10 Fit the fan belt and tension it as detailed in Section 15.

15 Fan belt – removal, refitting and tensioning

1 Loosen the alternator adjusting and mounting bolts and move the alternator towards the engine as far as possible.

2 Slip the belt over the edge of the alternator pulley. If the belt cannot be slid off with the fingers, do not attempt to lever it off, because this may damage the alternator pulley, but remove the alternator.

3 After detaching the belt from the alternator pulley, remove it from the fan and crankshaft pulleys. On the 2800 cc engine, it must also be removed from the water pump pulley (Fig. 2.5).

4 Pass the new belt round the crankshaft and fan pulleys, the water pump pulley if appropriate and finally the alternator pulley.

5 Refit the alternator if it has been removed and lever the alternator away from the engine until the belt can be deflected by finger pressure approximately 0.5 in (13 mm) at the centre of the longest span.

6 Tighten the alternator mounting and adjusting bolts and recheck the belt tension.

7 It is important to maintain correct belt tension. The belt being too slack will result in its slipping and reducing the efficiency of the alternator and of the cooling system. A belt too tight will cause excessive wear to the water pump and alternator bearings.

16 Temperature gauge sender unit – removal and refitting

1 For details of the removal and refitting of the temperature gauge, see Chapter 10.

2 To remove the sender unit, detach the Lucar connector from the unit.

3 Drain the cooling system, then unscrew the sender unit and remove it.

4 When fitting a new sender unit, apply a small quantity of jointing compound to the threads and screw it in so that it is firm, but not tight.

5 Reconnect the wire to the sender terminal and refill the cooling system.

17 Antifreeze

1 The cooling system is designed to operate with a 50% concentration of antifreeze at all times and water alone must never be used.

2 The recommended antifreeze is one which meets Ford Specification M97B 18-C and this may be left in the engine for two years, before being drained out and replaced by fresh antifreeze.

3 When topping up, always use an antifreeze mixture of 50% concentration.

a

EXH. EMISSION AIR PUMP

68 TO 79 LBS.

WATER PUMP

68 TO 79 LBS.

ALTER-NATOR

CRANK-SHAFT

b

EXH. EMISSION AIR PUMP

68 TO 79 LBS.

WATER PUMP

79 TO 90 LBS.

ALTER-NATOR

CRANK-SHAFT

POWER STEERING

c

EXH. EMISSION AIR PUMP

62 TO 73 LBS.

WATER PUMP

68 TO 79 LBS.

ALTER-NATOR

AIR CONDITION-ING

CRANK-SHAFT

99 TO110 LBS.

d

EXH. EMISSION AIR PUMP

62 TO 73 LBS.

WATER PUMP

ALTER-NATOR

AIR CONDITION-ING

CRANK-SHAFT

POWER STEERING

99 TO 110 LBS.

79 TO 90 LBS.

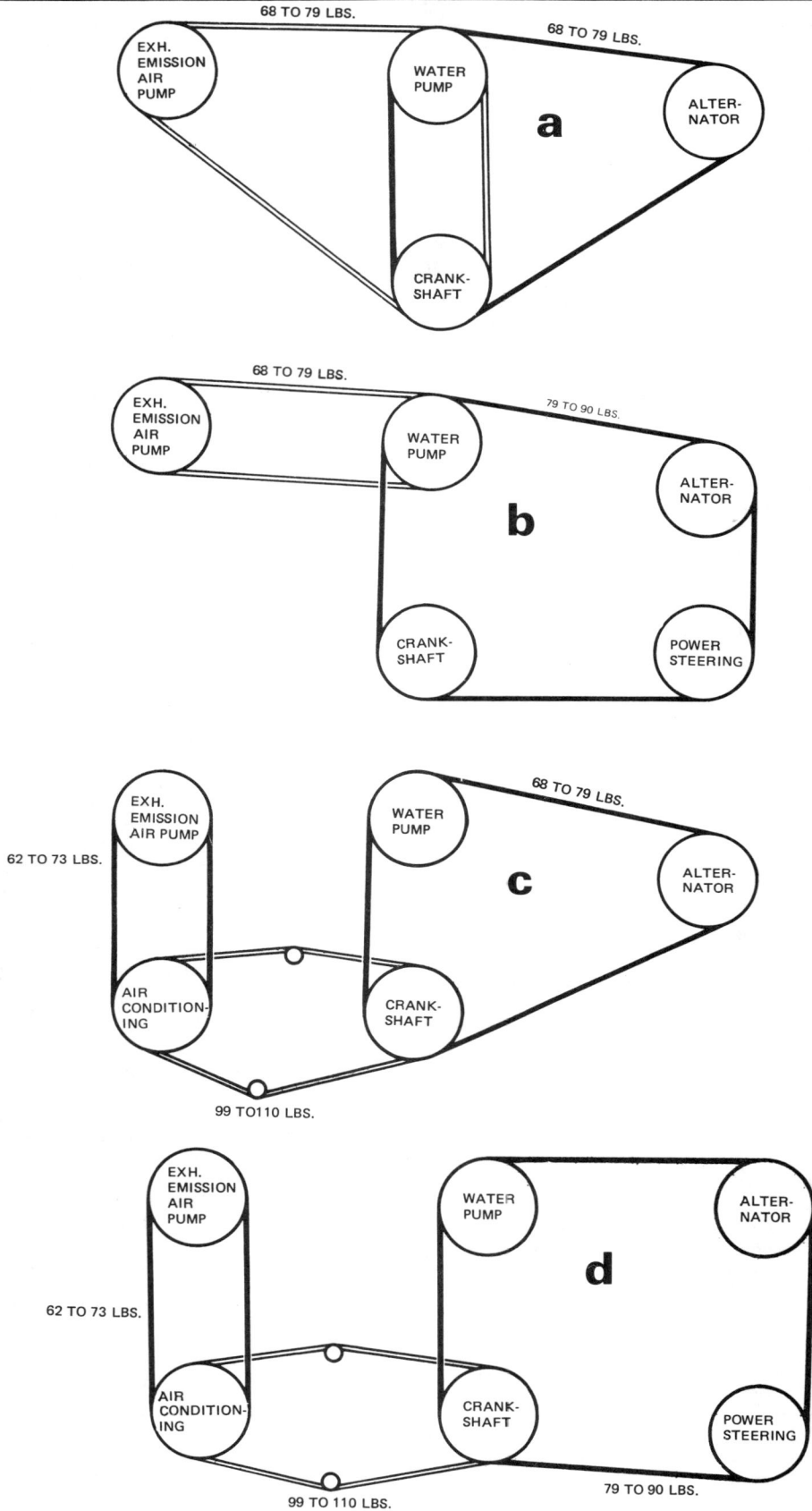

Fig. 2.5 Mercury Capri II drive belts and belt tension

a Manual steering without air conditioning   c Manual steering with air conditioning
b Power steering without air conditioning   d Power steering with air conditioning

18 Fault diagnosis – cooling system

Symptom	Reason/s
Overheating	Insufficient coolant
	Fan belt slipping
	Radiator core blocked, or grille restricted
	Air lock in cooling system
	Water hose collapsed, or kinked, impeding flow
	Thermostat defective
	Ignition timing incorrect
	Carburettor incorrectly adjusted
	Incorrect, or defective pressure cap
Engine runs too cool	Thermostat defective, or no thermostat
	Wrong thermostat fitted
Loss of coolant	Defective pressure cap
	Leaking hoses
	Leak in radiator, or heater core
	Thermostat or pump gasket leak
	Blown cylinder head gasket
	Cracked cylinder block, or head

Chapter 3 Carburation; fuel, exhaust and emission control systems

For modifications, and information applicable to later models, see Supplement at end of manual

Contents

Specifications

Mercury Capri II

Fuel pump
Type	Mechanical, driven from the camshaft
Delivery pressure	3·5 to 5·5 psi at curb idle speed
Volume flow	1 US pint in 25 seconds at curb idle speed

Fuel tank
Capacity	12·3 Imp gall, 15·3 US gall

Fuel filter
Renewable filter in fuel line to carburettor

Air cleaner
Renewable paper element

Carburettor
Type	Motorcraft double venturi with electrically assisted automatic choke
Model	2150 2–V
Throttle bore diameter	1·56 in
Venturi diameter	1·21 in
Float setting (dry)	$\frac{7}{16}$ in $\pm \frac{1}{32}$ in
Fuel level (wet)	$\frac{13}{16}$ in $\pm \frac{1}{16}$ in

Capri II

Fuel pump
Type .... Mechanical, driven by pushrod from eccentric on camshaft
Delivery pressure .... 3·5 to 5 psi

Fuel tank
Capacity .... 12·7 Imp gall (58 litres)

Fuel filter .... Nylon mesh, located in fuel pump

Air cleaner .... Renewable paper element

Carburettor
Type .... Weber dual venturi with automatic choke
Model 9510
Throttle barrel diameter .... 38 mm
Venturi diameter .... 27 mm
Main jet 145
Idling speed .... 800 ± 20 rpm
Fast idle .... 3200 ± 100 rpm
Float level .... 40 ± 0·3 mm
Float travel .... 12·5 ± 0·49 mm
Choke plate pull down .... 3·0 ± 0·25 mm

Torque wrench settings

Mercury Capri II	lbf ft	kgf m
Air cleaner wing nuts	15 to 25	2·1 to 2·9
Carburettor to manifold	12 to 15	1·7 to 2·1
Fuel pump to engine	12 to 15	1·7 to 2·1
Exhaust manifold to downpipe	15 to 20	2·1 to 2·5
U-bolts and clamps	28 to 33	3·9 to 4·6
Muffler box clamps	9 to 12	1·2 to 1·6
Fuel pump to engine	15 to 18	2·1 to 2·5

Capri II		
Air cleaner to carburettor	2 to 3	0·3 to 0·4
Air cleaner cover to body	5 to 7	0·7 to 1·0
Carburettor fixing nuts	15 to 18	2·1 to 2·5
Fuel pump to engine	15 to 18	2·1 to 2·5
U-bolts and clamps	28 to 33	3·9 to 4·5
Strap-type clamps	9 to 12	1·2 to 1·6

1 General description

The fuel system on all models consists of a rear mounted fuel tank, a mechanically operated fuel pump which is driven from the camshaft, a fuel filter and a carburettor.

Mercury Capri II models use a Motorcraft double-venturi carburettor, with an electrically assisted automatic choke. Capri II models are fitted with a Weber double-venturi carburettor, with automatic choke.

It is important that the correct grade of fuel is used. Only unleaded fuel should be used in the Mercury Capri II and the Capri II should use fuel of 97 octane rating (UK 4-star).

Part A: Mercury Capri II

2 Air cleaner – general

The air cleaner on the 2800 cc engine incorporated a renewable crankcase ventilation system filter in addition to the normal carburettor air intake filter.

On some models there is a vacuum modulator to operate the cold weather modulation system. This system ensures that the temperature of the carburettor intake air is above ambient if the ambient temperature is below 55°F.

Engines with Cold Temperature Actuated Vacuum Systems and Thermactor systems are equipped with a temperature sensitive switch, which is mounted in the air cleaner housing.

To avoid inadvertently dropping dirt into the carburettor, always remove the air cleaner as an assembly and then dismantle it to remove the filter element.

3 Air cleaner – removal and refitting

1   To avoid inadvertently dropping dirt into the carburettor, always remove the air cleaner as an assembly and then dismantle it.
2   Remove the wing nuts attaching the air cleaner body to the carburettor air horn studs. Disconnect the crankcase ventilation system hose at the air cleaner body. Disconnect the evaporative emission control system hose at the air cleaner body.
3   Disconnect the clip of the flexible tube.
4   Disconnect the sensor switch by removing its retaining clip, or by removing the cable connectors on switches which are riveted to the air cleaner.
5   Remove the air cleaner with two vacuum hoses connected.
6   Remove the air cleaner cover and take out the filter element (Fig. 3.1).
7   Wipe all the inside surfaces of the air cleaner with a lint-free cloth and fit a new filter element, ensuring that it seats properly.
8   Inspect the air cleaner gasket and fit a new one if necessary.
9   Refit the air cleaner, making sure that the air intake duct and hot air intake tube are properly aligned.
10   Connect the flexible tube and vacuum hose to the duct valve.
11   Connect the sensor switch.
12   Refit the cleaner cover and tighten the wing nuts.
13   Connect the crankcase ventilation system hose to the air cleaner body and connect the evaporative emission control system hose.

4 Crankcase ventilation filter – renewing

1   Disconnect the oil filter cap to air cleaner hose at the air cleaner, by unsnapping the elbow from the retainer clip (Fig. 3.2).

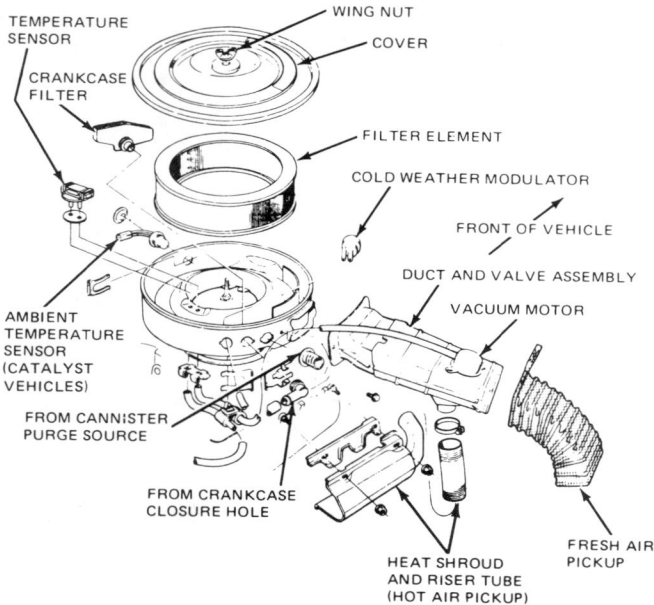

Fig. 3.1 Air cleaner assembly (typical)

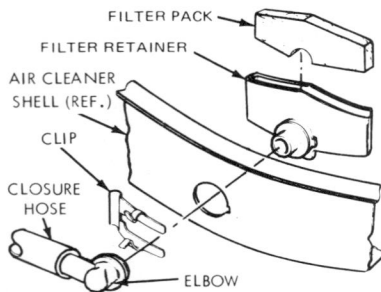

Fig. 3.2 Crankcase ventilation filter

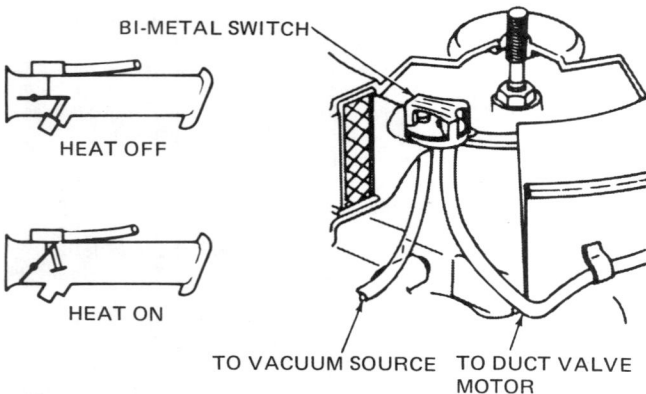

Fig. 3.3 Operation of the duct and valve assembly

2   Remove the air cleaner assembly as detailed in Section 3 and remove the air cleaner cover.
3   Remove the filter pack from the retainer, clean out the retainer and fit a new filter pack.
4   Reassembly is the reverse sequence to dismantling.

5   Cold weather modulator – operation

1   During engine operation at cold ambient temperatures the air cleaner duct door is prevented from admitting air which has not been preheated (Fig. 3.3). When air at the normal air intake is above 55°F, the cold weather modulator does not operate.
2   Normally, the duct air door will be closed to outside air any time that vacuum is applied by the bi-metal sensor. This occurs when the outside temperature is low enough to require heated air for the carburettor air intake.
3   When the temperature rises high enough to operate the bi-metal sensor, the vacuum is cut off and the door opens.
4   If vacuum is reduced due to acceleration and the temperature is low, a check valve on the bi-metal modulator seats to trap the vacuum in the vacuum motor, so that the entry of cold air is prevented.
5   The operation of the system under the various conditions is shown in Fig. 4.4.

6   Fuel pump – description

1   The mechanically operated pump is mounted on the left-hand side of the engine (Fig. 3.5) and is driven by an eccentric on the camshaft. The pump cannot be dismantled for repair. If the pump is suspect, test it as described in Section 8 and if it is found to be defective, fit a new pump.

7   Fuel pump – removal and refitting

1   Disconnect the battery.
2   Remove the inlet and outlet hoses to the pump, after unclamping the hose clips. If the crimped type of hose clips are fitted they should be cut off and renewed by a screw type clip.
3   Remove the fuel pump attachment screws, remove the pump and discard the gasket.
4   When refitting the pump, scrape both the pump and the cylinder block mounting surface free of old gasket and jointing compound.
5   Apply oil-resistant jointing compound to both faces of a new gasket and fit the gasket to the pump.
6   Insert the fixing bolts through the pump flange to keep the gasket in place and position the pump on the cylinder block, making sure that the pump rocker arm is riding on the camshaft eccentric.
7   Tighten the retaining bolts to the torque wrench setting given in the Specifications.
8   Fit the pump inlet hose and clamp it.
9   Position a suitable container over the end of the pump outlet. Reconnect the battery and crank the engine until petrol is seen to issue from the pump.
10   Reconnect and clamp the pump outlet hose.

8   Fuel pump – testing

1   Incorrect fuel pump pressure and low output will affect engine performance. Low pressure will result in lean mixture and fuel starvation at high speeds; and excessive pressure will cause carburettor flooding and high fuel consumption. Low pump output will cause fuel starvation at high speeds.
2   With the pump fitted to the engine and the engine at normal operating temperature, remove the air cleaner assembly and disconnect the fuel inlet line, or the fuel filter at the carburettor. Take care not to ignite any fuel which may be spilled.
3   Connect a pressure gauge, a restrictor and a flexible hose (Fig. 3.6) between the fuel filter and the carburettor.
4   Position the flexible hose and the restrictor so that the fuel can be discharged into a suitably graduated container.
5   Run the engine at idling speed and open the hose restrictor momentarily, to vent the system.
6   With the restrictor closed, allow the pressure to stabilise and note the reading. If it is not within the limits given in the Specifications, a new pump should be fitted.
7   If the pressure test is satisfactory, open the restrictor with the engine running at idling speed and allow fuel to flow into the graduated container, measuring the time which it takes for one pint to flow into the container. If this is a time longer than 25 seconds, the output is not satisfactory.
8   Repeat the test using an auxiliary fuel supply and with a new fuel filter. If still unsatisfactory, fit a new pump. If the test is satisfactory

TO BI-METAL SENSOR

TO DUCT VALVE
VACUUM MOTOR

COLD START OPERATION

BI-METAL
SENSOR

(2) MODULATOR
BI-METAL SEATS

O-RING SEAL

COLD WEATHER MODULATOR

VACUUM MOTOR

DUCT

(1) MANIFOLD VACUUM IS
HIGH (ABOVE 8 INCHES).

(3) CHECK VALVE OPENS

(4) FULL VACUUM
TO MOTOR

(5) VALVE OPEN FOR FULL HEAT
(BLOCKS FRESH AIR INLET).

HEATED AIR FROM HEAT SHROUD

ACCELERATION (MODULATOR TEMPERATURE BELOW 55° F.)

(3) BI-METAL
REMAINS SEATED

O-RING SEAL

(4) VACUUM IS TRAPPED

(1) MANIFOLD VACUUM IS
LOW (BELOW 8 INCHES)

(2) CHECK VALVE SEATS

(5) VALVE STAYS ON FULL HEAT
(BLOCKS FRESH AIR INLET)

HEATED AIR FROM HEAT SHROUD

WARM ENGINE (MODULATOR TEMPERATURE ABOVE 55° F.)

O-RING SEAL

(3) BI-METAL UNSEATED

(4) CONTROLLED VACUUM
TO MOTOR

(5) VALVE CLOSES TO ALLOW
ENTRY OF FRESH AIR

(1) MANIFOLD VACUUM
ABOVE 8 INCHES

(2) CHECK VALVE
REMAINS SEATED

(6) NORMAL TEMPERATURE
CONTROL

HEATED AIR FROM HEAT SHROUD

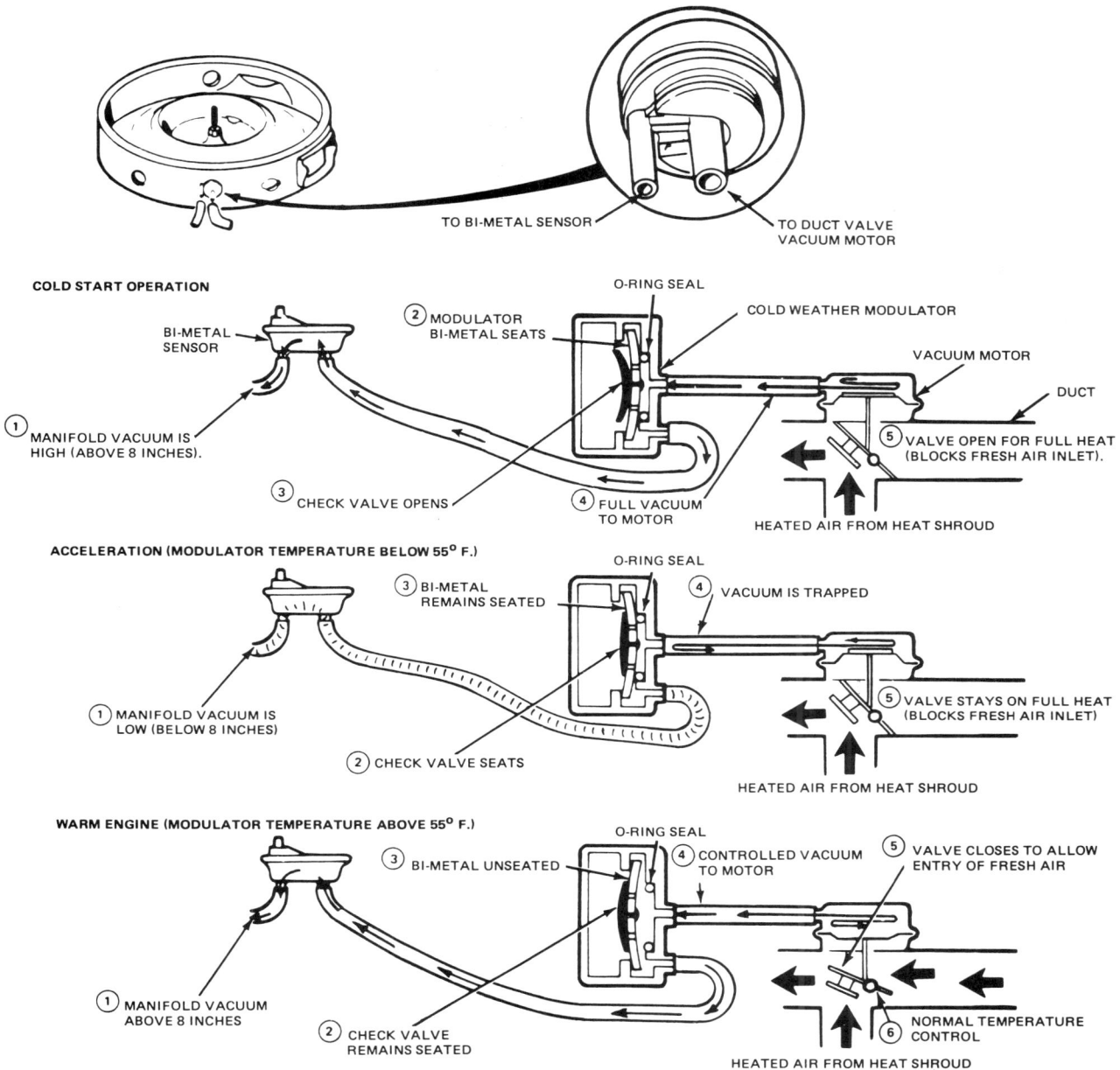

Fig. 3.4 Thermostatic air cleaner – cold weather modulator system

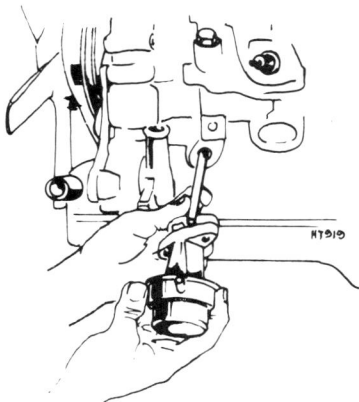

Fig. 3.5 Fuel pump

using an auxiliary fuel supply, check for fuel restrictions in the fuel from the tank to the pump.

9 Fuel filter – renewal

1   Remove the carburettor air cleaner.
2   Loosen the fuel line clips at the filter, pull off the fuel lines and discard the filter. On some models, unscrew the filter from the carburettor.
3   Fit a new filter, using new clips, taking care to fit the filter the right way round if it is marked to show the direction of fuel flow.
4   Start the engine and check for leaks. When satisfactory, refit the air cleaner.

10 Carburettor adjustments – general

1   Before making any alterations or adjustments to the carburettor and emission control systems, it is necessary to ensure that such

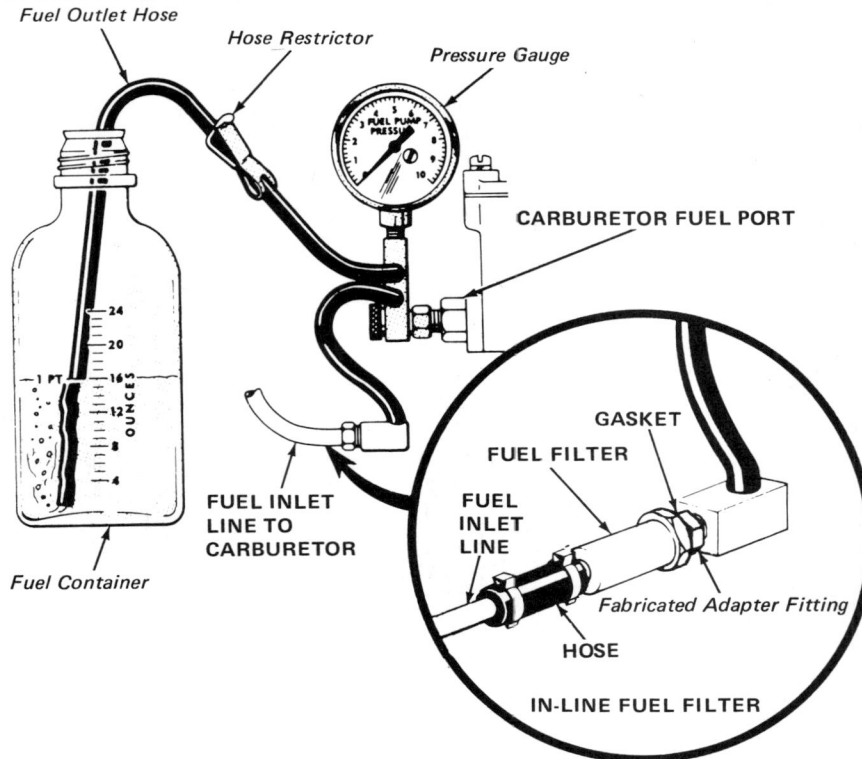

Fig. 3.6 Testing the fuel pump

action will not violate any Federal, State or Provincial laws.

2 Setting dimensions and specifications are given in this Chapter where relevant to adjustment procedures. Where these differ from those given on the engine tune-up decal, the decal information should be used.

3 Where the use of special test equipment is required to check exhaust gas analysis, adjustments made without its use must only be regarded as a temporary measure and should be checked at the earliest opportunity by a suitably equipped garage.

4 Before making any adjustments to the carburettor, check that the following items are serviceable and set correctly:-

(a) All vacuum hoses and connections
(b) Ignition system timing and contact breaker gap
(c) Spark plug gaps

5 If satisfactory carburation cannot be achieved, check the following:-

(a) Float chamber fuel level
(b) Crankcase ventilation system
(c) Valve clearances
(d) Engine compression
(e) Idle mixture

11 Carburettor – general description

1 The Motorcraft model 2150 2-V carburettor (Figs. 3.7 and 3.8) consists of two main assemblies, the air horn and the main body.

2 The air horn assembly, which is also the cover of the main body, contains the choke plate and fuel bowl vent valve. It contains the pullover enrichment system, which provides additional fuel flow at high air speeds through the air horn, by drawing fuel through metering orifices from the fuel bowl. It also contains a fuel decelerating metering system comprising a metered pick-up orifice in the fuel bowl and fuel/air mixing orifices and bleeds.

3 The main body contains the throttle plate, the accelerator pump assembly, the fuel bowl and the mechanical high speed bleed assembly.

4 Attached to the main body is the automatic choke (Fig. 3.9) and

choke pulldown diaphragm. The choke consists of a choke cap, thermostatic spring, bi-metallic switch and a heater powered by the alternator.

5 A thermostatically controlled hot idle compensator is located on the rear wall of the carburettor. As the temperature of the carburettor rises, the hot idle compensator opens and allows additional air to mix with the idle fuel-air mixture. This additional air improves idling stability and reduces the risk of rich mixture resulting from increased vaporisation and hot air entering the engine.

12 Carburettor – removal and refitting

1 Remove the air cleaner as described in Section 3.

2 Remove the throttle cable from the throttle lever. Disconnect all vacuum lines and emission hoses.

3 Unclamp the hose clip and pull off the fuel line.

4 Remove the choke heat tube.

5 Remove the carburettor retaining nuts and lift the carburettor off taking care not to spill the contents of the fuel bowl.

6 Remove the carburettor gasket, the spacer if fitted and the lower gasket from the manifold.

7 When refitting the carburettor, clean the gasket mounting surfaces. Place the spacer between two new gaskets and position the spacer and gaskets on the intake manifold.

8 Position the carburettor on the gasket and fit the choke heat tube, taking care not to damage the tube nut.

9 Fit the carburettor retaining nuts finger tight, then progressively and alternately tighten them half a turn at a time to the torque wrench setting given in the Specifications.

10 Refit the fuel pipe and clamp it. Reconnect the throttle and the vacuum lines. Note that the vacuum lines are colour coded and connect them accordingly.

11 Adjust the engine idling speed, and fuel mixture. If necessary adjust the stroke of the accelerator pump.

13 Carburettor – dismantling and reassembly

1 To facilitate working on the carburettor and to prevent damage to the throttle plates use four bolts about $2\frac{1}{4}$ inches long and of the

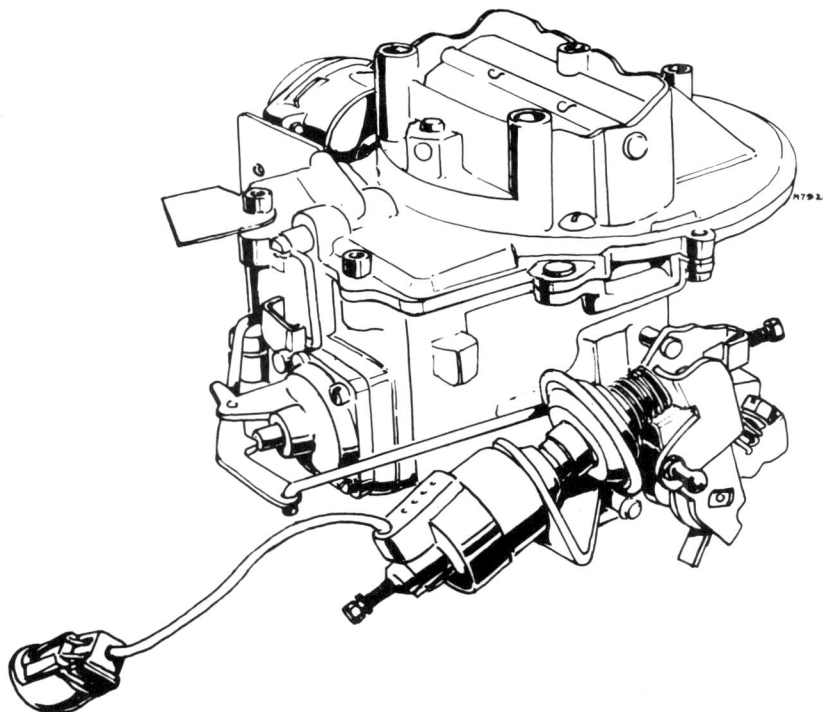

Fig. 3.7 Model 2150 – 2V carburettor – Left front $\frac{3}{4}$ view

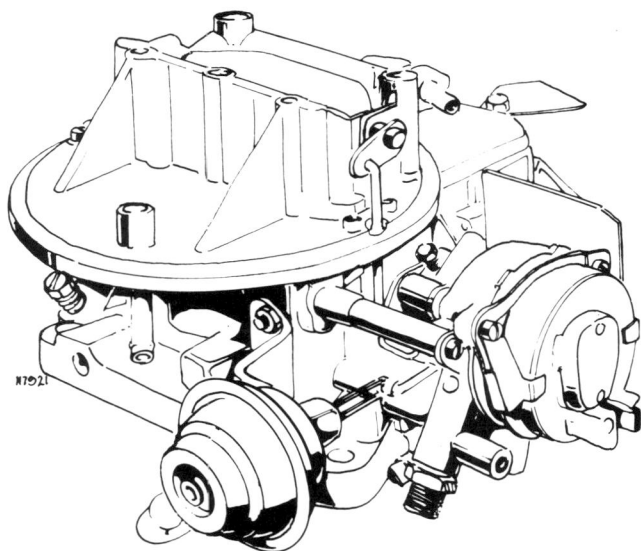

Fig. 3.8 Model 2150 – 2V carburettor – Right rear $\frac{3}{4}$ view

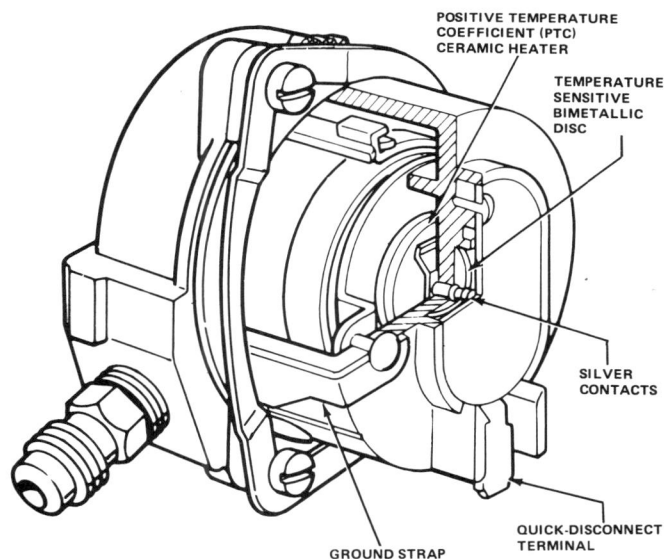

Fig. 3.9 Electrically assisted automatic choke

correct diameter and eight nuts to make temporary legs.

2   Use a separate container for the component parts of each assembly and take great care to use correctly fitting tools to avoid damage to nuts and screws.

3   The following is a step-by-step sequence of operations for a complete overhaul. Certain components may be serviced without a complete overhaul and for a partial overhaul, or the fitting of a new gasket, follow the appropriate steps.

Air horn

4   Remove the air cleaner anchor screw.

5   Remove the automatic choke control rod retainer (Fig. 3.11).

6   Remove the air horn attachment screws, lock washers and carburettor identification tag. Remove the air horn and air horn gasket.

7   Loosen the screw that secures the choke shaft lever to the choke shaft and remove the choke control rod from the air horn. Slide the plastic dust seal out of the air horn.

8   If it is necessary to remove the choke plate, remove the staking marks on the choke plate attachment screws and remove the screws. Remove the plate by taking it out of the shaft from the top of the air horn. Remove any burrs on the choke shaft and extract it from the air horn.

Choke pulldown diaphragm assembly

9   Disconnect the choke pulldown link, by removing the rod retainer and pulling the rod out of the diaphragm link slot.

10 Remove the two attachment screws from the bracket, disconnect the vacuum supply tube and remove the pulldown diaphragm.

HIGH-SPEED BLEED METERING ROD YOKE AND LIFT ROD

BOOSTER VENTURI SCREW

GASKET

WEIGHT

ACCELERATING PUMP DISCHARGE BALL CHECK

NOZZLE BAR, HIGH-SPEED BLEED AND BOOSTER VENTURI ASSEMBLY

GASKET

BOOSTER VENTURI

MAIN BODY

SPRING

RETAINER

IDLE MIXTURE NEEDLE

ELASTOMER VALVE

THROTTLE SHAFT LEVER ASSEMBLY

KICKDOWN ADJUSTMENT SCREW

IDLE LIMITER CAP

KICKDOWN LEVER

ACCELERATING PUMP DIAPHRAGM

ACCELERATING PUMP COVER

VENT VALVE ACTUATING LEVER

RETURN SPRING

SPRING

THROTTLE PLATES

ACCELERATING PUMP ROD

RETAINING CLIP

ACCELERATING PUMP OVER-TRAVEL SPRING

UPPER BODY

GASKET

DECEL VALVE CONNECTION (SOME MODELS)

FUEL BOWL VENT VALVE

THROTTLE SOLENOID POSITIONER (SOLENOID-DASHPOT)

CHOKE PLATE

CHOKE PLATE SHAFT

CHOKE PLATE LEVER

CURB IDLE RPM ADJUSTING NUT

CHOKE CLEAN AIR TUBE

CHOKE PLATE ROD

GASKET

DUST SHIELD

FLOAT

RETAINER

FLOAT SHAFT

MAIN JETS

SHAFT RETAINER

SOLENOID OFF IDLE (HOT ENGINE) SPEED ADJUSTING SCREW

SPRING

FUEL INLET NEEDLE

FUEL INLET NEEDLE SEAT

SHIELD

FILTER SCREEN

FAST IDLE CAM

DIAPHRAGM LINK

RETAINER

HOT IDLE COMPENSATOR

CHOKE LINKAGE

LINK

SHIELD

CHOKE PULLDOWN DIAPHRAGM ASSEMBLY

CHOKE HOUSING

CHOKE LEVER

PULLDOWN VACUUM SUPPLY TUBE

GASKET

GASKET

THERMOSTATIC SPRING HOUSING

ENRICHMENT VALVE

GASKET

RETAINER

COVER

SCREW

FAST IDLE ADJUSTING SCREW

SPRING

FAST IDLE ADJUSTING LEVER

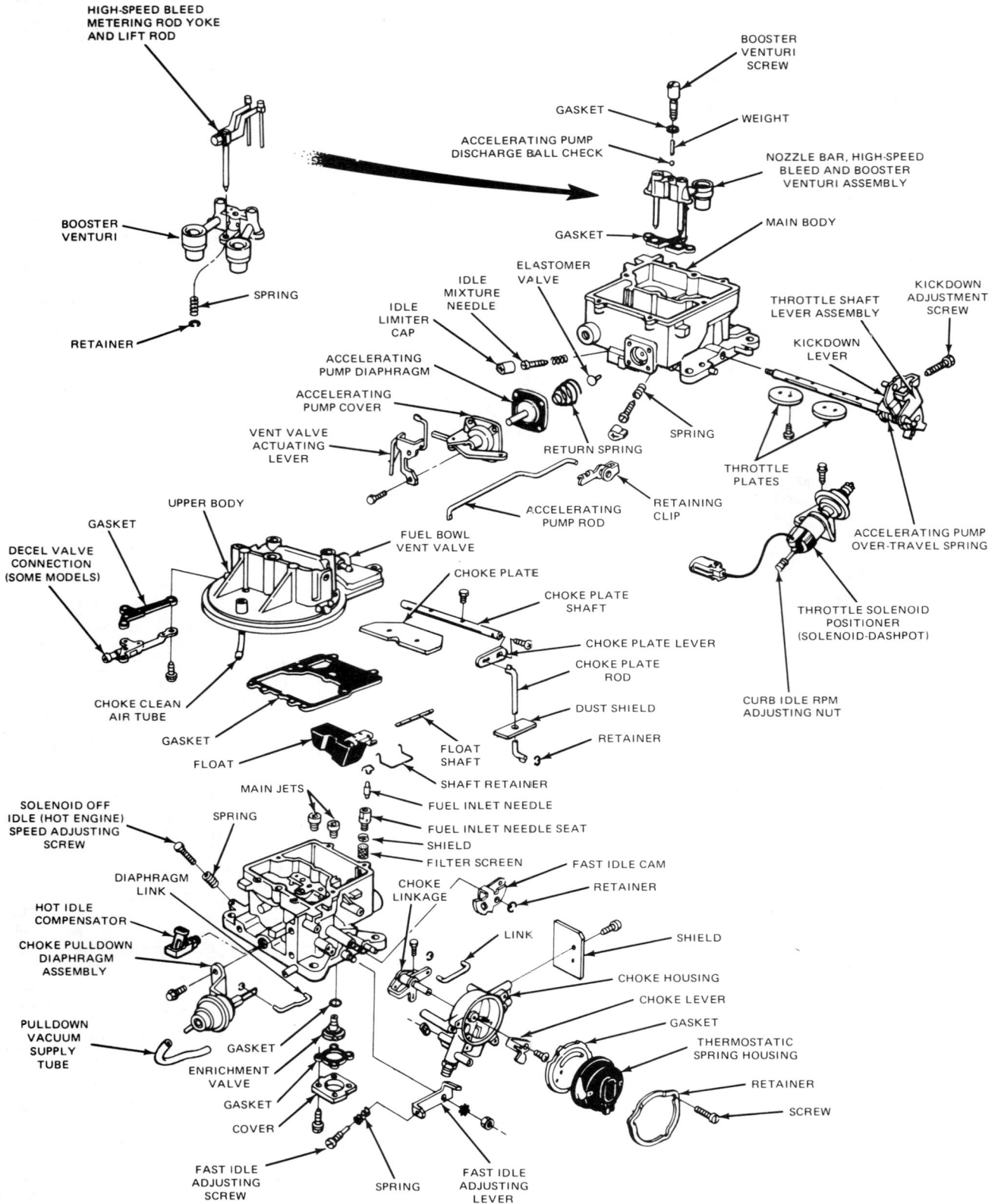

Fig. 3.10 Model 2150-2V carburettor – exploded view

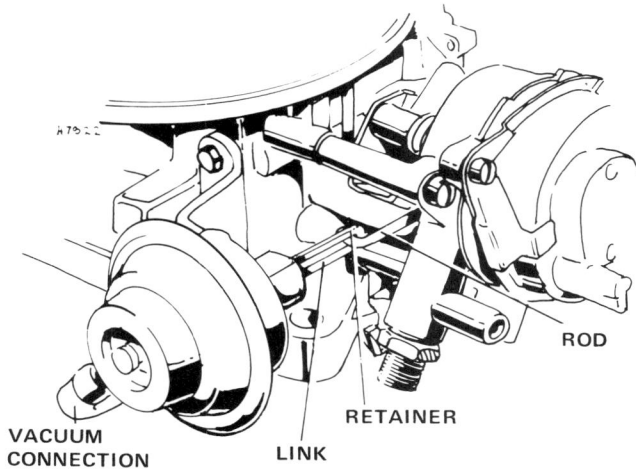

Fig. 3.11 Automatic choke pulldown assembly

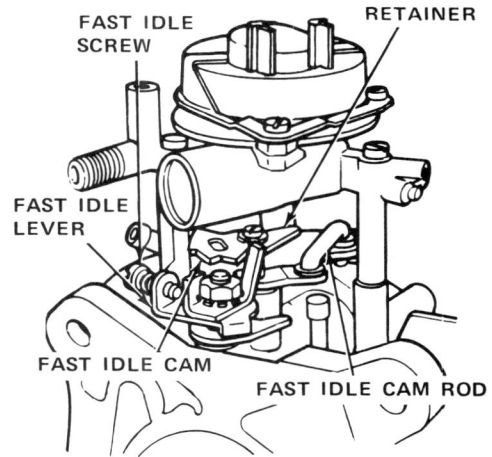

Fig. 3.12 Fast idle cam and fast idle lever

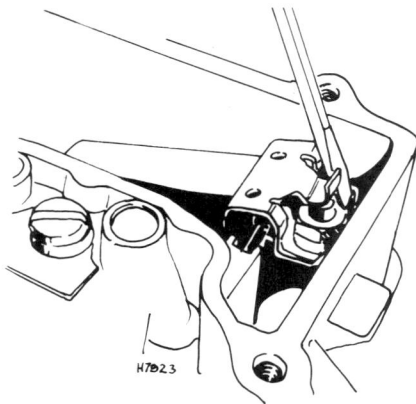

Fig. 3.13 Removing the float shaft retainer

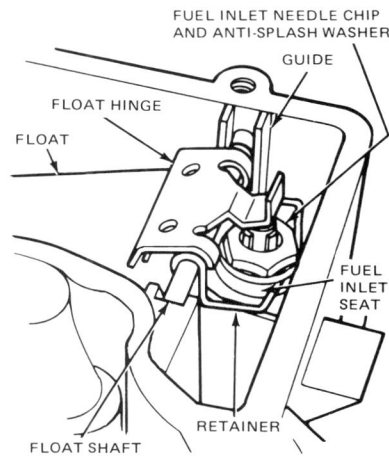

Fig. 3.14 Float assembly

Automatic choke

11 Remove the fast idle cam retainer (Fig. 3.12).

12 Remove the thermostatic choke spring housing retaining screws, then remove the clamp, housing and gasket.

13 Remove the retaining screws of the choke housing assembly. Remove the choke control rod retainer, if not already removed. Remove the choke housing assembly, gasket and the fast idle cam and rod from the fast idle cam lever.

14 Remove the retaining screw and washer from the choke lever and disconnect the choke control rod from the lever. Remove the choke lever and fast idle cam lever from the choke housing.

Main body

15 Use a screwdriver to prise the float shaft retainer from the fuel inlet seat (Fig. 3.13). Remove the float, float shaft retainer and fuel inlet needle assembly. Remove the retainer and float shaft from the float lever (Fig. 3.14).

16 Remove the fuel inlet needle, seat and filter screen. Using a jet wrench, remove the main jets.

17 Remove the booster venturi screw (accelerator pump discharge), air distribution plate, the booster venturi and metering rod assembly and gasket. Turn the main body upside down and let the accelerator pump discharge weight and ball fall out.

18 Remove the accelerator pump operating lever from the overtravel lever and retainer. To release the operating rod from the overtravel lever retainer, press upward on that part of the retainer which snaps over the rod. Disengage the rod from the retainer and from the overtravel lever. Remove the rod and retainer.

19 Remove the accelerator pump cover attachment screws. Remove the accelerator pump cover, diaphragm assembly and spring (Fig. 3.15).

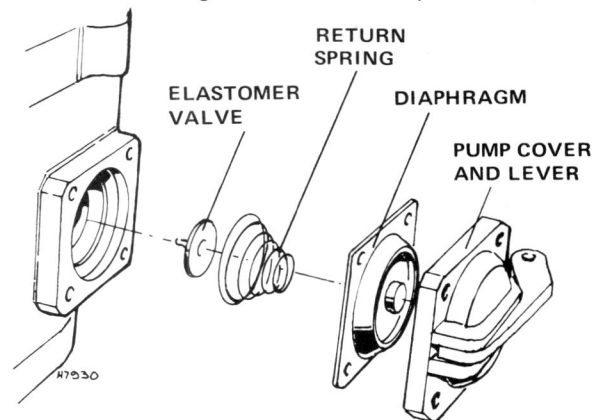

Fig. 3.15 Accelerator pump assembly

20 If it is necessary to remove the Elastomer valve, grasp it firmly and pull it out. Check that the tip of the valve did not break off during removal and if necessary recover it from the fuel bowl. When an Elastomer valve has been removed, it must be discarded and a new one fitted.

21 Invert the main body and remove the enrichment valve cover and gasket (Fig. 3.16). Use a box spanner to remove the enrichment valve, then remove its gasket and discard it.

22 Remove the idle fuel mixture adjusting screws and springs and take the limiters off the adjusting screws.

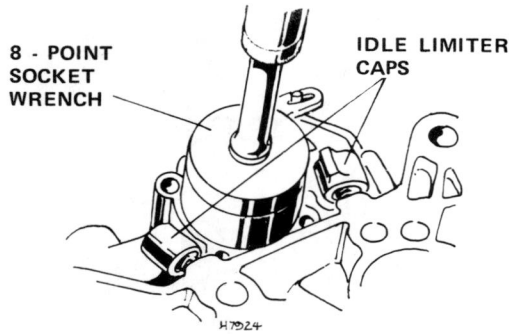

Fig. 3.16 Removing the enrichment valve

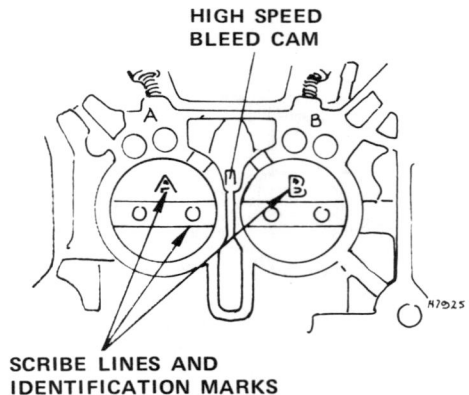

Fig. 3.17 Scribing the throttle plates

23 If necessary, remove the nut and washer securing the fast idle adjusting lever assembly to the throttle shaft and remove the lever assembly. If necessary, remove the idle screw and the spring from the fast idle adjusting lever.

24 If fitted, remove the anti-stall dashpot, or solenoid.

25 If it is necessary to remove the throttle plate, lightly scribe the plates on each side of the throttle shaft to ensure that they are refitted centrally and mark each plate so that it will be refitted in the same bore and in the same position as before removal (Fig. 3.17).

26 Slide the throttle shaft out of the main body, taking care to catch the mechanical high speed bleed actuator located on the throttle shaft between the throttle plates.

Reassembly

27 Before starting the reassembly procedure, wash all the parts in lead-free fuel, or methylated spirit. Make sure that all the holes in the new gaskets have been punched properly and that the accelerator pump diaphragm is not cut or torn.

Main body

28 Slide the throttle shaft assembly into the main body, until it begins to enter the high speed bleed cam slot in the body.

29 Holding the cam by the edge of the point, hold it in the slot and rotate the throttle shaft until the shaft will pass through the cam. Rotate the shaft clockwise until the throttle lever clears the boss for the Throttle Solenoid Positioner 'OFF' idle speed screw. Continue inserting the shaft, rotating it as necessary until both the shaft and the cam are in their proper positions.

30 Fit the throttle plates into their correct positions by using the marks scribed on them before dismantling. Secure the throttle plates with new screws, but do not tighten the screws fully.

31 Close the throttle plates and hold the carburettor up to the light to ensure that the plates are properly seated, with little, or no light showing between the plates and the throttle bores. If necessary, tap the plates lightly with the handle of a screwdriver to seat them.

32 While holding the throttles closed, tighten the attaching screws and stake them by lightly centre-punching the ends of the slots in the heads, or by burring the exposed threads with a pair of side cutters.

33 If necessary, fit the fast idle screw and spring and the screw on the fast idle adjusting lever.

34 Fit the anti-stall dashpot and solenoid, or the solenoid-dashpot as appropriate.

35 Fit the fast idling adjusting lever assembly onto the throttle shaft and refit the retaining washer and nut.

36 If the Elastomer valve was removed, lubricate the tip of a new Elastomer valve and insert the tip into the accelerator pump cavity central hole. Use a pair of fine snipe-nosed pliers to grip the valve tip inside the fuel bowl and pull the valve in until it seats in the pump cavity wall. Cut the tip off forward of the retaining shoulder and remove the cut off piece from the bowl.

37 Fit the accelerator pump diaphragm return spring onto the boss in the chamber. Insert the diaphragm assembly in the cover and place the diaphragm and cover assembly in position on the main body. Fit the cover retaining screws and tighten them.

38 Insert the accelerator pump operating rod into the hole in the accelerator pump actuating lever. Position the accelerator pump

operating rod retainer over the specified hole in the over-travel lever. Insert the operating rod through the retainer and the hole in the over-travel lever and snap the retainer down over the rod.

39 Insert the main body and fit the enrichment valve and a new gasket. Use a properly fitting spanner to tighten the valve securely.

40 Fit the idle mixture adjusting screws and springs, screwing the needles in gently with the fingers until the needles touch their seatings. From this position, unscrew each screw half a turn, to provide a preliminary idle fuel mixture adjustment. Do not fit the idle mixture limiters at this time.

41 Fit the enrichment valve cover, using a new gasket. The cover must be fitted with the limiter stops on the cover positioned so that they provide a positive stop for the tabs on the idle mixture adjusting screw limiters.

42 Fit the main jets, taking care to insert them in their correct positions. Fit the fuel inlet seat and baffle, using a new gasket.

43 Fit the fuel inlet needle assembly into the fuel inlet seat.

44 Slide the float shaft into the float lever. Position the float shaft retainer on the float shaft.

45 Insert the float assembly into the fuel bowl and hook the float lever tab under the fuel inlet needle assembly. Insert the float shaft into its guides in the side of the fuel bowl.

46 With a screwdriver, position the float shaft retainer in the groove on the fuel inlet needle seat. Check the float setting as detailed in Section 16.

47 Drop the accelerator pump discharge ball and weight into the passage in the main body.

48 Position the new booster assembly gasket and the booster venturi assembly in the main body. Fit the air distribution plate and the accelerator pump discharge screw. Tighten the screw.

Automatic choke

49 Position the fast idle cam lever on the thermostatic choke shaft and lever assembly. The bottom of the fast idle cam lever adjusting screw must rest against the tang on the choke lever. Insert the choke lever into the rear of the choke housing and position the choke lever so that the hole in the lever is towards the left side of the choke housing.

50 Fit the fast idle cam rod onto the fast idle cam lever. Place the fast idle cam on the fast idle cam rod and fit the retainer. Place the choke housing vacuum pick-up port, to main body gasket, on the choke housing flange.

51 Position the choke housing on the main body and at the same time, fit the fast idle cam on to the hub on the main body. Position the gasket and fit the choke housing attachment screws. Fit the fast idle cam retainer and the thermostatic spring housing.

Choke pulldown diaphragm assembly

52 Position the choke pulldown diaphragm mounting bracket against the main body casting and fit the two attachment screws.

53 Connect the vacuum supply tube to the vacuum base tube connection.

54 Insert the choke pulldown control rod through the slot in the diaphragm link and fit the retainer clip over the end of the rod, in the slot.

55 Carry out the automatic choke pulldown and fast idle cam adjustments as described in Section 15 and 17.

56 Fit the air cleaner assembly.

Air horn

57 If the choke plate shaft was removed, position the shaft in the air horn, then fit the choke plate rod to the end of the choke shaft.

58 If the choke plate was removed, insert the choke plate into the choke plate shaft. Fit the choke plate screws so that they are firm, but not tight. Check that the plate fits properly and does not bind, by moving the plate from the closed position to the open position. If necessary remove the choke plate and carefully file away the edge of the plate where it is binding, or scraping on the wall of the air horn. When the choke plate and shaft move freely, tighten the choke plate screws fully, while holding the plate in the fully closed position.

59 Position the fuel bowl gasket a d the choie rod plastic seal on the main body. Position the air horn on the main body and gasket, so that the choke plate rod fits through the seal and the opening in the main body.

60 Fit the end of the choke plate rod into the automatic choke lever. Fit the air horn attachment screws and the carburettor identification tag. Tighten the attachment screws.

61 Fit the choke plate rod retainer and the air cleaner anchor screw. Tighten the air cleaner anchor screw to a torque of 1.3 to 2.0 lbf ft (0.18 to 0.28 kgf m).

14 Accelerator pump – stroke adjustment

1 The accelerator pump stroke is factory set for a particular application and should not be changed. If the stroke has been changed from the specified hole, reset to specification as follows.

2 Release the rod from the retaining clip by lifting upwards on the portion of the clip which snaps over the shaft (Fig. 3.18) and then disengage the rod.

3 Position the clip over the specified hole in the overtravel lever and insert the operating rod through the clip and the overtravel lever. Snap the end of the clip over the rod to secure it.

15 Choke plate pulldown – adjustment

1 The Model 2150 2-V carburettor is equipped with a remotely-mounted choke pulldown diaphragm assembly. Vacuum is metered to the diaphragm through internal passages in the carburettor from an external connecting tube. As the vacuum bleeds through the orifices in the carburettor, the choke diaphragm pulls the choke plate to the pulldown position (Fig. 3.11).

2 To check the pulldown position, set the throttle on the fast idle cam top step.

3 Note the index position of the choke bi-metallic cap. Loosen its retaining screws and rotate the cap 90° in the rich (closing) direction (Fig. 3.19).

4 Operate the choke plate pulldown motor, by manually forcing the pulldown control diaphragm link in the direction of applied vacuum, or by applying vacuum to the external vacuum tube (Fig. 3.20).

5 Check the clearance between the edge of the choke plate and the air horn wall by inserting the shank of a $\frac{5}{32}$ in twist drill (Fig. 3.11). If necessary adjust the clearance by turning the adjustment screw on the end of the choke pulldown diaphragm.

6 After completing the check, reset the choke bi-metallic cap to the index position specified on the engine tune-up decal.

7 Check and if necessary adjust the fast idle speed to 1600 rpm.

16 Carburettor float – adjustment

1 Make an initial setting with the float dry and then obtain a final setting with the float wet as follows.

2 With no fuel in the fuel bowl and with the air horn removed, seat the fuel inlet needle by depressing the float tab and measure the distance between the top surface of the main body (gasket removed) and the top surface of the float. If this is not within the limits $\frac{13}{32}$ to $\frac{15}{32}$ in, bend the float tab to achieve the necessary correction.

3 Perform the final check at normal engine operating temperature and with the vehicle on a flat level surface.

4 With the engine not running, remove the carburettor air cleaner assembly. Remove the air horn attachment screws and the carburettor

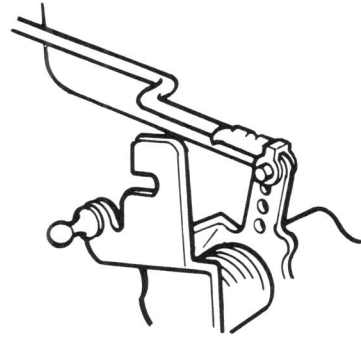

Fig. 3.18 Accelerator pump stroke adjustment

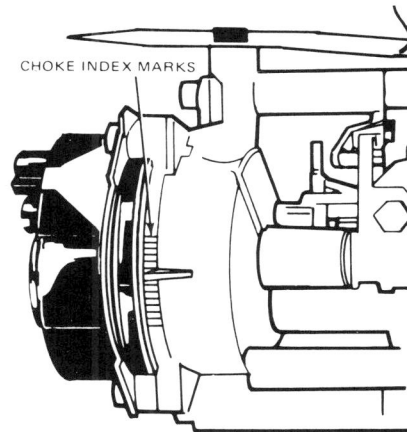

CHOKE INDEX MARKS

Fig. 3.19 Automatic choke thermostatic spring housing adjustment solenoid

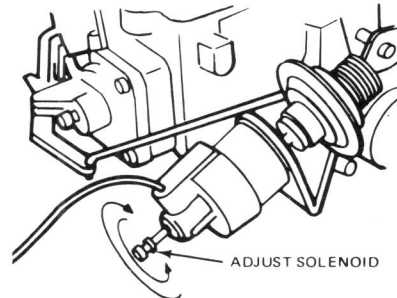

ADJUST SOLENOID

Fig. 3.20 Solenoid dashpot throttle positioner (TSP) adjustment

identification tag.

5 Temporarily leave the air horn and gasket in position on the carburettor body and start the engine. Leave the engine to idle for a few minutes, then remove the air cleaner stud, the air horn and gasket, to give access to the float assembly.

6 While the engine is idling, measure the vertical distance from the top machined surface of the carburettor main body to the surface of the fuel in the fuel bowl at its point of contact with the float. This distance should be between the limits $\frac{3}{4}$ and $\frac{7}{8}$ in.

7 If any adjustment is required, stop the engine to minimise the danger of fire if any fuel is spilled when the float setting is disturbed. Bend the float tab upward to raise the fuel level and bend it downwards to lower the level.

8 After each adjustment, the air horn must be refitted and secured in place with the engine air cleaner assembly stud. The engine must be started and run for a few minutes to stabilise fuel level, then stopped and the air horn removed to check the fuel level.

9 When the level is correct, fit a new air horn gasket, fit the air horn, the carburettor identification tag and the attachment screws.

10 Check that a plastic dust seal on the choke operating rod is

positioned correctly and does not cause the rod to bind, then tighten the attachment screws. Fit the air cleaner anchor stud and tighten it to a torque of 1.3 to 2.0 lbf ft (0.18 to 0.28 kgf m).

11 Check the idle fuel mixture, idle speed adjustment and the carburettor throttle positioner adjustment (if one is fitted) and make any necessary adjustments.

12 Fit the air cleaner.

17 Fast idle, curb idle and TSP - off idle speed – adjustment

1 A solenoid throttle positioner (TSP) (Fig. 3.20 and 3.21) is fitted to some models to prevent dieseling (running on) after the ignition has been switched off, by allowing the throttle to close beyond the point necessary for idling.

2 Remove the EGR vacuum line and air cleaner and plug both vacuum lines.

3 Connect a timing light and a tachometer to the engine.

4 With the transmission in neutral and the handbrake fully on, start the engine and allow it to run until it reaches the normal operating temperature.

5 Check the timing and if necessary adjust it (Chapter 4).

6 Remove the spark delay valve, if fitted, and connect the throttle vacuum signal directly to the advance side of the distributor. If the distributor is of the dual diaphragm type, leave the manifold vacuum line connected to the retard side of the distributor.

7 Set the throttle to the kickdown step on the choke cam (Fig. 3.22), making sure that the adjusting screw is against the shoulder of the kickdown step, then adjust the fast idle speed to 1600 rpm.

8 Kick the throttle off the kickdown step, allowing the engine to return to idling speed then repeat step 7 and 8 until the specified idle speed can be repeated each time the kickdown is operated.

9 Increase the engine speed to 2000 rpm for 10 seconds and then allow it to return to idle.

10 Collapse the solenoid plunger by forcing the throttle linkage against the solenoid stem.

11 With the transmission in neutral, turn the throttle arm adjusting screw on the carburettor body to obtain a TSP - off idle speed of 550 rpm.

12 Increase the engine speed to 2000 rpm for 10 seconds and then allow it to drop to idling speed.

13 If applicable, wait at least 5 seconds for the dashpot to bottom, before checking the curb idle speed. Place automatic transmission vehicles in 'Drive' and manual transmission vehicles in neutral. Turn the hexagon headed adjusting screw on the TSP plunger to obtain the specified curb idle speed.

14 If adjustment has to be made, repeat steps 12 and 13 until the proper idle speed can be obtained repeatedly.

15 Fit the spark delay valve (if removed) and reconnect the vacuum line to the EGR valve.

16 Stop the engine and remove the timing light and tachometer.

17 Refit the air cleaner and reconnect the vacuum line.

18 Idle mixture – adjustment

1 Idle mixture adjustment can only be carried out satisfactorily using special test equipment. The following procedure gives an approximate setting and can be used as a temporary setting after carburettor overhaul. Refer to Section 10 before making any adjustments.

2 Obtain the best possible idling speed using the method detailed in Section 17. If the idling speed is unstable, it should be increased just enough to get the engine running steadily.

3 Rotate the idle mixture screws (Fig. 3.23) by increments of $\frac{1}{8}$ th turn, to obtain the most satisfactory idle speed. When the idle mixture is too rich, indicated by sooty exhaust smoke, rotate the screws clockwise. When the mixture is too lean, indicated by the engine running unevenly and tending to stop, rotate the screws anti-clockwise. It should be expected that both screws will need to be turned by the same amount.

4 After making the adjustment, fit the idle mixture limiters, if these were removed from the adjuster screws and ensure that the setting is checked by a dealer with specialist carburettor emission control equipment at the earliest opportunity.

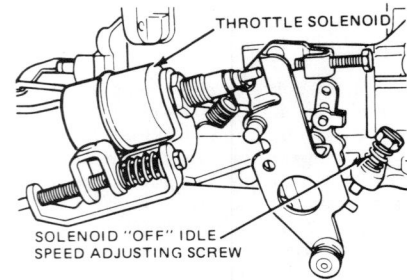

Fig. 3.21 Idle speed adjustment (vehicles with TSP)

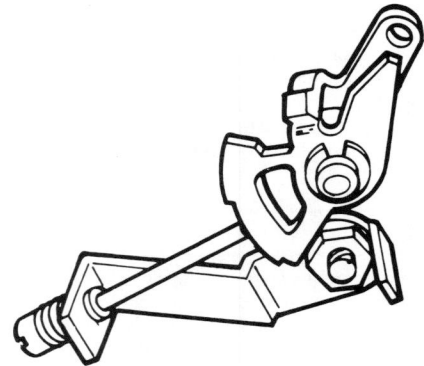

Fig. 3.22 Fast idle screw and stepped cam

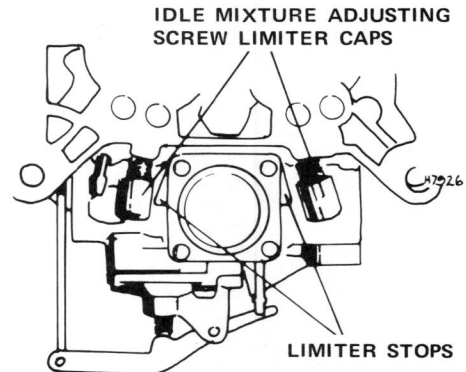

Fig. 3.23 Idle mixture adjusting screws and stops

19 Accelerator pedal assembly – removal and refitting

1 Disconnect the battery leads from the battery terminals.

2 Disconnect the accelerator cable retaining clip at the ball stud. Pull the cable slightly and at the same time depress the tangs on the bracket clip one at a time with a screwdriver and remove the throttle cable.

3 Loosen the bolt and detach the shaft extension rod (Fig. 3.24).

4 Use a punch to tap out the retaining clip, then slide the shaft assembly out until it butts against the heater.

5 Remove the bushing from the right-hand side of the pedal and remove the pedal assembly.

6 Detach the pedal, bushing and spring clip from the shaft.

7 Refitting the assembly is a reverse of the operations necessary for removal.

20 Charcoal canister – removal and refitting

1 The charcoal canister of the fuel evaporative system is fitted in the engine compartment, on the right-hand side of the dash panel.

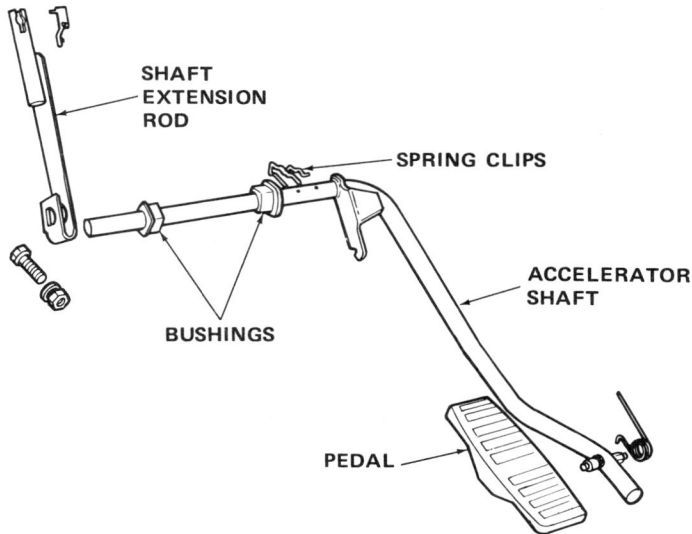

Fig. 3.24 Accelerator pedal assembly

2   Open the bonnet and disconnect the two vapour hoses from the canister, noting to which port each of the hoses is connected.
3   Remove the two Phillips head screws securing the canister to the dash panel and remove the canister and its bracket.
4   Refit the canister by reversing the operations necessary for removing it, taking care to connect the hoses to the correct ports on the canister.

21 Fuel tank – removal and refitting

1   Great care is necessary when working on any part of the fuel system and it is safer to do the work outside if possible. Avoid having the car over a pit, where explosive vapour can accumulate. Take care to avoid naked flames and any other sources of ignition.
2   Disconnect the battery leads.
3   Syphon any petrol remaining in the tank into a metal container suitable for storing petrol. Label the container clearly and store it in a well ventilated place.
4   Remove the screw securing the filler neck to the car body (Fig. 3.25).
5   Jack up the rear of the car, support it on firmly based axle stands, or on blocks. Disconnect the fuel feed pipe and return fuel line if fitted. Unclip the fuel lines from the front of the tank.
6   Disconnect the fuel gauge wires from the sender unit on the tank, marking each wire and terminal so that the wires will be reconnected correctly.
7   Disconnect the vapour line from the T connector on the vent hose and unclip the vent pipe from the chassis (Fig. 3.26).
8   Loosen the straps holding the tank. Hold the tank with one hand while unclipping the straps. Loosen the clamp between the tank and the filler pipe and remove the tank, leaving the filler pipe in position on the car.
9   When refitting the tank, make sure that the vent pipe passes behind the fuel tank straps.
10   Reconnect the filler pipe joint.
11   Reconnect the fuel feed pipe and the return fuel line if fitted, attaching them to the clips along the front of the tank.
12   Reconnect the fuel gauge wires to the terminals from which they were removed.
13   Reconnect the vapour line to the T connector on the vent pipe and clip the pipe into position along the chassis.
14   Check that all hoses are fitted properly, then lower the car to the ground.
15   Refit the screw securing the filler neck and reconnect the battery leads.
16   Put fuel back into the tank. It is preferable not to re-use the fuel which was taken out of the tank. If this is unavoidable, filter the fuel before putting it back.

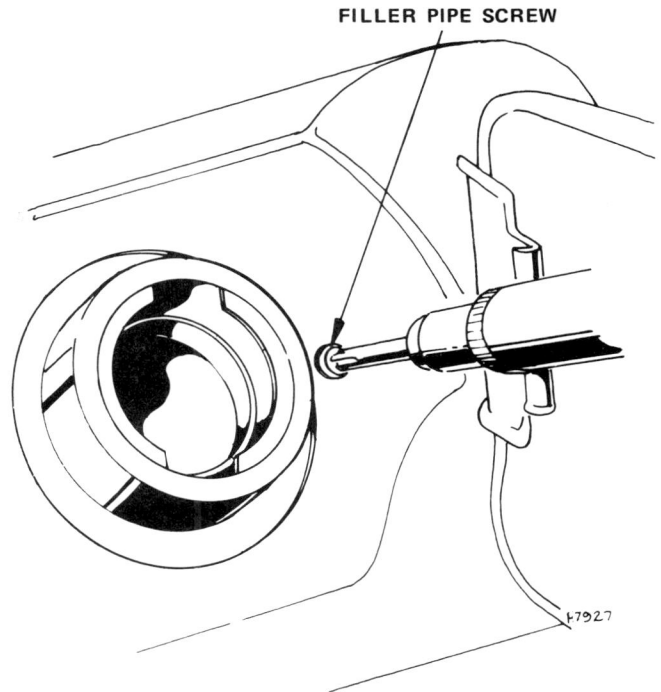

Fig. 3.25 Removing the filler pipe neck screw

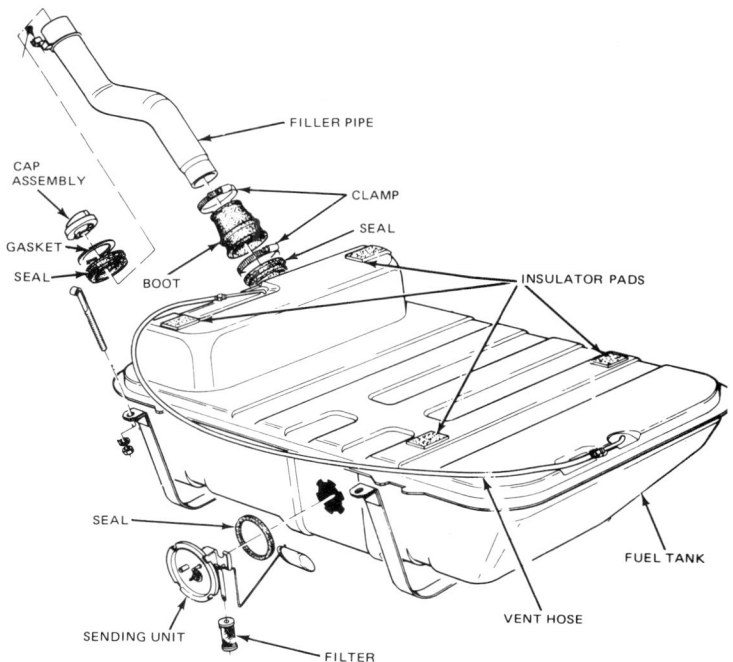

Fig. 3.26 Fuel tank assembly

22 Fuel tank – cleaning and repair

1   Remove the fuel tank as described in Section 21, then remove the fuel tank sender unit, the tank to filler pipe seal and the four insulator pads.
2   Before attempting any repair to the tank, steam the tank, or boil it in water containing alkali or detergent for at least two hours.
3   When refitting the tank, stick the four insulating pads onto the tank, refit the tank to filler pipe seal and refit the tank sender unit, using a new gasket.

23 Fuel tank filler pipe – removal and refitting

1   Remove the cap from the filler pipe.
2   Remove the right-hand side trim panel (Chapter 12).
3   Peel back the insulation clear of the pipe cover panel (Ghia only).
4   Lift out the panel covering the spare wheel.
5   Remove two screws from inside the car (Fig. 3.27) and remove the filler pipe door (Fig. 3.28).
6   Loosen the clamp of the pipe to floor boot and pull the gaiter up clear of the floor.
7   Remove the fuel tank as described in Section 21.
8   Remove the filler pipe with gaiter attached.
9   When refitting the pipe, first refit the boot if it has been removed, position the clamp on it, but do not tighten the clamp.
10 Position the neck assembly, align the holes for the neck securing screw and insert the screw, but do not tighten it.
11 Refit the fuel tank, fit the boot to the floor and tighten the screws of both clamps.
12 Tighten the screw securing the filler pipe neck to the body.
13 Refit the filler pipe door.
14 Refit the spare wheel cover panel.
15 Put the insulation back into position (Ghia only).
16 Refit the rear trim panel.
17 Refit the filler cap.

24 Throttle cable – removal, refitting and adjustment

1   Remove the clip at the ball-stud and then remove the throttle cable from the throttle lever ball-stud.
2   Remove the cable from the bracket by pulling on the cable slightly and then depressing the cable clip tabs one at a time, using a screwdriver (Fig. 3.29).
3   Remove the cable from the accelerator pedal.
4   Fit the cable by first threading it through the dash panel and attaching the cable ferrule to the accelerator pedal.
5   Fit the cable retainer to the dash panel.
6   Push the throttle cable clip into the opening and snap it into place.
7   Position the cable on the throttle lever ball-stud and fit the clip.
8   Place a weight on the accelerator pedal to hold it in its fully depressed position.
9   Open the bonnet. Make a sketch of the hoses running from the air cleaner and remove the air cleaner as described in Section 3.
10 Turn the throttle cable adjusting nut (Fig. 3.30) anti-clockwise until the carburettor throttle is just at its fully open position.
11 Operate the throttle several times to make sure that full throttle can be achieved, adjusting the cable if necessary.
12 Refit the air cleaner and emission hoses and then close the bonnet.

25 Kickdown cable – removal, refitting and adjustment

1   Remove the split cotter from the clevis assembly on the carburettor throttle arm, remove the clevis pin and slide the cable from the bracket arm.
2   Slacken the two cable adjusting nuts on the bracket (Fig. 3.30) and slide the cable out of the bracket.
3   Jack the car and support it on firmly based axlestands, or on blocks and disconnect the cable from the transmission.
4   Remove the cable from the car.
5   When fitting a cable, jack and support the car, then fit the transmission end of the cable.

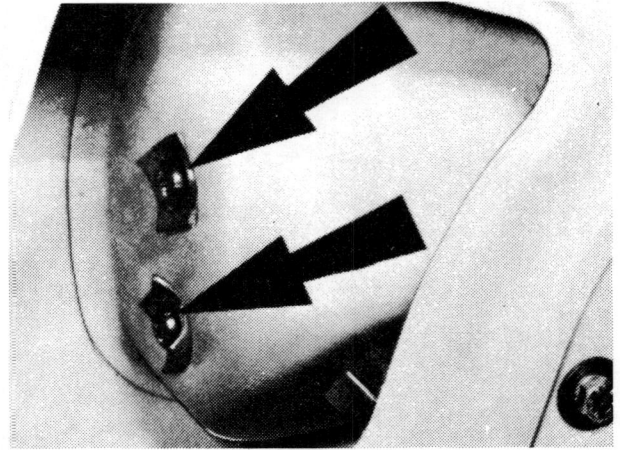

Fig. 3.27 Filler pipe door screws (arrowed)

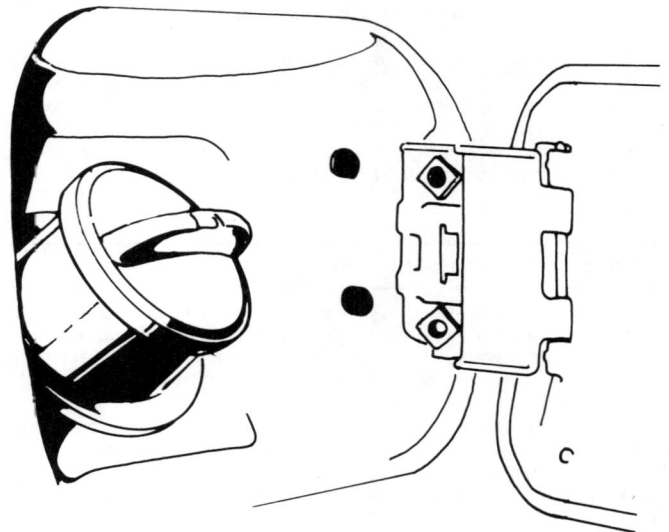

Fig. 3.28 Removing the filler pipe door

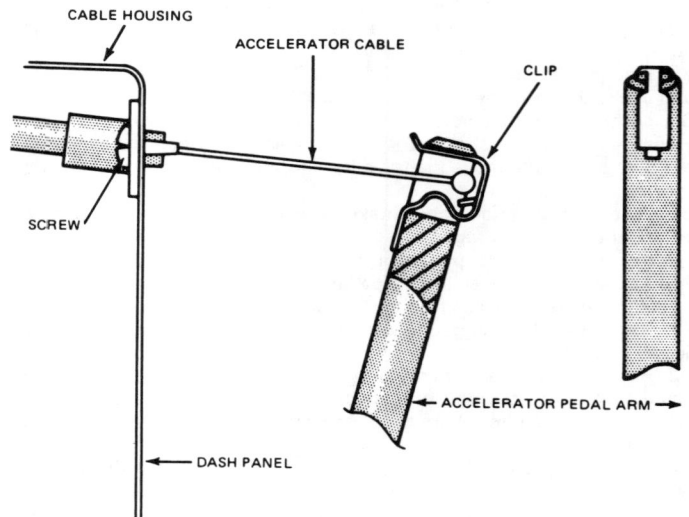

Fig. 3.29 Throttle cable to pedal connection

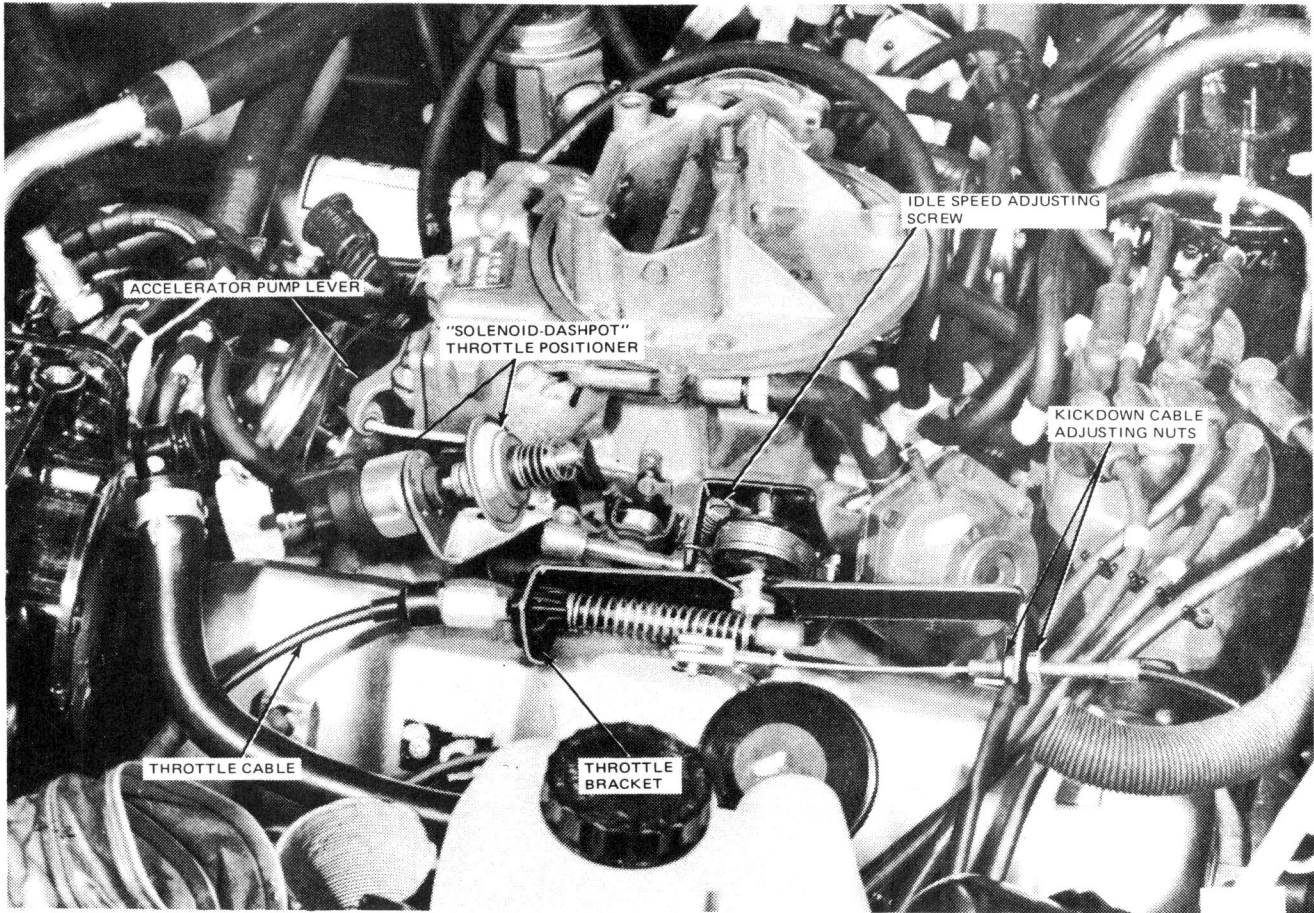

Fig. 3.30 Throttle linkage

6   Slide the screwed adjuster into the bracket adjacent to the carburettor, but do not tighten the adjusting nuts.

7   Fit the cable to the bracket arm, insert the clevis pin and fit a new split cotter.

26 Exhaust system – general description

The exhaust system for the 2800 V6 engine consists of two front pipe assemblies, two catalytic converters with heat shields, two intermediate pipes and two front and rear muffler assemblies (Fig. 3.31).

The entire exhaust system is supported on eight insulators, two at the top of each front muffler, one at the top of each rear muffler and one at the front of each catalytic converter.

27 Exhaust system – removal and refitting

1   Position the car over an inspection pit, or jack the car and support it securely on blocks, or stands.

2   Lift up the front muffler and pull the rubber insulator off each side of the bracket.

3   Saturate all the clamp nuts with penetrating oil, or a proprietary corrosion inhibitor. Loosen the clamp nuts of the clamp immediately in front of the front muffler and slide the clamp forward on to the intermediate pipe.

4   Remove the nuts and bolts from the catalytic converter grass shield clamps and remove the clamps and grass shield.

5   Remove the bolt securing the front pipe bracket to the body. Remove the bolts from the exhaust pipe flange and remove the front pipe, catalytic converter and intermediate pipe.

6   Use a hacksaw to cut through the rear exhaust pipe, about $9\frac{1}{2}$ in (240 mm) from the rear of the front muffler (Fig. 3.32) and remove the front muffler.

7   Remove the nut and bolt from the rear muffler support bracket and remove the rear exhaust assembly.

8   Remove the rubber insulator from the rear muffler bracket. Remove the rear muffler body to bracket bolt and remove the bracket.

9   If fitted, remove the tail pipe trim.

10   Remove the bracket from the front muffler. Remove the nuts and bolts from the converter flange, disconnect the converter from the front pipe and discard the gasket.

11   Start refitting by scribing a mark 1.8 in (45 mm) from the cut ends of the front muffler to rear muffler pipe.

12   Position the front muffler bracket directly below the body bracket and connect them with rubber insulators.

13   Fit the bracket to the front muffler and insert the bracket bolts, but do not tighten them at this stage.

14   Position the exhaust pipe flange on the manifold and fit the nuts, but do not tighten them.

15   Fit the front pipe bracket to the body, insert the bolt, but do not tighten it.

16   Fit the intermediate pipe into the front muffler and position the clamp, then screw on the nuts finger tight.

17   Position the converter pipe on the front flange, using a new gasket. Fit the nuts and bolts and tighten them. Fit the grass shield to the converter and tighten its fixing bolts.

18   Slide a junction sleeve (Part No 5K 256) on to the exhaust pipe at the rear of the front muffler. Fit the rear muffler bracket to the body and position the rear muffler in the bracket. Fit the nut and bolt, but do not tighten it.

19   Position the junction sleeve so that the ends of the sleeve align with the scribed marks on each of the pipe ends. Fit the U-bolt clamps and tighten the nuts to the torque wrench setting given in the Specifications.

20   Align the exhaust system so that at no point is it nearer than 1 in

C

D

E

F

G

H

J

K

RUBBER INSULATORS

REAR MUFFLERS

L

D

N

C

REAR PIPES

RUBBER INSULATORS

CATALYTIC CONVERTERS

K

FRONT EXHAUST
PIPES

H

J

F

G

E

K

J

G

H

FRONT MUFFLERS

Q

M

INTERMEDIATE PIPES

EXHAUST MANIFOLD
FLANGES

RUBBER INSULATORS

L

M

N

Q

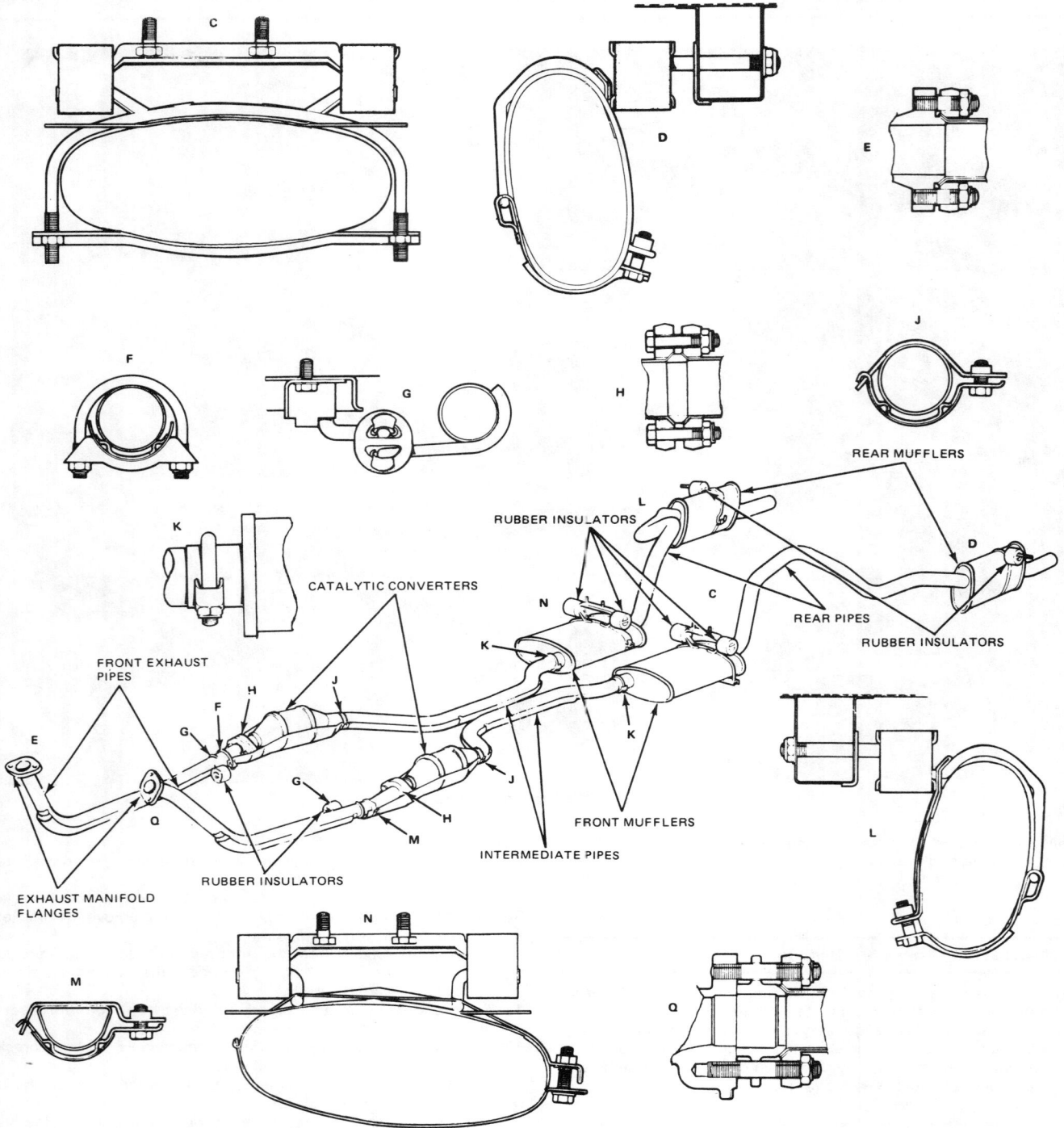

Fig. 3.31 Exhaust system

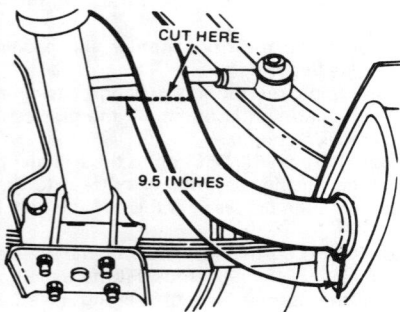

CUT HERE

9.5 INCHES

**Fig. 3.32 Cutting
point on rear
exhaust pipe**

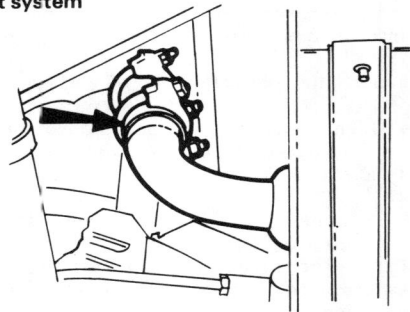

**Fig. 3.33 Junction
sleeve and U-bolt
clamps**

(25 mm) to any component, or part of the bodywork, then tighten the pipe bracket bolts and the muffler nuts and bolts.

21 If a tail pipe trim was removed, refit it.

28 Front, or rear muffler – removal and refitting

1   To remove part of the exhaust system, proceed as detailed in paragraphs 1 to 6 of the preceding Section. Having cut through the intermediate pipe, remove the selected part.

2   Refit in accordance with the details specified in the previous Section, paragraphs 11 to 21.

29 Catalytic converter – removal and refitting

1   Position the car over an inspection pit, or jack the car and support it securely on blocks, or stands.

2 Remove the clamps securing the grass shield to the catalytic converter and remove the shield.

3 Loosen the clamp at the front of the front muffler and remove the nuts from the catalytic converter flange.

4   Remove the converter and discard the gasket.

5   When refitting, first fit the intermediate pipe into the front muffler and screw the nuts on finger tight.

6   Fit a new gasket to the converter flange. Fit the converter flange to the front pipe flange and screw the nuts on finger tight.

7   Align the exhaust system so that at no point is it nearer than 1 in (25 mm) to any component, or part of the bodywork, then, starting at the front of the system, tighten all the nuts and bolts.

8   Check the system for leaks, refit the grass shield and then lower the car to the ground.

PART B: Capri II

30 Air cleaner – removal and refitting

1   Disconnect the battery.

2   Remove the two nuts securing the air cleaner lid and remove the lid, then take out the air cleaner element.

3   Knock back the four lock tabs and remove the four nuts securing the air cleaner to the carburettor body.

4   Lift the air cleaner body off the carburettor.

5   Refitting is the reverse of removal. Use new locktabs if the original ones are suspect and fit a new paper element unless the existing one is very clean.

31 Air cleaner element – removal and refitting

Note. *Some models are fitted with the thermostatically-controlled type air cleaner. This is very similar to the system used for the Mercury Capri II and a description is given in Section 2.*

1   Disconnect the battery.

2   Remove the two nuts securing the air cleaner lid and remove the lid.

3   Lift out the paper element and discard it.

4   Carefully clean the inside of the air cleaner body, ensuring that no dirt is allowed to drop into the carburettor.

5   Fit a new element and refit the air cleaner lid.

6   Reconnect the battery.

32 Fuel pump – description

The mechanical fuel pump is mounted on the left-hand side of the timing cover. The pump cannot be dismantled except for the removal of the cap to clean the filter. Should the pump be suspect, its output should be tested (Section 35) and if not to specification, a new pump must be fitted.

33 Fuel pump – removal and refitting

1   Loosen the hose clamps from the two pipe connections on the pump and remove the pump.

2   Undo and remove the two nuts and spring washers securing the pump to the timing cover and lift the pump off (Fig. 3.35).

3   Refitting the pump is the reverse of removal. Check the fuel lines and pump casing for leaks.

34 Fuel pump – cleaning

1   Detach the fuel pipe from the pump inlet tube.

2   Undo and remove the centre screw and O-ring and lift off the sediment cap, filter and seal.

3   Thoroughly clean the sediment cap, filter and pumping chamber using a paintbrush and clean petrol to remove any sediment.

4   To reassemble is the reverse sequence to dismantling. Do not overtighten the centre screw as it could distort the sediment cap.

35 Fuel pump – testing

1   If there are no obvious leaks, a preliminary check of fuel pump operation can be made by disconnecting the outlet pipe of the fuel pump and connecting the pump outlet by a length of tube to a glass jar.

2   Crank the engine and observe whether a spurt of petrol emerges from the pump outlet about every second.

3   To check that the pump is within its specification, connect a pressure gauge to the pump outlet. Disconnect the HT lead from the coil, crank the engine and observe whether the outlet pressure is between 5.5 and 7.7 lbf/in^2 (0.39 and 0.54 kgf/cm^2). The pump should deliver 1 pint (0.57 litres) in 20 seconds.

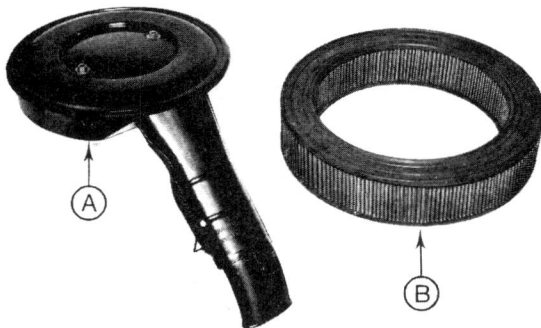

Fig. 3.34 Air cleaner assembly and element

A – Air cleaner   B – Element

Fig. 3.35 Removing the fuel pump

36 Carburettor – general description

The carburettor is of the Weber dual venturi downdraught type with an automatic choke to ensure easy starting from cold. The main and idling systems are duplicated, each barrel having separate systems supplied from a common float chamber.

A single accelerator pump of the diaphragm type supplies both barrels.

The main body of the carburettor incorporates the float chamber, throttle barrels, main venturi and accelerator pump body.

There are two throttle spindles, which are interconnected by gear quadrants to operate the throttle plates simultaneously. Each bank of cylinders is fed from a separate throttle barrel through ducts cast in the

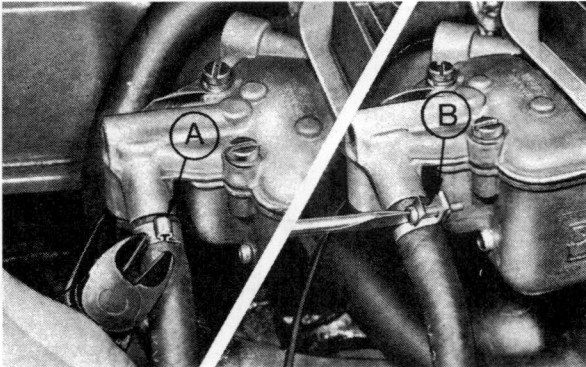

Fig. 3.36 Disconnecting and reconnecting the fuel supply pipe

A – Crimped type hose clamp   B – Screw type hose clamp

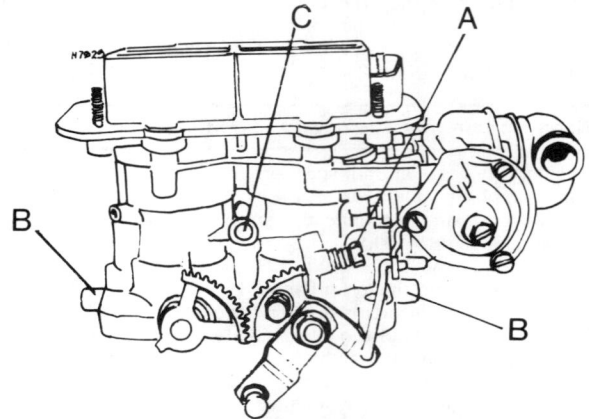

Fig. 3.37 Later type of carburettor

A – Idle screw
B – Mixture screws (covered by plastic caps)
C – Idle 'by-pass' screw

Fig. 3.38 Choke link U-clip (arrowed)

Fig. 3.39 Removing the carburettor upper body

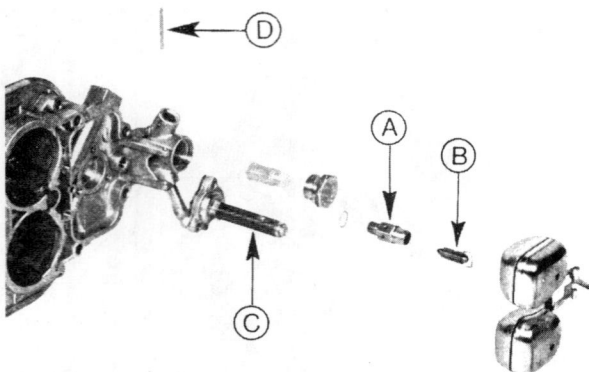

Fig. 3.40 Carburettor upper body components

A – Valve housing   C – Power valve diaphragm
B – Needle valve   D – Float retaining pin

Fig. 3.41 Carburettor jet positions (arrowed)

X – Main correction jets

inlet manifold.

Incorporated in the float chamber cover is the fuel feed inlet connection and the twin air intakes for the two barrels.

The fully automatic choke system is located on the right-hand side of the carburettor body and comprises a bi-metallic spring and a linkage to two off-set choke plates mounted on a common spindle. The choke housing is heated by engine coolant.

37 Carburettor – removal and refitting

1   Disconnect the battery
2   Remove the air cleaner assembly as detailed in Section 30.
3   Make sure that the cooling system is not under pressure, by removing the radiator cap and refitting it again. With the radiator cap in position, disconnect the two hoses from the automatic choke and secure them with their open ends upwards. This will ensure only a very small quantity of coolant will be lost.
4   Disconnect the fuel feed pipe from the carburettor. If a crimped type hose clamp is fitted, cut the clamp to remove it and renew it with a screw type hose clamp (Fig. 3.36).
5   Disconnect the vacuum pipe from the carburettor to the distributor.
6   Remove the four nuts and detach the carburettor assembly and gasket from the intake manifold.
7   Refitting is the reverse of the removal procedure, but first ensure that the joint faces are clean and undamaged. Use a new gasket, tighten the securing nuts to the torque wrench setting given in the Specifications and refit all the hoses.

38 Weber dual venturi carburettor – dismantling and reassembly

Note *On 1977 models onwards the carburettor has a 'by-pass' idle adjusting screw which is sealed in production with a white or gray plastic cap. Under no circumstances should this screw be tampered with (Fig. 3.37).*
1   Remove the carburettor from the engine, as detailed in Section 37 and clean the carburettor exterior with petrol or a water soluble proprietary cleaner.
2   Carefully prise out the U-circlip with a screwdriver and disconnect the choke plate operating link (Fig. 3.38).
3   Remove the six screws and detach the carburettor upper body (Fig. 3.39).
4   Unscrew the brass nut located at the fuel intake and detach the fuel filter.
5   Tap out the float retaining pin, and detach the float and needle valve.
6   Remove the three screws and detach the power valve diaphragm assembly.
7   Unscrew the needle valve housing.
8   Unscrew the jet and jets plugs from the carburettor body, noting the positions in which they are fitted (Fig. 3.40).
9   From beneath the carburettor remove the two primary diffuser tubes after removing the two main correction jets (Figs. 3.41 and 3.43).
10 Remove four screws, take off the accelerator pump cover and remove the diaphragm and spring (Fig. 3.42).
11 Clean the parts illustrated in Fig. 3.43 and then ensure that the jets are unobstructed by blowing through them.
12 Carefully screw in the mixture screws until each of them contacts its sealing. Note and record the number of turns, so that the screws can be refitted to their original settings. Unscrew each screw fully and remove it and its spring.
13 Check the float assembly for signs of damage and ensure that the floats do not leak. Leaking floats can be detected by submerging the float in a pan of water. When heating the water, leaks will be indicated by bubbles rising from the float. Inspect the power valve, pump diaphragm and gaskets for splits. Check that the throttle plates and mixture screw needles are not worn, or damaged (Fig. 3.44). Fit new parts where necessary.
14 Start reassembly by refitting the parts of the accelerator pump in the order shown in Fig. 3.45.
15 Fit the two mixture screws and springs, setting each screw to its original position and refit the jets and jet plugs.
16 Refit the power valve diaphragm assembly (Fig. 3.46) as follows.

Fig. 3.42 Removing the accelerator pump diaphragm

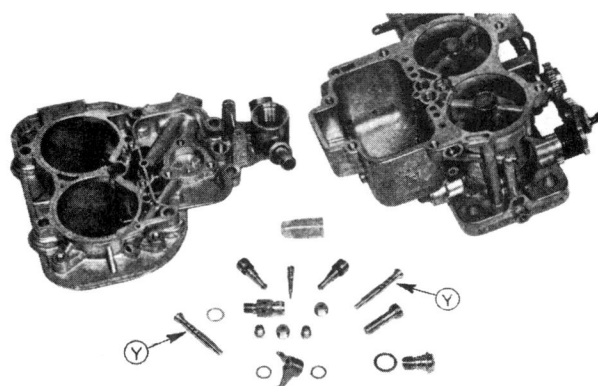

Fig. 3.43 Parts of carburettor to be cleaned

Y – Diffuser tubes

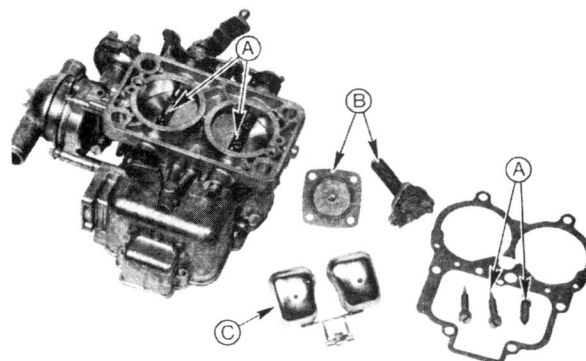

Fig. 3.44 Items to be checked

A – Check for damage, or wear
B – Check for splitting
C – Check for leaks

Loosely fit the three diaphragm retaining screws, compress the return spring ensuring that the diaphragm is not twisted or distorted then tighten the screws and release the spring. Check for correct functioning by pushing the diaphragm down and then blocking the air bleed hole with a finger. Release the diaphragm while still keeping the air hole blocked. If the diaphragm stays down, it has sealed properly to its housing.
17 Refit the needle valve housing, needle valve and float assembly to

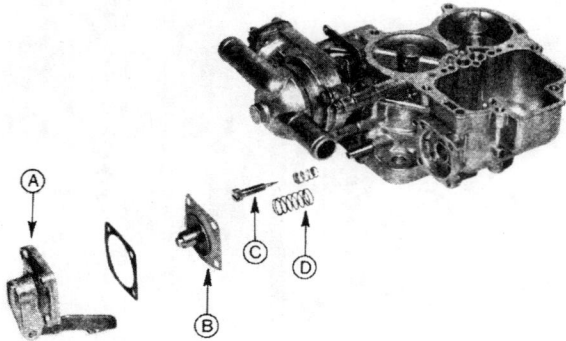

Fig. 3.45 Accelerator pump components

A – Pump housing   B – Pump diaphragm

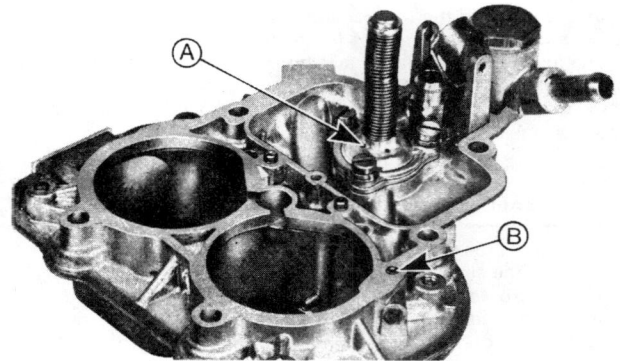

Fig. 3.46 Power valve diaphragm assembly

A – Power valve   B – Diaphragm bleed hole

Fig. 3.47 Float level adjustment (adjusting tag arrowed)

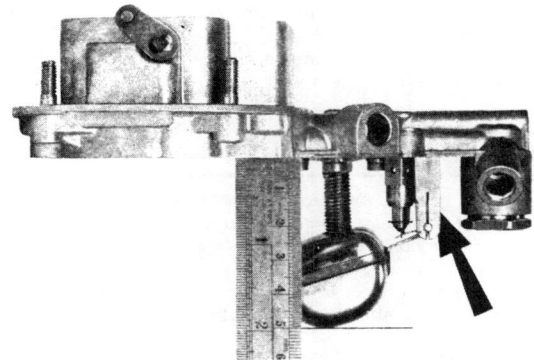

Fig. 3.48 Float travel adjustment (adjusting tag arrowed)

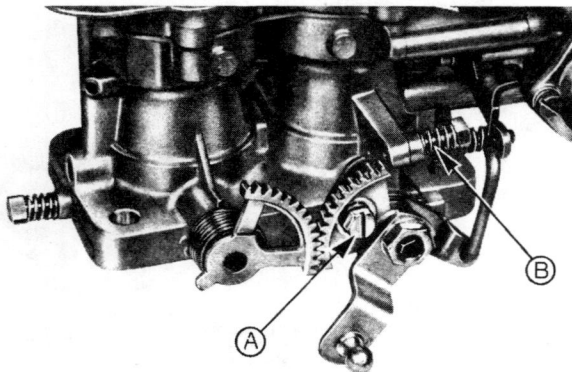

Fig. 3.49 Throttle plate synchronization adjustment

A – Synchronization adjustment screw   B – Idle screw

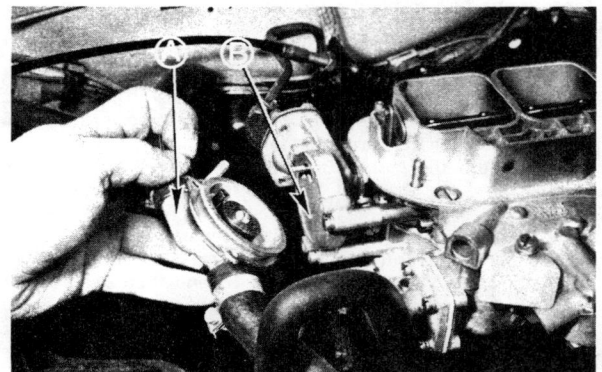

Fig. 3.50 Removal of auto-choke outer housing

A – Choke housing and bi-metal spring assembly
B – Internal heat shield

the upper body.

18 Adjust the float level settings, firstly with the upper body vertical and the needle valve shut off (Fig. 3.47). If the measurement is outside the limits 1.56 to 1.58 in (39.7 to 40.3 mm), bend the tag until the setting is correct and recheck.

19 Check the float travel by measuring from the body face when the upper body is horizontal (Fig. 3.48). If the measurement is outside the limits 2.05 to 2.07 in (52.2 to 52.8 mm), bend the tag until the setting

is correct and recheck. For both the float level adjustments the upper body gasket must be removed.

20 Refit the fuel intake filter and locating nut.

21 Position the gasket and refit the carburettor upper body. Make sure that the choke link locates through the upper body correctly.

22 Reconnect the choke link and secure it with the U-clip.

23 Adjust the throttle plates for synchronization. Wind back the idle screw (Fig. 3.49) until it is clear of the throttle mechanism and then

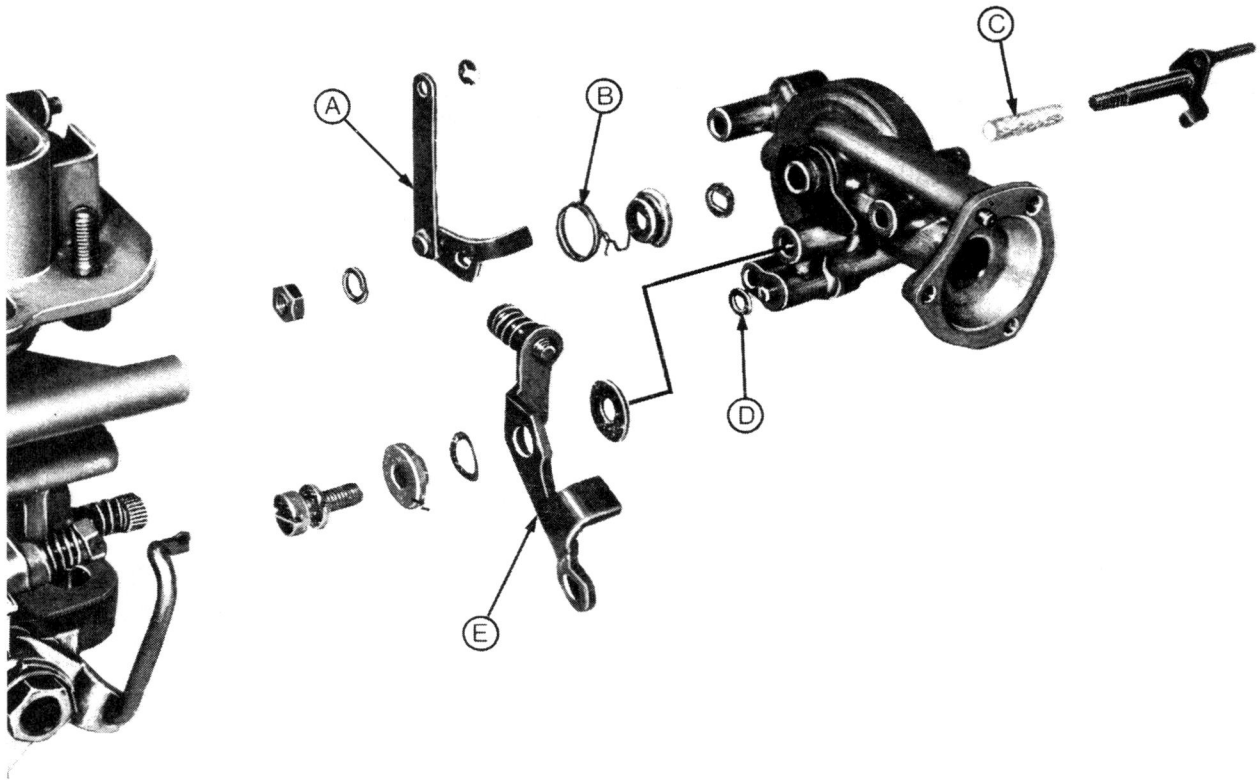

Fig. 3.51 Auto-choke assembly

A – Upper choke operating link   C – Spindle sleeve   E – Choke link with adjusting screw
B – Fast idle cam return spring   D – Sealing ring

loosen the synchronization adjusting screw. Hold the auto-choke plates in an open position, flick the throttle and allow both plates to close fully. Tap both plates to ensure that they have closed completely and then tighten the synchronization screw. To check, partially open the throttle using the idle screw, so that there is a clearance of 0.02 in (0.05 mm) between one of the throttle plates and its bore. Check that the other plate has the same opening.

39 Weber dual venturi carburettor automatic choke – removal, overhaul and refitting

1   Disconnect the battery.
2   Remove the air cleaner, as described in Section 30.
3   Remove the three screws, detach the cover and move it clear of the carburettor (Fig. 3.50). For access to the lower screw it will be necessary to make up a suitably cranked screwdriver.
4   Detach the internal heat shield.
5   Remove the single U-clip and disconnect the choke plate operating link.
6   Remove the three screws, disconnect the choke link at the operating lever and detach the choke assembly.
7   Remove the three screws and detach the vacuum diaphragm assembly.
8   Dismantle the remaining parts of the choke mechanism.
9   Clean all the components, inspect them for wear and damage and wipe them dry with a lint-free cloth. Do not use any lubricants during reassembly.
10   Reassemble the choke mechanism (Fig. 3.51).
11   Refit the vacuum diaphragm and housing, ensuring that the diaphragm is flat before the housing is fitted (Fig. 3.52).
12   Ensure that the O-ring is correctly located in the choke housing

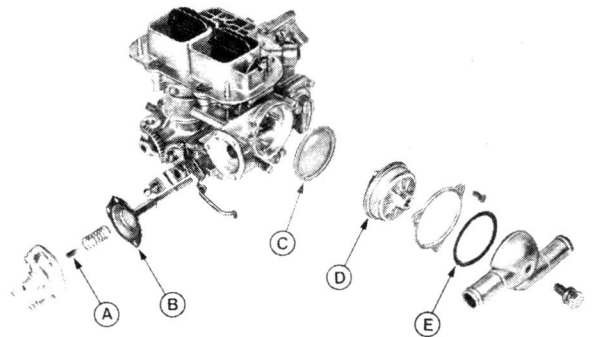

Fig. 3.52 Vacuum diaphragm and outer housing assembly

A – Diaphragm adjusting screw   D – Bi-metal spring and housing
B – Vacuum diaphragm   assembly
C – Internal heat shield   E – Outer sealing gasket

then reconnect the lower choke link. Position the assembly and secure it with the three screws; ensure that the upper choke link locates correctly through the carburettor body.
13   Reconnect the upper choke link to the choke spindle.
14   Check the vacuum pull-down and choke phasing, as described in Section 40.
15   Refit the internal heat shield ensuring that the hole in the cover locates correctly onto the peg cast in the housing (Fig. 3.53).

Fig. 3.53 Installation of internal heat shield

A – Internal heat shield   B – Locating peg

Fig. 3.54 Choke housing alignment marks

Fig. 3.55 Vacuum diaphragm held fully open

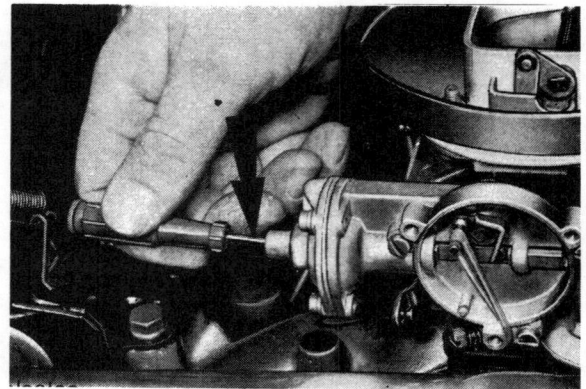

Fig. 3.56 Vacuum pull-down adjustment

16 Connect the bi-metal spring to the choke lever, position the choke cover and loosely fit the three retaining screws.
17 Rotate the cover until the marks are aligned, then tighten the three screws (Fig. 3.54).
18 Reconnect the battery, run the engine and adjust the fast idle speed, as described in Section 40.
19 Refit the air cleaner.

---

40 Weber dual venturi carburettor automatic choke – adjustment

Note: *The procedure is described for a carburettor which is fitted in the car but with the exception of fast idle speed adjustment, can be carried out on the bench if required where the carburettor has been removed.*
1   Disconnect the battery.
2   Remove the air cleaner, as described in Section 30.
3   Remove the three screws, detach the choke cover and move it clear of the carburettor.
4   Detach the internal heat shield.
5   *Vacuum pull-down:* Fit an elastic band to the choke plate lever and position it so that the choke plates are held closed. Open, then release the throttle to ensure that the choke plates close fully. Unscrew the plug from the diaphragm unit then manually push open the diaphragm up to its stop from inside the choke housing (Fig. 3.55). Do not push on the rod as it is spring loaded but push on the diaphragm plug body. The choke plate pull-down should now be measured, using an unmarked twist drill shank between the edge of the choke plate and the air horn wall, and compared with the specified torque. Adjust, if necessary, by screwing the adjusting screw in or out (Fig. 3.56). Refit the end plug and detach the elastic band on completion.
6   *Choke phasing:* Hold the throttle partly open and position the fast idle cam so that the fast idle adjusting screw locates on the upper

Fig. 3.57 Checking choke phasing

section of the cam (Fig. 3.57). Release the throttle to hold the cam in this position then push the choke plates down until the step on the cam jams against the adjusting screw. Measure the clearance between the edge of the choke plate and the air horn wall using an unmarked 0.08 in (2 mm) twist drill shank (a No 46 drill is 0.081 in). Adjust if necessary, by bending the tag arrowed in Fig. 3.58.
7   Refit the internal heat shield ensuring that the hole in the cover locates correctly onto the peg cast in the housing.
8   Connect the bi-metal spring to the choke lever, position the choke cover and loosely fit the three retaining screws.
9   Rotate the cover until the marks are aligned then tighten the three screws.

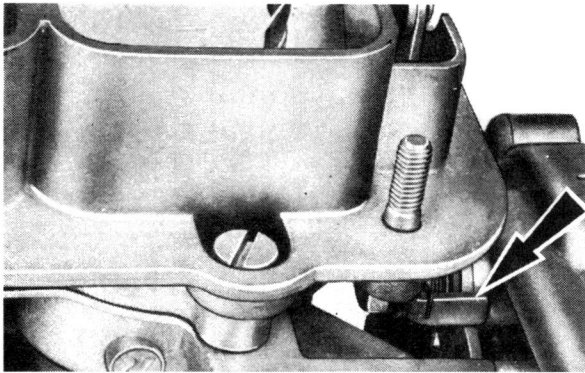

Fig. 3.58 Choke phasing adjustment tag (arrowed)

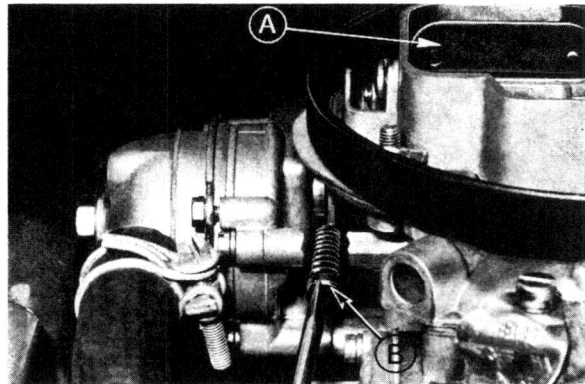

Fig. 3.59 Fast idle adjustment

A – Choke plates in open position
B – Fast idle adjusting screw

10 Reconnect the battery, run the engine and adjust the fast idle speed as described in the following paragraph.

Fast idle speed adjustment
11 **Note**: *Ideally a tachometer will be required in order to set the fast idle rpm to the specified value.* Run the engine up to normal operating temperature, then switch off and connect the tachometer (where available). Open the throttle partially, hold the choke plates fully closed then release the throttle so that the choke mechanism is held in the fast idle position (Fig. 3.59). Release the choke plates, checking that they are fully open (if they are not open, the assembly is faulty or the engine is not at operating temperature). Without touching the accelerator pedal, start the engine and adjust the fast idle screw as necessary to obtain the correct fast idle rpm.
12 Finally refit the air cleaner.

41 Weber dual venturi carburettor – idle mixture adjustment

Note: *On 1977 models onwards the carburettor has a 'by-pass' idle adjusting screw which is sealed in production with a white or grey plastic cap. Under no circumstances should this screw be tampered with (Fig. 3.37).*
1 Accurate setting of the idle mixture requires the use of an exhaust gas analyser, but an approximate setting can be obtained as follows.
2 Start the engine and allow it to run at a fast idling speed until it reaches normal operating temperature.
3 Adjust the engine idling speed screw (Fig. 3.60) until the engine runs at about 800 rpm.
4 Remove the plastic cap covering each mixture screw (where applicable) by punching a small hole in the centre of each cap and prising out with a screwdriver. Fully wind in the two mixture screws until they stop and then wind out three full turns on each screw. Turn

Fig. 3.60 Positions of carburettor adjusting screws

A – Mixture adjusting screws
B – Idle speed adjusting screw

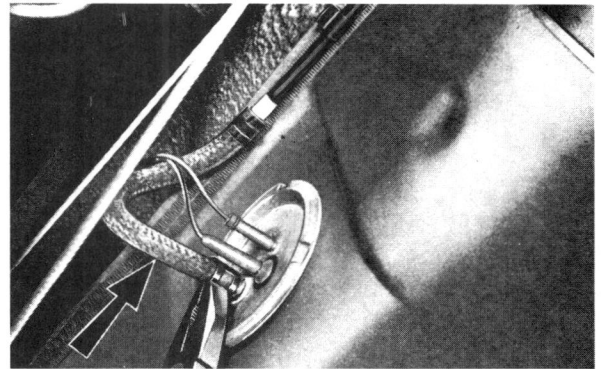

Fig. 3.61 Removing the fuel feed pipe

each screw both in and out by increments of a quarter of a turn at a time until the best running conditions are obtained. It is important that both screws are turned in the same direction and by the same amount each time.
5 When the best position has been found, recheck the idling speed and adjust it if necessary.
6 Where applicable fit new plastic caps to the mixture screws.

42 Fuel tank – removal and refitting

1 Great care is necessary when working on any part of the fuel system and it is safer to do the work outside if possible. Avoid having the car over a pit, where explosive vapour can accumulate and take care to avoid naked flames and any other sources of ignition.
2 Disconnect the battery leads.
3 Syphon any petrol remaining in the tank into a metal container suitable for storing petrol. Label the container clearly and store it in a well ventilated place.
4 Chock the front wheels securely. Jack up the rear of the car and support it on blocks, or firmly based stands.
5 Disconnect the fuel feed pipe at the tank and free it from the clips along the front edge of the tank (Fig. 3.61).
6 Remove the wiring connectors from the tank sender unit, noting their positions so that they can be reconnected correctly.
7 Unclip the vent pipe from the chassis and disconnect the breather pipe at the T-connection (Fig. 3.62).
8 Loosen the tank straps, support the tank in position and while still supporting the tank, remove the straps. Carefully remove the tank assembly and tank guard, if fitted, leaving the fuel filler pipe in position.
9 Before refitting the tank, ensure that the four insulator pads (B in Fig. 3.62) are stuck to the tank in the positions shown.
10 Smear grease round the exterior of the filler pipe base, to facilitate

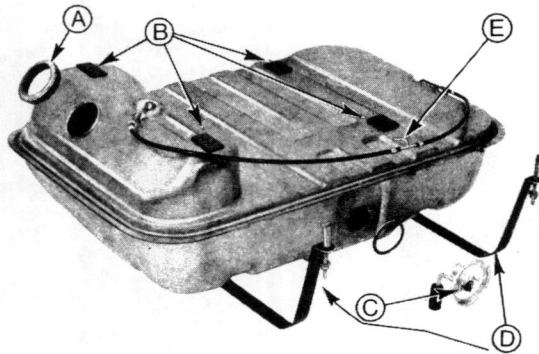

Fig. 3.62 Fuel tank assembly

A – Seal   D – Securing straps
B – Rubber insulators   E – T-connection
C – Sender unit

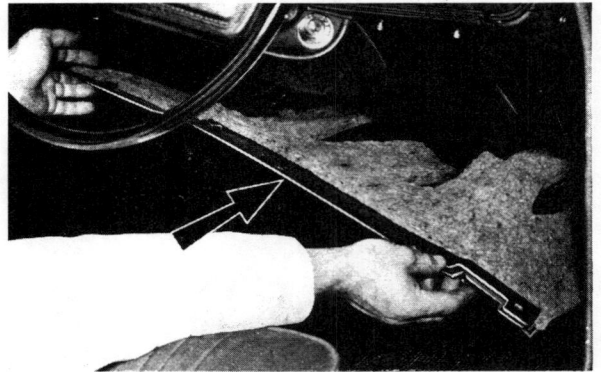

Fig. 3.63 Removal of dash panel lower insulating pad

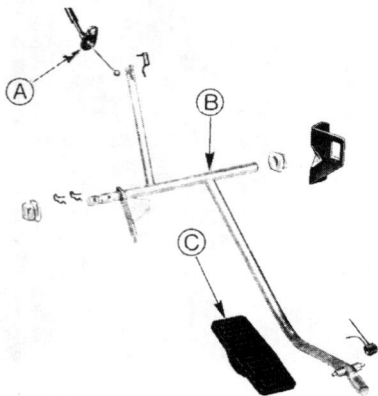

Fig. 3.64 Accelerator shaft assembly (RHD)

A – Throttle cable   B – Accelerator shaft   C – Throttle pedal

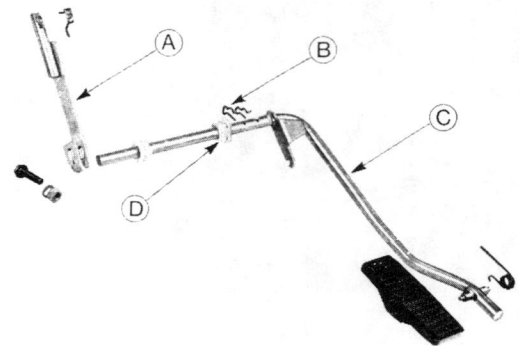

Fig. 3.65 Accelerator shaft assembly (LHD)

A – Shaft extension rod   C – Accelerator shaft
B – Retaining spring clip   D – End mounting bush

its entry into the fuel tank seal. Position the tank and support it, then refit the two tank clips after reconnecting the fuel and vent pipes.
11   Ensure that the vent pipe is clipped into position and is not kinked or trapped.
12   Tighten the tank strap nuts until 1.4 to 1.6 in (35 to 40 mm) of thread is protruding through the nut.

43 Fuel tank – cleaning and repair

The precautions are identical with those detailed in Section 22.

44 Fuel tank filler pipe – removal and refitting

The procedure is the same as that for the Mercury Capri II, as described in Section 23.

45 Kickdown cable – removal, refitting and adjustment

The procedure is the same as that for the Mercury Capri II, as described in Section 25.

46 Throttle cable – removal, refitting and adjustment

The procedure is the same as that for the Mercury Capri II, as described in Section 24.

47 Accelerator and pedal shaft – removal and refitting

Note: *If the pedal only is to be removed refer to paragraph 12.*
1   Disconnect the battery leads.
2   From inside the car remove the dash lower insulator panel. It is retained by five screws (rhd) or three screws (lhd) along the rear edge and can be unclipped from the front edge (Fig. 3.63).
3   Remove the accelerator cable from the pedal shaft as described in Section 24.

Rhd variants (Fig. 3.64)
4   Disconnect the brake operating rod at the brake pedal, then remove the master cylinder and servo unit. Refer to Chapter 9 for further information.
5   Working through the rear bulkhead in the engine compartment, pull out the shaft end securing clip.
6   Rotate the right-hand shaft mounting bush through 45° in either direction and pull it out.
7   Detach the accelerator shaft assembly.

Lhd variants (Fig. 3.65)
8   Loosen the clamp and detach the shaft extension rod.
9   Carefully drive out the right-hand mounting bush retaining clip from the shaft, then slide out the shaft until it touches the heater box.
10   Detach the right-hand mounting bush from the pedal box by rotating through 45° in either direction, then pulling it out. The accelerator shaft assembly can now be removed.

All models

11 Detach the reaming bush and clip from the shaft.

12 To remove the pedal, prise the flange away from the spigot on the shaft, then remove the pedal and spring.

13 When refitting the pedal, locate the spring on the spigot shaft, then clip the flanges onto the spigots and check that the pedal pivots correctly.

14 Refitting the pedal shaft is the reverse of the removal procedure, following which it will be necessary to adjust the cable, as described in Section 24. On rhd variants, check that the pedal has 0.24 to 0.55 in (6 to 14 mm) lift from the idle position. If necessary adjust the pedal lift-up stop to achieve this.

48 Ported Vacuum Switch – general

The Ported Vacuum Switch (PVS) is designed to prevent flat spots and misfiring occurring when the engine is cold and running with full or partial choke.

When the engine is cold (below 71°C (160°F)) the PVS is closed. In this condition, carburettor vacuum is applied directly to the distributor via the non-return valve, which allows the vacuum advance to be maintained under acceleration, preventing flat spots or misfiring.

When the engine has reached its normal operating temperature the PVS is open. In this condition the carburettor is connected to the distributor via the PVS.

49 Exhaust system – general description

There are two separate exhaust assemblies (Fig. 3.66), one routed down each side of the car. Each system consists of a single piece, comprising a front pipe, front resonator and rear muffler.

The resonator and muffler are flexibly supported from the floor pan, the resonator having two attachments and the muffler one.

At six monthly intervals the system should be checked for corrosion, leaks and the security and flexibility of its mountings.

50 Exhaust system – removal and refitting

1 Position the car over an inspection pit, or jack the car and support it securely on blocks, or stands.

2 Disconnect the battery.

3 Lift up the resonator box and pull the rubber insulator off each side bracket.

4 Saturate all the clamp nuts with penetrating oil, or a proprietary corrosion inhibitor.

5 Disconnect the front pipe from the manifold, detach the sealing ring and lower the front section of the exhaust.

6 Use a hacksaw to cut through the rear exhaust pipe about $9\frac{1}{2}$ in (240 mm) from the rear of the front resonator (Fig. 3.67).

7 Remove the nut securing the rear silencer bracket clamp (Fig. 3.68), swing the bracket clear of the silencer and detach the rear exhaust section.

8 Detach and remove the rear mounting rubber and bracket clamp.

9 Remove the front pipe U-clamp and drift off the front pipe. Detach the resonator mounting bracket and the tail pipe trim, if fitted.

10 Start refitting by scribing a mark 1.8 in (45 mm) from the cut ends of the resonator to silencer pipe.

11 Position the resonator and front pipe assembly, loosely secure it to the bracket and manifold connection.

12 Slide a service sleeve (Fig. 3.69) onto the resonator pipe, positioning its end in line with the scribed mark made previously.

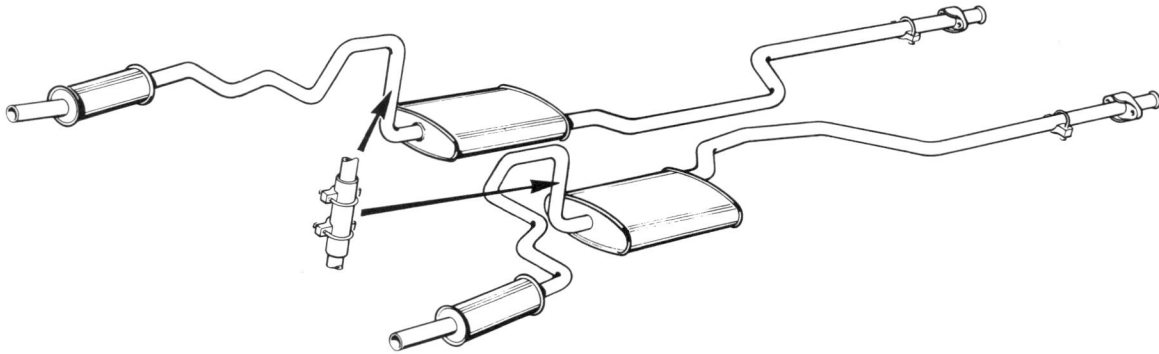

Fig. 3.66 Exhaust system layout

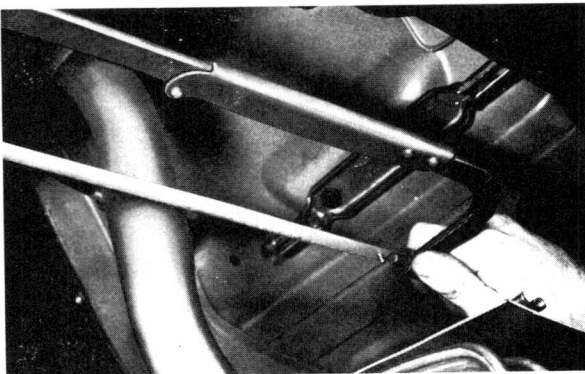

Fig. 3.67 Cutting through the exhaust pipe

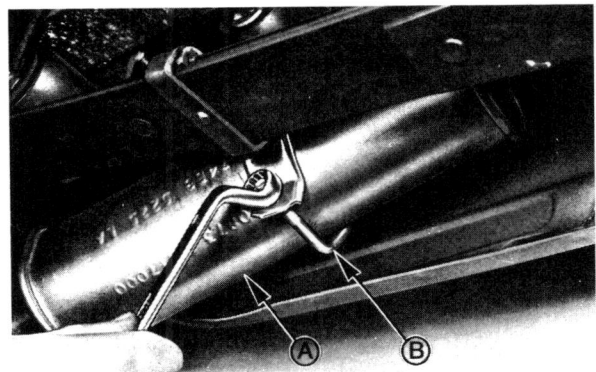

Fig. 3.68 Exhaust rear mounting

A – Silencer
B – Silencer support clamp

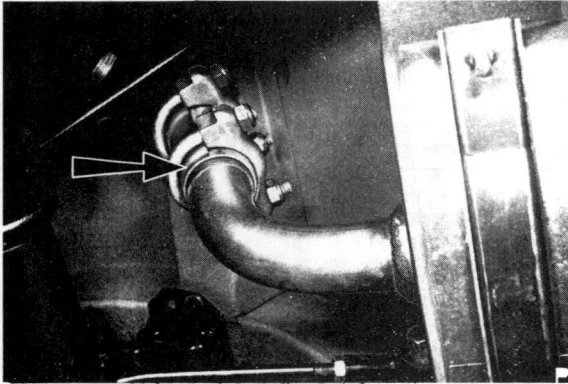

Fig. 3.69 Exhaust system service sleeve and U-clamps

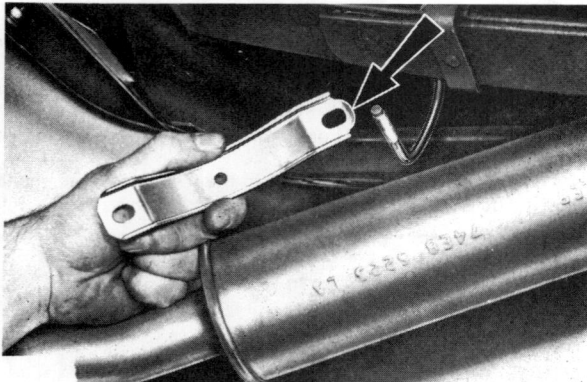

Fig. 3.70 Silencer support clamp

Angled end (arrowed) to be fitted uppermost

13 Fit the silencer pipe into the sleeve up to its scribed mark and refit the rear silencer clamp loosely. When fitting the clamp, ensure that its angled end is uppermost (Fig. 3.70).

14 Align the exhaust system so that at no point is it nearer than 1 in (25 mm) to any component, or part of the bodywork. Tighten the manifold connection and then screw on the nuts of the resonator clamp until 0.5 in (13 mm) of thread protrudes through the nuts.

15 Position the two U-clamps on the service sleeve and tighten the nuts to the torque wrench setting given in the Specifications.

16 Refit the tail pipe trim if appropriate then reconnect the battery, start the engine and check for leaks.

17 If satisfactory, switch off the engine and lower the car to the ground.

Part C Emission control

51 Emission control system – general description

Note: *The information given in this Section is not generally applicable to Capri II models, although for some markets certain items may be relevant. It must also be appreciated that applicability for Mercury Capri II models will be dependent upon the operating territory.*

1 In order to reduce the emission pollutants to a minimum, a comprehensive emission control system is incorporated on many vehicles. This system can be broken down into the following sub-sections:

Improved combustion (IMCO) system

2 The main features of this system are covered by the design of the engine and carburettor and therefore require no special information. An electrically assisted choke heater is used as an aid to fast choke release, for better emission characteristics during engine warm-up.

3 The heater is a constant temperature, positive temperature coefficient (PTC) unit, energised from the alternator field (IND) terminal, and is energised when the engine is running.

4 Incorporated with the unit is a fast idle cam latch, which holds the cam on the high position until the choke heats up and the bi-metal latch backs off, to allow the latch pin and fast idle cam to rotate to the normal run position.

5 An overcentre spring assists in closing the choke plate for initial starting of a cold engine in high ambient temperatures. This spring has no effect after initial choke pull-down occurs.

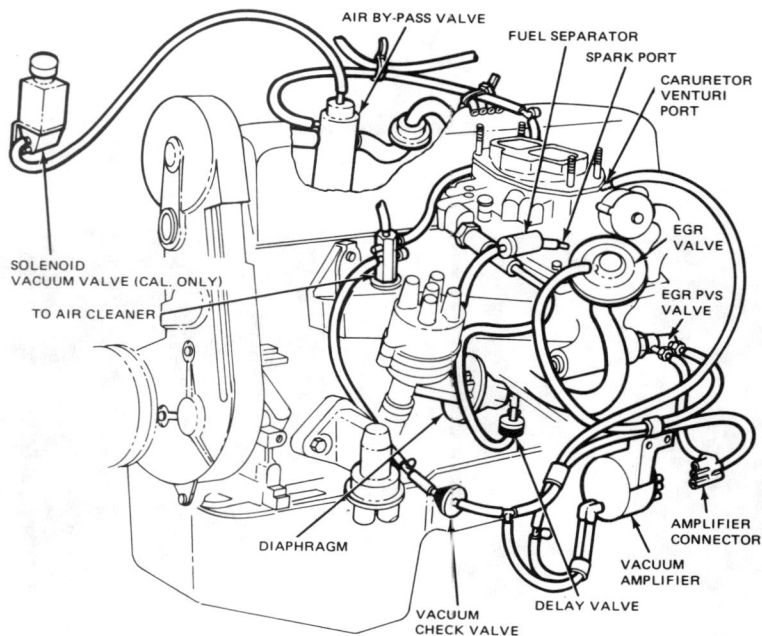

Fig. 3.71 Layout of the emission control system (typical)

Positive crankcase ventilation (PCV) system

6 The PCV system operates by drawing in air and mixing it with vapours which have escaped past the piston rings (blow-by vapours). This mixture is then drawn into the combustion chamber through an oil separator and PCV valve.

Evaporative emission control

7 This system is designed to limit the emission of fuel vapours to the atmosphere. It comprises the fuel tank, pressure and vacuum sensitive fuel filter cap, a restrictor bleed orifice, a charcoal canister and the associated connecting lines (Fig. 3.73).

8 When the fuel tank is filled, vapours are discharged to atmosphere through the filler tube and a space between the inner filler tube and the outer neck. When fuel covers the filler control tube, vapours can no longer escape and a vapour lock is created by the orifice, so that there can be no flow to the charcoal canister.

9 When thermal expansion occurs in the fuel tank, vapour is forced through the orifice to the canister, where it is stored when the engine is not running and is drawn into the carburettor intake system as soon as the engine is started.

Exhaust gas recirculation (EGR) system

10 This system is designed to reintroduce small amounts of exhaust gas into the combustion cycle, to reduce the generation of oxides of nitrogen. The amount of gas reintroduced is governed by engine vacuum and temperature.

11 The EGR valve (Fig. 3.74) is mounted on a spacer block between the carburettor and manifold. A venturi vacuum amplifier (VVA) (Figs. 3.75 and 3.76) is used to change the relatively weak vacuum signal in the carburettor throat, to a strong signal for operation of the EGR valve.

12 A relief valve is also used to modify the output EGR signal whenever venturi vacuum is equal to, or greater than, manifold vacuum. This allows the EGR valve to close at or near, wide open throttle, then maximum engine power is required.

13 The EGR/CSC (cold start cyle) regulates the distributor spark advance and EGR valve operation according to the engine coolant temperature, by sequentially switching the vacuum signals. When the

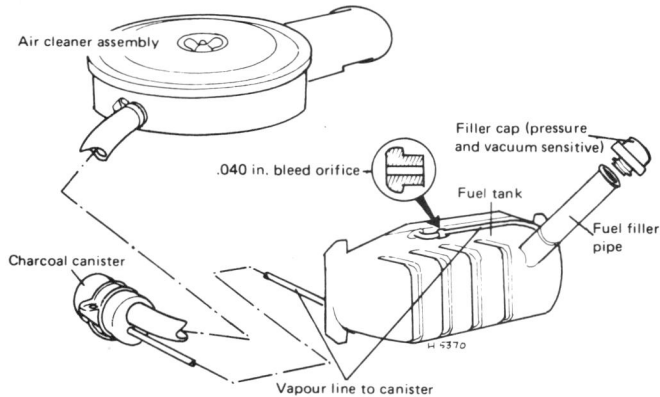

Fig. 3.72 Electrically assisted choke

A Overcentre spring   B Fast idle cam latch   P Latch pin

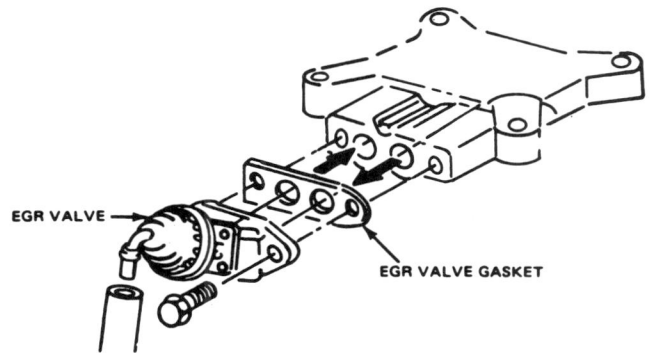

Fig. 3.74 Components of a typical EGR system

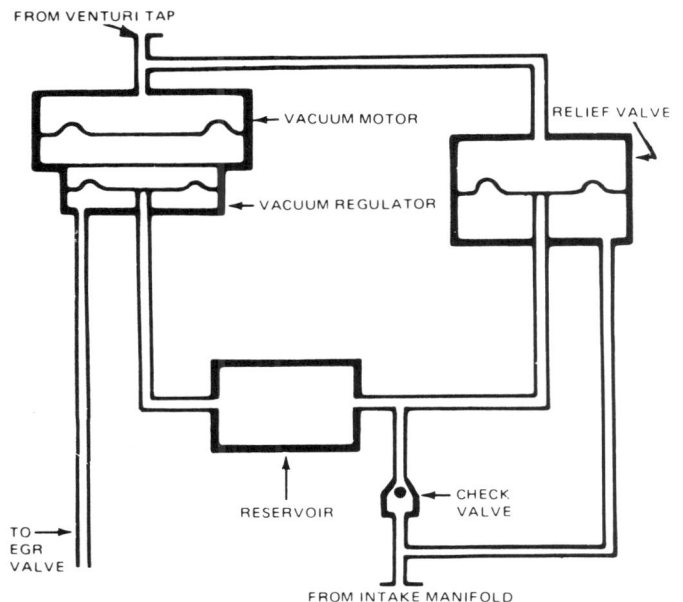

Fig. 3.73 Evaporative emission control system – typical

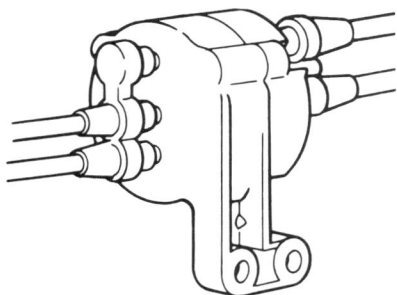

Fig. 3.75 The venturi vacuum amplifier

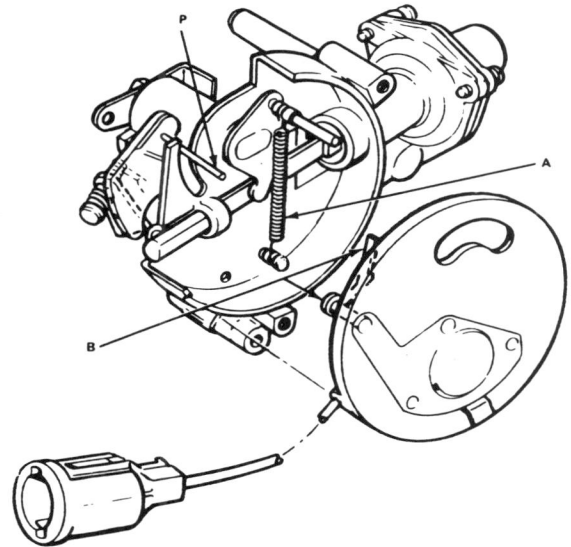

Fig. 3.76 Schematic diagram of a venturi vacuum amplifier

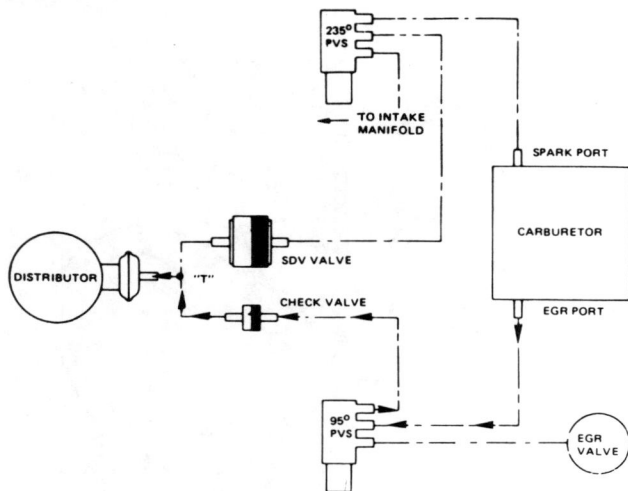

Fig. 3.77 EGR/CSC system operation below 82°F

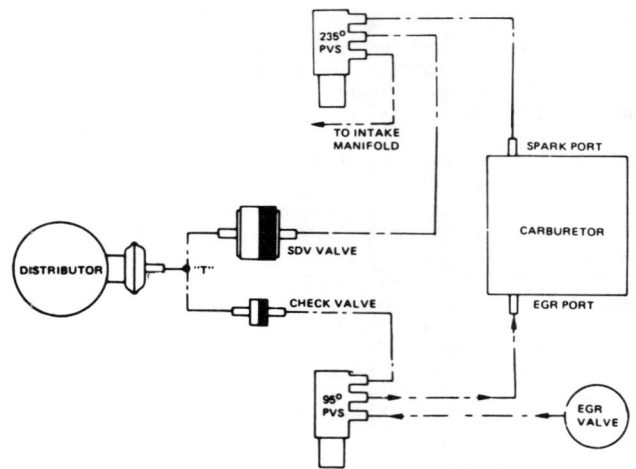

Fig. 3.78 EGR/CSC system operation above 95°F

Fig. 3.79 Typical ported vacuum switch (PVS)

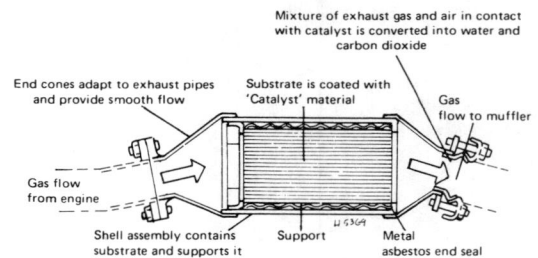

Fig. 3.80 Typical spark delay valve (SDV)

coolant temperature is below 82°F (27.8°C), the EGR ported vacuum switch (PVS) (Fig. 3.79) admits carburettor EGR port vacuum (which occurs at approximately 2500 rpm) directly to the distributor advance diaphragm through the one-way check valve. At the same time the PVS shuts off the carburettor vacuum to the EGR valve (Figs. 3.77 and 3.78).

14 When the engine coolant is 95°F (35°C) or above, the EGR-PVS directs carburettor vacuum to the EGR valve.

15 At temperatures between 82 and 95°F (27.8 and 35°C), the EGR-PVS may be closed, open or in the mid-position.

16 A spark delay valve (SDV) (Fig. 3.80) is incorporated in the system to delay the carburettor spark vacuum to the distributor diaphragm unit for a predetermined time. During acceleration, little or no vacuum is admitted to the distributor diaphragm unit until acceleration is completed, because of the time delay of the SDV and the re-routing of the EGR port vacuum at temperatures above 95°F (32°C). The check valve blocks the vacuum signal from the SDV to the EGR-PVS, so that carburettor spark vacuum will not be dissipated at temperatures above 95°F.

17 The 235°F (113°C) PVS is not strictly part of the EGR system, but is connected to the distributor vacuum advance unit to prevent over-heating while idling with a hot engine. At idle speeds, no vacuum is generated at either of the carburettor ports and the engine timing is fully retarded. However, when the coolant temperature reaches 235°F (113°C) the PVS is actuated to admit intake manifold vacuum to the distributor advance diaphragm. The engine timing is thus advanced, idling speed is correspondingly increased and the engine temperature is lowered due to increased fan speed and coolant flow.

Catalytic converter

18 On some models a catalytic converter is incorporated upstream of the exhaust front silencer (Fig. 3.81). The converter comprises a ceramic, honeycomb-like core, housed in a stainless steel pipe. The core is coated with a platinum and palladium catalyst, which converts unburned carbon monoxide and hydrocarbons into carbon dioxide and

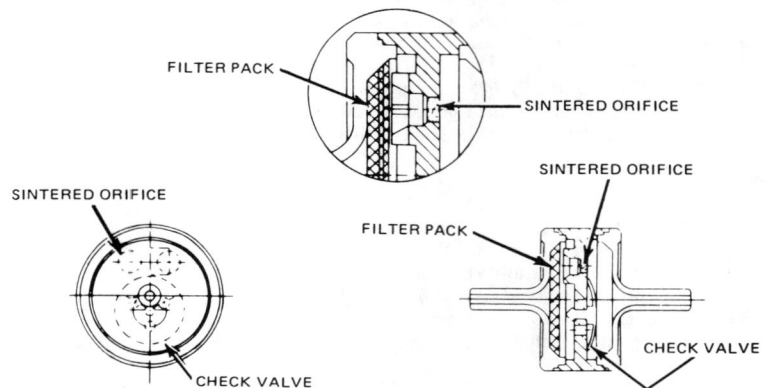

Fig. 3.81 Typical catalytic converter

water, by a chemical reaction.

19 No special maintenance of the converter is required, but it can be damaged by the use of leaded fuels, engine misfiring, excessive richness of the carburettor or mixture, incorrect operation of the Ther-mactor system, or running out of petrol.

Inlet air temperature regulation

20 Inlet air temperature regulation is accomplished by the use of a thermostatic air cleaner and duct system.

21 An additional feature, incorporated on some models, is the cold temperature actuated vacuum (CTAV) (Figs. 3.82 and 3) system. This is designed to select either carburettor spark or spark port vacuum, or carburettor EGR port vacuum, as a function of ambient air temperature. The selected vacuum source is used to control the distributor diaphragm unit.

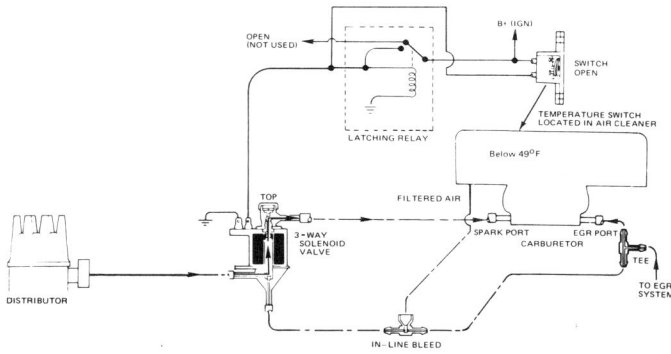

Fig. 3.82 Typical CTAV system operation below 49°F

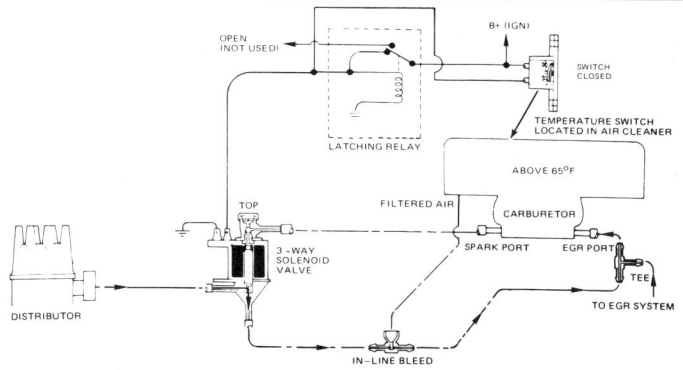

Fig. 3.83 Typical CTAV system operation above 65°F

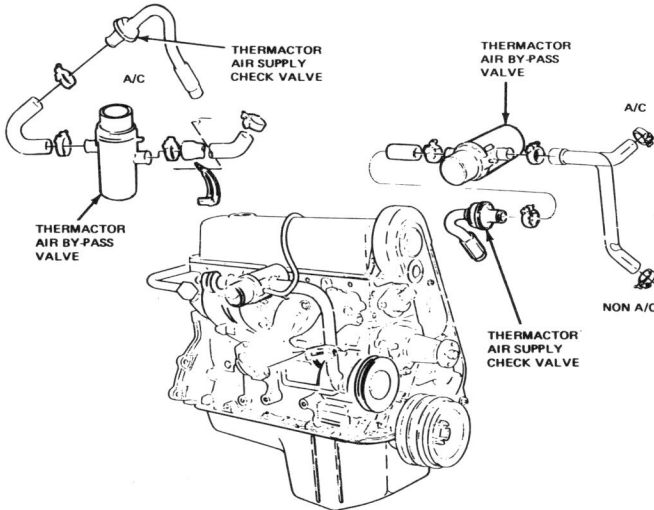

Fig. 3.84 Basic thermactor system (typical)

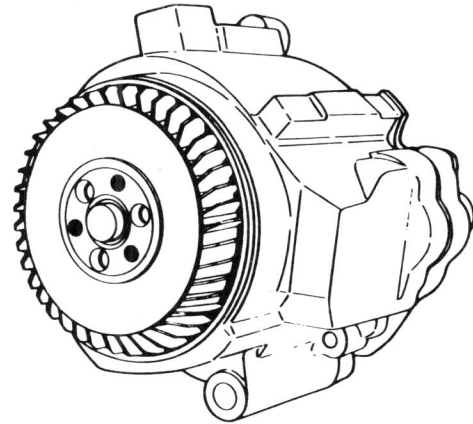

Fig. 3.85 Thermactor air pump

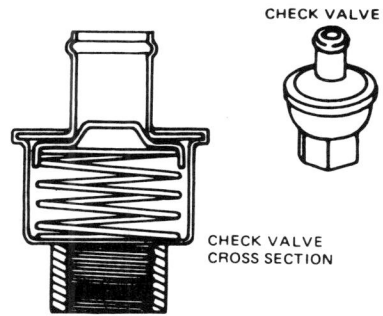

Fig. 3.86 Exhaust check valve

22 The system comprises an ambient temperature switch, a three-way solenoid valve, an external vacuum bleed and a latching relay.

23 The temperature switch activates the solenoid, which is open at temperatures below 49°F (9.5°C) and is closed above 65°F (18.3°C). Within this temperature range, the solenoid valve may be open, or closed.

24 Below 49°F (9.5°C), the system is inoperative and the distributor diaphragm receives carburettor spark port vacuum, while the EGR valve receives EGR port vacuum.

25 When the temperature switch closes, (above 65°F/18.3°C) the three way solenoid valve is energized from the ignition switch and the carburettor EGR port vacuum is delivered to the distributor advance diaphragm, as well as to the EGR valve. The latching relay is also energized by the temperature switch closing, and will remain energized until the ignition switch is turned off, regardless of the temperature switch being open or closed.

Thermactor exhaust control system

26 This system is designed to reduce the hydrocarbon and carbon monoxide content of the exhaust gases by continuing the oxidation of unburnt gases after they leave the combustion chamber. This is achieved by using an engine driven air pump to inject fresh air into the hot exhaust stream after it leaves the combustion chamber. This air mixes with the hot exhaust gases and promotes further oxidation, thus reducing their concentration and converting some of them into carbon dioxide and water.

27 The air pump draws in air through an impeller type, centrifugal fan and exhausts it from the exhaust manifold through a vacuum controlled air bypass valve and check valve. Under normal conditions thermactor air passes straight through the bypass valve, but during deceleration, when there is a high level of intake manifold vacuum, the diaphragm check valve operates to shut off the thermactor air to the air supply check valve and exhaust it to atmosphere. The air supply check valve is a non-return valve which will allow thermactor air to pass to the exhaust manifold but will not allow exhaust gases to flow in the reverse direction.

28 A slightly modified system may be used on some later vehicles which have catalytic converters in the exhaust system; this may incorporate a vacuum delay valve (VDV). A typical system is shown in the illustrations.

52 Emission control system – maintenance and testing

1 In view of the special test equipment and procedures, there is little that can be done in the way of maintenance and testing for the emission control system. In the event of a suspected malfunction of the system, check the security and condition of all pneumatic and electrical connections then, where applicable, refer to the following paragraphs for further information.

Electrically assisted choke heater

2 The only test that can be carried out on this assembly, without

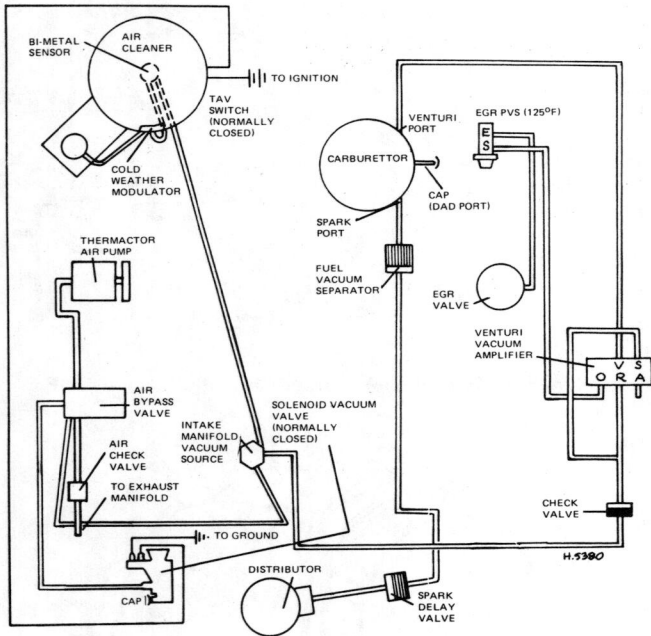

Vacuum diagram - A

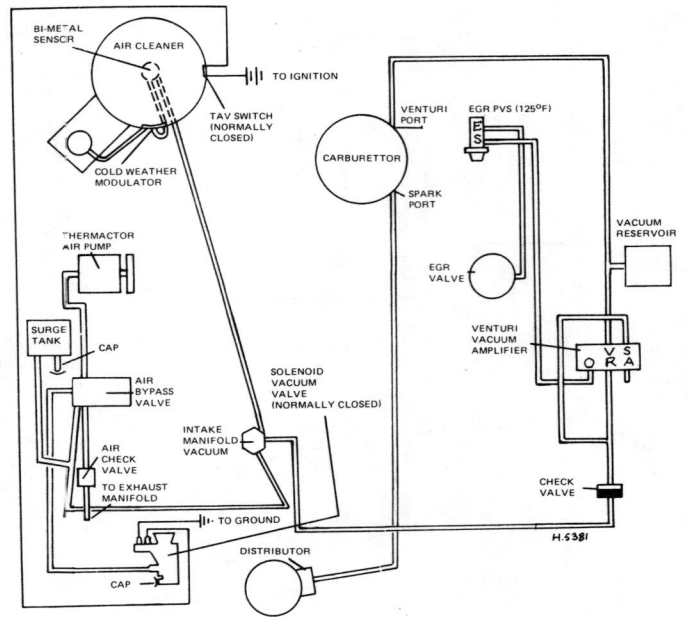

Vacuum diagram - B

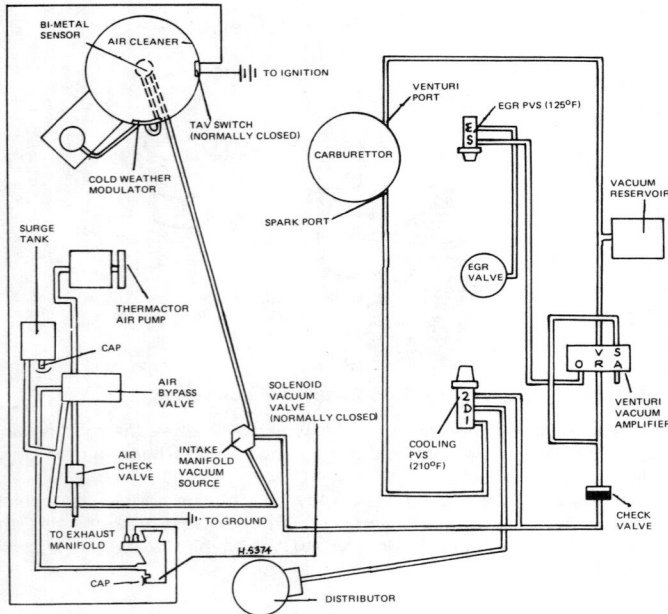

Vacuum diagram - C

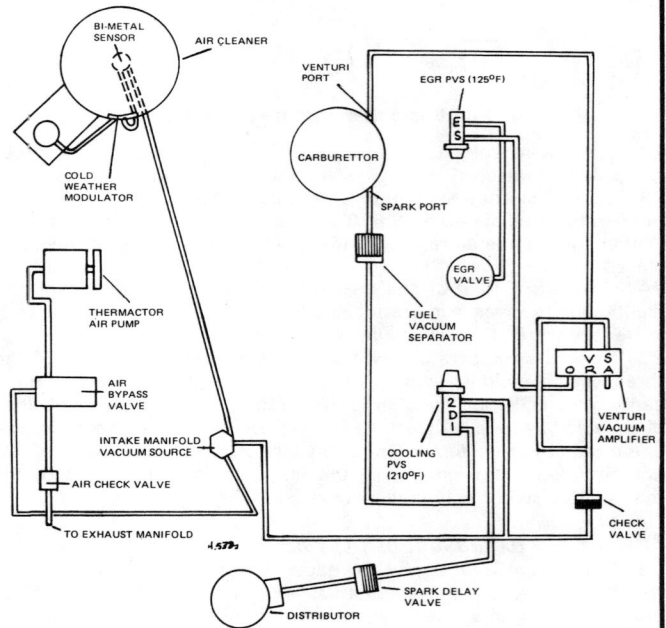

Vacuum diagram - D

Fig. 3.87a Typical vacuum diagrams

These diagrams are reproduced as a guide only, and do not necessarily cover all models or systems

A *California, automatic transmission, no air conditioning*
B *California, manual transmission, no air conditioning*
C *California, manual transmission, air conditioning*
D *Federal, automatic transmission, air conditioning*

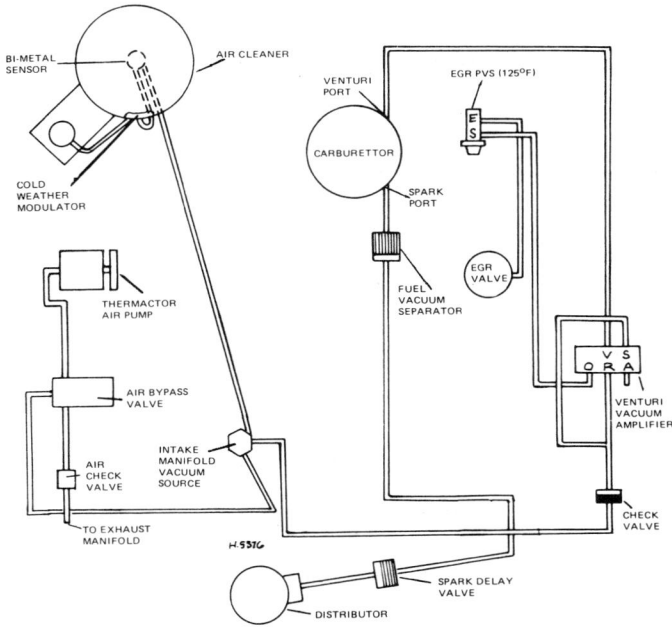

Vacuum diagram - E

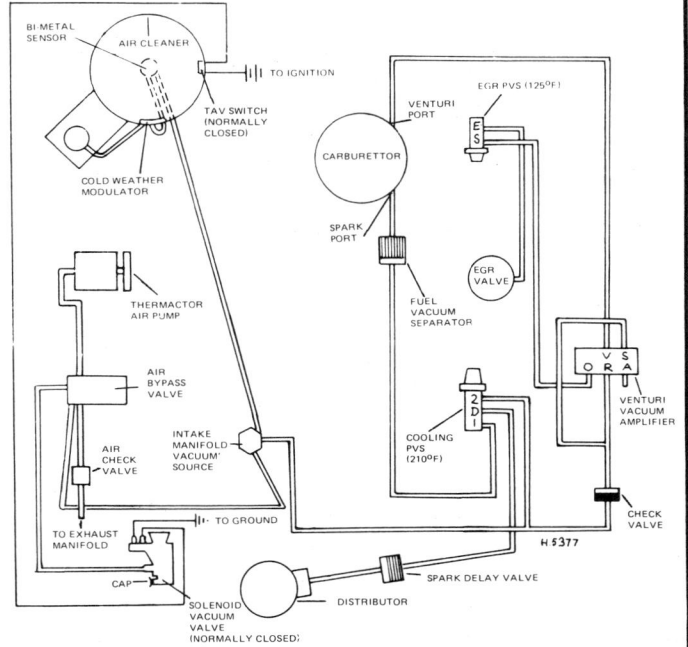

Vacuum diagram - F

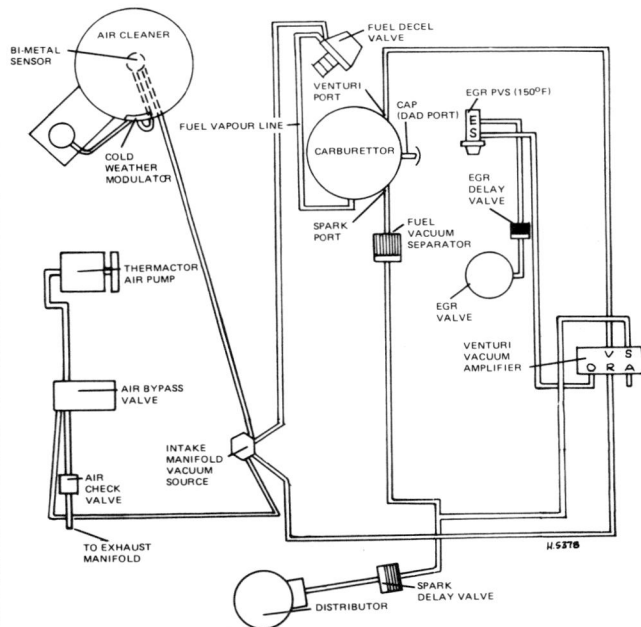

Vacuum diagram - G

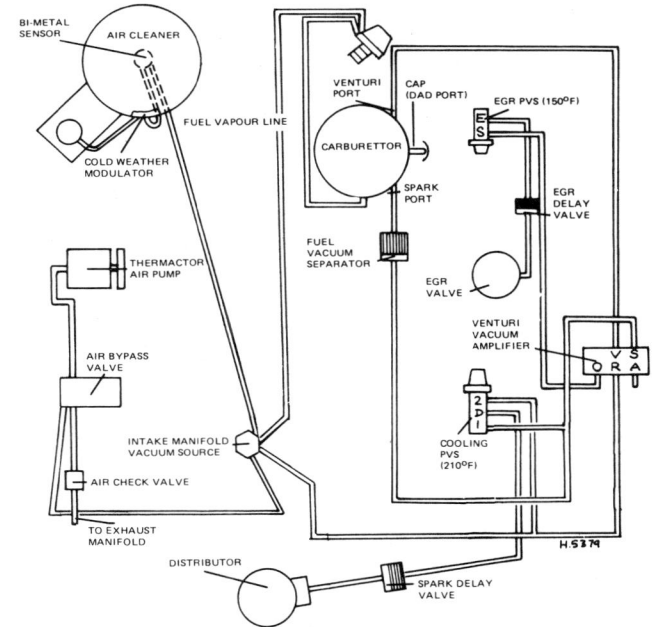

Vacuum diagram - H

Fig. 3.87b Typical vacuum diagrams

E *Federal, automatic transmission, no air conditioning*
F *California, automatic transmission, air conditioning*

G *Federal, manual transmission, no air conditioning*
H *Federal, manual transmission, air conditioning*

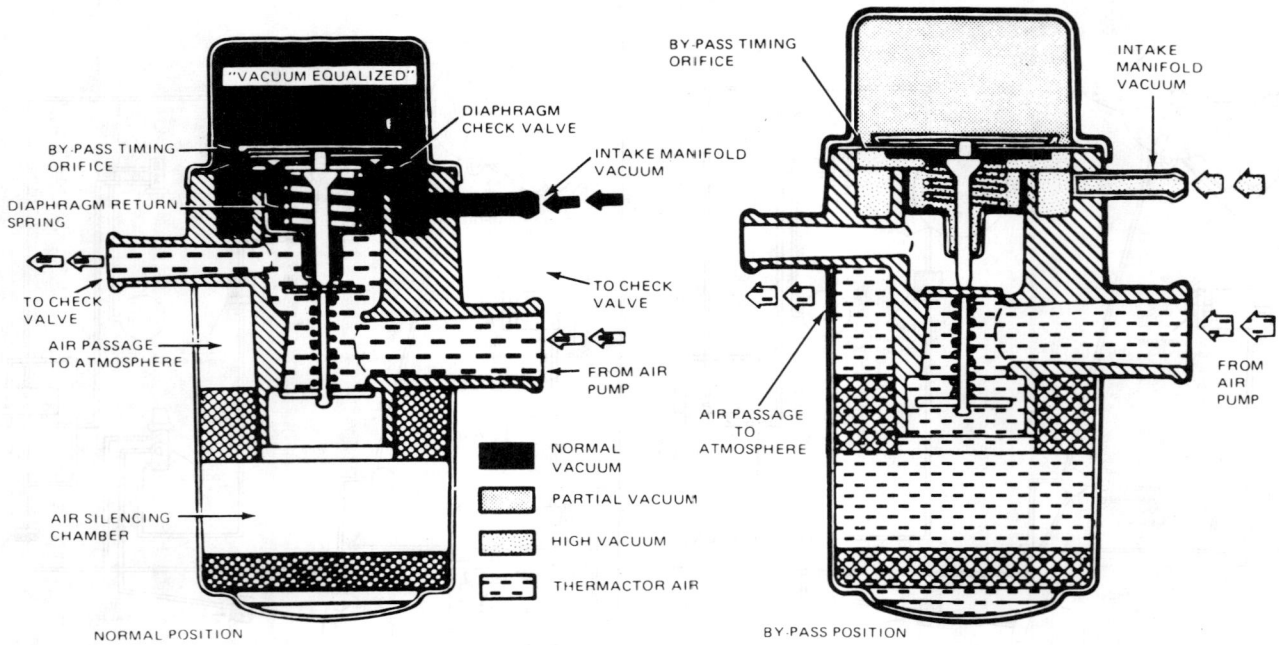

NORMAL POSITION

BY-PASS POSITION

Fig. 3.88 Thermactor system by-pass valve

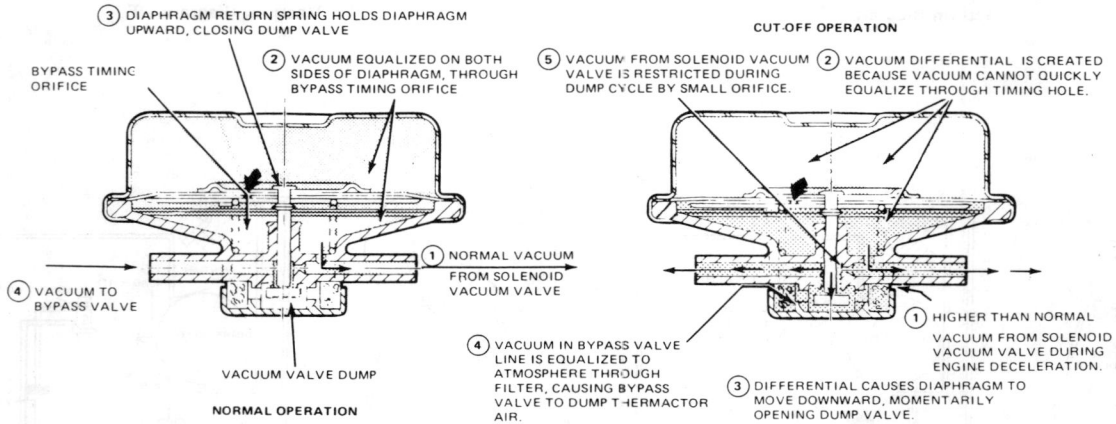

NORMAL OPERATION

CUT-OFF OPERATION

Fig. 3.89 Later type thermactor system by-pass valve

special test equipment, is a continuity check of the heater coil. If an ohmmeter is available, check for the specified resistance. If no ohmmeter is available, disconnect the stator lead from the choke cap terminal and connect one terminal of a 12V low wattage bulb (eg instrument panel bulb). Earth the other terminal of the bulb and check that it illuminates when the engine is running. If it fails to illuminate, check the alternator output and the choke lead for continuity. If the bulb illuminates, disconnect the bulb earth terminal and reconnect it to the choke lead. If the bulb does not illuminate when the engine is warm, a faulty choke is indicated.

PCV system

3   Remove all the hoses and components of the system and clean them in paraffin or petrol. Ensure that all hoses are free from any obstruction and are in a serviceable condition. Where applicable, similarly clean the crankcase breather cap and shake it dry. Renew parts as necessary then refit them to the car.

Charcoal canister

4   The charcoal canister is located on the right-hand dash panel in the engine compartment. To remove it, disconnect the two hoses, then remove the three nuts securing the canister bracket to the dash panel. Remove the canister and bracket. Refitting is the reverse of the removal procedure.

EGR system

5   The EGR valve can be removed for cleaning, but where it is damaged, corroded or extremely dirty it is preferable to fit a new unit. If the valve is to be cleaned, check that the orifice in the body is clear but take care not to enlarge it. If the valve can be dismantled, internal deposits can be removed with a small power driven rotary wire brush. Deposits around the valve stem and disc can be removed by using a steel blade or shim approximately 0.028 in (7 mm) thick in a sawing motion around the stem shoulder at both sides of the disc. Clean the cavity and passages in the main body; ensure that the poppet wobbles and moves axially before reassembly.

CTAV system

6   Without special equipment it is only possible to carry out electrical tests of the system circuitry. Connect one terminal of a 12V low wattage bulb (eg instrument panel bulb) to the car earth. Connect the other terminal to point 'B' (Fig. 3.92) and remove the connector at point 'D'. Turn on the ignition if the light illuminates, renew the latching relay. If there is no light, reconnect at point 'D'; there should now be a light. If there is none, check the temperature switch and the wiring back to the ignition switch. Provided that there is a light, disconnect at point 'D' again. There should now be a light; if there is none, renew the latching relay. If it is possible to cool the temperature switch below 49°F (9.5°C), check that the contacts are open at or

CONTROL VACUUM PORT

AIR INLET FROM THERMACTOR PUMP

AIR OUTPUT TO EXHAUST MANIFOLD

SILENCER AND VENT OPENINGS

NORMAL OPERATION

① MANIFOLD VACUUM PULLS DIAPHRAGM UP

② VALVE IS UNSEATED

③ AIR FROM THERMACTOR PUMP FLOWS FREELY TO EXHAUST MANIFOLD

④ VENT PORT SEALED OFF

"DUMP" OPERATION

① WHEN VACUUM SIGNAL DROPS

④ VALVE SEATS AND BLOCKS THERMACTOR AIR FLOW TO EXHAUST MANIFOLD.

③ VALVE OPENS TO ALLOW THERMACTOR AIR FLOW TO ATMOSPHERE.

② SPRING PULLS STEM DOWN

PRESSURE RELIEF OPERATION

① EXCESSIVE PRESSURE UNSEATS RELIEF VALVE.

③ PARTIAL THERMACTOR AIR FLOW TO EXHAUST MANIFOLD TO MEET SYSTEM REQUIREMENTS

② PARTIAL THERMACTOR AIR FLOW TO ATMOSPHERE

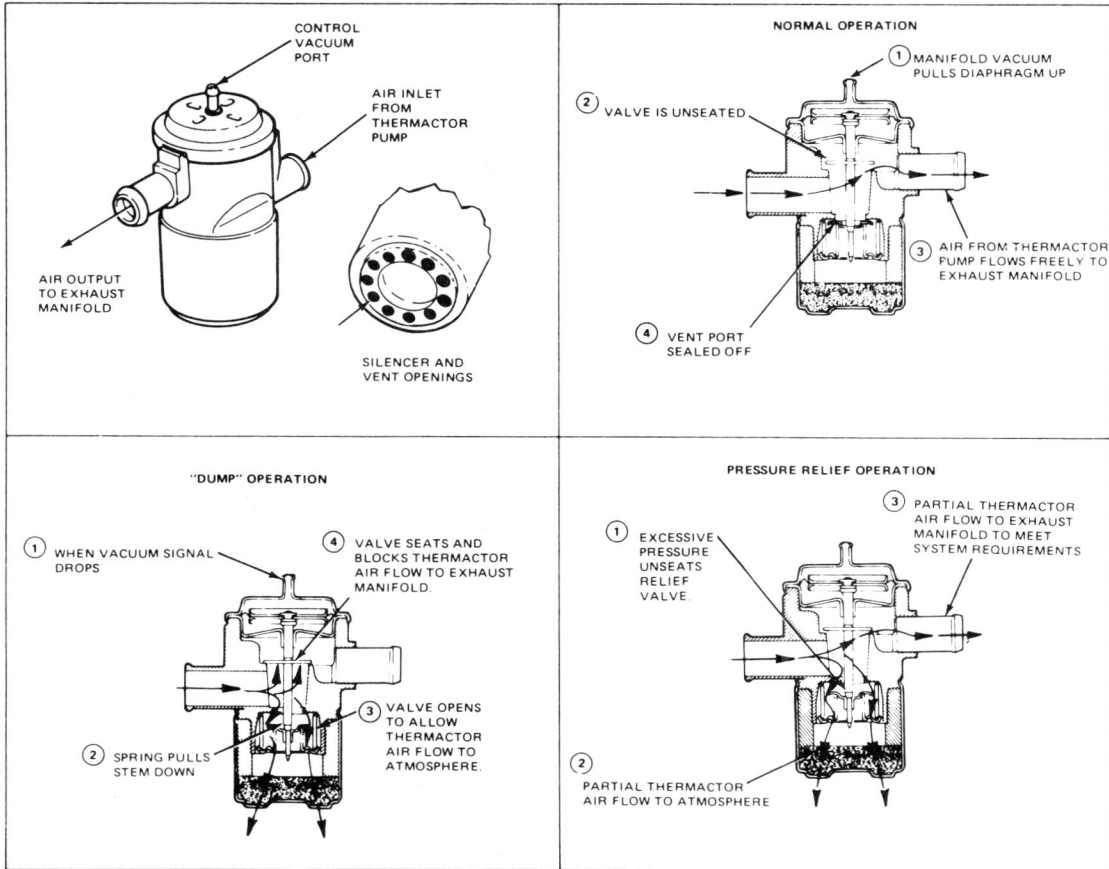

Fig. 3.90 Vacuum differential valve used on some systems

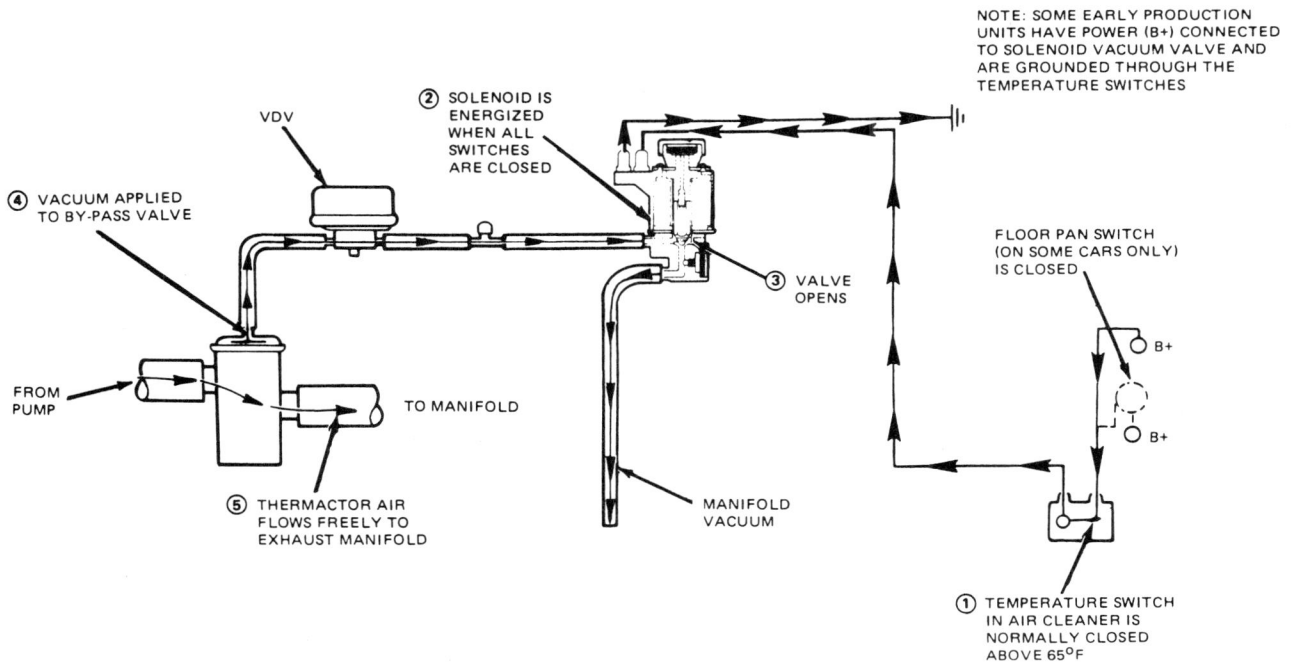

NOTE: SOME EARLY PRODUCTION UNITS HAVE POWER (B+) CONNECTED TO SOLENOID VACUUM VALVE AND ARE GROUNDED THROUGH THE TEMPERATURE SWITCHES

VDV

② SOLENOID IS ENERGIZED WHEN ALL SWITCHES ARE CLOSED

④ VACUUM APPLIED TO BY-PASS VALVE

③ VALVE OPENS

FLOOR PAN SWITCH (ON SOME CARS ONLY) IS CLOSED

B+

B+

FROM PUMP

TO MANIFOLD

⑤ THERMACTOR AIR FLOWS FREELY TO EXHAUST MANIFOLD

MANIFOLD VACUUM

① TEMPERATURE SWITCH IN AIR CLEANER IS NORMALLY CLOSED ABOVE 65°F

Fig. 3.91 Schematic diagram of typical thermactor system

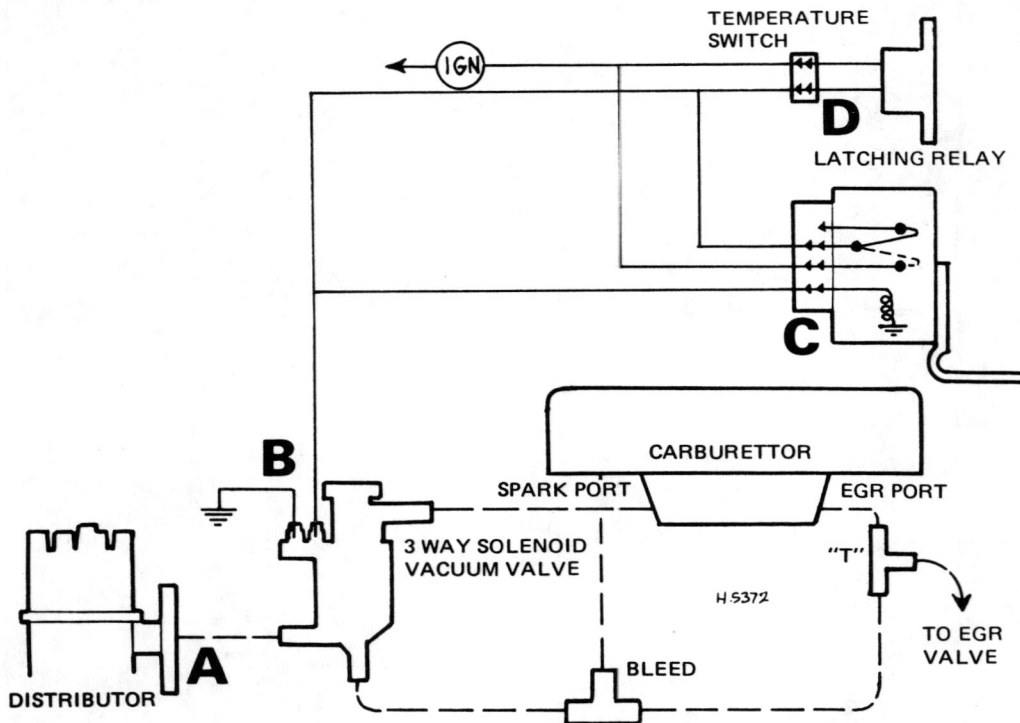

Fig. 3.92 Test connection points for the CTAV system

below this temperature.

Thermactor system

7   Apart from checking the condition of the drivebelt and pipe connections, and checking the pump drivebelt tension, there is little that can be done without the use of special test equipment. Drivebelt tension should be checked using a special tension gauge, the tension reading being as given in Chapter 2. This is approximately equal to $\frac{1}{2}$ in (13 mm) of belt movement between the longest pulley run under moderate hand pressure.

Part D: Fault diagnosis

53 Fault diagnosis – Fuel system

Symptom	Reason/s
Excessive fuel consumption*	Air cleaner choked or inlet duct system inoperative General leaks from fuel system Float chamber fuel level too high Rich mixture Incorrect valve clearances Dragging brakes Tyres under-inflated Faulty choke operation

* May also be due to faulty condenser or advance/retard system in distributor OR an emission control system fault

Symptom	Reason/s
Insufficient fuel delivery or weak mixture	Clogged fuel line or carburettor filter Fuel inlet needle valve stuck Faulty fuel pump Leaking pipe connections Leaking inlet manifold gasket Leaking carburettor mounting flange gasket Weak carburettor mixture setting

54 Fault diagnosis – Emission control system

The following list is for guidance only, since a combination of faults may produce symptoms which are difficult to diagnose. It is therefore essential that a Ford dealer or emission control specialist is consulted in the event of problems occurring.

Symptom	Reason/s
Electrically assisted choke heater Long engine warm-up time	Faulty choke heater
PCV system Fumes escaping from engine	Clogged PCV valve Split or collapsed hoses
Evaporative control system Fuel odour or rough engine running	Choked carbon canister Stuck filler cap valve Split or collapsed hoses
Thermactor system Fume emission from exhaust	Air pump drivebelt incorrectly tensioned Damaged air supply pipes Split or collapsed sensing hoses Defective air pump Faulty pressure relief valve
EGR system Rough idling	Faulty or dirty EGR valve Split of collapsed hoses Leaking valve gasket
Catalytic converter Fume emission from exhaust	Damaged or clogged catalyst

Chapter 4 Ignition system

Contents

Specifications

Mercury Capri II

Spark plugs
Type .... See engine decal
Electrode gap .... See engine decal

Firing order 1-4-2-5-3-6

Distributor .... Bosch, breakerless
Rotation (viewed from top) .... Clockwise
Automatic advance .... Centrifugal, with advance and retard diaphragm vacuum unit

Ignition timing (static) .... See engine decal
Capri II

Spark plugs
Type .... Motorcraft AGR22 (14 mm)
Electrode gap .... 0.025 in (0.64 mm)

Firing order 1-4-2-5-3-6

Distributor
Type .... Motorcraft or Bosch
Rotation (viewed from top) .... Clockwise
Automatic advance .... Centrifugal and single diaphragm vacuum unit
Condenser capacity .... 0.21 to 0.25 mfd

Contact breaker gap:
   Motorcraft .... 0.025 in (0.64 mm)
   Bosch .... 0.012 to 0.018 in (0.3 to 0.45 mm)
Dwell angle .... 38° to 40°

Ignition timing (static) .... 10° BTDC

Torque wrench settings

	lbf ft	kgf m
Spark plugs 2800 cc engine	15 to 20	2.1 to 2.8
3000 cc engine	22 to 29	3.0 to 4.0

1 General description

To achieve the best performance from an engine, it is necessary that the fuel/air mixture in the combustion chamber is ignited at exactly the right moment for the particular conditions of engine load and speed. The ignition system provides the spark necessary to start the mixture burning and the instant at which ignition occurs is varied automatically as engine operating conditions change.

The ignition system consists of a primary (low voltage) circuit which feeds current from the battery, through the ignition switch and contact breaker to the primary winding of the ignition coil. The ignition coil also has a secondary (high voltage winding) which, together with the distributor rotor, cap, the high tension leads and the spark plugs, forms the secondary circuit (Fig. 4.1). When the distributor contact breaker breaks the primary circuit, a very high voltage is induced in the secondary circuit of the ignition coil. This high voltage is routed to the appropriate cylinder by the rotor arm and the contacts in the distributor cap. The way in which the primary current is switched is different on the 2800 cc engine and the 3000 cc engine. The 2800 cc engine has an armature with magnetic spokes in place of the usual contact breaker cam (Fig. 4.2). As the armature rotates, the spokes pass in front of a magnetic pick-up and each time the pick-up senses the presence of a spoke, it sends a signal to an amplifier module

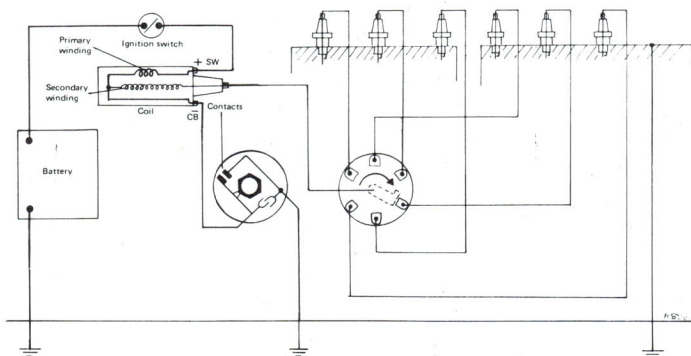

Fig. 4.1 Ignition primary and secondary circuits (typical)

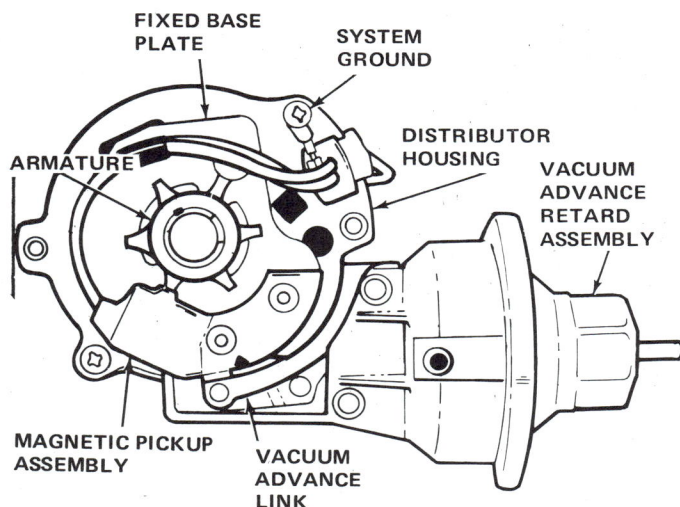

Fig. 4.2 Breakerless type distributor (Mercury Capri II)

causing the amplifier to switch the primary circuit off, to collapse the magnetic field produced by the primary circuit of the ignition coil and so induce a high voltage in the coil's secondary winding. After allowing sufficient time for the primary circuit to collapse, the amplifier switches the primary circuit on again, so that the cycle can be repeated when the next magnetic spoke passes the pick-up coil.

Part A   Mercury Capri II

2   Ignition timing (initial advance)

1   Refer to the engine decal to obtain the ignition timing initial advance. Locate the appropriate timing mark on the engine vibration damper on the crankshaft pulley (Fig. 4.3) and highlight it with a white chalk, or paint mark.

2   Disconnect the vacuum lines from the distributor and temporarily plug the pipes (Fig. 4.4).

3   Connect a proprietary ignition timing light in accordance with the manufacturer's instructions to the spark plug wire to No 1 cylinder. Start the engine and run it at an idling speed of 600 rpm, while shining the timing light onto the vibration damper. Note the position of the highlighted mark with respect to the timing pointer. If the line and the pointer do not coincide, stop the engine, slacken the distributor clamp bolt and start the engine. With the engine again idling, turn the distributor until the timing marks do coincide. If the timing marks cannot be made to coincide, or if it is suspected that the ignition is incorrect, check that the distributor has been fitted correctly by referring to Section 3.

4   Having set the timing, stop the engine and tighten the distributor clamp bolt.

5   Start the engine and while increasing its speed from idling to about 2500 rpm, check that the ignition timing advances and then returns to its lower setting when the engine returns to idling speed. If the ignition advances as speed increases and becomes less advanced when the speed falls again, it indicates that the centrifugal advance mechanism is working satisfactorily.

6   Remove the plugs from the vacuum lines and reconnect the vacuum lines to the vacuum unit, noting that the pipe from the intake manifold is connected to the inner diaphragm and the pipe from the carburettor is connected to the end of the vacuum unit. Repeat the test of paragraph 3 and check that with the pipes fitted, the ignition advances even more than under the influence of the centrifugal mechanism alone.

7   If a satisfactory result is not obtained in the tests of paragraphs 3 and 5, the distributor should be checked by a suitably equipped Ford dealer, or an ignition system specialist. Overhaul kits are not available for this type of distributor and in the event of failure, a new distributor must be fitted.

8   After completing the tests, disconnect and remove the timing light.

3   Distributor – removal and refitting

1   Remove the air cleaner as detailed in Chapter 3.

2   Disconnect the vacuum advance pipe from the distributor, then remove the distributor cap and place it and the wires to one side.

3   Scribe a mark on the distributor body and on to the cylinder block, to indicate the position of the rotor in the distributor and the position of the distributor in the cylinder block. These marks are to ensure that the distributor is refitted without altering the ignition timing.

4   Remove the distributor fixing bolt and clamp and lift the distributor out of the block. Do not rotate the engine while the distributor is out of the block, or it will be necessary to retime the engine.

5   If the engine has not been rotated while the distributor was removed, align the rotor with the mark which was scribed on the body to show rotor position. Insert the distributor into the block and if necessary move it to and fro slightly until the shaft engages. Align the scribed marks on the distributor body and the block, then insert and tighten fixing bolt.

6   If the crankshaft was rotated while the distributor was removed from the engine, it will be necessary to time the engine as follows. Rotate the crankshaft until No1 piston is on TDC after the compression

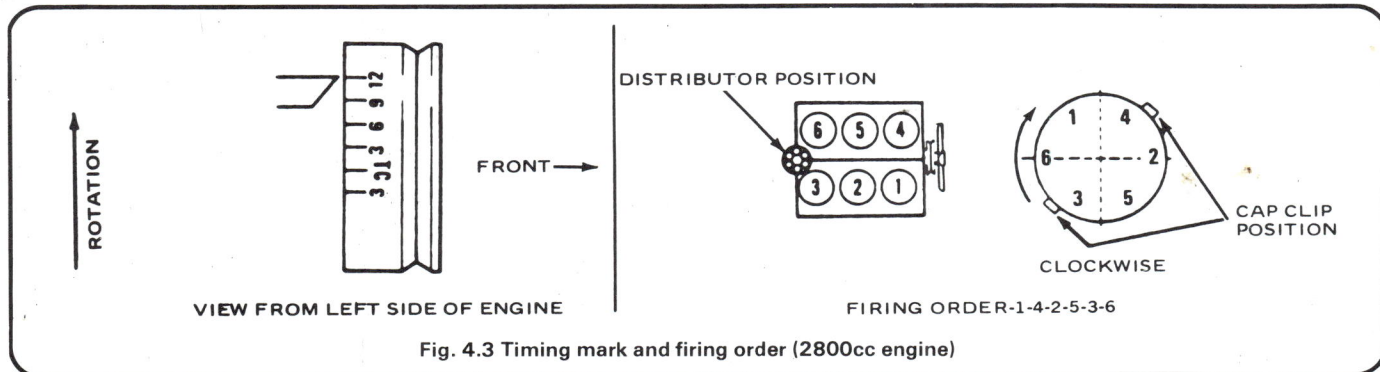

Fig. 4.3 Timing mark and firing order (2800cc engine)

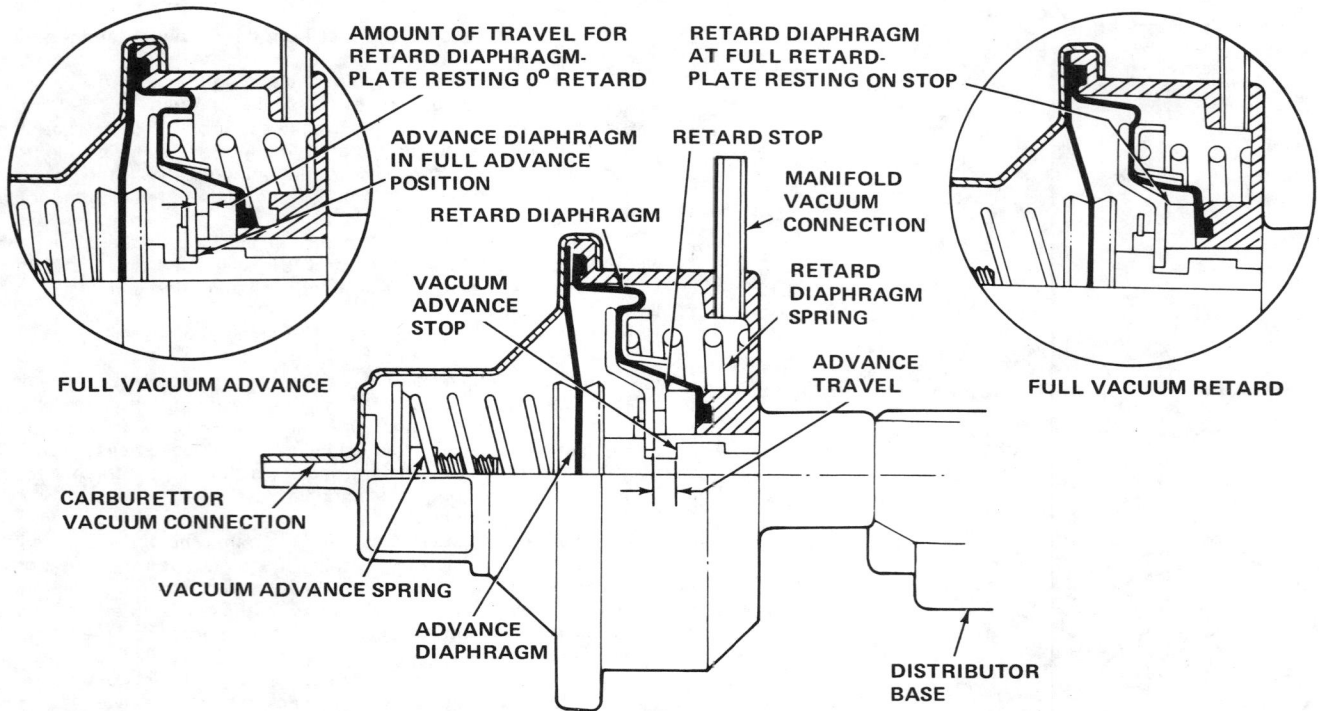

Fig. 4.4 Dual diaphragm vacuum advance unit (2800cc engine)

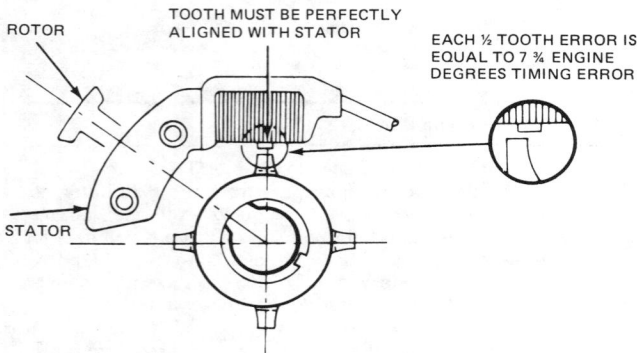

Fig. 4.5 The armature position for setting static timing (typical)

stroke. Align the correct initial timing mark on the timing pointer with the timing pointer on the crankshaft damper. Position the distributor in the block with one of the armature segments as shown in Fig. 4.5 and the rotor at the position for firing No 1 cylinder. Make sure that the oil pump intermediate shaft properly engages the distributor shaft. If necessary, crank the engine after the distributor gear is partially engaged, in order to engage the oil pump intermediate shaft. Fit, but do not tighten the retaining clamp and bolt, then rotate the distributor to advance the timing to a point where the armature tooth is perfectly aligned with the stator pole.

7   Tighten the distributor clamp. Fit the distributor cap and wires, including the connection of the distributor to the vehicle wiring harness.

8   Check the ignition timing light as detailed in Section 2.

Part B Capri II

---

4   Ignition timing (initial advance)

1   If the distributor has not been removed, or if the distributor has been removed and refitted without the crankshaft having been turned

while it was removed, the ignition timing can be checked with a timing light as detailed in Section 2.

2   Turn the engine until No 1 piston is approaching TDC on the compression stroke. This can be checked by removing No 1 spark plug and putting a finger over the hole to feel the compression as the engine is turned. If this check is not made and the piston is not on its compression stroke, the timing will be 180° out and the engine will not start.

3   Having found TDC on the compression stroke, turn the engine backwards until the timing mark on the crankshaft pulley is at 14° before TDC (Fig. 4.6).

4   With the vacuum advance unit pointing towards the front of the engine and with the rotor arm pointing towards the contact for No 1 cylinder (Fig. 4.7), insert the distributor. As the gears mesh, the distributor rotor will turn and it may be necessary to remove the distributor and rotate the shaft one or more teeth, so that when the teeth are fully engaged, the rotor is in the correct position. When it points in the required direction, with the assembly fully home, fit the distributor clamp plate bolt, washer and nut and tighten until the clamp just grips the distributor.

5   Turn the distributor so that the contact breaker points just begin to open, then tighten the clamp, so that it is firm, but do not overtighten (Fig. 4.8). If it is not possible to turn the distributor so that the points begin to open when the rotor arm is pointing towards the contact for

Fig. 4.6 Crankshaft pulley and timing marks

Measuring plug gap. A feeler gauge of the correct size (see ignition system specifications) should have a slight 'drag' when slid between the electrodes. Adjust gap if necessary

Adjusting plug gap. The plug gap is adjusted by bending the earth electrode inwards, or outwards, as necessary until the correct clearance is obtained. Note the use of the correct tool

Normal. Grey-brown deposits, lightly coated core nose. Gap increasing by around 0.001 in (0.025 mm) per 1000 miles (1600 km). Plugs ideally suited to engine, and engine in good condition

Carbon fouling. Dry, black, sooty deposits. Will cause weak spark and eventually misfire. Fault: over-rich fuel mixture. Check: carburettor mixture settings, float level and jet sizes; choke operation and cleanliness of air filter. Plugs can be re-used after cleaning

Oil fouling. Wet, oily deposits. Will cause weak spark and eventually misfire. Fault: worn bores/piston rings or valve guides; sometimes occurs (temporarily) during running-in period. Plugs can be re-used after thorough cleaning

Overheating. Electrodes have glazed appearance, core nose very white — few deposits. Fault: plug overheating. Check: plug value, ignition timing, fuel octane rating (too low) and fuel mixture (too weak). Discard plugs and cure fault immediately

Electrode damage. Electrodes burned away; core nose has burned, glazed appearance. Fault: pre-ignition. Check: as for 'Overheating' but may be more severe. Discard plugs and remedy fault before piston or valve damage occurs

Split core nose (may appear initially as a crack). Damage is self-evident, but cracks will only show after cleaning. Fault: pre-ignition or wrong gap-setting technique. Check: ignition timing, cooling system, fuel octane rating (too low) and fuel mixture (too weak). Discard plugs, rectify fault immediately

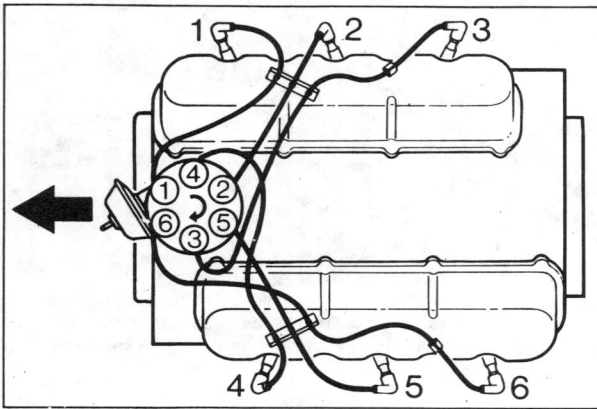

Fig. 4.7 Position of HT leads and firing order (Capri II)

Fig. 4.8 Tightening the distributor clamp

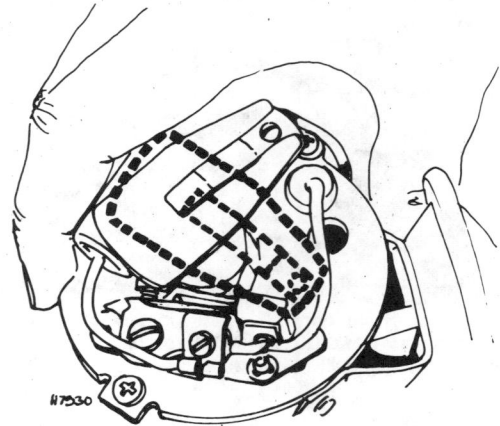

Fig. 4.10 Correct position of rotor arm for distributor refitment

2   Disconnect the high tension lead from the centre of the distributor cap, by gripping the end cap and pulling. Now disconnect the low tension lead.

3   Pull off the rubber connector joining the vacuum pipe to the carburettor vacuum unit.

4   Mark the position of the rotor arm relative to the distributor body and also make mating marks on the distributor body and the clamping plate, so that the distributor can be refitted without the ignition timing being altered.

5   Remove the bolt from the distributor body clamp and lift out the distributor.

6   Set the engine with its correct timing mark on the timing cover, in line with the notch in the crankshaft pulley as No 1 piston comes up on its compression stroke.

7   Align the tip of the rotor arm as shown in Fig. 4.10.

8   Fit the distributor to the engine so that the vacuum unit is facing forwards and is parallel to the centre line of the engine. It may be necessary to turn the rotor a few degrees to get the gear teeth to mesh.

9   Fit the distributor retaining bolt.

10   Refit the low tension lead.

11   Refit the distributor cap, the HT lead to the centre of the cap and the spark plug leads.

12   Reconnect the vacuum pipe to the carburettor vacuum unit.

13   Check the initial advance as described in Section 4.

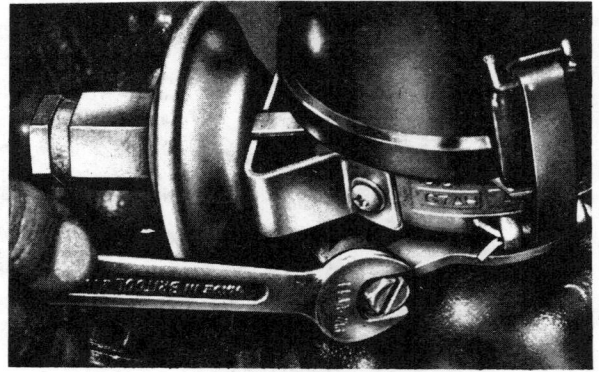

Fig. 4.9 Using a timing light

No 1 cylinder, the distributor must be removed and the mesh of the gear teeth changed.

6   This method of setting the timing is not as accurate as that obtained by using a timing light when the engine is running and this latter method should be used if possible (Fig. 4.9).

7   The setting given is for the recommended fuel of 97 octane (4 star) rating. For a lower grade fuel the timing must be retarded by about 1° for every reduction in octane number, with a similar advancing of the timing if a higher octane fuel is used.

5   Distributor – removal and refitting

1   Mark the six plug leads to ensure that they are refitted correctly, then pull off the connectors from the spark plugs.

6   Contact breaker points – adjustment

1   Release the two clips securing the distributor cap to the distributor body and lift the cap off with the HT leads attached. Wipe the inside of the cap with a clean dry cloth, look for signs of tracking on the plastic and ensure that the carbon brush in the centre of the distributor cap is in good condition.

2   Lift the rotor arm off and check that its spring contact is clean and in good condition.

3   Gently prise the contact breaker points apart to examine the condition of their faces. If they are burned or pitted, they can be removed and refaced, but it is much better to reject them and fit a new contact breaker assembly.

4   If the points are satisfactory, turn the crankshaft until the heel of the contact breaker arm is on the highest part of the cam and the points are at their maximum separation. Measure the gap with a feeler gauge. The gap should be 0.025 in (0.64 mm) and if it differs from this by more than 0.001 in (0.025 mm) the gap should be adjusted.

5   To adjust the gap, slacken the two clamping screws (photo) and insert a screwdriver into the notched hole in the contact breaker plate. Turn the screwdriver clockwise to increase the gap and anti-clockwise to decrease it (photo). When the gap is correct, tighten the damping screws and then check the gap again.

6   Refit the rotor arm and distributor cap, refitting the two clips to secure the cap.

7   Contact breaker – removal and refitting

1   The contact breaker points are mounted on the contact breaker plate and the assembly must be removed and refitted as a unit.

2   Remove the distributor cap and pull the rotor arm off.

3   Slacken the self-tapping screw which secures the condenser and low tension leads to the contact breaker assembly and slide out the forked cable terminations.

4   Undo and remove the two screws which secure the contact breaker base plate to the distributor and lift off the contact breaker assembly.

5   Before refitting the contact breaker assembly, smear the distributor cam with a trace of Vaseline, or grease to Specification ESF – MI C66 – A.

6   Fit the contact breaker and its clamping screws, but do not fully tighten the screws until the contact breaker gap has been adjusted as described in Section 6.

7   Refit the rotor arm and distributor cap, refitting the two clips to secure the cap.

8   Distributor – dismantling and reassembly

1   With the distributor removed from the engine, remove the rotor arm and the contact breaker assembly (Fig. 4.11).

2   Prise the small circlip from the vacuum unit pivot post.

3   Remove the two screws which secure the breaker plate to the distributor body and lift the plate off.

4   Slacken the self-tapping screw which secures the condenser and low tension leads to the contact breaker assembly and slide out the forked cable terminations.

5   Undo and the remove the condenser retaining screw and remove the condenser.

6   Remove the circlip, flat washer and wavy washer from the pivot post. Separate the two plates by bringing the holding down screw through the keyhole slot in the lower plate. Take care not to lose the earth spring on the pivot post.

7   Remove the two screws securing the vacuum unit to the distributor body and remove the vacuum unit.

8   To dismantle the vacuum unit, remove the plug from the end of the unit and withdraw the spring, vacuum stop and shims.

9   Before dismantling the centrifugal advance mechanism, note that the two springs are different and mark them so that they are refitted in their original places. Remove the springs, prise off the circlips securing the centrifugal weights, mark the weights to identify their original positions and then remove them.

10 Mark which of the end slots in the mechanical advance plate engages with the stop in the action plate. If this is not done, it is possible to have the rotor arm 180° from its correct position.

11 Remove the felt pad from the centre of the cam, expand the circlip which is then exposed and remove it. Lift off the cam and advance plate assembly.

12 Do not remove the distributor spindle unless it is necessary to fit a new gear, or spindle. To remove the gear, use a punch and hammer to drive out the lock pin and then pull the gear from the spindle. Take care to retain any shims, or washers which may be fitted. With the gear removed, the spindle assembly can be withdrawn from the distributor.

13 Before reassembling, carefully clean the body of the distributor and all its component parts. If the spindle has been removed, lubricate it with engine oil before reassembly .

14 Reassembly is a straightforward reversal of dismantling but there are several points which should be noted.

15 Lubricate the centrifugal weights and other parts of the centrifugal advance mechanism, the distributor shaft and the part of the spindle which carries the cam assembly, using engine oil. Do not oil excessively.

16 If the drive shaft has been removed, first refit the thrust washers below the action plate, before inserting the shaft into the distributor body. Fit the wavy washer and thrust washer to the lower end of the shaft and then refit the gear, securing it with a new spring pin. If a new gear, or a new drive shaft have been fitted, a new hole should be drilled at 90° to the existing hole.

17 After assembling the centrifugal weights and springs, check that they move freely, without binding.

18 Before assembling the breaker plates, make sure that the three nylon bearing studs are located in the holes in the upper bearing plate and that the earthing spring is fitted to the pivot post.

19 On completion of assembly, adjust the contact breaker gap to 0.025 in (0.64 mm).

6.5a Contact breaker plate clamp screw

6.5b Adjusting the contact breaker gap

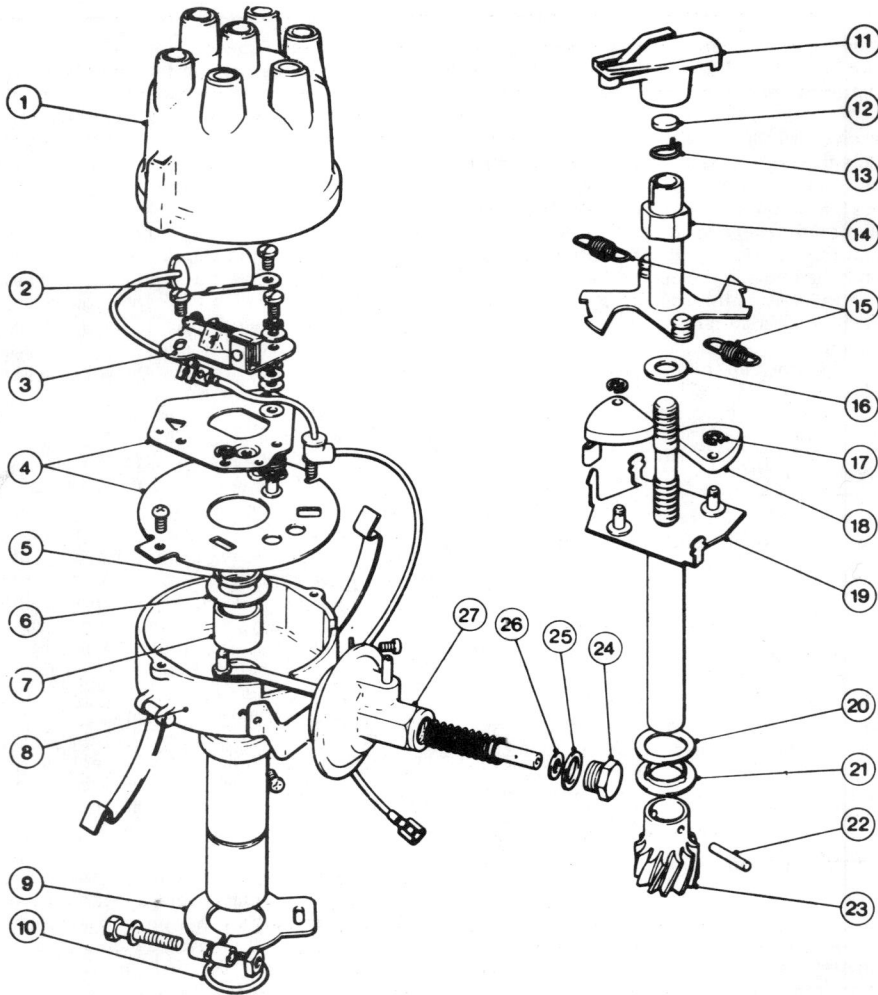

Fig. 4.11 Distributor components (typical)

1	Cap	8	Body
2	Condenser	9	Clamp plate
3	Points assembly	10	Seal
4	Base plate	11	Rotor
5	Thrust washers	12	Felt wick
6	Thrust washers	13	Circlip
7	Bush	14	Cam

15	Advance springs	22	Pin
16	Washers	23	Gear
17	Circlip	24	Nut
18	Advance weight	25	Washer
19	Shaft	26	Plate
20	Spacer	27	Vacuum unit
21	Washer		

Fig. 4.12 Lubricating the distributor cam

Fig. 4.13 Lubricating the distributor cam spindle pad

9 Distributor – lubrication

1 It is important that the distributor cam is smeared with petroleum jelly, or grease, at intervals of 6000 miles (10 000 km), or every six months (Fig. 4.12). At the same time, the cam spindle should be lubricated with engine oil.

2 Lubricate sparingly, because excess oil and grease may contaminate the contact breaker points and cause misfiring, or engine failure.

3 To gain access to the cam spindle, remove the distributor cap and rotor arm. Apply no more than two drops of oil to the felt pad (Fig. 4.13) and when the engine is hot, oil will run down the spindle and lubricate it.

4 Although the automatic advance mechanism can be lubricated by allowing a few drops of oil to pass through the gap between the cam and the contact breaker base, it is more satisfactory to dismantle the distributor as described in the previous Section.

5 Lubricate the pivot of the moving contact by applying not more than one drop of oil to the pivot post and then wiping away any excess.

6 After finishing the lubrication of the distributor, refit the rotor arm and the distributor cap.

10 Spark plugs and HT leads

1 The correct functioning of the spark plugs is vital for the correct performance of an engine and the wrong grade of plug, an incorrect gap, or dirty plugs will tend to result in reduced performance and increased fuel consumption.

2 At intervals of 6000 miles (10 000 km) the plugs should be removed, cleaned and if they are in poor condition, they should be rejected and a new set fitted.

3 Plugs should be cleaned by a sand blasting machine, which will clean them more thoroughly and with less risk of damage than cleaning by hand. The machine will also test the operation of the plug under pressure and any plug which fails the pressure test should be rejected.

4 If the correct grade of plug is fitted, the engine is in good condition and the fuel/air mixture and ignition timing are correct, the plug insulators should show a light greyish brown deposit when they are removed from the engine. The appearance of the insulator as a result of a variety of causes is shown in the colour illustrations on page 91.

5 A spark plug gap which is too large, or too small, will affect the ignition timing, as well as reduce the efficiency of the spark. Check the plug gap with a feeler gauge and set the correct gap by bending the outer electrode. Do not attempt to alter the plug gap by bending the central electrode, because this may crack the insulator and damage the plug.

6 Always keep the plug leads and the porcelain plug insulators free of dirt and oil, by wiping them with a clean rag at regular intervals. Dirty plug insulators are the most common cause of bad starting in damp weather.

11 Fault diagnosis – ignition system

There are two main divisions indicating ignition faults. Either the engine will not start or fire, or it is difficult to start and then runs intermittently, or unevenly. If the car stops suddenly, or will not start at all, it is likely that the fault is in the low tension circuit.

Engine will not start

If the engine spins at normal speed, indicating that the battery is in good condition and that the battery connections are making good electrical contact, first check that a spark is being produced. Remove one of the spark plugs and lay it with its lead attached in a place where the body of the plug is in electrical contact with the engine. Operate the starter and look to see whether there is a spark at the plug. Alternatively, remove the cap from the distributor and remove the high tension lead, connecting the coil to the distributor, from the top of the distributor cap. Hold the HT lead with a piece of dry rag so that the end of the lead is about $\frac{1}{4}$ in (6 mm) from some part of the cylinder block. Using an insulated screwdriver, separate the contact breaker points while the ignition is switched on and observe whether a spark jumps across from the end of the HT lead to the cylinder block. If a spark is not obtained, check that a test lamp will light when connected between the negative terminal of the coil and chassis earth. The lamp lighting indicates that the primary circuit of the coil and the ignition switch circuit are satisfactory and the fault is likely to be that the contact breaker is not making contact, or the condenser is defective. For a conventional contact breaker either clean the contacts, or fit a new contact breaker assembly and then check the gap setting. If the fault persists, change the condenser. For a breakerless distributor remove the distributor and amplifier module and have them checked by a Ford dealer.

Engine misfires

If the engine misfires regularly, run it at fast idling speed and short out each of the plugs in turn by placing the blade of a screwdriver with an insulated handle between the plug terminal and the cylinder head. No difference in engine running will be noticed in short circuiting a plug which is defective, while short circuiting a working plug will accentuate the misfiring. If a plug is suspect, change its position to another cylinder and recheck to see whether it is the plug, or the lead to it, which is defective.

If the misfiring cannot be attributed to a single cylinder, examine the inside of the distributor cover to ensure that the central brush is making satisfactory contact with the rotor arm and that there is no sign of tracking of the spark across the insulation of the distributor cover. On a distributor with a conventional contact breaker, an intermittent fault on the contact breaker condenser, or a loose condenser contact, can cause intermittent misfiring.

Chapter 5 Clutch

Contents

Specifications

Clutch type	Single dry plate, diaphragm spring
Actuation	Cable
Manufacturer	Borg and Beck, or Fichtel and Sachs
Size	9.5 in (242 mm)
Lining thickness	0.150 in (3.81 mm)
Clutch pedal free travel	1.06 ± 0.16 in (27 ± 4 mm)

Torque wrench settings

	lbf ft	kgf m
Clutch pressure plate-to-flywheel	12 to 15	1.64 to 2.05
Clutch housing to transmission case	40 to 47	5.5 to 6.5
Clutch bellhousing to engine	25 to 35	3.9 to 4.8

1 General description

All manual transmission models covered by this manual are fitted with a single dry plate disc, with a diaphragm spring pressure plate which is bolted to the engine flywheel. The clutch is operated by a cable connection from the clutch pedal (Fig. 5.1).

The diaphragm spring is pivoted on specially shouldered pins and is sandwiched between two annular rings, which act as fulcrums. As the centre of the spring is pushed in, the outside of the spring moves out, moving the pressure plate backwards and freeing the friction plate from contact with the driven plate. When the clutch pedal is released, the diaphragm spring forces the pressure plate forward until the friction plate is sandwiched between the driven plate and the flywheel.

The clutch release mechanism consists of a release fork and a bearing which is in permanent contact with the release fingers of the pressure plate assembly. Contact between the pressure plate and the release bearing will not damage the clutch, or the bearing, and there should never be any free play between them.

2 Clutch – adjustment

1 Improper adjustment of the clutch pedal is one of the most frequent causes of clutch failure and can be a contributory factor in some transmission failures. Adjust the clutch pedal free travel whenever the clutch does not disengage properly or whenever new clutch parts are fitted.

2 Pull the clutch pedal back until it is hard against its back stop and secure it in this position by placing a wood block between the pedal and the floor.

3 Jack up the front of the car and support it on blocks or stands.

4 Ensure that the clutch cable is not kinked, then pull the outer cable forward until the adjusting nut is pulled out of its recess in the clutch cable bushing, or free of the face of the bushing, depending on model (Fig. 5.2 and 5.3). If the clutch is badly in need of adjustment, it may be necessary to remove the boot from the side of the clutch housing and manually pull the release lever forward to assist in freeing the cable nut from the recess.

5 Pull the outer cable forward to take up any free play and turn the adjuster nut until it is up against the abutment face of the clutch housing or until the nut just enters the shaped recess in the bushing.

6 Remove the wood block from beneath the clutch pedal and press the pedal to the floor by hand three or four times and allow it to slowly return to its normal position. The pedal must not be allowed to spring back, because this may give a wrong indication of its normal rest position.

7 With the clutch pedal held firmly against the back stop, measure the distance A (Fig. 5.2).

8 Depress the pedal fully and release it gently. Measure the distance from the pedal to the floor, (dimension B in the figure). The difference between A and B should be 1.06 ± 0.16 in (27 ± 4 mm)

9 If the pedal lift is too small, the setting at the clutch housing should be increased. If pedal lift is too great, the setting at the clutch housing should be decreased. On no account should any attempt be made to alter the pedal back stop.

10 When the setting is correct, lock the adjuster nut, depress the pedal by hand and release it slowly. Recheck the pedal lift.

11 Remove the stands and lower the car to the ground.

---

3 Clutch – removal

1 Remove the gearbox and bellhousing as described in Chapter 6.

2 Scribe a mark on the clutch casing and the flywheel so that the

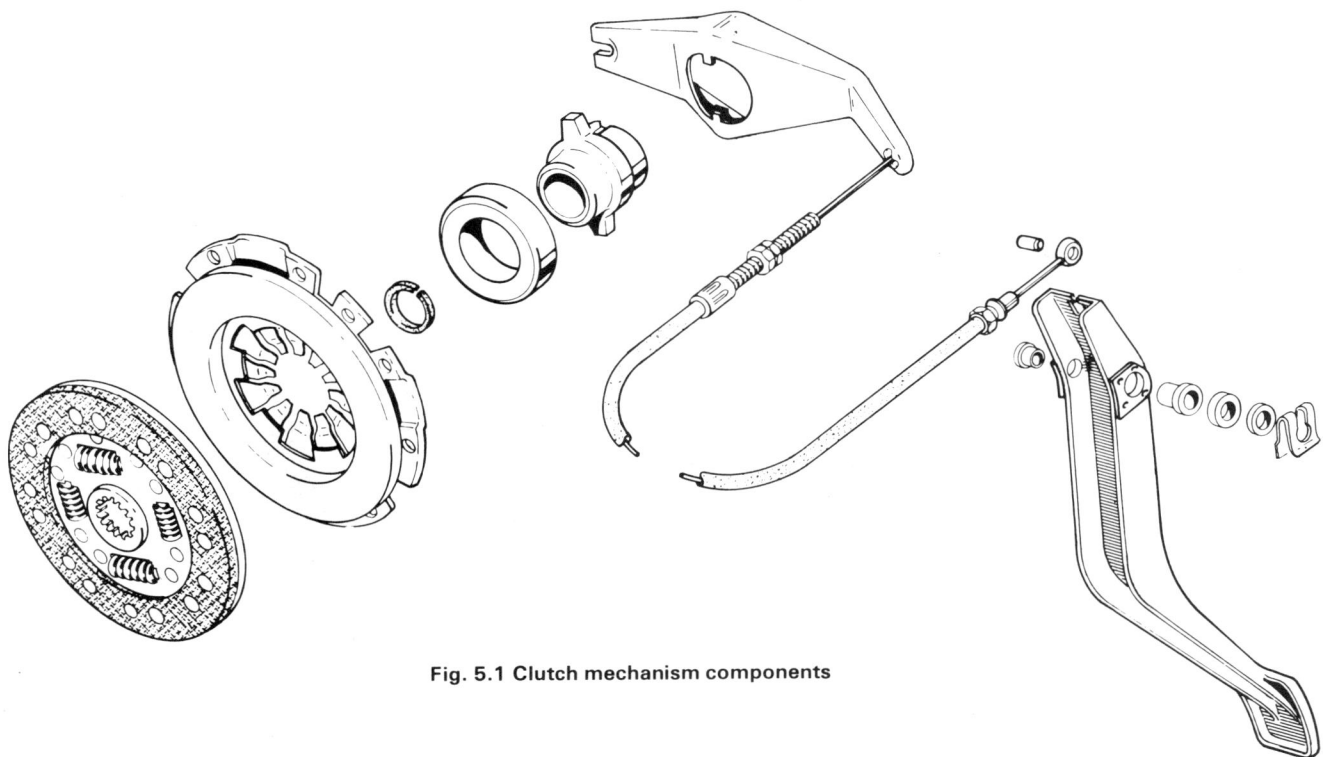

Fig. 5.1 Clutch mechanism components

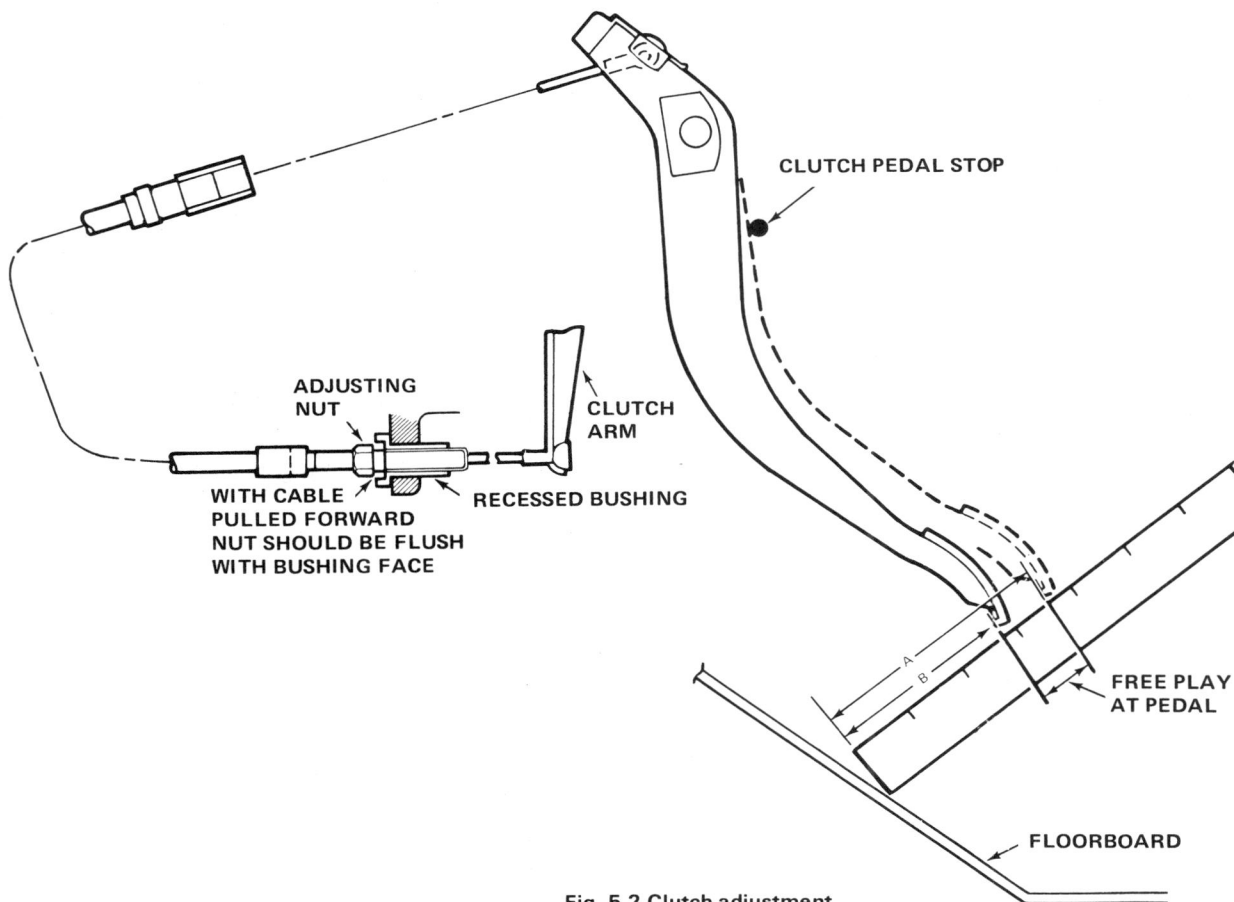

ADJUSTING
NUT

CLUTCH
ARM

CLUTCH PEDAL STOP

WITH CABLE
PULLED FORWARD
NUT SHOULD BE FLUSH
WITH BUSHING FACE

RECESSED BUSHING

FREE PLAY
AT PEDAL

FLOORBOARD

Fig. 5.2 Clutch adjustment

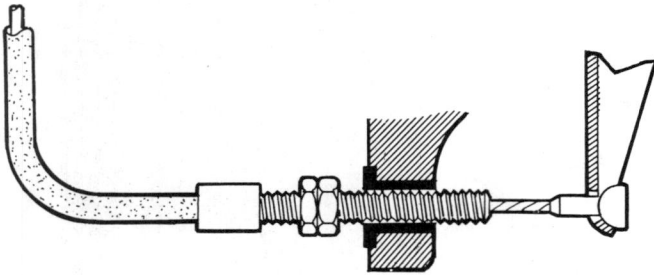

Fig. 5.3 Clutch adjuster

Fig. 5.4 Centralising the clutch friction plate

6.3 Clutch release arm and bearing

clutch will be refitted in its original position.

3   Release the clutch attachment bolts in stages, working in a diagonal sequence.

4   Remove the bolts and then lift off the pressure plate assembly, taking care not to allow the friction plate to drop out.

4   Clutch – inspection

1   Examine the friction plate for wear on the friction material, for broken hub springs, distortion of the rim and wear on the splines. Unless the clutch plate is in very good condition it is a false economy not to fit a new one.

2   The friction plate should be renewed as an assembly. It is advised that this course is preferable to trying to fit a new friction lining.

3   Check the machined faces of the flywheel and pressure plate. If the flywheel is scored, it should be removed and machined. If the pressure plate is scored, a new assembly should be fitted.

4   Examine the clutch assembly for any signs of oil leakage into the clutch and if signs of leaks are found, rectify the leaks before fitting the clutch.

5   Examine the diaphragm spring for wear and damage. If the diaphragm spring is unserviceable, a new pressure plate assembly must be fitted.

6   Check the release bearing for smoothness of operation. It should be reasonably free, bearing in mind that it is pre-packed with grease and there should not be any roughness, or slackness, in it.

7   Check the condition of the clutch pilot bearing in the end of the crankshaft. Further information on this is given in Chapter 1.

5   Clutch – refitting

1   It is important that no oil or grease gets onto the friction material of the driven plate, or on to the faces of the flywheel and pressure plate. It is advisable to have clean hands when refitting the clutch and to wipe the flywheel and pressure plate surfaces with clean rag before reassembly is started.

2   The friction plate is marked Flywheel side and it is important that this face, which can also be identified by its having the longer central boss, is placed against the flywheel.

3   Align the mating marks on the clutch assembly and the flywheel, which were made before removing the clutch, and locate the pressure plate assembly, with the friction plate resting inside it, onto the locating dowels. Insert the clutch retaining bolts, finger tight.

4   Apply a light coat of molybdenum-based grease (Ford chassis lube) to the splines of the friction plate and centralise the friction plate in the clutch assembly (Fig. 5.4). If a clutch centraliser, or a spare first motion shaft is not available, use a piece of wooden dowel which fits inside the bearing in the end of the crankshaft. On that portion of the dowel upon which the clutch friction plate rests, wind masking tape, or insulating tape, until the bore of the clutch plate is a snug fit on the tape.

5   Tighten the clutch attachment bolts progressively, in a diagonal sequence, until all the bolts are at the torque wrench setting given in the Specifications.

6   Refit the gearbox and bellhousing.

6   Clutch release bearing – removal and refitting

1   With the gearbox and bellhousing removed from the engine access to the clutch release arm and bearing is possible.

2   To remove the release bearing, first remove the rubber gaiter from the release arm.

3   Withdraw the release lever and bearing assembly from the clutch housing (photo).

4   Unhook the bearing from the release arm and with the aid of a vice and two blocks of wood, press the release bearing off its hub.

5   When refitting the clutch release mechanism, apply a daub of molybdenum-based grease (Ford chassis lube) to the hub bore and release lever fingers' ends, then engage the lever in the slots in the hub and release bearing assembly.

6   Pass the release lever through the aperture in the clutch housing. Lubricate the front bearing retainer and slide on the release bearing.

7   Refit the clutch arm boot and refit the transmission and bellhousing.

7   Clutch cable – renewal

1   Jack up the front of the car and support the front crossmember securely.

2   Release the locknut on the outer cable at the bellhousing and back off both the locknut and the adjuster nut or only the adjuster nut depending on model.

3   Remove the rubber gaiter from the bellhousing and unhook the end of the cable (Fig. 5.5).

4   Where applicable, remove the cowl trim from the instrument panel (6 self-tapping screws).

5   Disconnect the clutch cable from the pedal by pushing the pin out of the cable eye and then remove the cable.

6   When fitting a new cable pass the top end of the cable through the dash panel, so that it is near the clutch pedal.

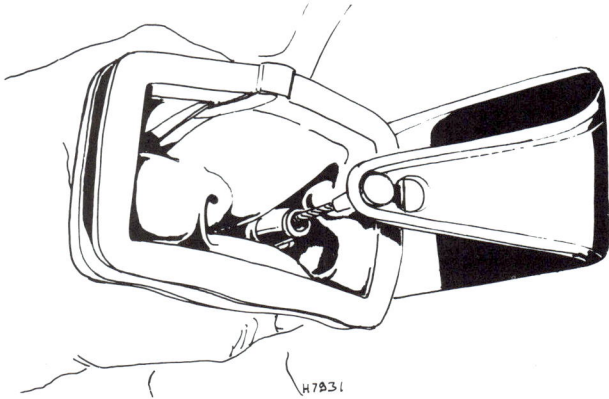

Fig. 5.5 Clutch release arm gaiter and cable attachment

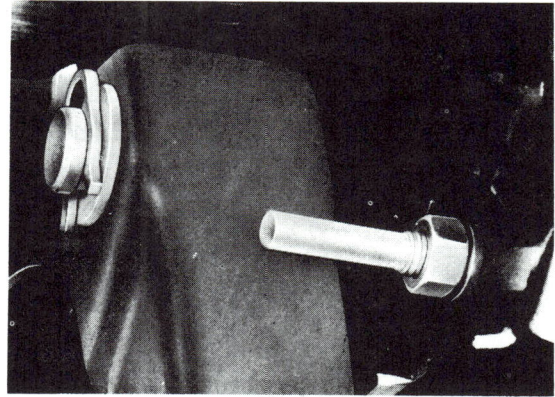

Fig. 5.6 Clutch pedal stop and pivot

7   Assemble the cable to the pedal, lubricate the pivot pin and fit it.
8   Daub the ball end of the cable with lubricant and then fit the ball into the clutch release lever. Fit the rubber boot in the aperture of the bellhousing.
9   Adjust the clutch as described in Section 2.

8   Clutch pedal – removal and refitting

1   Where applicable, remove the cowl trim from the instrument panel (6 self-tapping screws).
2   Remove the left-hand spring clip and its washer from the pedal pivot shaft (Fig. 5.6).
3   Unhook the clutch pedal return spring.
4   Push the pedal shaft to the right until it is clear of the pedal and remove the pedal.
5   Push the pin out of the eye in the end of the clutch cable to disconnect the cable.
6   Remove the clutch pedal pivot bush.
7   Refit the pedal by reversing the operations necessary for removal. Fit a new spring clip to the pivot and lubricate the pivot before refitting it. If the pivot bush is worn, fit a new one.
8   Refit the pedal and adjust the clutch as described in Section 2.

9   Fault diagnosis – clutch

There are four main faults to which the clutch and release mechanism is prone. They may occur by themselves, or in conjunction with any of the other faults. They are clutch squeal, slip, spin and judder.

Clutch squeal – diagnosis and remedy
1   If, on taking up the drive or when changing gear, the clutch squeals, this is indicative of a badly worn clutch release bearing.
2   As well as regular wear due to normal use, wear of the clutch release bearing is much accentuated if the clutch is ridden or held down for long periods in gear, with the engine running. To minimise wear of this component the car should always be taken out of gear at traffic lights and for similar hold-ups.
3   The clutch release bearing is not an expensive item, but it is difficult to get at.

Clutch slip – diagnosis and remedy
4   Clutch slip is a self-evident condition which occurs when the clutch driven plate is badly worn, oil or grease have got onto the flywheel or pressure plate faces, or the pressure plate itself is faulty.
5   The reason for clutch slip is that due to one of the faults above,

there is either insufficient pressure from the pressure plate, or insufficient friction from the driven plate, to ensure solid drive.
6   If small amounts of oil get onto the clutch, they will be burnt off under the heat of the clutch engagement, and in the process, gradually darken the linings. Excessive oil on the clutch will burn off leaving a carbon deposit which can cause quite bad slip, or fierceness, spin and judder.
7   If clutch slip is suspected, and confirmation of this condition is required, there are several tests which can be made.
8   With the engine in second or third gear and pulling lightly, sudden depression of the accelerator pedal may cause the engine to increase its speed without any increase in road speed. Easing off on the accelerator will then give a definite drop in engine speed without the car slowing.
9   In extreme cases of clutch slip the engine will race under normal acceleration conditions.
10   If slip is due to oil or grease on the linings a temporary cure can sometimes be effected by squirting carbon tetrachloride into the clutch. The permanent cure is, of course, to renew the clutch driven plate and trace and rectify the oil leak.

Clutch spin – diagnosis and remedy
11   Clutch spin is a condition which occurs when there is an obstruction in the clutch, either in the gearbox input shaft or in the operating lever itself, or oil may have partially burnt off the clutch lining and have left a resinous deposit which is causing the clutch disc to stick to the pressure plate or flywheel.
12   The reason for clutch spin is that due to any, or a combination of, the faults just listed, the clutch pressure plate is not completely freeing from the driven plate even with the clutch pedal fully depressed.
13   If clutch spin is suspected, the condition can be confirmed by extreme difficulty in engaging first gear from rest, difficulty in changing gear, and sudden take up of the clutch drive at the fully depressed end of the clutch pedal travel as the clutch is released.
14   Check the clutch cable adjustment (Section 2).
15   If these points are checked and found to be in order then the fault lies internally in the clutch, and it will be necessary to remove the clutch for examination.

Clutch judder – diagnosis and cure
16   Clutch judder is a self-evident condition which occurs when the gearbox or engine mountings are loose or too flexible, when there is oil on the face of the clutch friction plate, or when the clutch pressure plate has been incorrectly adjusted.
17   The reason for clutch judder is that due to one of the faults just listed, the clutch pressure plate is not freeing smoothly from the driven plate and is snatching.
18   Clutch judder normally occurs when the clutch pedal is released in first or reverse gears, and the whole car shudders as it moves backward or forward.

Chapter 6 Manual gearbox and automatic transmission

For modifications, and information applicable to later models, see Supplement at end of manual

Contents

Specifications

Manual gearbox

Number of gears .... 4 forward, 1 reverse

Type of gears .... Helical, constant mesh

Synchromesh .... All forward gears

Gearbox type designation .... Type E or type H

Gearbox application
Type E .... Capri II
Type H .... Mercury Capri II

Gear ratios

	Type E	Type H
First	3·16 : 1	3·65 : 1
Second	1·94 : 1	1·97 : 1
Third	1·41 : 1	1·37 : 1
Fourth	1 : 1	1 : 1
Reverse	3·346 : 1	3·66 : 1

Lubricant type .... SQM2C 9008 A (SAE 80 EP)

Lubricant capacity
Type E .... 3·5 Imp pints (2 litres, 3·9 US pints)
Type H .... 2·6 Imp pints (1·5 litres, 2·9 US pints)

Countershaft cluster gear
Endfloat .... 0·006 to 0·018 in (0·15 to 0·45 mm)
Thickness of thrust washer .... 0·061 to 0·063 in (1·55 to 1·60 mm)

Automatic transmission

Manufacturer .... Ford

Type .... Borceaux C3

Gear ratios:
First .... 2.47 : 1
Second .... 1.47 : 1
Third .... 1 : 1
Reverse .... 2.11 : 1

Transmission fluid specification

Early models (with black dipstick)	SQM-2C9007-AA
Later models (with red dipstick/filler tube)	SQM-2C9010-A

Fluid capacity of transmission, converter and oil cooler

13.2 Imp pints (7.5 litres, 15.0 US pints)

Converter ratio

2.22 : 1

Torque wrench settings (manual transmission)
Type E

	lbf ft	kgf m
Clutch housing to transmission	29 to 35	3.9 to 4.8
Clutch housing to engine	22 to 27	3.0 to 3.7
Transmission mainshaft nut	26 to 30	3.5 to 4.1
Drive gear bearing retainer to transmission case	12 to 15	1.67 to 2.06
Extension housing to transmission case	40 to 45	5.39 to 6.08
Selector shaft bracket	5 to 7	0.69 to 0.96
Selector housing cover to extension housing	12 to 15	1.57 to 2.06
Cover to extension housing	7 to 8	0.9 to 1.1
Cover to transmission case	12 to 15	1.67 to 2.06

Type H

	lbf ft	kgf m
Clutch housing to transmission	43 to 51	5.8 to 6.9
Clutch housing to engine	29 to 35	3.9 to 4.8
Drive gear bearing retainer to transmission case	15 to 18	2.1 to 2.5
Extension housing to transmission case	33 to 36	4.5 to 4.9
Selector housing cover to transmission case	15 to 18	2.1 to 2.5

Torque wrench settings (automatic transmission)

	lbf ft	kgf m
Torque converter housing to transmission	27 to 39	3.6 to 5.3
Disc to converter	27 to 30	3.6 to 4.1
Oil sump bolts	12 to 17	1.6 to 2.4
Downshift cable bracket	12 to 17	1.6 to 2.4
Downshift lever nut:		
Outer	7 to 11	1.0 to 1.5
Inner	30 to 40	4.1 to 5.4
Inhibitor switch	12 to 15	1.6 to 2.0
Brake band adjusting screw locknut	35 to 45	4.7 to 6.1
Fluid line to connector	7 to 10	0.9 to 1.4
Connector to transmission housing	10 to 15	1.4 to 2.0
Torque converter housing to engine	22 to 27	3.0 to 3.7
Torque converter drain plug	20 to 29	2.7 to 4.0
Oil cooler line to connector	12 to 15	1.6 to 2.0

---

1 Manual gearbox – general description

The manual gearboxes used on the models covered by this manual are equipped with four forward and one reverse gear.

All forward gears are engaged through blocker ring synchromesh units, to obtain smooth, silent, gearchanges. All forward gears on the mainshaft are in constant mesh with their corresponding gears on the countershaft gear cluster and are helically cut, to achieve quiet running.

The countershaft reverse gear has straight-cut spur teeth and drives the 1st/2nd gear synchronizer hub on the mainshaft through an interposed sliding idler gear.

Gears are engaged either by a single selector rail and forks, or by levers in the gearbox side cover and forks. Control of the gears is from a floor-mounted shift lever which connects either with the single shift rail, or the three selector levers and link rods.

Where close limits are required during assembly of the gearbox, selective shims are used to eliminate excessive endfloat, or backlash, without the need of using matched assemblies.

---

2 Gearbox (type E) – removal and refitting

1 If the gearbox is to be removed from the car without removing the engine, the gearbox is removed from beneath the car and a large ground clearance is required. If an inspection pit or ramps are not available, jack the car as high as possible, support itn securely on blocks or stands and chock the wheels.

2 Disconnect the battery.

3 Unscrew the gear lever knob and remove the cover and rubber gaiter. If a package tray or centre console is fitted, these must be removed (refer to Chapter 12 if necessary).

4 Bend back the lock tab on the gear lever retainer and either use a suitably cranked spanner (Fig. 6.2) to unscrew the retainer, or tap it undone with a hammer and drift. Lift out the gear lever.

5 Place a drip tray beneath the gearbox, remove the drain plug and when the oil has drained, refit the plug and tighten it.

6 Put mating marks on the two faces of the rear axle joint flange. Remove the four bolts from the rear axle pinion flange and the two bolts from the driveshaft centre bearing support and withdraw the driveshaft assembly from the extension housing. Tie a polythene bag round the end of the gearbox extension to keep out dirt and to catch any oil which has not drained.

7 Pull back the rubber boot over the clutch release lever and slacken the adjuster, so that the end of the clutch cable can be unhooked from the clutch release lever (Fig. 6.3).

8 Remove the screw and lock plate securing the speedometer drive and disconnect the drive.

9 Remove the cover from the reversing light switch. Note which way the leads are fitted and then remove them (Fig. 6.4).

10 Detach the exhaust pipe from the exhaust manifold and tie the pipe out of the way, so that the engine and transmission can be lowered.

11 Support the gearbox on a jack, or with blocks and remove the bolt securing the transmission to the rear engine mounting and the four bolts securing the gearbox crossmember to the floor (Fig. 6.5). Remove the crossmember.

12 Lower the transmission a little and insert a block of wood between

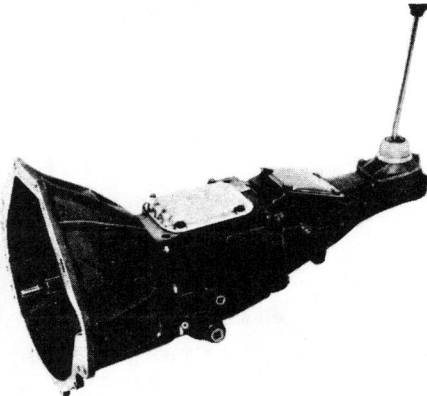

Fig. 6.1 Type E transmission

Fig. 6.2 Using a cranked spanner to remove the gear lever retainer

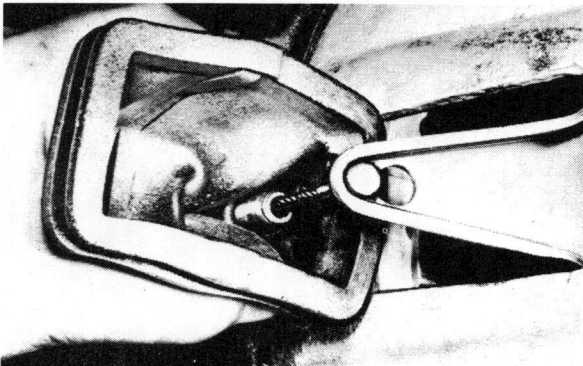

Fig. 6.3 Clutch release lever and cable

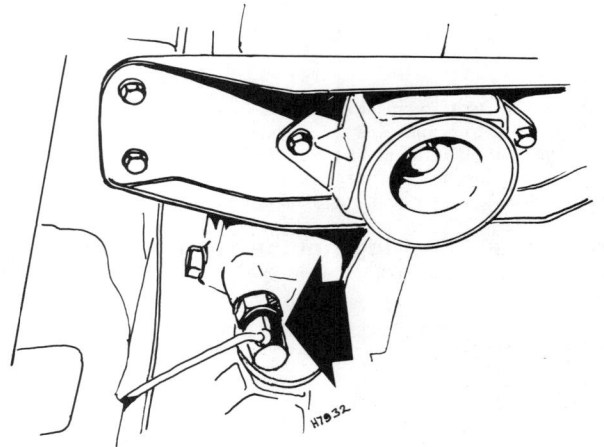

Fig. 6.4 Reversing light switch

Fig. 6.5 Gearbox crossmember fixings

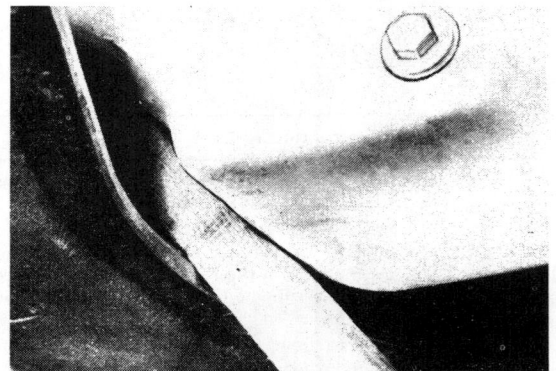

Fig. 6.6 Wooden block between sump and engine mounting

the sump and the front engine mounting so that the engine does not drop too far when the transmission is removed (Fig. 6.6).

13 Remove the six bolts securing the clutch housing to the engine. Pull the transmission assembly to the rear to disengage the gearbox driveshaft from the clutch pilot bearing and clutch friction plate. It is important that the engine and transmission are kept in line while this is being done, otherwise the gearbox shaft may be strained and damaged.

14 When the gearbox shaft is clear of the clutch, remove the transmission assembly from beneath the car.

15 When refitting, ensure that the two clutch housing guide bushes are fitted to the engine (Fig. 6.7) and that the clutch pilot bearing in the end of the crankshaft is in place and is serviceable. Tie the clutch lever to the clutch housing, to prevent the release lever from slipping out

while the transmission assembly is being fitted.

16 Smear some molybdenum-based grease (Ford chassis lube) onto the end and splines of the gearbox input shaft and refit the gearbox by reversing the removal procedure.

17 It is important when offering up the gearbox, that it is exactly in line with the crankshaft, otherwise the gearbox input shaft will not enter the clutch driven plate and the crankshaft. If there is difficulty in mating the splines of the gearbox shaft and the clutch plate, select a gear to restrain the movement of the gearbox shaft and turn the gearbox slightly until the splines enter. Do not attempt to force the transmission onto the engine. This may damage the splines and make fitting impossible.

18 After refitting has been completed, check the oil level in the transmission and top up as necessary with SAE 80 EP gear oil.

Fig. 6.7 Clutch housing guide bush (arrowed)

3 Gearbox (type H) – removal and refitting

1 If the gearbox is to be removed from the car without removing the engine, the gearbox is removed from beneath the car and a large clearance is required. If an inspection pit or ramps are not available, jack the car as high as possible, support it securely on blocks or stands and chock the wheels.

2 Disconnect the battery.

3 Place a drip tray beneath the gearbox, remove the drain plug (for which a square-section wrench is required) and when the oil has drained, refit the plug and tighten it.

4 Remove the starter motor (refer to Chapter 10, if necessary).

5 Put mating marks on the two faces of the rear axle joint flange.

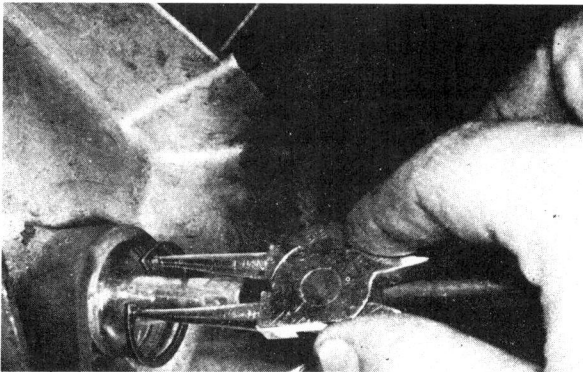

Fig. 6.8 Removing the speedometer drive circlip

Fig. 6.9 Oil level plug (H transmission)

Remove the four bolts from the rear axle pinion flange and the two bolts from the driveshaft bearing support and withdraw the driveshaft assembly from the extension housing. Tie a polythene bag round the end of the gearbox extension, to keep out dirt and to catch any oil which has not drained.

6 Pull back the rubber boot over the clutch release lever and slacken the adjuster, so that the end of the clutch cable can be unhooked from the clutch release lever.

7 Unhook the three selector shafts from the transmission.

8 Using suitable pliers, remove the circlip from the speedometer cable connection to the transmission (Fig. 6.8) and withdraw the cable.

9 Remove the cover from the reversing light switch. Note which way the leads are fitted and then remove them.

10 Support the gearbox on a jack, or on blocks and remove the bolt securing the transmission to the rear engine mounting and the four bolts securing the gearbox crossmember to the floor. Remove the crossmember.

11 Lower the transmission a little and insert a block of wood between the sump and the front engine mounting so that the engine does not drop too far when the transmission is removed.

12 Remove the bolt securing the adaptor plate and the six bolts from the transmission flange. Pull the engine free of the guide bushes on the engine, then turn the transmission through 90° and remove it rearwards to disengage the gearbox driveshaft from the clutch pilot bearing and clutch friction plate. It is important that the engine and transmission are kept in line while this is being done, otherwise the gearbox shaft may be strained and damaged.

13 When the gearbox shaft is clear of the clutch, remove the transmission assembly from beneath the car.

14 When refitting, ensure that the two clutch housing guide bushes are fitted to the engine, so that the adapter plate cannot slip while the transmission is being fitted. Check that the clutch pilot bearing is in the end of the crankshaft and that its condition is satisfactory. Tie the clutch lever to the clutch housing to prevent the release arm from slipping out while the transmission assembly is being fitted.

15 Smear some molybdenum-based grease (Ford chassis lube) on to the end and splines of the gearbox input shaft and refit the gearbox by reversing the removal procedure.

16 Fit the transmission with it turned at 90° to its fitted position, then turn it to its correct position to insert it fully.

17 It is important that, when offering up the gearbox, it is exactly in line with the crankshaft, otherwise the gearbox input shaft will not enter the clutch driven plate and the crankshaft. If there is difficulty in mating the splines of the gearbox shaft and the clutch plate, select a gear to restrain the motion of the gearbox shaft and turn the gearbox slightly until the splines enter. Do not attempt to force the transmission onto the engine. This may damage the splines and make fitting impossible.

18 After refitting has been completed, fill the gearbox to the correct level with SAE 80 EP gear oil (Fig. 6.9).

4 Gearbox (type E) – dismantling

1 Remove the four bolts from the top cover of the transmission extension housing and from the transmission case. Remove the covers, taking care not to lose the three springs under the transmission case cover.

2 Use a magnet to remove the three selector detent balls.

3 Remove the bolt from the selector finger and withdraw the finger from the selector shaft.

4 Remove the two bolts from the selector shaft bearing support and remove it (Fig. 6.11).

5 Remove the three bolts from the selector housing cover. Remove the cover with the shaft, then rotate the selector shaft slightly and withdraw it from the selector housing cover.

6 Drive out the roll pin at the side of the extension housing and remove the reverse gear relay lever.

7 Using a pin punch and a hammer, drive out the three roll pins from the 1st/2nd, 3rd/top and reverse gears sufficiently to release the selector forks (Fig. 6.12). Remove 3rd/top gear selector rail circlip and then withdraw the selector rails towards the extension housing. Note the plunger in the 3rd/top selector rail.

8 Remove the three selector forks.

9 Remove the plug from the side of the case and use a magnet to

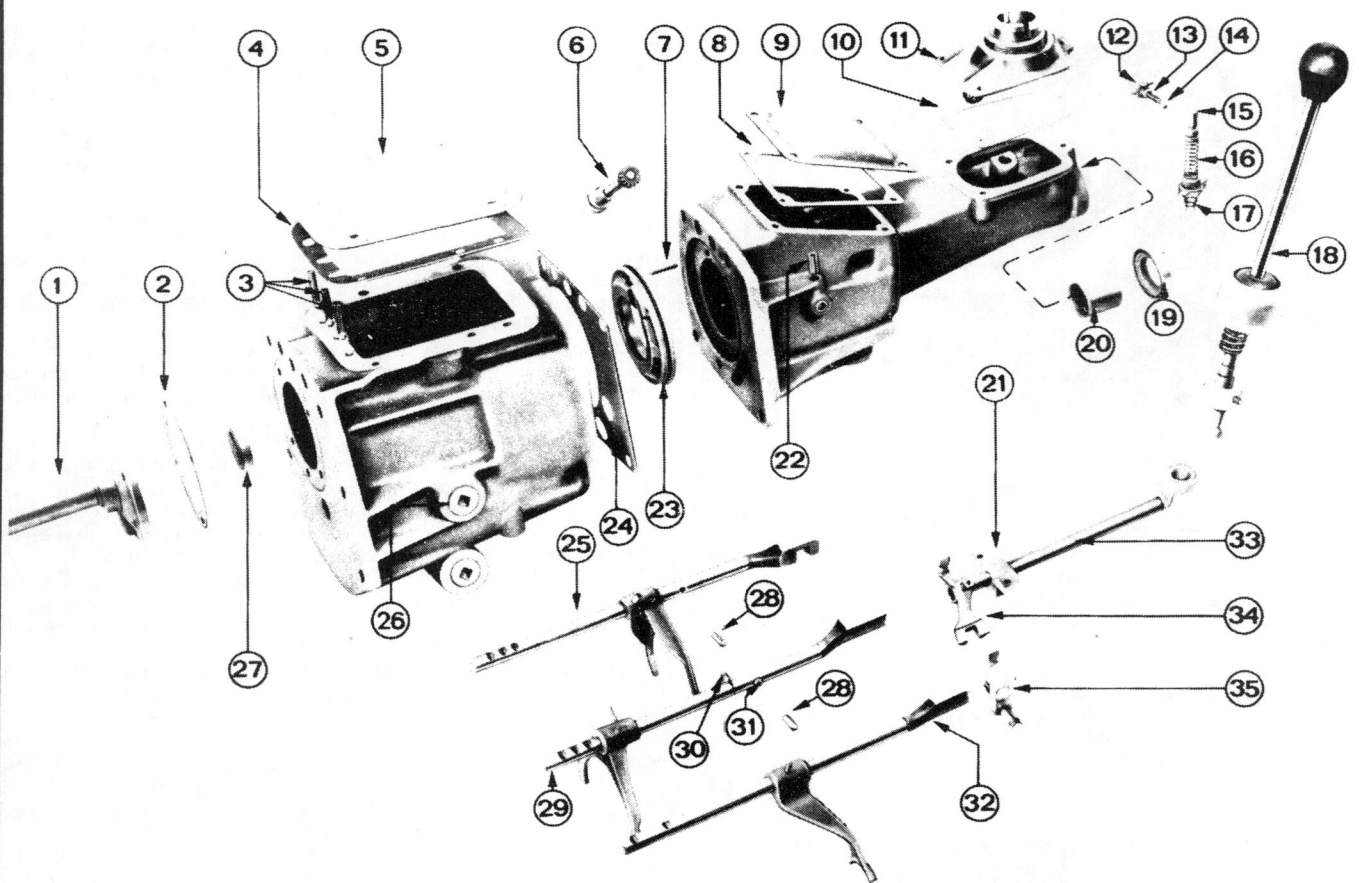

Fig. 6.10 Gear case components (E transmission)

1   Main drive gear bearing retainer
2   Gasket
3   Detent balls with springs
4   Transmission case gasket
5   Transmission case cover
6   Speedometer pinion
7   Dowel
8   Extension housing cover gasket
9   Extension housing top cover
10 Selector housing gasket
11 Selector housing cover
12 Banjo bolt with lock plate
13 Spring

14 Detent ball
15 Plunger
16 Spring
17 Reversing light switch
18 Gear lever assembly
19 Oil seal
20 Extension housing bush
21 Selector shaft bearing support
22 Reverse relay arm roll pin
23 Bearing support
24 Extension housing gasket
25 Selector rail with 1st/2nd gear selector fork

26 Filler plug
27 Drive gear bearing retainer oil seal
28 Plunger
29 Selector rail with 3rd/top gear selector fork
30 Circlip
31 Plunger
32 Selector rail with reverse gear selector fork
33 Selector shaft
34 Selector finger
35 Reverse gear relay lever

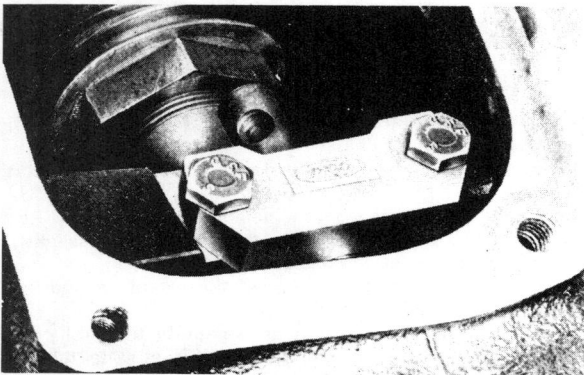

Fig. 6.11 Selector shaft bearing support

Fig. 6.12 Removing the selector fork roll pins

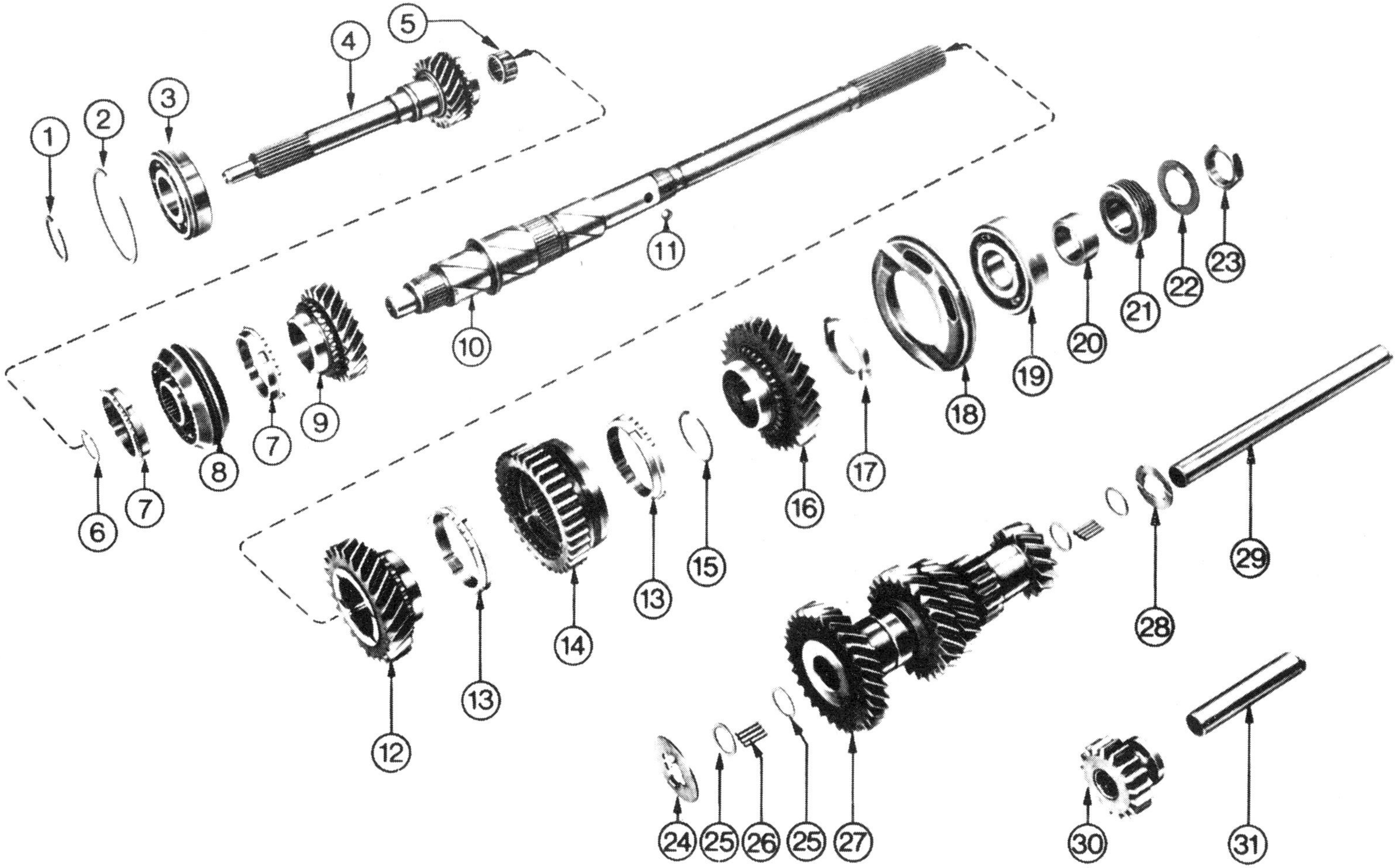

Fig. 6.13 Gear train components (E transmission)

1 Circlip
2 Circlip
3 Grooved ball bearing
4 Input shaft
5 Needle roller bearing
6 Circlip

7 3rd/top gear synchroniser
  blocker ring
8 3rd/top gear synchroniser hub
9 3rd gear
10 Transmission mainshaft
11 Speedometer drive ball

12 2nd gear
13 1st/2nd gear synchroniser
  blocker ring
14 1st/2nd gear synchroniser hub
15 Circlip
16 1st gear
17 Oil scoop ring

18 Intermediate bearing support
19 Ball bearing
20 Spacer
21 Speedometer worm gear
22 Lock plate
23 Mainshaft nut
24 Thrust washer

25 Shim
26 Needle rollers (22)
27 Countershaft cluster gear
28 Thrust washer
29 Countershaft
30 Reverse idler gear
31 Idler shaft

extract the plunger beneath it.

10 Bend back the tabs of the washers of the two bolts on the extension housing. Remove the banjo bolt, spring and ball and the reversing light switch, spring and plunger.

11 Use two screwdrivers and carefully push the speedometer out of the extension housing.

12 If there has been no sign of leaking from the extension housing oil seal, take care not to damage it. If the seal is defective, lever it out, taking care not to damage its seating.

13 Remove the four attachment bolts and detach the extension housing from the transmission case.

14 Using a long thin drift, tap out the countershaft from the front to the rear. Allow the laygear cluster to drop into the bottom of the box, out of mesh with the mainshaft gears.

15 Withdraw the mainshaft and extension assembly from the gearbox casing, pushing the 3rd/top synchronizer hub forward slightly to obtain the necessary clearance. A small roller bearing should be on the nose of the mainshaft, but if it is not there it will be found in its recess in the input shaft and should be removed.

16 Remove the four bolts securing the drive gear bearing retainer to the front of the gearbox (Fig. 6.15) and slide the retainer off the input shaft.

17 Remove the circlip from the outside of the front bearing and tap the outer race of the bearing to drive the input shaft and bearing assembly into the gearbox, then lift them out of the box.

18 Remove the countershaft gear cluster, the two thrust washers and any loose needle rollers.

19 Remove the reverse idler shaft by screwing a suitable bolt into the end of the shaft and then levering the shaft out using two open-ended spanners.

---

5 Mainshaft (type E) – dismantling and reassembly

1 Remove 3rd/top gear synchronizer hub circlip. Ease the hub and third gear forward by levering them gently with a pair of snipe-nosed pliers.

2 Remove the hub, the synchronizer ring and 3rd gear from the front of the mainshaft.

3 Mount the plain part of the mainshaft in a soft jawed vice, unlock the mainshaft nut and remove it.

4 Remove the lock plate, speedometer drive gear, its drive ball (Fig. 6.16) and then lever off the rear bearing, complete with bearing retainer. Separate the bearing and its retainer.

5 Remove the oil scoop ring and first gear.

6 Remove 1st/2nd gear synchronizer circlip and pull off the hub with the blocker rings and second gear.

7 Check that there is a mark to align the selector sleeve in relation to the hub. If no mark can be seen, make one with a dab of paint and then dismantle the synchronizer hubs.

8 Before starting reassembly, clean all parts thoroughly and check their condition. Smear all parts with transmission oil before fitting.

9 Reassemble the synchronizer sleeve and hub so that the marks on them align. Insert the blocker bars and fit the blocker bar springs so that their open ends are staggered relative to each other.

10 Place the synchronizer blocker ring onto the cone of second gear and slide it onto the mainshaft together with 1st/2nd gear synchronizer hub. The gear on the hub should face forward (Fig. 6.17).

11 Fit the synchronizer blocker ring and the circlip which holds the synchronizer hub in place.

12 Slide on first gear, so that the synchronizing cone portion lies inside the synchronizing ring which has just been fitted.

13 Fit the oil scoop, with the oil groove facing rearwards (Fig. 6.18).

14 Apply multi-purpose grease to the ball bearing seat of the bearing retainer. Refit the retainer with the bearing inserted and then slide on the spacer.

15 Insert the drive ball of the speedometer gear into the shaft and slide the speedometer worm gear over it.

16 Fit the lock plate so that the two tabs fit into the speedometer worm gear recess. Screw on the nut and tighten it to the torque

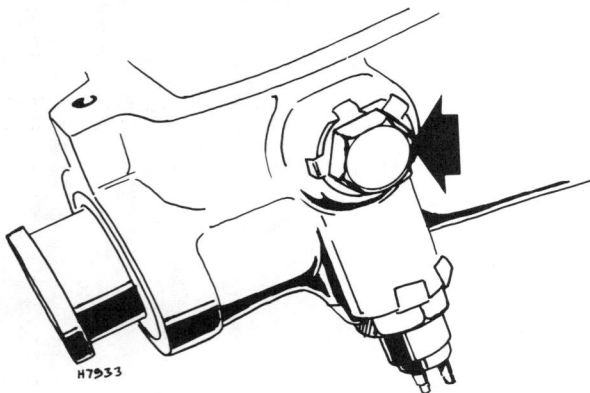
Fig. 6.14 Reverse gear interlock

Fig. 6.15 Front drive gear bearing retainer

Fig. 6.16 Speedometer gear and ball

Fig. 6.17 Reverse gearing facing forwards

Fig. 6.18 Oil scoop ring with oil groove facing rear

Fig. 6.19 Synchroniser hub with wide boss facing rear

Fig. 6.20 Laygear, shaft and bearings

wrench setting given in the Specifications, then lock the nut by bending the tab washer.

17 Fit the synchronizer blocker ring to the cone of third gear and fit them to the front of the mainshaft. Fit the 3rd/top gear synchronizer hub, with its wide boss towards the rear (Fig. 6.19) and then retain it in place by fitting the circlip.

6 Input shaft (type E) – dismantling and reassembly

1   It is not necessary to dismantle the input shaft unless a new bearing or a new shaft is being fitted.
2   With a pair of circlip pliers, expand and remove the small circlip which secures the bearing to the input shaft.

3   With a soft headed hammer, gently tap the bearing forward until it can be pulled from the shaft.
4   When fitting the bearing, ensure that the groove in the periphery of the outer bearing track is away from the gear, otherwise it will not be possible to fit the large circlip which retains the bearing in place in the housing.
5   Either stand the input shaft upright on a bench and tap the bearing into place using a piece of tube of suitable diameter, or use the jaws of a vice to support the bearing and tap the rear of the input shaft with a soft faced hammer.
6   When the bearing is fully home, fit the circlip which retains the bearing on the shaft.

7 Laygear (type E) – dismantling and reassembly

1   Remove a shim from each end of the laygear, remove 22 needle rollers from each end of the gear (Fig. 6.20).
2   When reassembling, insert a shim into the bottom of the bore. Daub the bore with general purpose grease and insert the 22 needle rollers. When all the rollers are in place, smear grease over them to retain them and then secure the shim over the ends of the rollers with grease.

8 Gearbox (type E) – examination and renovation

1   Carefully clean and then examine all the component parts for signs of excessive wear, damage, distortion or damage to machined faces and threads.
2   Examine the gears for excessive wear and broken or chipped teeth. It is not satisfactory to fit a new gear unless its mating gear is also renewed and if the condition of gears is bad, an exchange gearbox should be fitted.
3   Examine the layshaft for wear on the ends which are in contact with the needle rollers and if there is a wear step, a new layshaft should be fitted.
4   The four synchronizer rings are certain to be worn and it is a false economy not to renew them. New rings will improve the smoothness of gear changing considerably.
5   The needle roller bearing between the nose of the mainshaft and the bore of the input shaft should be discarded and a new one fitted.
6   Check the condition of the bearing on the input shaft and the one on the mainshaft. It is worth renewing these having dismantled the gearbox.
7   If there is excessive wear in the synchronizer units they must be renewed as an assembly, because parts are not sold individually. These units are expensive and as the selector forks are also likely to need renewing, an exchange gearbox may be a more satisfactory solution. If possible compare the synchronizer rings and selector forks with new ones, before deciding what to do.
8   If the bush bearing in the gearbox extension is badly worn, it is best to take the extension to a Ford garage to have the bearing pulled out and a new one fitted. The gearbox needs to be assembled and the mainshaft refitted for this to be done.
9   The oil seals in the extension housing and the front bearing retainer should be renewed. Drive out the old seal with a screwdriver and tap in a new seal with a hammer and piece of wood. Make sure that the seal has entered its bore squarely before attempting to tap it in.

9 Gearbox (type E) – reassembly

1   When any bolt screws into a through bore, jointing compound should be applied to the threads of the bolt before it is inserted.
2   Fit the reverse idler gear with the groove on the gear towards the rear. Insert the idler shaft and drive it in with a plastic headed hammer until the bottom of the step on the end of the shaft is flush with the end of the gearbox. The milled flats should be proud of the gearbox face and should be aligned with the countershaft bore (Fig. 6.21).
3   Fit the large thrust washer to the countershaft bore at the front of the gearbox and the small thrust washer to the countershaft bore at the rear of the box. The tabs on the washers should be towards the case and the washers should be greased to retain them in place.
4   Check that the needle rollers and end washers of the countershaft

Fig. 6.21 Position of reverse gear idler shaft when fitted

Fig. 6.22 Front bearing retainer oil return bore

Fig. 6.23 Fitted position of countershaft

Fig. 6.24 Alignment of bearing support and dowel

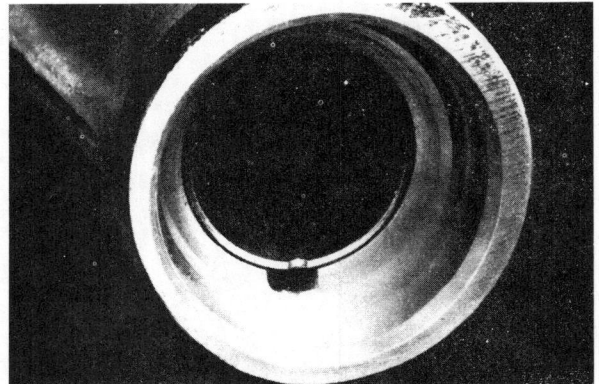

Fig. 6.25 Alignment of extension housing bush oil groove

gear are in place, then lower the gear cluster into the case carefully, making sure that the thrust washers are not displaced.

5   Push the input shaft, together with its ball bearing, into the front of the gearbox until the circlip round the bearing bears against the front of the gearbox case.

6   Fit the drive bearing retainer, using a new gasket, making sure that the oil return bore of the gasket and bearing retainer are aligned as in Fig. 6.22. Apply jointing compound to the threads of the bolts, insert them and tighten to the torque wrench setting given in the Specifications.

7   Oil the new input shaft needle roller bearing and push it into the bore of the input shaft. Slide the top gear synchronizer blocker ring on to the cone of the input shaft.

8   Fit the extension housing gasket, then insert the assembled mainshaft into the rear of the box and drive it in until the nose of the mainshaft is fully engaged in the bore of the front driveshaft bearing.

9   Carefully turn the gearbox upside down, so that the countershaft gear cluster drops into engagement with the mainshaft. Check that the gear and the two thrust washers are in line and then carefully push in the countershaft from the rear. If necessary tap the shaft in with a plastic headed hammer, but take great care not to dislodge the thrust washers or needle rollers. When fully home, the bottom of the step on the idler shaft should be in line with the face of the box and the milled flats should be in line with the idler shaft bore (Fig. 6.23).

10   Turn the gearbox the right way up and align the hole in the ball bearing support with the dowel on the extension housing (Fig. 6.24). Fit the extension housing. Apply jointing compound to the threads of the bolts, insert them and tighten to the torque wrench setting given in the Specifications.

11   If a new extension housing bush has been fitted, check that the notch or oil groove in it aligns with the oil return groove in the extension housing (Fig. 6.25). If the new extension housing oil seal has not already been fitted, slide it over the extension shaft and carefully tap it in with a hammer and a block of wood.

12   Fit a new O-ring to the speedometer pinion assembly (Fig. 6.26),

refit the assembly (Fig. 6.27) and fit the circlip to secure it.

13   Insert the reverse gear interlock plunger, ball and spring. Fit the bolt with a lock plate and insert the bolt. Tighten the bolt and bend the lock plates to secure it (Fig. 6.28).

14   Insert all three selector forks into their positions in the gearbox.

15   Slide 1st/2nd gear selector rail through the right-hand bore in the case, then thread it through the 1st/2nd gear selector fork (Fig. 6.29). Align the holes in the fork and rail and tap in the roll pin. Insert the plunger into the case.

16   Fit the plunger into the 3rd/top gear selector rail, insert the rail through the centre bore in the case and thread the rail through the 3rd/top gear selector fork (Fig. 6.30). Fit the circlip to the groove in the selector rail. Align the holes in the selector fork and rail, insert the roll pin and tap it home.

Fig. 6.26 Speedometer drive components

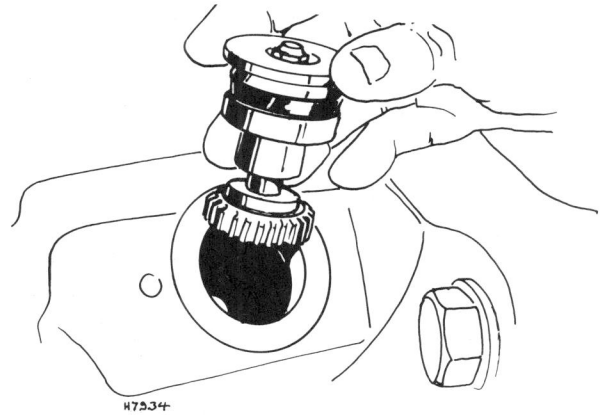

Fig. 6.27 Refitting the speedometer drive

Fig. 6.28 Reverse gear interlock

Fig. 6.29 1st/2nd gear selector fork and rail

Fig. 6.30 3rd/top gear selector fork and rail

Fig. 6.31 Reverse gear selector fork and rail

17 Push reverse gear selector rail through the left-hand bore in the housing, and then thread it through the reverse gear selector fork (Fig. 6.31). Align the holes in the fork and rail, insert a roll pin and tap it home.

18 Fit the interlock plunger, apply sealing compound to the plug and drive in the plug.

19 Insert reverse gear relay lever and secure it with a roll pin.

20 Insert the selector shaft through the selector housing cover and fit the cover using a new gasket. Insert the cover retaining bolts and screw them in finger-tight.

21 Fit the selector shaft bracket (Fig. 6.32).

22 Slide the selector finger onto the selector shaft (Fig. 6.33). Engage the screw in the recess in the shaft and tighten the screw.

23 Drop the three detent balls into their bores in the case, grease the

three springs and insert them into the recesses of the gearbox cover (Fig. 6.34). Fit a new cover gasket and position the cover onto it. Insert the cover bolts and tighten them to the torque wrench setting given in the Specifications.

24 Check the play between the selector finger and 3rd/top gear selector rail (Fig. 6.35). This dimension should be 0.35 in (0.9 mm). To make the check, move the selector lever up to the reverse gear stop. Using a lever, push 3rd/top gear selector rail to the rear and then measure the clearance by inserting feeler gauges between 3rd/top gear selector rail and selector finger. If the clearance is not as specified, it should be corrected by changing the reverse interlock gear plunger for one which will give the appropriate clearance.

25 Fit a new gasket to the extension housing cover. Position the cover, insert the fixing bolts (Fig. 6.36) and tighten them to the torque

Fig. 6.32 Selector shaft bearing bracket

Fig. 6.33 Selector finger (A) on selector shaft

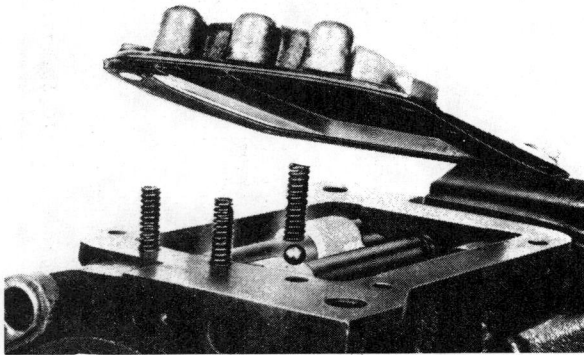

Fig. 6.34 Cover, detent springs and balls

Fig. 6.36 Extension housing cover in position

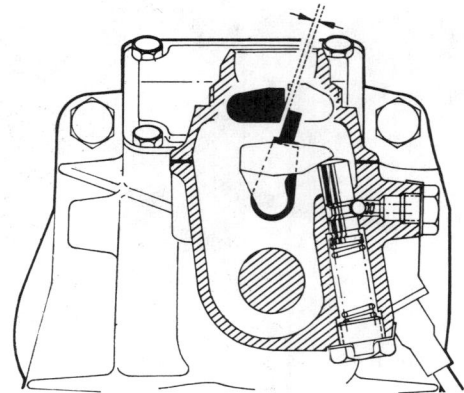

Fig. 6.35 Play between selector finger and 3rd/top selector rail

4   Turn the gearbox upside down over a tray and allow the oil to drain out.
5   Remove the four bolts from the extension housing, pull the extension housing to disengage its spigot and then turn the extension housing until the end of the countershaft is unobstructed (Fig. 6.42).
6   Using a drift or wooden dowel 7 in (177 mm) long and the same diameter as the countershaft, drive out the countershaft from the front of the gearbox, towards the rear.
7   Remove the three bolts from the main drive gear bearing retainer (Fig. 6.43) and pull the retainer off the driveshaft.
8   Push the countershaft gear cluster to one side and tap the input shaft assembly out of the front of the gearbox.
9   Withdraw the gearbox extension complete with the mainshaft assembly.
10   Lift out the countershaft gear cluster and the two thrust washers. Check that the spacer is in place in each end of the countershaft cluster and that none of the needle rollers have fallen out.
11   Insert a bolt into the end of the shaft of the reverse idler gear and lever the shaft out as in Section 4, paragraph 19.
12   Fit a spanner on the hexagon of the speedometer drive assembly and unscrew the assembly from the extension housing (Fig. 6.44).

wrench setting given in the Specifications.
26   Make sure that the gearbox drain plug is fitted and tightened, then fill the gearbox to the correct level by pouring in 3·5 pints (2 litres) of oil to specification SQM2C 9008A (SAE 80 EP).

10   Gearbox (type H) – dismantling

1   Remove the clutch release lever and bearing. Remove four bolts and detach the clutch housing from the gearbox (Fig. 6.39).
2   Remove seven bolts from the selector housing cover and remove the supports for the reverse gear return spring, the reversing light switch (Fig. 6.40) and then the housing cover (Fig. 6.41).
3   Take out the three selector forks and lay them out in order.

11   Mainshaft (type H) – dismantling and reassembly

1   Remove the mainshaft bearing circlip from its groove in the extension housing (Fig. 6.45) and drive out the mainshaft assembly with a plastic headed hammer.
2   Remove the circlip from the 3rd/top gear synchronizer hub (Fig. 6.46). Pull off the synchronizer assembly and third gear by hand, or use a sprocket puller.
3   Remove 2nd gear circlip (Fig. 6.47) and remove the thrust washer and then second gear.
4   Put spots of paint as mating marks on one face of the hub and sleeve of the 1st/2nd gear synchronizer assembly. Take off the sleeve

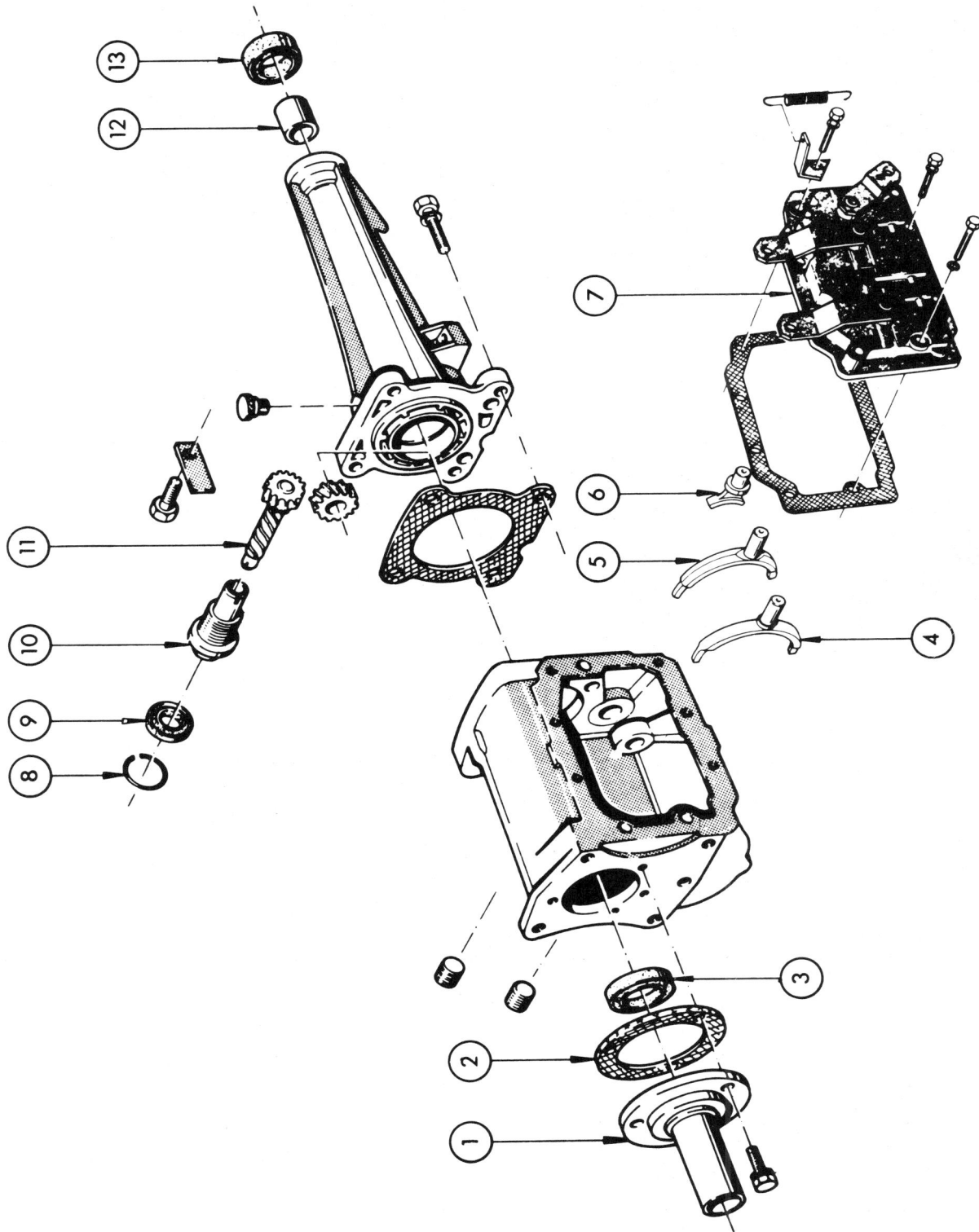

Fig. 6.37 Gearbox casing components (H transmission)

1 Main drive gear bearing retainer
2 Gasket
3 Oil seal
4 3rd/top gear selector fork
5 1st/2nd gear selector fork
6 Reverse gear selector fork
7 Selector housing cover
8 Circlip
9 Oil seal
10 Speedometer pinion bearing
11 Speedometer pinion
12 Extension housing bush
13 Extension housing oil seal

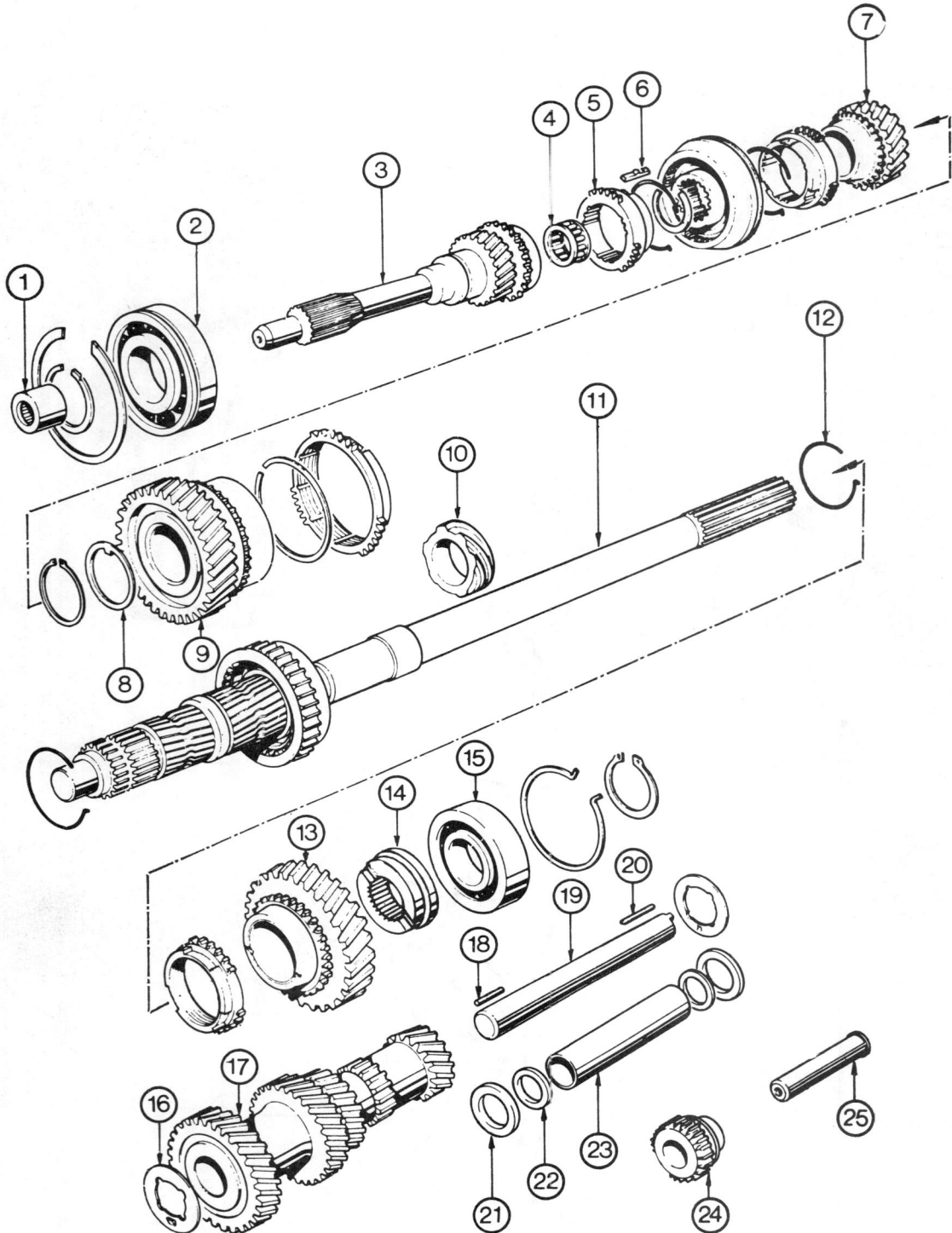

Fig. 6.38 Gear train components (H transmission)

1	Input shaft bearing	10	Speedometer worm gear	17	Countershaft cluster gear
2	Grooved ball bearing	11	Mainshaft complete with	18	Front needle rollers – 19 off
3	Input shaft		1st/2nd gear synchroniser hub	19	Countershaft
4	Needle roller bearing	12	1st/2nd gear synchroniser	20	Rear needle rollers – 19 off
5	Synchroniser blocker ring		spring	21	Thrust washer
6	Blocker bar	13	1st gear	22	Shim
7	3rd gear	14	Oil scoop ring	23	Spacer tube
8	Thrust washer	15	Grooved ball bearing	24	Reverse idler gear
9	2nd gear	16	Thrust washer	25	Idler shaft

Fig. 6.39 Clutch release lever and bearing

Fig. 6.40 Selector housing cover and fittings

Fig. 6.41 Selector housing cover removed

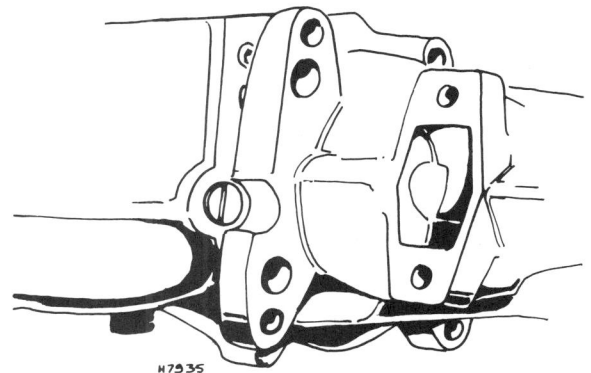

Fig. 6.42 Gearbox extension turned for removal of countershaft

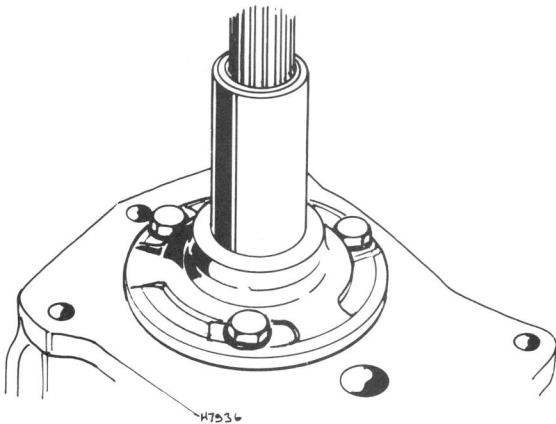

Fig. 6.43 Main drive gear bearing retainer

Fig. 6.44 Withdrawing the speedometer gear

and remove the three blocker bars and two springs. The synchronizer hub and mainshaft form a unit and should not be dismantled further (Fig. 6.48).

5   Carefully draw or tap off the speedometer drive gear from the rear of the mainshaft.

6   Remove the mainshaft rear bearing circlip by supporting first gear and pressing or driving the shaft from the bearing. By this means the bearing, oil scoop, first gear and the extension housing circlip are removed.

7   Put mating marks on one face of the 3rd/top gear synchronizer assembly and then withdraw the hub, blocker bars and springs.

8   Before starting to assemble the mainshaft, clean all parts thoroughly, check their condition and lubricate them with transmission oil.

9   Reassemble the 3rd/top gear synchronizer assembly by aligning the mating marks on the hub and sleeve and inserting the blocker bars. Starting from one blocker bar, fit the spring on one side, then fit the other spring, staggered in relation to it (Fig. 6.49).

10 Insert the 1st gear blocker bars and springs into the hub on the mainshaft.

11 Slide the first gear blocker ring, first gear and the oil scoop ring on to the rear end of the mainshaft. The larger diameter of the oil scoop ring should be towards the ball bearing (Fig. 6.50).

12 If a new bearing is being fitted, it is necessary to determine the thickness of the extension housing circlip as follows. Insert a circlip in the groove of the extension housing and pull it as far as possible towards the gearbox mating face. Accurately measure the distance from the bottom of the bearing recess in the extension housing to the

Fig. 6.45 Remove mainshaft bearing circlip

Fig. 6.46 Remove 3rd/top gear synchroniser circlip

Fig. 6.47 Remove 2nd gear circlip

Fig. 6.48 1st/2nd gear synchroniser hub and mainshaft

Fig. 6.49 Correct reassembly of 3rd/top gear synchroniser springs

Fig. 6.50 1st gear, blocker ring and oil scoop ring

top surface of the circlip. This dimension is the total thickness of bearing plus circlip required if there is to be no end play. Measure the width of the bearing which is being fitted and subtract this from the total dimension to find the thickness of circlip required.

13 Slide the selected circlip over the shaft, lubricate the bore and outside surface of the bearing, then drive the bearing onto the mainshaft.

14 Fit a circlip to the mainshaft, the circlip thickness being selected so that all endfloat between the bearing inner track and the circlip is eliminated.

15 Press on the speedometer drive gear to obtain a dimension A of 3·24 in (62·25 mm) as shown in Fig. 6.51.

16 On the forward end of the mainshaft, fit the second gear with its blocker ring and then the thrust washer and retaining circlip (Fig. 6.52).

17 Slide the third gear and its synchronizer blocker ring onto the mainshaft, followed by the third/top synchronizer assembly with its longer hub facing forward. Fit the circlip to retain the synchronizer hub.

18 Fit the needle roller bearing to the nose of the mainshaft.

12 Input shaft (type H) – dismantling and reassembly

The dismantling and reassembly is similar to that of the type E transmission described in Section 6.

Fig. 6.51 Correct setting of speedometer worm gear

Fig. 6.52 2nd gear blocker ring, gear, bearing and circlips fitted

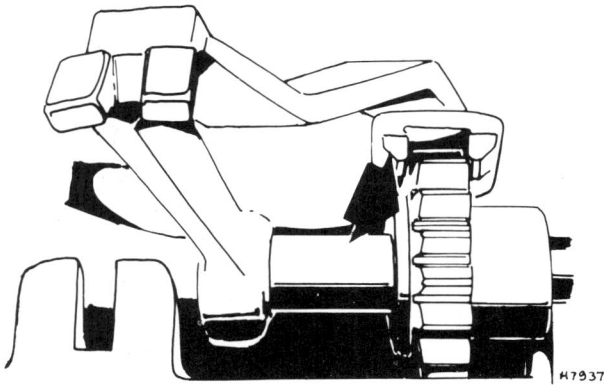

Fig. 6.53 Reverse idler gear with groove towards rear

Fig. 6.54 Fitting the input shaft

13 Laygear (type H) – dismantling and reassembly

The dismantling and reassembly is similar to that of the type E laygear, described in Section 7.

14 Gearbox (type H) – examination and renovation

The examination and renovation of the type H gearbox is the same as for type E, described in Section 8.

15 Gearbox (type H) – reassembly

1   When any bolt screws into a through bore, jointing compound should be applied to the threads of the bolt before it is inserted.
2   Fit the reverse idler gear with its groove towards the rear of the gearbox (Fig. 6.53). Grease the shaft, insert it into the end of the gearbox and the gear, then drive it in until the end of the shaft is recessed by 0·008 to 0·032 in (0·2 to 0·8 mm).
3   Fit the laygear thrust washers into their recesses in the ends of the gearbox and retain them in place with grease. If a dummy shaft is available insert it in the laygear, otherwise position the spacers and needle rollers securely with grease and position the laygear carefully between the thrust washers.
4   Use grease to stick a new gasket to the face of the extension housing, then fit the extension housing to the gearbox casing, but turn it slightly to expose the hole for the countershaft.
5   Fit the top gear synchronizer blocker ring onto the mainshaft then enter the mainshaft, taking care that the needle roller bearing on the nose of the mainshaft enters the recess in the input shaft.
6   Push in the input shaft until the circlip on the bearing is against the front face of the gearbox (Fig. 6.54).
7   Lightly grease the lip of the drive gear bearing oil seal. Fit a new

Fig. 6.55 Flat on the end of the countershaft horizontal

gasket taking care to position the gasket so that the oil return bore is not obstructed. Cover the splines of the input shaft with adhesive tape to prevent them damaging the oil seal and slide the oil seal retainer over the input shaft. Position the seal retainer, apply jointing compound to the bolt threads, insert the bolts and tighten them to the torque wrench setting given in the Specifications.
8   Push the countershaft gear cluster so that its gears mesh with those of the mainshaft. Check that the bore of the gear cluster is aligned with the layshaft holes in the end of the gearbox. Insert the layshaft from the rear of the gearbox, easing it in slowly so as not to displace the needle rollers, spacers or thrust washers. Finally tap the shaft until its end is flush with the front of the case. Align the flat on the rear end of the countershaft so that it is horizontal (Fig. 6.55).
9   Align the bolt holes of the gearbox and the extension housing,

apply jointing compound to the threads of the bolts, insert them and tighten to the torque wrench setting given in the Specifications.

10 If a new extension housing bush has been fitted, check that the notch or oil groove in it aligns with the oil return groove in the extension housing. If a new extension oil seal has not already been fitted, slide it over the extension shaft and carefully tap it in with a hammer and a block of wood.

11 Screw in and tighten the speedometer pinion assembly.

12 Fit the first/second and third/top selector forks into the selector housing cover so that the numbers on them are facing forward. Fit the reverse selector fork so that the number is facing towards the rear.

13 Fit the selector housing cover, using a new gasket and ensuring that the forks are properly fitted into the grooves of the synchronizer assemblies. Coat the threads of the bolts with jointing compound before fitting them and tighten them to the torque wrench setting given in the Specifications. When fitting the cover, make sure that the two brackets, reverse gear lever return spring and reversing light switch are fitted to their correct places.

14 Fit the clutch housing, coat the threads of the bolts with jointing compound, insert them and tighten to the torque wrench setting given in the Specifications.

15 Refit the clutch release fork and bearing.

16 Gearshift mechanism (type H) – removal and refitting

1 Drive the vehicle over a pit, or raise it on a ramp to gain access to the selector rods at the side of the gearbox (Fig. 6.56).

2 Unhook the three selector shafts from the gear lever.

3 Release the locknut on the gear lever knob and screw off the knob and the locknut.

4 If a clock is fitted, carefully lever it out of its housing. Disconnect the battery and then remove the cable from the clock. If a parcel tray or centre console is fitted, this must also be removed (see Chapter 12).

5 Remove the three bolts from the selector housing cover, lift out the selector mechanism assembly and remove the gasket from beneath it (Fig. 6.57).

6 When refitting the assembly, first position the gasket, insert the selector mechanism assembly and cover. Insert the three fixing screws and tighten them.

7 Refit the parcel tray or centre console if applicable.

8 Reconnect the clock, press it back into its housing and reconnect the battery leads.

9 Screw the locknut onto the gear lever, screw on the knob and align it so that the engraving on the knob indicates the correct position of

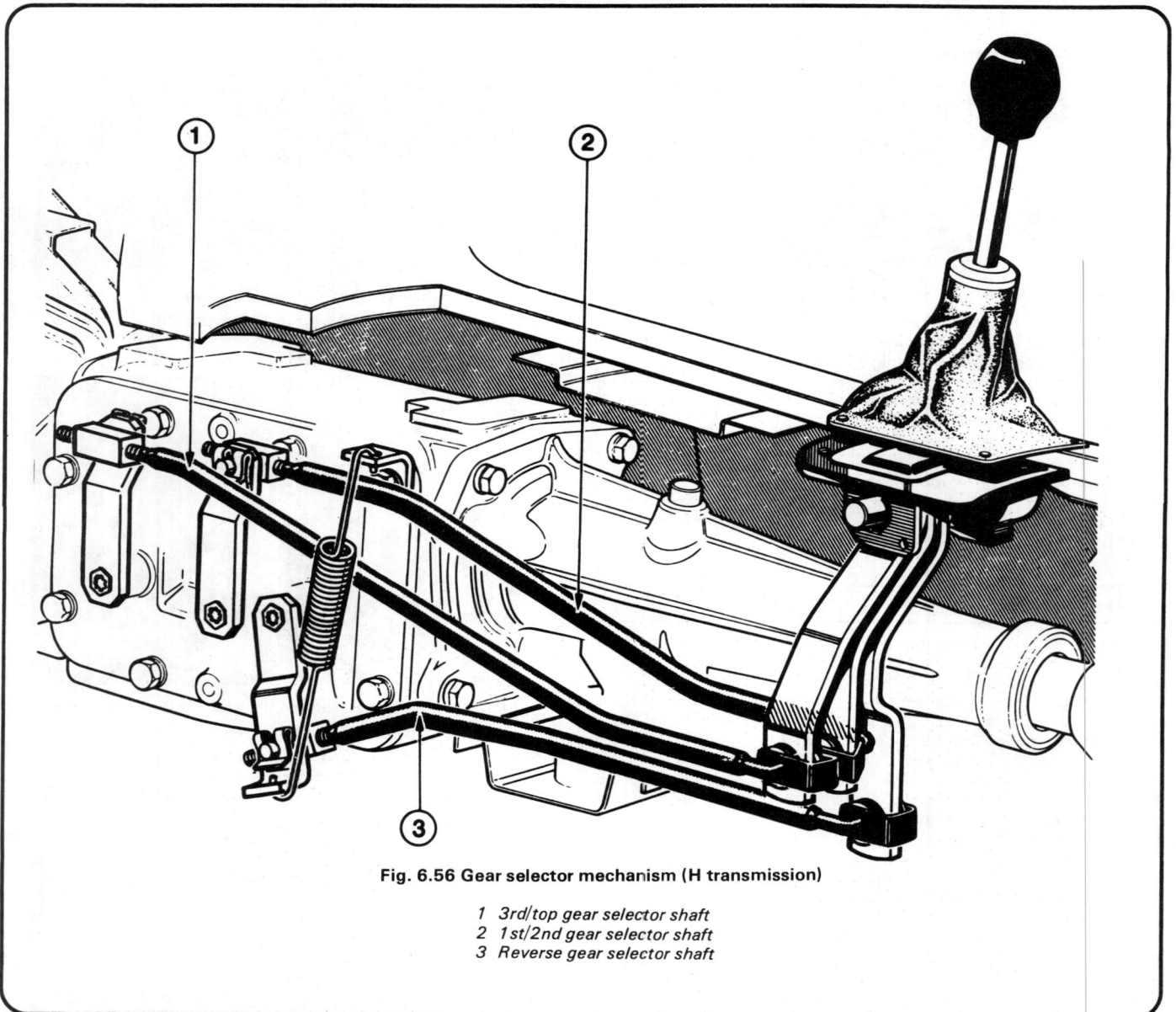

Fig. 6.56 Gear selector mechanism (H transmission)

1 3rd/top gear selector shaft
2 1st/2nd gear selector shaft
3 Reverse gear selector shaft

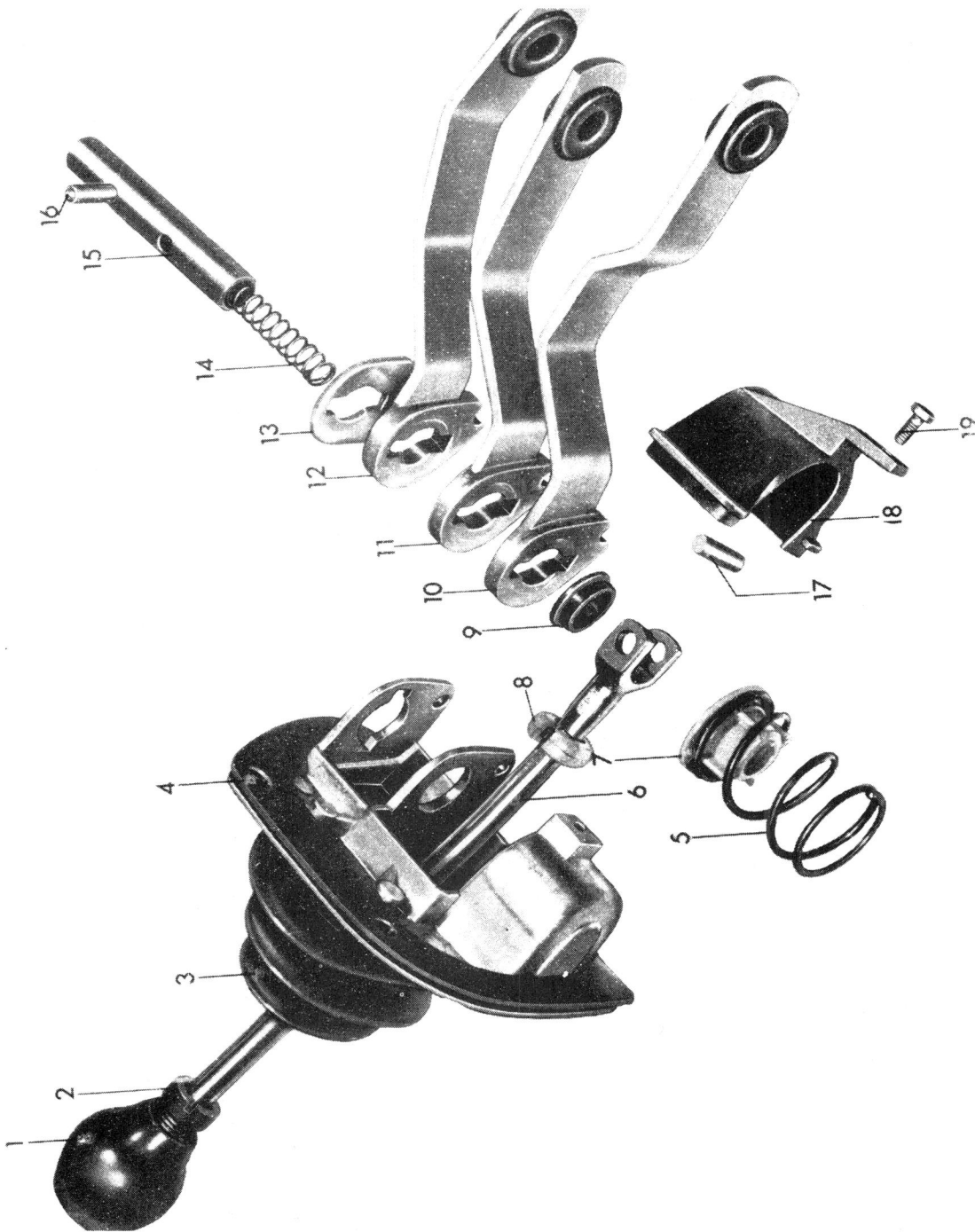

Fig. 6.57 Gearchange lever mechanism – exploded view

1 Gear lever knob
2 Locknut
3 Gaiter
4 Selector housing cover and gasket

5 Reverse gear spring
6 Gear lever
7 Spring retainer
8 Sphere

9 Bush
10 Lever for reverse gear
11 Lever for 1st/2nd gear
12 Lever for 3rd/4th gear

13 Damping washer
14 Spring
15 Gearchange shaft
16 Selector pin

17 Selector pin
18 Gearchange housing cover
19 Mounting screw

the gears. Lock the knob in this position.

10 Reconnect the selector shafts by first inserting a 0·2 in (5 mm) diameter pin into the lock hole of the gear lever to fix it in its neutral position. Adjust the rods if necessary, so that they can be reconnected without any strain and then remove the locking pin.

17 Gearshift mechanism (type H) – dismantling and reassembly

1 Remove one screw and take off the cover of the gearchange housing.

2 Drive the pin out of the gearchange shaft (Fig 6.58), remove the shaft (Fig. 6.59) and withdraw the gear lever assembly from the selector channel (Fig. 6.60).

3 Remove the gear knob and locknut, pull out the gear lever and remove the sphere from its shaft.

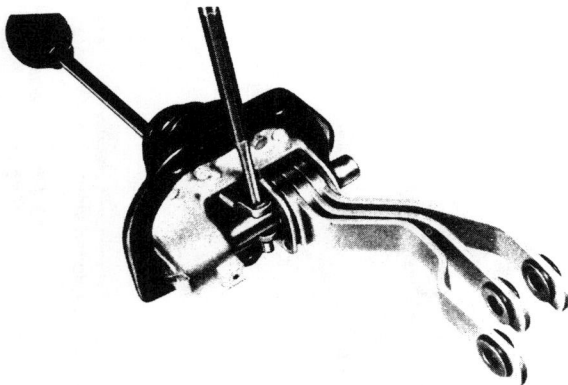

Fig. 6.58 Drive out the pin

4 Push the gear selector levers to the rear, withdraw the gearchange shaft and press the selector pin out of the gearchange shaft.

5 Remove the three selector levers and the damping washer.

6 Remove the small bush from the selector lever bracket and then remove the reverse gear spring and its retainer.

7 Before starting reassembly, smear general purpose grease on all sliding surfaces.

8 Insert the reverse gear spring and its retainer, the small spring and the selector lever bracket bush.

9 Assemble the three selector levers in their correct relative positions. Place the damping washer against the 3rd/4th gear lever, the flat part of the damping washer being towards the mounting plate of the assembly.

10 Fit the lever assembly, having first inserted the selector pin into its guide bore. When the pin is in place, turn a selector lever to retain the pin.

11 Fit the sphere to the gearchange shaft. Insert the selector lever into the selector channel, fit the fork of the lever over the gearchange shaft and drive in the pin to secure it.

12 Fit the gearchange housing cover and retain it with its fixing screw.

13 Screw on the gear lever locknut. Screw on the gear knob and lock it in place after aligning the knob.

18 Reversing light switch (type E and type H gearboxes)

1 On type E transmissions the reversing light switch is mounted below the rear end of the gearbox extension. To remove the switch, disconnect the leads, unscrew the switch and remove the switch, spring and plunger. When refitting the switch, apply a smear of gasket sealant to the screw threads and refit the plunger, spring and switch.

2 On type H transmissions, the reversing light switch is mounted on a bracket on the gearshift housing cover. If necessary the switch can be adjusted by using washers when mounting it on its bracket, or by loosening the two bracket fixing screws and moving the bracket.

Fig. 6.59 Withdraw the gearchange shaft

Fig. 6.60 Withdraw the lever assembly

19 Fault diagnosis – manual transmission

Symptom	Reason/s
Weak or ineffective synchromesh	Synchronizing cones worn or damaged Baulk ring synchromesh dogs worn, or damaged Blocker bar spring displaced or broken
Jumps out of gear	Shift rod out of adjustment (type H) Broken gearchange fork rod spring Worn selector fork or synchromesh sleeve
Excessive noise	Insufficient oil, or wrong grade of oil Worn bearings and needle rollers Worn or damaged gear teeth
Gears difficult to engage	Clutch not disengaging fully, due to incorrect adjustment

20 Automatic transmission – general description

1   The automatic transmission fitted to both the Mercury Capri II and the Capri II is the Bordeaux model C3 (Fig. 6.63). It is a three speed unit, capable of providing automatic upshift and downshift through three forward gear ratios. It also provides manual selection of first and second gears.
2   The transmission consists of a torque converter, a planetary gear train, two multiple disc clutches, a one-way clutch and an hydraulic control system.
3   The only maintenance adjustment required by the transmission is the adjustment of the front band. Because of the complexity of the automatic transmission unit and the need for special equipment, overhaul and the diagnosis and rectification of faults should be entrusted to a Ford main agent. The content of the following Sections is therefore confined to supplying general information and any service information which can be used by the owner.

21 Automatic transmission – general precautions

Towing

If a vehicle with automatic transmission has to be towed, put the selector lever in the 'N' position. The car may be towed for a distance of no more than 12 miles (20 km) at a speed of 20 to 25 mph (30 to 40 kph). If the distance to be towed is greater than 12 miles (20 km), the driveshaft from the transmission to the rear axle must be removed before towing is started, or alternatively the vehicle can be towed with its rear wheels off the ground.

Safety

Before any carburettor checks are carried out with the engine running, on a vehicle with automatic transmission, it is esential that the selector lever is in the P or N position and the handbrake is applied hard.

When either P or N is selected, the engine must never be run at a speed greater than 4500 rpm, otherwise the transmission will be damaged.

22 Automatic transmission – fluid level checking

1   Before attempting to check the fluid level, the fluid must be at its normal operating temperature (approximately 65°C/150°F). This is best accomplished by driving the car for about 5 miles (8 km) under normal running conditions.
2   Park the car on level ground, apply the handbrake and depress the brake pedal.
3   Allow the engine to idle, then move the selector through all the positions three times.
4   Select 'P' and wait for 1 to 2 minutes with the engine still idling.
5   Now withdraw the dipstick (Fig. 6.61) (engine still idling), wipe it clean with a lint-free cloth, refit it and withdraw it again. Note the oil level and, if necessary, top-up to maintain between the 'MAX' and 'MIN' dipstick markings. Only fluid meeting the stated specification should be used; this is applied through the dipstick tube.

23 Automatic transmission – removal and refitting

1   If possible, raise the car on a hoist or place it over an inspection pit. Alternatively, it will be necessary to jack up the car to obtain the maximum possible amount of working room underneath.
2   Place a large drain pan beneath the transmission sump (oil pan) then, working from the rear, loosen the attaching bolts and allow the fluid to drain. Remove all the bolts except the two front ones to drain as much fluid as possible, then temporarily refit two bolts at the rear to hold it in place.
3   Remove the torque converter drain plug access cover and adapter plate bolts from the lower end of the converter housing.
4   Remove the three flywheel-to-converter attaching bolts, cranking the engine as necessary to gain access by means of a spanner on the crankshaft pulley attaching bolt. **Caution:** *Do not rotate the engine backwards.*
5   Rotate the engine until the converter drain plug is accessible, then remove the plug, catching the fluid in the drain pan. Fit and tighten the drain plug afterwards.

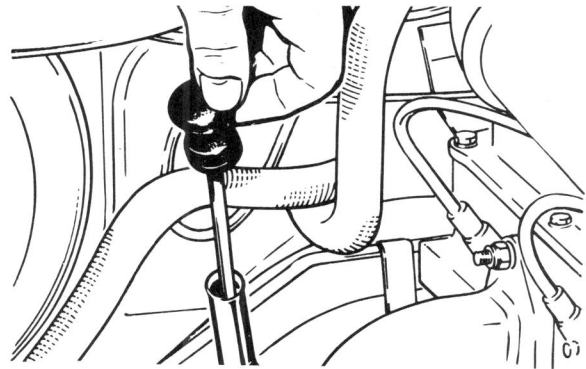

Fig. 6.61 Checking the automatic transmission fluid level

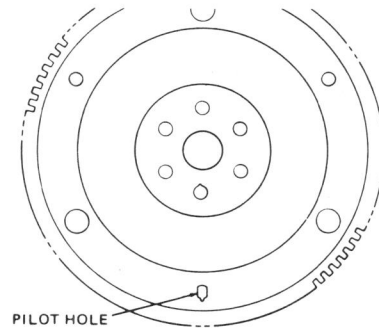

PILOT HOLE

Fig. 6.62 Flywheel pilot hole

6   Remove the propeller shaft, referring to Chapter 7, as necessary. Place a polythene bag over the end of the transmission to prevent dirt from entering.
7   Detach the speedometer cable from the extension housing.
8   Disconnect the shift rod at the transmission manual lever, and the downshift rod at the transmission downshift lever.
9   Remove the starter motor retaining bolts and position the motor out of the way.
10 Disconnect the starter inhibitor (neutral start) switch leads.
11 Disconnect the vacuum lines from the vacuum unit.
12 Position a trolley jack beneath the transmission and raise it to *just* take the transmission weight.
13 Remove the engine rear support to crossmember nut and the transmission extension housing crossmember.
14 Remove the inlet steady pipe rest from the inlet pipe and rear engine support. Disconnect the exhaust pipes at the manifolds and support them to one side.
15 Lower the trolley jack slightly, then place another jack to the front end of the engine. Raise the engine to gain access to the upper converter housing-to-engine attaching bolts.
16 Disconnect the oil cooler lines at the transmission and plug them to prevent dirt from entering.
17 Remove the lower converter housing-to-engine bolts, and the transmission filler tube.
18 Ensure that the transmission is securely mounted on the trolley jack, then remove the two upper converter housing-to-engine bolts.
19 Carefully move the transmission rearwards and downwards, and away from the car.
20 Refitting the transmission is essentially the reverse of the removal procedure, but the following points should be noted:

a) *Rotate the converter to align the bolt drive lugs and drain plug with the holes in the flywheel.*
b) *Do not allow the front of the transmission to drop below the horizontal because this may cause the converter to move forward and disengage from the pump gear.*
c) *When fitting the three flywheel-to-converter bolts, position the flywheel so that the pilot hole is in the six o'clock position (Fig. 6.62). Fit one bolt first and tighten it, then fit the other two bolts in turn. Do not attempt to fit it in any other way.*

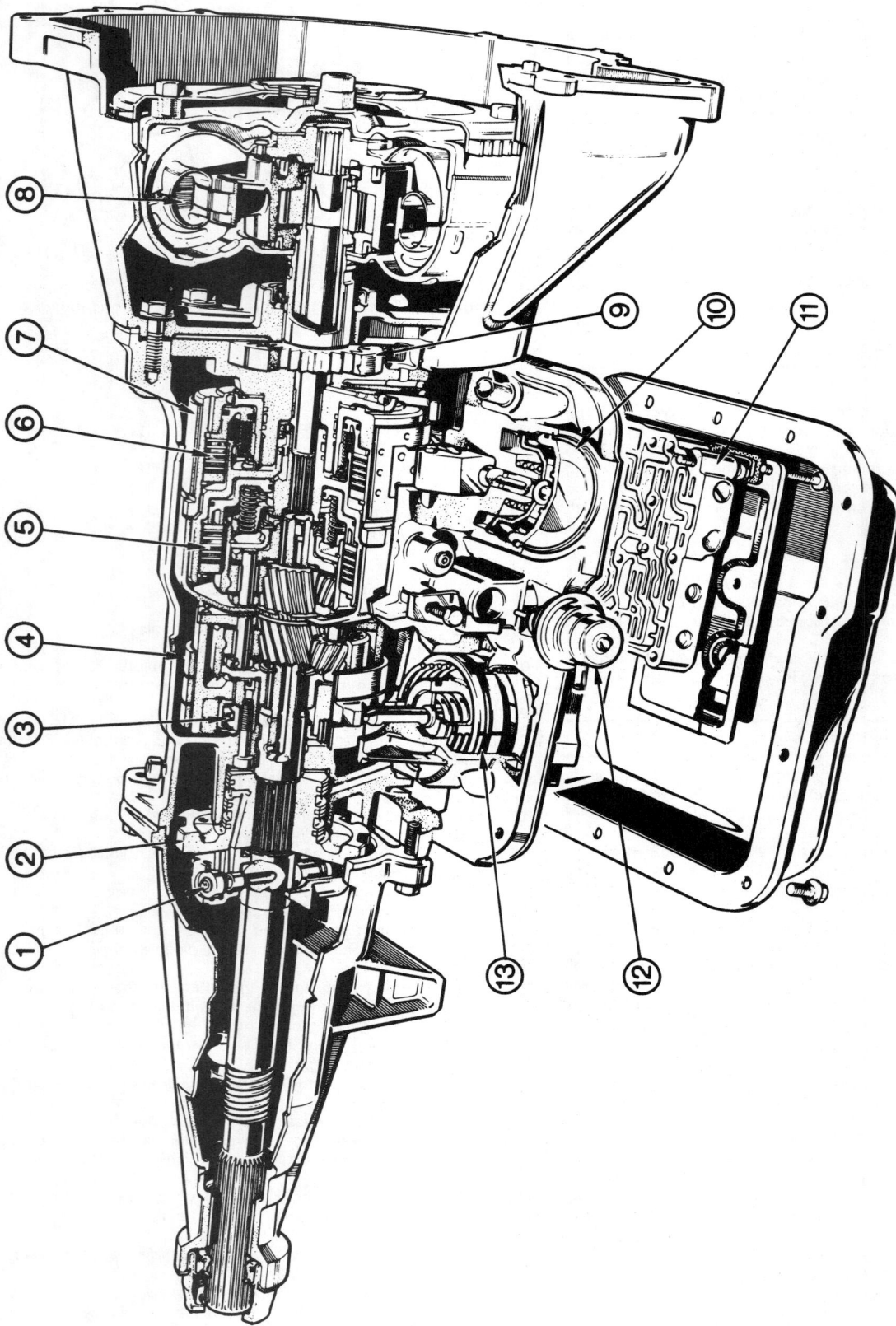

Fig. 6.63 C3 automatic transmission

1 Governor assembly
2 Governor hub
3 One-way clutch

4 Rear brake band
5 Forward clutch
6 Reverse and top gear clutch

7 Front brake band
8 Torque converter
9 Hydraulic pump

10 Front servo
11 Valve body

12 Vacuum diaphragm
13 Rear servo

d) *Adjust the downshift cable and selector linkage as necessary (see Sections 26 and 28).*

e) *When the car has been lowered to the ground, add sufficient fluid to bring the level up to the MAX mark on the dipstick when the engine is not running. Afterwards, check the fluid level as detailed in the previous Section.*

24 Front band – adjustment

The intermediate or front band is used to hold the sun gear stationary so as to give the second gear ratio. If it is not correctly adjusted there will be noticeable slip during first to second gearchange or from third to second gearchange. The first symptoms of these conditions will be a very sluggish gearchange instead of the usual crisp action.

To adjust the intermediate band, undo and remove the adjustment screw locknut located on the left-hand side of the transmission case (Fig. 6.64). Tighten the adjusting screw using a torque wrench set to 10 lbf ft (1·4 kgf m) and then slacken off the adjustment screw 1½ turns. A new locknut should be fitted and tightened to a torque wrench setting of 35 – 45 lbf ft (4·8 – 6·22 kgf m).

25 Gear selector mechanism – removal and refitting

1   Chock the front wheels, jack up the rear of the car and support it

securely on axle stands or blocks.

2   Undo and remove the manual lever control rod nut from the side of the transmission underneath the car (Fig. 6.65). Detach the rod from the stud.

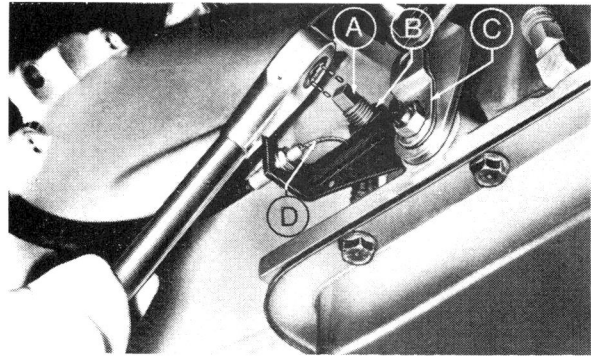

Fig. 6.64 Brake band adjustment

A – Adjustment screw   C – Downshift lever
B – Locknut   D – Downshift cable

Fig. 6.65 Gear selector mechanism components

A – Selector pawl
B – Operating cable
C – Push button (RHD)
D – Selector lever handle
E – Adjusting link
F – Gearshift rod

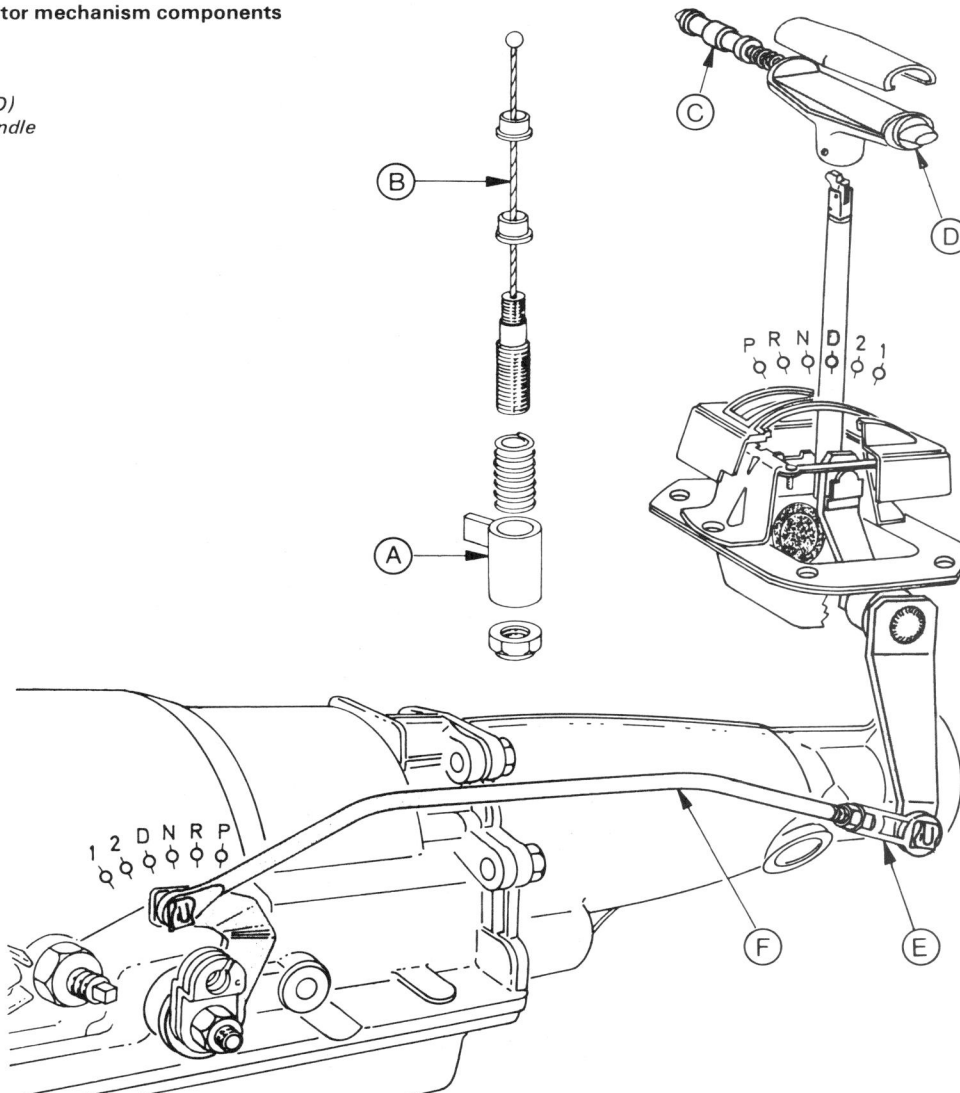

3 Inside the car, undo and remove the selector lever handle securing screw.

4 Undo and remove the screws securing the dial housing to the selector lever assembly and lift off the dial housing.

5 Undo and remove the two screws securing the pointer back up shield to the selector lever assembly and remove the shield.

6 Undo and remove the two screws securing the dial indicator light to the selector lever. Remove the lamp assembly.

7 Undo and remove the selector housing and lever assembly securing bolts and remove the selector lever and housing.

8 To remove the selector lever from the housing, undo and remove the securing nut and separate the lever from the housing.

9 To reassemble, first refit the selector lever to the housing and secure it with the nut.

10 Fit the handle to the selector lever.

11 Check the clearance between the detent pawl and plate. When correctly adjusted, the detent pawl should just clear the highest point on the detent plate (dimension Y in Fig. 6.66).

12 To adjust the height of the pawl, hold the adjustment screw stationary and turn the locknut (X in Fig. 6.66) until the correct clearance is obtained.

13 Remove the handle from the selector lever again.

14 Complete the reassembly as the reversal of dismantling and if necessary adjust the selector linkage as described in the following Section.

26 Selector linkage – adjustment

1 Check that the selector lever is adjusted correctly by measuring the end clearance between the lever pawl and the quadrant notch (Fig. 6.67) . This should be between 0·004 and 0·008 in (0·1 and 0·2 mm)

and can be adjusted by turning the cable locknut which is accessible after removing the selector lever housing plug.

2 Disconnect the shift rod from the shift lever at the adjustable end of the shift rod.

3 Place the hand control lever in D.

4 Place the selector lever on the side of the transmission housing at D. This can be determined by counting two clicks back from the fully forward position.

5 Connect the shift rod to the hand control lever by inserting the clevis pin. The pin should slide in freely, but if it does not, lengthen or shorten the rod adjuster until the pin can be inserted easily. After making the adjustment, tighten the locknut, making sure that the slot in the adjustable end remains vertical.

6 Connect the gear shift rod to the selector arm and secure it.

7 Check that the manual selector lever can be engaged in every selector position and that engagement can be felt. If necessary readjust the gear shift rod to achieve this.

27 Downshift cable – removal and refitting

1 Remove the split pin to disconnect the end of the cable from the carburettor linkage connecting lever.

2 Detach the cable sheath from the upper bracket, by unscrewing the adjusting nut from the threaded coupling. Pull the cable sheath right back and unhook the cable from the slot in the bracket.

3 Detach the cable sheath from the transmission bracket by unscrewing the nut from the threaded coupling and unhooking the cable from the slot in the bracket (Fig. 6.68).

4 Unhook the cable from the transmission downshift lever and remove it.

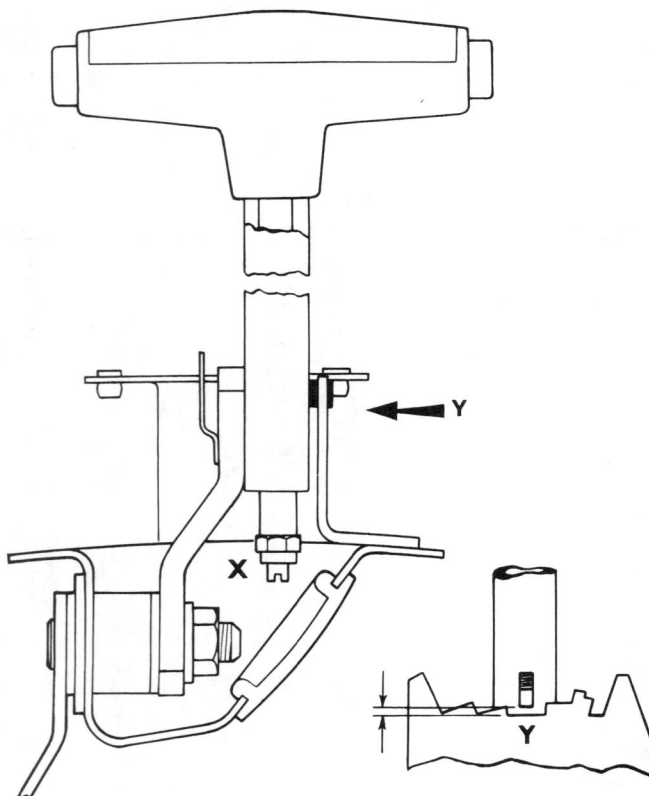

Fig. 6.66 Selector lever adjustment. Adjust the effective length of the selector cable at points 'X' to give clearance shown at 'Y'. (0.005-0.010 in /0.13-0.25mm)

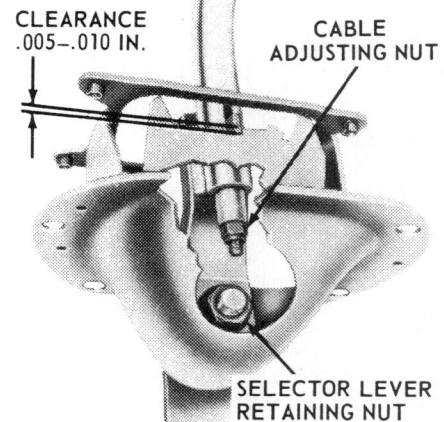

Fig. 6.67 Selector linkage adjustment

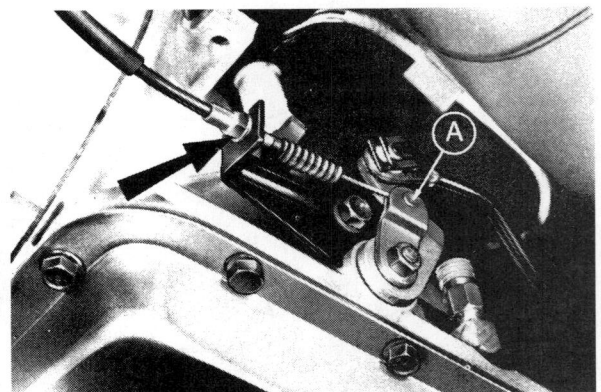

Fig. 6.68 Transmission end of kickdown cable

A – Transmission downshift lever

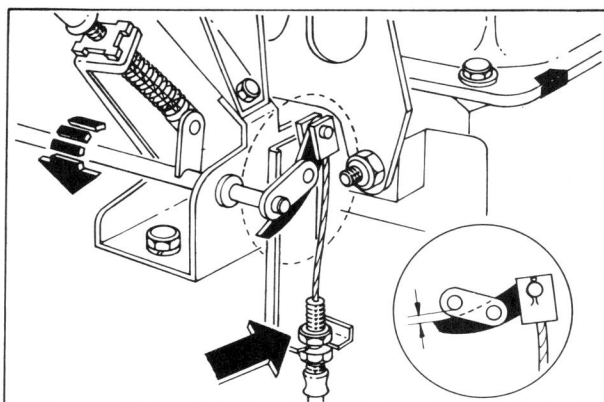

Fig. 6.69 Downshift cable adjustment

Specified clearance (inset) 0.02 to 0.05 in (0.5 to 1.3 mm)

5   When refitting, first hook the cable into the downshift lever.
6   Screw the cable sheath onto the bracket on the transmission and route the cable against the dash panel and up to the carburettor.
7   Insert the threaded coupling into the upper bracket with the inner nut screwed on fully and the outer nut screwed on only a few turns.
8   Adjust the cable as described in the following Section.

28 Downshift cable – adjustment

1   With the accelerator pedal held in the fully depressed position, check that the carburettor throttle plates are fully open.
2   Press the end of the downshift cable connecting lever with a screwdriver to ensure that the inner cable is taut and while keeping it under tension turn the adjuster nut on the outer cable until there is a clearance of 0·02 to 0·05 in (0·5 to 1·3 mm) between the operating shaft lever and the downshift cable connecting lever (Fig. 6.69).
3   Tighten the locknut and then recheck the clearance.

29 Inhibitor switch – removal and refitting

1   Pull the cable connector off the switch (Fig. 6.70).
2   Unscrew the starter inhibitor switch and remove the O-ring.
3   To refit the switch, fit a new O-ring and screw the switch into the housing finger-tight. Tighten the switch to the torque wrench setting given in the Specifications. It is important that this torque is not exceeded.
4   Refit the cable plug connector to the switch.

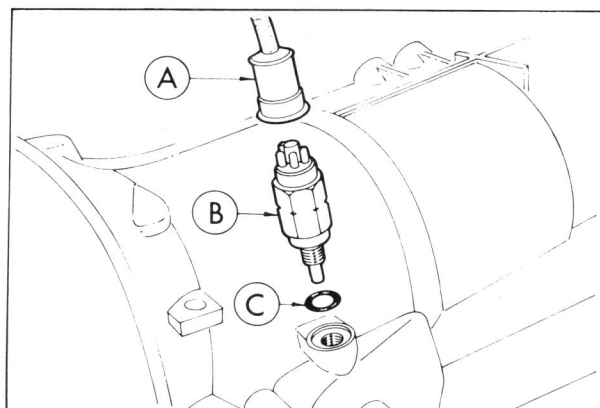

Fig. 6.70 Starter inhibitor switch

A – Connector   *B – Inhibitor switch*   *C – O-ring*

5   Check that the engine will start only with the lever in the P and N positions and in no other position.
6   Turn on the ignition without starting the engine. Check that the reversing light comes on in the R position, but not in any other position.

30 Automatic transmission extension housing oil seal – renewal

1   Remove the propeller shaft, as described in Chapter 7.
2   Jack the rear of the car to minimise the loss of oil from the transmission, then carefully prise out the oil seal, being careful not to damage the machined recess into which the seal fits.
3   Ensure that the recess is clean and undamaged, then press in a new seal with the lip of the seal inwards. Tap the seal home fully with a tube of suitable diameter, or with a hammer and a block of wood, being careful that the seal is inserted squarely.
4   Refit the propeller shaft, lower the car to the ground and then check the level of the transmission fluid as described in Section 19.

31 Fault diagnosis – automatic transmission

Faults in these units are most commonly the result of low fluid level, incorrect adjustment of the selector linkage, or downshift cable, or a faulty inhibitor switch. If the problem still exists after these points have been checked, it will be necessary to take the car to a dealer with equipment to diagnose internal faults.

Chapter 7 Propeller shaft

Contents

Specifications

Type (Capri II) .... Two piece tubular, with rubber mounted centre bearing. Universal joints are Hardy-Spicer type, with an alternative constant velocity (CV) centre joint on some models.

Type (Mercury Capri II) .... Single piece tubular, with Hardy-Spicer universal joints

Torque wrench settings

	lbf ft	kgf m
Centre bearing to floor assembly	13 to 17	1.8 to 2.3
Propeller shaft to drive pinion flange	44 to 48	6.0 to 6.5

1 General description

On Capri II models, drive is transmitted from the gearbox to the rear axle by means of a finely balanced tubular propeller shaft, split into two halves and supported at the centre by a rubber-mounted bearing. On some models, a constant velocity type centre joint is used.

Fitted to the front, centre and rear of the propeller shaft assembly are universal joints, which allow vertical movement of the rear axle and slight movement of the complete power unit on its rubber mountings. Each universal joint comprises a four-legged centre spider, four needle roller bearings and two yokes.

Fore and aft movement of the rear axle is absorbed by a sliding spline located at the gearbox end. The yoke flange of the rear universal joint is fitted to the rear axle and is secured to the pinion flange by four bolts and lock washers.

On Mercury Capri II models a one-piece propeller shaft is used.

The propeller shaft universal joints cannot be renewed without special equipment because the joint spiders are staked into the yokes in a position determined during electronic balancing. When joint wear is detected (see Section 4), either a new propeller shaft should be obtained, or the complete propeller shaft should be passed to a suitably equipped engineering workshop for repair.

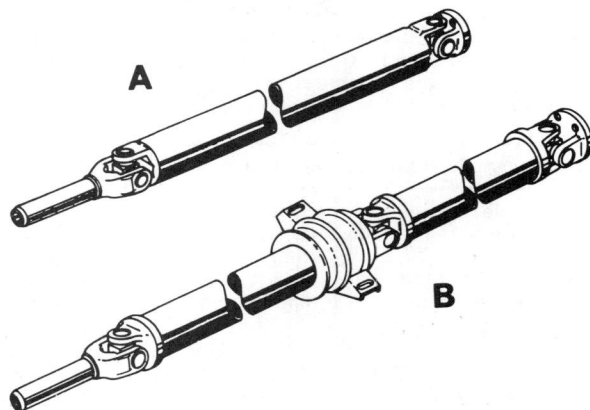

Fig. 7.1 Single piece (A) and two-piece (B) propeller shafts

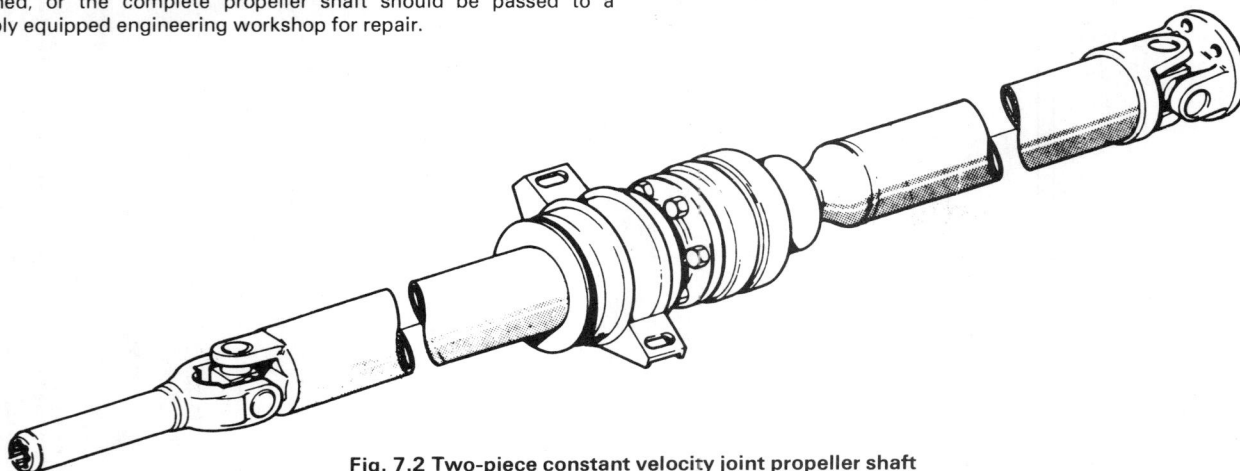

Fig. 7.2 Two-piece constant velocity joint propeller shaft

2 Propeller shaft – removal and refitting

1   Jack up the rear of the car, or position the rear of the car over a pit, or on a ramp.

2   If the rear of the car is jacked up, supplement the jack with support blocks, so that danger is minimised should the jack collapse.

3   If the rear wheels are off the ground, place the car in gear, or put the handbrake on, to ensure that the propeller shaft does not turn when an attempt is made to loosen the four bolts securing the propeller shaft to the rear axle flange.

4   The propeller shaft is carefully balanced to fine limits and it is important that it is refitted in exactly the same position it was in prior to its removal. Scratch a mark on the propeller shaft and rear axle flanges, to ensure accurate mating when the time comes for reassembly.

5   Unscrew and remove the four lock bolts and securing washers which hold the flange of the propeller shaft to the flange on the rear axle (Fig. 7.3).

6   Where applicable, undo and remove the two bolts holding the centre bearing housing to the underframe. Note the position and number of any shims which are fitted (Fig. 7.4).

7   Push the shaft forward slightly to separate the two flanges at the rear, then lower the end of the shaft and pull it rearwards to disengage it from the gearbox mainshaft splines.

8   Place a large can, or tray, under the rear of the gearbox extension to catch any oil which is likely to leak through the spline lubricating holes when the propeller shaft is removed.

9   Refitting the propeller shaft is a reversal of the above procedure. Ensure that the mating marks scratched on the propeller shaft and rear axle flanges line up, and that any shims at the centre bearing are refitted.

10 Note the method of securing the flanges, either nuts and bolts, or setscrews, according to type of rear axle.

3 Propeller shaft centre bearing – renewal

1   Prior to removing the centre bearing from the section of the two-piece propeller shaft, carefully scratch marks on the rear yoke and on the shaft just forward of the bearing housing, to ensure correct alignment on reassembly.

2   Knock back the tab washer on the centre bolt located in the jaws of the rear yoke. Slacken off the nut and remove the U-washer from under it.

3   With the U-washer removed, the rear yoke can now be drawn off the splines of the front section. The centre bolt and its washer remain attached to the splined front section.

4   Slide the bearing housing with its rubber insulator from the shaft. Bend back the six metal tabs on the housing and remove the rubber insulator.

5   The bearing and its protective caps should now be withdrawn from the splined section of the propeller shaft, by careful levering with two large screwdrivers, or tyre levers. If a suitable puller tool is available, this should always be used in preference to any other method as it is less likely to cause damage to the bearing (Fig. 7.5).

6   To refit the bearing, first fill the space between the bearing and caps with a general purpose grease. Select a piece of piping or tubing that is just a fraction smaller in diameter than the bearing, place the splined part of the drive shaft upright in a vice, position the bearing on the shaft and, using a soft hammer on the end of the piece of tubing, drive the bearing firmly and squarely onto the shaft.

7   Refit the rubber insulator in the bearing housing, ensuring that the boss on the insulator is at the top of the housing and will be adjacent to the under-frame when the propeller shafts are refitted.

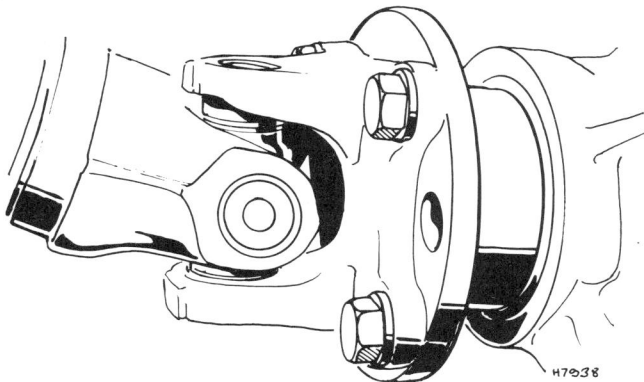

Fig. 7.3 Propeller shaft to rear axle fixing bolts

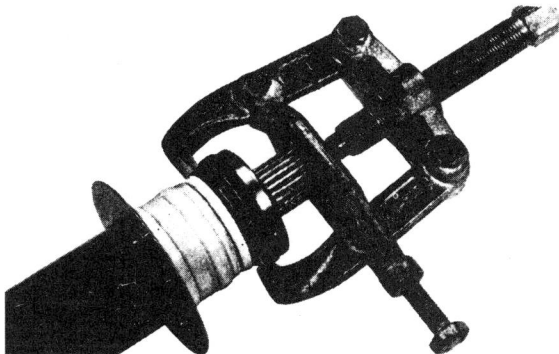

Fig. 7.4 Attachment of centre bearing to floor

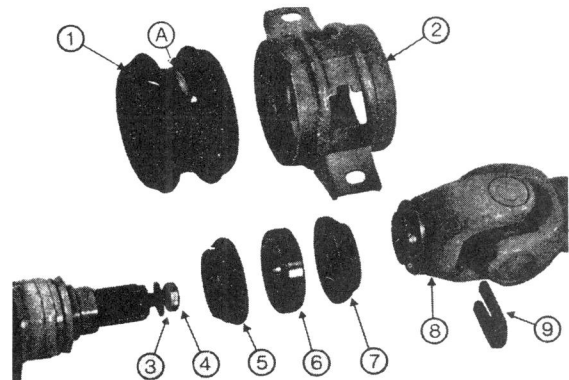

Fig. 7.5 Withdrawing a centre drive shaft bearing and cap

Fig. 7.6 Components of the centre bearing

A Mark for position of rubber insulator   4 Bolt   8 Yoke
1 Rubber insulator   5 Cap   9 U-retainer
2 Retainer   6 Bearing
3 Lock plate   7 Cap

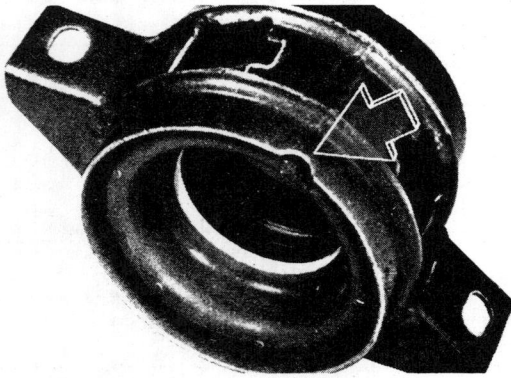

Fig. 7.7 Retainer mark in centre bearing (arrowed)

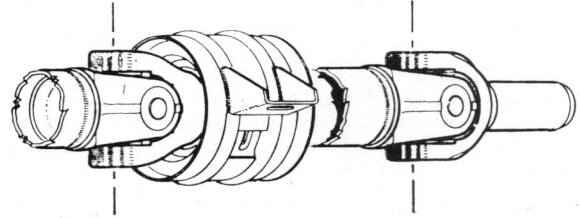

Fig. 7.8 Correct installed position of forward and rear driveshaft parts

8   When the insulator is correctly positioned, bend back the six metal tabs and slide the housing and insulator assembly over the bearing, so that the recess (Fig. 7.7) faces towards the front of the car.
9   Slide the splined end of the shaft into the rear yoke, ensuring that the previously scribed mating marks are correctly aligned (Fig. 7.8).
10 Refit the U-washer under the centre bolt, with its smooth surface facing the front section of the propeller shaft (Fig. 7.9). Tighten down the centre bolt to the specified torque and bend up its tab washer to secure it.

4   Universal joints – inspection

1   Wear in the needle roller bearings is characterised by vibration in the transmission, 'clonks' on taking up the drive, and in extreme cases of lack of lubrication, metallic squeaking, and ultimately grating and shrieking sounds as the bearings break up.
2   It is easy to check if the needle roller bearings are worn with the propeller shaft in position, by trying to turn the shaft with one hand, the other holding the rear axle flange when the rear universal is being checked, and the front half coupling when the front universal is being

Fig. 7.9 Centre bearing U-retainer

checked. Any movement between the propeller shaft and the front and the rear half couplings, is indicative of considerable wear. If worn, a new propeller shaft must be obtained, or the existing shaft overhauled by a suitably equipped engineering workshop.

5   Fault diagnosis – propeller shaft

Symptom	Reason/s
Vibration	Wear in sliding sleeve splines
	Worn universal joint bearings
	Propeller shaft out of balance
	Propeller shaft distorted
Knock, or clunk when taking up drive	Worn universal joint bearings
	Worn rear axle drive pinion splines
	Loose rear drive flange bolts
	Excessive backlash in rear axle gears

Chapter 8 Rear axle

Contents

Specifications

Axle designation	D (Salisbury)
Type	Hypoid, semi-floating, integral differential
Ratio	Capri II 3.09 : 1 Mercury Capri II (except California) 3.09 : 1 Mercury Capri II (California only) 3.22 : 1
Lubricant capacity	1.9 Imp pints, 2.3 US pints, 1.1 litre
Lubricant type	SQM – 2C 9002 AA (SAE 90 EP)

Torque wrench settings

	lbf ft	kgf m
Bearing cap-to-axle casing	44 to 50	6.0 to 6.8
Cover-to-axle casing	26 to 33	3.5 to 4.5
Crownwheel-to-differential case	59 to 64	8.0 to 8.7
Drive pinion flange bolts	44 to 48	6.0 to 6.5
Halfshaft retainer plate-to-axle flange	20 to 23	2.7 to 3.1
Drive pinion self-locking nut (early axle type)	74 to 88	10.0 to 12.0

1 General description

1   The rear axle is of the hypoid semi-floating type and is located by semi-elliptic road springs, in conjunction with a stabilizer bar.
2   The differential is integral with the axle housing and the rear axle must be removed to carry out any repairs to the differential which may become necessary.
3   The drive pinion runs in two tapered roller bearings, which are pre-loaded by a spacer. Early axles have a fixed length spacer and later ones a collapsible spacer (Figs. 8.1 and 8.2). Both types of spacer are interchangeable, but care must be taken to ensure that the appropriate method of determining drive pinion bearing preload is used.
4   The correct depth of mesh of the pinion in the crownwheel is obtained by the use of selected shims inserted between the pinion and rear tapered roller bearing.
5   The ring gear is bolted to the differential case, which is mounted on two tapered roller bearings. These bearings are preloaded by selective fit shims, positioned on either side of the differential housing. The differential assembly is of the two pinion type.
6   The axleshafts are splined to the differential side gears and supported at the outer ends by ball bearings. Oil seals are fitted at each end of the axle housing.
7   Overhauling the rear axle requires a variety of special tools and it is not recommended that any attempt should be made to do this. If a rear axle is defective it should be replaced by an exchange unit.

2 Rear axle – removal and refitting

1   Remove the rear wheel hub caps (if fitted) and slacken the wheel nuts. Jack up the car, fit stands or blocks under the side members and remove the rear wheels.
2   Remove the four bolts and detach the driveshaft from the drive

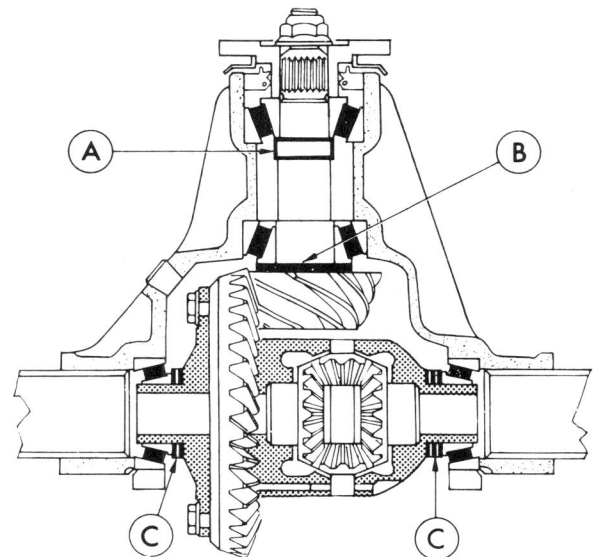

Fig. 8.1 Sectional view of the integral differential axle (early type with fixed length spacer)

A Spacer   *B Shim*   *C Shims*

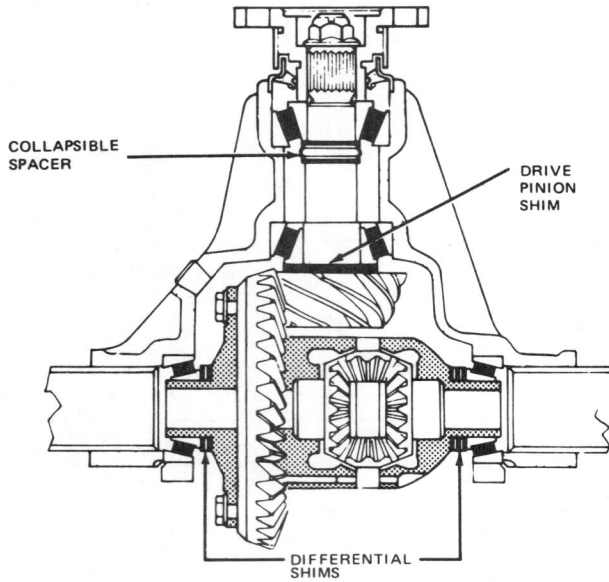

Fig. 8.2 Sectional view of the integral differential axle (later type with collapsible spacer)

COLLAPSIBLE SPACER

DRIVE PINION SHIM

DIFFERENTIAL SHIMS

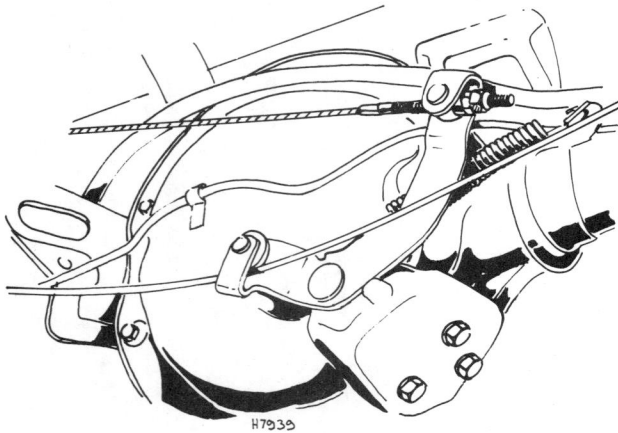

Fig. 8.3 Driveshaft mounting to drive pinion flange

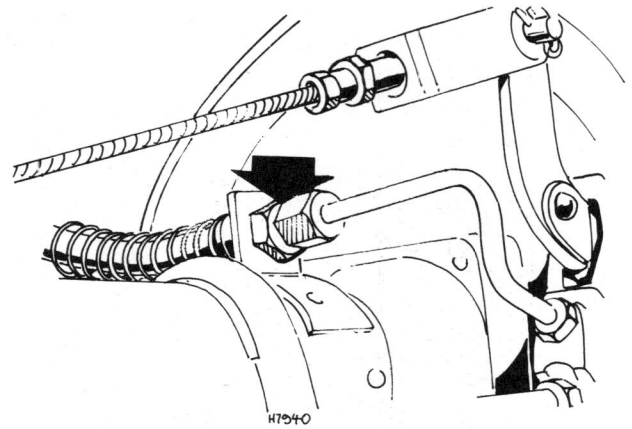

Fig. 8.4 Brake cable adjuster and relay lever

Fig. 8.5 Brake hose connection

Fig. 8.6 Shock absorber to rear axle mounting

Fig. 8.7 Disconnecting the rear stabiliser

pinion flange (Fig. 8.3).

3   Unscrew and remove the locknut from the brake cable at the relay lever on the rear axle. Unscrew the adjuster and release the cable (Fig. 8.4).

4   Disconnect the brake hose from the brake pipe on the right-hand side and plug the pipes to avoid losing brake fluid (Fig. 8.5).

5   Place a jack under the differential casing, raise the axle, then detach the shock absorbers from the axle (Fig. 8.6).

6   Pull the stabiliser bar to the rear to release the force on its fixing, (Fig. 8.7) then remove the attachment bolt from each end.

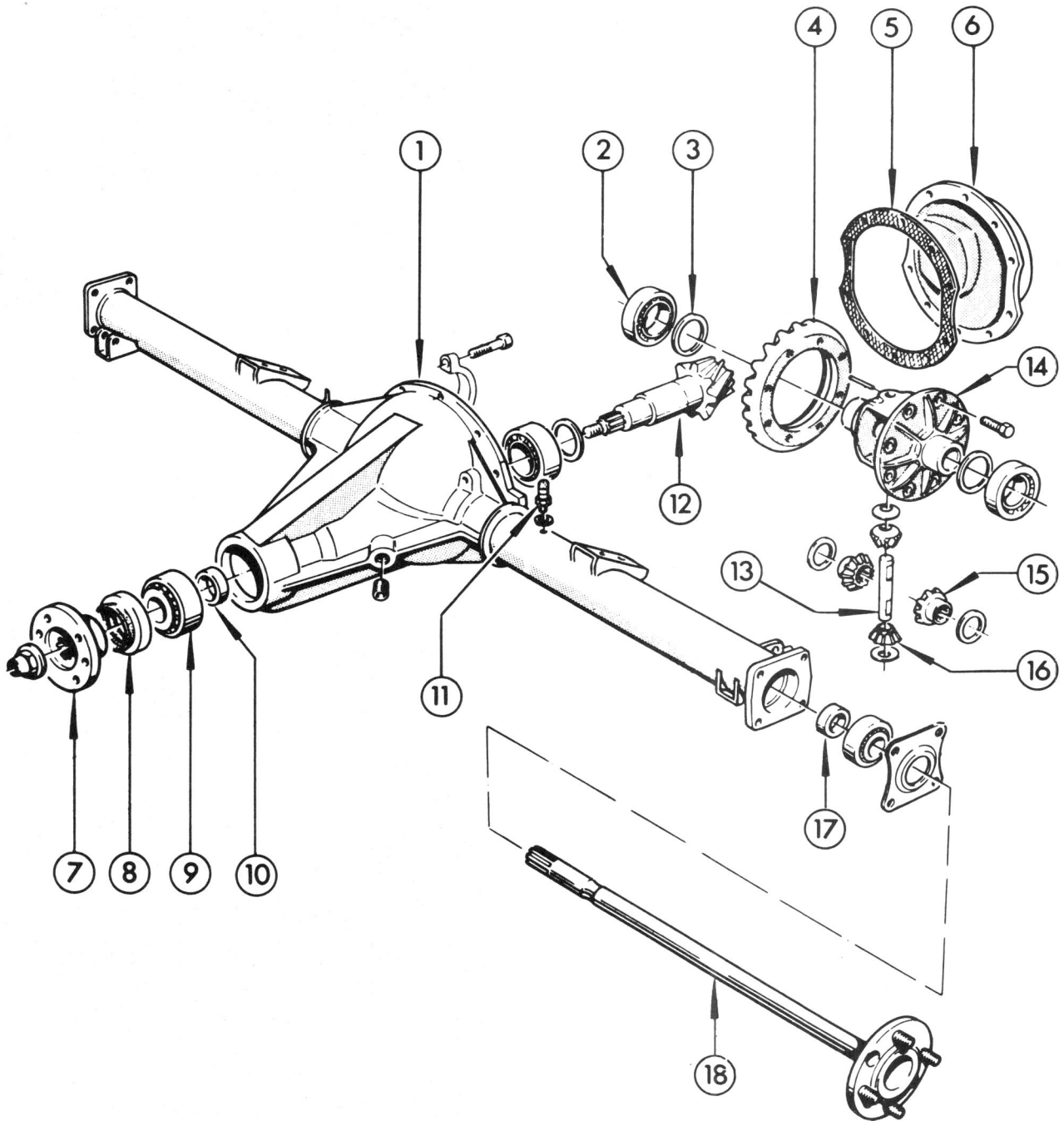

Fig. 8.8 Component parts of integral differential (Type D Salisbury) axle

1 Axle housing	8 Oil seal	13 Pinion gear shaft
2 Differential case taper roller bearing	9 Drive pinion taper roller bearing	14 Differential case
3 Differential case shim	10 Drive pinion spacer – (fixed length	15 Side gear
4 Crown wheel	or collapsible)	16 Differential pinion
5 Gasket	11 Vent valve	17 Retaining ring
6 Cover	12 Drive pinion	18 Half shaft
7 Drive pinion flange		

7   Remove the four nuts from the attachment plate (Fig. 8.9) and remove the two U-bolts from each of the spring attachments.

8   With the help of an assistant, lift the axle clear of the rear springs and remove it from the side of the car.

9   When refitting, first lift the axle and position it on the rear springs, ensuring that the upper rubber insulators (Fig. 8.10) and the centre eye bolts are positioned correctly.

10   Attach the driveshaft to the drive pinion flange. Fit the bolts and new lock washers, but do not tighten the bolts at this stage.

11   Fit the lower rubber insulators of the axle mountings, the plates and U-bolts. Make sure that the mountings are in the same position as when they were removed, then fit new self-locking nuts to the U-bolts and tighten them to a torque of 18 to 27 lbf ft (2.5 to 3.6 kgf m).

12   Fit the brackets over the rubber insulators on the stabilizer bar. Press the stabilizer bar so that the bolts can be inserted without strain and tighten the bolts to a torque of 29 to 37 lbf ft (4.0 to 5.0 kgf m) before releasing the stabilizer bar.

13   Jack the rear axle until the shock absorbers can be fitted, then insert the bolts and tighten them to a torque of 39 to 46 lbf ft (5.3 to 6.3 kgf m).

14   Reconnect the brake hose to the brake pipe and bleed the brakes, as described in Chapter 9.

15   Reconnect the handbrake cable to the relay lever and adjust the cable so that the lever is raised slightly off its stop.

16   Tighten the bolts connecting the driveshaft to the drive pinion, to a torque of 44 to 48 lbf ft (6.0 to 6.5 kgf m).

17   Fit the rear wheels, remove the jack from beneath the rear axle, lower the car to the ground and tighten the wheel nuts.

18   Check the level of oil in the rear axle and top up if necessary.

3   Halfshaft – removal and refitting

1   Slacken the wheel nuts, jack up the rear of the car and fit stands, or blocks securely under the body jacking points. Remove the road wheel.

2   Ensure that the handbrake is off. Remove the brake drum retaining screw and using a soft-faced hammer on the outer circumference of the brake drum, tap the drum off.

3   Remove the four bolts securing the backplate. The bolts are accessible through the holes in the halfshaft flange (Fig. 8.11).

4   If it is not possible to pull the shaft assembly out, because the ball bearing on the axleshaft is too tight, screw two long bolts from behind the axleshaft at diametrically opposite points. Use these two bolts as jacking screws to push the shaft out (Fig. 8.12).

5   When refitting the halfshaft, enter it into the axle tube carefully and ensure that the splined end of the shaft enters the differential assembly.

6   Ensure that the backplate is properly seated and aligned, then insert the four retaining bolts and tighten them to the torque wrench setting given in the Specifications.

7   Refit the brake drum, insert the retaining screw and tighten it.

8   Refit the road wheel, lower the car to the ground and tighten the wheel nuts.

S   Check the oil level in the rear axle casing and top up if necessary.

Fig. 8.9 Attachment of rear axle to rear springs

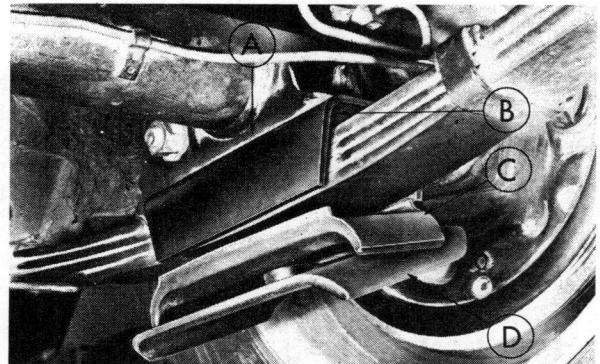

Fig. 8.10 Components of rear axle mounting

A—Rubber pad retainer plate   B—Upper rubber pad
C—Lower rubber pad   D—Attachment plate

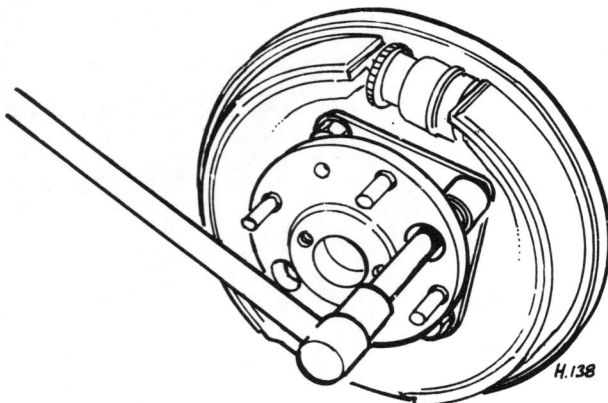

Fig. 8.11 Removal of bearing retainer plate securing bolts

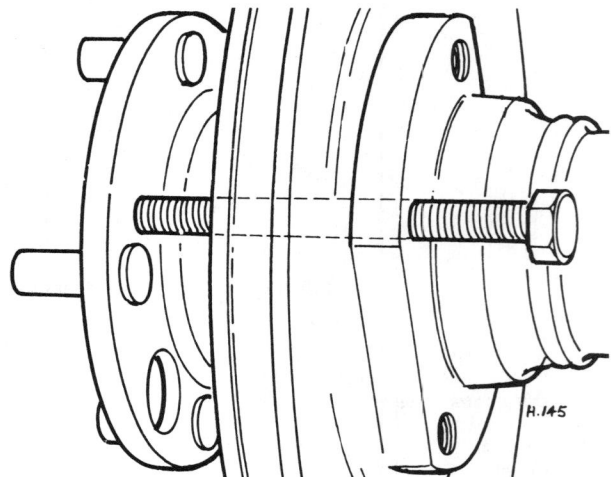

Fig. 8.12 Using long bolts to withdraw the halfshaft

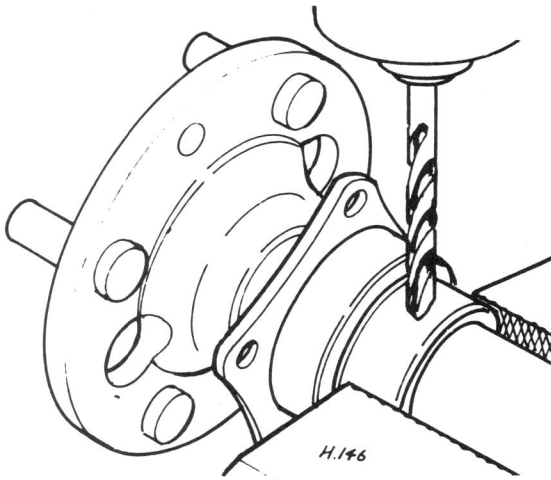

Fig. 8.13 Drilling hole in bearing inner ring prior to cutting with chisel

Fig. 8.14 Removing the retaining ring

Fig. 8.15 Fitting a rear axle bearing and retainer, using the special axle shaft tool

Fig. 8.16 Using a wheel nut and washers to fit a new wheel stud

4   Rear axleshaft bearing – removal and refitting

1   Because this operation requires either a special axle shaft tool, or a press, it should not be attempted unless one of these is available.
2   Withdraw the half shaft as described in the previous Section.
3   Using a $\frac{5}{16}$ in or 8 mm drill, make a hole through the bearing inner ring (Fig. 8.13). Using a sharp cold chisel, cut the ring across the hole (Fig. 8.14), taking care not to damage the shaft and then slide the ring off. A new ring will be required for reassembly.
4   Press the old bearing off the shaft, using a press or an axle shaft tool.
5   To reassemble, slide the axle shaft retaining plate onto the axle, then the new bearing (with the oil seal in the bearing facing away from the axle shaft flange). Finally, slide on a new bearing retaining ring onto the axle shaft.
6   Press the bearing and retaining ring onto the shaft, until the retain-ing ring is firmly against the bearing (Fig. 8.15).
7   Before fitting the axle shaft, apply some lithium grease to the outer bearing cup, or the bearing seat in the axle tube.

5   Wheel stud – removal and refitting

1   Remove the road wheel and brake drum as described in the first two paragraphs of Section 3.
2   Saturate the stud to be removed with penetrating oil, or a proprietary anti-corrosion fluid and allow time for it to penetrate.
3   Press, or drive, the defective stud towards the brake back plate until it is free of the wheel hub flange and can be removed.
4   Insert a new stud from the back of the wheel flange and turn it backwards and forwards slightly until the splines are felt to engage.
5   Pull the new stud fully into the flange by using a wheel nut and washers as shown in Fig. 8.16.

See overleaf for 'Fault diagnosis – rear axle.

6   Fault diagnosis – rear axle

Symptom	Reason/s
Vibration	Worn axleshaft bearings Loose drive flange bolts Out of balance propeller shaft Wheels out of balance Defective tyre
Noise	Insufficient lubricant Excessive wear of gears and bearings
Clunk on acceleration or deceleration	Incorrect mesh of crownwheel and pinion Excessive backlash due to wear of crownwheel and pinion teeth Worn axleshaft or differential side gear splines Loose drive flange bolts Worn drive pinion flange splines
Oil leakage	Defective or worn pinion or axleshaft oil seal Blocked axle housing breather

Chapter 9 Braking system

For modifications, and information applicable to later models, see Supplement at end of manual

Contents

Specifications

General
System type .... Dual line hydraulic, with servo assistance
Front brakes .... Disc, self-adjusting
Rear brakes .... Drum, self-adjusting
Handbrake (parking brake) .... Self-adjusting, cable operated (rear wheels only)

Front brakes
Disc thickness
    New .... 0·5 in (12·7 mm)
    Minimum .... 0·45 in (11·4 mm)
Disc run-out (max. including hub) .... 0·0035 in (0·09 mm)
Minimum permissible pad thickness .... 0·125 in (3·2 mm)

Rear brakes
Minimum permissible thickness (bonded linings) .... 0·03 in (0·8 mm)

Servo boost ratio .... 4·3 : 1

Brake fluid specification
Capri II .... ESEA-M6C-1001A (Green) or SAM-6C 9101-A (Amber)
Mercury Capri II ESA–M6C25–A

Torque wrench settings
Capri II

	lbf ft	kgf m
Caliper to front suspension unit	35 to 50	4·8 to 6·9
Brake disc to hub	30 to 34	4·2 to 4·7
Backplate to axle housing	20 to 23	2·7 to 3·2
Hydraulic unions	5 to 7	0·7 to 1·0
Bleed valve	8 max	1·0 max
Master cylinder stop screw (FoG)	4·3 to 7	0·6 to 1·0

Mercury Capri II

Caliper to front suspension	45 to 50	6·2 to 6·9
Rear back plate to axle housing	15 to 18	2·1 to 2·5
Hydraulic unions	5 to 7	0·7 to 1·0
Bleed valves	5 to 7	0·7 to 1·0

1 General description

Disc brakes are fitted to the front wheels of all models and single leading shoe drum brakes at the rear. The mechanically operated handbrake works on the rear wheels only.

All models use a floor mounted handbrake (parking brake) lever located between the front seats.

The Capri II models use either the handbrake system described in this paragraph or is similar to the system used for the Mercury Capri II model. A single cable runs from the lever to a compensator mechanism on the back of the rear axle casing. From the compensator a single cable runs to the rear brake drums. As the rear brake shoes wear, the handbrake cables operate a self-adjusting mechanism in the rear brake drums, thus doing away with the necessity for the owner to adjust the brakes.

On Mercury Capri II models, a cable runs from the parking brake lever through an abutment bracket on the rear axle, to the right-hand brake backplate. A transverse rod connects from the abutment to the left-hand brake backplate.

All models have the dual-line braking system, with a separate hydraulic system for the front and rear brakes, so that if failure of the hydraulic pipes to the front or rear brakes occurs, half the braking system still operates. Servo assistance in this condition is still available. On some models a warning light is fitted on the facia, which illuminates should either circuit fail. The bulb is connected to a pressure differential switch in the hydraulic line.

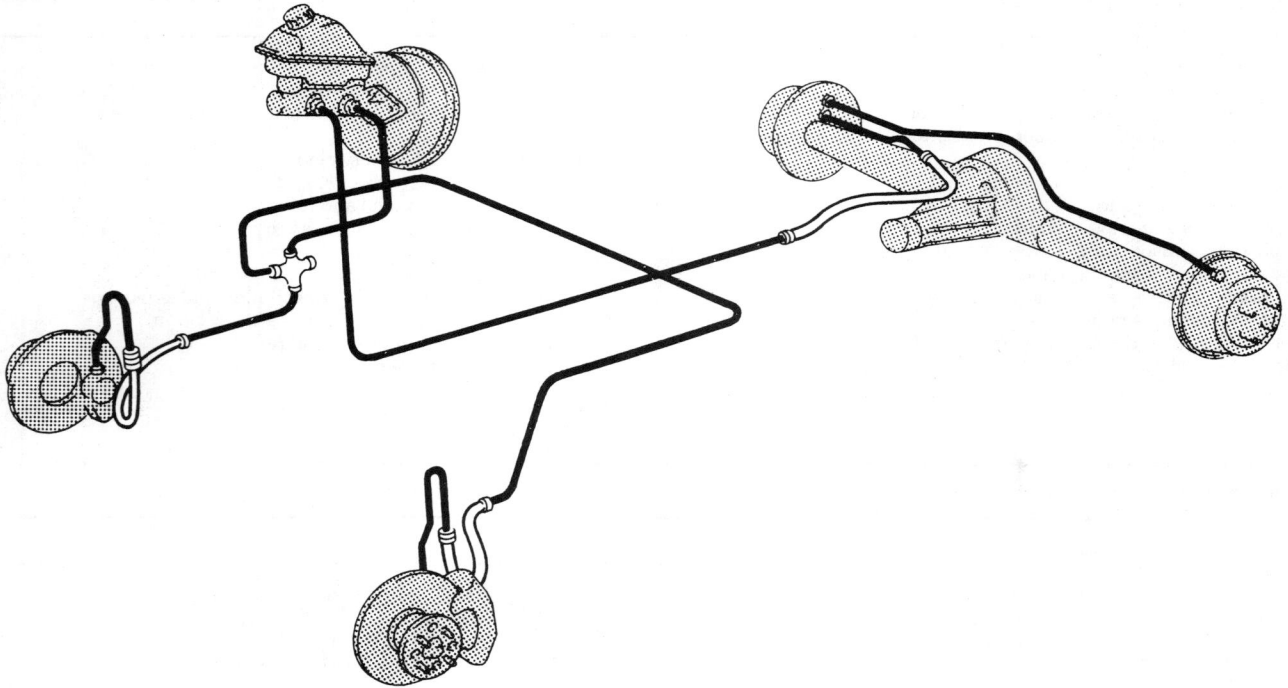

Fig. 9.1 Brake line layout (rhd)

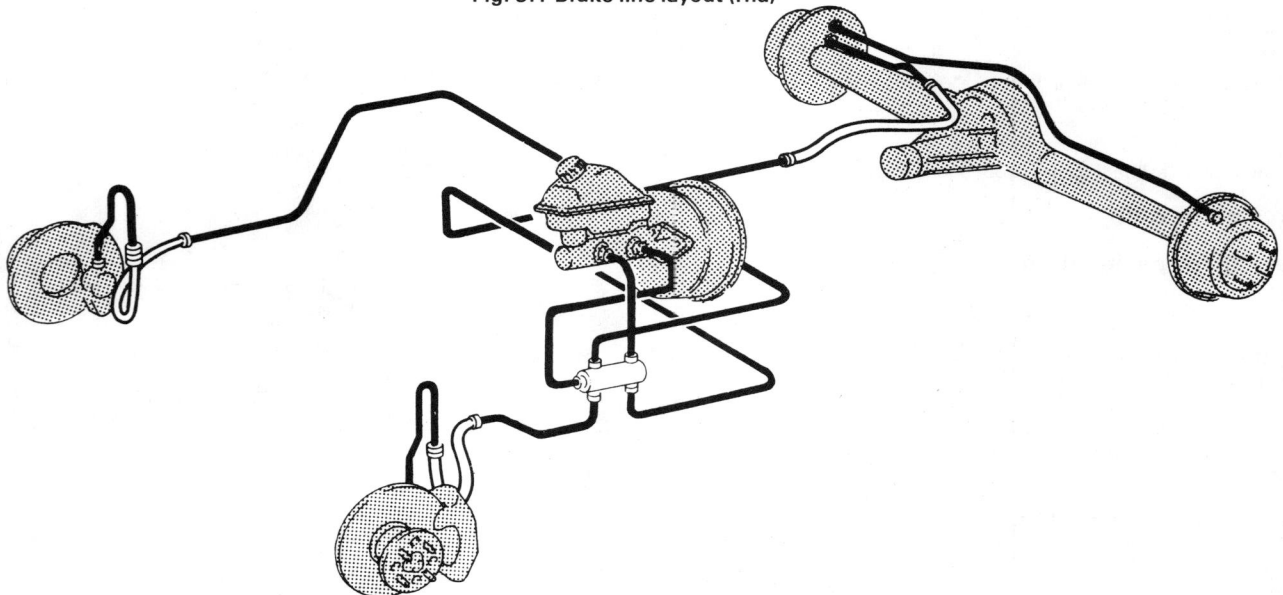

Fig. 9.2 Brake line layout (lhd)

2 Front disc pads – inspection and renewal

1 Apply the handbrake, remove the front wheel trim (where applicable), slacken the wheel nuts, jack up the front of the car and place on firmly based axle stands. Remove the front wheel.

2 Inspect the amount of friction material left on the pads. The pads must be renewed when the thickness of the friction material has been reduced to a minimum of 0.12 inches (3.00 mm).

3 If the fluid level in the master cylinder reservoir is high, when the pistons are moved into their respective bores to accommodate new pads, the level could rise sufficiently for the fluid to overflow. Place absorbent cloth around the reservoir, or syphon a little fluid out, so preventing paintwork damage being caused by the hydraulic fluid.

4 Using a pair of long nosed pliers, extract the two small clips that hold the main retaining pins in place (photo).

5 Remove the main retaining pins which run through the caliper and the metal backing of the pads and the shims (Fig. 9.3).

6 The friction pads can now be removed from the caliper. If they prove difficult to remove by hand, a pair of long nosed pliers can be used. Lift away the shims and tension springs (where fitted).

7 Carefully clean the recesses in the caliper in which the friction pads and shims lie, and the exposed faces of each piston, removing all traces of dirt or rust.

8 Using a piece of wood, carefully retract the pistons.

9 Place the brake pad tension springs on the brake pads and shims and locate in the caliper (Fig. 9.4). Insert the main pad retaining pins, making sure that the tangs of the tension springs are under the retaining pins. Secure the pins with the small wire clips.

10 Refit the roadwheel and lower the car. Tighten the wheel nuts securely and refit the wheel trim.

11 To correctly seat the pistons, pump the brake pedal several times and finally top up the hydraulic fluid level in the master cylinder reservoir as necessary.

3 Front brake caliper – removal and refitting

1 Apply the handbrake, remove the front wheel trim, slacken the wheel nuts, jack up the front of the car and place on firmly based axle stands. Remove the front wheel.

2 Wipe the top of the master cylinder reservoir and unscrew the cap. Place a piece of polythene sheet over the top of the reservoir and refit the cap.

3 Remove the friction pads, as described in Section 2.

4 If it is intended to fit new caliper pistons and/or seals, depress the brake pedal, to bring the pistons into contact with the disc and assist subsequent removal of the pistons.

5 Wipe the area clean around the flexible hose bracket and detach the pipes as described in Section 13. Tape up the end of the pipe to stop the possibility of dirt ingress.

6 Using a screwdriver, or chisel, bend back the tabs on the locking

2.4 Brake pad pin retaining clips (arrowed)

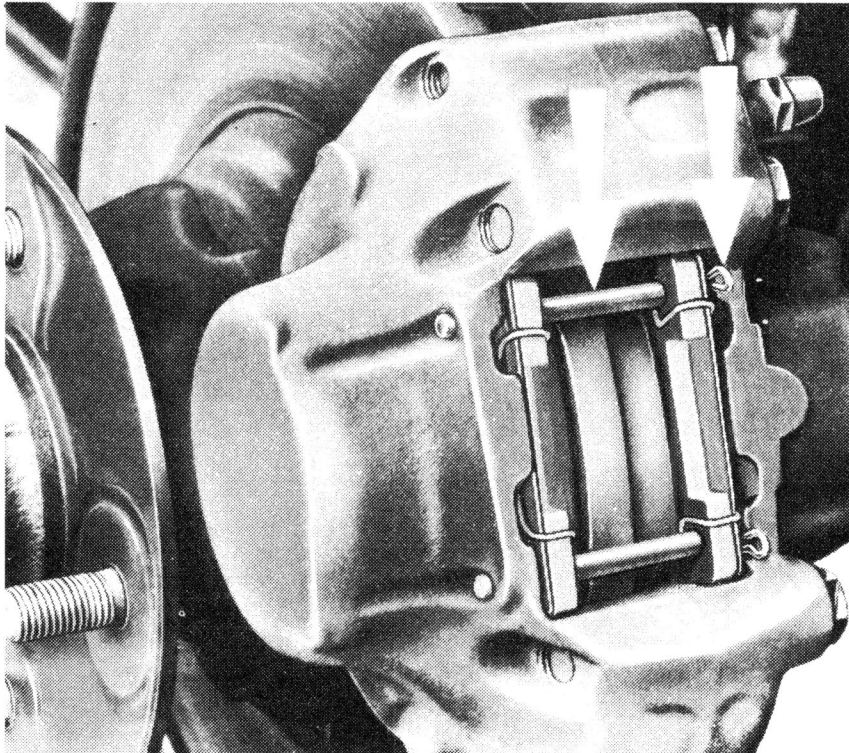

Fig. 9.3 Brake pad retaining pins and clips (arrowed)

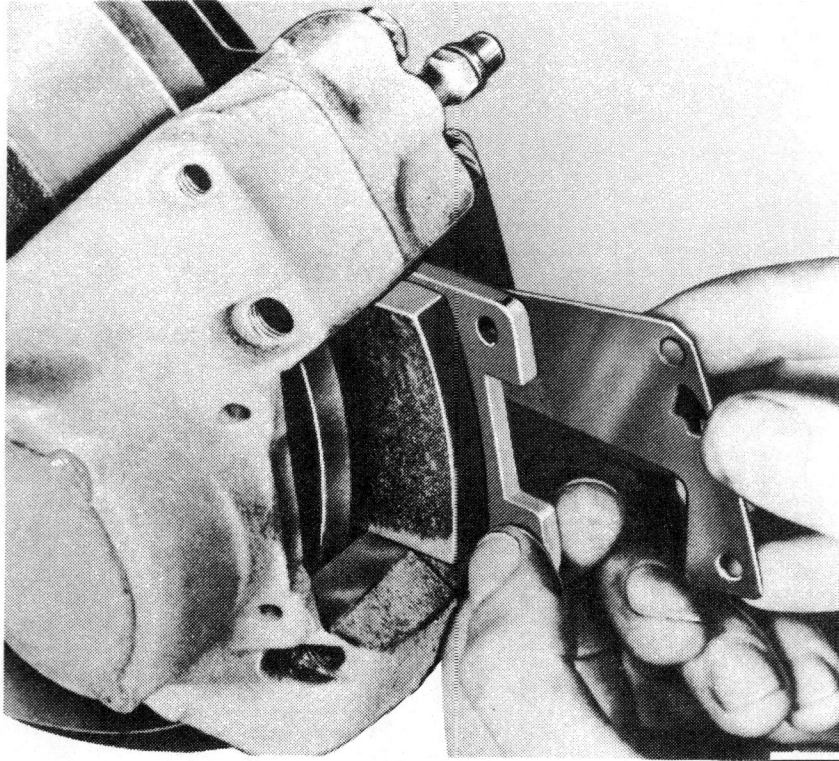

Fig. 9.4 Fitting brake pads and shims

plate and undo the two caliper body mounting bolts (Fig. 9.5). Lift away the caliper from its mounting flange on the suspension leg.

7   To refit the caliper, position it over the disc and move it until the mounting bolt holes are in line with the two front holes in the suspension leg mounting flange.

8   Fit the caliper retaining bolts through the two holes in a new locking plate and insert the bolts through the caliper body. Tighten the bolts to the specified torque wrench setting.

9   Using a screwdriver, pliers, or chisel, bend up the locking plate tabs so as to lock the bolts.

10 Remove the tape from the end of the flexible hydraulic pipe and reconnect it to the union on the hose bracket. Be careful not to cross the thread of the union nut during the initial turns. The union nut should be tightened securely using a spanner of short length.

11 Push the pistons into their respective bores so as to accommodate the pads. Watch the level of hydraulic fluid in the master cylinder reservoir as it can overflow whilst the pistons are being retracted. Place absorbent cloth around the reservoir, or syphon a little fluid out, so preventing paintwork damage.

12 Fit the pads, shims and tension springs, as described in Section 2.

13 Bleed the hydraulic system, as described in Section 14. Refit the roadwheel and lower the car.

4   Front brake caliper – servicing

1   The pistons should be removed first. To do this, half withdraw one piston from its bore in the caliper body.

2   Carefully remove the securing circlip and extract the sealing boot from its location in the lower part of the piston skirt. Completely remove the piston.

3   If difficulty is experienced in withdrawing the pistons, use a jet of compressed air or foot pump to move it out of its bore.

4   Remove the sealing bellows from its location in the annular ring which is machined in the cylinder bore.

5   Remove the piston sealing ring from the cylinder bore, using a small screwdriver, but take care not to scratch the fine finish of the bore.

6   To remove the second piston, repeat paragraphs 1 to 5 inclusive.

7   It is important that the two halves of the caliper are not separated

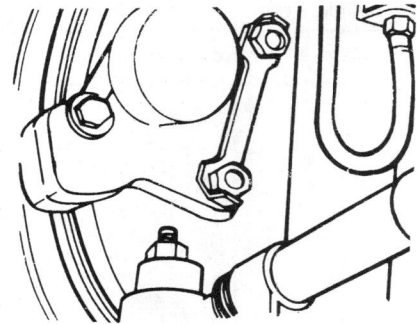

Fig. 9.5 Brake caliper mounting bolts and locking plate

under any circumstances. If hydraulic fluid leaks are evident from the joint, the caliper must be renewed complete.

8   Thoroughly wash all parts in methylated spirits, or clean hydraulic fluid. During reassembly, new rubber seals must be fitted. These should be well lubricated, with clean hydraulic fluid.

9   Inspect the pistons and bores for signs of wear, score marks, or damage and if evident, new parts should be obtained ready for fitting, or a new caliper obtained.

10 To reassemble, fit one of the piston seals into the annular groove in the cylinder bore.

11 Fit the rubber boot to the cylinder bore groove, so that the lip is turned outward.

12 Lubricate the seal and rubber boot with clean hydraulic fluid. Push the piston, crown first, through the rubber sealing bellows and then into the cylinder bore. Take care, as it is easy for the piston to damage the rubber boot.

13 With the piston half-inserted into the cylinder bore, fit the inner edge of the boot into the annular groove in the piston skirt.

14 Push the piston down the bore as far as it will go. Secure the rubber boot to the caliper with the circlip.

15 Repeat paragraphs 10 to 14 inclusive for the second piston.

16 Before refitting the caliper, plug the ends of the hydraulic pipes, so that no dirt enters them.

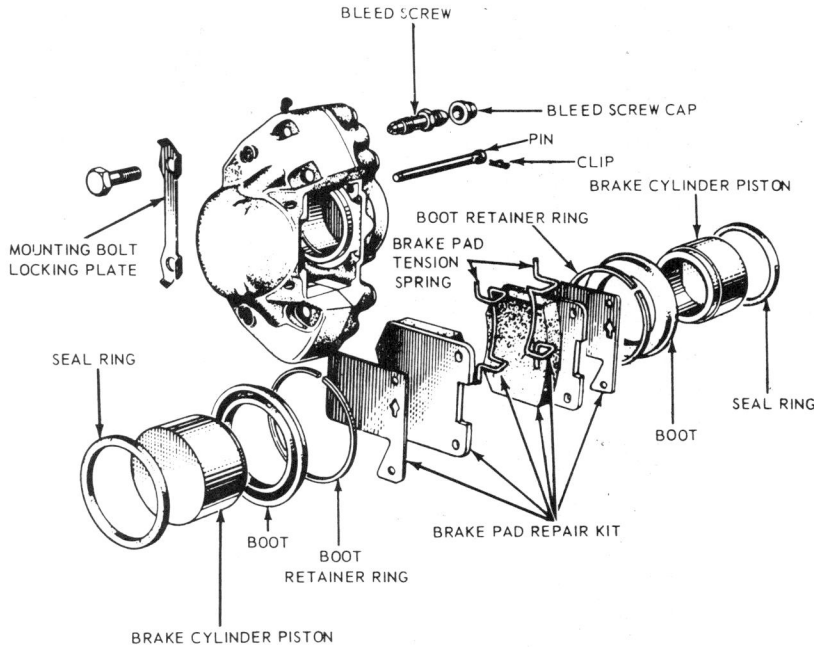

Fig. 9.6 Brake caliper components

17 After fitting the caliper remove the plugs from the hydraulic pipes and make the hydraulic connections.

5 Front disc (rotor) and hub – removal and installation

Note: *Brake discs (rotors) are fitted as matched pairs and should therefore never be renewed or reground as single items.*

1 After jacking up the car and removing the front wheel, remove the caliper, as described in Section 4.
2 Tap off the dust cap from the centre of the hub.
3 Remove the split pin from the nut retainer and lift the retainer away.
4 Unscrew the adjusting nut and lift away the thrust washer and outer taper bearing.
5 Pull off the complete hub and disc assembly from the stub axle.
6 From the back of the hub assembly, carefully prise out the grease seal and lift away the inner tapered bearing.
7 Carefully clean out the hub and wash the bearings with petrol, making sure that no grease, or oil, is allowed to get onto the brake disc.
8 Should it be necessary to separate the disc from the hub, for renewal or regrinding, first bend back the locking tabs and undo the four securing bolts. With a scriber, mark the relative positions of the hub and disc, to ensure refitting in their original positions. Separate the disc from the hub.
9 Thoroughly clean the disc and inspect for signs of deep scoring, cracks, or excessive corrosion. If these are evident, the discs may be reground, but no more than a maximum of 0.05 in (1.2 mm) from the original thickness may be removed. It is however, desirable to fit new discs.
10 To reassemble, make quite sure that the mating faces of the disc and hub are clean and place the disc on the hub, lining up any previously made marks.
11 Fit the four securing bolts and two new tab washers and tighten the bolts in a progressive and diagonal manner to the specified torque wrench setting. Bend up the locking tabs.
12 Work some grease well into the bearing, fully pack the bearing cages and rollers. **Note**: *Leave the hub and grease seal empty, to allow for subsequent expansion of the grease.*
13 To reassemble the hub, first fit the inner bearing and then gently tap the grease seal into the hub. A new seal must always be fitted, as during removal, it was probably damaged or distorted. The lip must face inwards to the hub.
14 Refit the hub and disc assembly on the stub axle and slide in the outer bearing and thrust washer.
15 Refit the adjusting nut and tighten it to a torque of 27 lbf ft (3.7

kgf m), whilst rotating the hub and disc, to ensure free movement and centralisation of the bearings. Slacken the nut back by 90°, which will give the required endfloat of 0.001 – 0.005 in (0.03 – 0.13 mm). Fit the nut retainer and a new split pin, but at this stage do not lock the split pin.
16 If a dial indicator gauge is available, it is advisable to check the disc for run-out. The measurement should be taken as near to the edge of the worn, yet smooth, part of the disc as possible, and must not exceed 0.002 in (0.05 mm). If the figure obtained is found to be excessive, check the mating surfaces of the disc and hub for dirt or damage and check the bearing and cups for excessive wear or damage.
17 If a dial indicator gauge is not available, the run-out can be checked by means of a feeler gauge placed between the casting of the caliper and the disc. Establish a reasonably tight fit with the feeler gauge between the top of the casting and the disc and rotate the disc and hub. Any high or low spots will immediately become obvious by extra tightness or looseness of the fit of the feeler gauge. The amount of run-out can be checked, by adding or subtracting feeler gauges as necessary.
18 Once the disc run-out has been checked and found to be correct, bend the ends of the split pin back and replace the dust cap.
19 Reconnect the brake hydraulic pipe and bleed the brakes as described in Section 14 of this Chapter.

6 Drum brake shoes – inspection and renewal

After high mileages, it will be necessary to fit replacement shoes. Refitting new brake linings to shoes is not considered economic, or possible, without the use of special equipment. However, if the services of a local garage or workshop having brake relining equipment are available, then there is no reason why the original shoes should not be relined successfully. Ensure that the correct specification linings are fitted to the shoes.

1 Chock the front wheels, jack up the rear of the car and place on firmly based axle stands. Remove the roadwheel and release the handbrake.
2 Release the brake drum retaining screw and, using a soft-faced hammer on the outer circumference of the brake drum, remove the brake drum (photo).
3 The brake linings should be renewed if they are so worn that the rivet heads are flush with the surface of the lining. If bonded linings are fitted, they must be renewed when the lining material has worn down to the minimum specified thickness.
4 Depress each shoe holding down spring and rotate the spring retaining washer through 90°, to disengage it from the pin secured to

6.2 Rear brake with drum removed (Capri II)

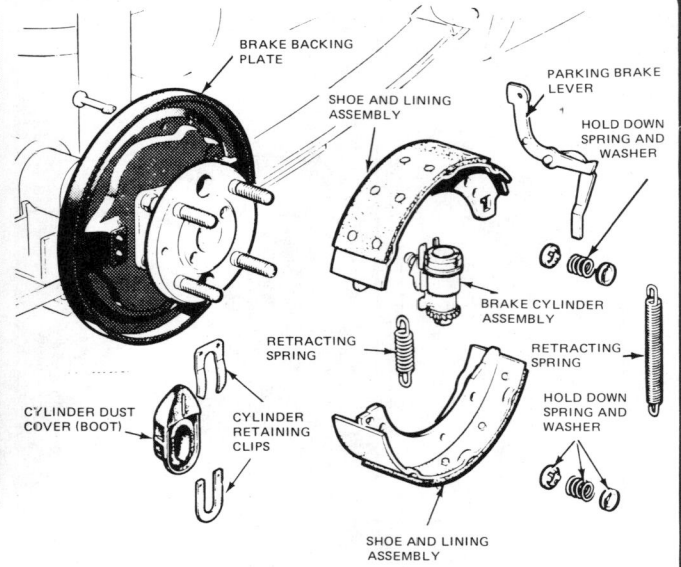

Fig. 9.7 Rear brake assembly (Capri II) – exploded view

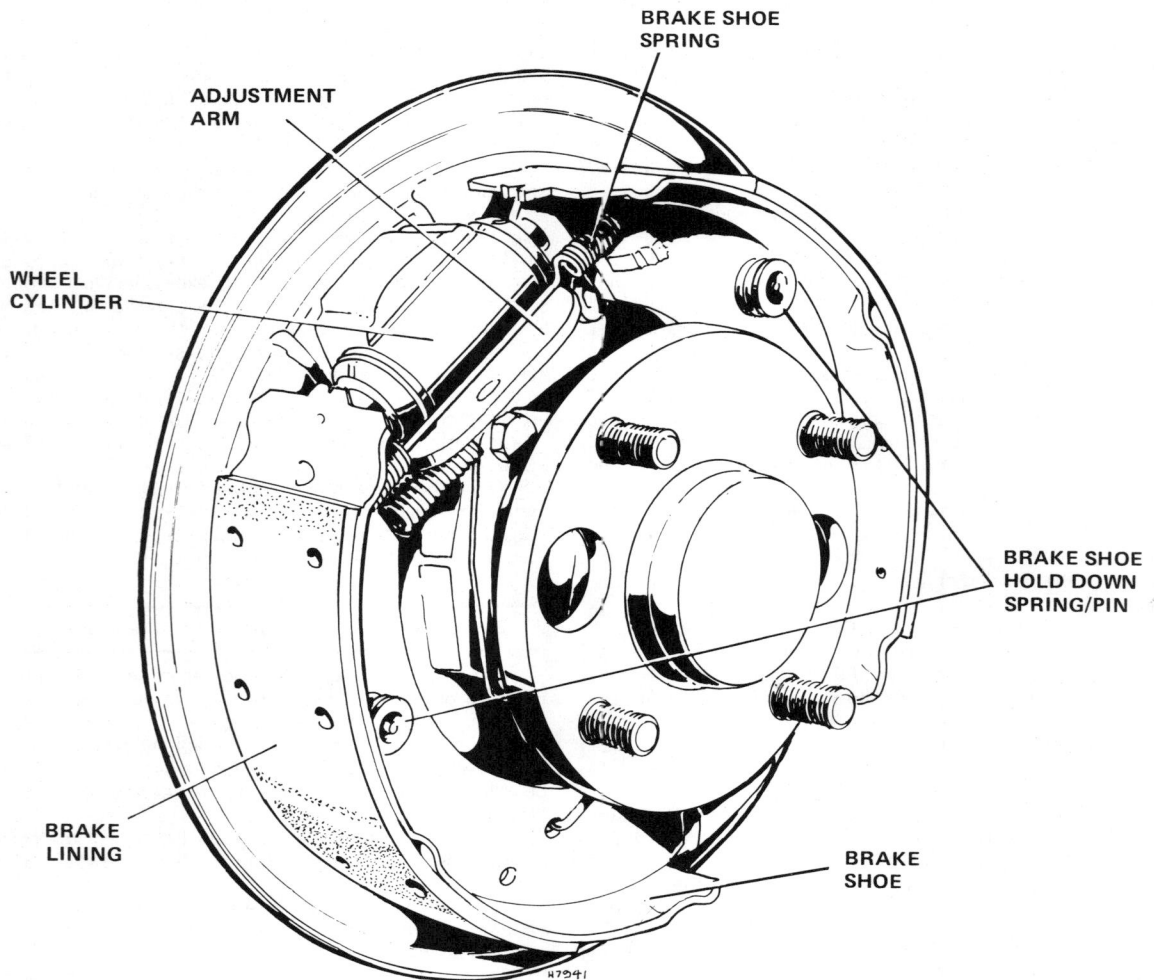

BRAKE BACKING PLATE

SHOE AND LINING ASSEMBLY

PARKING BRAKE LEVER

HOLD DOWN SPRING AND WASHER

BRAKE CYLINDER ASSEMBLY

RETRACTING SPRING

RETRACTING SPRING

CYLINDER DUST COVER (BOOT)

CYLINDER RETAINING CLIPS

HOLD DOWN SPRING AND WASHER

SHOE AND LINING ASSEMBLY

ADJUSTMENT ARM

BRAKE SHOE SPRING

WHEEL CYLINDER

BRAKE SHOE HOLD DOWN SPRING/PIN

BRAKE LINING

BRAKE SHOE

Fig. 9.8 Rear brake assembly (Mercury Capri II)

the backplate. Lift away the washer and spring.

5 Ease each shoe from its location slot in the fixed pivot and then detach the other end of each shoe from the wheel cylinder.

6 Note which way round and into which holes in the shoes the two retracting springs fit.

7 Lift away the two brake shoes and retracting springs.

8 If the shoes are left off, make sure that the brake pedal is not operated. Place an elastic band round the wheel cylinder to stop the piston falling out.

9 *Capri II:* Withdraw the ratchet wheel assembly from the wheel cylinder and rotate the wheel until it abuts the slot head bolt shoulder. If this is not done, difficulty will arise in refitting the brake drum.

10 Thoroughly clean all traces of dust from the shoes, backplates and brake drums using a brush. Do not blow the dust out and be careful not to inhale any. Brake dust causes a reduction in braking efficiency, so that it is important that it is cleaned out.

11 Check that the piston is free in the cylinder, that the rubber dust covers are undamaged and in position, and that there are no hydraulic leaks.

12 Prior to reassembly, smear a trace of brake grease on the shoe support pads, brake shoe pivots and on the ratchet wheel face and threads.

13 To reassemble, first fit the retracting springs to the shoe webs in the same position as was noted during removal.

14 Fit the shoe assembly to the backplate by first positioning the rear shoe in its location on the fixed pivot and over the parking brake link. Follow this with the front shoe.

15 Secure each shoe to the backplate with the spring and dished washer (dish facing inwards) and turned through 90° to lock it in position. Make sure that each shoe is firmly seated on the backplate.

16 *Mercury Capri II:* Reset the self-adjuster unit to its minimum setting by gently prising the adjuster arm from the adjuster wheel with a small screwdriver. Push the adjuster arm towards the backplate until the arm reaches the top of its arc.

17 Refit the brake drum, aligning the paint mark on the drum with that on one of the studs, and push it along the studs as far as it will go. Secure with retaining screw.

18 The shoes must next be centralised, by the brake being depressed firmly several times.

19 Pull on and then release the handbrake several times, to reset the adjuster mechanism on Capri II models. It is important to note that with the ratchet wheel in the fully off adjustment position, it is possible for the indexing lever on the parking brake link to over-ride the ratchet and stay in this position. When operating the link lever it is necessary to ensure that it always returns to the fully off position each time.

20 Refit the roadwheel and lower the car. Road test to ensure correct operation of the brakes.

7 Drum brake wheel cylinder (Capri II) – removal, inspection and servicing

1 Refer to Section 6 and remove the brake drum and shoes. Clean down the rear of the backplate, using a stiff brush. Place a quantity of rag under the backplate to catch any hydraulic fluid that may issue from the open pipe or wheel cylinder.

2 Wipe the top of the brake master cylinder reservoir and unscrew the cap. Place a piece of polythene sheet over the top of the reservoir and refit the cap.

3 Using an open ended spanner, carefully unscrew the hydraulic pipe connection union at the rear of the wheel cylinder. To prevent dirt entering, tape over the end of the pipe.

4 Withdraw the split pin and clevis pin from the handbrake lever at the rear of the backplate.

5 Using a screwdriver, carefully ease the rubber dust cover from the rear of the backplate and lift away.

6 Pull off the two U-shaped retainers holding the wheel cylinder to the backplate, noting that the spring retainer is fitted from the hand-brake link end of the wheel cylinder and the flat retainer from the other end, the flat retainer being located between the spring retainer and the wheel cylinder.

7 The wheel cylinder and handbrake link can now be removed from the brake backplate.

8 To dismantle the wheel cylinder, first remove the small metal clip holding the rubber dust cap in place, then prise off the dust cap.

9 Take the piston complete with its seal out of the cylinder bore and then withdraw the spring. Should the piston and seal prove difficult to remove, gentle pressure will push it out of the bore.

10 Inspect the cylinder bore for score marks caused by impurities in hydraulic fluid. If any are found, the cylinder and piston will require renewal as an assembly.

11 If the cylinder bore is sound, thoroughly clean it out with fresh hydraulic fluid.

12 The old rubber seal will probably be visibly worn or swollen. Detach it from the piston, smear a new rubber seal with hydraulic fluid and assemble it to the piston with the flat face of the seal next to the piston rear shoulder.

13 Reassembly is a direct reversal of the dismantling procedure. If the rubber dust cap appears to be worn, or damaged, it should also be renewed.

14 Before commencing refitting, smear the area where the cylinder slides on the backplate and the brake shoe support pads, brake shoe pivots, ratchet wheel face and threads with brake grease.

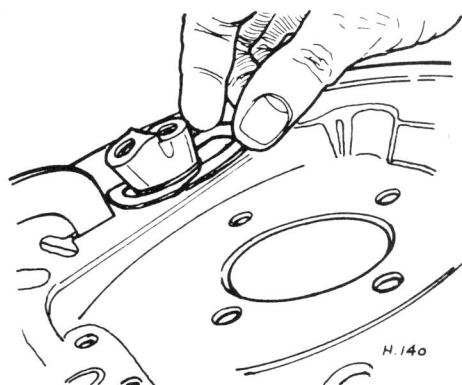

Fig. 9.9 Removing the retaining plate of the rear wheel cylinder (Capri II)

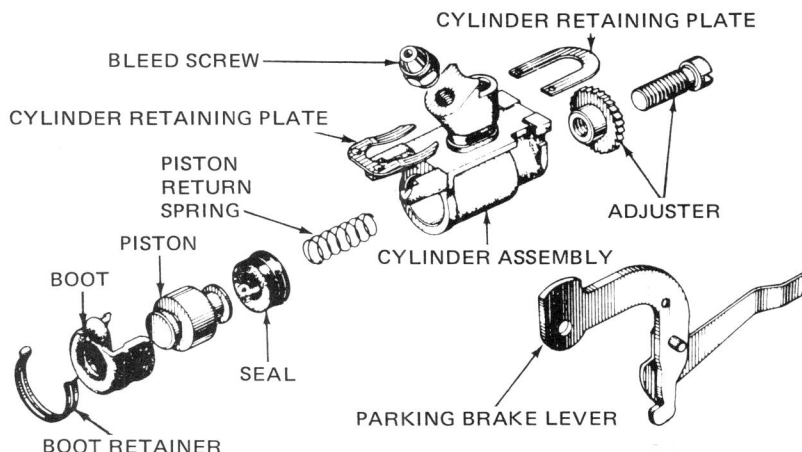

Fig. 9.10 Rear wheel cylinder components (Capri II)

15 Refitting is a straightforward reversal of the removal sequence, but the following parts should be checked with extra care.

16 After fitting the rubber boot, check that the wheel cylinder can slide freely in the backplate and that the handbrake link operates the self-adjusting mechanism correctly.

17 It is important to note that the self-adjusting ratchet mechanism on the right-hand rear brake is right-hand threaded and the mechanism on the left-hand rear brake is left-hand threaded.

18 When refitting is complete, bleed the braking system as described in Section 14.

8 Drum brake wheel cylinder (Mercury Capri II) — removal, inspection and servicing

1 Initially proceed as described in paragraphs 1 to 3 of the previous Section, but do not pull the hydraulic pipe out of the rear of the wheel cylinder, as it may bend and be difficult to refit later.

2 Remove the wheel cylinder attaching bolts and washers. Remove the cylinder and tape over the end of the hydraulic pipe.

3 To dismantle the wheel cylinder, first remove the rubber dust covers.

4 Slide out the piston assemblies and remove the spring from the cylinder bore.

5 Where applicable, unscrew the bleed nipple.

6 Refer to the procedure given in paragraphs 10 to 12 in the previous Section, bearing in mind that there are two pistons and seals.

7 Reassembly of the wheel cylinder is the reverse of the dismantling procedure. Ensure that the parts are adequately lubricated with hydraulic fluid.

8 The wheel cylinder can now be refitted to the backplate, following the reverse of the removal procedure. On completion, bleed the brakes, as described in Section 14.

9 Drum brake backplate — removal and refitting

1 To remove the backplate, refer to Chapter 8 and remove the half-shaft.

2 Detach the handbrake cable from the handbrake relay lever on the backplate.

3 Wipe off the top of the master cylinder reservoir and unscrew the cap. Place a piece of polythene sheet over the top of the reservoir and refit the cap.

4 Using an open ended spanner, carefully unscrew the hydraulic pipe connection union at the rear of the wheel cylinder. To prevent dirt entering, tape over the pipe ends.

5 The brake backplate may now be lifted away.

6 Refitting is the reverse sequence to removal. It will be necessary to bleed the brake hydraulic system, as described in Section 14.

10 Master cylinder — removal and refitting

1 Apply the handbrake and chock the front wheels. Drain the fluid from the master cylinder reservoir and master cylinder, by attaching a plastic bleed tube to one of the front brake bleed screws. Undo the screw one turn and then pump the fluid out into a clean glass container by means of the brake pedal. Hold the brake pedal against the floor at the end of each stroke and tighten the bleed screw. When the pedal has returned to its normal position, loosen the bleed screw and repeat the process. The above sequence should now be carried out on one of the rear brake bleed screws.

2 Wipe the area around the two union nuts on the side of the master cylinder body and using an open ended spanner, undo the two union nuts. Tape over the ends of the pipes to stop dirt entering.

3 Undo and remove the two nuts and spring washers that secure the master cylinder to the rear of the servo unit. Lift away the master cylinder, taking care not to damage the servo unit and ensure that no hydraulic fluid is allowed to drip onto the paintwork.

4 Refitting the master cylinder is the reverse sequence to removal. Always start the union nuts before finally tightening the master cylinder nuts. It will be necessary to bleed the complete hydraulic system; full details will be found in Section 14.

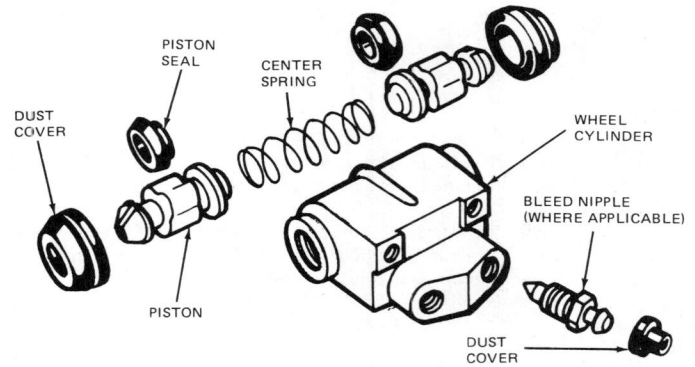

Fig. 9.11 Rear wheel cylinder components (Mercury Capri II)

11 Master cylinder (FoG) — servicing

If a new master cylinder is to be fitted, it will be necessary to lubricate the seals before fitting to the car as they have a protective coating when originally assembled. Remove the blanking plugs from the hydraulic pipe union seatings. Inject clean hydraulic fluid into the master cylinder and operate the primary piston several times so that the fluid spreads over all the internal working surfaces.

If the master cylinder is to be dismantled after removal, proceed as follows:

1 The component parts are shown in Fig. 9.12.

2 Prior to dismantling, wipe the exterior of the master cylinder clean.

3 Using a clean metal rod of suitable diameter, depress the primary piston until it reaches the stop, so that the pressure of the intermediate piston is removed from the stop screw.

4 Unscrew the stop screw and remove the sealing washer. Release the pressure on the piston.

5 Lightly depress the primary piston again, to relieve the pressure on the circlip located in the bore at the flanged end of the cylinder. With a pair of pointed pliers, remove the circlip, taking care not to scratch the finely finished bore.

6 Lift away the stop washer and withdraw the primary piston assembly.

7 Undo and remove the connecting screw and withdraw the deep spring retainer, spring, flat spring retainer, seal retainer, primary seal, seal protector and secondary seal from the piston.

8 The intermediate piston assembly may now be removed, by lightly tapping on the master cylinder against a wooden base.

9 Withdraw the spring, spring retainer, seal retainer, primary cup seal, seal protector and the two secondary seals from the piston.

10 Thoroughly wash all parts in either methylated spirit, or clean approved hydraulic fluid and place in order ready for inspection.

11 Examine the bores of the master cylinder carefully for any signs of scoring, ridges or corrosion and, if it is found to be smooth all over, new seals can be fitted. If there is any doubt as to the condition of the bore, a new assembly must be obtained.

12 If examination of the seals shows them to be apparently oversize or very loose on their seats, suspect oil contamination in the system. Oil will swell these rubber seals, and if one is found to be swollen it is reasonable to assume that all seals in the braking system will require attention.

13 Before reassembly, wash all parts in methylated spirit, or clean approved hydraulic fluid. **Do not** use any other type of oil or cleaning fluid or the seals will be damaged.

14 Reassemble according to the piston assembly diagram, noting the following points:

Dip all seals in clean hydraulic fluid before fitting.
Secondary seals are identified by a silver band.
Tighten the stop screw to the specified torque setting.

12 Master cylinder (FoB) — servicing

1 Refer to the introduction in Section 11.

2 The component parts are shown in Fig. 9.14.

3 Prior to dismantling, wipe the exterior of the master cylinder clean.

SPRING SEAT DISC PRIMARY CUP WASHER PISTON SECONDARY CUP PRIMARY CUP RETAINER SCREW SPRING RETAINER SPRING SEAT DISC PRIMARY CUP STOP WASHER SECONDARY CUP INTERMEDIATE RING WASHER SNAP RING SECONDARY CUP PISTON WASHER STOP SCREW SEAL

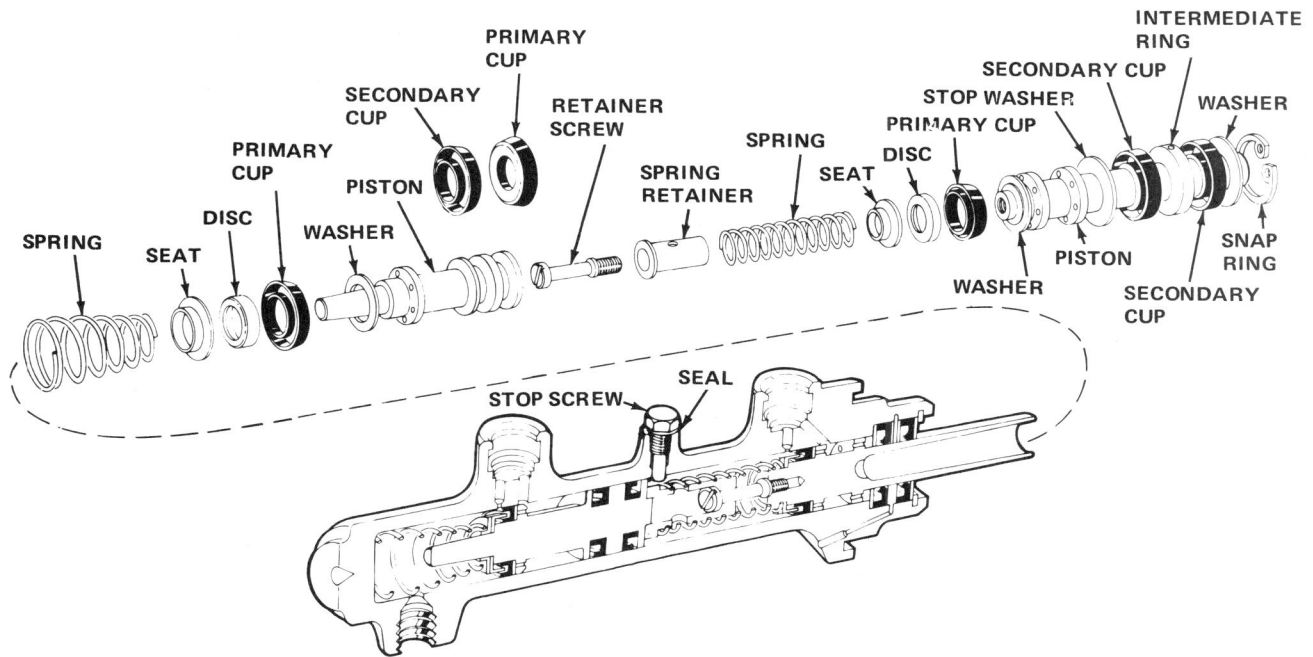

Fig. 9.12 Master cylinder components (FoG)

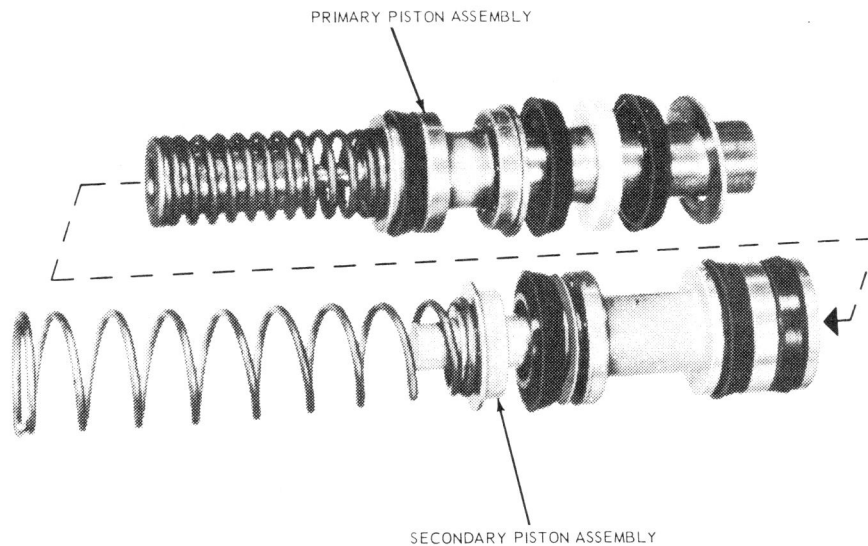

PRIMARY PISTON ASSEMBLY

SECONDARY PISTON ASSEMBLY

Fig. 9.13 Master cylinder piston assembly (FoG)

4   Undo and remove the two screws and spring washers holding the reservoir to the master cylinder body. Lift away the reservoir. Using an Allen key, or wrench, unscrew the tipping valve nut and lift away the seal. Using a suitable diameter rod, push the primary plunger down the bore, this operation enabling the tipping valve to be withdrawn.

5   Using a compressed air jet, very carefully applied to the rear outlet connection, blow out all the master cylinder internal components. Alternatively, shake out the parts. Take care that adequate precautions are taken to ensure all parts are caught as they emerge.

6   Separate the primary and secondary plungers from the intermediate spring. Use the fingers to remove the gland seal from the primary plunger.

7   The secondary plunger assembly should be separated by lifting the thimble leaf over the shouldered end of the plunger. Using the fingers, remove the seal from the secondary plunger.

8   Depress the secondary spring, allowing the valve stem to slide through the keyhole in the thimble, thus releasing the tension on the spring.

9   Detach the valve spacer, taking care of the spring washer which

will be found located under the valve head.

10 For information on inspection, refer to Section 11, paragraphs 10 to 13 inclusive.

11 All components should be assembled wet, by dipping in clean brake fluid. Using fingers only, fit new seals to the primary and secondary plungers, ensuring that they are the correct way round. Place the dished washer with the dome against the underside of the valve seat. Hold it in position with the valve spacer, ensuring that the legs face towards the valve seal.

12 Refit the plunger return spring centrally on the spacer, insert the thimble into the spring and depress until the valve stem engages in the keyhole of the thimble.

13 Insert the reduced end of the plunger into the thimble, until the thimble engages under the shoulder of the plunger and press home the thimble leaf. Refit the intermediate spring between the primary and secondary plungers.

14 Check that the master cylinder bore is clean and smear with clean brake fluid. With the complete assembly suitably wetted with brake fluid, carefully insert the assembly into the bore. Ease the lips of the

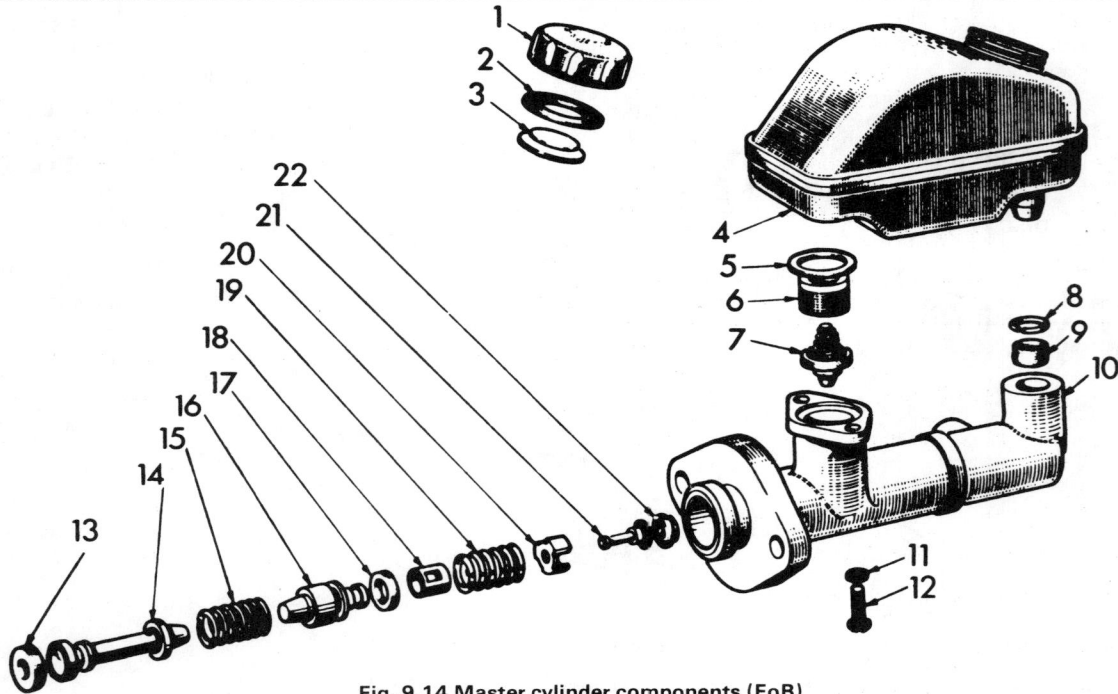

Fig. 9.14 Master cylinder components (FoB)

1 Reservoir cap	7 Tipping valve	13 Seal	18 Spring retainer
2 Cap seal	8 Circlip	14 Primary piston	19 Spring
3 Seal retainer	9 Gasket	15 Spring	20 Spring retainer
4 Reservoir	10 Master cylinder body	16 Secondary piston	21 Valve
5 Sealing ring	11 Washer	17 Seal	22 Seal
6 Tipping valve retainer	12 Screw		

piston seals into the bore, taking care that they do not roll over. Push the assembly fully home.

15 Refit the tipping valve assembly and seal to the cylinder bore, and tighten the securing nut to a torque wrench setting of 27 to 35 lbf ft (4.8 to 6.22 kgf m).

16 Using a clean screwdriver, push the primary piston in and out, checking that the recuperating valve opens when the screwdriver is withdrawn and closes again when it is pushed in.

17 Check the condition of the front and rear reservoir gaskets and if there is any doubt as to their condition, they must be renewed.

18 Refit the hydraulic fluid reservoir and tighten the two retaining screws.

19 The master cylinder is now ready for refitting to the servo unit. Bleed the complete hydraulic system and road test the car.

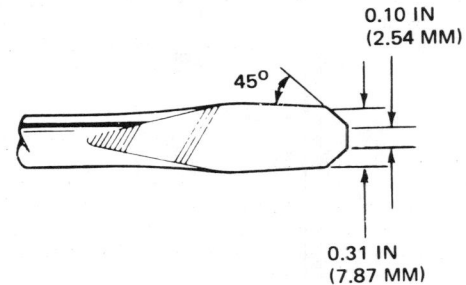

Fig. 9.15 Centralising tool for valve and switch assembly

13 Flexible hose – inspection, removal and refitting

1 Inspect the condition of the flexible hydraulic hoses leading from under the front wings to the brackets on the front suspension units, and also the single hose on the rear axle casing. If they are swollen, damaged or chafed, they must be renewed.

2 Undo the locknuts at both ends of the flexible hoses and then holding the hexagon nut on the flexible hose steady, undo the other union nut and remove the flexible hose and washer.

3 Refitting is a reversal of the removal procedure, but carefully check that all the securing brackets are in sound condition and that the locknuts are tight.

14 Bleeding the hydraulic system

1 Removal of all the air from the hydraulic system is essential to the correct working of the braking system. Before undertaking this, examine the fluid reservoir cap to ensure that both vent holes, one on top and the second underneath but not in line, are clear; check the

level of fluid and top-up if required.

2 Check all brake line unions and connections for possible seepage, and at the same time check the condition of the rubber hoses, which may be perished.

3 If the condition of the wheel cylinders is in doubt, check for possible signs of fluid leakage.

4 If there is any possibility of incorrect fluid having been put into the system, drain all the fluid out and flush through with methylated spirits. Renew all piston seals and cups since these will be affected and could possibly fail under pressure.

5 Gather together a clean jar, a 9 inch (230 mm) length of tubing which fits tightly over the bleed nipples, and a tin of the correct brake fluid.

6 Centralise the piston in the pressure differential valve (see Section 15). To do this, modify the blade of a screwdriver as shown and after removing the rubber cover from the hose of the valve, insert the screwdriver and wedge it to hold the piston centralised (Fig. 9.15).

7 Clean the dirt from around the front caliper bleed nipple which is furthest from the master cylinder (see Figs. 9.1 and 9.2).

8 Open the bleed valve with a spanner and then have an assistant quickly depress the brake pedal. After slowly releasing the pedal for a

moment, to allow the fluid to refill in the master cylinder, depress it again. This will force air from the system. Continue until no more air bubbles can be seen coming from the tube. At intervals, make certain that the reservoir is kept topped up, otherwise air will enter at this point again.

9   Repeat this operation on the other front brake and the rear brakes (some models have one bleed nipple only on the rear brakes). When completed, check the level of the fluid in the reservoir and then check the feel of the brake pedal, which should be firm and free from any 'spongy' action, which is normally associated with air in the system.

15 Pressure differential switch – description and servicing

1   This device is incorporated in the hydraulic circuit on some models. It is a switch in which a piston is kept 'in balance' when the hydraulic pressure in the independent front and rear hydraulic brake circuits is equal. In the event of a drop in pressure in either circuit, the piston is displaced and makes an electrical contact to illuminate a warning light on the instrument panel.

2   To dismantle the switch, first disconnect the hydraulic pipes at their unions on the switch body. To prevent a loss of hydraulic fluid, either place a piece of polythene under the cap of the master cylinder and screw it down tightly, or plug the ends of the two pipes leading from the master cylinder.

3   Referring to Fig. 9.16, disconnect the wiring from the switch assembly.

4   Undo the single bolt holding the assembly to the rear of the engine compartment and remove it from the car.

5   To dismantle the assembly, start by undoing the end plug and discarding the gasket.

6   Unscrew the switch assembly from the top of the unit then push the piston out of the bore, taking extreme care not to damage the bore during this operation.

7   Take the small seals from the piston, followed by the sleeves.

8   Carefully examine the piston and the bore of the actuator for score marks, scratches or damage. If any are found the complete unit must be exchanged for a new one. Also check that the piston retaining clips are secure and undamaged.

9   Reassembly of the unit is the reverse of the removal procedure. Ensure that all parts are adequately lubricated with hydraulic brake fluid.

16 Vacuum servo unit – description

1   A vacuum servo unit is fitted into the brake hydraulic circuit, in series with the master cylinder, to provide assistance to the driver when the brake pedal is depressed. This reduces the effort required by the driver to operate the brakes, under all braking conditions.

2   This unit operates by vacuum, obtained from the induction manifold and comprises basically a booster diaphragm and check valve. The servo unit and hydraulic master cylinder are connected together so that the servo unit piston rod acts as the master cylinder pushrod. The driver's braking effort is transmitted through another pushrod to the servo unit piston and its built-in control system. The servo unit piston does not fit tightly into the cylinder, but has a strong diaphragm to keep its edges in constant contact with the cylinder wall, so ensuring an air-tight seal between the two parts. The forward chamber is held under vacuum conditions created in the inlet manifold of the engine and during periods when the brake pedal is not in use, the controls open a passage to the rear chamber, so placing it under vacuum conditions as well. When the brake pedal is depressed, the vacuum passage to the rear chamber is cut off and the chamber exposed to atmospheric pressure. The consequent rush of air pushes the servo piston forward in the vacuum chamber and operates the main pushrod to the master cylinder.

3   The controls are designed so that assistance is given under all conditions. When the brakes are not required, vacuum in the rear chamber is established when the brake pedal is released. All air from the atmosphere entering the rear chamber is passed through a small air filter.

4   Under normal operating conditions the vacuum servo unit is very reliable and does not require overhaul except at very high mileages. In this case it is far better to obtain a service exchange unit, rather than repair the original unit.

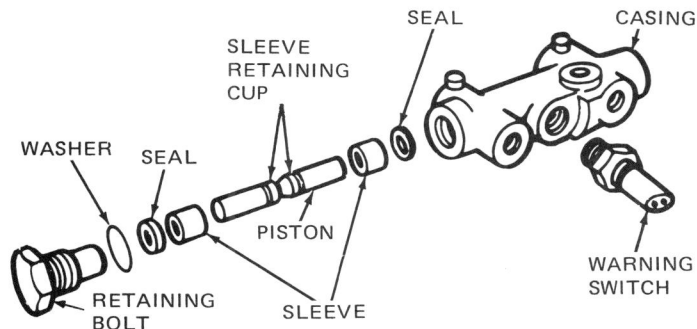
Fig. 9.16 Pressure differential valve – exploded view

17 Vacuum servo unit – removal and refitting

1   Slacken the clip securing the vacuum hose to the servo unit and carefully draw the hose from its union.

2   Refer to Section 10 and remove the master cylinder.

3   Using a pair of pliers, remove the spring clip in the end of the brake pedal to pushrod clevis pin. Lift away the clevis pin and bushes.

4   Undo and remove the nuts and spring washers, securing the servo union mounting bracket to the bulkhead. Lift away the servo unit and bracket.

5   Undo and remove the four nuts and spring washers, that secure the bracket to the servo unit.

6   Refitting the servo unit is the reverse sequence to removal. It will be necessary to bleed the brake hydraulic system as described in Section 14.

18 Vacuum servo unit – servicing

Thoroughly clean the outside of the unit using a stiff brush and wipe with a non-fluffy rag. It cannot be too strongly emphasised that cleanliness is important when working on the servo. Before any attempt be made to dismantle, refer to Fig. 9.18, where it will be seen that two items of equipment are required. Firstly, a base plate must be made to enable the unit to be safely held in a vice. Secondly, a lever must be made similar to the form shown. Without these items it is impossible to dismantle satisfactorily.

To dismantle the unit proceed as follows:

1   Refer to Fig. 9.18 and using a file, or scriber, make a line across the two halves of the unit to act as a datum for alignment.

2   Fit the previously made base plate into a firm vice and attach the unit to the plate, using the master cylinder studs.

3   Fit the lever to the four studs on the rear shell as shown.

4   Use a piece of long rubber hose and connect one end to the adapter on the engine inlet manifold and the other end to the non-return valve. Start the engine and this will create a vacuum in the unit, so drawing the two halves together.

5   Rotate the lever in an anti-clockwise direction until the front shell indentations are in line with the recesses in the rim of the rear shell. Press the lever assembly down firmly, whilst an assistant stops the engine and quickly removes the vacuum pipe from the inlet manifold connector. Depress the operating rod so as to release the vacuum, whereupon the front and rear halves should part. If necessary, use a soft-faced hammer and lightly tap the front half to break the bond.

6   Lift away the rear shell, followed by the diaphragm return spring, the dust cap, end cap and the filter. Also, withdraw the diaphragm. Press down the valve rod and shake out the valve retaining plate. Then separate the valve rod assembly from the diaphragm plate.

7   Gently ease the spring washer from the diaphragm plate and withdraw the pushrod and reaction disc.

8   The seal and plate assembly in the end of the front shell are a press fit. It is recommended that, unless the seal is to be renewed, they are left undisturbed.

9   Thoroughly clean all parts. Inspect them for signs of damage, stripped threads etc., and obtain new ones as necessary. All seals should be renewed and for this a 'Major Repair Kit' should be purchased. This kit will also contain two separate greases, which must be used as directed and not interchanged.

10 To reassemble, first smear the seal and bearing with Ford grease

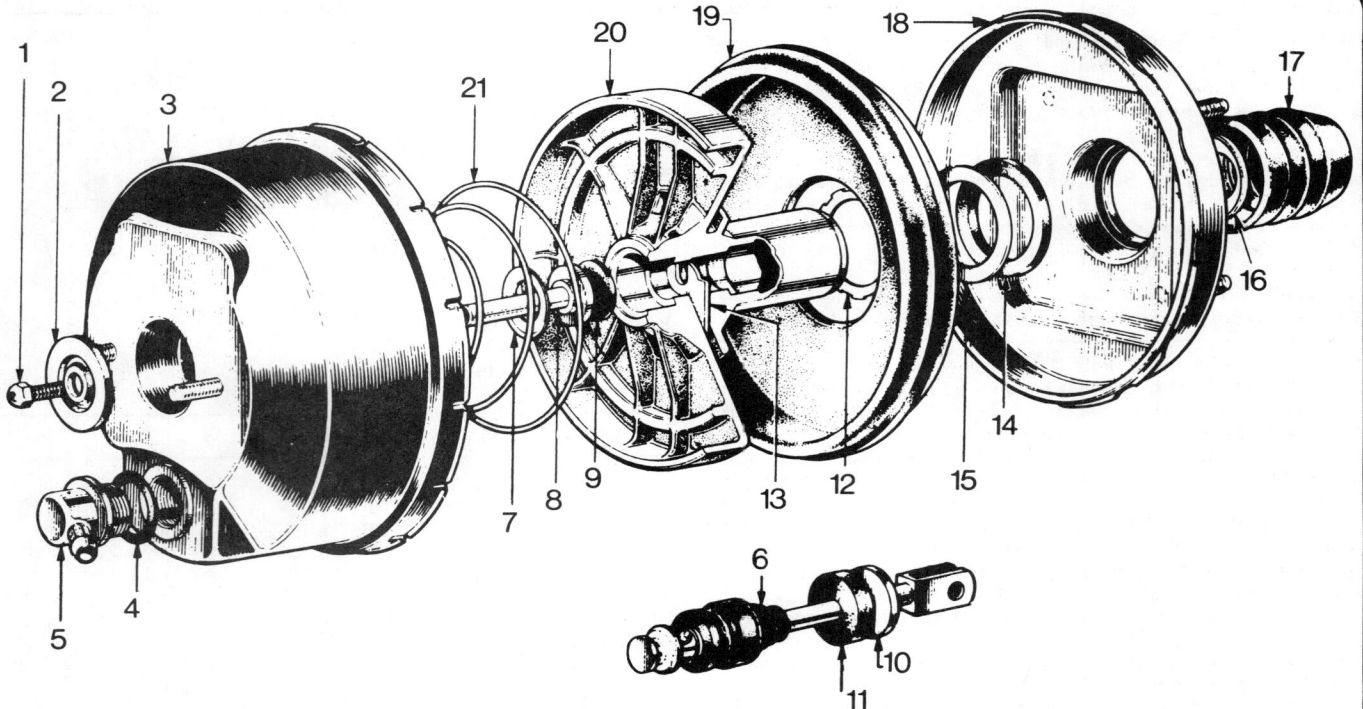

Fig. 9.17 Brake servo (booster) components

1	Bolt	8	Brake servo pushrod	15	Piston guide
2	Seat assembly	9	Reaction disc	16	Filter retainer
3	Front shell	10	Washer	17	Dust cover
4	Seal	11	Filter	18	Rear shell
5	Valve assembly	12	Castellated washer	19	Diaphragm
6	Pushrod assembly	13	Stop key	20	Diaphragm plate
7	Dished washer	14	Seal	21	Spring

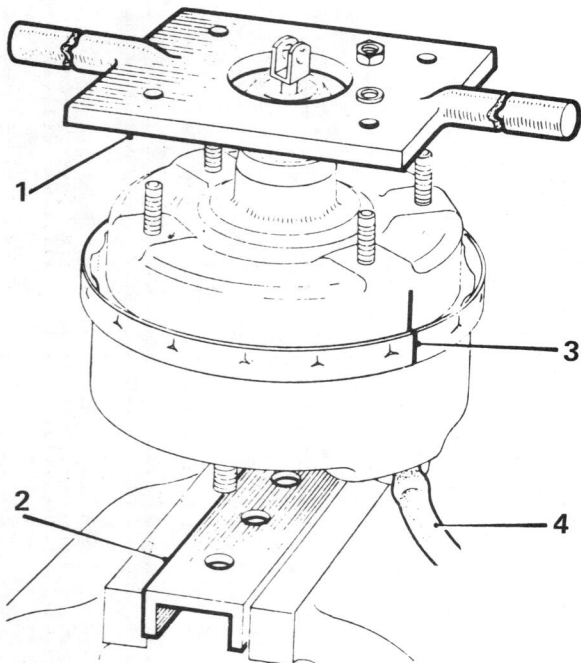

Fig. 9.18 Special tools for dismantling brake servo

1	Lever	4	Vacuum
2	Base plate		connection
3	Scribed line		

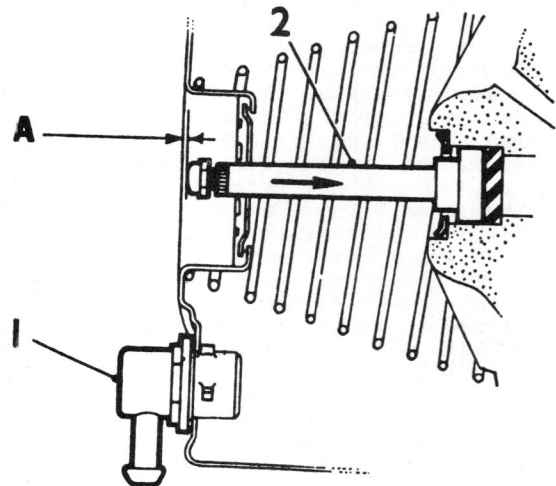

Fig. 9.19 Brake servo pushrod setting

A Setting gap 0.011 to 0.016 in (0.28 to 0.40 mm)
1 Vacuum applied to connection
2 Pushrod against reaction disc

numbered '64949008 EM - 1C - 14' and refit the rear shell, positioning it so that the flat face of the seal is towards the bearing. Press into position and refit the retainer.

11 Lightly smear the disc and hydraulic pushrod with Ford grease number '64949008 EM - 1C - 14'. Refit the reaction disc and pushrod to the diaphragm plate and press in the large spring washer. The small spring washer supplied in the 'Major Repair Kit' is not required. It is important that the length of pushrod is not altered in any way and any attempt to move the adjustment bolt will strip the threads. If a new hydraulic pushrod has been required, the length will have to be reset. Details of this operation are given at the end of this Section.

12 Lightly smear the outer diameter of the diaphragm plate neck and the bearing surfaces of the valve plunger with Ford grease number '64949008 EM - 1C - 14'. Carefully fit the valve rod assembly into the neck of the diaphragm and fix it with the retaining plate.

13 Fit the diaphragm into position and the non-return valve to the front shell. Smear the seal and plate assembly with Ford grease numbered '64949008 EM - 1C - 15' and press into the front shell with the plate facing inwards.

14 Fit the front shell to the base plate and the lever to the rear shell. Reconnect the vacuum hose to the non-return valve and the adaptor on the engine inlet manifold. Position the diaphragm return spring in the front shell. Lightly smear the outer bead of the diaphragm with Ford grease numbered '64949008 EM-1C-14' and locate the diaphragm assembly in the rear shell. Position the rear shell assembly on the return spring and line up the previously made scribe marks.

15 The assistant should start the engine. Very carefully, press the two halves of the unit together and, using the lever tool, turn clockwise to lock the two halves together. Stop the engine and disconnect the hose.

16 Press a new filter into the neck of the diaphragm plate, refit the end cap and position the dust cover onto the special lugs of the rear shell.

17 Hydraulic pushrod adjustment only applies if a new pushrod has been fitted. It will be seen from Fig. 9.19 that there is a bolt screwed into the end of the pushrod. The amount of protrusion has to be adjusted in the following manner: Remove the bolt and coat the threaded portion with Loctite Grade B. Reconnect the vacuum hose to the adaptor on the inlet valve and non-return valve. Start the engine and screw the prepared bolt into the end of the pushrod. Adjust the position of the bolt head so that it is 0.011 to 0.016 inch (0.28 to 0.40 mm) below the face of the front shell as shown by dimension A in Fig. 9.19. Leave the unit for a minimum of 24 hours to allow the Loctite to set hard.

18 Refit the servo unit to the car, as described in the previous Section. To test the servo unit for correct operation after overhaul, start the engine and run for a period of two minutes and then switch off. Wait for ten minutes and apply the footbrake very carefully, listening to hear the rush of air into the servo unit. This will indicate that vacuum was retained and the servo operating correctly.

19 Handbrake (Capri II) – adjustment

Note: *Some models are fitted with a similar system to that used by the Mercury Capri II. For details see Section 20.*

1 Adjustment of the handbrake is normally carried out by the action of the rear brake automatic adjusters. When new components have been fitted, or where the handbrake cable has stretched, then the following operations should be carried out.

2 Chock the front wheels, jack up the rear of the car and support on firmly based axle-stands. Release the handbrake.

3 Slide under the car and check that the primary cable follows its correct run and is correctly in its guide.The cable guides must be kept well greased at all times.

4 Adjust the effective length of the primary cable by slackening the locknut on the end of the cable adjacent to the relay lever on the rear axle (Fig. 9.21).

5 Adjust the nut until the primary cable has no slack in it and the relay lever is just clear of the slot in the banjo casing. Retighten the locknut.

6 Slacken the locknut on the end of the transverse cable adjacent to the right-hand rear brake (Fig. 9.22). Check that the parking brake operating levers are in the fully off position, that is, back on their stops and adjust the cable so that there is no slack. Check that the operating

levers are still on their stops and tighten the locknut.

7 Lower the car to the ground.

20 Parking brake (Mercury Capri II) – adjustment

1 Adjustment of the parking brake is normally carried out by the action of the rear brake automatic adjusters. When new components have been fitted, or where the parking brake cable has stretched, then the following operations should be carried out.

2 Chock the front wheels, jack up the rear of the car and support on firmly based axle-stands. Release the parking brake.

3 Ensure that the primary cable is properly located, then engage the

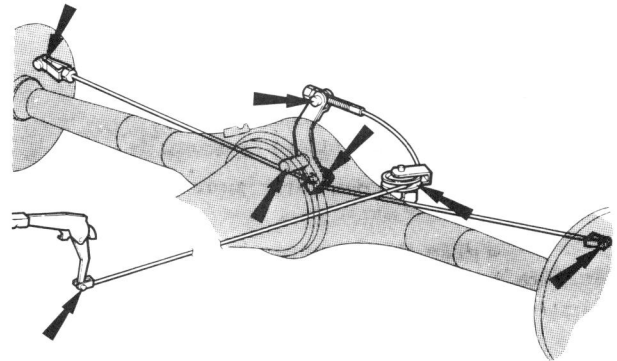

Fig. 9.20 Handbrake cable layout (Capri II). Arrows indicate lubrication points

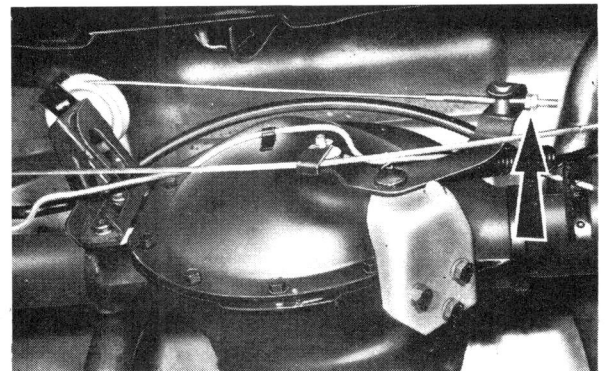

Fig. 9.21 Primary cable adjustment (Capri II)

Fig. 9.22 Transverse cable adjustment (Capri II)

keyed sleeve 'A' into the abutment slot 'B' (Fig.9.23).
4   Turn the adjuster nut 'C' until all cable slack is eliminated and a clearance of 0.039 to 0.059 in (1 to 1·5 mm) exists between the parking brake lever stop and the brake backplate.
5   Lower the car to the ground.

21 Handbrake (parking brake) control lever – removal and refitting

1   Chock the front wheels, jack up the rear of the car and support on firmly based axle-stands. Release the handbrake.
2   Working inside the car, remove the carpeting from around the area of the handbrake lever.
3   *Models fitted with a console:* Refer to Chapter 12 and remove the console.
4   Remove the split pin and withdraw the clevis pin that connects the primary cable to the lower end of the handbrake lever. This protrudes under the floor panels. **Note:** *On some models, the cable hooks onto the end of the handbrake lever* (photo).
5   Undo and remove the six self-tapping screws which secure the handbrake lever rubber boot to the floor. Draw the rubber boot up the lever.
6   Undo and remove the two bolts that secure the handbrake lever assembly to the floor. Lift away the lever assembly.
7   Refitting the lever assembly is the reverse sequence of removal. The following additional points should be noted:

(a)   Apply some grease to the primary cable clevis pin.
(b)   Adjust the primary cable as described in Section 20.

22 Handbrake cables (Capri II) – removal and refitting

Note: *Some models are fitted with a similar system to that fitted to the Mercury Capri II. For details see Section 23.*

Primary cable

1   Chock the front wheels, jack up the rear of the car and support on firmly based axle-stands. Release the handbrake.
2   Working under the car, unscrew and remove the nuts that secure the end of the primary cable to the relay lever located at the rear of the axle casing.
3   Detach the primary cable from the end of the handbrake lever, by removing the split pin and withdrawing the clevis pin. **Note:** *On some models, the cable hooks onto the end of the handbrake lever.*
4   Detach the cable from its underbody guides and lift away.
5   Refitting the primary cable is the reverse sequence of removal, but

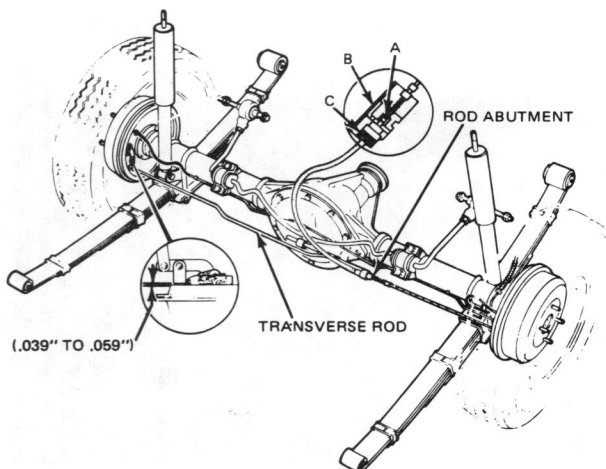

the following additional points should be noted:

(a)   Apply some grease to the cable guides and insert the cable. Also lubricate the front clevis pin.
(b)   Refer to Section 19 and adjust the primary cable.

Transverse cable

1   Chock the front wheels, jack up the front of the car and support on firmly based axle-stands. Release the handbrake.
2   Working under the car, remove the split pin and withdraw the clevis pin that secures the transverse cable to the left-hand backplate.
3   Detach the cable from the right-hand rear backplate, by removing the locknut and unscrewing the cable from the clevis.
4   Remove the pulley pins, split pin and withdraw the pulley pin. Lift away the little pulley wheel and transverse cable.
5   Refitting the transverse cable is the reverse sequence of removal, but the following additional points should be noted:

(a)   Apply some grease to the pulley and pivot pin, the threaded end of the cable and the clevis pin.
(b)   Adjust the transverse cable as described in Section 19.

23 Parking brake cable and rod (Mercury Capri II) – removal and refitting

Primary cable

1   Chock the front wheels, jack up the rear of the car and support on firmly based axle-stands. Release the parking brake.
2   Remove the spring clip and clevis pin, connecting the parking brake cable to the lever of the parking brake handle.
3   Remove the spring clip and clevis pin from the right-hand rear brake lever and disconnect the cable.
4   Remove the parking brake cable-to-transverse rod retaining clip, then slide the cable clear of the rod bracket.
5   Slide the cable, adjusting nut and guide clear of the abutment bracket and remove the assembly from the car.
6   Refitting is the reverse of the removal procedure. Apply a little general purpose grease to the rubbing and pivoting parts, then check the adjustment (Section 20).

Transverse rod

7   Proceed as described in paragraphs 1 and 2.
8   Remove the spring retaining clip which secures the parking brake cable to the transverse rod and slide the cable assembly clear.
9   Remove the spring clip and clevis pin, then disconnect the rod from the left-hand rear brake lever.
10 Slide the rod out of the bushing on the axle casing.
11 Refitting is the reverse of the removal procedure. Apply a little general purpose grease to the rubbing and pivoting parts, then check the adjustment (Section 20).

Fig. 9.23 Handbrake assembly (Mercury Capri II)

21.4 Primary brake cable hooked end

24 Fault diagnosis – Braking system

Before diagnosing faults from the following chart, check that braking irregularities are not caused by:

1 *Uneven and incorrect tyre pressures.*
2 *Incorrect 'mix' of radial and crossply tyres.*
3 *Wear in the steering mechanism.*
4 *Defects in the suspension and dampers.*
5 *Misalignment of the bodyframe.*

Symptom	Reason/s
Pedal travels a long way before the brakes operate	Brake shoes set too far from the drums (auto. adjusters seized)
Stopping ability poor, even though pedal pressure is firm	Linings, discs or drums badly worn or scored One or more wheel hydraulic cylinders seized, resulting in some brake shoes not pressing against the drums (or pads against discs) Brake linings contaminated with oil Wrong type of linings fitted (too hard) Brake shoes wrongly assembled Servo unit not functioning
Car veers to one side when the brakes are applied	Brake pads or linings on one side are contaminated with oil Hydraulic wheel cylinder(s) on one side partially or fully seized A mixture of lining materials fitted between sides Brake discs not matched Unequal wear between sides caused by partially seized wheel cylinders Front suspension stabilizer bar bushes worn
Pedal feels spongy when the brakes are applied	Air is present in the hydraulic system
Pedal feels springy when the brakes are applied	Brake linings not bedded into the drums (after fitting new ones) Master cylinder or brake backplate mounting bolts loose Severe wear in brake drums, causing distortion when brakes are applied Discs out of true
Pedal travels right down with little or no resistance and brakes are virtually non-operative	Leak in hydraulic system, resulting in lack of pressure for operating wheel cylinders If no signs of leakage are apparent, the master cylinder internal seals are failing to sustain pressure
Binding, juddering, overheating	One, or a combination of, reasons given in the foregoing Sections

Chapter 10 Electrical system

For modifications, and information applicable to later models, see Supplement at end of manual

Contents

Specifications

System type .... 12 volt, negative earth

Battery

Battery type .... Lead acid, 12 volt
Capacity (amp hr):
    3·0 Manual transmission (FoB) 44
    3·0 Automatic transmission (FoB) 55
    3·0 Manual transmission (FoG) 55
    3·0 Automatic transmission (FoG) 66
    Mercury Capri II. All models 66

Note: *A battery of higher capacity may be fitted for some markets, and in most cases is available as an optional fitment.*

Starter motor (Bosch manufacture)

Type	EF 0·7	GF 1·0
Minimum brush length	0·4 in (10 mm)	0·4 in (10 mm)
Brush spring pressure	32 to 46 oz (900 to 1300 g)	32 to 46 oz (900 to 1300 g)
Commutator:		
Minimum diameter	1·291 in (32·8 mm)	1·291 in (32·8 mm)
Maximum out-of-round	0·012 in (0·3 mm)	0·012 in (0·3 mm)
Armature endfloat	0·004 to 0·012 in (0·1 to 0·3 mm)	0·004 to 0·012 in (0·1 to 0·3 mm)

Note: *Starter motors used on Mercury Capri II may differ slightly from the above Specifications*

Starter motor (Lucas manufacture)

Type	M35J	5M90
Minimum brush length	0·374 in (9·5 mm)	0·354 in (9·0 mm)
Brush spring pressure	16·94 oz (480 g)	30 oz (850 g)
Commutator:		
Minimum diameter	1·339 in (34 mm)	—
Maximum out-of-round	0·003 in (0·075 mm)	—
Armature endfloat	0·004 to 0·012 in (0·1 to 0·3 mm)	0·004 to 0·012 in (0·1 to 0·3 mm)

Alternator (Bosch manufacture)

Type	G1–28A	L1–35A	K1–55A
Output at 13·5V and 6000 rpm (nominal)	28 amp	35 amp	55 amp
Stator winding resistance per phase	0·2 to 0·21 ohms	0·13 to 0·137 ohms	0·01 to 0·017 ohms
Rotor winding resistance at 20°C (68°F)	4 to 4·4 ohms	4 to 4·4 ohms	4 to 4·4 ohms
Minimum protrusion of brushes in free position	0·197 in (5 mm)	0·197 in (5 mm)	0·197 in (5 mm)
Regulating voltage (model A01) 4000 rpm, 3 to 7 amp load	13·7 to 14·5 volt	13·7 to 14·5 volt	13·7 to 14·5 volt

Alternator (Femsa manufacture)

Type	ALD 12–32 or ALD 12–33
Output at 13·5V and 6000 rpm (nominal)	32 amp
Stator winding resistance per phase	0·173 ± 0·01 ohms
Rotor winding resistance at 20°C (68°F)	5·0 ± 0·15 ohms
Minimum protrusion of brushes in free position	0·28 in (7 mm)
Regulating voltage (model GRK 12–16), 4000 rpm, 3 to 7 amp load	13·7 to 14·5 volt
Field relay closing voltage	2·0 to 2·8 volt

Alternator (Lucas manufacture)

Type	15 ACR	17 ACR
Output at 13·5V and 6000 rpm (nominal)	28 amp	35 amp
Stator winding resistance per phase	0·198 ± 0·01 ohms	0·133 ± 0·007 ohms
Rotor winding resistance at 20°C (68°F)	3·27 ohms ± 5%	3·201 ohms ± 5%
Minimum protrusion of brushes in free position	0·2 in (5 mm)	0·2 in (5 mm)
Regulating voltage (model 14TR) 4000 rpm, 3 to 7 amp load	14·2 to 14·6 volt	14·2 to 14·6 volt

Windscreen wipers (front)

Type	Two speed electric, self parking

Windscreen wiper (rear – optional and Ghia)

Type	Single speed electric, self parking

Horn

Type	4 in (102 mm) beep or projector
Current draw	4·5 to 5·0 amp

Bulb chart (Capri II)

Headlamp, except Ghia	45/40W
Headlamp, Ghia	60/55W halogen
Fog lamps	55W
Driving lamps	55W
Direction indicators	21W, bayonet
Stoplights	21W, bayonet
Front side and licence plate lights	4W, bayonet
Reverse lamps	21W, bayonet
Interior lights:	
Front	6W, festoon
Rear (GT)	6W, festoon
Instrument panel warning lights	2W, wedge base

Instrument panel illumination	2W, wedge base
Electric clock	1·2W
Heated rear screen switch	1·2W

Bulb chart (Mercury Capri II)

Headlights (sealed beam)	5¾ inch S.B. Type 1 (high beam)
	5¾ inch S.B. Type 2 (high and low beam)
Side lights/front direction indicators	32 CP/4CP bayonet 15d/19
Rear direction indicator	32 CP bayonet 15d
Rear/stoplights	32 CP/4CP bayonet 15d/19
Rear number plate light	3 CP bayonet
Interior light	10W bayonet
Instrument panel lights	1 CP wedge base
Side marker lights	2 CP wedge base
Back-up light	32 CP bayonet 15d

For lamps not listed consult your Ford dealer.

Fuses (Capri II)

	Fuse and rating	Circuits protected
Main fusebox on engine compartment bulkhead on driver's side	1 – 16 amp	Cigar lighter, clock, interior light
	2 – 8 amp	Licence plate lights, instrument panel illumination
	3 – 8 amp	RH tail and side lights
	4 – 8 amp	LH tail and side lights
	5 – 16 amp	Horn, blower motor
	6 – 16 amp	Wiper motor, reversing lights
	7 – 8 amp	Direction indicators, stoplights, instrument cluster
Fuses in dipper relay housing	8 – 16 amp	LH dipped headlamp
	9 – 16 amp	RH dipped headlamp
	10 – 16 amp	RH main beam
	11 – 16 amp	LH main beam
Fuses mounted under facia	12 – 8 amp	Within relay for heated rear screen
	13 – 2 amp	Radio circuit (medium-slow blow)
	14 – 8 amp	Within relay for driving lamps (RPO)
	15 – 8 amp	Within relay for fog lamps (RPO)

Fuses (Mercury Capri II)

	Fuse and rating	Circuits protected
Main fusebox on left-hand side of engine compartment on driver's side	1 – 8 amp	Clock, cigar lighter, interior light, hazard flasher
	2 – 8 amp	Licence plate lamp, map reading lamp, instrument illumination
	3 – 8 amp	RH tail, parking and side marker lights
	4 – 8 amp	LH tail, parking and side marker lights
	5 – 8 amp	Heater blower, horn
	6 – 16 amp	Wiper motors, back-up light, instrument cluster
	7 – 8 amp	Stoplights, turn signals

Torque wrench settings

	lbf ft	kgf m
Alternator pulley nut	25 to 29	3·5 to 4·0
Alternator mounting bolts	15 to 18	2·1 to 2·5
Alternator mounting bracket	20 to 25	2·8 to 3·5
Starter motor retaining bolts	20 to 25	2·8 to 3·5

1 General description

The major components of the 12 volt negative earth system comprise a 12 volt battery, an alternator (driven from the crankshaft pulley), and a starter motor.

The battery supplies a steady amount of current for the ignition, lighting and other electrical circuits and provides a reserve of power when the current consumed by the electrical equipment exceeds that being produced by the alternator.

The alternator has its own regulator which ensures a high output if the battery is in a low state of charge and the demand from the electrical equipment is high, and a low output if the battery is fully charged and there is little demand from the electrical equipment.

When fitting electrical accessories to cars with a negative earth system it is important, if they contain silicon diodes, or transistors, that they are connected correctly; otherwise serious damage may result to the components concerned. Items such as radios, tape players,

electronic ignition systems, electric tachometer, automatic dipping etc, should all be checked for correct polarity.

It is important that the battery positive lead is always disconnected if the battery is to be boost charged; also, if body repairs are to be carried out using electric welding equipment the alternator must be disconnected otherwise serious damage can be caused. Whenever the battery has to be disconnected it must always be reconnected with the negative terminal earthed.

2 Battery – removal and refitting

1   The battery is on a carrier fitted to the left-hand wing valance of the engine compartment. Disconnect the negative and then the positive leads from the battery terminals by undoing and removing the plated nuts and bolts. Note that two cables are attached to the positive terminal.

2   Unscrew and remove the bolt, and plain washer that secures the

battery clamp plate to the carrier. Lift away the clamp plate. Carefully lift the battery from its carrier, holding it vertically to ensure that none of the electrolyte is spilled.

3   Refitting is a direct reversal of this procedure. **Note:** *Refit the positive lead before the negative lead and smear the terminals with petroleum jelly to prevent corrosion.* **Never** *use an ordinary grease.*

3   Battery – maintenance and inspection

1   Normal weekly battery maintenance consists of checking the electrolyte level of each cell to ensure that the separators are covered by $\frac{1}{4}$ inch (6.35 mm) of electrolyte. If the level has fallen top up the battery using distilled water only. Do not overfill. If a battery is over-filled or any electrolyte spilled, immediately wipe away and neutralize, as electrolyte attacks and corrodes any metal it comes into contact with very rapidly.

2   If the battery has the Auto-fil device fitted, a special topping up sequence is required. The white balls in the Auto-fil battery are part of the automatic topping up device which ensures correct electrolyte level. The vent chamber should remain in position at all times except when topping up or taking specific gravity readings. If the electrolyte level in any of the cells is below the bottom of the filling tube top up as follows:

(a) *Lift off the vent chamber cover.*
(b) *With the battery level, pour distilled water into the trough until all the filling tubes and trough are full.*
(c) *Immediately refit the cover to allow the water in the trough and tubes to flow into the cells. Each cell will automatically receive the correct amount of water.*

3   As well as keeping the terminals clean and covered with petroleum jelly, the top of the battery, and especially the top of the cells, should be kept clean and dry. This helps prevent corrosion.

4   Once every three months remove the battery and inspect the battery securing bolts, the battery clamp plate, tray and battery leads for corrosion (white fluffy deposits on the metal which are brittle to touch).If any corrosion is found, clean off the deposits with ammonia and paint over the clean metal with an anti-rust/anti-acid paint.

4   Battery – electrolyte replenishment

1   If the battery is in a fully charged state and one of the cells maintains a specific gravity reading which is 0.025 or more lower than the others, and a check of each cell has been made with a voltmeter to check for short circuits (a four to seven second test should give a steady reading of between 12 to 18 volts) then it is likely that electrolyte has been lost from the cell with the low reading.

2   Top-up the cell with a solution of 1 part sulphuric acid to 2.5 parts of water. If the cell is already topped-up draw some electrolyte out of it with a pipette.

3   When mixing the sulphuric acid and water **never add water to sulphuric acid** – always pour the acid slowly onto the water in a glass container. **If water is added to sulphuric acid it will explode.**

4   Continue to top-up the cell with the freshly made electrolyte and then recharge the battery and check the hydrometer readings.

5   Battery – charging

1   In winter time when heavy demand is placed upon the battery, such as when starting from cold, and much electrical equipment is continually in use, it is a good idea to occasionally have the battery fully charged from an external source at the rate of 3.5 to 4 amps.

2   Continue to charge the battery at this rate until no further rise in specific gravity is noted over a four hour period.

3   Alternatively, a trickle charger charging at the rate of 1.5 amps can be safely used overnight.

4   Special rapid 'boost' chargers which are claimed to restore the power of the battery in 1 to 2 hours are most dangerous as they can cause serious damage to the battery plates through over-heating.

5   While charging the battery, note that the temperature of the electrolyte should never exceed 100°F (37.8°C).

6   Alternator – general

The alternator may be of Lucas, Femsa or Bosch manufacture according to the vehicle and production source (Fig. 10.1).

The main advantage of the alternator over its predecessor, the dynamo, lies in its ability to provide a high charge at low revolutions. Driving slowly in heavy traffic with a dynamo invariably means no charge is reaching the battery. In similar conditions even with the wiper, heater, lights and perhaps radio switched on, the alternator will ensure a charge reaches the battery.

7   Alternator – routine maintenance

1   The equipment has been designed for the minimum amount of maintenance in service, the only items subject to wear being the brushes and bearings.

2   Brushes should be examined after about 75000 miles (120000 km) and renewed if necessary. The bearings are prepacked with grease for life, and should not require further attention.

3   Check the fan belt every 3000 miles (5000 km) for correct adjustment which should be 0.5 inch (13 mm) total movement at the centre of the longest run between pulleys.

8   Alternator – special procedures

Whenever the electrical system of the car is being attended to, or an external means of starting the engine is used, there are certain precautions that must be taken, otherwise serious and expensive damage can result.

1   Always make sure that the negative terminal of the battery is earthed. If the terminal connections are accidentally reversed or if the battery has been reverse charged, the alternator diodes will be damaged.

2   The output terminal on the alternator marked 'BAT' or 'B+' must never be earthed, but should always be connected directly to the positive terminal of the battery.

3   Whenever the alternator is to be removed, or when disconnecting the terminals of the alternator circuit, always disconnect the battery terminal earth first.

4   The alternator must never be operated without the battery to alternator cable connected.

5   If the battery is to be charged by external means, always disconnect both battery cables before the external charger is connected.

6   Should it be necessary to use a booster charger or booster battery to start the engine, always double check that the negative cable is connected to negative terminal and the positive cable to positive terminal.

9   Alternator – removal and refitting

1   Disconnect the battery leads.

2   Note the terminal connections at the rear of the alternator and disconnect the plug or multi pin connector. On Mercury Capri II models disconnect the heater hose bracket at the alternator.

3   Undo and remove the alternator adjustment arm bolt, slacken the alternator mounting bolts and push the alternator inward towards the engine. Lift the fan belt from the pulley.

4   Remove the remaining two mounting bolts and carefully lift the alternator away from the car.

5   Take care not to knock, or drop the alternator, otherwise this can cause irreparable damage.

6   Refitting the alternator is the reverse sequence to removal.

7   Adjust the fan belt so that it has 0.5 inch (13 mm) total movement at the centre of the longest run between pulleys.

10   Alternator – fault diagnosis and repair

Due to the specialist knowledge and equipment required to test, or service, an alternator it is recommended that if the performance is suspect, the car be taken to an automobile electrician who will have the facilities for such work. Because of this recommendation, information is limited to the inspection and renewal of the brushes. Should the

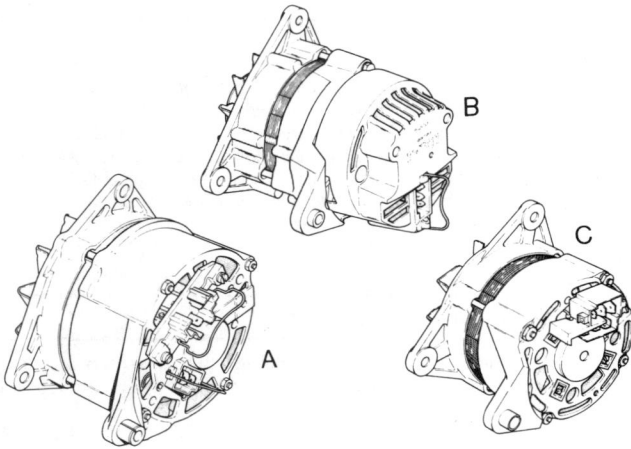

Fig. 10.1 Alternator recognition

A Bosch
B Lucas
C Femsa

alternator not charge, or the system be suspect, the following points may be checked before seeking further assistance:

1 Check the fan belt tension, as described in Section 7.
2 Check the battery, as described in Section 3.
3 Check all electrical cable connections for cleanliness and security.

11 Alternator brushes (Lucas) – inspection, removal and refitting

1 Undo and remove the two screws and washers securing the end cover.
2 To inspect the brushes, the brush holder mountings should be removed complete by undoing the two bolts and disconnecting the 'Lucar' connection to the diode plates (Figs. 10.5 and 10.6).
3 With the brush holder moulding removed and the brush assemblies still in position, check that they protrude from the face of the moulding by at least 0.2 inches (5 mm). Also check that when depressed, the spring pressure is 7 to 10 ozs. when the end of the brush is flush with the face of the brush moulding. To be done with any accuracy, this requires a push type spring gauge.
4 Should either of the foregoing requirements not be fulfilled, the spring assemblies should be refitted.
5 This can be done by simply removing the holding screws of each assembly and fitting a new assembly.
6 With the brush holder moulding removed, the slip rings on the face end of the rotor are exposed. These can be cleaned with a petrol-soaked cloth and any signs of burning may be removed with fine glass paper. On no account should any other abrasive be used, or any attempt at machining be made.
7 When the brushes are refitted, they should slide smoothly in their holders. Any sticking tendency may first be rectified by wiping with a petrol soaked cloth or, if this fails, by carefully polishing with a very fine file where any binding marks appear.
8 Reassemble in the reverse order of dismantling. Ensure that leads which may have been connected to any of the screws are reconnected correctly. Note:-

(a) If the charging system is suspect, first check the fan belt tension and condition – refer to Section 7 for details.
(b) Check the battery – refer to Section 3 for details.
(c) With an alternator, the ignition warning light control feed comes from the centre point of a pair of diodes in the alternator via a control unit similar in appearance to an indicator flasher unit. Should the warning light indicate lack of charge, check this unit and if suspect renew it.
(d) Should all the above prove negative, then have the alternator checked.

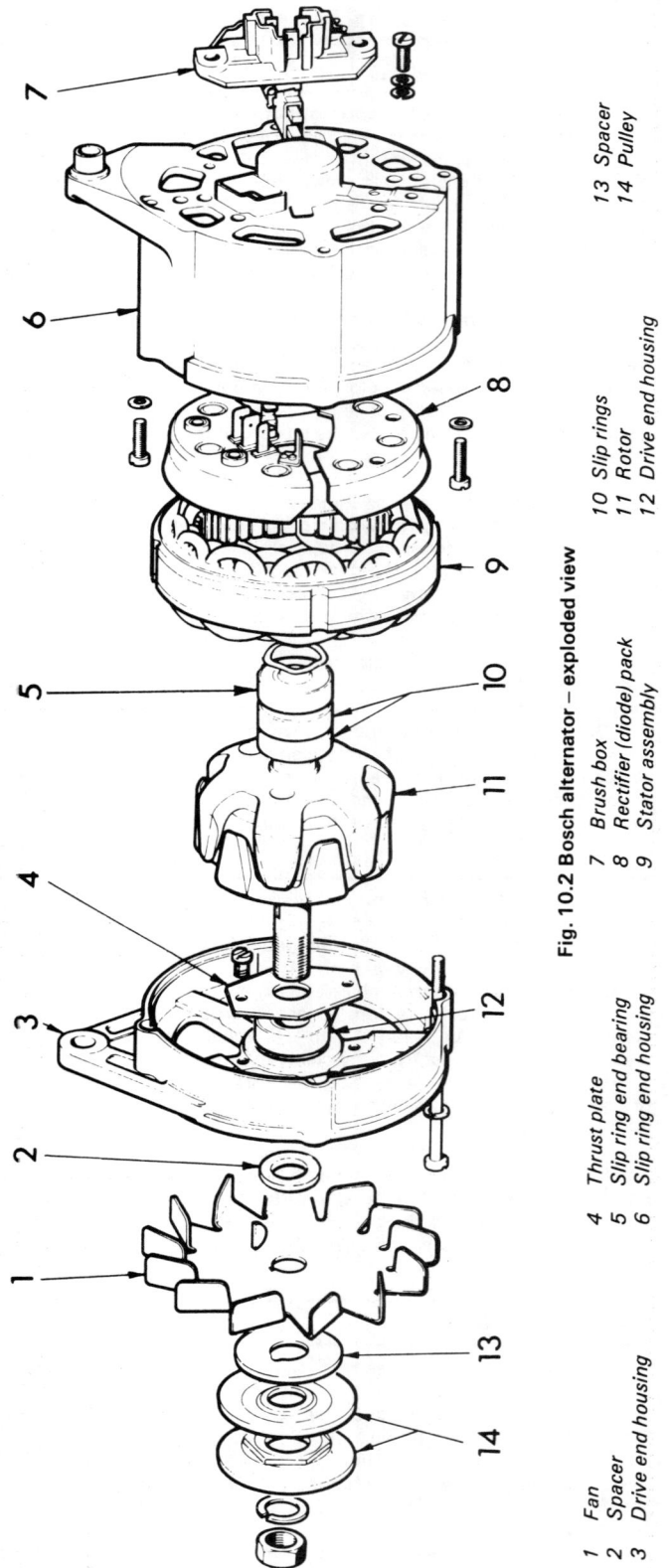

Fig. 10.2 Bosch alternator – exploded view

1 Fan
2 Spacer
3 Drive end housing
4 Thrust plate
5 Slip ring end bearing
6 Slip ring end housing
7 Brush box
8 Rectifier (diode) pack
9 Stator assembly
10 Slip rings
11 Rotor
12 Drive end housing
13 Spacer
14 Pulley

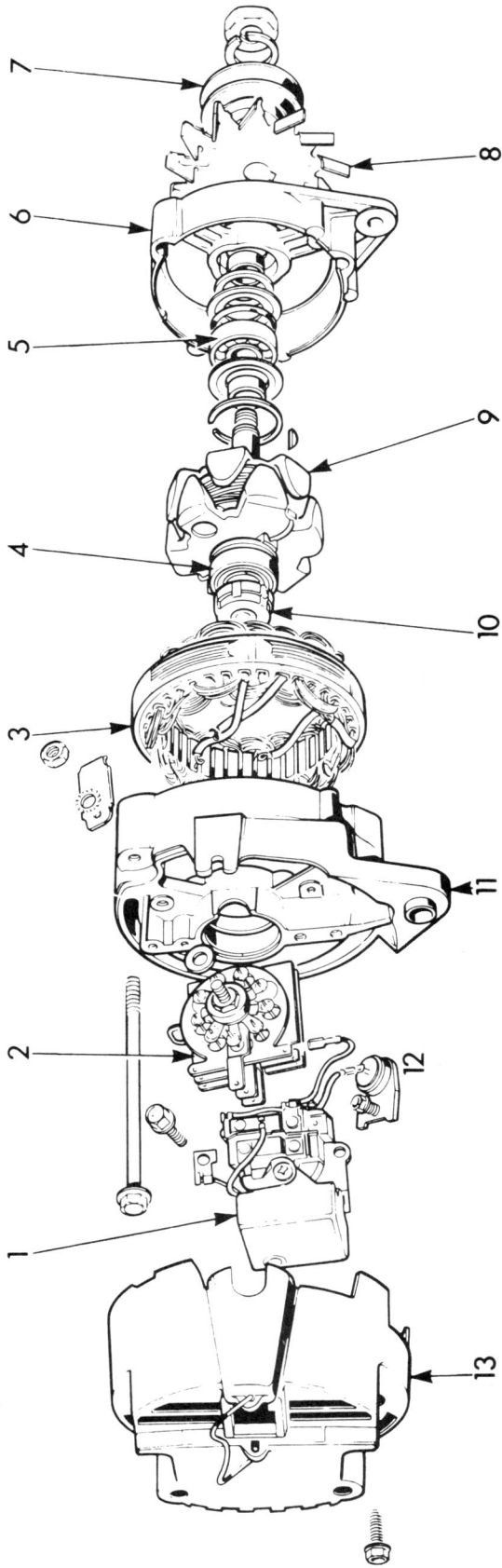

Fig. 10.3 Lucas alternator – exploded view

1 Regulator
2 Rectifier (diode) pack
3 Stator assembly

4 Slip ring end bearing
5 Drive end bearing
6 Drive end housing

7 Pulley
8 Fan
9 Rotor

10 Slip ring
11 Slip ring end housing

12 Surge protection diode
13 End cover

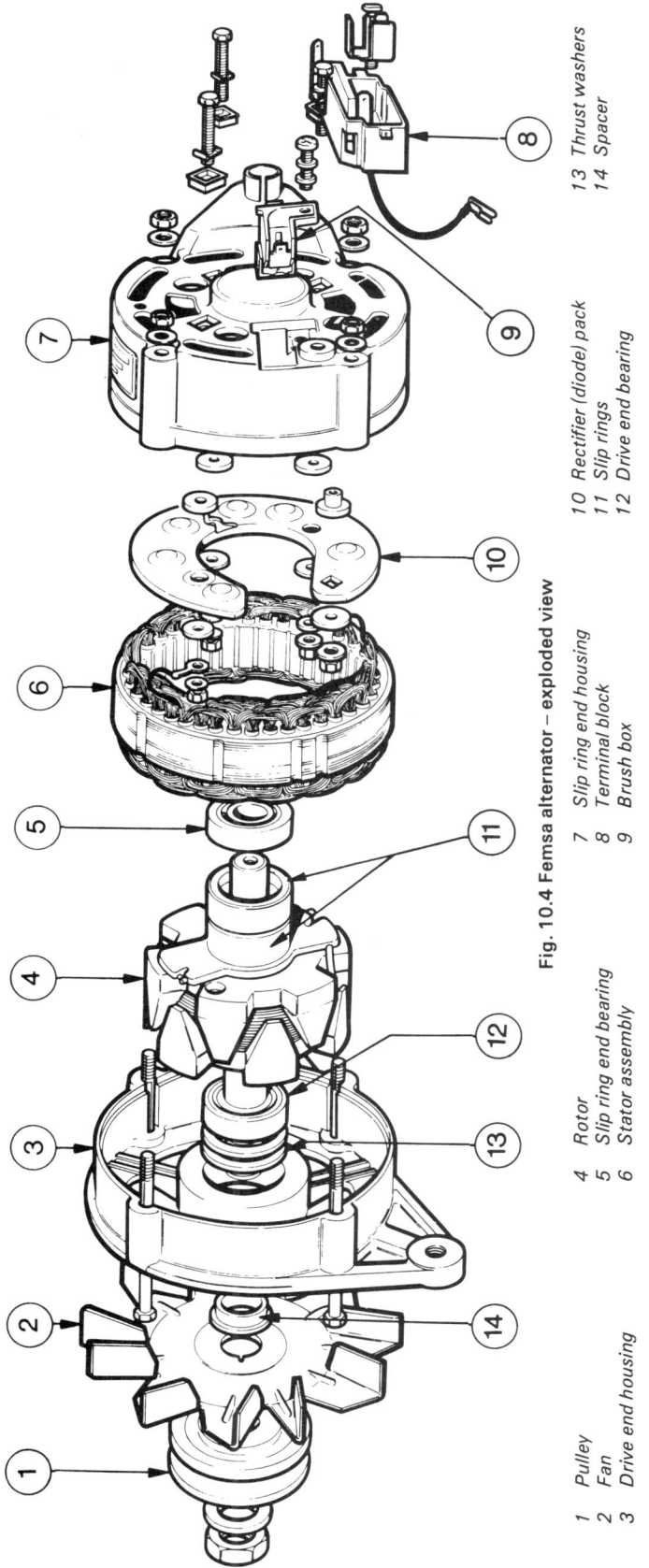

Fig. 10.4 Femsa alternator – exploded view

1 Pulley
2 Fan
3 Drive end housing

4 Rotor
5 Slip ring end bearing
6 Stator assembly

7 Slip ring end housing
8 Terminal block
9 Brush box

10 Rectifier (diode) pack
11 Slip rings
12 Drive end bearing

13 Thrust washers
14 Spacer

12 Alternator brushes (Bosch) – inspection, removal and refitting

1   Undo and remove the two screws, spring and plain washers that secure the brush box to the rear of the brush end housing. Lift away the brush box.
2   Check that the carbon brushes are able to slide smoothly in their guides without any sign of binding.
3   Measure the length of brushes and if they have worn down to 0.35 inch (9 mm) or less, they must be renewed.
4   Hold the brushwire with a pair of engineer's pliers and unsolder it from the brush box. Lift away the two brushes.
5   Insert the new brushes and check to make sure that they are free to move in their guides. If they bind, lightly polish with a very fine file.
6   Solder the brushwire ends to the brush box, taking care that solder is allowed to pass to the stranded wire.
7   Whenever new brushes are fitted, new springs should also be fitted.
8   Refitting the brush box is the reverse sequence to removal.

13 Alternator brushes (Femsa) – inspection, removal and refitting

1   Disconnect the single wire from the brush box.
2   Remove the crosshead retaining screw, then withdraw the brush box.
3   Check that the carbon brushes are able to slide smoothly in their guides without any sign of binding.
4   Measure the amount by which the brushes protrude from the brush box. If this is less than 0.28 inch (7 mm), obtain and fit new brushes.
5   Refitting the brush box is a straightforward reversal of the removal procedure.

14 Starter motor – general description

The starter motor fitted to engines covered by this manual may be either of the inertia or pre-engaged type.
The pre-engaged type is recognisable by the solenoid assembly mounted on the motor body.
The principle of operation of the inertia type starter motor is as follows: When the ignition is switched on and the switch operated, current flows from the battery to the starter motor solenoid switch which causes it to become energised. Its internal plunger moves inwards and closes an internal switch, so allowing full starting current to flow from the battery to the starter motor. This causes a powerful magnetic field to be induced into the field coils which causes the armature to rotate.
Mounted on helical spines is the drive pinion which, because of the sudden rotation of the armature, is thrown forward along the armature shaft and so into engagement with the flywheel ring gear. The engine crankshaft will then be rotated until the engine starts to operate on its own and at this point, the drive pinion is thrown out of mesh with the flywheel ring gear.
The method of engagement on the pre-engaged starter differs considerably in that the drive pinion is brought into mesh with the starter ring gear before the main starter current is applied.
When the ignition is switched on, current flows from the battery to the solenoid which is mounted on the top of the starter motor. The plunger in the solenoid moves inwards, so causing a centrally pivoted engagement lever to move in such a manner that the forked end pushes the drive pinion into mesh with the starter ring gear. When the solenoid reaches the end of its travel, it closes an internal contact and full starting current flows to the starter field coils. The armature is then able to rotate the crankshaft, so starting the engine.
A special one way clutch is fitted to the starter drive pinion, so that when the engine just fires and starts to operate on its own, it does not drive the starter motor.

Fig. 10.5 Lucas alternator – brush box retaining screws

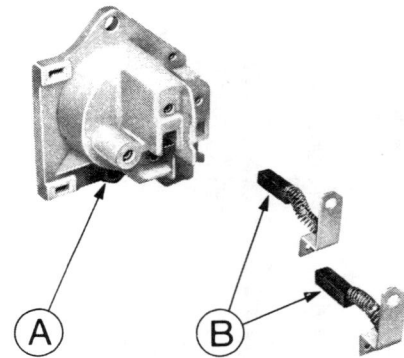

Fig. 10.6 Lucas alternator – brush gear

A Brush box   B Brush assemblies

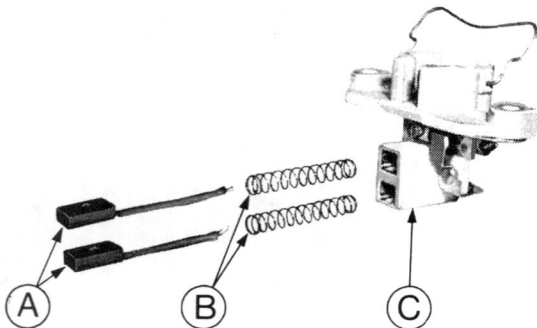

Fig. 10.7 Bosch alternator – brush gear

A Brushes   B Spring   C Brush box

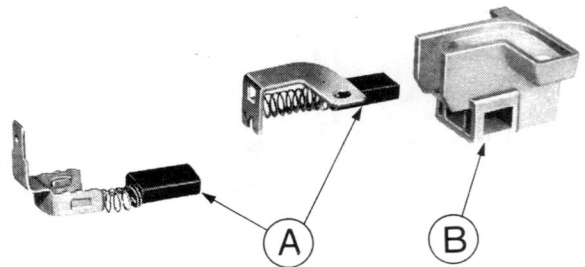

Fig. 10.8 Femsa alternator – brush gear

A Brush assemblies   B Brush box

15 Starter motor (inertia) – testing on engine

1   If the starter motor fails to operate, check the condition of the battery, by turning on the headlamps. If they glow brightly for several seconds and then gradually dim, the battery is in an uncharged condition.

2   If the headlamps continue to glow brightly and it is obvious that the battery is in good condition, check the tightness of the battery terminal to its connection on the body frame. Check the tightness of the connections at the relay switch and at the starter motor. Check the wiring with a meter for breaks or shorts.

3   If the wiring is in order, check the starter motor switch is operating. To do this, press the rubber covered button in the centre of the relay switch under the bonnet. If it is working, the starter motor will be heard to 'click', as it tries to rotate. Alternatively, check it with a voltmeter.

4   If the battery is fully charged, the wiring in order, and the switch working, but the starter motor fails to operate, it will have to be removed from the car for examination.

16 Starter motor (inertia) – removal and refitting

1   Disconnect the positive and then the negative terminals from the battery. Also disconnect the starter motor cable from the terminal on the starter motor end cover.

2   Undo and remove the nuts, bolts and spring washers which secure the starter motor to the clutch and the flywheel housing. Lift the starter motor away by manipulating the drive gear out from the ring gear area and then from the engine compartment.

3   Refitting is the reverse procedure to removal. Make sure that the starter motor cable, when secured in position by its terminal, does not touch any part of the body, or power unit, which could damage the insulation.

17 Starter motor (inertia) – dismantling, overhaul and reassembly

1   With the starter motor on the bench, loosen the screw on the cover band and slip the cover band off. With a piece of wire bent into the shape of a hook, lift back each of the brush springs in turn and check the movement of the brushes in their holders by pulling on the flexible connectors. If the brushes are so worn that their faces do not rest against the commutator, or if the ends of the brush leads are exposed on their working faces, they must be renewed.

2   If any of the brushes tend to stick in their holders, wash them with a petrol moistened cloth and, if necessary, lightly polish the sides of the brush with a very fine file until it moves quite freely in its holder.

3   If the surface of the commutator is dirty, or blackened, clean it with a petrol dampened rag. Secure the starter motor in a vice and check it by connecting a heavy gauge cable between the starter motor terminal and a 12 volt battery.

4   Connect the cable from the other battery terminal to the starter motor body. If the motor turns at high speed it is in good order.

5   If the starter motor still fails to function, or if it wished to renew the brushes, then it is necessary to further dismantle the motor.

6   Lift the brush springs with the wire hook, and lift all four brushes out of their holders one at a time.

7   Remove the terminal nuts and washers from the terminal post on the commutator end bracket.

8   Unscrew the two through bolts which hold the end plates together and pull off the commutator end bracket. Also remove the driving end bracket which will come away complete with the armature.

9   At this stage, if the brushes are to be renewed, their flexible connectors must be unsoldered and the connectors of new brushes soldered in their place. Check that the new brushes move freely in their holders as detailed above. If cleaning the commutator with petrol fails to remove all the burnt areas and spots, then wrap a piece of glass paper round the commutator and rotate the armature.

10 If the commutator is very badly worn, remove the drive gear as

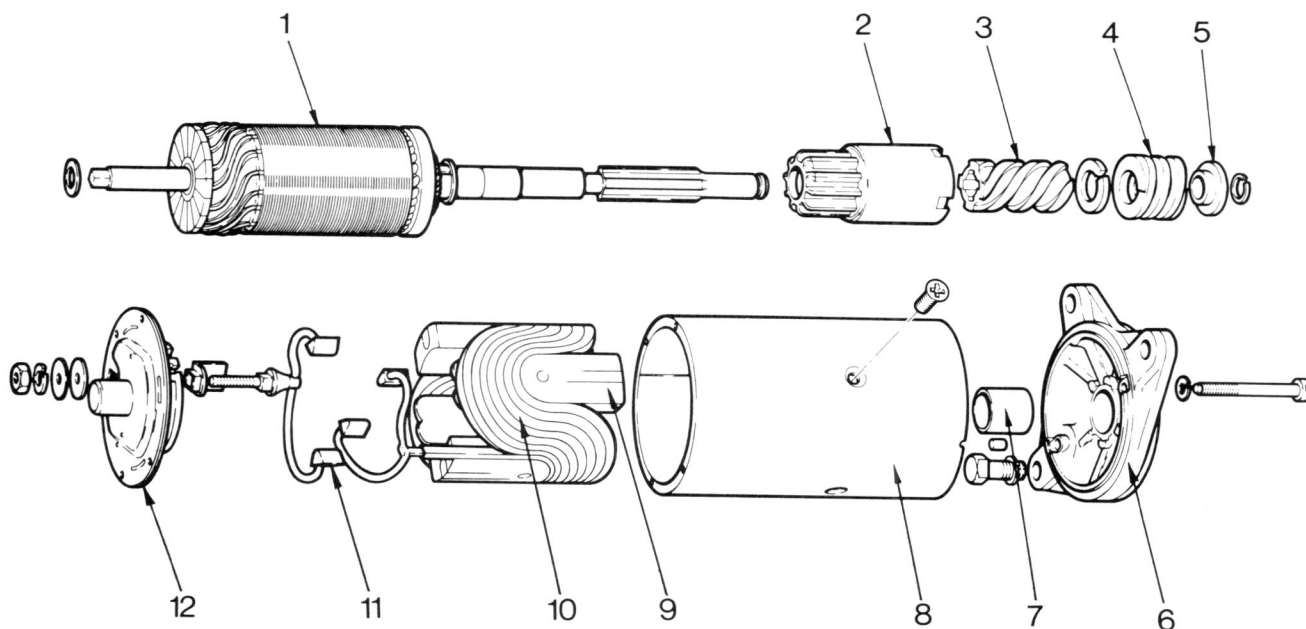

Fig. 10.9 Lucas starter motor (inertia type)

1 Armature	4 Spring	7 Drive end bush	10 Field coils
2 Pinion	5 Sleeve nut	8 Yoke	11 Brushes
3 Bendix	6 Drive end housing	9 Pole segments	12 Commutator end housing

detailed below. Mount the armature in a lathe and with the lathe turning at high speed, take a very fine cut out of the commutator and finish the surface by polishing with glass paper. **Do not undercut the insulators between the commutator segments.**

11 With the starter motor dismantle, test the four field coils for an open circuit. Connect a 12 volt battery with a 12 volt bulb in one of the leads between the field terminal post and the tapping point of the field coils to which the brushes are connected. An open circuit is proved by the bulb not lighting.

12 If the bulb lights, it does not necessarily mean that the field coils are in order, as there is a possibility that one of the coils will be earthed to the starter yoke or pole shoes. To check this, remove the lead from the brush connector and place it against a clean portion of the starter yoke. If the bulb lights, the field coils are earthing. Renewal of the field coils calls for the use of a wheel operated screwdriver, a soldering iron, caulking and riveting operations and is beyond the scope of the majority of owners. The starter yoke should be taken to a reputable electrical engineering works for new field coils to be fitted. Alternatively purchase an exchange Lucas starter motor.

13 If the armature is damaged, this will be evident after visual inspection. Look for signs of burning, discolouration, and for conductors that have lifted away from the commutator.

14 With the starter motor stripped down, check the condition of the bushes. They should be renewed when they are sufficiently worn to allow visible side movement of the armature shaft.

15 The old bushes are simply driven out with a suitable drift and the new bushes inserted by the same method. As the bushes are of the porous bronze type, it is essential that they are allowed to stand in engine oil for at least 24 hours before fitment. Alternatively soak in oil at 100°C (212°F) for 2 hours.

16 To dismantle the starter motor drive, first use a press to push the retainer clear of the circlip, which can then be removed. Lift away the retainer and mainspring.

17 Slide the remaining parts with a rotary action out of the armature shaft.

18 It is most important that the drive gear is completely free from oil, grease and dirt. With the drive gear removed, clean all parts thoroughly in paraffin. **Under no circumstances oil the drive components.**
Lubrication of the drive components could easily cause the pinion to stick.

19 Reassembly of the starter motor drive is the revers sequence of dismantling. Use a press to compress the spring and retainer sufficiently to allow a new circlip to be fitted to its groove on the shaft. Remove the drive from the press.

20 Reassembly of the starter motor is the reverse sequence to dismantling.

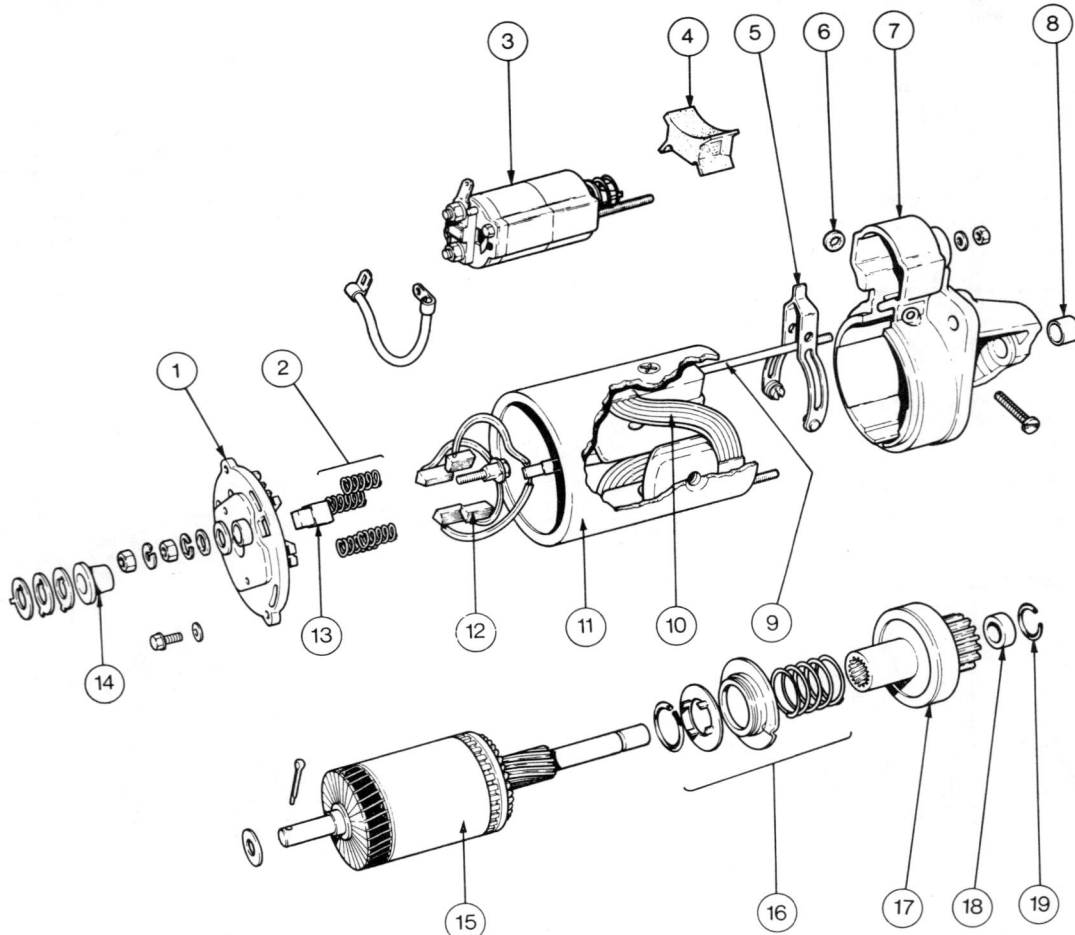

Fig. 10.10 Lucas starter motor (pre-engaged type)

1 Commutator end housing	8 Drive end bush	14 Commutator end bearing
2 Brush springs	9 Through bolt	15 Armature assembly
3 Solenoid assembly	10 Field coil	16 Drive plate and springs
4 Grommet	11 Yoke	17 Pinion
5 Pivot lever	12 Brushes	18 Thrust collar
6 Pivot pin retaining clip	13 Insulator	19 Ring
7 Drive end housing		

18 Starter motor (pre-engaged) – testing on engine

1   If the starter motor fails to operate, check the condition of the battery by turning on the headlamps. If they glow brightly for several seconds and then gradually dim, the battery is in an uncharged condition.

2   If the headlights continue to glow brightly and it is obvious that the battery is in good condition, check the tightness of the battery wiring connections (and in particular the earth lead from the battery terminal to its connection on the body frame). If a terminal on the battery becomes hot when an attempt is made to work the starter this is a sure sign of a poor connection. To rectify remove the terminal, clean the mating faces thoroughly and reconnect. Check the connections on the rear of the starter solenoid. Check the wiring with a meter, or test lamp, for breaks or shorts.

3   Test the continuity of the solenoid windings, by connecting a test lamp circuit comprising a 12 volt battery and low wattage bulb between the 'STA' terminal and the solenoid body. If the two windings are in order the lamp will light. Next connect the test lamp between the solenoid main terminals. Energise the solenoid by applying a 12 volt supply between the unmarked Lucar terminal and the solenoid body. The solenoid should be heard to operate and the test bulb light. This indicates full closure of the solenoid contacts.

4   If the battery is fully charged, the wiring in order, the starter/ignition switch working and the starter motor still fails to operate, it will have to be removed from the car for examination. Before this is done ensure that the starter motor pinion has not jammed in mesh with the flywheel by engaging a gear (not automatic) and rocking the car to and fro. This should free the pinion if it is stuck in mesh with the flywheel teeth.

19 Starter motor (pre-engaged) – removal and refitting

Removal is basically identical to that for the inertia type starter motor with the exception of the cables at the rear of the solenoid. Note these connections and then detach the cable terminal from the solenoid.

20 Starter motor (Lucas pre engaged) – dismantling, overhaul and reassembly

1   Detach the heavy duty cable linking the solenoid 'STA' terminal to the starter motor terminal, by undoing and removing the securing nuts and washers.

2   Undo and remove the two nuts and spring washers securing the solenoid to the drive end bracket.

3   Carefully withdraw the solenoid coil unit from the drive end bracket.

4   Lift off the solenoid plunger and return spring from the engagement lever.

5   Remove the rubber sealing block from the drive end bracket.

6   Remove the retaining ring (spire nut) from the engagement lever pivot pin and withdraw the pin.

7   Unscrew and remove the two drive end bracket securing nuts and spring washers and withdraw the bracket.

8   Lift away the engagement lever from the drive operating plate.

9   Extract the split pin from the end of the armature and remove the shim washers and thrust plate from the commutator end of the armature shaft.

10   Remove the armature, together with its internal thrust washer.

11   Withdraw the thrust washer from the armature.

12   Undo and remove the two screws securing the commutator end bracket to the starter motor body yoke.

13   Carefully detach the end bracket from the yoke, at the same time disengaging the field brushes from the brush gear. Lift away the end bracket.

14   Remove the thrust collar clear of the jump ring and then remove the jump ring. Withdraw the drive assembly from the armature shaft.

15   At this stage, if the brushes are renewed, their flexible connectors must be unsoldered and the connectors of the new brushes soldered in their place. Check that the new brushes move freely in their holders as detailed above. If cleaning the commutator with petrol fails to remove

all the burnt areas and spots, wrap a piece of glass paper around the commutator and rotate the armature.

16   If the commutator is very badly worn, remove the drive gear, mount the armature in a lathe and with the lathe turning at high speed, take a very fine cut out of the commutator and finish the surface by polishing with glass paper. **Do not undercut the insulators between the commutator segments.**

17   With the starter motor dismantled, test the four field coils for an open circuit. Connect a 12 volt battery with a 12 volt bulb in one of the leads between the field terminal post and the tapping point of the field coils to which the brushes are connected. An open circuit is proved by the bulb not lighting.

18   If the bulb lights, it does not necessarily mean that the field coils are in order, as there is a possibility that one of the coils will be earthes to the starter yoke or pole shoes. To check this, remove the lead from the brush connector and place it against a clean portion of the starter yoke. If the bulb lights, the field coils are earthing. Replacement of the field coils calls for the use of a wheel operated screwdriver, a soldering iron, caulking and riveting operations, and is beyond the scope of the majority of owners. The starter yoke should be taken to a reputable electrical engineering works for new field coils to be fitted. Alternatively purchase an exchange Lucas starter motor.

19   If the armature is damaged, this will be evident on inspection. Look for signs of burning, discolouration and for conductors that have lifted away from the commutator. Reassembly is a straightforward reversal of the dismantling procedure.

20   If a bearing is worn, allowing excessive side play of the armature shaft, the bearing bush must be renewed. Drift out the old bush with a piece of suitable diameter rod, preferably with a shoulder on it to stop the bush collapsing.

21   Soak a new bush in engine oil for 24 hours or, if time does not permit, heat in an oil bath at 100°C (212°F) for two hours prior to fitting.

22   As new bushes must not be reamed after fitting, it must be pressed into position using a small mandrel of the same internal diameter as the bush and with with a shoulder on it. Place the bush on the mandrel and press into position using a bench vice.

23   Using a test lamp and battery, test the continuity of the coil winding between terminal 'STA' and a good earth point on the solenoid body. If the lamp fails to light, the solenoid should be renewed.

24   To test the solenoid contacts for correct opening and closing, connect a 12 volt battery and a 60 watt test lamp between the main unmarked Lucar terminal and the 'STA' terminal. The lamp should not light.

25   Energise the solenoid with a separate 12 volt supply connected to the small unmarked Lucar terminal and a good earth on the solenoid body.

26   As the coil is energised the solenoid should be heard to operate and the test lamp should light with full brilliance.

27   The contacts may only be renewed as a set (ie moving and fixed contacts). The fixed contacts are part of the moulded cover.

28   To fit a new set of contacts, first undo and remove the moulded cover securing screws.

29   Unsolder the coil connections from the cover terminals.

30   Lift away the cover and moving contact assembly.

31   Fit a new cover and moving contact assembly, soldering the connections to the cover terminals.

32   Refit the moulded cover securing screws.

33   Whilst the motor is apart, check the operation of the drive clutch. It must provide instantaneous take up of the drive in one direction and rotate easily and smoothly in the opposite direction.

34   Make sure the drive moves freely on the armature shaft splines, without binding or sticking.

35   To reassemble the starter motor is the reverse sequence of dismantling. The following additional points should be noted:

(a)   When assembling the drive always use a new retaining ring (spire nut) to secure the engagement lever pivot pin.

(b)   Make sure that the internal thrust washer is fitted to the commutator end of the armature shaft before the armature is fitted.

(c)   Make sure that the thrust washers and plate are assembled in the correct order and are prevented from rotating separately, by engaging the collar pin with the locking piece on the thrust plate.

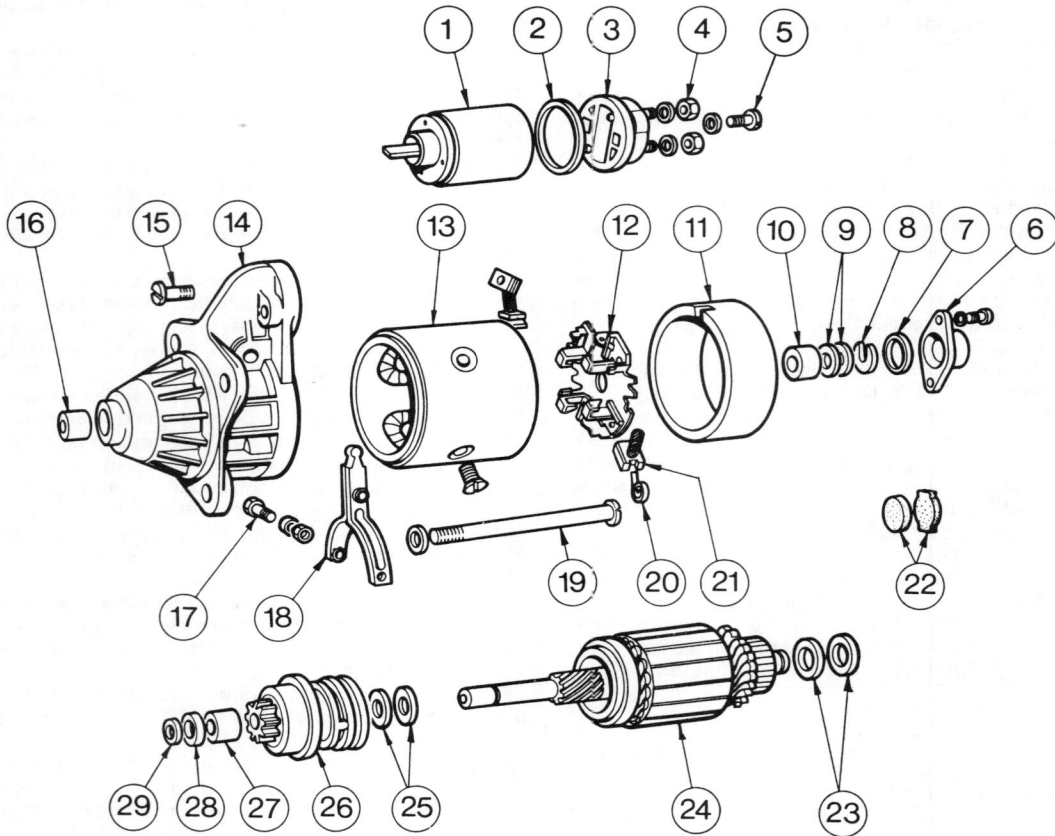

Fig. 10.11 Bosch starter motor (pre-engaged type)

1	Solenoid assembly	9	Thrust washer
2	Packing ring	10	Commutator end bearing
3	Switch contacts and cover	11	Commutator end housing
4	Nut	12	Brush plate
5	Screw	13	Yoke
6	Cover	14	Drive end housing
7	Washer	15	Screw
8	'U' shoe		

16	Bush	23	Thrust washers
17	Pivot pin	24	Armature assembly
18	Pivot lever	25	Packing rings
19	Bolt	26	Drive assembly
20	Brush spring	27	Bush
21	Brush	28	Stop ring
22	Lubricating pads	29	Stop ring

21 Starter motor (Bosch pre-engaged) – dismantling, overhaul and reassembly

1 The procedure is similar to that described in the preceding Section, but refer to the illustration for detail differences in component design (Fig 10.11).

22 Headlamp assembly – removal and refitting

Capri II

1 Disconnect the battery earth lead and remove the headlamp cover plate (photo).
2 Disengage the spring clip, then pull off the cap and multi-plug assembly (photo).
3 Remove the headlamp bulb retainer and bulb (photos).
4 Pull out the parking lamp bulb holder.
5 Remove the retaining screw and withdraw the headlamp assembly. If necessary, remove the adjusters and retaining clips from the lens and reflector assembly (photo).
6 Refitting is the reverse of the removal procedure, but it is recommended that beam alignment is checked, and adjusted if necessary as described in Section 23.

Mercury Capri II

7 Open the hood then remove the 4 bezel retaining screws (two at the top, two at the bottom).

8 Remove the bezel and the three foam insulators (Fig. 10.13)
9 Loosen the three screws from the headlamp retaining ring and remove the ring.
10 Withdraw the headlamp and disconnect the multi-way connector (Fig. 10.14).
11 Refitting is the reverse of the removal procedure, but it is recommended that beam alignment is checked, and adjusted if necessary.

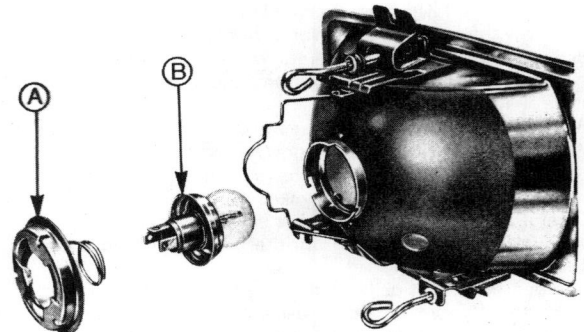

Fig. 10.12 Headlamp assembly (Capri II)

A Bulb retainer   B Bulb

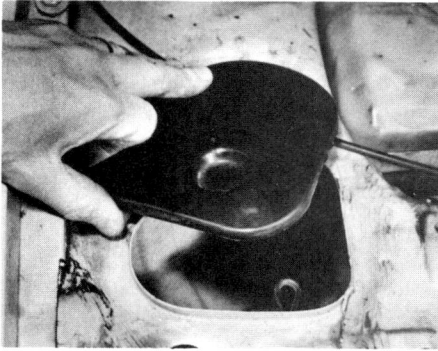
22.1 Removing the headlamp cover plate

22.2 Headlamp cap and multi-plug

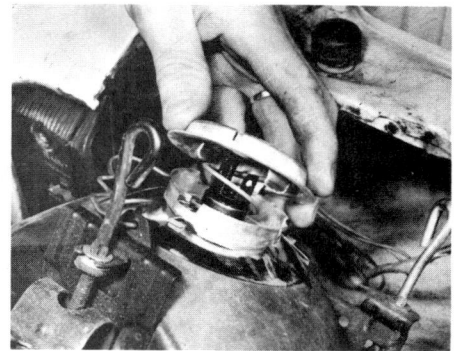
22.3a Remove the bulb retainer ...

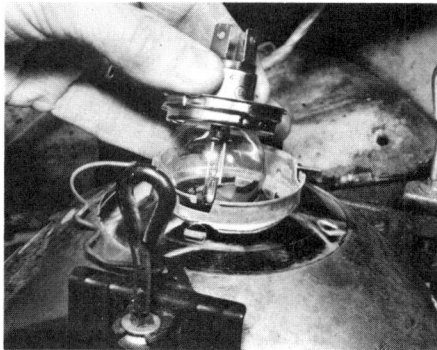
22.3b ... and bulb

22.5 The headlamp retaining screw

HEADLAMP
BEZEL

Fig. 10.13 Headlamp bezel removal (Mercury Capri II)

23 Headlamp beam – alignment

1 The procedure given in this Section is satisfactory for most practical purposes, although it is not intended to replace the alignment procedure used by many dealers and motor factors who would use beam setting equipment.

2 Refer to Fig 10.15 which shows a beam setting chart for right-hand drive vehicles (for left-hand drive vehicles the chart is a mirror image).

3 Position the vehicle on flat, level ground 33 ft (10 m) from a wall on which the aiming chart is to be fixed. A suitable chart can be drawn using white chalk on any convenient flat surface, such as a garage wall or door.

4 Bounce the front of the vehicle, to ensure that the suspension has settled and measure the height from the headlamp centre to the ground (H).

5 Mark the centre of the front and rear windows (outside if a heated rear screen is fitted) using a soft wax crayon or masking tape and position the car at right-angles to the chart so that:

    (a) The vertical centre line and the window markings are exactly in line when viewed through the rear window and

    (b) the horizontal line is at height 'H-X' above the ground.

6 Remove the headlamp cover plate (Capri II), or the bezels (Mercury Capri II), cover the right headlamp and switch on the main beam.

7 Adjust the horizontal alignment of the left-hand headlamp, so that the intersection of the horizontal and angled light pattern coincides with the vertical line on the aiming chart.

8 Adjust the vertical alignment so that the light/dark intersection of the beam pattern coincides with the dotted line on the aiming board.

9 Repeat the procedure for the left headlamp.

10 On completion, switch off the headlamps and refit the cover plates.

24 Parking lamp bulb (Capri II) — removal and refitting

1 Disconnect the battery earth lead and remove the headlamp cover plate.

2 Pull out the parking lamp bulb holder from the rear of the headlamp assembly.

3 Remove the parking lamp bulb.

4 Refitting is the reverse of the removal procedure.

25 Front direction indicator assembly (Capri II) — removal and refitting

1 Disconnect the battery earth lead and remove the headlamp cover plate.

2 Remove the indicator lens (2 screws) and remove the bulb (photo).

3 Remove the reflector. The lower retaining screw is accessible by inserting a screwdriver between the headlamp and reflector body. Disconnect the wiring, to permit the assembly to be withdrawn.

4 Refitting is the reverse of the removal procedure.

26 Front parking and turn signal lights (Mercury Capri II) — removal and refitting

1 To renew a bulb only, remove the two crosshead lens retaining screws and take off the lens. The bayonet fitting bulb can then be removed.

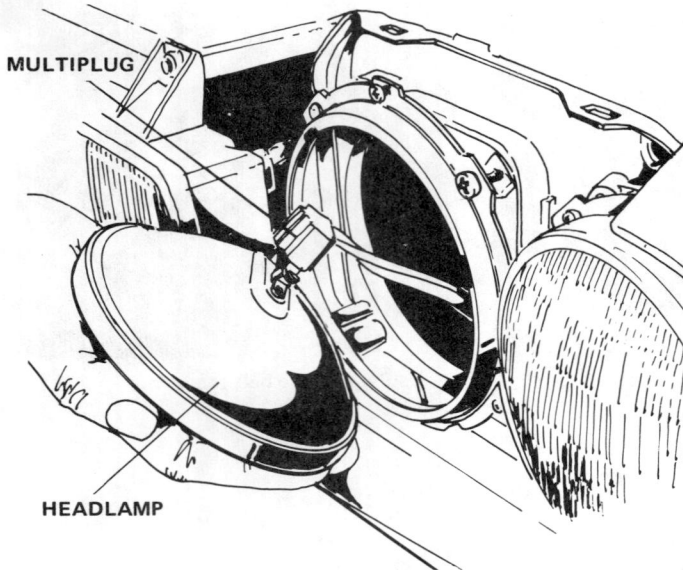

Fig. 10.14 Headlamp removal (Mercury Capri II)

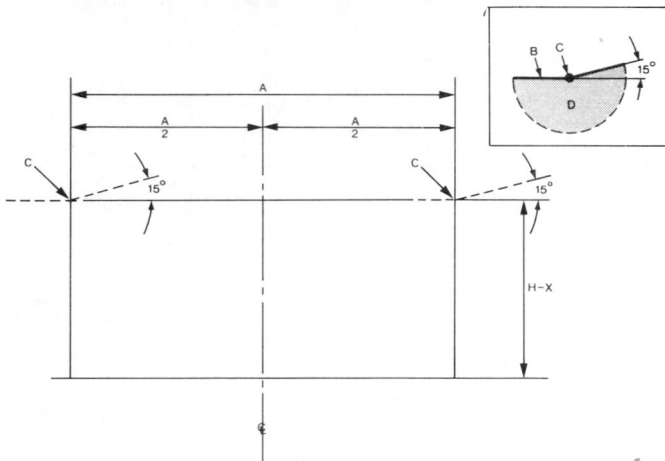

Fig. 10.15 Headlamp beam alignment chart (right-hand drive)

A Distance between headlamp   D Dipped beam pattern
  centres   H Height from ground to centre
B Light/dark boundary   of headlamps
C Dipped beam centre   X 8 in (20 cm)

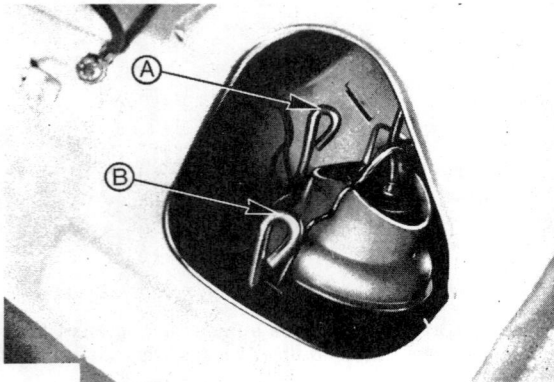

Fig. 10.16 Beam adjusting screws (Capri II)

A Horizontal   B Vertical

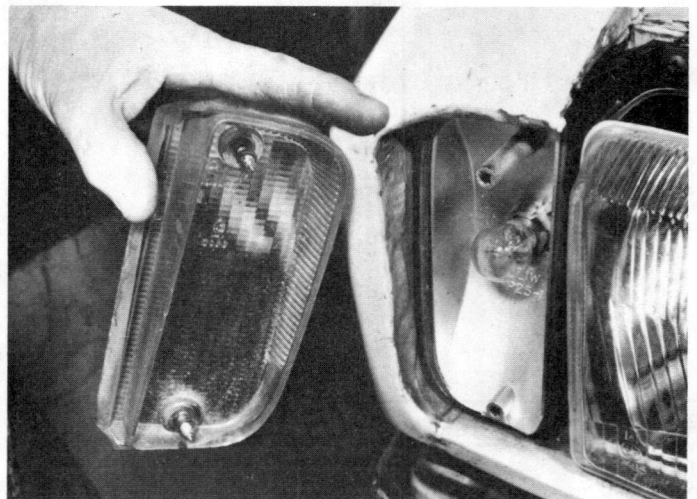

25.2 The indicator lens removed (Capri II)

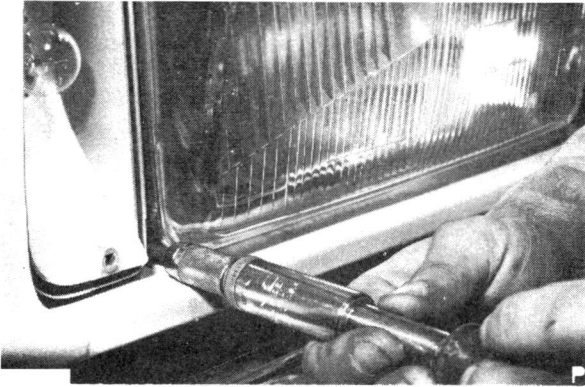

Fig. 10.17 Access to the direction indicator lamp lower screw

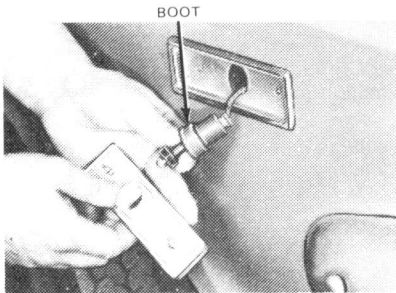

Fig. 10.19 Rear lamp assembly retaining screws

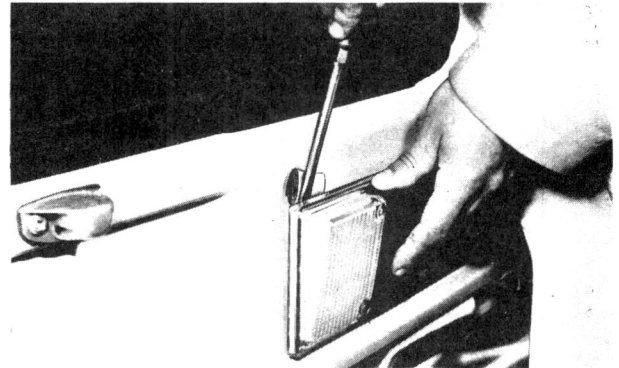

Fig. 10.18 Front side marker light (Mercury Capri II)

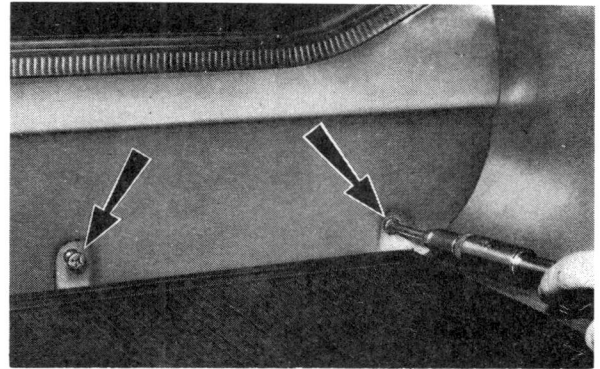

Fig. 10.20 Rear lamp assembly removal

2   If the complete light assembly is to be removed, remove the radiator grille as described in Chapter 12.
3   Remove the bulb socket from the rear of the light body, then the two body retaining nuts.
4   Refitting is the reverse of the removal procedure.

27 Side marker lights (Mercury Capri II) – removal and refitting

Bulbs renewal – front
1   From behind the fender (wing) pull back the bulb holder protective boot.
2   Turn the bulb holder counter-clockwise and pull the lamp from the body. Pull the bulb out of its holder.
3   Refitting is the reverse of the removal procedure.

Bulb renewal – rear
4   Open the tailgate door and remove the floor panel.
5   Reach under the side panel to the marker light bulb, turn the bulb counter-clockwise to remove it, then remove the dust cover and connector. (If a rear window washer is fitted, the reservoir will need to be removed on the left-hand side).
6   Refitting is the reverse of the removal procedure.

Light body – front
7   From behind the fender (wing), remove the securing nuts, clamps and washers, withdraw the light unit from the fender.
8   Slide back the rubber boot and disengage the bulb from the holder.
9   Refitting is the reverse of the removal procedure.

Light body – rear
10 Remove the rear panel trim, B post trim, and upper quarter window trim. Remove the side panel retaining screws, for access to the rear of the marker lamp (for further information on these operations, see Chapter 12).
11 Remove the two light retaining bolts, then remove the light body from outside the car.
12 Refitting is the reverse of the removal procedure

28 Rear lamp assembly – removal and refitting

1   Disconnect the battery earth lead.
2   Open the tailgate, where applicable remove the tailgate trim panel, and remove the rear lamp retaining screws (Fig. 10.19).
3   Carefully lever out the rear lamp assembly and disconnect the wiring. Take care that the paintwork is not damaged during this operation (Fig. 10.20)
4   Clean off any caulking compound from the lamp body.
5   Refitting is the reverse of the removal procedure, but to ensure a weather proof joint, a caulking compound should be applied around the lamp body prior to its fitting.

29 Rear lamp assembly – bulb renewal

1   Remove the four lens retaining screws and take off the lens (photo).
2   Remove and discard the bulbs.
3   Refitting is the reverse of the removal procedure.

30 Licence plates (number plates) lamp assembly – removal and refitting

1   Disconnect the battery earth lead.
2   Open the tailgate, lift up the carpet and remove the spare wheel cover.
3   Remove the lamp lens (2 screws).
4   Disconnect the wiring and attach a length of cord to the lamp assembly lead, so that the lead can be pulled through the body section when refitting. Remove the lamp body.

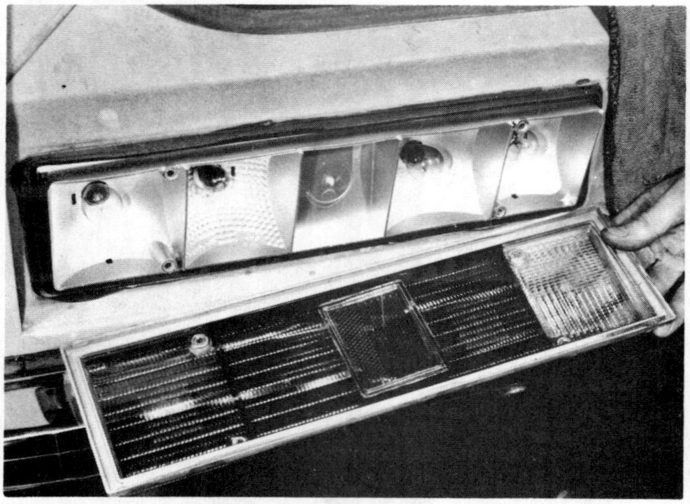

29.1 The rear lamp assembly with lens removed

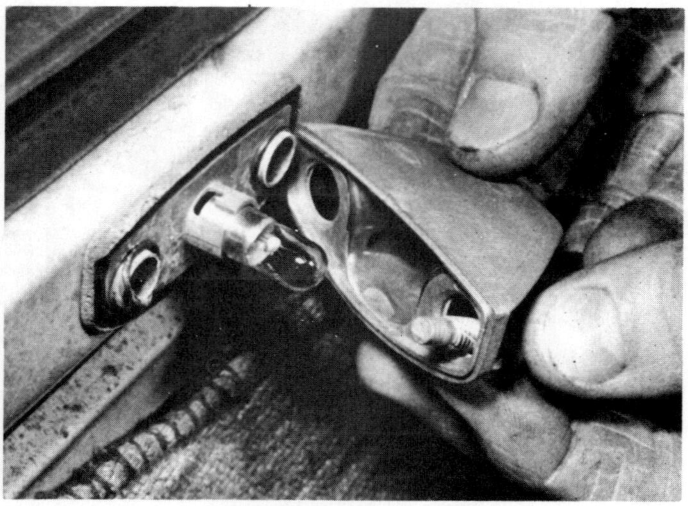

30.6 Access to the number plate lamp bulb

5   Refitting is the reverse of the removal procedure.
6   For access to the bulb only, remove the two crosshead screws and take off the lens (photo).

31 Windscreen wiper motor and linkage (rear) — removal and refitting

1   Disconnect the battery earth lead.

2   Remove the wiper arm and blade.
3   Open the tailgate, and remove the tailgate trim panel.
4   Disconnect the wiring at the wiper motor, noting the respective position of the leads.
5   Remove the wiper spindle retaining nut and the three motor bracket retaining screws. Remove the motor and linkage assembly from the tailgate.
6   Remove the drive spindle nut and the three retaining bolts to detach the motor from the bracket.

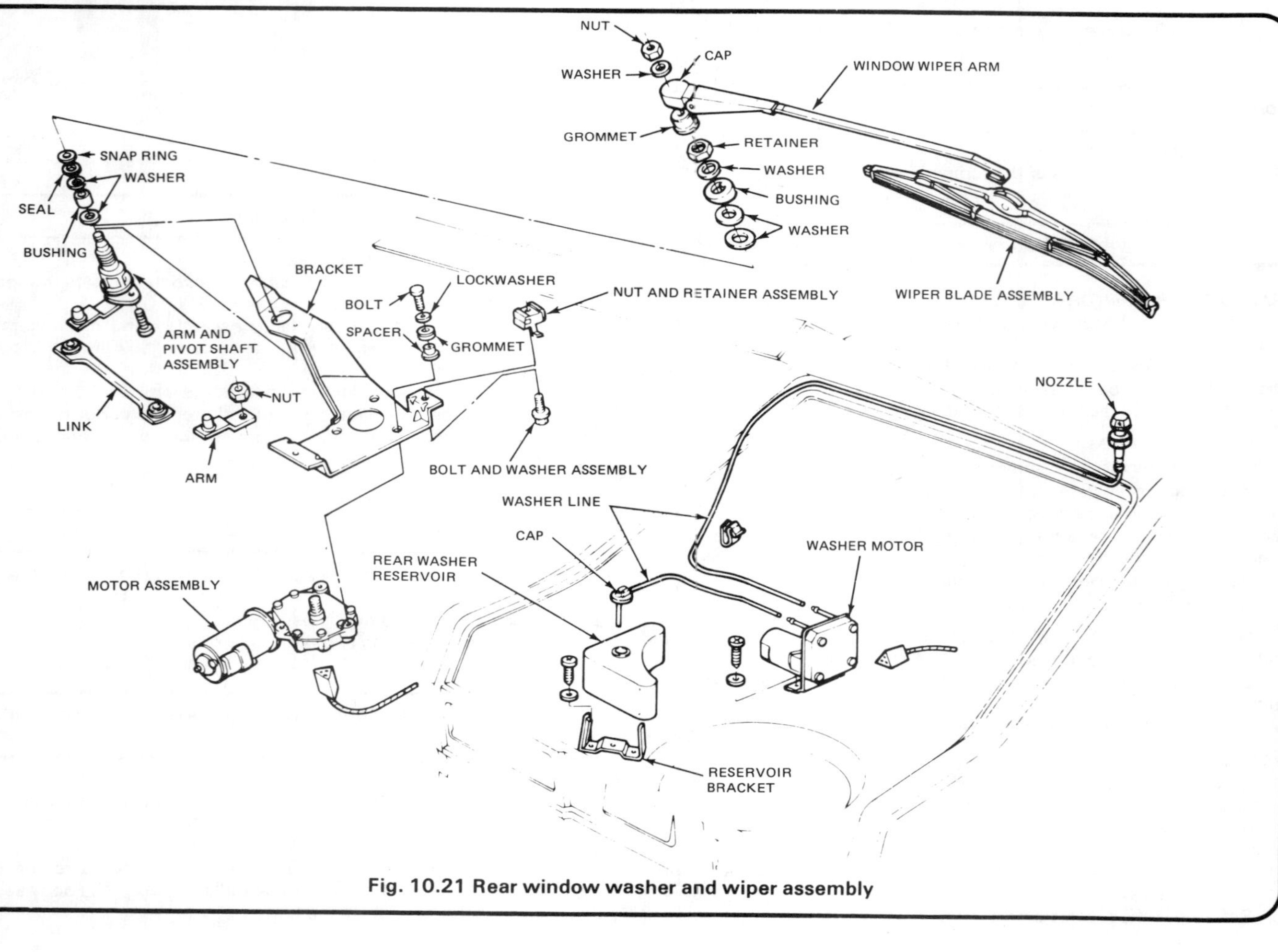

Fig. 10.21 Rear window washer and wiper assembly

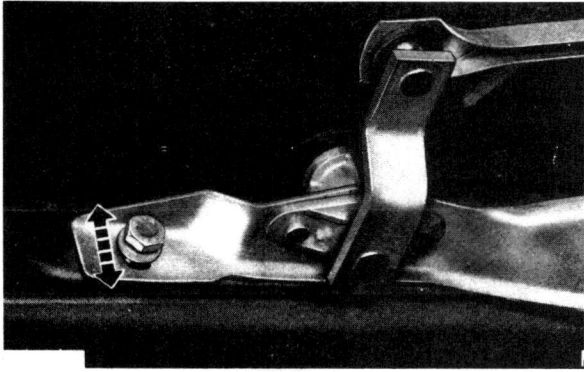

Fig. 10.22 Adjustment point for rear wiper assembly

7 Remove the circlip at the wiper spindle end and detach the linkage from the bracket.
8 Refitting is the reverse of the removal procedure, adjustment of the motor bracket being made before the bolts are finally tightened.

32 Windscreen washer pump (rear) – removal and refitting

1 Disconnect the battery earth lead.
2 Open the tailgate and remove the spare wheel cover.
3 Remove the washer pipes and leads, noting their installed positions to prevent mix-up when refitting.
4 Remove the pump mounting screws and lift off the pump.
5 Refitting is the reverse of the removal procedure.

33 Windscreen washer nozzle (rear) – removal and refitting

1 Open the tailgate, remove the weather strip and pull down the headlining for access to the washer nozzle. Remove the nozzle.
2 Refitting is the reverse of the removal procedure.

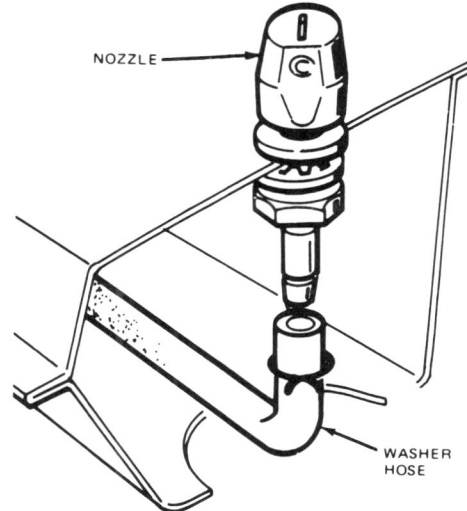

Fig. 10.23 Washer nozzle (rear window)

34 Windscreen wiper motor and linkage (front) – removal and refitting

1 Disconnect the battery earth lead.
2 Remove the windscreen wiper arm and blades. (Refer to Section 40, if necessary).
3 Remove the air cleaner and disconnect the choke cable at the carburettor (Capri II only).
4 Remove the steering column shroud.
5 Remove the retaining screws, and pull the lower dash insulating panel and cover panel assembly clear of the dash panel.
6 Disconnect the cigar lighter wiring and withdraw the panel assembly, complete with choke cable, away from the vehicle.
7 Remove the instrument cluster bezel and the instrument cluster.

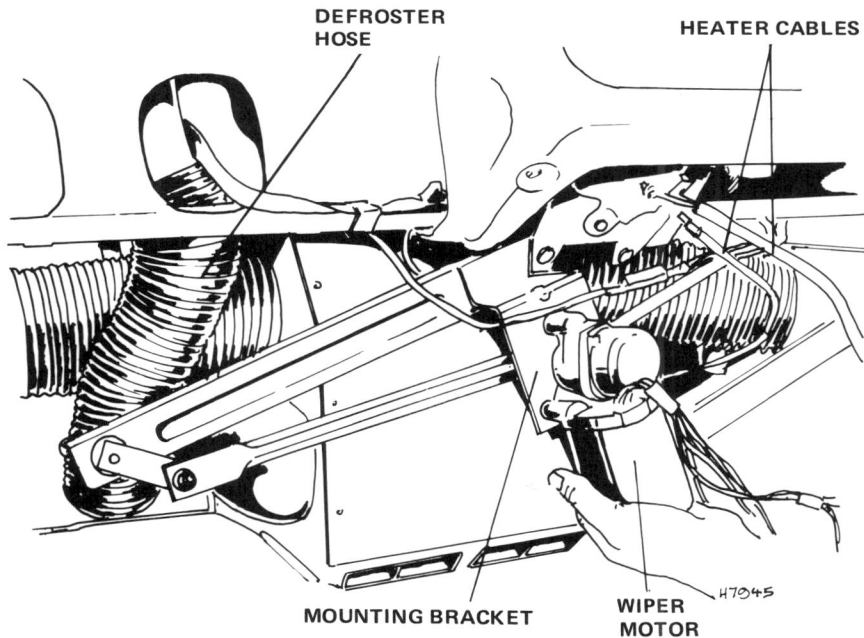

Fig. 10.24 Windscreen wiper motor removal

Refer to Section 43, if necessary.

8 Remove the glovebox catch striker and glovebox assembly. Disconnect the light wiring.

9 Disconnect the cable from the heater controls.

10 Disconnect the driver's side demister tube connector from the heater box and remove the connector and tube.

11 Disconnect and remove the driver's side face level vent tube.

12 Disconnect the wiring at the wiper motor and heater.

13 Remove the driver's side demister vent (1 screw).

14 Remove the wiper spindle retaining nuts and the motor bracket retaining screw. Remove the motor and linkage from the vehicle.

15 If necessary, separate the motor from the linkage.

16 Refitting is the reverse of the removal procedure, but ensure that the heater control cable and the choke operating cable are correctly adjusted.

35 Windscreen washer pump (front) – removal and refitting

1 The front windscreen washers on Capri II models are operated from a facia mounted wash/wipe switch (see Section 60), and an integral pump and reservoir, mounted at the front right-hand side of the engine compartment.

2 To remove the pump and reservoir, pull off the electrical connections, lift up the reservoir and disconnect the flexible pipe from the reservoir. The pump can be removed from the reservoir if necessary (photo).

3 The front windscreen washers on Mercury Capri II models are operated from a floor mounted wash/wipe foot pump. The reservoir is mounted in the engine compartment.

4 To remove the washer pump, disconnect the battery earth cable then pull back the floor covering from around the washer pump.

5 Remove the two crosshead screws, disconnect the flexible hose and lead and remove the pump.

6 Refitting is the reverse of the removal procedure.

36 Windscreen washer nozzles (front) – removal and refitting

1 Disconnect the battery earth lead.

2 Remove the retaining screws, withdraw the nozzles and disconnect the pipes.

3 Refitting is the reverse of the removal procedure.

37 Windscreen wiper mechanism – fault diagnosis and rectification

1 Should the windscreen wipers fail, or work very slowly, check the terminals on the motor for loose connections, and make sure the insulation of all the wiring is not cracked, or broken, thus causing a short circuit. If this is in order, check the current the motor is taking by connecting an ammeter in the circuit and turning on the wiper switch. Consumption should be between 2.3 and 3.1 amps.

2 If no current is passing through the motor, check that the switch is operating correctly.

3 If the wiper motor takes a very high current, check the wiper blades for freedom of movement. If this is satisfactory, check the gearbox cover and gear assembly for damage.

4 If the motor takes a very low current, ensure that the battery is fully charged. Check the brush gear and ensure the brushes are bearing on the commutator. If not, check the brushes for freedom of movement and if necessary, renew the tension springs. If the brushes are very worn they should be replaced with new ones. Check the armature by substitution if this unit is suspect.

38 Windscreen wiper motor – brush renewal

1 Remove the two motor case/gear housing screws and withdraw

35.2 Removing the front washer pump leads (Capri II)

the case and armature together.

2 Withdraw the brushes from the holders and remove the springs.

3 Remove the three brush mounting plate to wiper gear housing screws. Pull the wiring plug out of the side of the housing and remove the brush mounting plate.

4 Remove the screw and earth wire in the gear housing cover plate. Loosen the second screw and slide the cover plate away.

5 Disconnect the white/green and black/green leads from the terminals on the switch cover assembly, then remove the wiring assembly from the motor.

6 Disconnect the motor multi-pin connector from the harness and remove the motor feed wires and brushes.

7 Connect the replacement motor feed wire and brush assembly into the harness via the multi-pin connector.

8 Connect the black/green wire to the terminal marked 'black' and the white/green wire to the terminal marked 'green' on the switch cover assembly.

9 Slide the gear housing cover plate into position, ensuring that the wires are correctly positioned in the cut-out on the cover plate.

39 Windscreen wiper motor – dismantling and reassembly

1 Separate the motor from the linkage.

2 Remove the brushes, wiring harness and brush mounting plate, referring to the previous Section as necessary.

3 Remove the remaining screw securing the gear housing cover plate and switch cover assembly. Remove the assembly.

4 Remove the spring steel armature stop from the gear housing.

5 Remove the spring clip and washer, which secure the pinion gear. Withdraw the gear and washers.

6 Remove the nut securing the motor output arm. Remove the arm, spring and flat washers.

7 Remove the output gear, the parking switch assembly and washer from the gear housing.

8 Reassembly is the reverse of the removal procedure, referring to the previous Section as necessary for the brush gear connections.

40 Windscreen wiper arms and blades – removal and refitting

1 To remove a wiper blade, raise the wiper arm away from the windscreen then, either slide the blade out of the hooked end of the arm or remove it from the spring clip in the centre of the blade. Refitting of the blade is straightforward (photo).

2 To remove a wiper arm, lift up the cap at the spindle, remove the nut and carefully prise off the arm. When refitting, position the arm as necessary to obtain a satisfactory sweep on the windscreen (photo).

CAP

NUT

WASHER

WIPER ARM

BLADE FRAME
ASSEMBLY

BLADE

GROMMET

LOCKWASHER

WASHER

PIVOT SHAFT

SPACER

WASHER

SPACER

LOCKNUT

EXTERNAL TOOTH
WASHER

WASHER

PIVOT ARM

BUSHING

WASHER

GROMMET

CAP

LOCK WASHER

SPACER

NUT

WASHER

WASHERS

SPACER

PIVOT SHAFT

EXTERNAL TOOTH
WASHER

LOCKNUT

WASHER

PIVOT ARM

CLIP

WASHER

BRACKET

BUSHING

WASHER

BOLT

ARM

WIRE LOOM

ARM

OUTPUT ARM

BUSHING

WIPER
MOTOR
ASSEMBLY

GEAR

GEAR

CLIP

BRUSH SPRING

BRUSH PLATE

THRU BOLT

ARMATURE

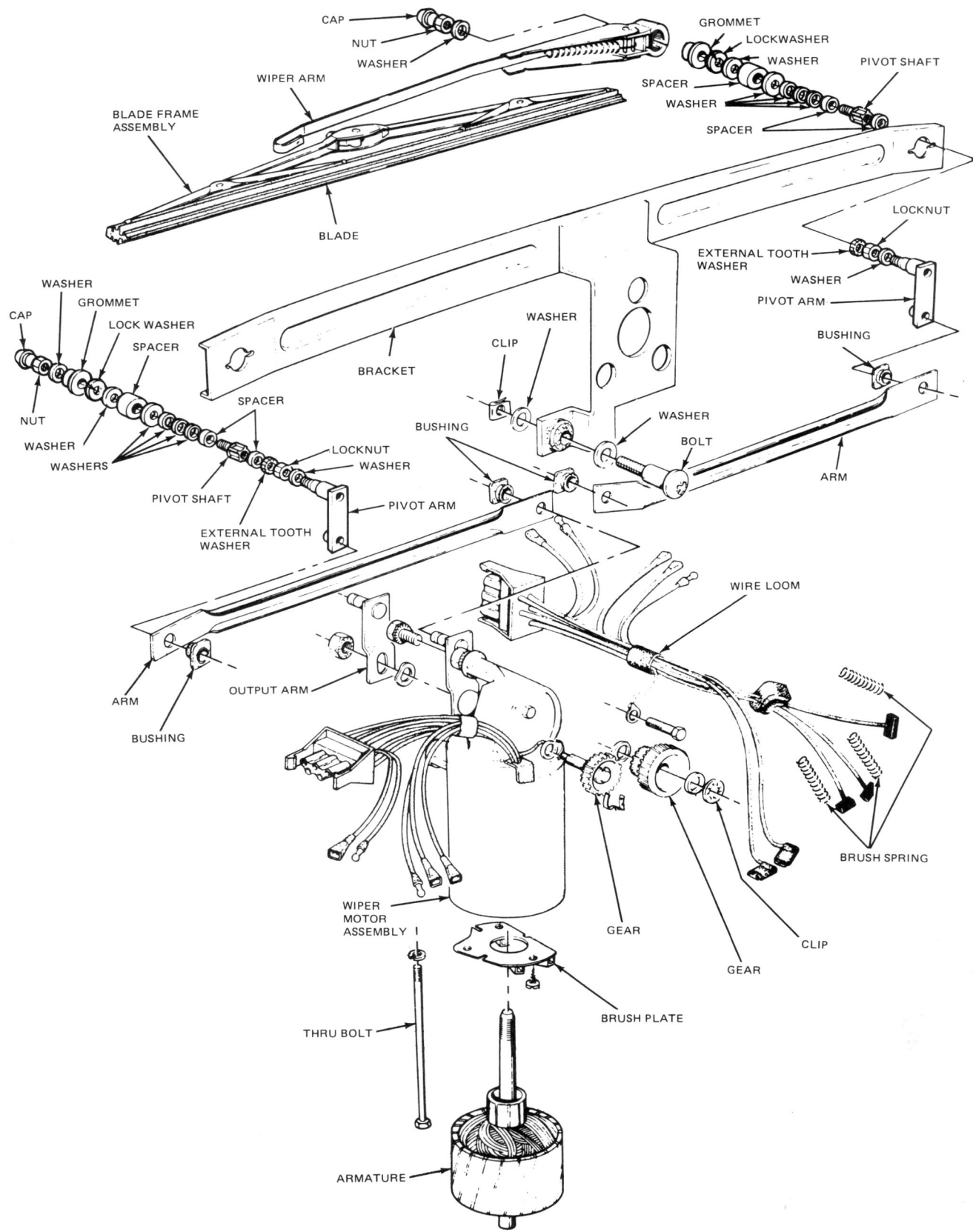

Fig. 10.25 Windscreen wiper assembly — major parts

40.1 Spring clip type wiper blade attachment

40.2 Wiper arm securing nut

41 Horn – fault finding and rectification

1   If the horn works badly or fails completely, check the wiring leading to the horn plug located on the body panel next to the horn itself. Also check that the plug is properly pushed home and is in a clean condition, free from corrosion etc.
2   Check that the horn is secure on its mounting and that there is nothing lying on the horn body.
3   If the fault is not an external one, remove the horn cover and check the leads inside the horn. If they are sound, check the contact breaker contacts. If these are burnt, or dirty, clean them with a fine file and wipe all traces of dirt and dust away with a petrol moistened rag.

42 Fuses

1   If a fuse blows, always trace and rectify the cause before renewing it with one of the same rating.
2   The fuse block is located within the engine compartment on the side apron.
3   The fuse ratings and circuits protected vary according to model and reference should be made to 'Specifications' Section at the beginning of this Chapter.

43 Instrument cluster – removal and refitting

Capri II
1   Disconnect the battery earth lead.
2   Remove the steering column shroud. The bottom half is retained by two screws and the top half can then be pushed out.
3   Remove eight screws from the lower dash trim panel, ease the panel over the ignition switch and allow it to hang freely.
4   Where applicable, pull out the two radio control knobs, remove three screws and disconnect the switch multi-plugs. Remove the facia panel.
5   Remove the four instrument cluster retaining screws and ease the cluster forwards. Disconnect the speedometer cable, oil pressure gauge feed pipe (where applicable) and the wiring loom multi-plug.
6   Refitting is the reverse of the removal procedure.

Mercury Capri II (without air conditioning) (Fig. 10.26)
7   Follow the procedure given for the Capri II models with the following additions:

(a) *Take out the ashtray.*
(b) *Withdraw the hazard flasher switch and disconnect the wiring.*
(c) *Remove the direction indicator switch and allow it to hang by its leads.*

(d) *Disconnect the cigar lighter and clock cable connectors, and completely remove the lower trim panel.*
(e) *Pull off the instrument panel illumination control knob.*
(f) *Remove the lower screws securing the instrument cluster bezel and release the bezel from its upper location by pulling down. Also disconnect the seat belt warning light at the connector.*

8   Refitting is the reverse of the removal procedure.

Mercury Capri II (with air conditioning) (Fig. 10.27)
9   Initially refer to paragraphs 1 and 2 of this Section.
10   Remove the lower left side dash trim panel screws. Withdraw the hazard switch and disconnect the cable connector.
11   Remove the turn signal switch screws, leaving the switch hanging by the wiring harness.
12   Remove the two bottom screws on the right lower dash trim panel. Remove the air-conditioning panel assembly and remove the two screws securing the assembly to the dash.
13   Where applicable, pull the trim panel forwards and down, then remove the cigar lighter and rear window wash/wiper switch connectors. Remove the trim panel.
14   Pull off the panel illumination control knob and radio control knobs.
15   Now follow the procedure given in paragraph 7(f) followed by paragraph 5.
16   Refitting is the reverse of the removal procedure.

44 Clocks (console mounted) – removal and refitting

Refer to the procedure given for removing the centre console in Chapter 12, where this item is listed.

45 Hazard warning switch – removal and refitting

1   Pull the switch from the lower dash trim panel and disconnect the wiring harness.
2   When refitting, connect the wiring harness and press the switch into the trim panel to retain it.

46 Steering column multi-function switch – removal and refitting

1   Disconnect the battery earth lead.
2   Remove the steering column shroud. The bottom half is retained by two screws and the top half can then be pulled out.
3   Remove the switch retaining screws, disconnect the multi-plug, then detach the switch from the steering column.
4   Refitting is the reverse of the removal procedure.

LENS

INSTRUMENT CLUSTER HOUSING (FRONT)

OIL PRESSURE GAGE

AMMETER

SPEEDOMETER

MASK

TACHOMETER

GASKET

INSTRUMENT CLUSTER HOUSING (REAR)

PRINTED CIRCUIT

VOLTAGE REGULATOR ASSEMBLY

FUEL GAGE

LAMP

SOCKET ASSEMBLY

TEMPERATURE GAGE

OIL PRESSURE LINE

ODOMETER RESET KNOB

SELF TAPPING SCREWS

CLIP

ADAPTER

CLIP

RADIO HOLE COVER

COVER CLIP

LAMP ASSEMBLY

SCREW

LAMP

SELF-TAPPING SCREW

HEADLIGHT SWITCH

HAZARD FLASHER SWITCH

INSTRUMENT LIGHT SWITCH

HOLE COVER

HOLE COVER

CLOCK

INSTRUMENT CLUSTER BEZEL

PILLAR

HARNESS

BRACKET

CONSOLE

CLOCK HOUSING

CLOCK BULB

CIGAR LIGHTER ASSEMBLY

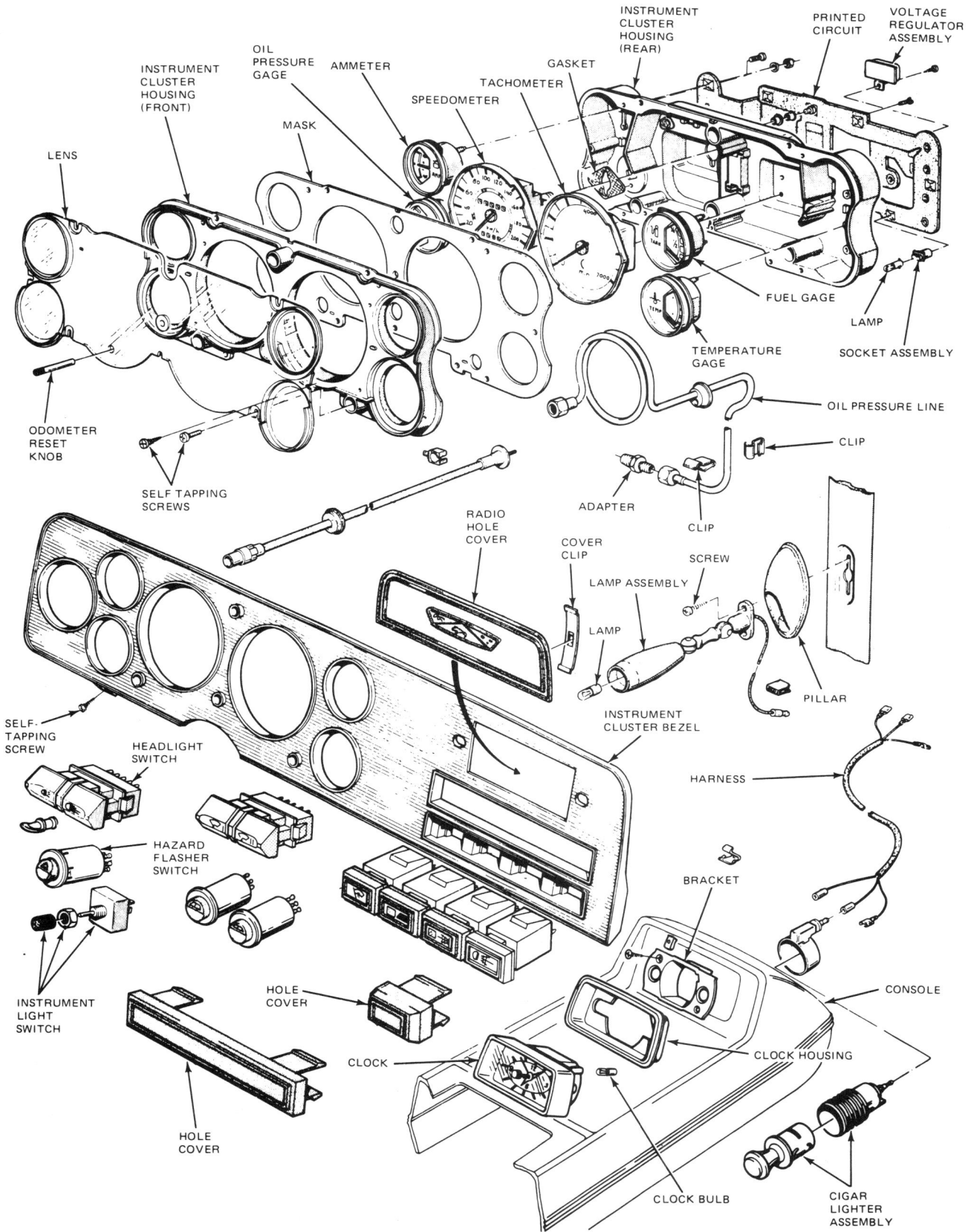

Fig. 10.26 Instrument cluster – Mercury Capri II, lhd, without air conditioning

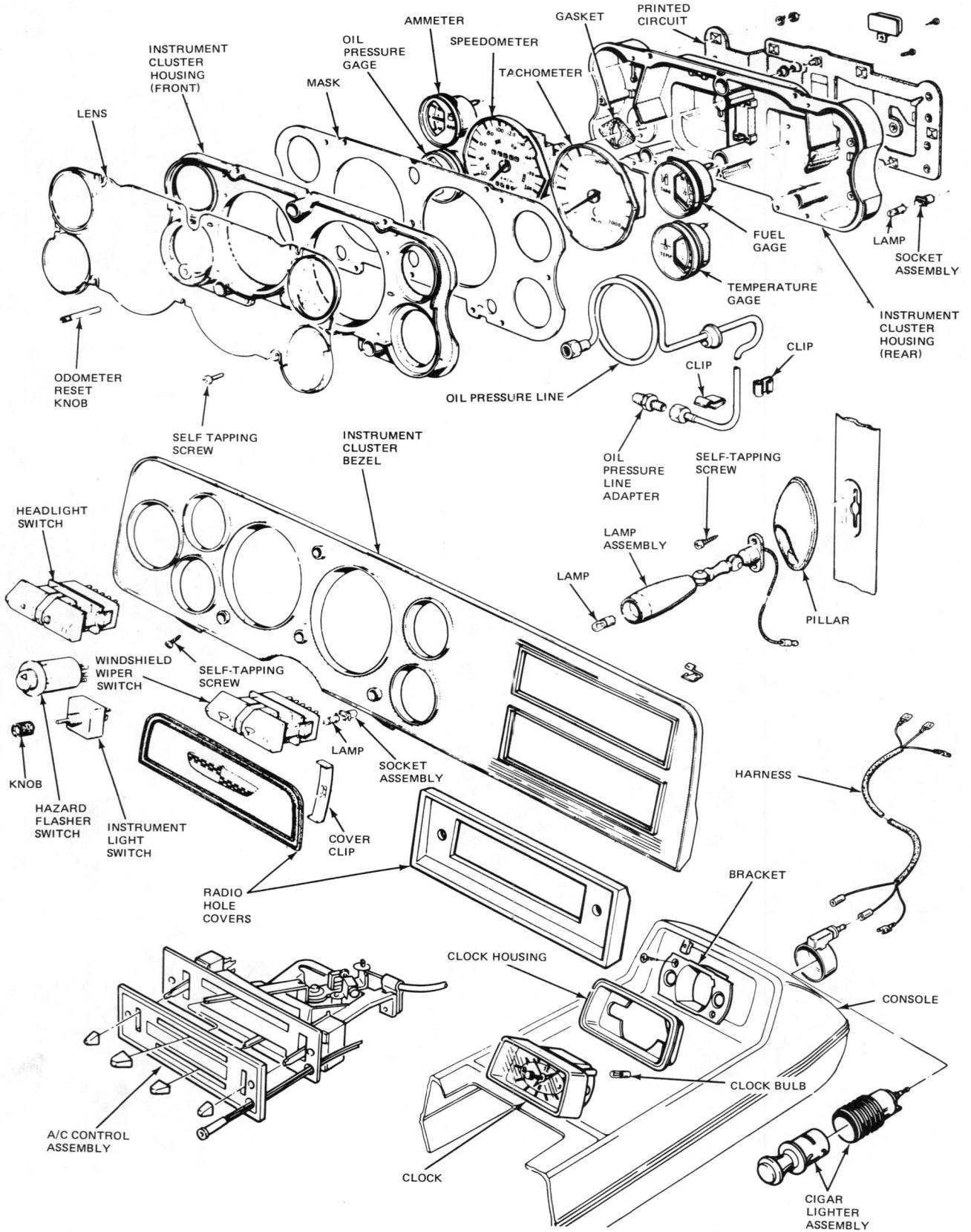

Fig. 10.27 Instrument cluster – Mercury Capri II, lhd, with air conditioning (The rhd model is opposite hand, but similar)

47 Flasher unit

1   The flasher unit is mounted behind the instrument cluster and access to it can be gained after drawing the panel forward (see Section 43).

2   In the event of failure of a particular piece of equipment, always check the connecting wiring, bulbs and fuses before assuming that it is the relay or flasher unit that is at fault. Take the relay or flasher unit to your dealer for testing, or check the circuit by substituting a new component.

48 Speedometer cable – renewal

1   Chock the front wheels, jack up the rear of the car and support on firmly based stands.

2   Working under the car carefully remove the snap-ring that secures the speedometer cable to the transmission. Detach the cable.

3   Working in the engine compartment, remove the speedometer cable clip located on the engine bulkhead.

4   Ease the speedometer cable rubber grommet from the engine bulkhead.

5   Refer to Section 43 and move the instrument cluster by a sufficient amount to gain access to the rear of the speedometer.

6   Detach the cable from the rear of the speedometer.

7   Refitting is the reverse sequence to removal. For reliable operation, it is very important that there are no sharp bends in the cable run.

49 Instrument voltage regulator – removal and refitting

1   Remove the instrument panel cluster as described in Section 43.

2   Unscrew and remove the single screw that retains the instrument voltage regulator to the rear of the instrument panel and withdraw the regulator.

3   Refitting is a reversal of the removal procedure.

50 Cigar lighter – removal and refitting

1   Initially proceed as described in paragraphs 1 to 4 of Section 56.

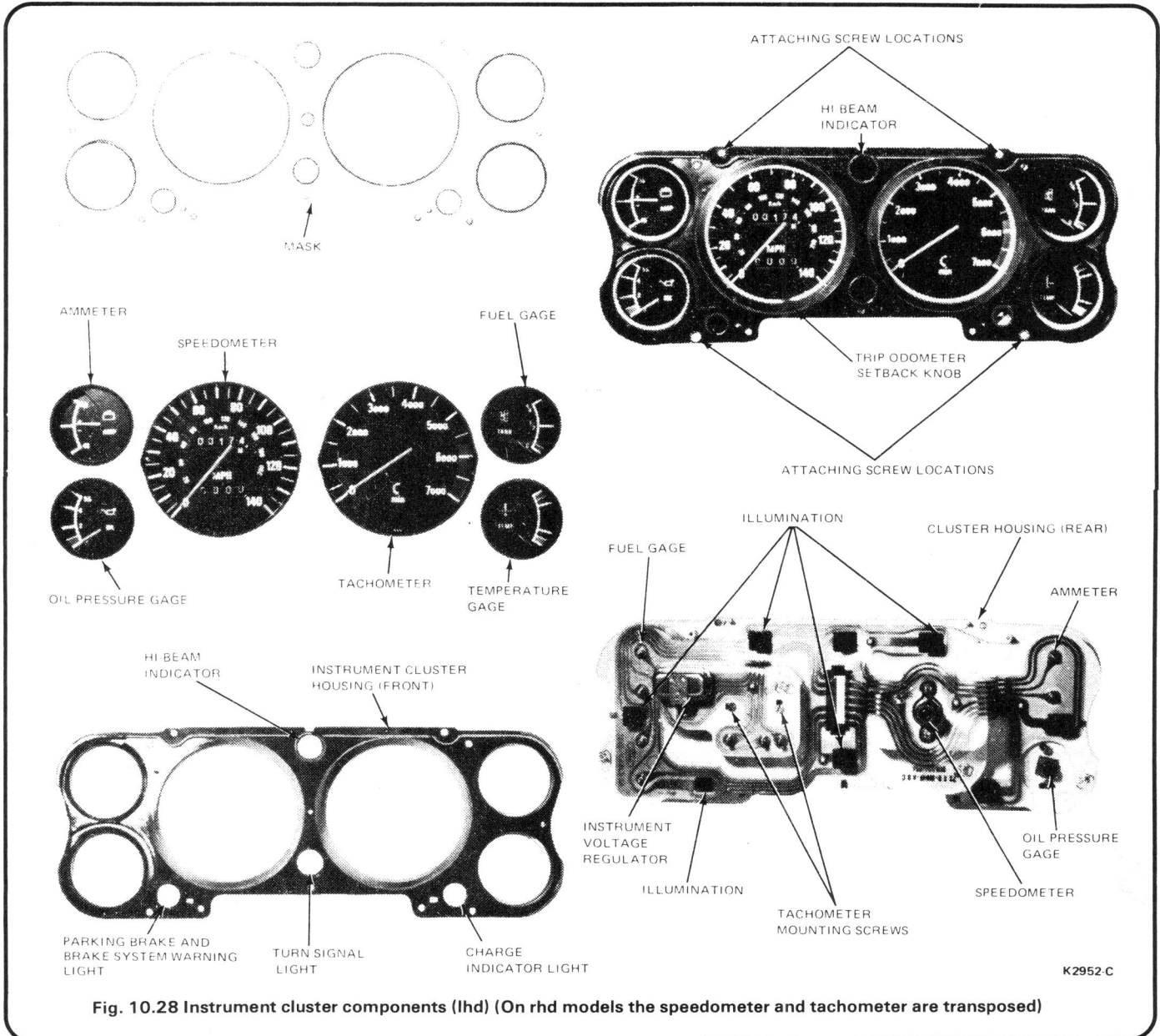

Fig. 10.28 Instrument cluster components (lhd) (On rhd models the speedometer and tachometer are transposed)

2   Unclip the cigar lighter illumination bulb from the unit body.
3   Working from behind the instrument panel, unscrew and remove the lighter body. Remove the front section through the instrument panel.
4   Refitting is the reverse of the removal procedure.

51 Ignition switch – removal and refitting

1   Disconnect the battery earth lead.
2   Remove the steering column shroud. The bottom half is retained by two screws and the top half can then be pulled out.
3   Set the ignition key to the 'O' position.
4   Note the location of the cables at the ignition switch and then detach the cables.
5   Undo and remove the two screws that secure the ignition switch to the lock. Lift away the switch.
6   Refitting the ignition switch is the reverse of the removal procedure.

52 Steering column lock – removal and refitting

1   Disconnect the battery earth lead.
2   Remove the steering column shroud. The bottom half is retained by two screws and the top half can then be pushed out.
3   Undo and remove the two screws that secure the upper steering column support bracket.
4   Turn the column until it is possible to gain access to the headless bolts.
5   Note the location of the cables to the ignition switch terminals and lock body and then detach the cables.
6   Using a suitable diameter drill remove the headless bolts that clamp the lock to the steering column. Alternatively, use a centre punch to rotate the bolts.
7   Lift away the lock assembly and clamp bracket.
8   Refitting the lock assembly is the reverse sequence to removal. Make sure that the pawl enters the steering shaft. It will be necessary to use new shear bolts, which must be tightened equally before the heads are separated from the shank.

53 Key-in-lock warning buzzer (Mercury Capri II) – removal and refitting

1   Disconnect the battery earth lead.
2   Remove the lower left-hand dash trim panel.
3   Disconnect the buzzer connector (located on the steering column bracket) and remove the buzzer retaining screw.
4   Refitting is the reverse of the removal procedure.

54 Door pillar switches – removal and refitting

1   Disconnect the battery earth lead.
2   Prise the switch out of the door pillar, disconnect the lead and remove the switch.
3   Refitting is the reverse of the removal procedure.

55 Interior light – removal and refitting

1   To remove the interior light lens, switch and/or body, carefully prise the lens away from the light body.

56 Map light (Mercury Capri II) – removal and refitting

1   Disconnect the battery earth lead.
2   Remove the steering column shroud. The bottom half is retained by two screws and the top half can then be pushed out.
3   Remove the screws retaining the direction indicator switch and allow the switch to hang by the wiring harness.
4   Remove the lower dash panel screws, pull the panel forward and down, to gain access to the clock and cigar lighter cable connectors. Disconnect the cables and remove the trim panel.

5   Remove the glovebox (refer to Chapter 12, if necessary).
6   Disconnect the map light harness at the harness connector under the instrument panel crash pad on the right-hand side.
7   Remove the retaining screws, and remove the map light, complete with harness. A length of cord can be tied to the end of the harness lead and drawn through the pillar to act as an aid to refitting.
8   Refitting is the reverse of the removal procedure.

57 Instrument illumination and warning lamp bulbs (general) – renewal

1   Refer to Section 43 and move the instrument cluster by a sufficient amount to gain access to the bulb holder(s).
2   Extract the bulb from its holder.
3   Refitting is the reverse of the removal procedure.

58 Handbrake warning light bulb – renewal

1   Disconnect the battery earth lead.
2   Remove the steering column shroud. The bottom half is retained by two screws and the top half can then be pushed out.
3   Remove the ashtray.
4   Remove all the screws along the upper edge and glove compartment edge of the lower panel, and also those on the lower edge (outboard of the steering column) so that the lower panel can be pulled down and clear of the steering lock.
5   Reach up under the facia panel and apply sideways pressure to the bulb holder to release it from the instrument cluster.
6   Refitting is the reverse of the removal procedure, but ensure that the bulb holder electrical contacts are horizontal to mate with the printed circuit contacts.

59 Facia mounted heated rear window warning light bulb – renewal

1   Using a piece of thick paper or a piece of card to prise against, use a screwdriver to prise out the switch assembly from the multi-plug.
2   Withdraw the bulb holder and remove the bulb.
3   Refitting is the reverse of the removal procedure.

60 Facia mounted heated rear window switch and windscreen washer switch (front) – removal and refitting

1   Follow the procedure given in the previous Section for warning light bulb renewal.

61 Rear window washer and wiper switches – removal and refitting

1   Remove the lower dash trim panel, as described in Section 43.
2   Disconnect the switch leads then press the switch(es) out of the trim panel.
3   Refitting is the reverse of the removal procedure.

62 Heated rear window switch (Mercury Capri II with air-conditioning) – removal and refitting

1   Remove the two screws securing the air-conditioning assembly to the lower dash panel.
2   Partially pull out the assembly, disconnect the bulb housing connectors and withdraw the plastic bulb housing.
3   Remove the switch knob, remove the switch retaining cap screw and remove the switch.
4   Refitting is the reverse of the removal procedure.

63 Luggage compartment lamp – removal and refitting

1   Disconnect the battery earth lead.

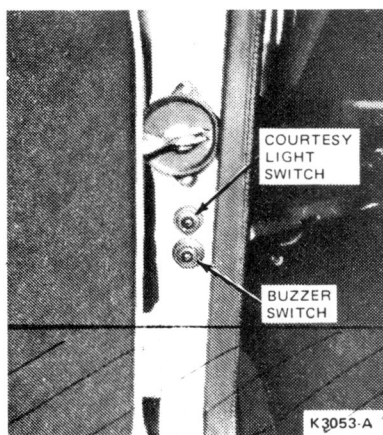

Fig. 10.29 Door pillar switches

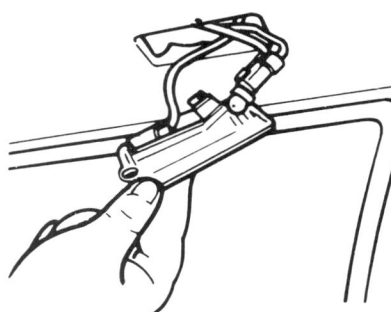

Fig. 10.30 Interior light

Fig. 10.31 Map light

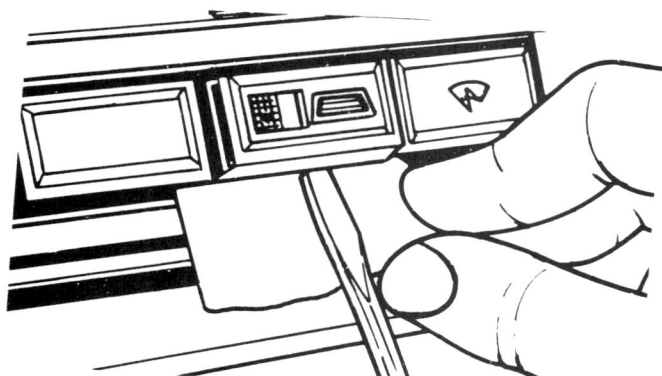

Fig. 10.32 Removing a facia-mounted heated rear window
warning light bulb, or a facia-mounted windscreen washer switch

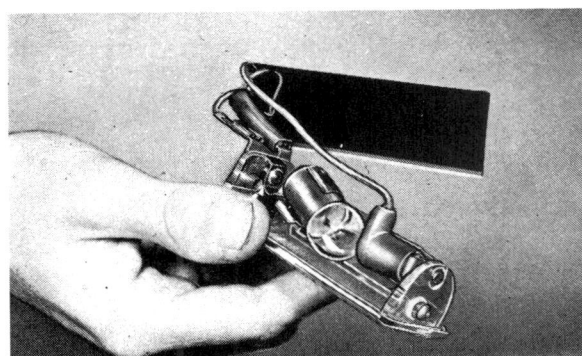

Fig. 10.33 Removing the luggage compartment lamp

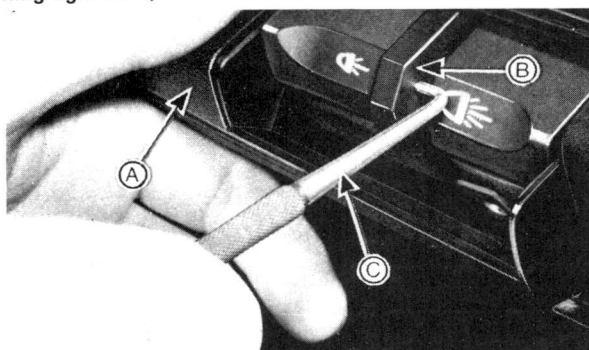

Fig. 10.34 Light and windscreen wiper switch removal

A Lower panel   B Centre web   C Cranked tool

2   Open the tailgate and pull out the lamp from the trim panel.
3   Note the relative positions of the electrical connections then
remove them from the lamp.
4   Refitting is the reverse of the removal procedure.

64 Light and windscreen wiper (front) switches – removal and refitting

1   Disconnect the battery earth lead.
2   Slacken the three screws on the lower panel.
3   Fully depress one of the switches of the pair to be removed, then
insert a suitably cranked tool such as a piece of bent welding rod into
the exposed hole in the switch centre web (Fig. 10.34).
4   Hold down the lower panel and gently pull out the switches.
5   When refitting, first connect the plug, then refit the switch and
tighten the parcel screws.
6   Finally reconnect the battery earth lead.

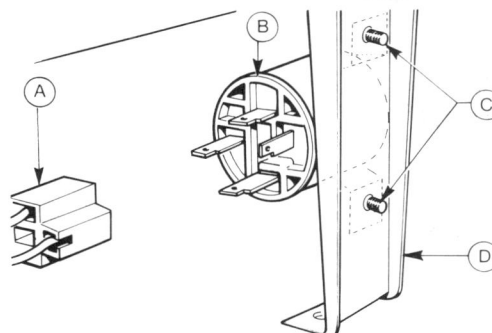

Fig. 10.35 Heated rear window relay

A Multi-plug   C Retaining screws
B Relay   D Bracket

65 Heated rear window relay – removal and refitting

1   Disconnect the battery earth lead.
2   Remove the steering column shroud. The bottom half is retained
by two screws and the top half can then be pushed out.
3   Remove the lower panel retaining screws, disconnect the cigar
lighter and remove the panel.
4   Disconnect the multi-plug and remove the relay.
5   Refitting is the reverse of the removal procedure.

66 Seat belt/starter interlock system

1   This system is fitted to North American cars (not Canada) and is
designed to prevent operation of the car unless the front seat belts
have been fastened.
2   If either of the front seats is occupied and the seat belts have not

been fastened, when the ignition key is turned to the 'II' (ignition on) position, a warning lamp will flash and a buzzer will sound.

3   If the warning is ignored, further turning of the key to the start position will not actuate the starter motor.

4   In an emergency, and in the event of a failure in the system, an over-ride switch is located under the bonnet. One depression of the switch will permit one starting sequence of the engine, without the front seat belts being fastened.

5   If a fault develops in the system, check the fuse and then the security of all leads and connections.

67 Seat belt warning buzzer (Mercury Capri II) – removal and refitting

1   Initially proceed as described in paragraphs 1 to 4 of Section 56.

2   Remove the buzzer-to-steering column mounting screw(s), disconnect the wiring and remove the buzzer.

3   Refitting is the reverse of the removal procedure.

68 Radios and tape players – fitting (general)

A radio or tape player is an expensive item to buy and will only give its best performance if fitted properly. If you do not wish to do the fitting yourself there are many in-car entertainment specialists who can do the fitting for you.

Make sure the unit purchased is of the same polarity as the car and ensure that units with adjustable polarity are correctly set before commencing installation.

It is difficult to give specific information with regard to fitting, as final positioning of the radio/tape player, speakers and aerial is entirely a matter of personal preference. However, the following paragraphs give guidelines, which are relevant to all installations.

Radios

Most radios are a standardised size of 7 inches wide, by 2 inches deep – this ensures that they will fit into the radio aperture provided in most cars. If your car does not have such an aperture, the radio must be fitted in a suitable position either in, or beneath, the dashpanel. Alternatively, a special console can be purchased which will fit between the dashpanel and the floor, or on the transmission tunnel. These consoles can also be used for additional switches and instrumentation if required. Where no radio aperture is provided, the following points should be borne in mind before deciding where to fit the unit:

a)   *The unit must be within easy reach of the driver wearing a seat belt.*

b)   *The unit must not be mounted in close proximity to an electric tachometer, the ignition switch and its wiring, or the flasher unit and associated wiring.*

c)   *The unit must be mounted within reach of the aerial lead, and in such a place that the aerial lead will not have to be routed near the components detailed in the preceding paragraph 'b'.*

d)   *The unit should not be positioned in a place where it might cause injury to the car occupants in an accident; for instance, under the dashpanel above the driver's or passengers' legs.*

e)   *The unit must be fitted really securely.*

Some radios have mounting brackets provided, together with instructions: others will need to be fitted using drilled and slotted metal strips, bent to form mounting brackets – these strips are available from most accessory shops. The unit must be properly earthed, by fitting a separate earthing lead between the casing of the radio and the vehicle frame.

Use the radio manufacturer's instructions when wiring the radio into the vehicle's electrical system. If no instructions are available, refer to the relevant wiring diagram to find the location of the radio 'feed' connection in the vehicle's wiring circuit. A 1-2 amp 'in-line' fuse must be fitted in the radio's 'feed' wire – a choke may also be necessary (see next Section).

The type of aerial used and its fitted position, is a matter of personal preference. In general, the taller the aerial, the better the reception. It is best to fit a fully retractable aerial – especially if a mechanical car-wash is used, or if you live in an area where cars tend to be vandalised. In this respect, electrical aerials which are raised and lowered automatically when switching the radio on or off are convenient, but are more likely to give trouble than the manual type.

When choosing a site for the aerial, the following points should be considered:

a)   *The aerial lead should be as short as possible – this means that the aerial should be mounted at the front of the car.*

b)   *The aerial must be mounted as far away from the distributor and HT leads as possible.*

c)   *The part of the aerial which protrudes beneath the mounting point must not foul the roadwheels, or anything else.*

d)   *If possible, the aerial should be positioned so that the coaxial lead does not have to be routed through the engine compartment.*

e)   *The plane to the panel on which the aerial is mounted should not be so steeply angled that the aerial cannot be mounted vertically (in relation to the 'end-on' aspect of the car). Most aerials have a small amount of adjustment available.*

Having decided on a mounting position, a relatively large hole will have to be made in the panel. The exact size of the hole will depend upon the specific aerial being fitted, although, generally, the hole required is of $\frac{3}{4}$ inch (19 mm) diameter. On metal bodied cars, a 'tank-cutter' of the relevant diameter is the best tool to use for making the hole. This tool needs a small diameter pilot hole drilled through the panel, through which, the tool clamping bolt is inserted. On GRP bodied cars, a 'hole-saw' is the best tool to use. Again, this tool will require the drilling of a small pilot hole. When the hole has been made, the raw edges should be de-burred with a file and then painted, to prevent corrosion.

Fit the aerial according to the manufacturer's instructions. If the aerial is very tall, or if it protrudes beneath the mounting panel for a considerable distance, it is a good idea to fit a stay between the aerial and the vehicle frame. This stay can be manufactured from the slotted and drilled metal strips previously mentioned. The stay should be securely screwed or bolted in place. For best reception it is advisable to fit an earth lead between the aerial and the vehicle frame.

It will probably be necessary to drill one or two holes through bodywork panels, in order to feed the aerial lead into the interior of the car. Where this is the case, ensure that the holes are fitted with rubber grommets to protect the cable and to stop entry of water.

Positioning and fitting of the speaker depends mainly on its type. Generally, the speaker is designed to fit directly into the aperture already provided in the car (usually in the shelf behind the rear seats, or in the top of the dashpanel). Where this is the case, fitting the speaker is just a matter of removing the protective grille from the aperture and screwing or bolting the speaker in place. Take great care not to damage the speaker diaphragm whilst doing this. It is a good idea to fit a 'gasket' between the speaker frame and the mounting panel, in order to prevent vibration – some speakers will already have such a gasket fitted.

When connecting a rear mounted speaker to the radio, the wires should be routed through the vehicle beneath the carpets, or floor mats – preferably the middle, or along the side of the floorpan, where they will not be trodden on by passengers. Make the relevant connections as directed by the radio manufacturer.

Ensure that all the electrical connections have been made properly, so that there is a good electrical contact and that all the wiring is installed neatly and secured to the car with wiring clips, or PVC tape.

After completing the installation of the radio, it will be necessary to trim the radio to suit the aerial. If specific instructions on this are not given by the manufacturer of the radio, proceed as follows. Find a medium waveband station with a low signal strength and turn the trim screw on the radio in or out until the signal is received at maximum strength.

Tape players

Fitting instructions for both cartridge and cassette stereo tape players are the same and in general, the same rules apply as when fitting a radio. Tape players are not usually prone to electrical interference like radio – although it can occur – so positioning is not so critical. If possible, the player should be mounted on an 'even-keel'. Also, it must be possible for a driver wearing a seat belt to reach the unit in order to change or turn over tapes.

For the best results from speakers designed to be recessed into a panel, mount them so that the back of the speaker protrudes into an enclosed chamber within the car (eg. door interiors or the boot cavity).

To fit recessed type speakers in the front doors, first check that there is sufficient room to mount the speakers in each door without their fouling the latch or window winding mechanism. Hold the speaker against the skin of the door, and draw a line around the periphery of the speaker. With the speaker removed, draw a second 'cutting' line, within the first, to allow enough room for the entry of the speaker back, but at the same time providing a broad seat for the speaker flange. When you are sure that the 'cutting-line' is correct, drill a series of holes around its periphery. Pass a hacksaw blade through one of the holes and then cut through the metal between the holes until the centre section of the panel falls out.

De-burr the edges of the hole and then paint the raw metal to prevent corrosion. Cut a corresponding hole in the door trim panel – ensuring that it will be completely covered by the speaker grille. Now drill a hole in the door edge and a corresponding hole in the door surround. These holes are to feed the speaker leads through – so fit grommets. Pass the speaker leads through the door trim, door skin and out through the holes in the side of the door and door surround. Refit the door trim panel and then secure the speaker to the door using self-tapping screws. **Note**: *If the speaker is fitted with a shield, to prevent water dripping on it, ensure that this shield is at the top.*

69 Radios and tape players – suppression of interference (general)

To eliminate unwanted noises costs very little and is not as difficult as is sometimes thought. With common sense and patience and following the instructions in the following paragraphs, interference can be virtually eliminated.

The first cause for concern is the generator. The noise this makes over the radio is like an electric mixer and the noise speeds up when you rev up (if you wish to prove the point, you can remove the drivebelt and try it). The remedy for this is to connect a 1.0 uf–3.0 uf capacitor between earth, probably the bolt that holds down the generator base, and the *large* terminal on the alternator. If you connect it to the small terminal, you will probably damage the generator permanently (see Fig. 10.36).

A second common cause of electrical interference is the ignition system. Here a 1.0 uf capacitor must be connected between earth and the 'SW' or '+' terminal on the coil (see Fig. 10.37). This may stop the tick-tick-tick sound that comes over the speaker. Next comes the spark itself.

There are several ways of curing interference from the ignition HT system. One is to use carbon film HT lead, but this is liable to internal breaks, causing erratic ignition. The second and more successful method, is to use resistive spark plug caps (see Fig. 10.38) of about 10000 ohm to 15000 ohm resistance. If, due to lack of room, these cannot be used, an alternative is to use 'in-line' suppressors (Fig. 10.38) – if the interference is not too bad, you may get away with only one suppressor in the coil to distributor line. If the interference continues (a 'clacking' noise), fit suppressor to all the HT leads.

Check that the case of the radio and the fixings for the aerial make good electrical contact with the metalwork of the car. Ensure that the aerial plug is pushed fully into the socket in the radio and that the radio has been trimmed (see preceding Section). Make sure that the radio has an in line fuse and that the rating of the fuse cartridge is not higher than 2 amps.

Although the ignition system is the principal cause of interference, unwanted noises on the radio can also be produced by the electric

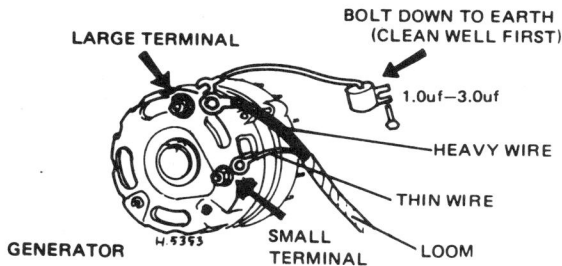

Fig. 10.36 The correct way to connect a capacitor to the generator

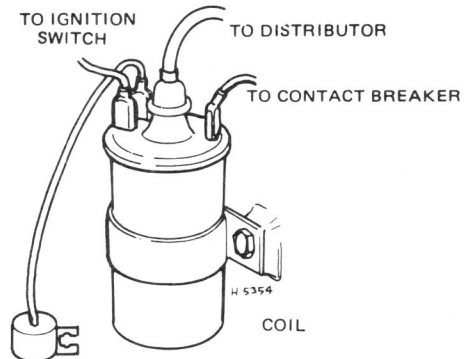

Fig. 10.37 The capacitor must be connected to the ignition switch side of the coil

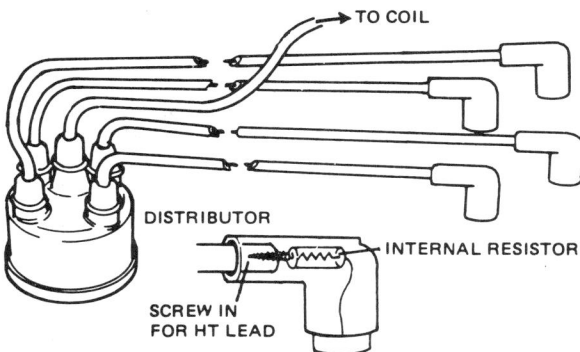

Resistive spark plug caps

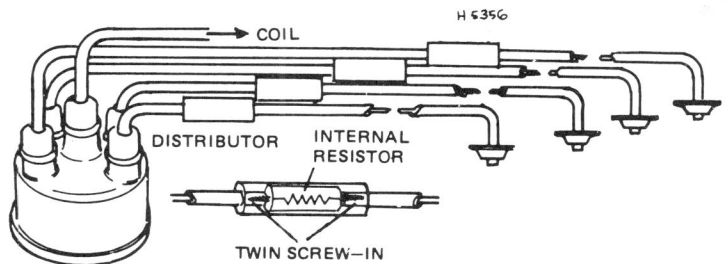

'In-line' suppressors

Fig. 10.38 Ignition HT lead suppressors

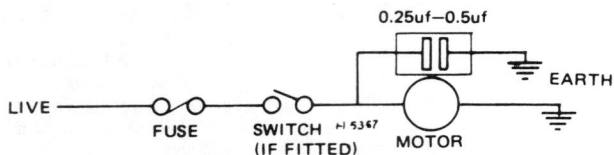

Fig. 10.39 Correct method of suppressing electric motors

Fig. 10.40 Method of suppressing instrument voltage controls

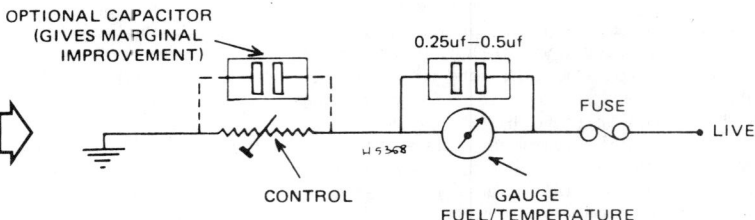

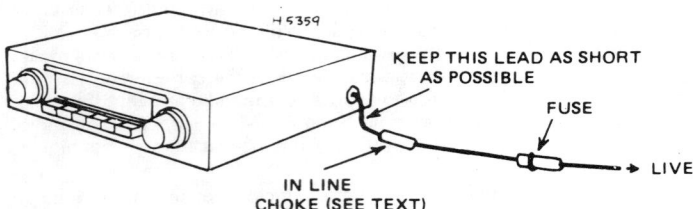

Fig. 10.41 Fitting an 'in-line' choke

motors of the windscreen wiper, windscreen washer, heater fan and electric aerial, if fitted. Other sources of interference are electric fuel pumps, flashing turn signals and instrument voltage stabilizers: Fig. 10.39 shows the way to suppress interference from an electric motor and Fig. 10.40 shows instrument voltage stabilizer suppression. Turn signals are not normally suppressed.

Modern car radios usually have a choke as well as a fuse in the live line, as shown in Fig. 10.41. If your installation lacks one of these, put one in as shown. For a transistor radio, a choke having a current carrying capacity of 2 amps is adequate. For any other equipment, use a choke of the same current rating as the protective fuse. Components for radio interference suppression are available from radio and car accessory shops.

An electric clock should be suppressed by connecting a 0.5 uf capacitor across it as shown for a motor in Fig. 10.39.

If the car is fitted with electronic ignition, it is not recommended that spark plug resistors and contact breaker capacitors are fitted. Most electronic ignition units have built-in suppression and the addition of external components may have adverse effects upon the operation of the ignition system.

70 Fault diagnosis – electrical system

Symptom	Reason/s
No voltage at starter motor	Battery discharged Battery defective internally Battery terminal leads loose, or earth lead not securely attached to body Loose or broken connections, in starter motor circuit Starter motor switch, or solenoid, faulty
Voltage at starter motor: faulty motor	Starter motor pinion jammed in mesh with flywheel gear ring Starter brushes badly worn, sticking, or brush wires loose Commutator dirty, worn or burnt Starter motor armature faulty Field coils earthed
Insufficient current flow to keep battery charged	Fan belt slipping Battery terminal connections loose or corroded Alternator not charging properly Short in lighting circuit causing continual battery drain Regulator unit not working correctly
Alternator not charging *	Fan belt loose and slipping, or broken Brushes worn, sticking, broken or dirty Brush springs weak or broken

* If all appears to be well but the alternator is still not charging, take the car to an automobile electrician for checking of the alternator and regulator

Symptom	Reason/s
Battery will not hold charge for more than a few days	Battery defective internally Electrolyte level too low Fan/alternator belt slipping Battery terminal connections loose or corroded Alternator not charging properly Regulator unit not working correctly
Ignition light fails to go out, battery runs flat in a few days	Fan belt loose and slipping, or broken Alternator faulty

Failure of individual electrical equipment to function correctly is dealt with alphabetically, below

Symptom	Reason/s
Fuel gauge gives no reading	Fuel tank empty! Electric cable between tank sender unit and gauge earthed, or loose Fuel gauge case not earthed Fuel gauge supply cable interrupted Fuel gauge unit broken
Fuel gauge registers full all the time	Electric cable between tank unit and gauge broken or disconnected
Horn operates all the time	Horn push either earthed, or stuck down Horn cable to horn push earthed
Horn fails to operate	Blown fuse Cable or cable connection loose, broken or disconnected Horn has an internal fault
Horn emits intermittent or unsatisfactory noise	Cable connections loose Horn incorrectly adjusted
Lights do not come on	If engine not running, battery discharged Light bulb filament burnt out, or bulbs broken Wire connections loose, disconnected, or broken Light switch shorting or otherwise faulty
Lights come on but fade out	If engine not running, battery discharged
Lights give very poor illumination	Lamp glasses dirty Lamps badly out of adjustment Incorrect bulb, with too low wattage fitted Existing bulbs old and badly discoloured
Lights work erratically – flashing on and off, especially over bumps	Battery terminals, or earth connections, loose Lights not earthing properly Contacts in light switch faulty
Wiper motor fails to work	Blown fuse Wire connections loose, disconnected or broken Brushes badly worn Armature worn or faulty Field coils faulty
Wiper motor works very slowly and takes excessive current	Commutator dirty, greasy or burnt Drive to spindles too bent, or unlubricated Drive spindle binding, or damaged Armature bearings dry, or unaligned Armature badly worn, or faulty
Wiper motor works slowly and takes little current	Brushes badly worn Commutator dirty, greasy or burnt Armature badly worn or faulty
Wiper motor works but wiper blades remain static	Linkage disengaged, or faulty Drive spindle damaged, or worn Wiper motor gearbox parts badly worn

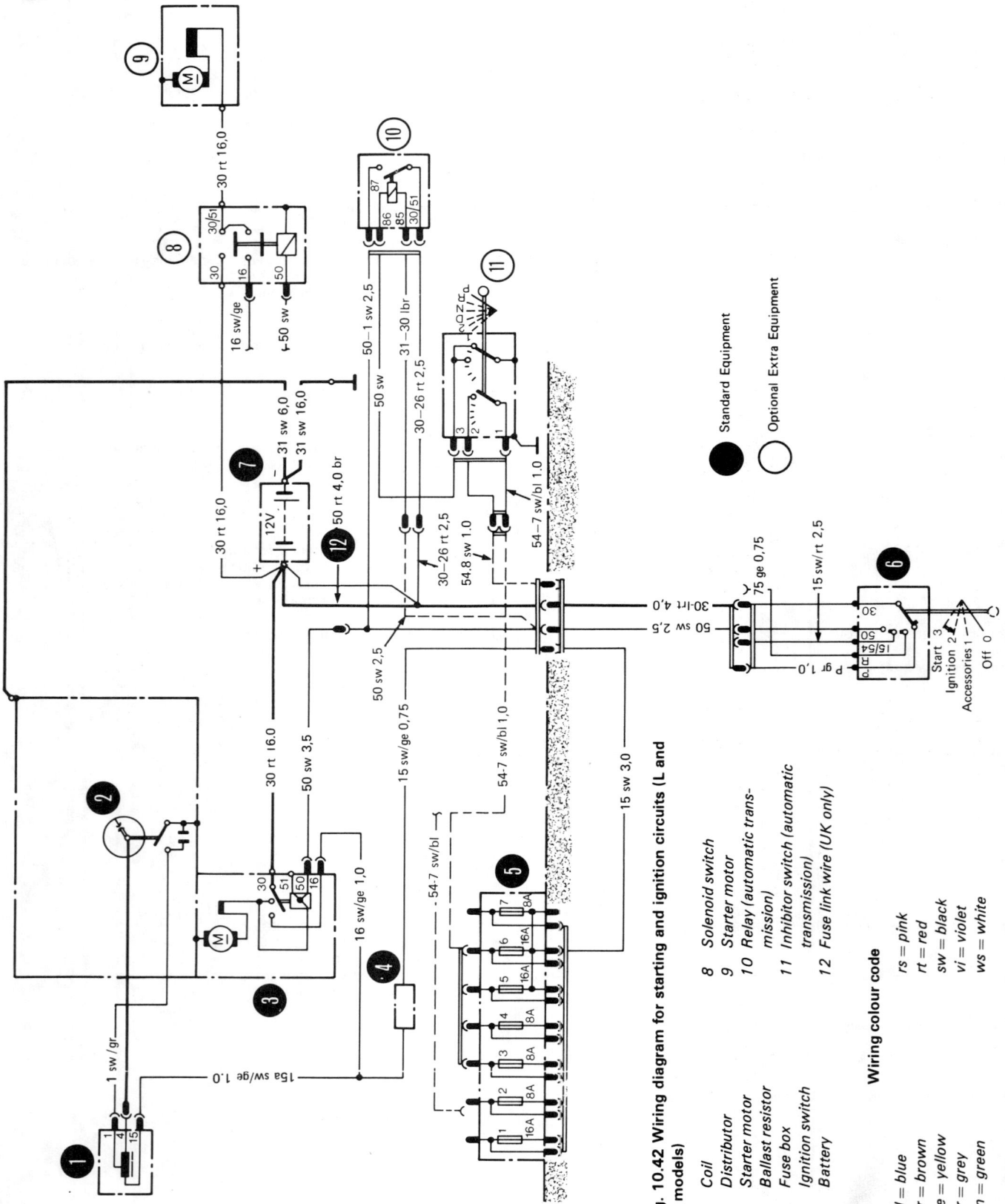

Fig. 10.42 Wiring diagram for starting and ignition circuits (L and XL models)

1 Coil
2 Distributor
3 Starter motor
4 Ballast resistor
5 Fuse box
6 Ignition switch
7 Battery

8 Solenoid switch
9 Starter motor
10 Relay (automatic transmission)
11 Inhibitor switch (automatic transmission)
12 Fuse link wire (UK only)

Wiring colour code

bl = blue
br = brown
ge = yellow
gr = grey
gn = green

rs = pink
rt = red
sw = black
vi = violet
ws = white

Standard Equipment

Optional Extra Equipment

Off 0
Accessories 1
Ignition 2
Start 3

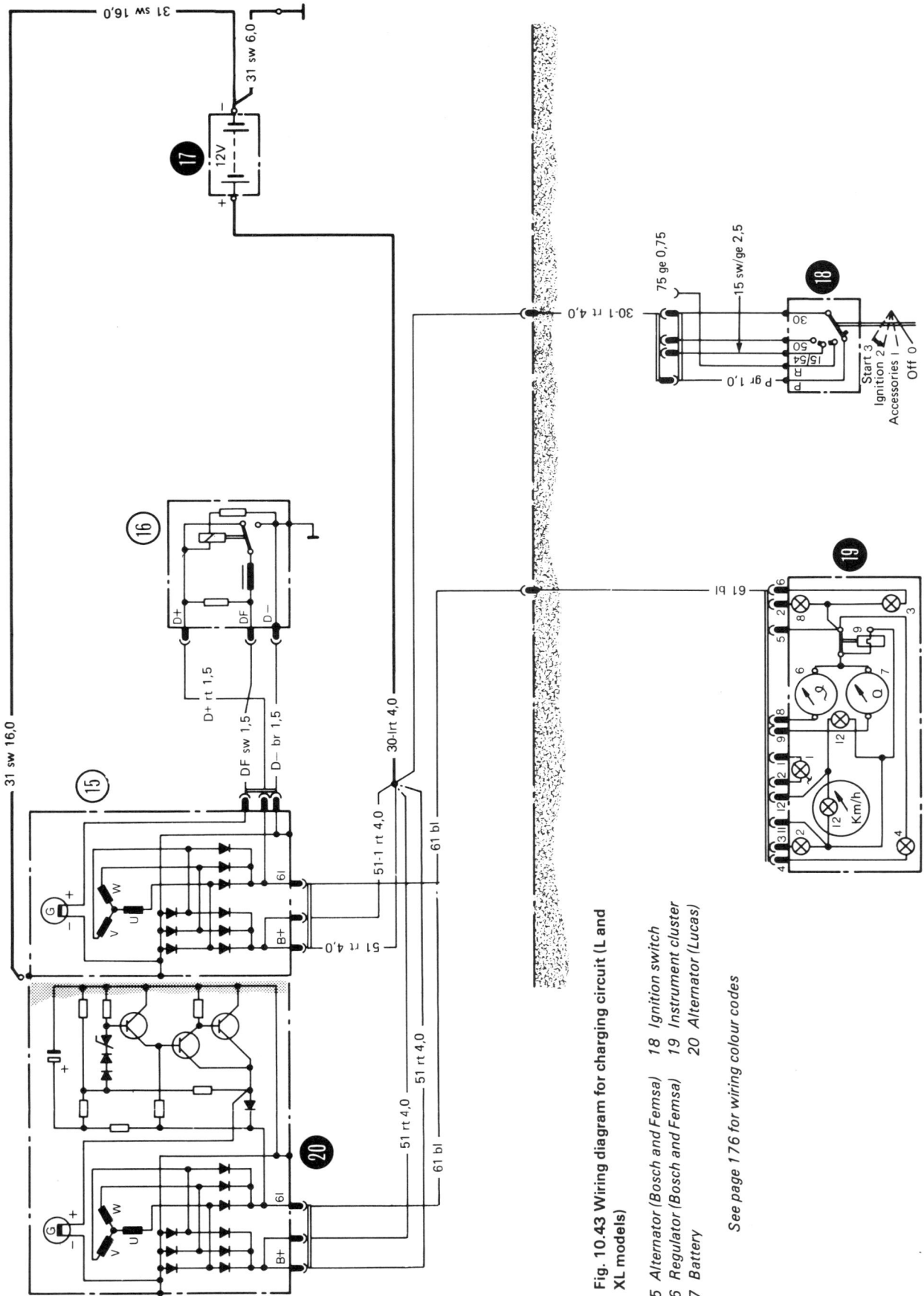

Fig. 10.43 Wiring diagram for charging circuit (L and XL models)

15 Alternator (Bosch and Femsa)   18 Ignition switch
16 Regulator (Bosch and Femsa)   19 Instrument cluster
17 Battery   20 Alternator (Lucas)

See page 176 for wiring colour codes

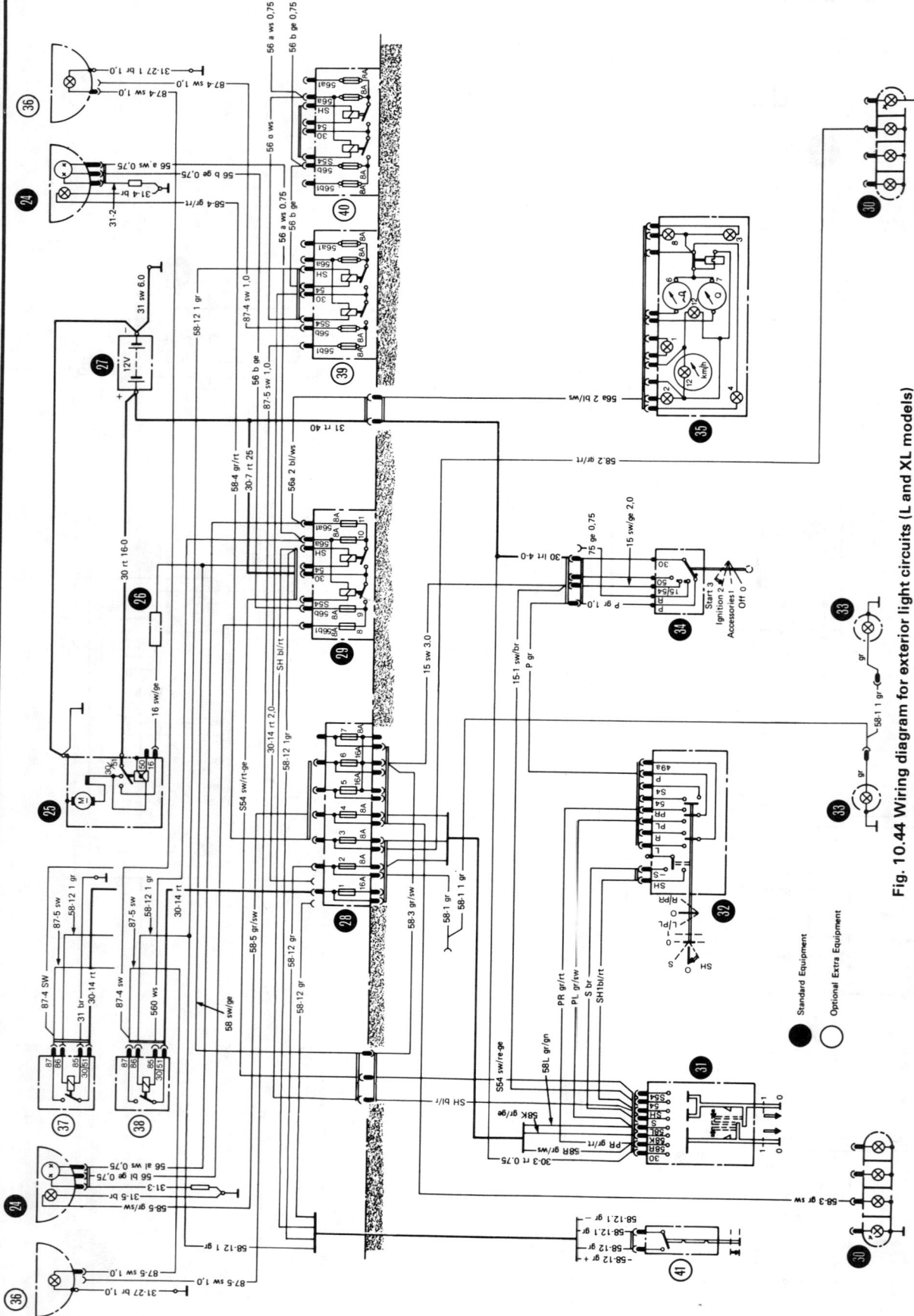

Fig. 10.44 Wiring diagram for exterior light circuits (L and XL models)

24 Headlamp
25 Starter motor
26 Ballast resistor
27 Battery
28 Fuse box
29 Headlamp dimmer/dipper relay
30 Rear lamp assembly
31 Light switch
32 Flasher switch
33 Number plate lamp
34 Ignition switch
35 Instrument cluster
36 Fog lamp
37 Relay (fog lamp)
38 Relay (fog lamp)
39 Dimmer/dipper relay (fog lamp)
40 Dimmer/dipper relay (headlamp)
41 Fog lamp switch

● Standard Equipment
○ Optional Extra Equipment

See page 176 for wiring colour codes

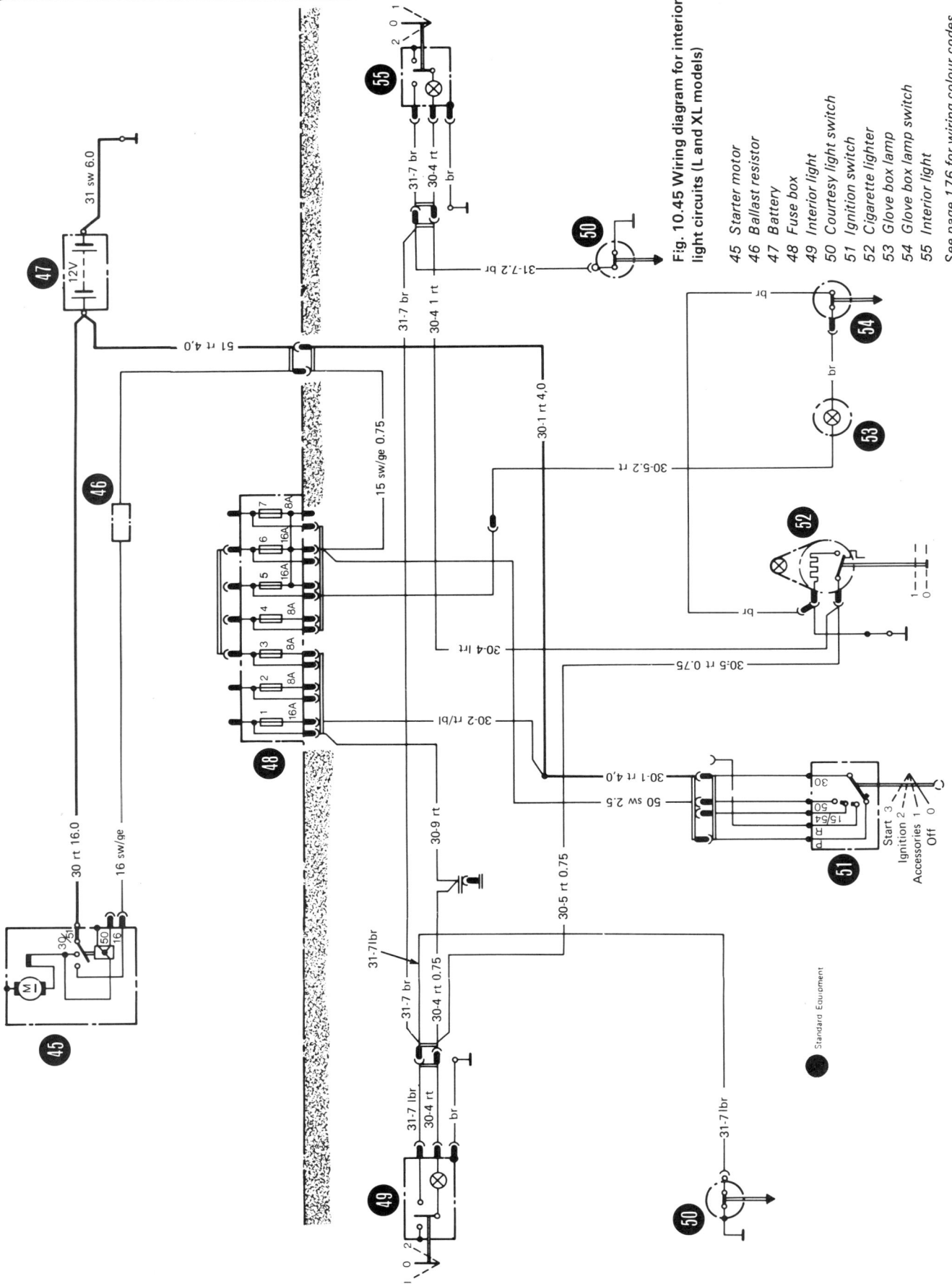

Fig. 10.45 Wiring diagram for interior light circuits (L and XL models)

45 Starter motor
46 Ballast resistor
47 Battery
48 Fuse box
49 Interior light
50 Courtesy light switch
51 Ignition switch
52 Cigarette lighter
53 Glove box lamp
54 Glove box lamp switch
55 Interior light

See page 176 for wiring colour codes

Standard Equipment

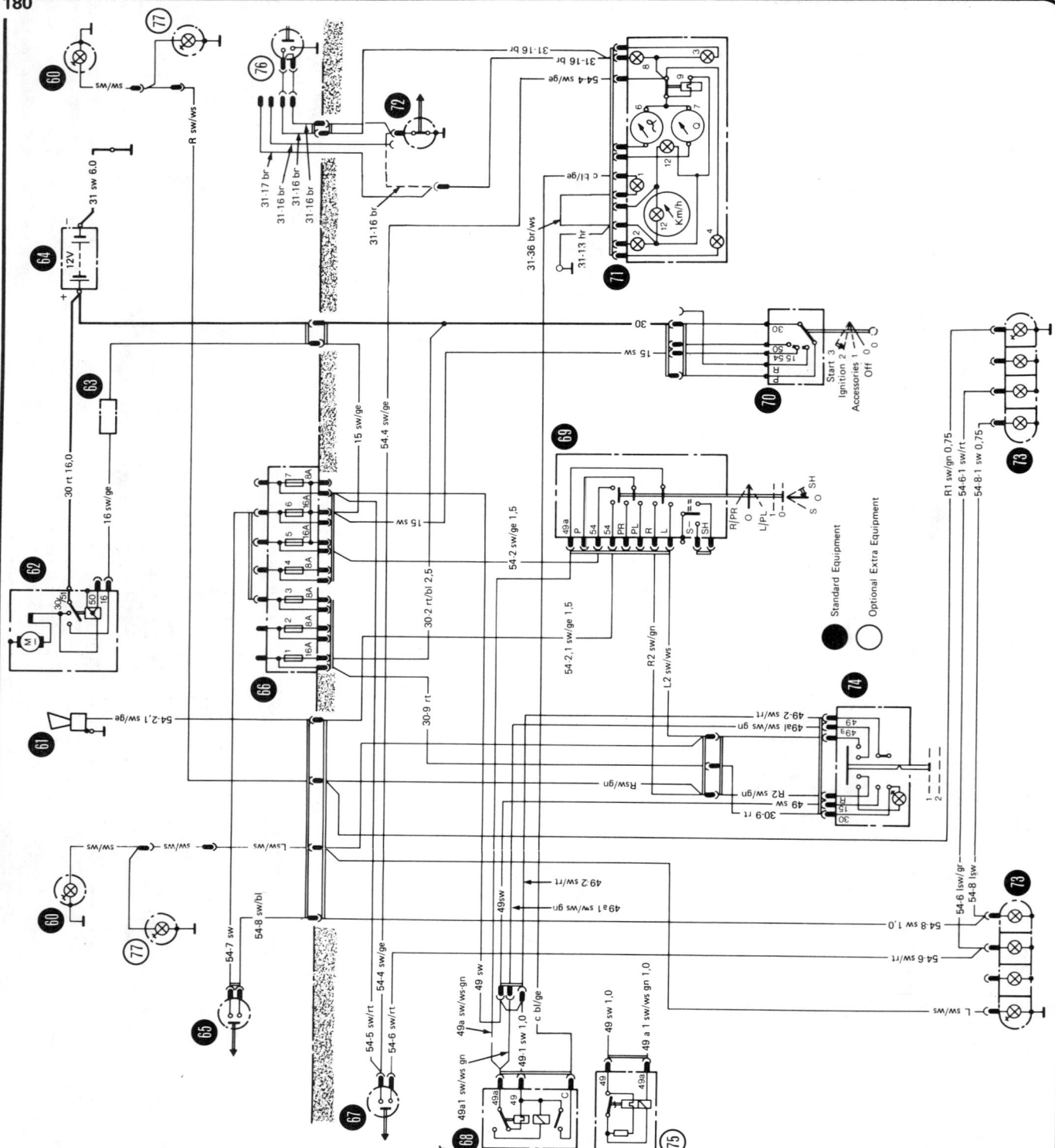

Fig. 10.46 Wiring diagram for horn, indicator and hazard light circuits (L and XL models)

60 Front flasher lamp
61 Horn
62 Starter motor
63 Ballast resistor
64 Battery
65 Reversing lamp switch
66 Fuse box
67 Stop light switch
68 Flasher unit
69 Indicator switch
70 Ignition switch
71 Instrument cluster
72 Handbrake warning light switch
73 Rear lamp assembly
74 Flasher switch warning system
75 Flasher unit (UK only)
76 Dual circuit brake warning system switch
77 Side repeater flasher lamp

See page 176 for wiring colour codes

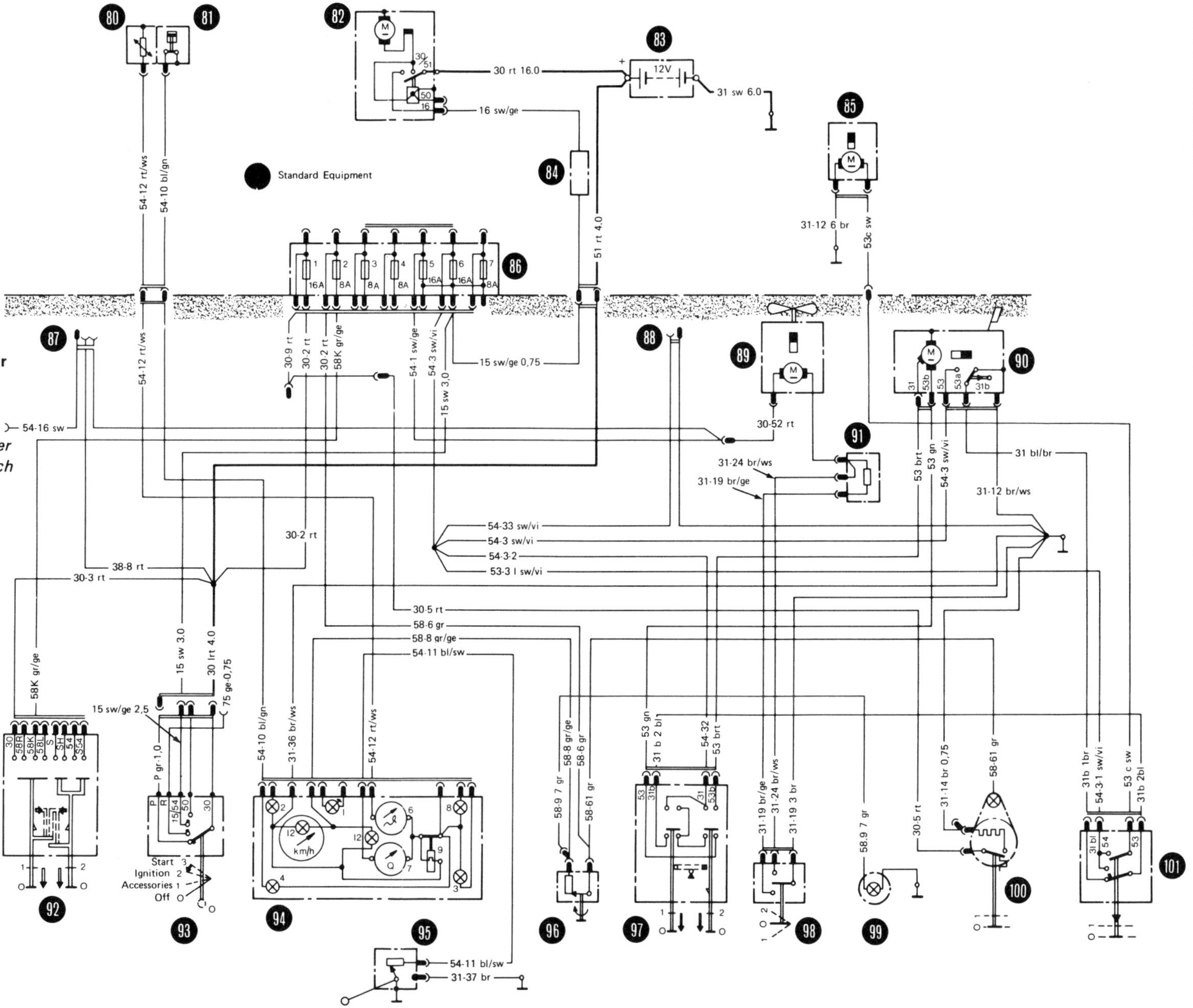

Fig. 10.47 Wiring diagram for heater, wiper and ancillary circuits (L and XL models)

80 Water temperature sender
81 Oil pressure control switch
82 Starter motor
83 Battery
84 Ballast resistor
85 Electric washer pump motor
86 Fuse box
87 Heated rear window
88 Wiper/wash system rear window
89 Heater blower motor
90 Wiper motor
91 Series resistor (heater motor)
92 Light switch
93 Ignition switch
94 Instrument cluster
95 Fuel gauge sender unit
96 Dimmer potentiometer
97 Wiper motor switch
98 Heater blower switch
99 Heater blower switch
100 Cigarette lighter
101 Electric wash pump switch

See page 176 for wiring colour codes

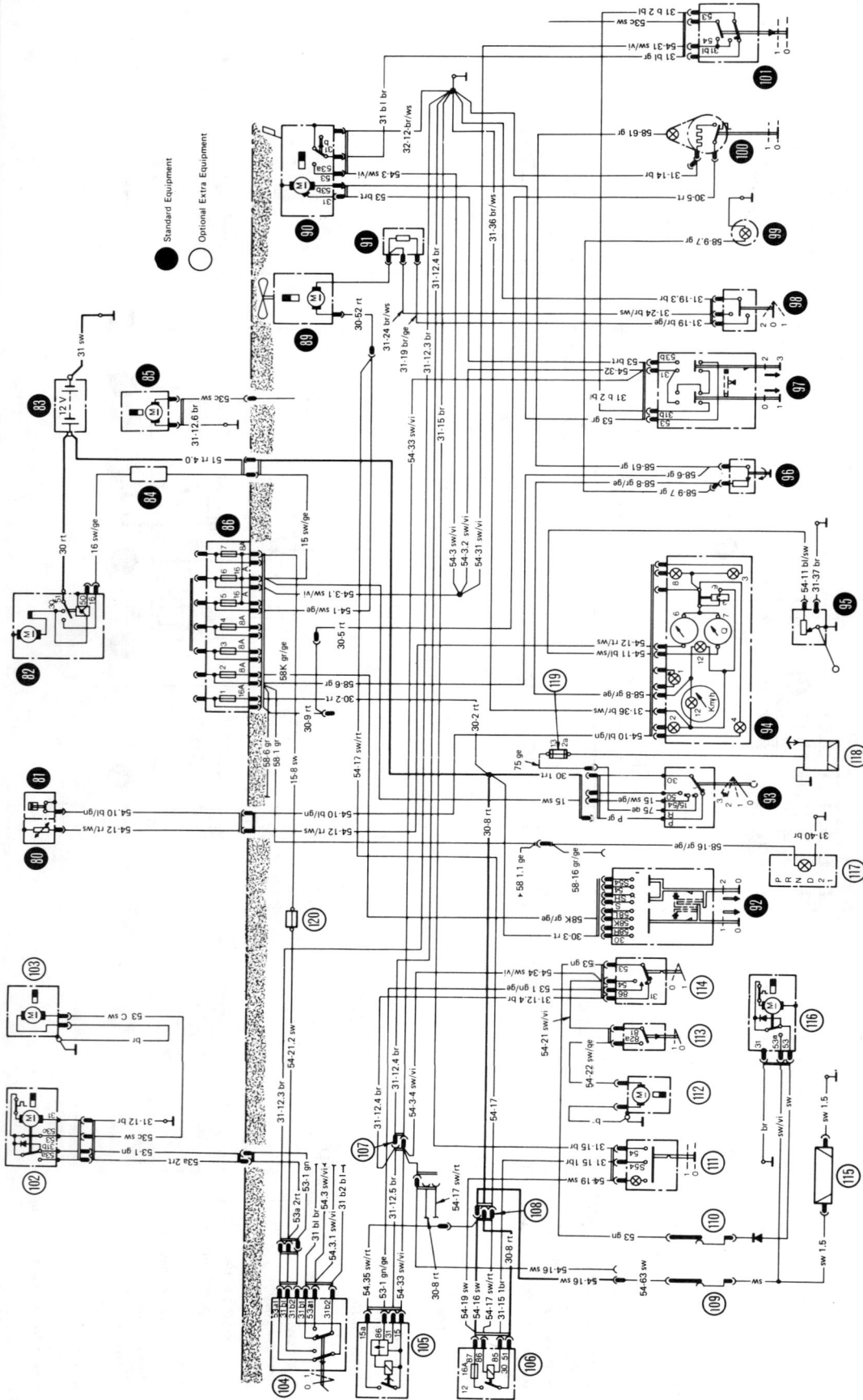

Fig. 10.48 Wiring diagram for Regular Production Option (RPO) circuits (additional to Fig. 10.47) (L and XL models)

Standard Equipment

Optional Extra Equipment

See page 176 for wiring colour codes

102	Wiper motor (headlamp)	107	Wiper/wash system (rear window connections)	111	Heated rear window switch	116	Rear window wiper motor
103	Front washer pump			112	Rear window washer pump	117	Selector illumination (automatic gearbox)
104	Foot switch (wiper/wash system)	108	Heated rear window connections	113	Rear window washer pump switch	118	Radio
105	Time relay (wiper motor, rear window)	109	Tailgate damper (left-hand)	114	Wiper motor rear window switch	119	Fuse sleeve for item 118
106	Relay (heated rear window)	110	Tailgate damper (right-hand)	115	Heated rear window	120	Fuse sleeve for item 104

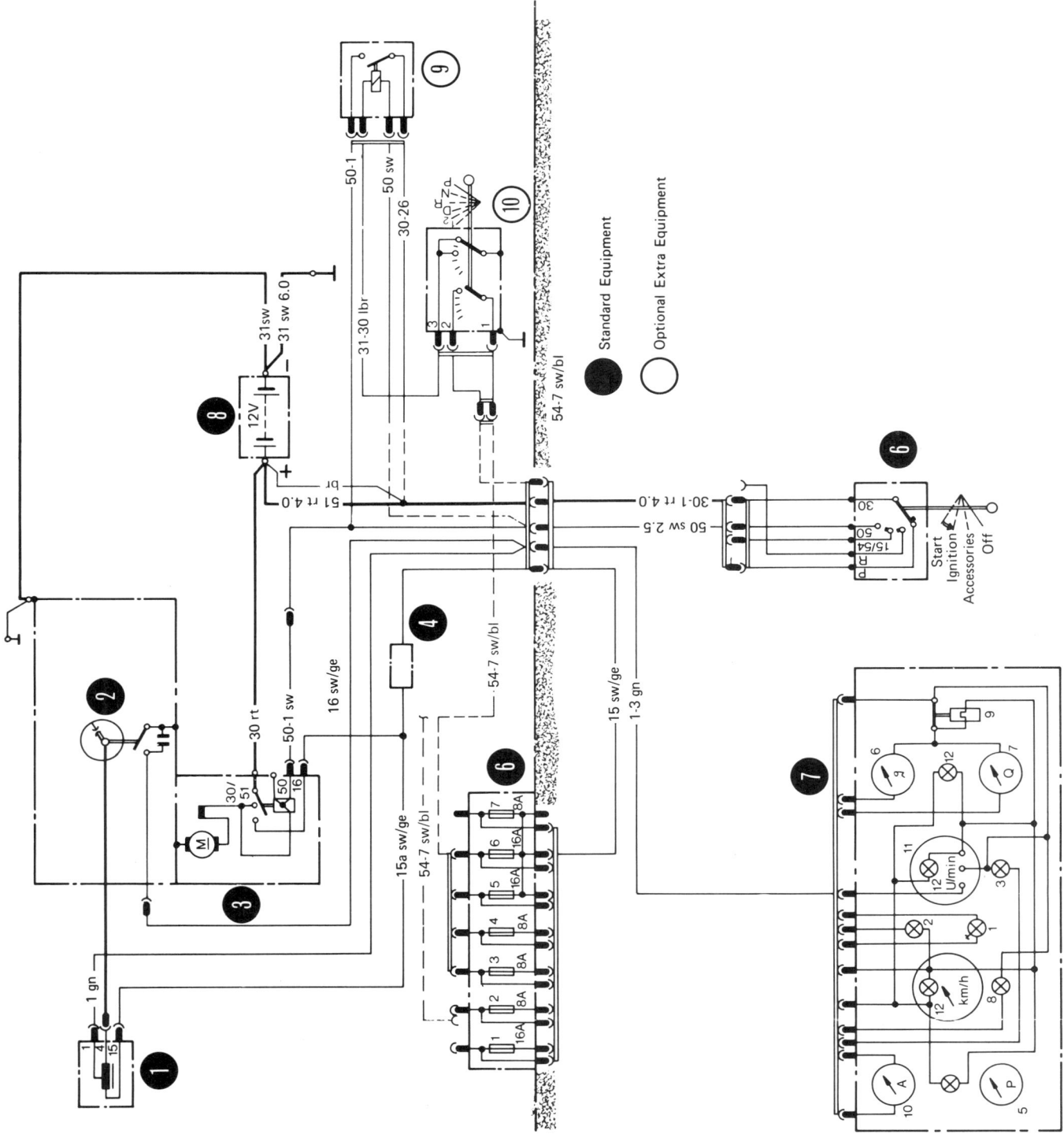

Fig. 10.49 Wiring diagram for starting and ignition circuits (GT and Ghia models)

1 Coil
2 Distributor
3 Starter motor
4 Ballast resistor
5 Instrument cluster
6 Fuse box
7 Ignition switch
8 Battery
9 Relay (automatic transmission)
10 Inhibitor switch (automatic transmission)
11 Fuse link wire (UK only)

See page 176 for wiring colour codes

Standard Equipment

Optional Extra Equipment

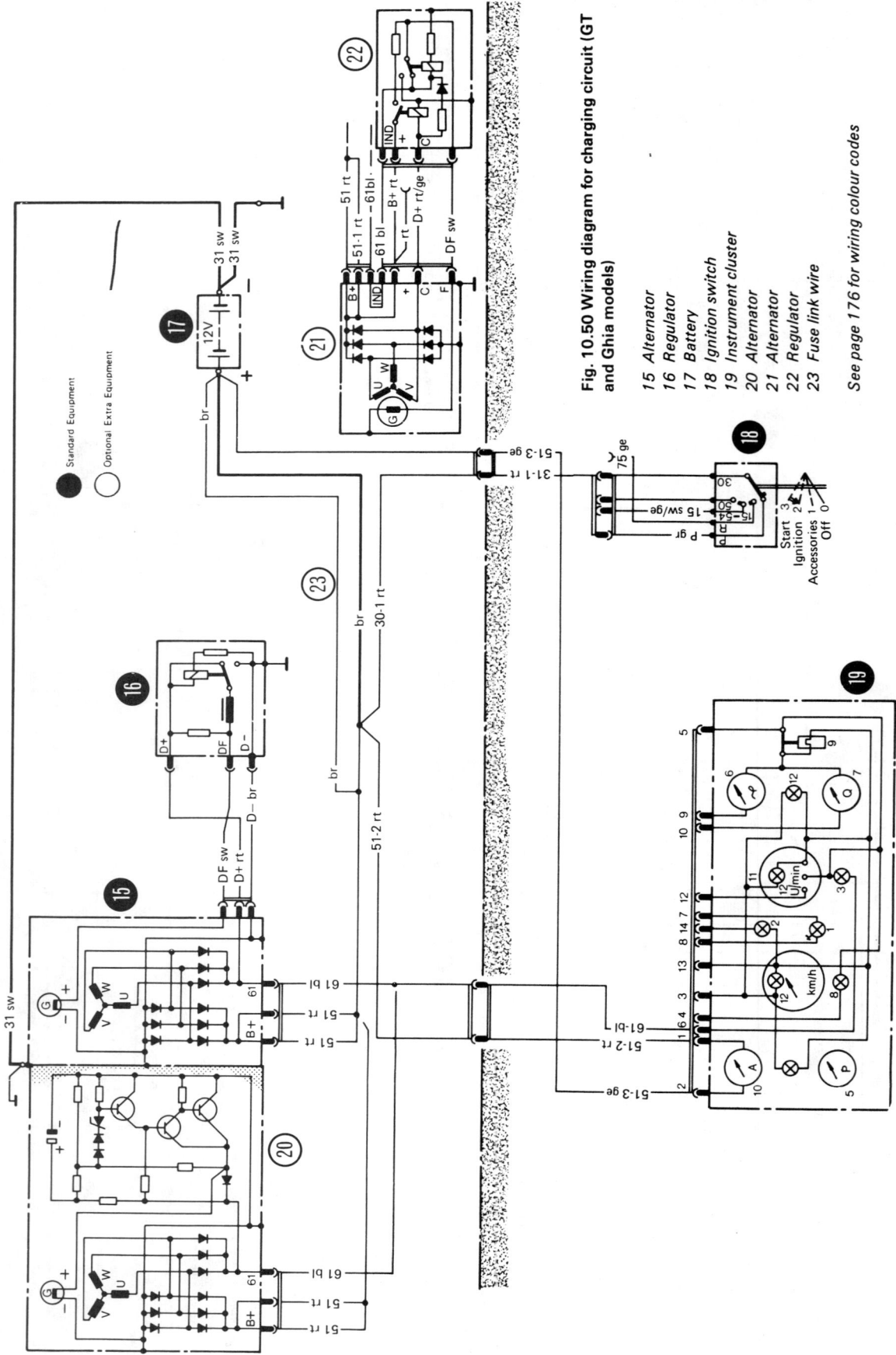

Fig. 10.50 Wiring diagram for charging circuit (GT and Ghia models)

15 Alternator
16 Regulator
17 Battery
18 Ignition switch
19 Instrument cluster
20 Alternator
21 Alternator
22 Regulator
23 Fuse link wire

See page 176 for wiring colour codes

Standard Equipment

Optional Extra Equipment

Start   3
Ignition   2
Accessories 1
Off   0

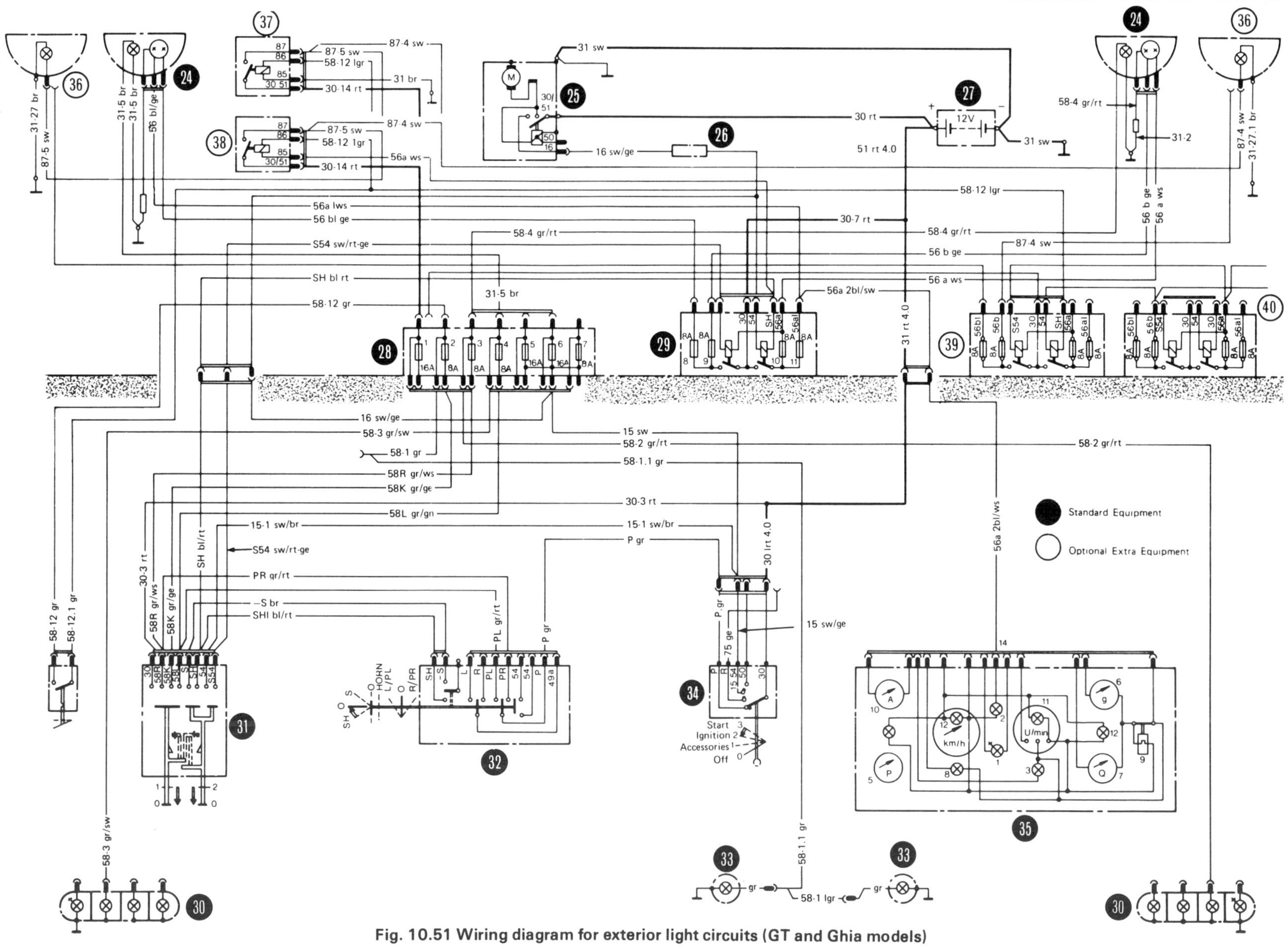

Fig. 10.51 Wiring diagram for exterior light circuits (GT and Ghia models)

Standard Equipment

Optional Extra Equipment

Start 3
Ignition 2
Accessories 1
Off 0

HORN

24 Headlamp
25 Starter motor
26 Ballast resistor
27 Battery
28 Fuse box

29 Headlamp dimmer/dipper relay
30 Rear lamp assembly
31 Light switch
32 Flasher switch
33 Number plate lamps

34 Ignition switch
35 Instrument cluster
36 Fog lamp
37 Relay (fog lamp)
38 Relay (fog lamp)

39 Dimmer/dipper relay (fog lamp)
40 Dimmer/dipper relay
41 Fog lamp switch

See page 176 for wiring colour codes

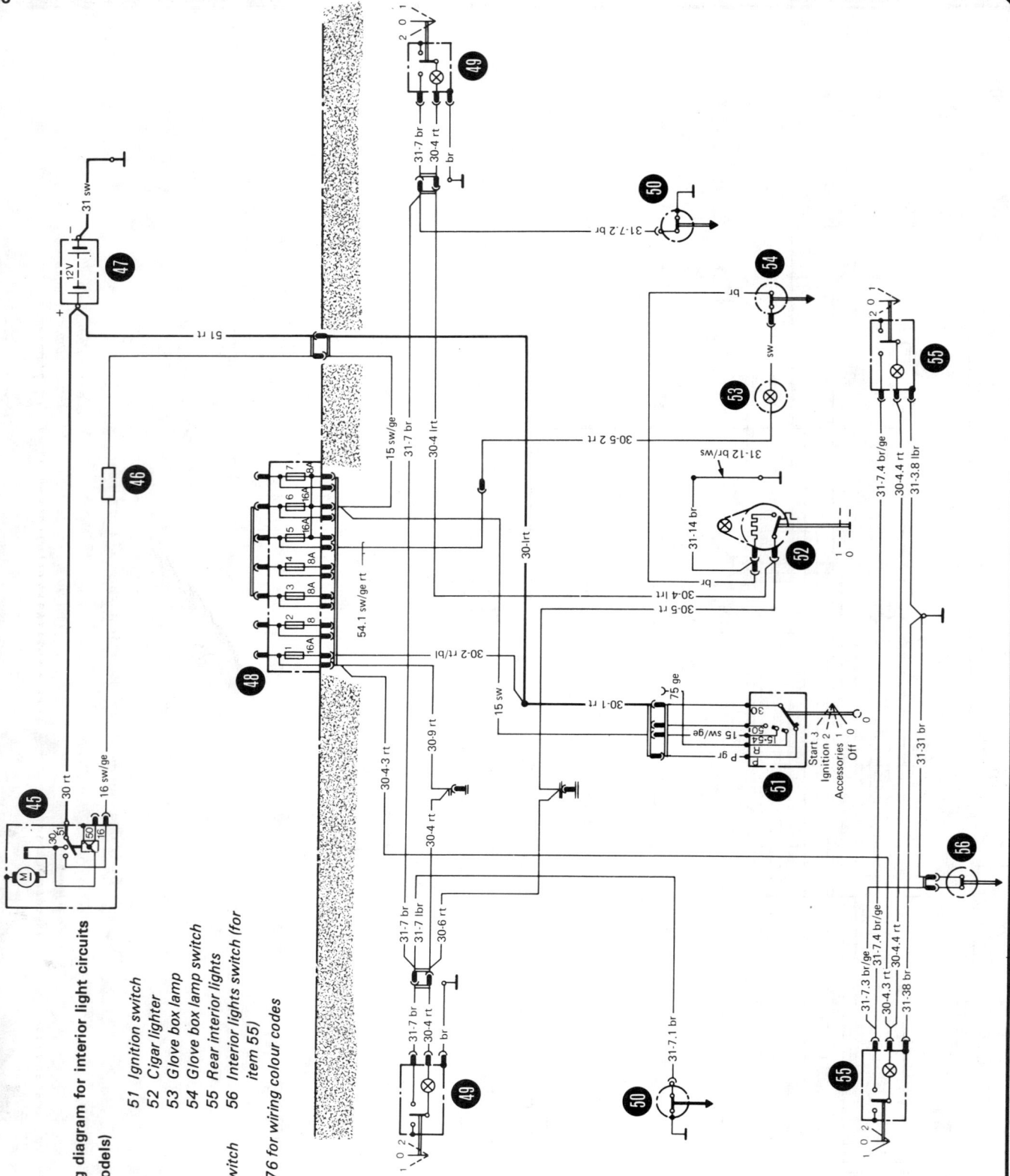

Fig. 10.52 Wiring diagram for interior light circuits
(GT and Ghia models)

45 Starter motor   51 Ignition switch
46 Ballast resistor   52 Cigar lighter
47 Battery   53 Glove box lamp
48 Fuse box   54 Glove box lamp switch
49 Interior light   55 Rear interior lights
50 Courtesy light switch   56 Interior lights switch (for
       item 55)

See page 176 for wiring colour codes

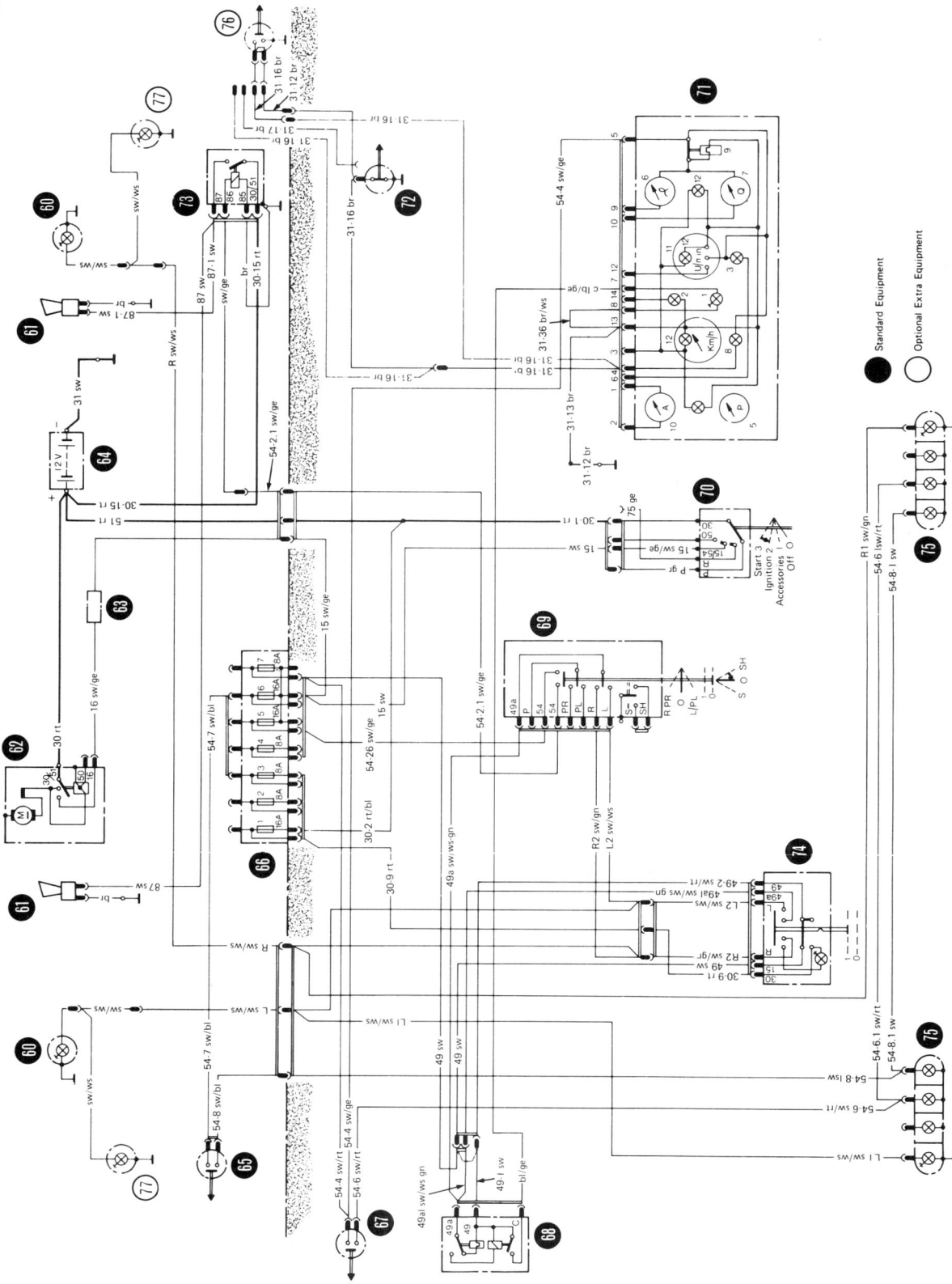

Fig. 10.53 Wiring diagram for horn, indicator and hazard light circuits (GT and Ghia models)

60 Front flasher lamp
61 Horn
62 Starter motor
63 Ballast resistor
64 Battery
65 Reversing lamp switch
66 Fuse box
67 Stop light switch
68 Flasher unit
69 Indicator switch
70 Ignition switch
71 Instrument cluster
72 Handbrake warning light switch
73 Horn relay
74 Flasher switch warning system
75 Rear lamp assembly
76 Dual circuit brake warning system switch
77 Side repeater flasher lamp
See page 176 for wiring colour codes

● Standard Equipment
○ Optional Extra Equipment

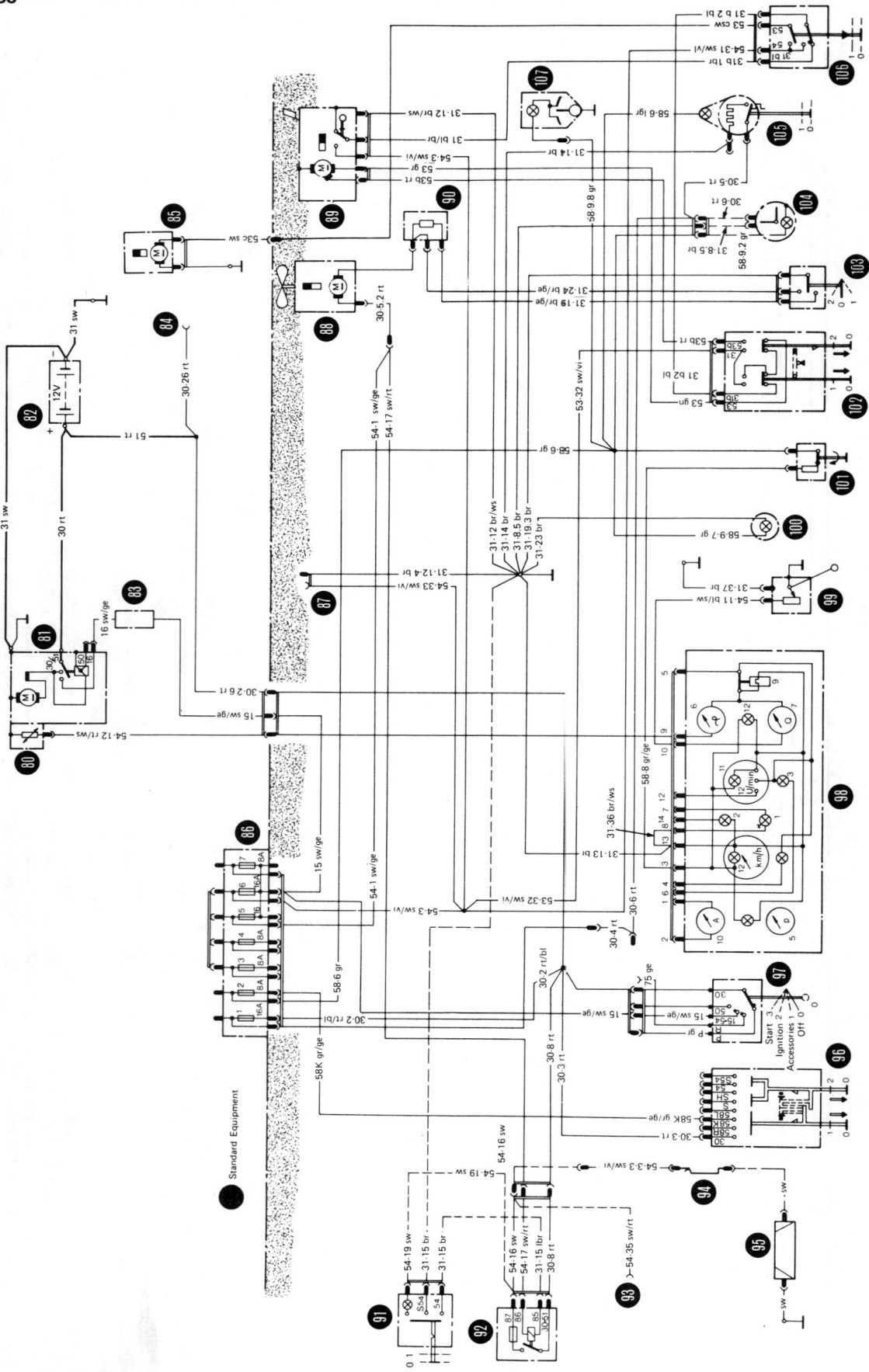

Fig. 10.54 Wiring diagram for heater, wiper and ancillary circuits (GT and Ghia models)

80	Water temperature sender
81	Starter motor
82	Battery
83	Ballast resistor
84	Relay (automatic transmission)
85	Electric washer pump motor
86	Fuse box

87	Wiper wash system rear window
88	Heater blower motor
89	Wiper motor
90	Series resistor (heater blower motor)
91	Heated rear window switch
92	Heated rear window relay
93	Rear window wiper/washer system

95	Heated rear window
96	Light switch
97	Ignition switch
98	Instrument cluster
99	Fuel gauge sender unit
100	Heater blower switch lamp
101	Dimmer potentiometer

102	Wiper motor switch
103	Heater blower switch
104	Clock
105	Cigarette lighter
106	Electric washer pump switch
107	Map reading lamp
	See page 176 for wiring colour codes

Standard Equipment

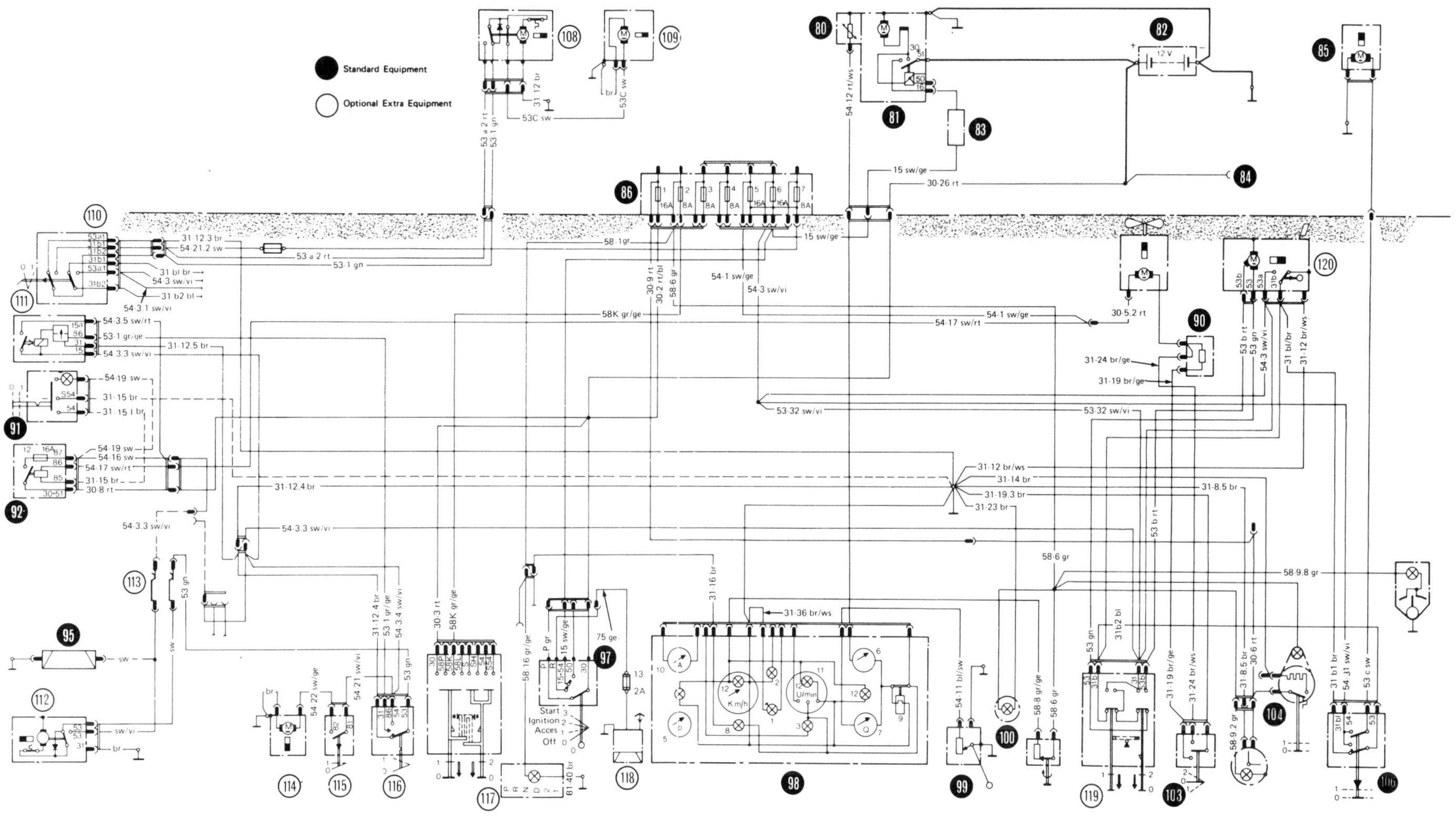

Fig. 10.55 Wiring diagram for Regular Production Option (RPO) circuits (additional to Fig. 10.54) (GT and Ghia models)

108 *Wiper motor (headlamp)*
109 *Headlamp washer pump*
110 *Foot operated switch (wipe/wash system)*
111 *Time relay (wiper motor, rear window)*
112 *Wiper motor (rear window)*
113 *Tailgate damper*
114 *Wash pump motor (rear window)*

115 *Wash pump motor switch (rear window)*
116 *Wiper motor switch (rear window)*
117 *Automatic gear shift indication lamp*
118 *Radio*
119 *Wiper motor switch (front screen)*
120 *Wiper motor*

See page 176 for wiring colour codes

Standard Equipment

Optional Extra Equipment

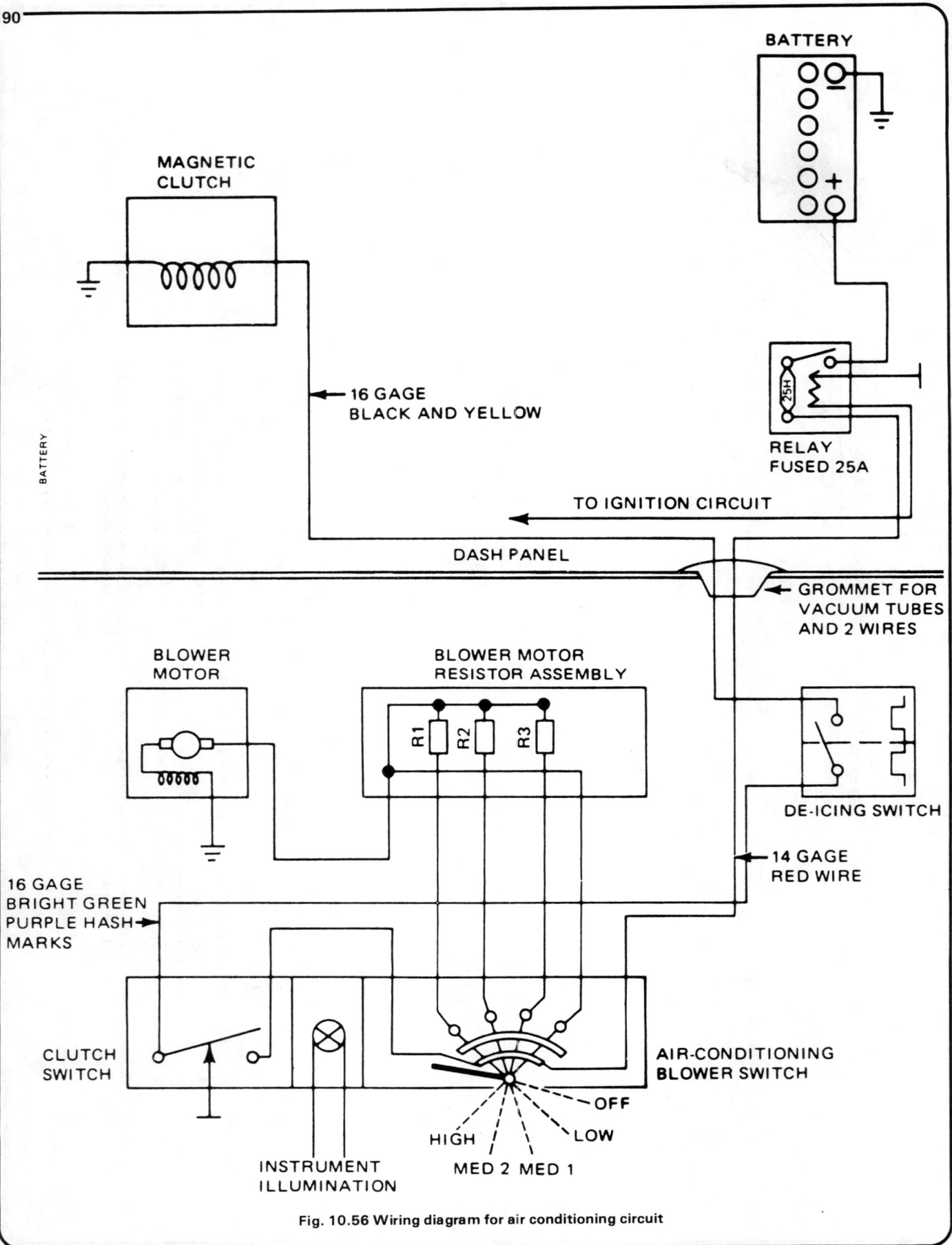

Fig. 10.56 Wiring diagram for air conditioning circuit

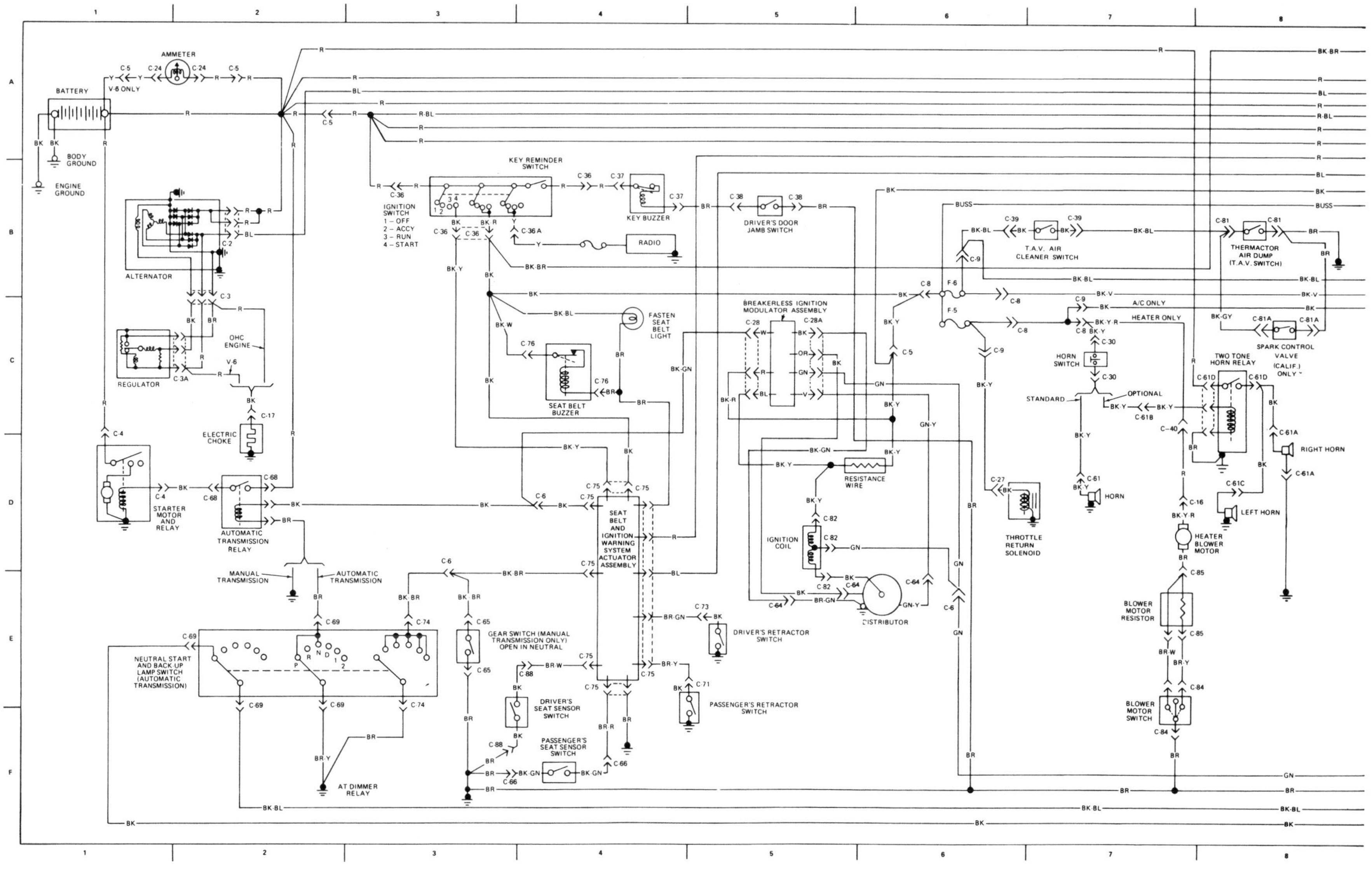

Fig. 10.57 Wiring diagram for Mercury Capri II (Part A). See page 195 for key

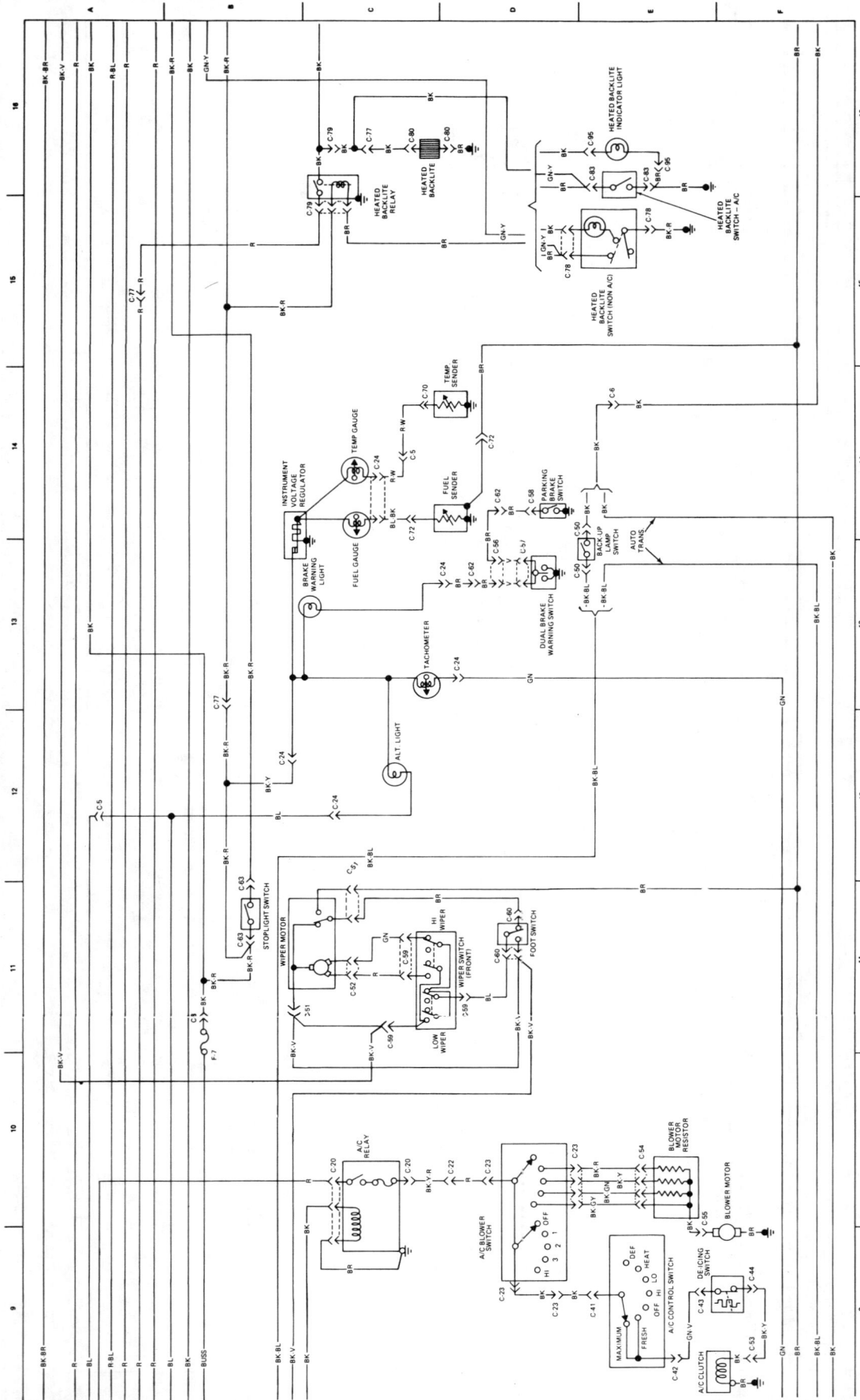

Fig. 10.57 Wiring diagram for Mercury Capri II (Part B). See page 195 for key

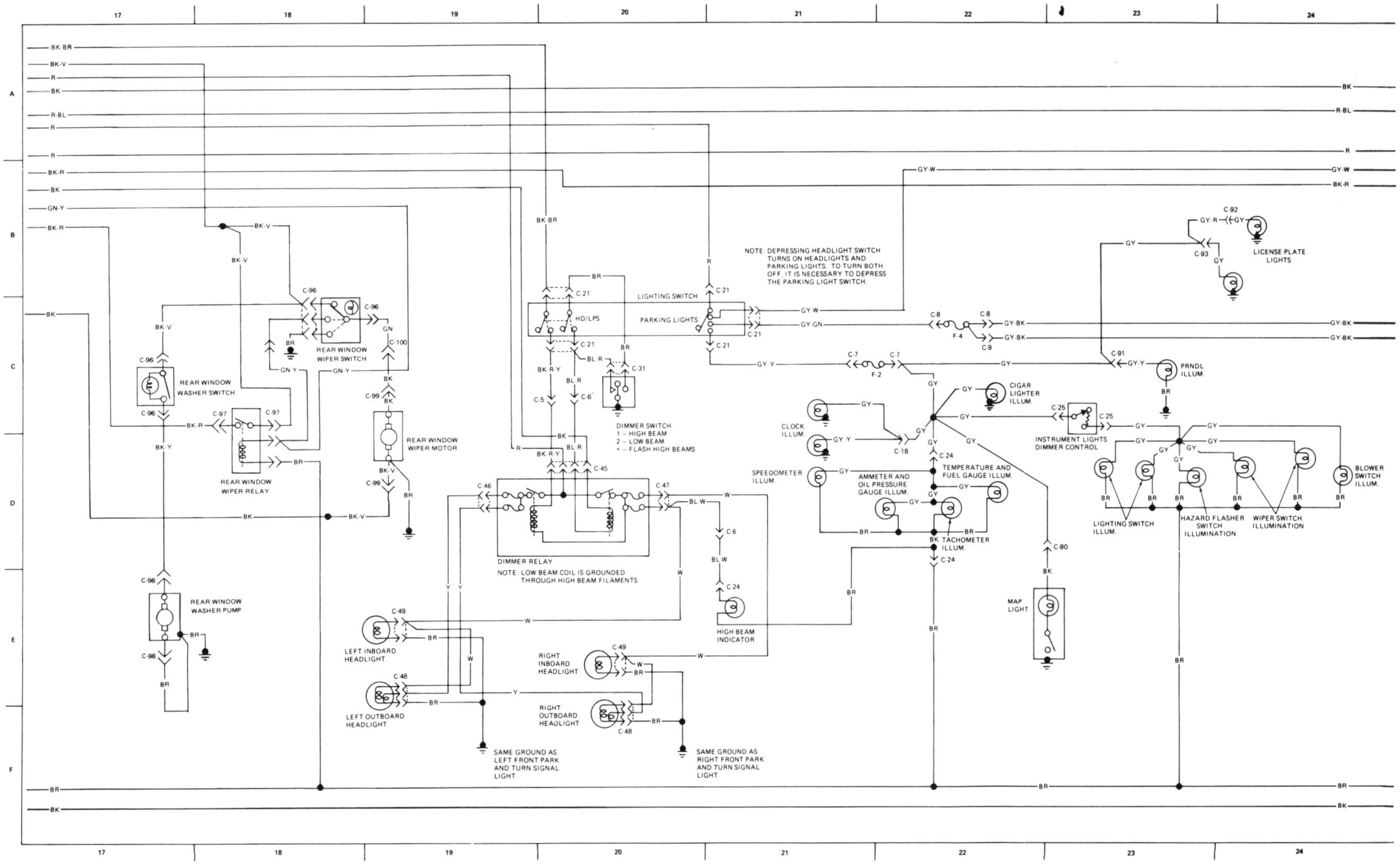

Fig. 10.57 Wiring diagram for Mercury Capri II (Part C). See page 195 for key

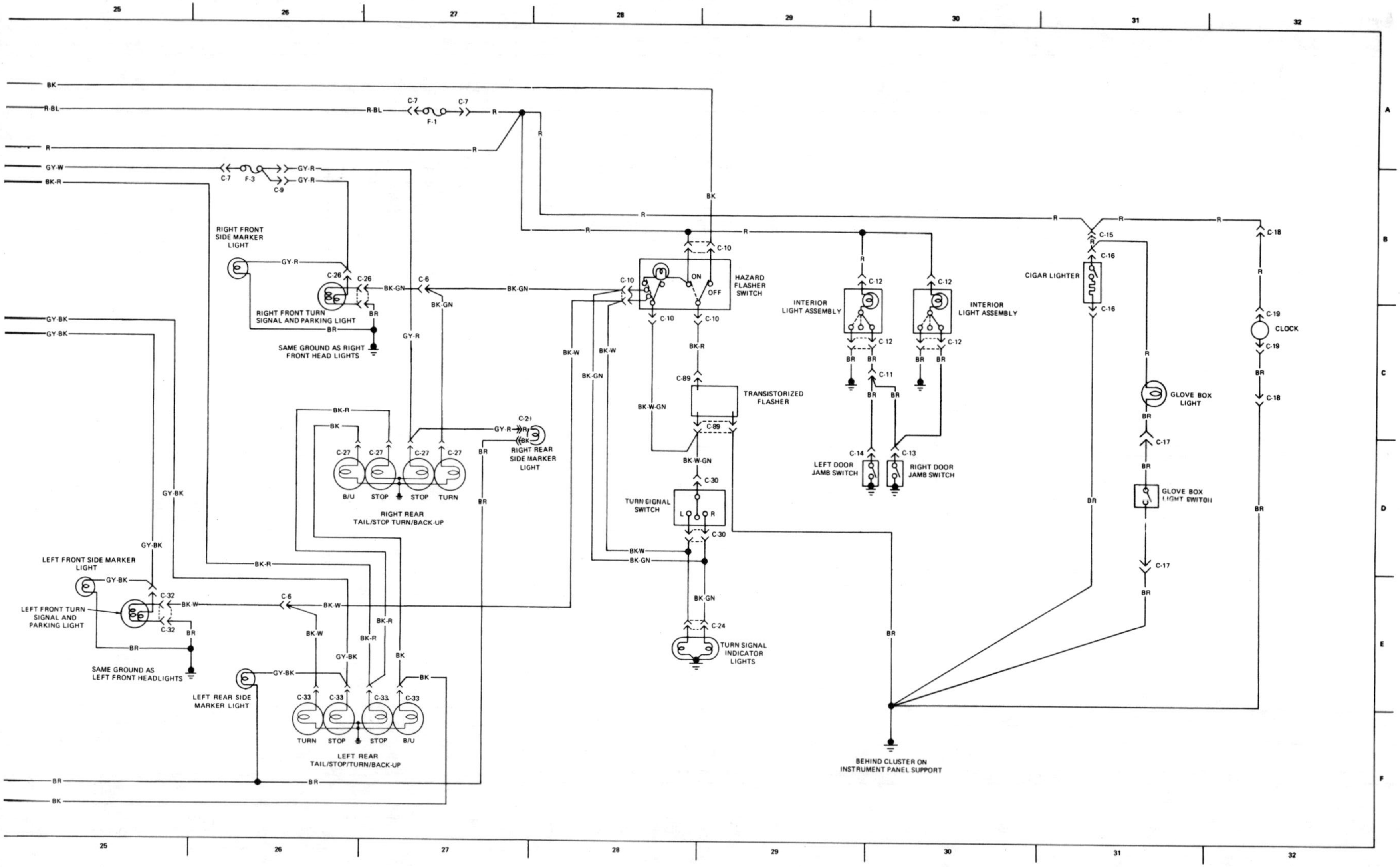

Fig. 10.57 Wiring diagram for Mercury Capri II (Part D). See page 195 for key

Key to Fig. 10.57 Parts A, B, C and D, pages 191 to 194

Component	Location	Component	Location
Air conditioner clutch	F–9	Alternator	C–12
Alternator	B–1	Brake warning	C–13
Alternator regulator	C–1	Heated backlight	E–16
Battery	A–1	High beam	E–21
Buzzers		Seat belt	C–4
Key reminder	B–4	Turn signal	E–28
Seat belt	C–4	Instrument voltage regulator	B–14
Cigar lighter	B–31	Motors	
Clock	C–32	A/C blower	F–8
Distributor	E–6	Heater blower	D–7
Exterior lights		Starter	D–1
Back-up	D–26, F–27	Windshield wiper (front)	B–11
Headlights		Windshield wiper (rear)	D–18
Left	E–19	Radio	B–4
Right	E–20	Relays	
License plate	B–24	Air conditioning	C–10
Park and turn signal		Automatic transmission	D–19
Left	E–25	Dimmer	C–15
Right	C–26	Heated backlight	C–16
Side marker		Starter motor	D–1
Left front	E–25	Two-tone horn and ignition warning	
Left rear	E–26	actuator	C–8
Right front	B–26	Seat belt logic box	D–4
Right rear	C–28	Senders	
Stop lights		Fuel gauge	D–14
Left	E–26	Water temperature gauge	D–14
Right	D–27	Switches	
Tail lights		A/C blower	D–9
Left	F–26	A/C control	E–9
Right	D–27	Dimmer	
Rear turn signal		Instrument panel illumination	C–23
Left	F–26	High beam	C–20
Right	D–27	Door jamb	
Flashers		Driver's	D–30
Hazard flasher	B–28	Passenger's	D–30
Turn signal	D–28	Door jamb – key buzzer	B–5
Gauges		Dual brake warning	D–13
Ammeter	A–2	Gear	E–3
Fuel	C–14	Glove box lamp	D–31
Tachometer	C–13	Hazard flasher	B–28
Temperature	C–14	Heated backlight	E–15
Heated backlight	C–16	Heater blower	F–7
Heater blower motor	D–7	Horn	C–7
Heater blower motor resistor	E–7	Ignition	B–3
Horns	D–7, D–8	Lighting	C–20
Ignition coil	D–5	Neutral start	E–2
Ignition resistor wire	D–5	Parking brake	D–13
Illumination lights		Seat belt retractor	
Ammeter and oil pressure gauge	D–21	Driver's	E–5
Blower switch	D–24	Passenger's	F–5
Cigar lighter	C–22	TAV air cleaner	B–7
Clock	D–21	Thermactor air dump	B–8
Dome	B–29	Throttle return	D–6
Fuel gauge	D–22	Turn signal	D–28
Glove box	C–31	Seat sensor	
Hazard flasher	B–28	Driver's	E–3
Lighting switch	D–23	Passenger's	F–4
Map	E–22	Spark control valve	
PRND21	C–23	Stop light	B–11
Tachometer	D–22	Windshield wiper (front)	D–11
Temperature gauge	D–22	Foot switch	D–11
Windshield wiper switch	D–24	Windshield wiper (rear)	C–18
Indicator lights		Rear washer switch	C–17

Wiring colour code

BK	Black	Y	Yellow	W	White	V	Violet	GY	Grey
R	Red	BL	Blue	GN	Green	O	Orange	BR	Brown

Chapter 11 Suspension and steering

For modifications, and information applicable to later models, see Supplement at end of manual

Contents

Specifications

Front suspension

Type	Independent, MacPherson strut
Lateral control	Track control arms
Longitudinal control	Stabilizer bar
Shock absorbers	Hydraulic, telescopic, double-acting
Fluid type:	
FoB	SM6C–1003–A
FoG	GES–M6C–4503–A
Fluid capacity:	
FoB	325 ± 15 cc (0·18 Imp. pint, approx/0·22 US pint approx.)
FoG	340 ± 15 cc (0·19 Imp. pint, approx/0·23 US pint approx.)

Rear suspension

Type	Semi-elliptic, leaf spring with rigid axle and stabilizer bar
Shock absorbers	Hydraulic, telescopic, double-acting

Steering gear

Type	Rack and pinion
Steering wheel turns (lock-to-lock)	3·36
Lubricant type	SAE 90 EP gear oil
Lubricant capacity	0·15 litre (0·25 Imp. pint/0·3 US pint)
Pinion bearing shim thicknesses	0·005, 0·007, 0·010, 0·090 in (0·127, 0·178, 0·254, 0·286 mm)
Rack slipper bearing shim thicknesses	0·002, 0·005, 0·010, 0·015, 0·020 in (0·051, 0·127, 0·254, 0·381, 0·508 mm)

Power steering gear

Pump type	Hobourn-Eaton roller pump
Steering wheel turns (lock-to-lock)	3·23
Lubricant type	SAE 40 or 20W/50 oil
Lubricant capacity	0·19 litre (0·33 Imp. pint/0·4 US pint)
Fluid type	Automatic transmission fluid, ESWM–2C–33E or SQM–2C9007 AA or D2AZ–19582–A
Fluid capacity	0·5 litre (0·9 Imp. pint/1·1 US pint)

Front wheel alignment (unladen)

Castor angle	0° 38′ to 1° 48′
Max. difference (side to side)	0° 45′
Camber angle	0° 15′ to 1° 45′
Max. difference, side to side	1° 0′
Toe-in	0 to 0·28 in (0 to 7 mm)

Tyres

Size	185/70 HR13	
Pressures:	**Front**	**Rear**
Load up to 3 persons	23 lbf/in² (1·6 kgf/cm²)	23 lbf/in² (1·6 kgf/cm²)
Load in excess of 3 persons	28 lbf/in² (2·0 kgf/cm²)	28 lbf/in² (2·0 kgf/cm²)

Note 1: For sustained high speeds in excess of 100 mph, consult the tyre manufacturer or a Ford dealer.
Note 2: Where there is a tyre chart on the inside of the glove compartment door, refer to this for recommended tyre pressures and loads.

Torque wrench settings

	lbf ft	kgf m
Suspension unit upper mounting bolts	15 to 18	2 to 2·4
Spindle to top mount assembly *	29 to 33	4·1 to 4·6
Track control arm ball stud nut	30 to 35	4·2 to 4·9
Stabilizer bar attachment clamps **	21 to 24·3	2·9 to 3·4
Stabilizer bar to track control arm nut **	14 to 45	2·1 to 6·2
Track control arm inner bushing **	18 to 22	2·5 to 3·1
Front suspension crossmember to body sidemember	29 to 37	4·1 to 5·1
Shock absorber to rear axle	39 to 46	5·3 to 6·3
Shock absorber to floor assembly	20 to 24	2·7 to 3·3
Stabilizer bar to axle tube	29 to 37	4 to 5
Stabilizer bar to sidemember	26 to 30	3·5 to 4·1
Locknut on stabilizer bar end-piece	29 to 37	4 to 5
Spring U-bolts	18 to 27	2·5 to 3·6
Front of rear spring	26 to 30	3·5 to 4·1
Rear of rear spring	8 to 10	1·1 to 1·4
Steering arm to suspension unit	30 to 34	4·1 to 4·7
Steering gear to crossmember	15 to 18	2·1 to 2·5
Trackrod-end to steering arm (Capri II)	18 to 22	2·5 to 3·0
(Mercury Capri II)	30 to 35	4·1 to 4·8
Coupling to pinion spline	12 to 15	1·7 to 2·1
Universal joint to steering shaft spline (Capri II)	17 to 22	2·3 to 3·00
(Mercury Capri II)	12 to 15	1·7 to 2·1
Steering wheel to shaft (Capri II)	20 to 25	2·8 to 3·5
(Mercury Capri II)	25 to 30	3·5 to 4·1
Steering column tube to pedal box	15 to 18	1·7 to 2·1
Power steering fluid pressure lines	19 to 23	2·6 to 3·2
Power steering fluid return lines	12 to 15	1·66 to 2·1
Pinion bearing cover plate bolts	7·5 to 9	1 to 1·2
Rack slipper cover plate bolts	7·5 to 9	1 to 1·2
Wheelnuts (steel wheels) (Capri II)	50 to 65	7·0 to 8·9
(Mercury Capri II)	50 to 55	7·0 to 7·6
Post August 1977 (Capri II)	50 to 67	7·0 to 9·0
Wheelnuts (aluminium wheels)	90 to 100	12·4 to 13·8
Post August 1977 (Capri II)	87 to 105	11·5 to 14·0

* These are to be tightened with the wheels in the 'straight-ahead' position and the weight of the car resting on its wheels. They are to be locked by punching the nut into the slot using a 0·10 in (3 mm) diameter ball ended punch.

** These are to be tightened with the weight of the car resting on its wheels.

1 General description

Each of the independent front suspension MacPherson strut units consists of a vertical strut, enclosing a double acting damper, surrounded by a coil spring.

The upper end of each strut is secured to the top of the wing valance under the bonnet by rubber mountings.

The wheel spindle carrying the brake assembly and wheel hub, is forged integrally with the suspension unit foot.

The steering arms are connected to each unit, which is in turn connected to trackrods and thence to the rack and pinion steering gear.

The lower end of each suspension unit is located by a track control arm. A stabilising torsion bar is fitted between the outer ends of each track control arm and secured at the front, to mountings on the body front member.

A rubber rebound stop is fitted inside each suspension unit, thus preventing the spring becoming over-extended and jumping out of its mounting plates. Upward movement of the wheel is limited by the spring becoming fully compressed, but this is damped by the addition of a rubber bump stop, fitted around the suspension unit piston rod, which comes into operation before the spring is fully compressed.

Whenever repairs have been carried out on a suspension unit, it is essential to check the wheel alignment, as the linkage could be altered, which will affect the correct front wheel settings.

Every time the car goes over a bump, vertical movement of a front wheel pushes the damper body upwards, against the combined resistance of the coil spring and the damper piston.

Hydraulic fluid in the damper is displaced and forced through the compression valve, into the space between the inner and outer cylinder. On the downward movement of the suspension, the road spring forces the damper body downwards against the pressure of the hydraulic fluid, which is forced back again through the rebound valve. In this way the natural oscillations of the spring are damped out and a comfortable ride is obtained.

On the front uprights there is a shroud inside the coil spring, which protects the machined surface of the piston rod from road dirt.

The steering gear is of the rack and pinion type and is located on the front crossmember by two U-shaped clamps. The pinion is connected to the steering column by a flexible coupling. On Mercury Capri II models, optional power steering is available.

The steering wheel is mounted on a convoluted collapsible cam which is designed to collapse progressively in the event of impact damage, thus protecting the driver to some degree.

Turning the steering wheel causes the rack to move in a lateral direction and the trackrods attached to each end of the rack pass this movement to the steering arms on the suspension/axle nuts, thereby moving the roadwheels.

Two adjustments are possible on the steering gear, rack damper adjustment and pinion bearing pre-load adjustment, but the steering gear must be removed from the car to carry out these adjustments. Both adjustments are made by varying the thickness of shim-packs.

At the rear, the axle is located by two inverted U-bolts at each end of the casing to underslung semi-elliptic leaf springs which provide both lateral and longitudinal location. Lateral movement of the rear axle is further controlled by fitting a stabilizer bar.

Double acting telescopic shock absorbers, are fitted between the spring plates on the rear axle and reinforced mountings in the boot of the car. These shock absorbers work on the same principle as the front shock asborbers.

In the interests of lessening noise and vibration, the spring and dampers are mounted on rubber bushes. A rubber spacer is also incorporated between the axle and the springs.

2 Front hub bearings – maintenance and adjustment

1   At the interval given in the Routine Maintenance Section at the beginning of the manual, clean and re-pack the front wheel bearings, then adjust them as described in the following paragraphs.

2   Apply the handbrake, jack up the front of the car and remove the roadwheels.

3   Disconnect the hydraulic brake at the union on the suspension unit and either plug the open ends of the pipes, or have a jar handy to catch the escaping fluid.

4   Bend back the locking tabs on the two bolts holding the brake caliper to the suspension unit, undo the bolts and remove the caliper.

5   By careful tapping and levering, remove the dust cap from the centre of the hub.

6   Remove the split pin from the nut retainer and undo the larger adjusting nut from the stub axle.

7   Withdraw the thrust washers and the outer tapered bearing.

8   Pull off the complete hub and disc assembly from the stub axle.

9   Carefully prise out the grease seal from the back of the hub assembly and remove the inner tapered bearing.

10 Carefully clean out the hub and wash the bearings with petrol making sure that no grease or oil is allowed to get onto the brake disc.

11 Working the grease well into the bearings, fully pack the bearing cages and rollers with wheel bearing grease. **Note:** *Leave the hub cavity half empty, to allow for subsequent expansion of the grease.*

12 To reassemble the hub assembly, first fit the inner bearing and then gently tap the grease seal back into the hub. If the seal was at all damaged during removal, a new one must be fitted.

13 Refit the hub and disc assembly onto the stub axle and slide on the outer bearing and the thrust washer.

14 If a torque wrench is available, tighten the centre adjusting nut to a torque of 27 lbf ft (3·37 kgf m), then slacken it off 120° (two flats). Refit the nut retainer and a new split pin.

15 If a torque wrench is not available, tighten up the centre nut until a slight drag is felt on rotating the wheel, then loosen the nut very slowly

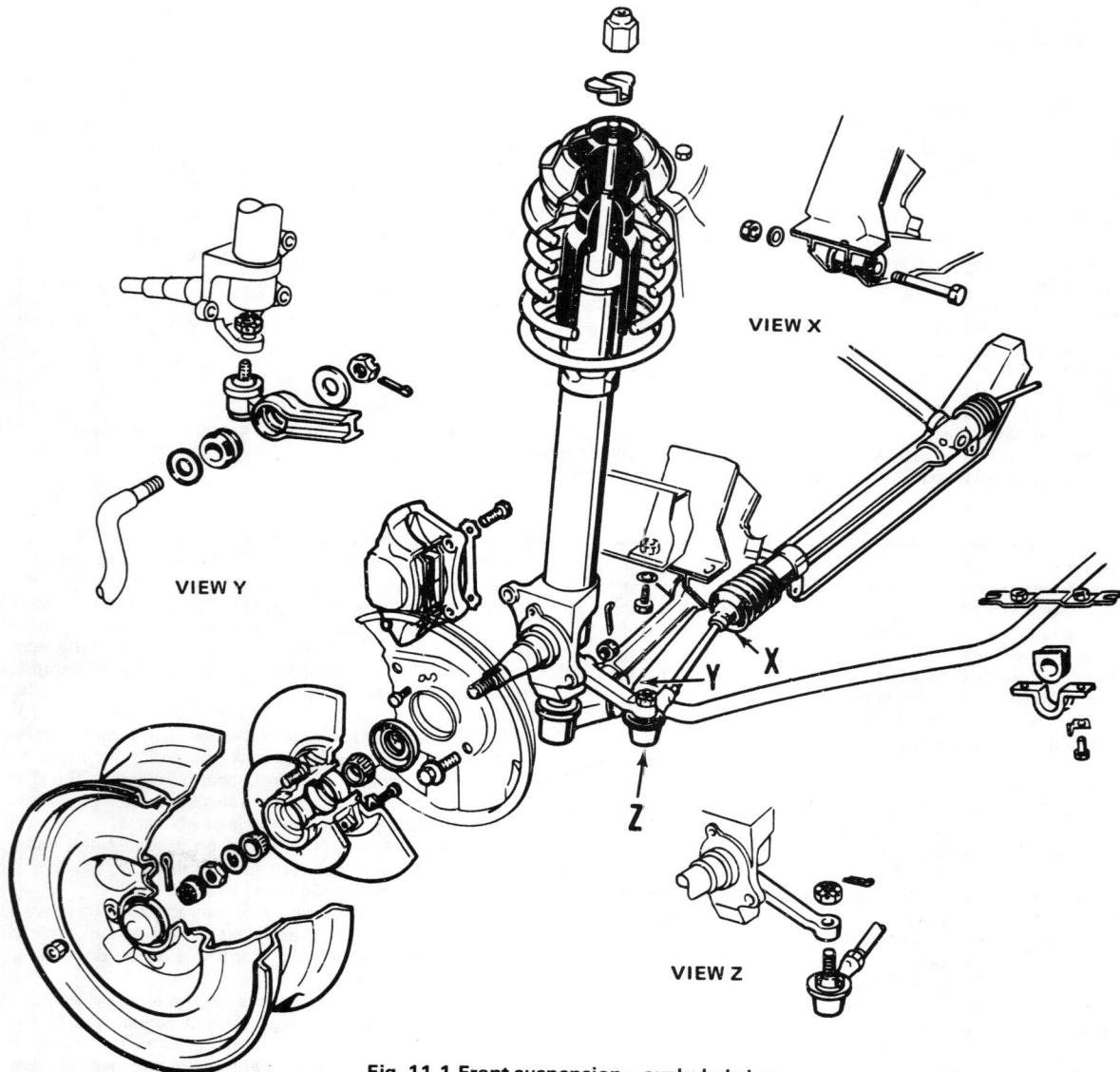

VIEW X

VIEW Y

VIEW Z

Fig. 11.1 Front suspension – exploded view

until the wheel turns freely again and there is just a perceptible end-float.

16 Refit the nut retainer, a new split pin and the dust cap.
17 Refit the caliper and connect the hydraulic brake line.
18 Bleed the brakes, as described in Chapter 9.

3 Front hub – dismantling and bearing renewal

1 Remove the hub/disc assembly, as described in Section 2.
2 Remove the oil seal and roller bearing races.
3 Using a brass drift, or bearing puller, remove the bearing tracks from the ends of the hub.
4 If the disc is to be renewed because of scoring, or distortion (see Chapter 9), bend down the lockplate tabs and unscrew and remove the bolts which connect the hub and disc.
5 Reassembly is a reversal of removal, but if all front wheel bearings are being renewed, take care not to mix up the bearings and their tracks. Keep them in their boxes as matched sets until required.
6 Use new locking plates under the disc to hub bolts and tighten all bolts to specifications.
7 Pack the bearings with grease and adjust them, as described in Section 2.

4 Front suspension strut – removal and refitting

1 It is difficult to work on the front suspension without one or two special tools, the most important of which is a set of adjustable spring clips which is Ford tool No. P.5045 (USA tool number T70P–5045). This tool, or similar clips or compressors, is vital and any attempt to dismantle the units without it may result in personal injury.
2 Get someone to sit on the wing of the car and with the spring partially compressed in this way, securely fit the spring clips.
3 Jack up the car and remove the roadwheel, then disconnect the brake pipe at the bracket on the suspension leg and plug the pipes. Alternatively have a jar handy to catch the escaping hydraulic fluid.
4 Disconnect the trackrod from the steering arm (see Section 11, paragraph 4), leaving the steering arm attached to the suspension unit.
5 Remove the outer end of the track control arm from the base of the suspension strut unit (for further information see Section 7).
6 Working under the bonnet, undo the three bolts holding the top end of the suspension strut to the side panel and lower the unit, complete with the brake caliper, away from the car.
7 Refitting is a direct reversal of the removal sequence, but use a

new split pin on the steering arm to track rod nut and also on the track control arm to suspension unit nut.
8 The top suspension unit mounting bolts, the track control arm to suspension strut nut and the steering arm to trackrod end nut, must all be tightened to the specified torque.

5 Front coil spring – removal and refitting

1 Get someone to sit on the front wing of the car and with the spring partially compressed in this way, securely fit spring clips, or a road-spring compressor (Fig. 11.2).
2 Jack up the front of the car, fit stands and remove the roadwheel.
3 Working under the bonnet, remove the piston nut and the cranked retainer.
4 Undo and remove the three bolts securing the top of the suspension unit to the side panel.
5 Push the piston rod downwards as far as it will go. It should now be possible to remove the top mounting assembly, the dished washer and the upper spring seat from the top of the spring.
6 The spring can now be lifted off its bottom seat and removed over the piston assembly.
7 If a new spring is being fitted, check extremely carefully that it is of the same rating as the spring on the other side of the car. The colour coding of the springs can be found in the Specifications at the beginning of this Chapter.
8 Before fitting a new spring, it must be compressed with the adjustable restrainers. Make sure that the clips are placed on the same number of coils and in the same position as on the spring that has been removed.
9 Place the new spring over the piston and locate it on its bottom seat, then pull the piston and fit the upper spring seat, so that it locates correctly on the flats cut on the piston rod.
10 Fit the dished washer to the piston rod, ensuring that the convex side faces upwards.
11 Fit the top mounting assembly. With the steering in the straight-ahead position, fit the cranked retainer, so that the ear on the retainer faces inwards and is at 90° to the centre-line of the car. Later models have retainers which incorporate two ears. Screw the piston rod nut on, having previously applied Loctite, or a similar compound, to the threads. Do not fully tighten the piston nut at this stage.
12 If necessary, pull the top end of the unit upward until it is possible to locate correctly the top mount bracket and fit the three retaining bolts from under the bonnet. These nuts must be tightened to the specified torque.
13 Remove the spring clips, fit the roadwheel and lower the car to the ground.
14 Finally slacken off the piston rod nut, get an assistant to hold the upper spring seat to prevent it turning and retighten the nut to the specified torque. Ensure that the cranked retainer faces inwards (ie; towards the engine) (photo).

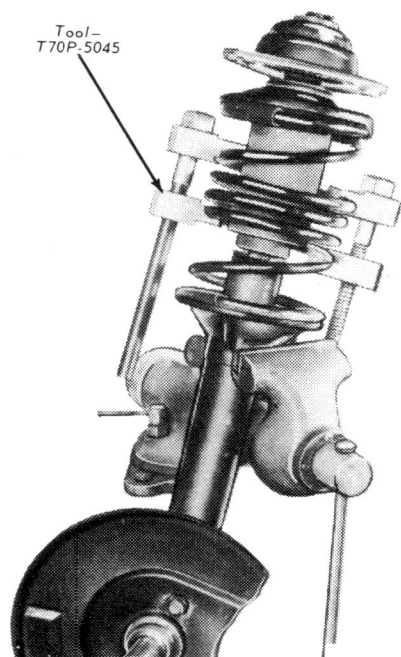

Fig. 11.2 Compressing a front spring using the special tool

5.14 Suspension unit cranked retainer – installed position

6   Front stabilizer bar – removal and refitting

1   Jack up the front of the car, support the car on suitable stands and remove both front roadwheels.
2   Working under the car at the front, knock back the locking tabs on the four bolts securing the two front clamps that hold the stabilizer bar to the frame and then undo the four bolts and remove the clamps and rubber insulators.
3   Remove the split pins from the castellated nuts retaining the stabilizer bar to the track control arms, then undo the nuts and pull off the large washers, carefully noting the way in which they are fitted.
4   Pull the stabilizer bar forward out of the two track control arms and remove from the car.
5   With the stabilizer bar out of the car, remove the sleeve and large washer from each end of the bar, again noting the correct fitting positions.
6   Reassembly is a reversal of the above procedure, but new locking tabs must be used on the front clamp bolts and new split pins on the castellated nuts. The nuts on the clamps and the castellated nuts on each end of the stabilizer bar must not be fully tightened down until the car is resting on its wheels.
7   Once the car is on its wheels, the castellated nuts on the ends of the stabilizer bar should be tightened down to the specified torque and new split pins fitted. The four clamp bolts on the front mounting points must be tightened to the specified torque and the locking tabs knocked up.

7   Track control arm (suspension arm) – removal and refitting

1   Jack up the front of the car, support it on suitable stands and remove the front wheel.
2   Working under the car, remove the split pin and unscrew the castellated nut that secures the track control arm to the stabilizer bar.
3   Lift away the large dished washer, noting which way round it is fitted.
4   Remove the self-lock nut and flat washer from the back of the track control arm pivot bolt. Release the inner end of the track control arm.
5   Withdraw the split pin and unscrew the nut securing the track control arm balljoint to the base of the suspension unit. Separate the joint, using a balljoint separator, or wedges.
6   To refit the track control arm, first assemble the track control arm ball stud to the base of the suspension unit.

7   Refit the nut and tighten to the specified torque. Secure with a new split pin.
8   Place the track control arm so that it correctly locates over the stabilizer bar and then secure the inner end.
9   Slide the pivot bolt into position from the front and secure with the flat washer and a new self-locking nut. The nut must be to the rear. Tighten the nut to the specified torque, when the car is on the ground.
10 Fit the dished washer to the end of the stabilizer bar, making sure it is the correct way round and secure with the castellated nut. This must be tightened when the car is on the ground, to the specified torque. Lock the castellated nut with a new split pin.

8   Rear shock absorber – removal and refitting

1   Remove the back seat, after having removed the two screws from the floor assembly crossmember.
2   Remove the screws securing the seat belt to the top of the B-pillar.
3   Detach the B-pillar cover (2 screws).
4   Remove the top trim from the side window (4 screws).
5   Remove the two screws from the rocker panel at the rear end and pull off the door weatherstrip, in the region of the side trim.
6   Take out the boot side trim (2 screws) and the carpet.
7   Remove the lining of the rear panel (5 screws) and of the side panel (10 screws), folding the rear seat forward for access.
8   Note the position of the steel and rubber washer at the wheel arch and axle mounting, then remove the shock absorber.
9   Refitting is a direct reversal of the removal procedure, but ensure that the rubber and steel washers are correctly positioned (where these are showing signs of deterioration, new items should be used). Commence the refitting by first connecting the shock absorber at the axle end, then extending it for fitting at the wheel arch end.

9   Rear stabilizer bar – removal, renewal of bushes and refitting

1   Chock the front wheels to prevent the car moving, then jack up the rear of the car for access to the rear axle and stabilizer bar mountings.
2   Using a multi-grip wrench, or similar tool, to hold the stabilizer bar towards the axle tube, remove the two bolts at each stabilizer bar-to-axle tube bracket.
3   Disconnect the nut and bolt at each end of the stabilizer bar, where it is attached to the floor assembly.

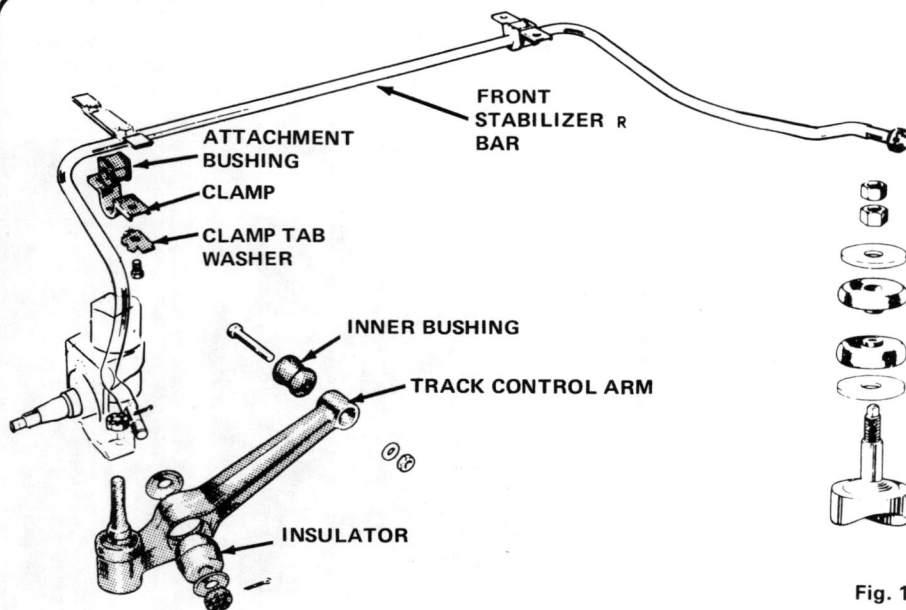

Fig. 11.3 Track control arm and stabilizer bar components

FRONT STABILIZER R BAR

ATTACHMENT BUSHING

CLAMP

CLAMP TAB WASHER

INNER BUSHING

TRACK CONTROL ARM

INSULATOR

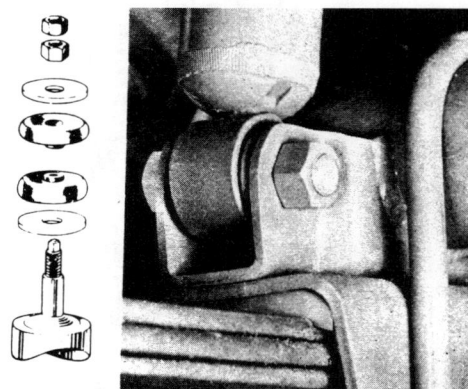

Fig. 11.4 Rear shock absorber mountings

4   To renew a stabilizer bar mounting bush, remove the locknut at one end and unscrew the end piece. Remove the nut and withdraw both rubber bushes from the stabilizer bar.

5   Dip the new rubber bushes in glycerine, or brake fluid; ensure that the stabilizer bar surface is clean and not scored, then slide on the bushes and refit the end piece. When fitted, the endpiece should be positioned as shown in Fig. 11.5. Dimension 'A' should be between 10·2 and 10·4 in (259·5 and 264·5 mm) and the difference between the two sides must not be greater than 0·1 inch (2·5 mm).

6   If the bushes in the end pieces require renewal, it may be found more convenient to remove the end pieces from the stabilizer bar, although this is not essential. The bushes can be pressed out using a suitable drift whilst the end piece is supported on a suitable diameter tube. Fitting is straightforward, the new bushes being pressed in until the steel case on the outside of the bush is flush with the inside of the end piece. Note the position of the semi-circular recess in the bush as shown in Fig. 11.7.

7   When refitting the stabilizer bar, it should be fitted at the floor end first, with the washers and self-locking nuts loosely installed.

8   The bar is then fitted to the axle tube, using a suitable tool to pull it towards the axle. The brackets, clamps and rubber insulators should now be fitted and the bolts tightened to the specified torque.

9   Lower the vehicle to the ground, then load the vehicle so that the centre of the axle tube and the spring rear eye are on the same horizontal level (the weight required is approximately that of two adults). The nuts and bolts securing the stabilizer bar to the floor can now be tightened to the specified torque.

10   Rear leaf spring – removal, renewal of bushes and refitting

1   Chock the front wheels to prevent the car moving, then jack up the rear of the car and support it on suitable stands. To make the springs more accessible remove the roadwheels.

2   Place a trolley jack underneath the differential housing to support the rear axle assembly when the springs are removed. Do not raise the jack under the differential housing so that the springs are flattened, but raise it just enough to take the full weight of the axle with the springs fully extended.

3   Undo the rear shackle nuts and remove the combined shackle bolt and plate assemblies, then remove the rubber bushes (Fig. 11.8).

4   Undo the nut from the front mounting and take out the bolt running through the mounting.

5   Undo the nuts on the ends of the four U-bolts and remove the U-bolts, together with the attachment plate and rubber spring insulators.

6   The rubber bushes can be pressed or driven out, and new bushes fitted as described for the bushes in the stabilizer bar and end pieces in the previous Section. A little glycerine, or brake fluid, will allow the bushes to be pressed in more easily. Note that the front bushes are $\frac{7}{16}$ inch (11 mm) diameter and the rear bushes are $\frac{5}{16}$ inch (8 mm) diameter.

7   Refitting the spring is the reverse of the removal procedure. The nuts on the U-bolts, spring front mounting and rear shackles must be torqued to the figures given in the Specifications at the beginning of this Chapter only **after** the car has been lowered onto its wheels.

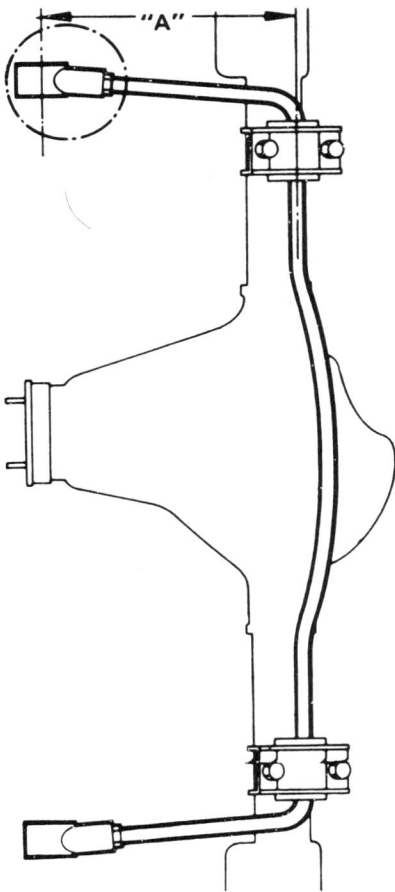

Fig. 11.6 Rear suspension layout

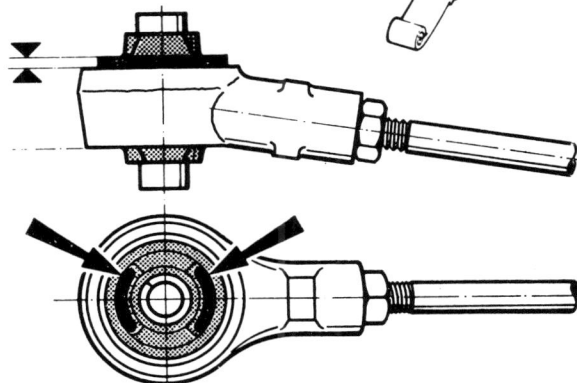

Fig. 11.5 Fitting the stabilizer bar

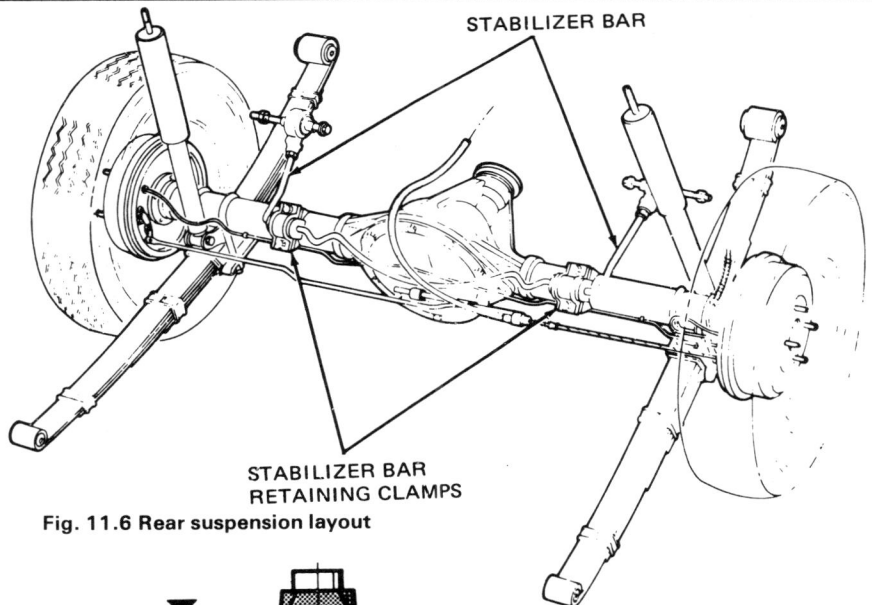

Fig. 11.7 Correct position for stabilizer rubber bush

Fig. 11.8 Rear suspension – exploded view

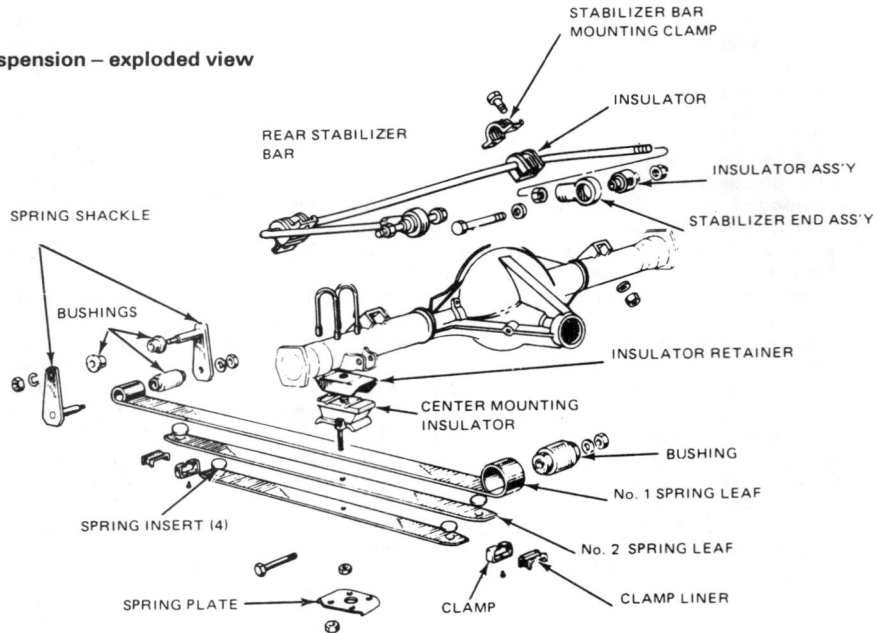

11 Steering gear – removal and refitting

1   Before starting set the front wheels in the straight-ahead position. Jack up the front of the car and place blocks under the wheels. Lower the car slightly on the jack, so that the trackrods are in a near-horizontal position.

2   Remove the nut and bolt from the clamp at the front of the flexible coupling on the steering column. This clamp holds the coupling to the pinion splines (photo).

3   Working on the front crossmember, knock back the locking tabs on the two nuts on each rack housing U-clamp, undo the nut and remove the locking tabs and clamps.

4   Remove the split pins and castellated nuts from the ends of each trackrod, where they join the steering arms. Separate the trackrods from the steering arms, using a ball joint separator or wedges and lower the steering gear downwards out of the car.

5   Before refitting the steering gear, make sure that the wheels have remained in the straight-ahead position. Also check the condition of the mounting rubbers round the housing and if they appear worn, or damaged, renew them.

6   Check that the steering gear is also in the straight-ahead position. This can be done by ensuring that the distances between the ends of both trackrods and the steering gear housing on both sides is the same.

7   Place the steering gear in its location on the crossmember and at the same time mate up the splines on the pinion, with the splines in the clamp on the steering column flexible coupling.

8   Refit the two U-clamps, using new locking tabs under the bolts. Tighten the bolts to the specified torque.

9   Refit the trackrod ends into the steering arms, refit the castellated nuts and tighten them to the specified torque. Use new split pins to retain the nuts.

10 Tighten the clamp bolt on the steering column flexible coupling to the specified torque, having first made sure that the pinion is correctly located in the splines.

11 Jack up the car, remove the blocks from under the wheels and lower the car to the ground. It is advisable to take the car to your local dealer and have the toe-in checked (see Section 19).

12 Steering gear – adjustments

1   For the steering gear to function correctly, two adjustments are necessary. These are pinion bearing preload and rack slipper adjustment. Ideally this will require the use of a dial gauge and mounting block, a surface table, a torque gauge and a splined adaptor. It is felt

11.2 Steering column clamp nut and bolt (arrowed)

that most people will be able to suitably improvise, using other equipment, but if this cannot be done and the equipment listed is not available, the job should be entrusted to your local vehicle Main Dealer.

2   To carry out these adjustments, remove the steering gear from the car, as described in the previous Section. Mount the assembly in a soft jawed vice, then remove the rack slipper cover plate, shim pack gasket and spring.

3   Remove the pinion bearing cover plate, shim pack and gasket.

Pinion bearing preload

4   Place the shim pack and cover plate on the bearing, tighten the bolts, then slacken them so that the cover plate touches the shim. The shim pack must comprise at least three shims, one of which must be 0·093 inch (2·35 mm), this being immediately against the cover plate.

5   Measure the cover plate-to-housing gap, and if outside the range 0·011 to 0·013 inch (0·28 to 0·33 mm) reduce the shim pack thickness (if the gap is too large), or increase it (if the gap is too small) until this gap is obtained. Remember that the 0·093 inch (2·35 mm) shim must remain immediately against the cover plate.

6   When the correct gap is obtained, remove the cover plate, install

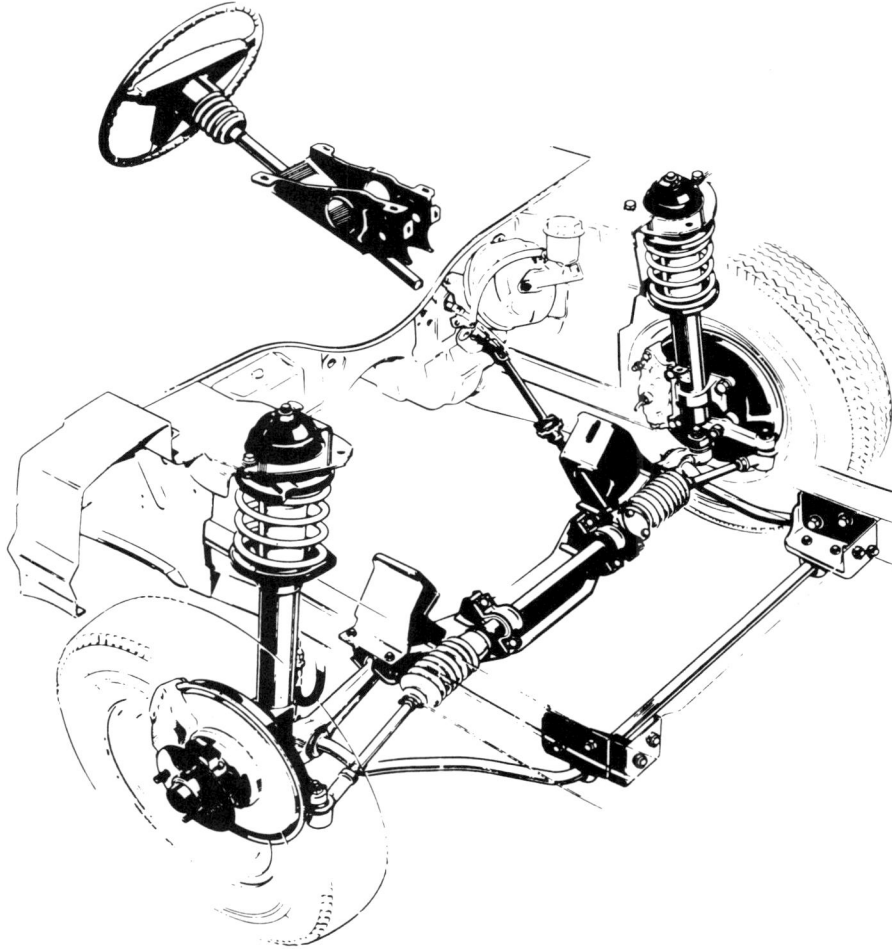

Fig. 11.9 Steering gear layout (left-hand drive)

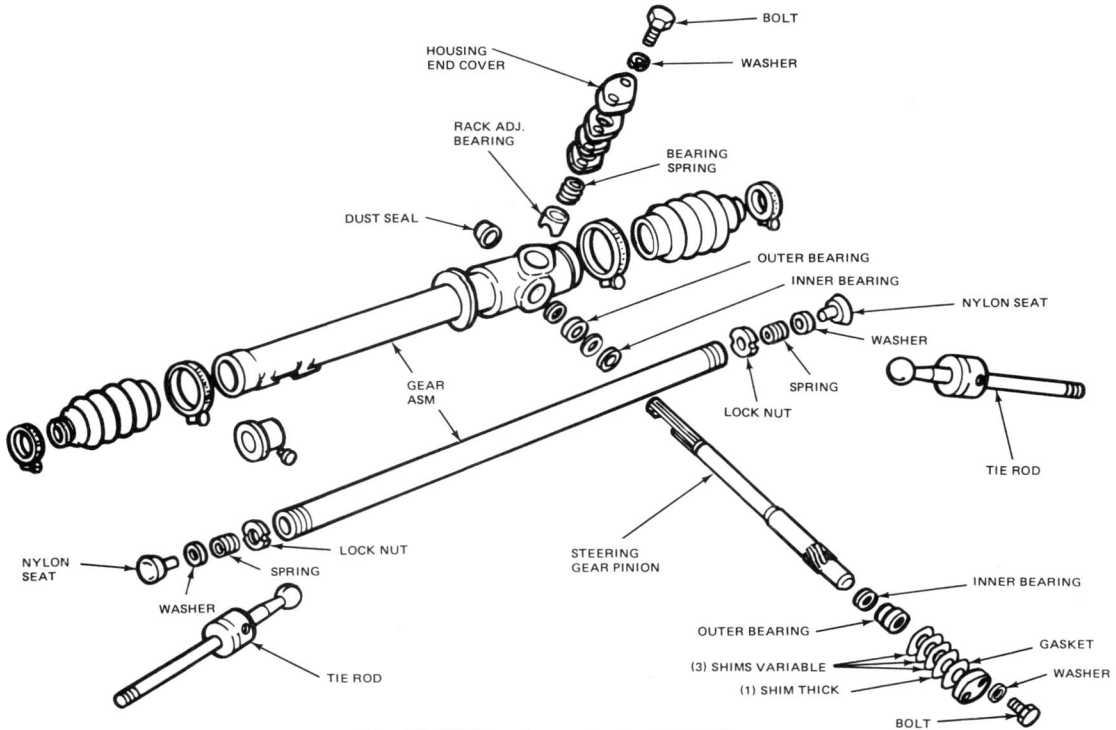

Fig. 11.10 Steering gear components

the gasket and refit the cover plate. Apply a sealer, such as Loctite, to the cover bolt threads, fit them and tighten to 6 to 8 lbf ft (0·83 to 1·1 kgf m).

Rack slipper adjustment

7   Having set the pinion bearing preload, measure the height of the slipper above the main body of the rack, as the rack is transversed from lock-to-lock by turning the pinion. Note the height reading obtained.
8   Prepare a shim pack which, including the thickness of the rack slipper bearing gasket, is 0·002 to 0·006 inch (0·05 to 0·15 mm) thicker than the dimension noted in paragraph 7.
9   Fit the spring, gasket, shim pack and cover plate to the rack housing (gasket nearest housing). Apply a sealer such as Loctite to the cover bolt threads, fit them and torque tighten to 6 to 8 lbf ft (0·83 to 1·1 kgf m).
10 Measure the torque required to turn the pinion throughout its range of travel. This should be 10 to 18 lbf inch (11·5 to 20·7 kgf cm); if outside this range, faulty components, lack of lubricant, etc., should be suspected.

13 Steering gear – dismantling, overhaul and reassembly

Note: *The procedure given may be beyond the capabilities of many d-i-y motorists. Read through the Section before commencing any work and if not considered to be feasible, entrust the job to your local vehicle Main Dealer.*

1   Remove and discard the wire retaining clips, remove the bellows and drain the lubricant.
2   Mount the steering gear in a soft-jawed vice and drill out the pins securing the trackrod housings to the locknuts. Centre-punch the pins before drilling them. Use a 4 mm ($\frac{5}{32}$ inch or No. 22) drill, but do not drill too deeply.
3   It is now necessary to unscrew the housings from the ball joints, so that the trackrods, housings, locknuts, ball seats, washers and springs can be removed. Ideally this requires the use of special tools which should be available from a vehicle Main Dealer, but if improvised grips or wrenches are used, take care that no parts are damaged (if parts are damaged, new items must be obtained).
4   Remove the rack slipper cover plate, shim pack, gasket and slipper.
5   Remove the pinion bearing preload cover plate, shim pack, gasket and lower bearing.
6   Using a screwdriver, or similar tool, prise out the pinion oil seal.
7   Clean all dirt and paint from the pinion shaft, then push the pinion out of the housing.
8   Take out the pinion upper bearing and washer.
9   Clean and inspect all the parts for damage and wear. Examine the bush in the end of the rack tube furthest from the pinion. If worn, it can be pressed out and a new bush fitted.
10 Commence reassembly by fitting the pinion upper bearing and washer into the housing.
11 Position the rack into the housing and leave it in the central position.
12 Fit the pinion, ensuring that after fitting the flat is towards the right-hand side of the vehicle (irrespective of right or left-hand drive vehicles).
13 Fit the pinion lower bearing cover plate and adjust the preload as described in the previous Section.
14 Assemble the rack slipper, spring, gasket, shim pack and cover plate, adjusting as described in the previous Section.
15 Lubricate the ball seats, balls and housings, with SAE 90 EP gear oil. Screw the locknuts onto the ends of the steering rack.
16 Assemble the springs, washers, ball seats, trackrod ends and housing. Tighten the housings, to obtain a rotational torque of 5 lbf ft (0·7 kgf m), then lock them with the locknuts. Recheck the torque after tightening the locknut.
17 Drill new holes (even if the old holes are in alignment), 4 mm ($\frac{5}{32}$ inch or No. 22 drill) diameter x9 mm (0·38 inch) deep along the break lines between the housing and the locknut, approximately opposite the spanner locating hole in the housing.
18 Fit new retaining pins and peen over the surrounding metal, to retain them.
19 Lightly grease the inside of the bellows, where they will contact the trackrods. Install one bellows, ensuring that it locates in the trackrod groove, then fit a new retaining clip. Do not tighten the clip

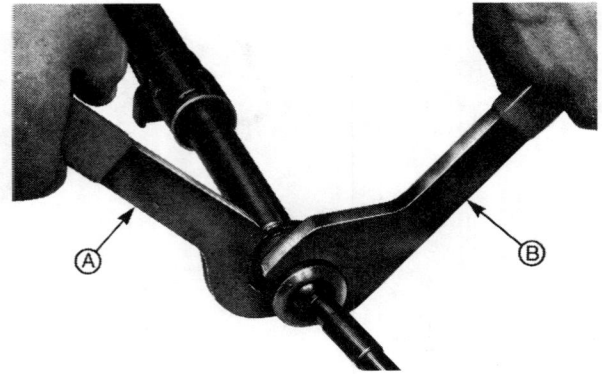

Fig. 11.11 Removing a track rod
(A and B are special tools available for the purpose)

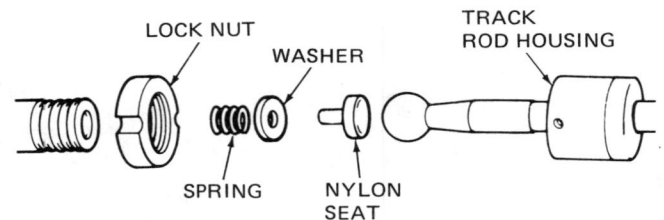

Fig. 11.12 Tie rod (track rod) end – exploded view

until the lock-in has been checked.
20 Add the specified quantity of steering gear oil, operating the rack over its range of travel to assist the lubricant in flowing. Do not overfill.
21 Fit the other bellows, but do not tighten the (new) clip yet.
22 Check the pinion turning torque, as described in paragraph 10 of the previous Section.

14 Power steering – general description

The power steering system available on Mercury Capri II cars has a pulley-driven Hobourn-Eaton series 110 roller pump. This pump delivers fluid to a servo assisted rack and pinion gear assembly.

Servo assistance is obtained through a piston, mounted on the rack and running in the rack tube. The degree of assistance is controlled by a spool valve, mounted concentrically with the input and pinion shaft.

The power steering system on the Capri II model is similar to that of the Mercury Capri but has a separate fluid reservoir.

Owing to the complexity of the power steering system, it is recommended that repair or overhaul is entrusted to a specialist in this type of work.

For maintenance details refer to Chapter 13.

15 Power steering – bleeding

1   The power steering system will only need bleeding in the event of air being introduced into the system, eg where pipes have been disconnected or where a leakage has occurred. To bleed the system proceed as described in the following paragraphs.
2   Open the bonnet (hood) and check the fluid level in the integral reservoir. Top-up if necessary using the specified type of fluid.
3   If fluid is added, allow two minutes, then run the engine at approximately 1500 rpm. Slowly turn the steering wheel from lock-to-lock, whilst checking and topping-up the fluid level until the level remains steady and no more bubbles appear in the reservoir.
4   Clean and refit the reservoir cap and close the bonnet.

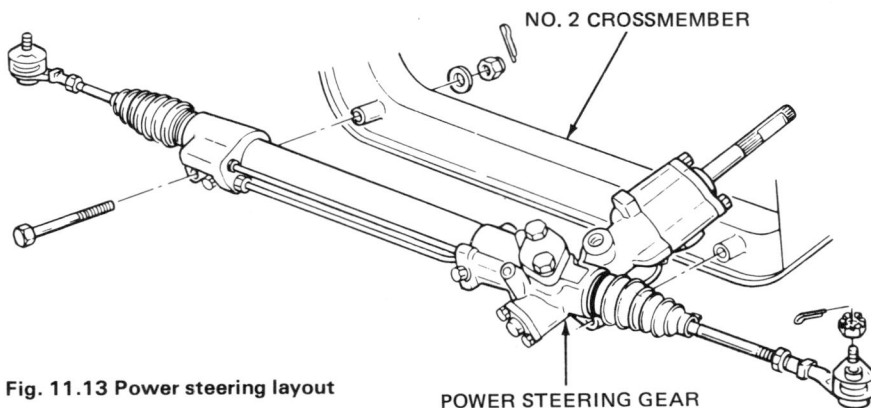

Fig. 11.13 Power steering layout

NO. 2 CROSSMEMBER

POWER STEERING GEAR

Fig. 11.14 Power steering reservoir and dipstick

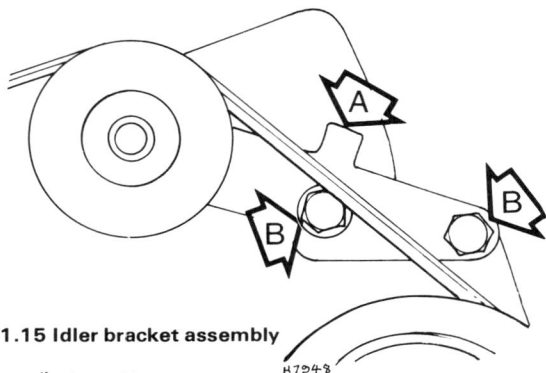

Fig. 11.15 Idler bracket assembly

A Idler adjustment tag
B Idler bolts

18.3 Removal of the steering wheel motif

16 Power steering pump – removal and refitting

1   Disconnect the battery earth lead.
2   Raise the car on a hoist, or place it over an inspection pit if possible. Alternatively, the car must be jacked up to provide the working room beneath.
3   Where applicable, remove the engine splash shield.
4   Loosen the alternator mounting bolts and remove the driveshaft (refer to Chapter 10 if necessary).

5   Disconnect the power system fluid lines and drain the fluid into a suitable container.
6   Remove the fuel pump from the engine, but do not disconnect the fuel lines. Move the pump away from the power steering bolts. (Refer to Chapter 3 for further information, if necessary).
7   Remove the power steering pump. As applicable, remove the pump pulley and adapter bracket.
8   Refitting is a direct reversal of the removal procedure. Ensure that the fluid lines are tightened to the specified torque, top up the system with an approved fluid, adjust the alternator drivebelt tension (see Chapter 10), or adjust the idler bracket assembly depending on model (Fig. 11.15), then bleed the system, as described in the previous Section 15.

17 Power steering gear – removal and refitting

1   The procedure for removing the power steering gear is similar to that described in Section 11 for the manual steering gear with the additional task of disconnecting the pump lines. When refitting, ensure that the fluid lines are tightened to the specified torque; top up the system with an approved fluid; adjust the alternator driveshaft tension (see Chapter 10), then bleed the system, as described in Section 15.

18 Steering column – removal, dismantling, reassembly and refitting

1   Disconnect the battery earth lead.
2   Remove the upper and lower steering coupling clamp bolts and tap the coupling shaft down the pinion shaft to disconnect the coupling shaft from the column.
3   Carefully prise out the motif from the centre of the steering wheel and then unscrew the wheel retaining nut (photo).
4   Ensure that the roadwheels are in the straight-ahead position, then pull off the steering wheel.
5   Remove the direction indicator actuator cam.
6   Remove the steering column shroud (2 screws at the bottom, then pull out at the top) and lower the dash panel trim.
7   Disconnect the direction indicator switch from the column (two bolts – see Fig. 11.16)
8   Disconnect the loom wiring from the ignition switch.
9   Remove the two steering column retaining bolts (see Fig. 11.17) and pull the column assembly from the vehicle. Push the grommet out of the floor pan.
10   Drill off the steering column lockbolt heads, or tap them round with a pin punch, then use suitable grips to pull out the bolt shanks. Remove the steering lock (refer to Chapter 10, if necessary).
11   Remove the circlip (snap-ring), washer and spring from the lower end of the column.
12   Tap the lower end of the shaft with a soft-faced hammer to remove the shaft and bearing from the top of the column.
13   Using the shaft as a drift, tap the lower bearing out of the column.
14   Inspect all the parts for wear and damage, renewing if necessary.
15   Commence reassembly by positioning the shaft in the column, then assemble the lower bearing (smaller diameter towards the

Fig. 11.16 Direction indicator switch retaining bolts (arrowed)

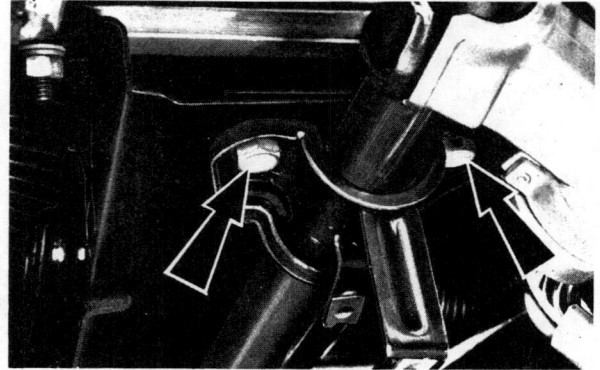

Fig. 11.17 Steering column retaining bolts (arrowed)

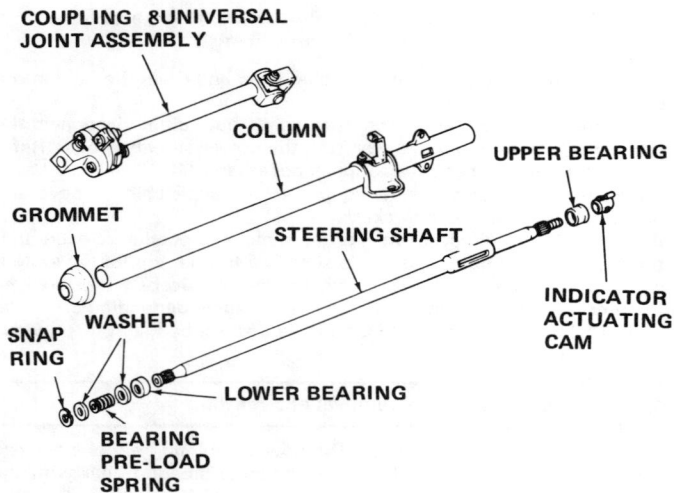

Fig. 11.18 Steering column assembly

column), spring, washer and circlip to the shaft. Push the assembly into the column to locate the bearing against the stops.

16 Press the upper bearing onto the column.

17 Secure the steering lock to the column and shear the bolts.

18 Use the steering lock to locate the shaft in the column, then fit the direction indicator actuating cam and steering wheel. Check that the roadwheels are still in the 'straight-ahead' position.

19 Install the steering column grommet at the lower end.

20 Locate the column assembly and secure it with the two mounting bolts.

21 The remainder of the refitting procedure is the reverse of the removal procedure.

19 Steering angles and front wheel alignment

1 Accurate front wheel alignment is essential for good steering and tyre wear. Before considering the steering angle, check that the tyres are correctly inflated, that the front wheels are not buckled, the hub bearings are not worn or incorrectly adjusted and that the steering linkage is in good order, without slackness or wear at the joints.

2 Wheel alignment consists of four factors:

Camber, is the angle at which the front wheels are set from the vertical when viewed from the front of the car. Positive camber is the amount (in degrees) that the wheels are tilted outwards at the top from the vertical.

Castor, is the angle between the steering axis and a vertical line when viewed from each side of the car. Positive castor is when the steering axis is inclined rearwards.

Steering axis inclination is the angle, when viewed from the front of the car, between the vertical and an imaginary line drawn between the upper and lower suspension strut pivots.

Toe-in is the amount by which the distance between the **front**

inside edges of the roadwheels (measured at hub height) is less than the distance measured between the **rear** inside edges.

3 The angles of camber, castor and steering axis are set in production and are not adjustable.

4 Front wheel alignment (toe-in) checks are best carried out with modern setting equipment, but a reasonably accurate alternative is by means of the following procedure.

5 Place the car on level ground with the wheels in the 'straight-ahead' position.

6 Obtain or make a toe-in gauge. One may easily be made from a length of rod or tubing, cranked to clear the sump or bellhousing and having a setscrew and locknut at one end.

7 With the gauge, measure the distance between the two inner wheel rims at hub height at the front of the wheel.

8 Rotate the roadwheel through 180° (half a turn), by pushing or pulling the car and then measure the distance again at hub height between the inner wheel rims at the rear of the roadwheel. This measurement should either be the same as the one just taken, or greater by not more than 0·28 inch (7 mm).

9 Where the toe-in is found to be incorrect, slacken the locknuts on each trackrod, also the flexible bellows clips and rotate each trackrod by an equal amount until the correct toe-in is obtained. Tighten the trackrod-end locknuts, while the ball joints are held in the centre of their arcs of travel. It is imperative that the lengths of the trackrods are always equal otherwise the wheel angles on turns will be incorrect. If new components have been fitted, set the roadwheels in the 'straight-ahead' position and also centralise the steering wheel. Adjust the lengths of the trackrods by turning them so that the trackrod-end ball joint studs will drop easily into the eyes of the steering arms. Measure the distances between the centres of the ball joints and the grooves on the inner ends of the trackrods and adjust, if necessary, so that they are equal. This is an initial setting only and precise adjustment must be carried out as described in earlier paragraphs of this Section.

20 Wheels and tyres

1 Check the tyre pressures weekly (when the tyres are cold).

2 Frequently inspect the tyre walls and treads for damage and pick out any large stones which have become trapped in the tread pattern.

3 If the wheels and tyres have been balanced on the car, they should not be moved to a different axle position. If they have been balanced off the car then, in the interests of extending tread life, they can be moved between front and rear on the same side of the car and the spare incorporated in the rotational pattern.

4 Never mix tyres of different construction, or very dissimilar tread patterns.

5 Always keep the roadwheels tightened to the specified torque and if the bolt holes become elongated or flattened, renew the wheel.

6 Occasionally, clean the inner faces of the roadwheels and if there is any sign of rust or corrosion, paint them with metal preservative paint.

Note: *Corrosion on aluminium alloy wheels may be evidence of a more serious problem which could lead to wheel failure. If corrosion is evident, consult your Ford dealer for advice.*

7 Before removing a roadwheel which has been balanced on the car, always mark one wheel stud and bolt hole, so that the roadwheel may be refitted in the same relative position, to maintain the balance.

21 Fault diagnosis – Suspension and steering

Before diagnosing faults from the following chart, check that any irregularities are not caused by:

1 *Binding brakes.*
2 *Incorrect 'mix' of radial and crossply tyres.*
3 *Incorrect tyre pressures.*
4 *Misalignment of the bodyframe.*

Symptom	Reason/s
Steering wheel can be moved considerably before any sign of movement of the roadwheels is apparent	Wear in the steering linkage, gear and column coupling
Vehicle difficult to steer in a consistent straight line – wandering	As above Wheel alignment incorrect (indicated by excessive or uneven tyre wear) Front wheel hub bearings loose or worn Worn ball joints
Steering stiff and heavy	Incorrect wheel alignment (indicated by excessive or uneven tyre wear) Excessive wear, or seizure, in one or more of the joints in the steering linkage or suspension Excessive wear in the steering gear Failure of power steering gear pump Low tyre pressures
Wheel wobble and vibration	Roadwheels out of balance Roadwheels buckled Wheel alignment incorrect Wear in the steering linkage, suspension ball joints or track control arm pivot Broken front spring
Excessive pitching and rolling on corners and during braking	Defective shock absorbers and/or broken spring

Chapter 12 Bodywork and fittings

For modifications, and information applicable to later models, see Supplement at end of manual

Contents

1 General description

The bodywork is of a monocoque, all-steel, welded construction with impact absorbing front and rear sections.

The car has 2 side doors and a full-length lifting tailgate, for easy access to the rear compartment. The side doors are fitted with anti-burst locks and incorporate a key operated lock in each handle. Window frames are adjustable for position. The tailgate hinges are bolted to the underside of the roof panel and to the tailgate itself. Gas-filled dampers support the tailgate in the open position. When closed, it is fastened by a key-operated lock incorporating a release pushbutton.

An automatic bonnet (hood) locking mechanism operates when the bonnet is closed, a release lever being fitted at the edge of the instrument panel on the driver's side. The bonnet (hood) is hinged at the rear and is held in the open position by a support stay.

A cable-operated sliding roof is available as an option, this being controlled by a handle fitted flush to the head lining.

Toughened safety glass is fitted to all windows, the windscreen having an additional 'zone' toughened band in front of the driver. In the event of the windscreen shattering, this zone crazes into large sections, to give a greater degree of visibility as a safety feature. An optional glass/plastic/glass laminated windscreen is available at extra cost. This has the advantage of cracking only, giving an even greater degree of visibility in the event of accidental damage. The front door windows have a conventional winding mechanism. On certain variants, frameless opening rear quarter windows are fitted. These are hinged at the forward edge and are operated from an 'over-centre' type latch. A heated rear window is available as an optional extra throughout the range.

All vehicles have individual reclining front bucket seats. GT versions have individual rear folding seats and a folding rear bench seat is used on other models. The standard seat and panel upholstery is of vinyl material, but a cloth fabric trim is available for all models.

A padded facia crash panel is standard equipment, as is deep pile wall-to-wall carpeting. Inertia reel seatbelts are fitted to all models.

To prevent damage under minor impacts, rubber faced bumpers are used, with rubber overriders on GT models.

All models are fitted with a heating and ventilating system which operates by ram air when the car is moving, or by a blower when stationary, or for increased airflow. The heater is operated from a central control panel and airflow is directed to the windscreen or car interior according to the control level settings. A heavy duty heater is available for some markets and USA models can be supplied with an optional air conditioning system.

2 Maintenance – bodywork and underframe

1 The general condition of a car's bodywork is the one thing that significantly affects its value. Maintenance is easy but needs to be regular. Neglect, particularly after minor damage can lead quickly to further deterioration and costly repair bills. It is important also to keep watch on those parts of the car not immediately visible, for instance, the underframe, inside all the wheel arches and the lower part of the engine compartment.

2 The basic maintenance routine for the bodywork is washing – preferably with a lot of water, from a hose. This will remove all the loose solids which may have stuck to the car. It is important to flush these off in such a way as to prevent grit from scratching the finish.

3 The wheel arches and underframe need washing in the same way to remove any accumulated mud which will retain moisture and tend to encourage rust. Paradoxically enough, the best time to clean the underframe and wheel arches is in wet weather when the mud is thoroughly wet and soft. In very wet weather the underframe is usually cleaned of large accumulations automatically and this is a good time for inspection.

4 Periodically it is a good idea to have the whole of the underframe of the car steam cleaned, engine compartment included, so that a thorough inspection can be carried out to see what minor repairs and renovations are necessary. Steam cleaning is available at many

garages and is necessary for removal of the accumulation of oil grime which sometimes is allowed to cake thick in certain areas near the engine, gearbox and back axle. If steam cleaning facilities are not available, there are one or two excellent grease solvents available which can be brush applied. The dirt can then be simply hosed off.

5 After washing paintwork, wipe off with a chamois leather to give an unspotted clear finish. A coat of clear protective wax polish will give added protection against chemical pollutants in the air. If the paintwork sheen has dulled or oxidised, use a cleaner/polisher combination to restore the brilliance of the shine. This requires a little effort, but is usually necessary because regular washing has been neglected. Always check that the door and ventilator opening drain holes and pipes are completely clear so that water can be drained out. Bright work should be treated the same way as paintwork. Windscreens and windows can be kept clear of the smeary film which often appears if a little ammonia is added to the water. If they are scratched, a good rub with a proprietary metal polish will often clear them. Never use any form of wax or other body or chromium polish on glass.

---

3   Maintenance – upholstery and carpets

1 Mats and carpets should be brushed or vacuum cleaned regularly to keep them free of grit. If they are badly stained remove them from the car for scrubbing or sponging and make quite sure they are dry before refitting. Seats and interior trim panels can be kept clean by a wipe over with a damp cloth. If they do become stained (which can be more apparent on light coloured upholstery) use a little liquid detergent and a soft nail brush to scour the grime out of the grain of the material. Do not forget to keep the head lining clean in the same way as the upholstery. When using liquid cleaners inside the vehicle do not over-wet the surfaces being cleaned. Excessive damp could get into the seams and padded interior causing stains, offensive odours or even rot. If the inside of the car gets wet accidentally it is worthwhile taking some trouble to dry it out properly, particularly where carpets are involved. *Do not leave oil or electric heaters inside the vehicle for this purpose.*

---

4   Minor body damage – repair

The photo sequence on pages 214 and 215 illustrates the operations detailed in the following sub-Sections.

Repair of minor scratches in the car's bodywork

If the scratch is very superficial, and does not penetrate to the metal of the bodywork, repair is very simple. Lightly rub the area of the scratch with a paintwork renovator, or a very fine cutting paste, to remove loose paint from the scratch and to clear the surrounding bodywork of wax polish. Rinse the area with clean water.

Apply touch-up paint to the scratch using a thin paint brush; continue to apply thin layers of paint until the surface of the paint in the scratch is level with the surrounding paintwork. Allow the new paint at least two weeks to harden; then blend it into the surrounding paintwork by rubbing the paintwork in the scratch area, with a paintwork renovator or a very fine cutting paste. Finally, apply wax polish.

An alternative to painting over the scratch is to use a paint patch. Use the same preparation for the affected area, then simply pick a patch of a suitable size to cover the scratch completely. Hold the patch against the scratch and burnish its backing paper; the paper will adhere to the paintwork, freeing itself from the backing paper at the same time. Polish the affected area to blend the patch into the surrounding paintwork.

Where the scratch has penetrated right through to the metal of the bodywork, causing the metal to rust, a different repair technique is required. Remove any loose rust from the bottom of the scratch with a penknife, then apply rust inhibiting paint to prevent the formation of rust in the future. Using a rubber or nylon applicator fill the scratch with bodystopper paste. If required, this paste can be mixed with cellulose thinners to provide a very thin paste which is ideal for filling narrow scratches. Before the stopper-paste in the scratch hardens, wrap a piece of smooth cotton rag around the top of a finger. Dip the finger in cellulose thinners and then quickly sweep it across the surface of the stopper-paste in the scratch; this will ensure that the surface of the stopper-paste is slightly hollowed. The scratch can now be painted

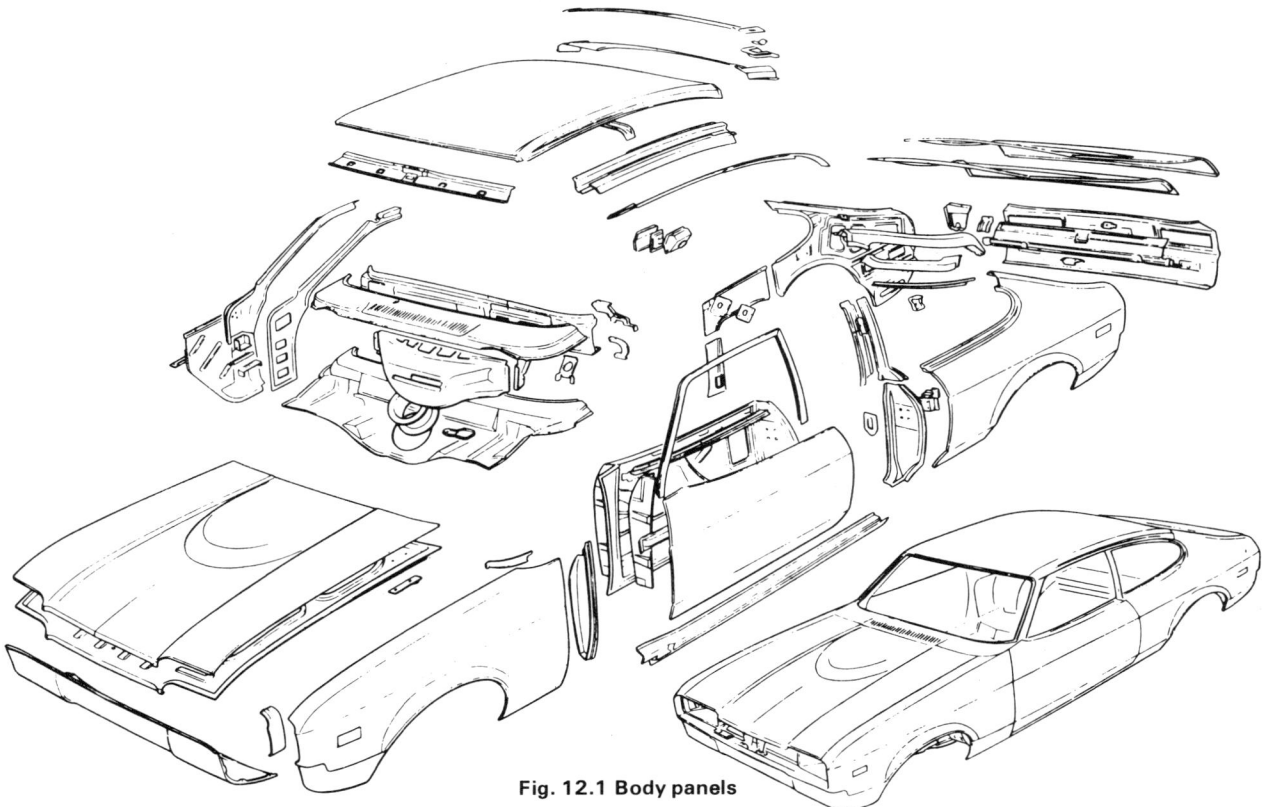

Fig. 12.1 Body panels

over as described earlier in this Section.

Repair of dents in the car's bodywork

When deep denting of the car's bodywork has taken place, the first task is to pull the dent out, until the affected bodywork almost attains its original shape. There is little point in trying to restore the original shape completely, as the metal in the damaged area will have stretched on impact and cannot be reshaped fully to its original contour. It is better to bring the level of the dent up to a point which is about $\frac{1}{8}$ in (3 mm) below the level of the surrounding bodywork. In cases where the dent is very shallow anyway, it is not worth trying to pull it out at all. If the underside of the dent is accessible, it can be hammered out gently from behind, using a mallet with a wooden or plastic head. Whilst doing this, hold a suitable block of wood firmly against the outside of the dent. This block will absorb the impact from the hammer blows and thus prevent a large area of the bodywork from being 'belled-out'.

Should the dent be in a section of the bodywork which has double skin or some other factor making it inaccessible from behind, a different technique is called for. Drill several small holes through the metal inside the dent area - particularly in the deeper sections. Then screw long self-tapping screws into the holes just sufficiently for them to gain a good purchase in the metal. Now the dent can be pulled out by pulling on the protruding heads of the screws with a pair of pliers.

The next stage of the repair is the removal of the paint from the damaged area, and from an inch or so of the surrounding 'sound' bodywork. This is accomplished most easily by using a wire brush or abrasive pad on a power drill, although it can be done just as effectively by hand using sheets of abrasive paper. To complete the preparation for filling, score the surface of the bare metal with a screwdriver or the tang of a file, or alternatively, drill small holes in the affected area. This will provide a really good 'key' for the filler paste.

To complete the repair see the Section on filling and respraying.

Repair of rust holes or gashes in the car's bodywork

Remove all paint from the affected area and from an inch or so of the surrounding 'sound' bodywork, using an abrasive pad or a wire brush on a power drill. If these are not available a few sheets of abrasive paper will do the job just as effectively. With the paint removed you will be able to gauge the severity of the corrosion and therefore decide whether to renew the whole panel (if this is possible) or to repair the affected area. New body panels are not as expensive as most people think and it is often quicker and more satisfactory to fit a new panel than to attempt to repair large areas of corrosion.

Remove all fittings from the affected area except those which will act as a guide to the original shape of the damaged bodywork (eg headlamp shells etc). Then, using tin snips or a hacksaw blade, remove all loose metal and any other metal badly affected by corrosion. Hammer the edges of the hole inwards in order to create a slight depression for the filler paste.

Wire brush the affected area to remove the powdery rust from the surface of the remaining metal. Paint the affected area with rust inhibiting paint; if the back of the rusted area is accessible treat this also.

Before filling can take place it will be necessary to block the hole in some way. This can be achieved by the use of one of the following materials: Zinc gauze, Aluminium tape or Polyurethane foam.

Zinc gauze is probably the best material to use for a large hole. Cut a piece to the approximate size and shape of the hole to be filled, then position it in the hole so that its edges are below the level of the surrounding bodywork. It can be retained in position by several blobs of filler paste around its periphery.

Aluminium tape should be used for small or very narrow holes. Pull a piece off the roll and trim it to the approximate size and shape required, then pull off the backing paper (if used) and stick the tape over the hole; it can be overlapped if the thickness of one piece is insufficient. Burnish down the edges of the tape with the handle of a screwdriver or similar, to ensure that the tape is securely attached to the metal underneath.

Polyurethane foam is best used where the hole is situated in a section of bodywork of complex shape, backed by a small box section (eg where the sill panel meets the rear wheel arch - most cars). The usual mixing procedure for this foam is as follows: Put equal amounts of fluid from each of the two cans provided in the kit into one container. Stir until the mixture begins to thicken, then quickly pour this mixture into the hole, and hold a piece of cardboard over the larger

apertures. Almost immediately the polyurethane will begin to expand, gushing out of any small holes left unblocked. When the foam hardens it can be cut back to just below the level of the surrounding bodywork with a hacksaw blade.

Bodywork repairs — filling and re-spraying

Before using this Section, see the Sections on dent, deep scratch, rust hole and gash repairs.

Many types of bodyfiller are available, but generally speaking those proprietary kits which contain a tin of filler paste and a tube of resin hardener are best for this type of repair. A wide, flexible plastic or nylon applicator will be found invaluable for imparting a smooth and well contoured finish to the surface of the filler.

Mix up a little filler on a clean piece of card or board — use the hardener sparingly (follow the maker's instructions on the pack) otherwise the filler will set very rapidly.

Using the applicator, apply the filler paste to the prepared area; draw the applicator across the surface of the filler to achieve the correct contour and to level the filler surface. As soon as a contour that approximates the correct one is achieved, stop working the paste — if you carry on too long the paste will become sticky and begin to 'pick-up' on the applicator. Continue to add thin layers of filler paste at twenty-minute intervals until the level of the filler is just 'proud' of the surrounding bodywork.

Once the filler has hardened, excess can be removed using a metal plane or file. From then on, progressively finer grades of abrasive paper should be used, starting with a 40 grade production paper and finishing with 400 grade 'wet-or-dry' paper. Always wrap the abrasive paper around a flat rubber, cork, or wooden block — otherwise the surface of the filler will not be completely flat. During the smoothing of the filler surface the 'wet-or-dry' paper should be periodically rinsed in water. This will ensure that a very smooth finish is imparted to the filler at the final stage.

At this stage the 'dent' should be surrounded by a ring of bare metal, which in turn should be encircled by the finely 'feathered' edge of the good paintwork. Rinse the repair area with clean water, until all of the dust produced by the rubbing-down operation has gone.

Spray the whole repair area with a light coat of primer — this will show up any imperfections in the surface of the filler. Repair these imperfections with fresh filler paste or bodystopper, and once more smooth the surface with abrasive paper. If bodystopper is used, it can be mixed with cellulose thinners to form a really thin paste which is ideal for filling small holes. Repeat this spray and repair procedure until you are satisfied that the surface of the filler, and the feathered edge of the paintwork are perfect. Clean the repair area with clean water and allow to dry fully.

The repair area is now ready for spraying. Paint spraying must be carried out in a warm, dry, windless and dust free atmosphere. This condition can be created artificially if you have access to a large indoor working area, but if you are forced to work in the open, you will have to pick your day very carefully. If you are working indoors, dousing the floor in the work area with water will 'lay' the dust which would otherwise be in the atmosphere. If the repair area is confined to one body panel, mask off the surrounding panels; this will help to minimise the effects of a slight mis-match in paint colours. Bodywork fittings (eg chrome strips, door handles etc) will also need to be masked off. Use genuine masking tape and several thicknesses of newspaper for the masking operations.

Before commencing to spray, agitate the aerosol can thoroughly, then spray a test area (an old tin, or similar) until the technique is mastered. Cover the repair area with a thick coat of primer; the thickness should be built up using several thin layers of paint rather than one thick one. Using 400 grade 'wet-or-dry' paper, rub down the surface of the primer until it is really smooth. While doing this, the work area should be thoroughly doused with water, and the 'wet-or-dry' paper periodically rinsed in water. Allow to dry before spraying on more paint.

Spray on the top coat, again building up the thickness by using several thin layers of paint. Start spraying in the centre of the repair area and then using a circular motion, work outwards until the whole repair area and about 2 inches of the surrounding original paintwork is covered. Remove all masking material 10 to 15 minutes after spraying on the final coat of paint.

Allow the new paint at least two weeks to harden fully, then, using a paintwork renovator or a very fine cutting paste, blend the edges of the new paint into the existing paintwork. Finally, apply wax polish.

5 Major body damage – repair

Where serious damage has occurred or large areas need renewal due to neglect, it means certainly that completely new sections or panels will need welding in and this is best left to professionals. If the damage is due to impact it will also be necessary to completely check the alignment of the bodyshell structure. Due to the principle of construction the strength and shape of the whole can be affected by damage to a part. In such instances the services of a Ford agent with specialist checking jigs are essential. If a frame is left misaligned it is first of all dangerous as the vehicle will not handle properly and secondly uneven stresses will be imposed on the steering, engine and transmission, causing abnormal wear or complete failure. Tyre wear may also be excessive.

6 Maintenance – vinyl roof covering

Under no circumstances try to clean any external vinyl roof covering with detergents, caustic soap or spirit cleaners. Plain soap and water is all that is required with a soft brush to clean dirt that may be ingrained. Wash the covering as frequently as the rest of the car.

7 Maintenance – locks and hinges

Once every 6 months or 6000 miles (10 000 km) the door, bonnet and tailgate hinges should be lubricated with a few drops of engine oil. Door striker plates can be given a thin smear of grease to reduce wear and ensure free movement.

8 Bumpers – removal and refitting

Front bumper (Capri II)
1 Disconnect the battery earth lead.
2 Remove the radiator cover which is retained by five screws.
3 Remove the four bumper retaining screws and lift away the bumper.
4 Refitting is the reverse of the removal procedure, but do not fully tighten the bolts until the bumper is correctly aligned.

Front bumper (Mercury Capri II)
5 Remove the nuts from the bolts securing the bumper to the bumper brackets and lift the bumper away.
6 Remove the front license plate brackets.

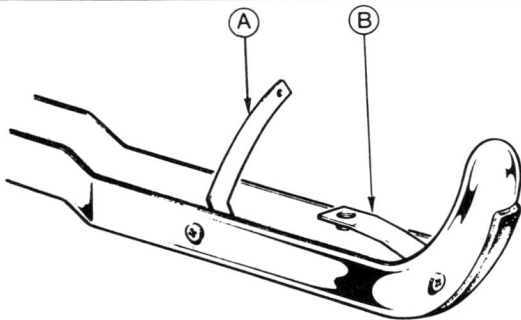

Fig. 12.2 Front bumper mounting (Capri II)

A Inner mounting bracket   B Outer mounting bracket

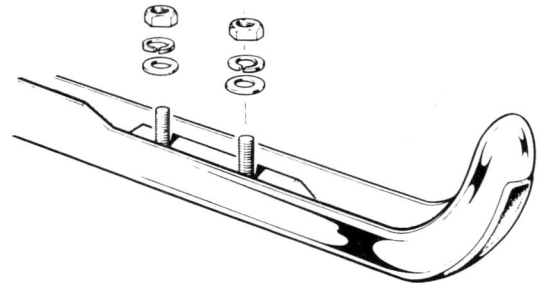

Fig. 12.3 Rear bumper mounting (Capri II)

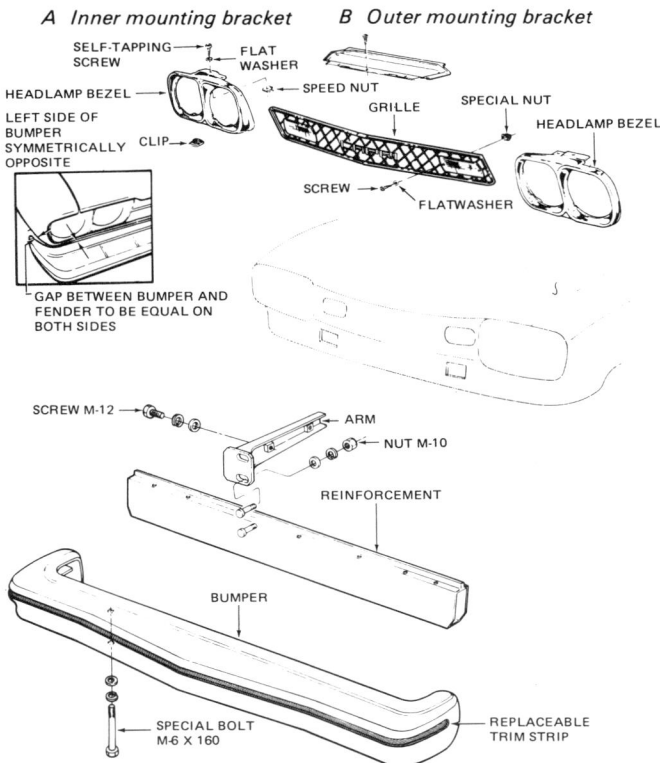

Fig. 12.4 Front bumper and grille (Mercury Capri II)

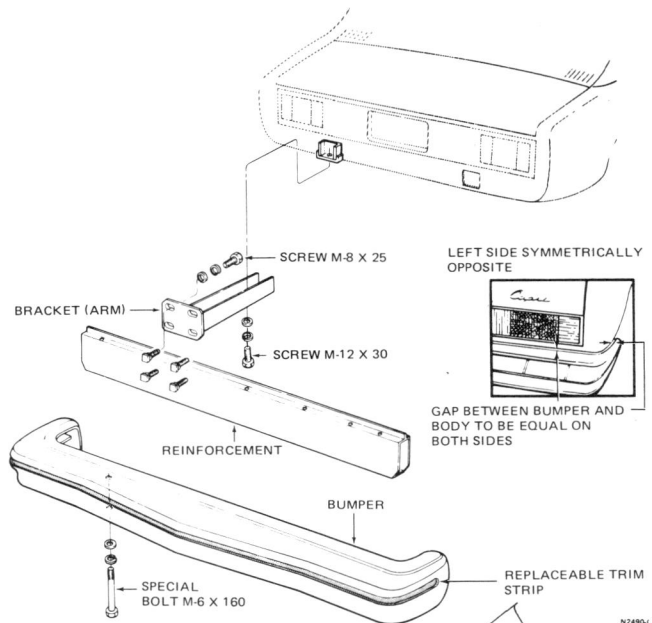

Fig. 12.5 Rear bumper (Mercury Capri II)

7   Remove the bolts securing the bumper reinforcement, then lift the reinforcement away.

8   Refitting is a direct reversal of the removal procedure but do not fully tighten the bolts until the bumper is correctly aligned.

Rear bumper (Capri II)

9   Open the tailgate, then remove the mat and the sub-floor.

10   Remove the jack and washer water reservoir (where applicable).

11   Remove the two nuts, spring washer and flat washers, at each end and lift away the bumper.

12   Refitting is the reverse of the removal procedure but do not fully tighten the nuts until the bumper is correctly aligned.

Rear bumper (Mercury Capri II)

13   Remove the eight bolts and washers securing the bumper assembly to the brackets, then remove the assembly.

14   Remove the special bolts securing the bumper reinforcement to the bumper.

15   Refitting is a direct reversal of the removal procedure but do not fully tighten the bolts until the bumper is correctly aligned.

Bumper trim strips

16   The bumper trim strips can be removed, and replacements fitted, by prising them in and out of the retaining grooves. The job is made a little easier if a soap and water solution is applied to the T-shaped retaining groove.

9   Radiator grille – removal and refitting

1   Disconnect the battery earth lead.

2   Remove the eight screws and washers and lift away the grille. On Mercury Capri II models it is necessary to disconnect the turn signal leads, before the grille can be removed fully.

3   When refitting, ensure that the eight special nuts are correctly positioned on the front and lower crossmembers, then align and secure the bumper with the screws and washers. On Mercury Capri II models the turn signal leads must be connected before the grille is fitted.

4   Reconnect the battery earth lead.

10   Windscreen – removal and refitting

1   If you are unfortunate enough to have a windscreen shatter, or should you wish to renew your present windscreen, fitting a replacement is one of the few jobs which the average owner is advised to leave to a professional, but for the owner who wishes to attempt the job himself, the following instructions are given.

2   Cover the bonnet with a blanket, or cloth to prevent accidental damage and remove the windscreen wiper blades and arms as detailed in Chapter 10.

3   Put on a pair of lightweight shoes and get into one of the front seats. With a piece of soft cloth between the sole of your shoes and the windscreen glass, place both feet in one top corner of the windscreen and push firmly (See Fig. 12.6).

4   When the weatherstrip has freed itself from the body flange in that area, repeat the process at frequent intervals along the top edge of the windscreen until, from outside the car, the glass and weatherstrip can be removed together.

5   If you are having to renew your windscreen due to a shattered screen, remove all traces of sealing compound and broken glass from the weatherstrip and body flange.

6   Gently prise out the clip which covers the joint of the chromium finisher strip and pull the finisher strip out of the weatherstrip. Then remove the weatherstrip from the glass or, if it is on the car (as in the case of a shattered screen) remove it from the body flange.

7   To fit a new windscreen start by fitting the weatherstrip around the new windscreen glass.

8   Apply a suitable sealer to the weatherstrip to body groove. Fit a fine, but strong, piece of cord right the way round the groove, allowing an overlap of about 6 in (15 cm) at the joint.

9   From outside the car, place the windscreen in its correct position, making sure that the loose end of the cord is inside the car.

10   With an assistant pressing firmly on the outside of the windscreen, get into the car and slowly pull the cord thus drawing the weatherstrip over the body flange (See Fig. 12.7).

11   Apply a further layer of sealer to the underside of the rubber to glass groove, from outside the car.

12   Refit the chromium finisher strip into its groove in the weatherstrip and fit the clip which covers the joint.

13   Carefully clean off any surplus sealer from the windscreen glass, before it has a chance to harden and then refit the windscreen wiper arms and blades.

11   Tailgate window glass – removal and refitting

1   Where applicable, remove the window glass wiper arm and blade, and carefully disconnect the heater element connections.

2   Carefully prise out the mylar insert from the rubber moulding.

3   If possible, obtain help from an assistant and carefully use a blunt bladed screwdriver to push the weatherstrip lip along the upper transverse section under the tailgate aperture flange. When approximately two thirds of the weatherstrip lip has been treated in this manner, pressure should be applied to the glass from inside the car. The glass and weatherstrip can then be removed from the outside.

4   Clean the lip of the window aperture and the glass and weatherstrip if they are to be used again. Do not use solvents such as petrol or white spirit on the weatherstrip, as these may cause deterioration of the rubber.

5   When refitting, fit the weatherstrip to the glass, then insert a drawcord in the rubber-to-body groove, so that the cord ends emerge at the bottom centre with approximately 6 in (15 cm) of overlap. During this operation it may help to retain the weatherstrip to the glass by using short lengths of masking tape.

Fig. 12.6 Windscreen removal

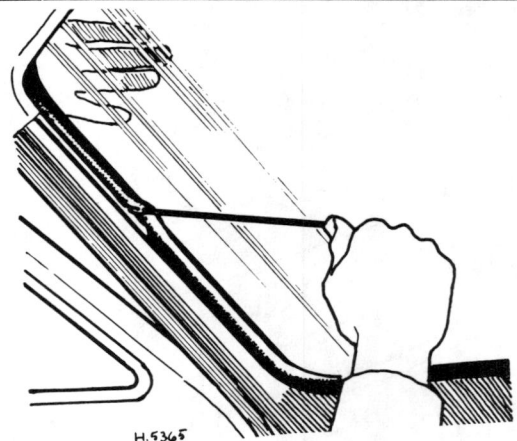

Fig. 12.7 Windscreen fitting, using a cord

6   On British built vehicles only, apply a suitable sealer to the body flange. Position the glass and weatherstrip assembly to the body aperture and push up until the weatherstrip groove engages the top tranverse flange of the body aperture. Ensure that the ends of the drawcord are inside the car, then get the assistant to push the window firmly at the base whilst one end of the drawcord is pulled from the weatherstrip groove. Ensure that the cord is pulled at right-angles to the flange (ie towards the centre of the glass) and that pressure is always being applied on the outside of the glass in the vicinity of the point where the drawcord is being pulled.

7   When the glass is in position, remove any masking tape which may have been used, then seal the weatherstrip to the glass.

8   Lubricate the mylar insert with a rubber lubricant and refit it.

9   Refit the wiper arm and blade (where applicable) and reconnect the heater element connections.

12 Door rattles – tracing and rectification

1   The most common cause of door rattles is a misaligned, loose or worn striker plate. Other causes may be:

    a) Loose door or window winder handles.
    b) Loose or misaligned door lock components.
    c) Loose or worn remote control mechanism.

2   It is quite possible for rattles to be the result of a combination of the above faults, so a careful examination should be made to determine the exact cause.

3   If it is found necessary to adjust the striker plate, close the door to the first of the two locking positions. Visually check the relative attitude of the striker outside edge to the lock support plate edge. The edges 'A' and 'B' (Fig. 12.8) should be parallel and can be checked by shining a torch through the door gap from above and below the striker.

4   Check the amount by which the door stands proud of the adjacent panel. Adjust the striker plate as necessary to obtain a dimension of 0.24 in (6mm).

5   With the lock in the open position, check the lock claw striker clearance (dimension 'A' in Fig. 12.9). This should be 0.28 in (7 mm) and can be checked by placing a small ball of plasticine, or similar material on the striker post and checking its height after gently closing the door. The striker plate can be repositioned vertically to obtain this dimension, but take care to not to disturb any previous initial settings of the plate.

13 Door remote control handle – removal and refitting

1   Remove the door trim panel, as described in Section 14.

2   Push the remote control handle assembly towards the front of the car and pull it out of the opening in the door inner panel (Fig. 12.10).

3   Lift the protective cap off the rear and twist the assembly to disengage it from the operating rod (photos).

4   Remove the protective cap from the operating rod (photo).

5   Refitting is the reverse of the removal procedure.

14 Door trim panel – removal and refitting

1   Carefully lift up and remove the window winder handle insert strip.

2   Remove the winder handle retaining screw and pull off the handle and escutcheon.

3   Remove the two armrest retaining screws, turn the armrest through 90° and pull out the top fixing.

4   Carefully prise out the remote control bezel and unscrew the private lock button (photo).

5   Taking care that no damage to the panel or paintwork occurs, carefully prise the trim panel from the door panel.

6   When refitting, press in the panel so that it is secured by its clips.

7   Refit the lock button, then position the bezel on the door remote control housing, push the trim pad clear of the housing and push the bezel rearwards to secure.

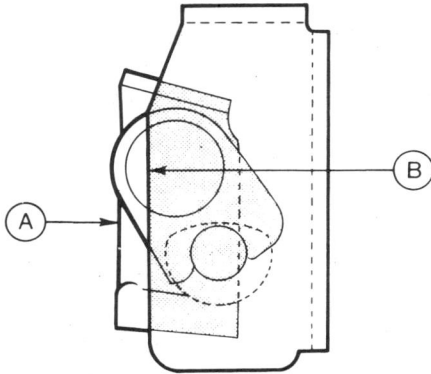

Fig. 12.8 Aligning the striker to lock support plate

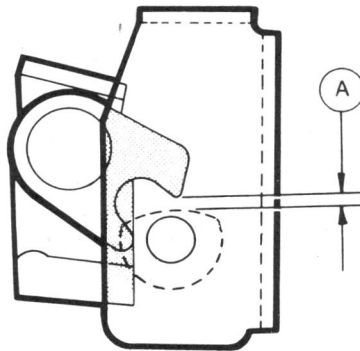

Fig. 12.9 Lock claw to striker clearance

13.3a Lift the protective cap off the rear of the remote control handle ...

13.3b ... and twist the assembly to disengage it from the operating rod

13.4 The remote control handle protective cap

14.4 Removing the remote control bezel

This sequence of photographs deals with the repair of the dent and paintwork damage shown in this photo. The procedure will be similar for the repair of a hole. It should be noted that the procedures given here are simplified — more explicit instructions will be found in the text

In the case of a dent the first job — after removing surrounding trim — is to hammer out the dent where access is possible. This will minimise filling. Here, the large dent having been hammered out, the damaged area is being made slightly concave

Now all paint must be removed from the damaged area, by rubbing with coarse abrasive paper. Alternatively, a wire brush or abrasive pad can be used in a power drill. Where the repair area meets good paintwork, the edge of the paintwork should be 'feathered', using a finer grade of abrasive paper

In the case of a hole caused by rusting, all damaged sheet-metal should be cut away before proceeding to this stage. Here, the damaged area is being treated with rust remover and inhibitor before being filled

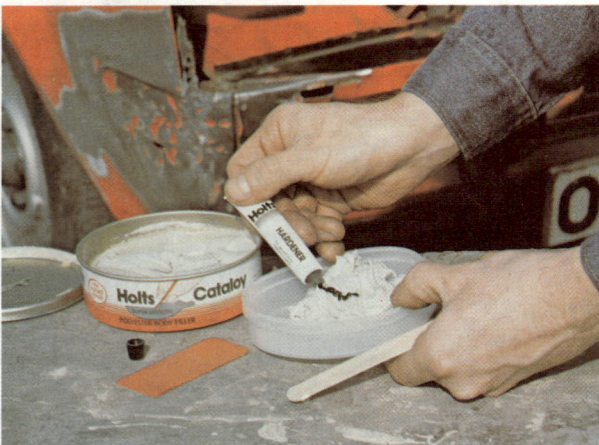

Mix the body filler according to its manufacturer's instructions. In the case of corrosion damage, it will be necessary to block off any large holes before filling — this can be done with zinc gauze or aluminium tape. Make sure the area is absolutely clean before...

...applying the filler. Filler should be applied with a flexible applicator, as shown, for best results; the wooden spatula being used for confined areas. Apply thin layers of filler at 20-minute intervals, until the surface of the filler is slightly proud of the surrounding bodywork

Initial shaping can be done with a Surform plane or Dreadnought file. Then, using progressively finer grades of wet-and-dry paper, wrapped around a sanding block, and copious amounts of clean water, rub down the filler until really smooth and flat. Again, feather the edges of adjoining paintwork

The whole repair area can now be sprayed or brush-painted with primer. If spraying, ensure adjoining areas are protected from over-spray. Note that at least one inch of the surrounding sound paintwork should be coated with primer. Primer has a 'thick' consistency, so will fill small imperfections

Again, using plenty of water, rub down the primer with a fine grade of wet-and-dry paper (400 grade is probably best) until it is really smooth and well blended into the surrounding paintwork. Any remaining imperfections can now be filled by carefully applied knifing stopper paste

When the stopper has hardened, rub down the repair area again before applying the final coat of primer. Before rubbing down this last coat of primer, ensure the repair area is blemish-free — use more stopper if necessary. To ensure that the surface of the primer is really smooth use some finishing compound

The top coat can now be applied. When working out of doors, pick a dry, warm and wind-free day. Ensure surrounding areas are protected from over-spray. Agitate the aerosol thoroughly, then spray the centre of the repair area, working outwards with a circular motion. Apply the paint as several thin coats

After a period of about two weeks, which the paint needs to harden fully, the surface of the repaired area can be 'cut' with a mild cutting compound prior to wax polishing. When carrying out bodywork repairs, remember that the quality of the finished job is proportional to the time and effort expended

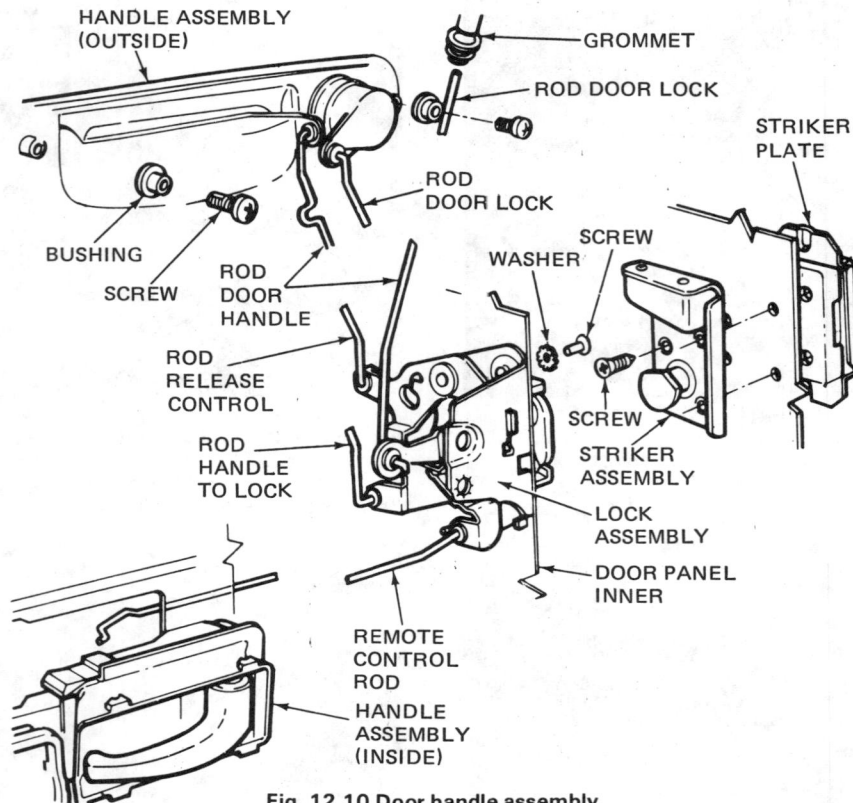

Fig. 12.10 Door handle assembly

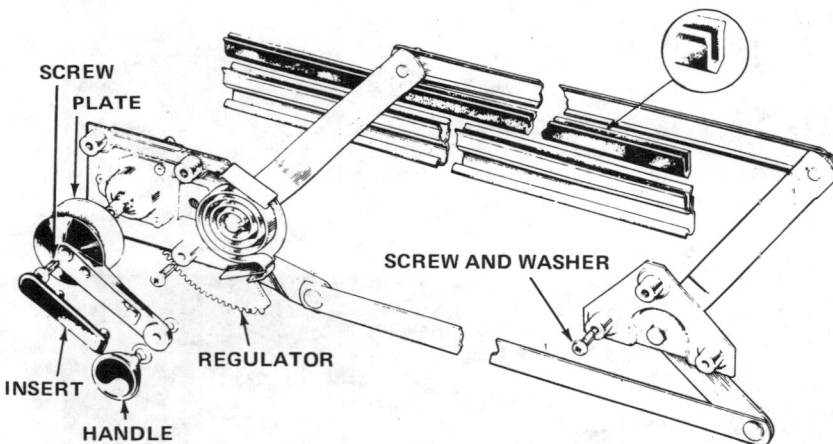

Fig. 12.11 Door window regulator assembly

8   Position the spacer over the armrest stud. Position the armrest to the door and push the stud to secure it. Secure the armrest with the two screws.
9   Assemble the escutcheon over the winder shaft and fit the winder so that when the window is closed, the winder is in the lower vertical position. Secure the winder with the screw and refit the insert strip.

15   Door window regulator assembly – removal and refitting

1   Remove the door trim panel, as described in the previous Section.
2   Peel off the plastic sheet.
3   Temporarily refit the winder handle and lower the window. Remove the four gear plate fixing screws and the three pivot plate screws.
4   Draw the regulator assembly towards the rear of the door, to disengage it from the runner at the base of the window.
5   Push the window glass up and use adhesive tape on each side of

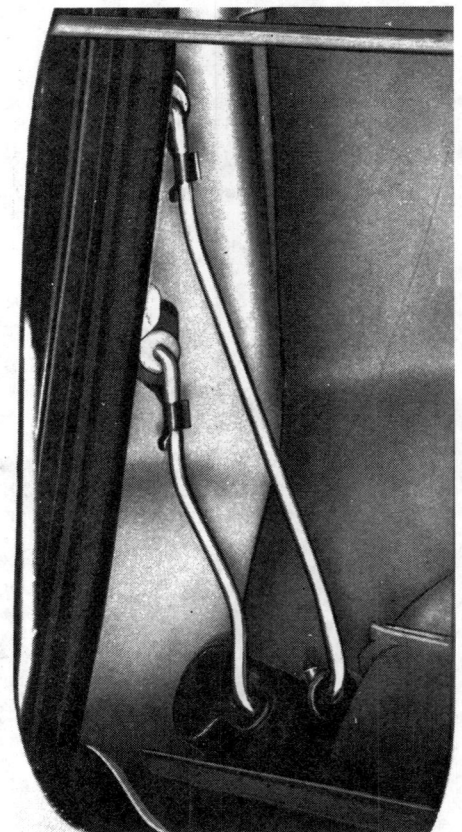

Fig. 12.12 Door lock to handle connecting links

the glass and over the window frame to retain it. If it is to be left for any length of time, use a wooden support as well.

6   Withdraw the regulator from the door.

7   Refitting is the reverse of the removal procedure, alignment being obtained by adjusting the pivot plate as necessary.

16 Exterior door handle – removal and refitting

1   Remove the door trim panel, as previously described.

2   Pull back the plastic sheet behind the exterior handle then disconnect the two connecting links from the door lock to the exterior handle.

3   Remove the two handle retaining bolts and withdraw the handle.

4   Refitting is the reverse of the removal procedure, but do not forget to install the bushes for the link rods. A little petroleum jelly on the rod ends will assist with their installation.

17 Door lock assembly – removal and refitting

1   Remove the door trim panel as previously described and remove the plastic sheeting.

2   Remove the remote control handle and two window frame bolts.

3   Using a screwdriver, prise the clips from the exterior handle rod and detach the rods from the lock.

4   Remove the crosshead screws securing the lock to the shell and the plastic clips securing the remote control rod to the inner panel.

5   Remove the lock from the door through the lower rear access aperture.

6   When refitting, insert the remote control rod through the door aperture, ensuring that the rod lies against the door inner panel. Locate the lock on the door shell, pushing the frame towards the outer panel, to enable the lock to be correctly positioned on the rear shell.

7   Secure the lock with the three screws and secure the remote control rod to the inner panel, with the two plastic clips.

8   Refit the exterior handle rods in their respective lock locations. Position the black bush A and white bushes B as shown in Fig. 12.13.

9   The remainder of the refitting procedure is the reverse of the removal procedure.

18 Door window glass – removal and refitting

1   Remove the door trim panel, as previously described, then peel the plastic sheeting away from the door panel apertures.

2   Remove the door belt moulding/weatherstrip assembly (see Fig. 12.14).

3   Wind up the window glass, then remove the pivot plate screws. Remove the four regulator gear plate securing screws. Disengage the studs and rollers of the regulator arms from the door glass channel and carefully lift out the glass. Allow the regulator to fall away, pivoting on the regulator handle shaft.

4   When refitting, initially insert a small block of wood in the bottom of the door assembly. Locate the glass in the door panel, so that it is resting on the wooden block.

5   Locate the studs and rollers of the regulator arm into the door glass channel, then temporarily install the window handle and turn it to align the gear plate with the panel fixings. Secure the plate to the inner panel.

6   Loosely assemble the pivot plate, then wind up the glass and align it in the frame. Tighten the pivot plate screws.

7   The remainder of the refitting procedure is the reverse of the removal procedure.

19 Door window frame – removal and refitting

1   Remove the door trim panel as previously described, then peel the plastic sheeting away from the lower door panel apertures.

2   Remove the door belt moulding/weatherstrip assembly (see Fig. 12.14).

3   Lower the window glass, then peel back the lower front corner of the plastic sheeting and remove the reflector (where applicable) to gain access to the front and rear lower fixing bolts.

4   Remove the five bolts and frame seals, to free the frame from the shell. Push the glass out of the frame at the rear of the door, so that

Fig. 12.13 The black (A) and white (B) door lock bushes

Fig. 12.14 Removing the door belt moulding

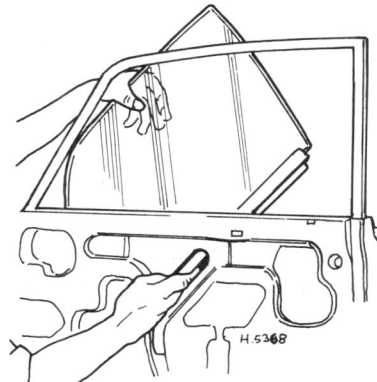

Fig. 12.15 Door window glass removal

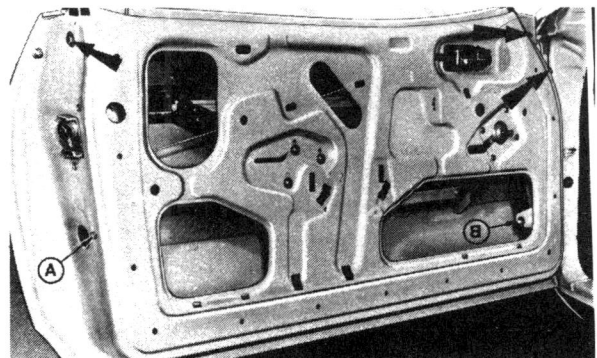

Fig. 12.16 Window frame retaining bolts at A and B (arrowed)

the frame lies between the glass and the outer panel. Repeat for the front of the door.

5   Pull the rear of the frame from the shell, whilst guiding the front of the frame rearwards past the first door bolt moulding retaining clip. This enables the frame to be lifted clear.

6   When refitting, insert the front of the frame so that the vertical leg lies to the rear of the first moulding clip.

7   Spring the rear of the frame into the shell, so that the frame lies between the glass and the outer panel, whilst springing the frame front vertical leg past the moulding clip, so that this also lies between the glass and the inner panel.

8   Spring the frame around the glass and secure it with the five bolts.

9   Pull the weatherstrip from the door aperture flange, then shut the door and adjust the frame to obtain a gap between the frame and flange (in and out) of 0.4 to 0.56 in (10 to 14 mm) and between the frame and the A-pillar (fore and aft) of 0.32 to 0.48 in (8 to 12 mm). Tighten the bolts.

10 The remainder of the refitting procedure is the reverse of the removal procedure.

20 Window frame moulding and door weatherstrips – removal and refitting

1   Where applicable, wind the window down to its fullest extent. Carefully prise the weatherstrip out of the groove in the door outer bright metal finish moulding.

2   When refitting, correctly position the weatherstrip over its groove. With the thumbs, carefully prise the strip fully into the groove.

3   Wind the window up (where applicable) and check that the weatherstrip is fitted correctly.

21 Rear quarter trim panel – removal and refitting

1   Remove the screws retaining the window quarter trim and lift

21.2 Removing the B pillar vertical trim

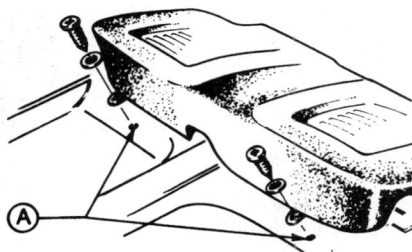

Fig. 12.19 Load space trim panel fixing screws

away the trim.

2   Remove the B-pillar vertical trim and the seatbelt screw (where applicable) (photo).

3   Remove the two screws (A in Fig. 12.17) and remove the rear seat cushion. Where applicable, feed the seatbelt and buckle assemblies through the opening in the cushion.

4   Remove the three trim panel screws and the step plate. Where applicable, remove the luggage compartment hook. Carefully prise away the trim panel.

5   Refitting is the reverse of the removal procedure, but on completion, tighten the seatbelt bolt to a torque of 15 to 20 lbf ft (2.1 to 2.9 kgf m).

22 Opening rear quarter glass assembly – removal and refitting

1   Remove the trim covers from the B-panel and the quarter window surround (trim).

2   Remove the two toggle retaining screws and remove the toggle from the rear C-pillar.

3   Remove the window frame weatherstrip, then drive out the toggle-to-catch retaining pin and remove the toggle.

4   Refitting is the reverse of the removal procedure, but lubricate the B-pillar hinge pivots with a soap solution prior to fitting the glass assembly. Adjust the toggle, or weatherstrip flange, to achieve 0.32 to 0.39 in (8 to 10 mm) gap between the glass and the weatherstrip flange.

23 Load space trim panel – removal and refitting

1   Remove the rear quarter trim panel, as previously described.

2   Pull the seat forward and remove the ten securing screws. It may also be necessary to detach the back trim panel (five screws).

3   Remove the interior light connection and the seatback lock knob

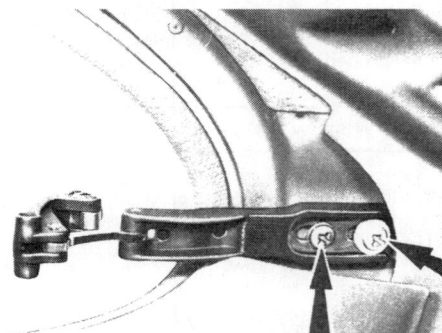

Fig. 12.17 Seat cushion securing screws

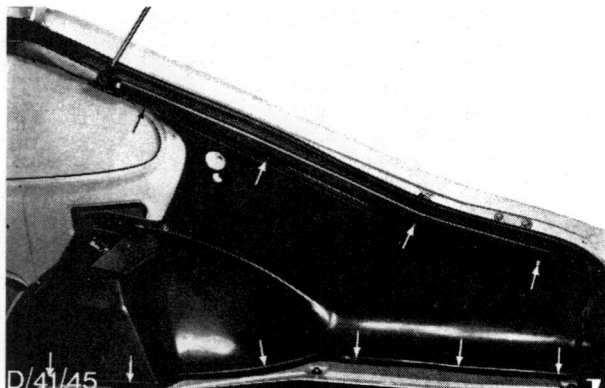

Fig. 12.18 Quarter window fixing screws (arrowed)

and then remove the panel.

4   Refitting is the reverse of the removal procedure. Ensure that the sound deadening material is correctly positioned and that the trim panel does not foul the seat release hinge mechanism.

24 Bonnet (hood) release cable – removal and refitting

1   In the event of the release cable breaking, it is possible to remove the radiator grille to operate the lock spring by hand. Grille removal is dealt with in Section 9, but since it is not possible to open the bonnet, it will be found a little difficult (though not impossible) to gain access to the upper retaining screws.

2   To remove the release cable in normal circumstances, remove the radiator upper cowl plate.

3   From inside the car, remove both the clevis pins and the spring and disconnect the release cable from the control lever.

4   Slacken the cable adjuster clamp and release the cable from the hood lock spring.

5   Remove the cable retaining clips, then pull the cable through the dashpanel to remove it.

6   Refitting of the cable is essentially the reverse of the removal

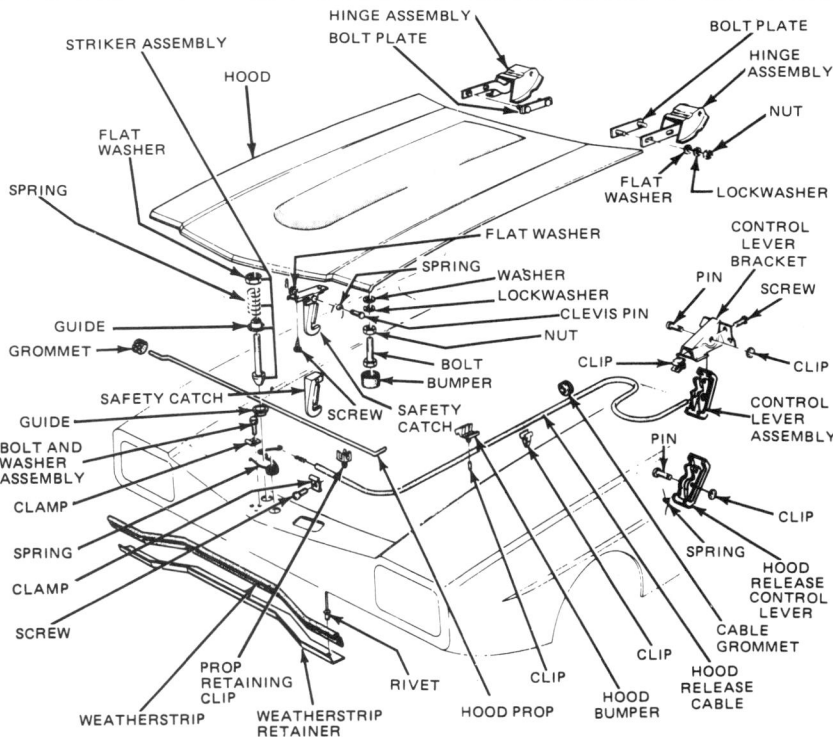

Fig. 12.20 Bonnet assembly components

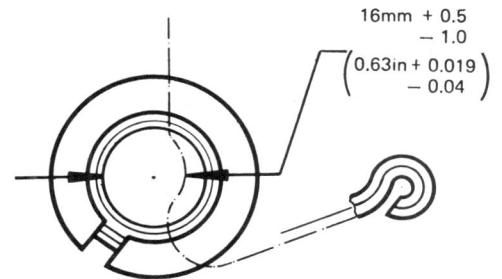

Fig. 12.22 Bonnet spring setting dimension

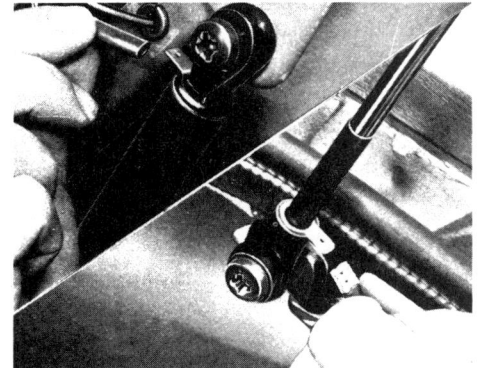

Fig. 12.23 The damper (strut) in-line connectors

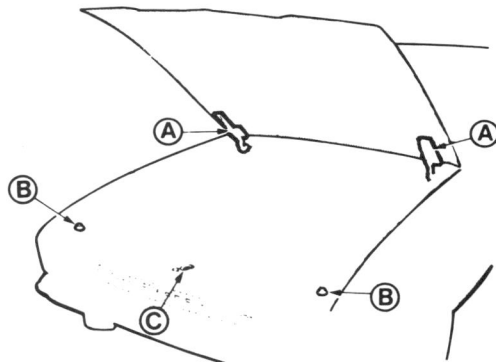

Fig. 12.21 Bonnet adjustment points

A Hinge   C Striker
B Bump rubber

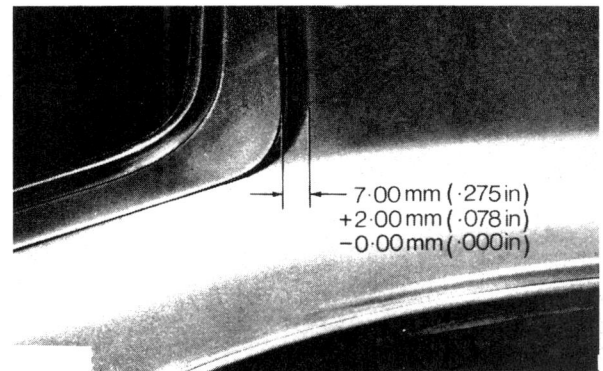

Fig. 12.24 Tailgate to roof edge alignment

procedure, adjusting as necessary, to remove any cable slack. For further information on this, refer to paragraph 6 of the following Section.

25 Bonnet (hood) – removal, refitting and adjustment

1   Open the bonnet to its fullest extent. Using a suitable implement, scribe a line around the hinges.
2   Remove the two bolts and washers securing each side of the bonnet to its hinges. With assistance, it can now be lifted off.
3   Refitting is a reversal of removal procedure. Before fully tightening the securing bolts, ensure that the hinges are aligned with the scribed marks. This will ensure correct alignment.
4   If it is found that the bonnet requires adjustment, this can be effected in the vertical plane by slackening the catch post locknut and screwing the catch post in or out. Fore-and-aft adjustment can be effected by slackening the hinge bolts.
5   Adjustable bump rubbers are also provided and these should be positioned as necessary to stop vibration, but at the same time must allow the bonnet to be closed easily.

6   Adjustment of the bonnet locking spring can be made by slackening the cable clamp on the upper crossmember and sliding the outer cable through the clip as necessary. When correctly positioned, the hood lock spring/cable setting dimension should be as shown in Fig. 12.22. Tighten the clamp screw when the adjustment is satisfactory.

26 Tailgate assembly – removal and refitting

1   Open the tailgate and detach the in-line connectors from the damper(s)/strut(s).
2   Detach each damper, by removing the securing bolt at each end.
3   With help from an assistant, support the tailgate and remove it by removing the hinge bolts.
4   When installing, align the tailgate so that the edges are flush with the rear of the roof and the C-pillar sides and the gap between the tailgate and the roof edge is 0.275 to 0.353 in (7 to 9 mm) – see Fig. 12.24.
5   Align the lower edges of the tailgate, so that it is flush with the rear corners of the body, with the striker plate in the upper central position.

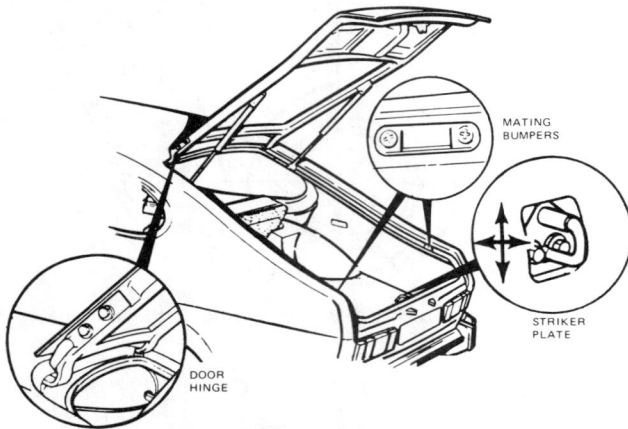

Fig. 12.25 Tailgate adjustment points

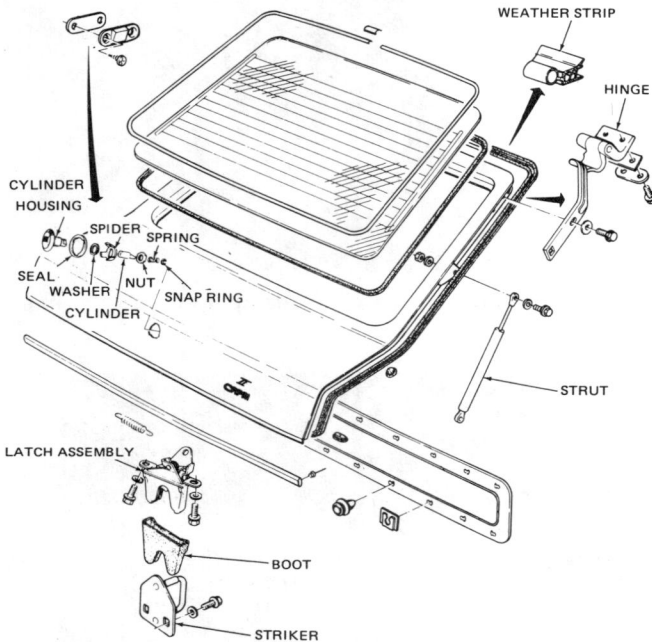

Fig. 12.26 Tailgate components

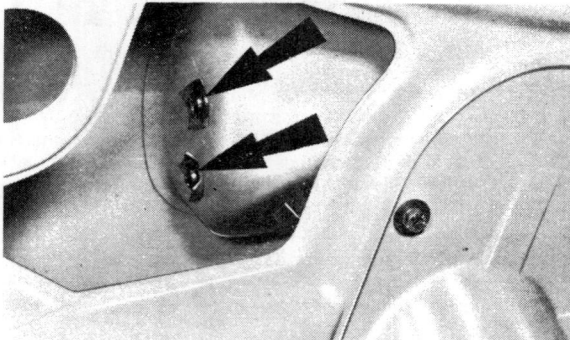

Fig. 12.27 Fuel filler flap retaining screws

6   Pads can be used beneath the C-pillar bumpers for alignment of the tailgate sides with the C-pillar slope. Note that the thick end of the bumper faces towards the front of the vehicle.
7   On completion, refit the dampers. Assemble the spacer to the screw, then locate the screw and spacer through the pushrod end of the damper. Secure the damper to the C-pillar bracket, with the terminals facing rearwards.
8   Align the damper to the tailgate bracket and secure it with the

remaining screw and spacer.
9   Reconnect the electrical connections to the dampers.

27 Tailgate lock assembly – removal and refitting (including removal of the lock barrel)

1   Open the tailgate and remove the latch (three bolts and washers).
2   Remove the lock cylinder retaining nut, then turn the lock spider, to detach it from the lock cylinder and outer panel.
3   Refitting is the reverse of the removal procedure.
4   If it is found necessary to remove the lock barrel, this can be done after it has been removed, by removing the circlip (snap-ring) from the barrel housing. The spring, barrel and spider can then be detached and a new barrel fitted by reversing this procedure.

28 Tailgate striker plate – removal and refitting

1   Open the tailgate then carefully scribe a mark around the striker to facilitate refitting.
2   Remove the single bolt and washer and take off the striker plate.
3   Refitting is the reverse of the removal procedure, following which adjustment can be made, if found necessary, to obtain satisfactory opening and closing of the tailgate.

29 Fuel filler flap – removal and refitting

1   Remove the loadspace trim panel, as previously described.
2   Remove the two screws indicated in Fig. 12.27 and lift away the filler flap.
3   Installation is the reverse of the removal procedure.

30 Instrument panel crash pad – removal and refitting

1   Disconnect the battery earth lead.
2   Remove the steering column shroud retaining screws. Remove the lower half and release the upper half retaining lug from its spring clip, by pulling sharply upwards.
3   Remove the instrument cluster, as described in Chapter 10.
4   Detach the flexible pipes from the dash panel vents and defrosters.
5   Remove the left and right-hand A-pillar trims (2 screws each) – also the grab handle, if fitted.
6   Remove the instrument panel pad retaining screws and lift the pad away. If appropriate, remove the dash panel vents and transfer them to the new instrument panel.
7   Installation is essentially the reverse of the removal procedure, but connect the flexible pipes to the vents and defrosters before the crash pad is fitted.

31 Centre console – removal and refitting

Basic type
1   Lift the carpet from around the front of the console, then push the clock and bezel out of the housing. Disconnect the clock leads.
2   Remove the two screws at the rear end and two more from the clock end, to release the console.
3   Remove the gear lever knob, or T-handle.
4   Lift off the console. As applicable, remove the clock mounting plate screws and/or gearshift lever boot.
5   Refitting is the reverse of the removal procedure.

Ghia type
6   Lift the carpet from around the front of the console.
7   Fabricate two small brackets from $\frac{1}{16}$ in (1.5 mm) sheet steel (see Fig. 12.31A) and insert these behind the black bezel, to remove the clock (Fig. 12.31B).
8   Remove the two console retaining screws, then prise out the cap in front of the gearshift lever and remove the screws beneath.
9   Carefully prise the handbrake lever boot and bezel assembly from the console and remove it.
10 Carefully prise out the centre panel cover from behind the gear lever.

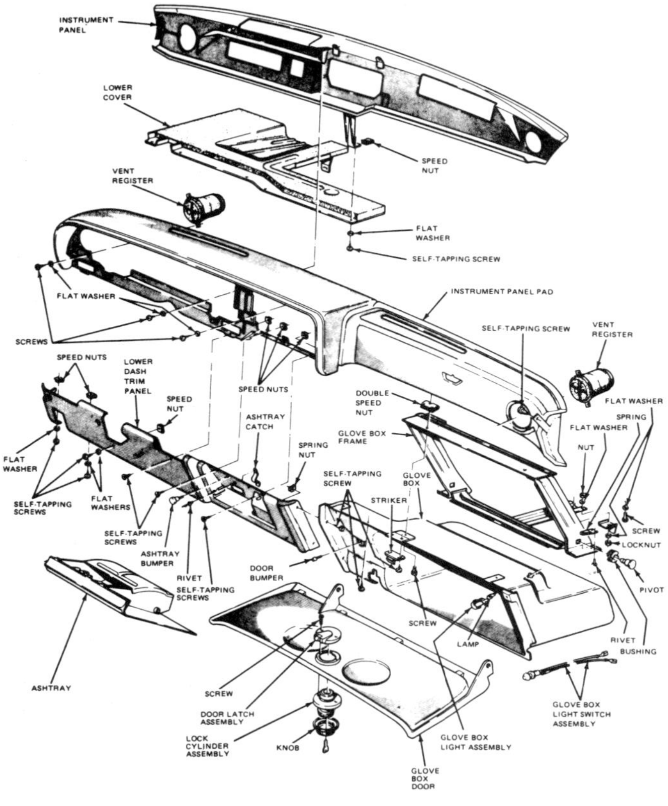

Fig. 12.28 Instrument panel, crash pad and glove box (cars without air conditioning)

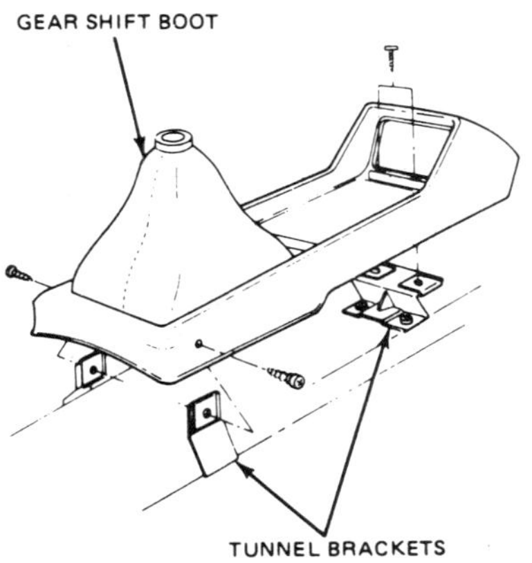

Fig. 12.29 Centre console – basic type

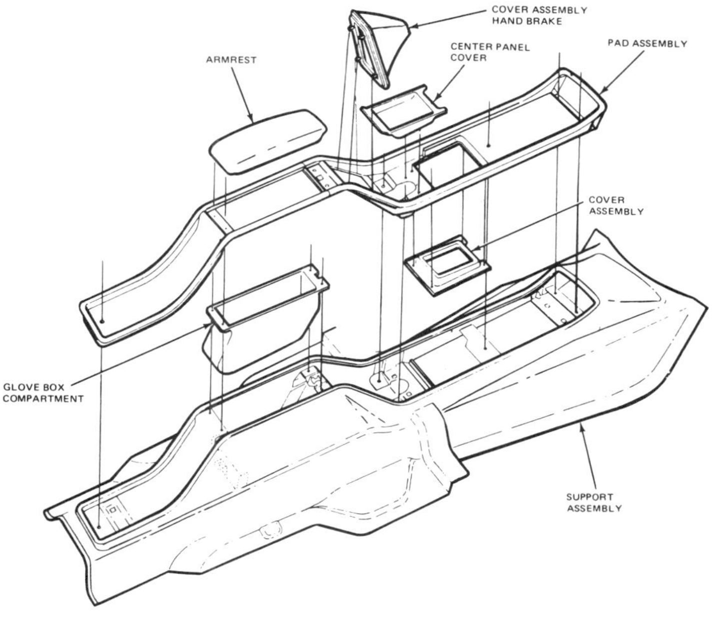

Fig. 12.30 Centre console – Ghia type

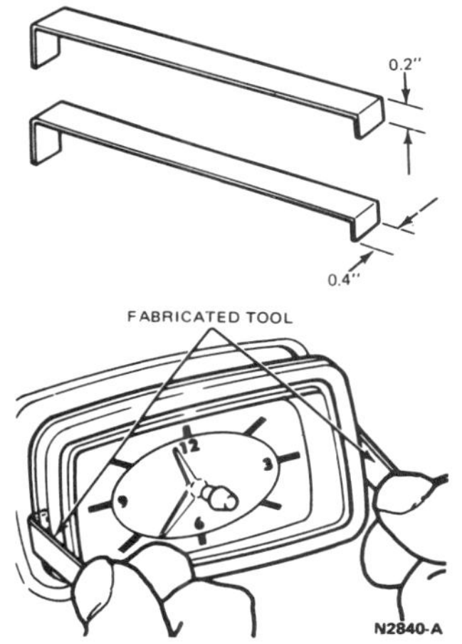

Fig. 12.31 Ghia clock removal

A *Tools required*
B *Tools in use*

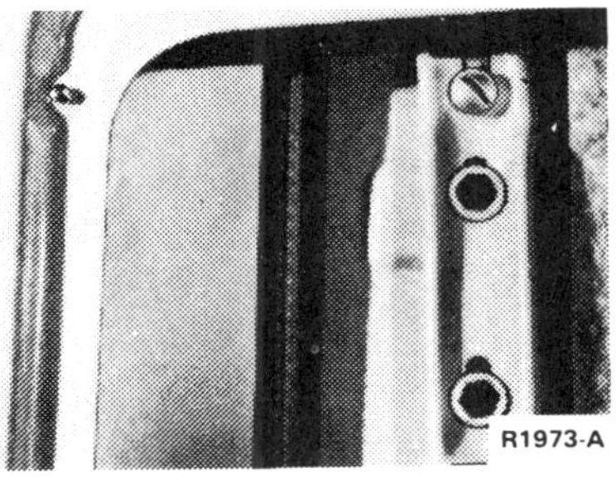

Fig. 12.32 Sunroof gap adjustment (front)

11 Lift up the centre armrest and remove the screw from the bottom of the compartment.
12 Remove the armrest hinge screws and place the armrest in the compartment.
13 Remove the two screws at the front end of the armrest.
14 Prise out the cap at the rear of the console and remove the screw.
15 Carefully lift out the rear section, front section and console compartment.
16 Remove the heat insulating pad from beneath the console compartment area.
17 As applicable, remove the electrical connector from the base of each seatbelt stalk and remove the stalk fixing bolt through the top of the console. Remove the stalk assembly through the inside console support.
18 Pull the carpet away from the sides of the support assembly, then detach the support by removing the eight securing screws.
19 Refitting is basically the reverse of the removal procedure, but first ensure that all the spire nuts are correctly located on the brackets. Tighten the seatbelt stalks to a torque of 26 to 31 lbf ft (3.6 to 4.3 kgf m).

32 Sunroof panel – adjustments

Gap adjustment
1 When closed, a gap of 0.23 to 0.27 in (5.8 to 6.9 mm) should exist between the sunroof and the car roof. If a vinyl roof cover is fitted, this gap should be reduced by 0.07 in (1.78 mm). If adjustment is required, proceed as detailed below.
2 With the sunroof half open, remove the sunroof headlining frame.

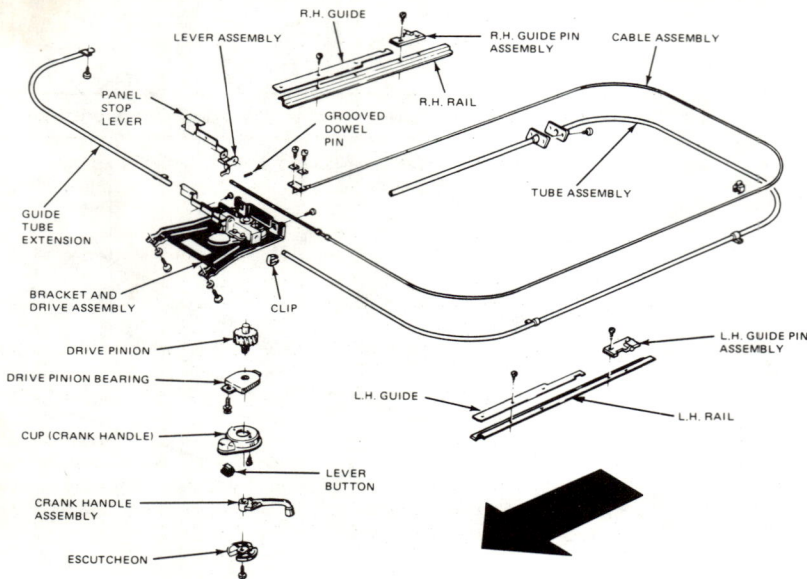

Fig. 12.33 Sunroof control mechanism

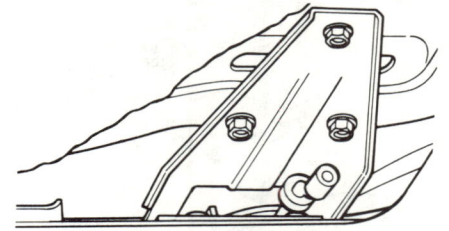

Fig. 12.34 Sunroof gap adjustment (rear)

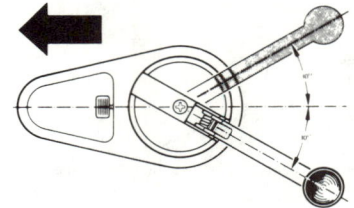

Fig. 12.35 Checking the handle alignment

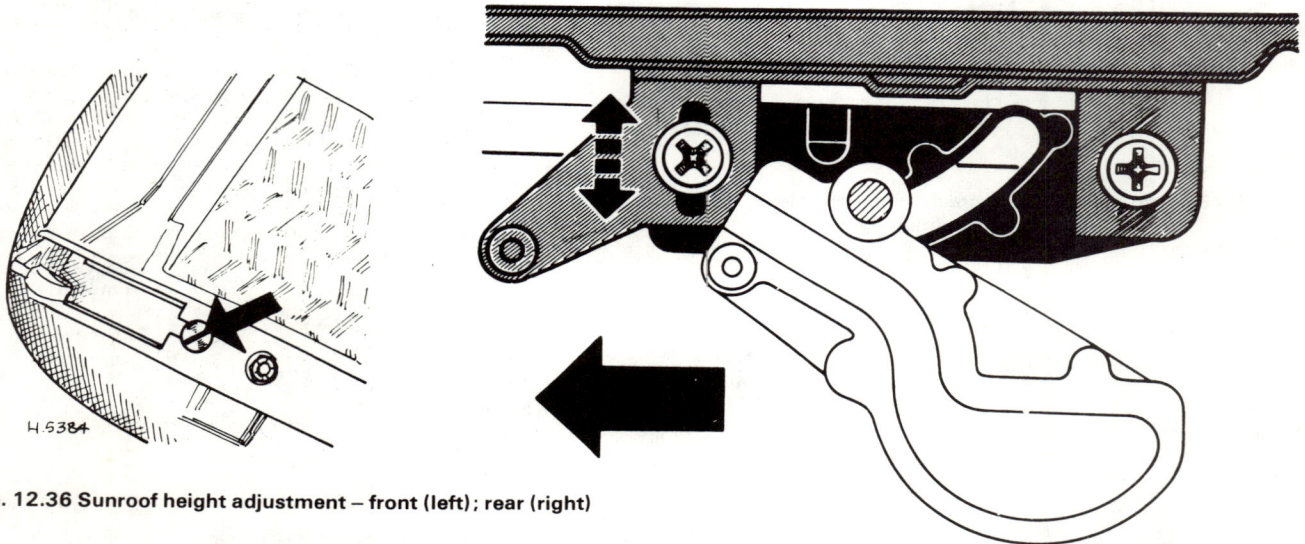

Fig. 12.36 Sunroof height adjustment – front (left); rear (right)

3   Close the sunroof, then pull the headlining from the rear and remove it.

4   To adjust the front of the sunroof, loosen the front guide retaining screws, then whilst pressing the guides inwards, tighten the screws.

5   To adjust the rear, loosen the two fixing screws at each side of the adjusting base, then press the rear slides inwards and tighten.

6   Fit the headlining and headlining frame.

7   If the adjustment is still incorrect, remove the weatherstrip from the roof panel and bend its mounting flange as necessary.

Height adjustment

8   The front edge of the sunroof should be flush with, or 0.04 in (1 mm) below the edge of the car roof. The rear edge should be flush with or 0.04 in (1 mm) above the car roof. If adjustment is required, proceed as described below.

9   Proceed as described in paragraphs 1 to 4 inclusive, but before tightening the screws, adjust the sunroof height by turning the adjusting screw (Fig. 12.36) as necessary. Tighten the guide retaining screws.

10   To adjust the rear end, loosen the adjusting screws on the link assemblies (on the inner side of the panel). Adjust the height and tighten the screws.

11   Check for leaks and noises, adjusting again, if necessary.

12   Fit the headlining and headlining frame.

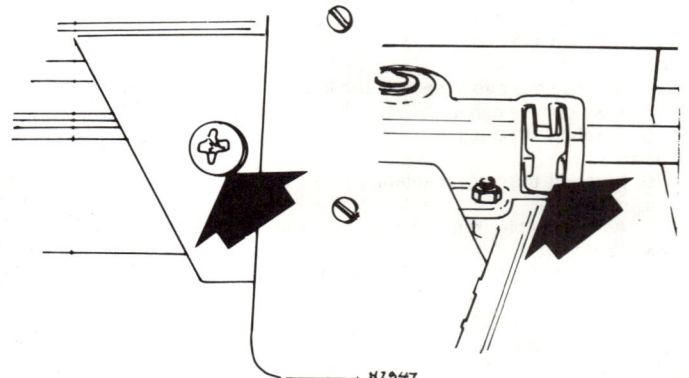

Fig. 12.37 Tube guide screw and clip (arrowed)

33 Sunroof – removal and refitting

1 Open the sunroof, then mark the position of both guide pin assemblies. Remove the guide pins and guides.
2 Close the sunroof, then push the button upwards to the tilt position.
3 Lift the front of the sunroof out of its opening, whilst turning the handle until the screws fastening the cable to the base assembly are accessible.
4 Unscrew the cable and lift out the complete sunroof, including the base assembly.
5 Unscrew the handle assembly, pull out the handle and escutcheon then remove the button control. Remove the cup.
6 Unscrew the gear bearing, then remove it, together with the pinion.
7 Move the cable so that the grooved dowel pin appears in the opening of the pinion. Pull out the pin and discard it. The operating cable can now be pulled out of the tube assembly.
8 To refit the sunroof, install the operating cable into the tube assembly. Turn the cable at its T-formed end and fit a new grooved dowel pin. Smear a little general purpose grease on the cable and where it will contact the pinion, then assemble the pinion and bearing.
9 Fit the handle cup and fit the button to the lever.
10 Fit the handle and escutcheon, then check the handle position as follows:

   (a) *Pull the button down and turn the handle fully clockwise, which should now be approximately 30 degrees ahead of its original position opposite the cup of the handle (Fig. 12.35).*
   (b) *Push the button up and turn the handle fully anticlockwise, which should now be approximately 30 degrees ahead of its original position. The handle can be reset on the pinion splines as necessary.*

11 Insert the sunroof into the opening and attach the cable to the base assembly.
12 Carefully move the sunroof to the rear, by turning the handle, then screw on the guide pin assemblies with the pin outwards, to coincide with the marks made when removed. Note that the left and right-hand guides are not interchangeable.
13 Adjust the roof, as described in the previous Section.

34 Sunroof bracket and drive assembly – removal and refitting

1 Remove the crank handle, the pinion drive and the bearing.
2 Remove the covering strip, then remove the mirror, courtesy light and sun visors.
3 Remove the windscreen, as described in Section 10.
4 Carefully remove the headlining from above the middle of the windscreen.
5 Pull the grooved dowel pin out of the actuating cable and discard it.
6 Pull back on the cable slightly, to clear the drive assembly of the cable.
7 Remove the tube guide screw (right-hand side) and clip (left-hand side), and remove the tubes.
8 Remove the screws, to release the bracket and drive assembly.
9 Refitting the bracket and drive assembly is the reverse of the removal procedure, using a new grooved dowel pin. Check the handle position, as described in paragraph 10 of the previous Section and adjust the roof, if necessary, as described in Section 32.

35 Seatbelts – general

1 Mercury Capri II models will normally be fitted with a seatbelt interlock and warning buzzer system. Further information on these will be found in Chapter 10.
2 All models are fitted with inertia reel seatbelts for the front seats. Rear seatbelts of a similar type are also available.
3 Fig. 12.38 shows the floor-mounted front seatbelt stalk. Removal of the basic type fixing is straightforward, but for Ghia models the centre console must be partly removed, as described in Section 31.
4 To remove the front seatbelt inertia reel, remove the rear quarter trim panel, as described in Section 21, then remove the three nuts from the anchor plate and lower the assembly through the aperture, whilst feeding the belt through the slot in the inner panel (photos).

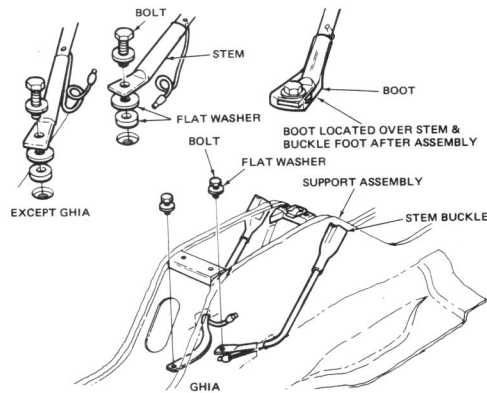

Fig. l2.38 Front seatbelt anchorage points

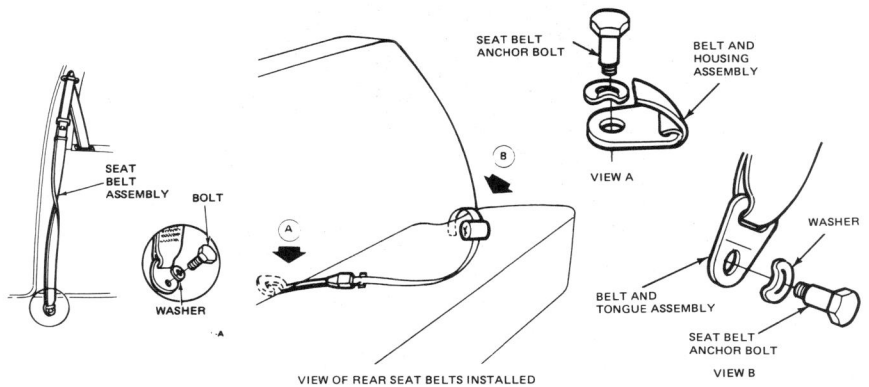

Fig. 12.39 Rear seatbelt anchorage points

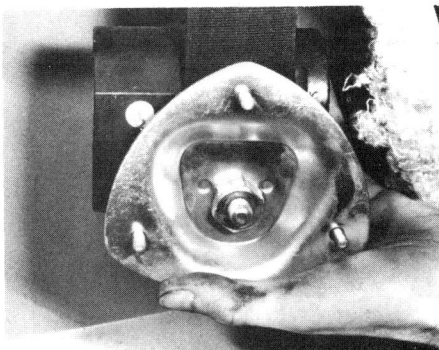

35.4a Anchor plate stud nuts

35.4b Feeding the belt through the slot in the inner panel

35.4c Lowering the inertia reel through the slot in the inner panel

5   If the seatbelt fixings are removed, they should be torque tightened to the following values on installation. (**Note:** *This does not include the inertia reel anchor plate*):

Front stalks   26 to 31 lbf ft (3.6 to 4.3 kgf m)
Other fixings   15 to 20 lbf ft (2.1 to 2.9 kgf m)

36 Heater controls – adjustment

1   Disconnect the battery earth lead, then remove the glove compartment by unscrewing 7 screws at the top and 2 nuts at the bottom. Also disconnect the glove compartment lighting leads (Fig. 12.40).
2   Move the heater controls to a point 0.08 in (2 mm) from the end position, then remove both outer cable clips (see Figs. 12.41, 12.42 or 12.43 as appropriate).
3   *Standard heater:* Check that the distributor and regulator flap levers are at the end of their travel and clamp the outer cables in this position (Fig. 12.41).
4   *Heavy duty heater:* Check that the distributor flap lever (Fig. 12.42) and water control lever (Fig. 12.43) are at the end of their travel and clamp the outer cables in this position.
5   On completion, reconnect the glove compartment lighting leads, then refit the glove compartment and reconnect the battery earth lead.

37 Heater controls – removal and refitting

1   Disconnect the battery earth lead.
2   Remove the steering column shroud (2 screws at the bottom, then pull out at the top). Lower the steering column (leaving the two bolts in position) sufficiently to allow the instrument cluster trim to be removed.

Fig. 12.40 Removing the glove compartment

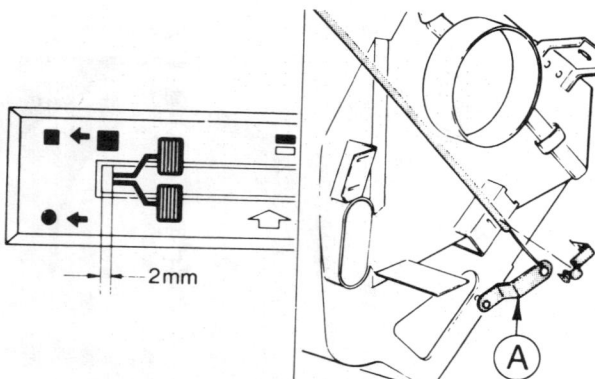

Fig. 12.42 Heavy duty heater, control cable adjustment

A Distributor flap control lever

3   Disconnect the switch leads and remove the instrument cluster trim, complete with cowl trim (11 screws). Remove the instrument cluster bezel (3 screws).
4   Using a large pair of pliers, break the heater control knobs and remove the controls (4 screws). Do not disconnect the control cables at the heater.
5   Remove the heater control panel (2 screws). Remove the blower switch and lighting leads.
6   Disconnect the cables from the heater controls.
7   Refitting is the reverse of the removal procedure, during which it will be necessary to adjust the cables, as described in the previous Section. Also it will be necessary to obtain new heater control knobs.

38 Heater water valve (heavy duty heater) – removal and refitting

1   Drain the engine coolant and disconnect the lower hose from the radiator (refer to Chapter 2, if necessary).
2   Disconnect the three water hoses from the water valve.
3   Remove the outer cable from the clip on the water valve bracket, then remove the assembly from the bulkhead (2 screws).
4   Twist the water valve, to disconnect the cable from the operating lever.
5   Refitting is the reverse of the removal procedure, during which adjustment should be made, as described in Section 36 for the heavy duty heater. On completion, refit the radiator hose and fill the cooling system, as described in Chapter 2.

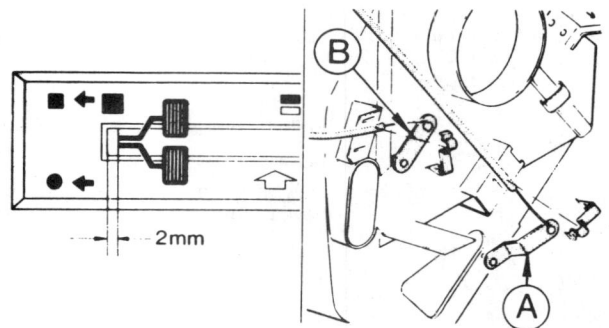

Fig. 12.41 Heater control cable adjustment (standard heater)

A Distributor flap control lever   B Regulator flap control lever

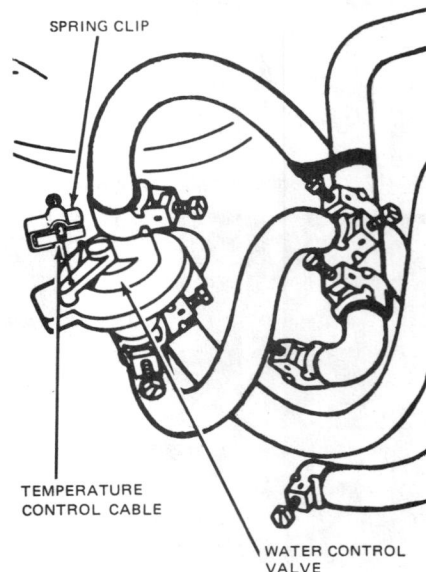

Fig. 12.43 Heavy duty heater, water valve

Fig. 12.44 The water valve hoses (arrowed)

39 Heater assembly – removal and refitting

1 Disconnect the battery earth lead.

2 Drain the coolant, referring to Chapter 2, if necessary.

3 Disconnect the water hoses from the heater heat exchanger. If practicable, blow through the heat exchanger with compressed air to remove any coolant remaining. Alternatively place cloths and/or newspapers beneath to absorb any spillage.

4 Remove the cover panel, together with the heat exchanger-to-water connection gasket, from the bulkhead (2 screws).

5 Slacken the gearlever locknut, then remove the gearlever. The locknut requires a special peg spanner, available from Ford, but it is not difficult to fabricate a tool which will do the job.

6 Remove the parcel tray (4 screws). Where there is a centre console, this must be removed also (refer to Section 31).

7 Remove the steering column shroud (2 screws at the bottom, then pull out at the top). Lower the steering column (leaving the two bolts in position), sufficiently to allow the instrument cluster to be removed.

8 Remove the lower dash panel, complete with cover panel (9 screws). Remove the ashtray and cigarette lighter and disconnect the switches.

9 Remove the glove compartment by unscrewing the 7 screws at the top and 2 nuts at the bottom. Also disconnect the glove compartment lighting leads.

10 Disconnect the demister nozzle hoses, together with their connections (1 screw each).

11 Disconnect the facia vent hoses from the heater. There are 2 on the standard heater and 4 on the heavy duty heater.

12 Remove the lower dash panel support stay (1 screw).

13 Disconnect the control cables from the heater and the heater blower leads.

14 Remove the demister nozzles (refer to Section 42, if necessary).

15 Remove the windscreen wiper motor bracket from its mounting.

16 Remove the 4 heater securing screws, then pull the heater far enough rearward for the water connection pipes to clear the bulkhead. Tilt the top of the heater upward and forward, and withdraw it sideways, then remove the foam gasket also.

17 Refitting is the reverse of the removal procedure, during which it will be necessary to adjust the heater controls as described in Section 36. Do not forget to tighten the gearlever locknut. On completion, fill the cooling system, as described in Chapter 2.

40 Heater assembly (Behr) – dismantling and reassembly

1 Remove the distributor flapshaft (1 clip). Note that the flap remains in the lower section of the housing.

2 Remove the clamps securing the two halves of the housing, using circlip pliers. Remove the upper section, complete with the motor, from the lower section.

3 Remove the heat exchanger and from frame the lower section of

the housing, then remove the heat exchanger from the frame and take off the foam packing.

4 To remove the distributor flap from the housing, remove the clip and withdraw the control lever sideways.

5 Remove the regulator flap from the lower section of the housing. Bend back the 2 clamping straps sufficiently to enable the control lever to be withdrawn after it has been turned towards the side, then remove the regulating flap.

6 Remove the retaining straps for the blower motor cap, by pressing outwards from the inside using a screwdriver (see Fig. 12.50).

7 Detach the motor from the upper section. Disconnect the motor leads, remove the 4 retaining clamps and remove the motor and fan inwards.

8 When reassembling, position the blower motor so that the

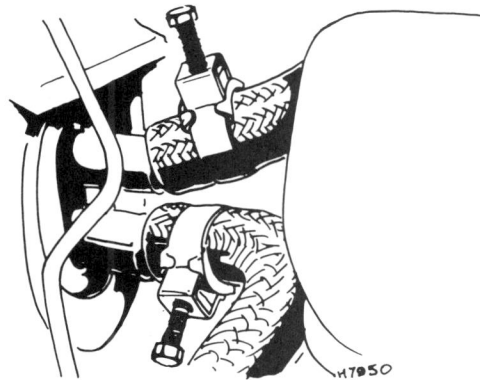

Fig. 12.45 Heat exchanger hoses

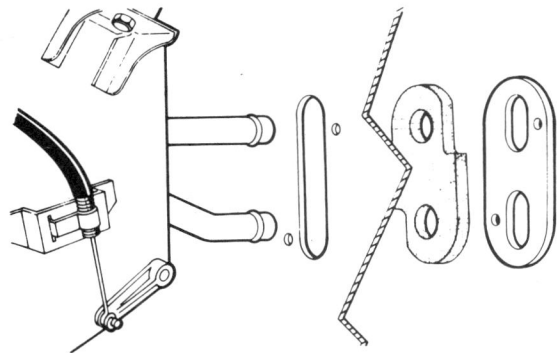

Fig. 12.46 Heat exchanger gasket and cover panel

Fig. 12.47 Blower motor cap retaining strap

electrical connections face towards the cable fastening at the upper section. Secure the motor and connect the leads, then fit the motor cap.

9   Position the regulating flap in the lower section and insert the control lever by turning it from the side as necessary and swing it round into the straps. Close the straps using pliers.

10 Position the distributor flap in the lower section and insert the control lever from the side.

11 The remainder of the reassembly procedure is the reverse of the removal procedure.

41 Heater assembly (Smiths standard and heavy duty) – dismantling and reassembly

1   *Standard heater:* Remove clips 'A' and 'B' (Fig. 12.52) and remove the heater housing side cover complete with flaps (15 screws).
2   *Heavy duty heater:* Remove clip 'A' (Fig. 12.52) and remove the

heater housing side cover complete with flaps (15 screws).
3   Remove the heat-exchanger and foam seal.
4   Prise off the circlip and remove the fan from the blower motor shaft.

Fig. 12.48 Installed position of blower motor

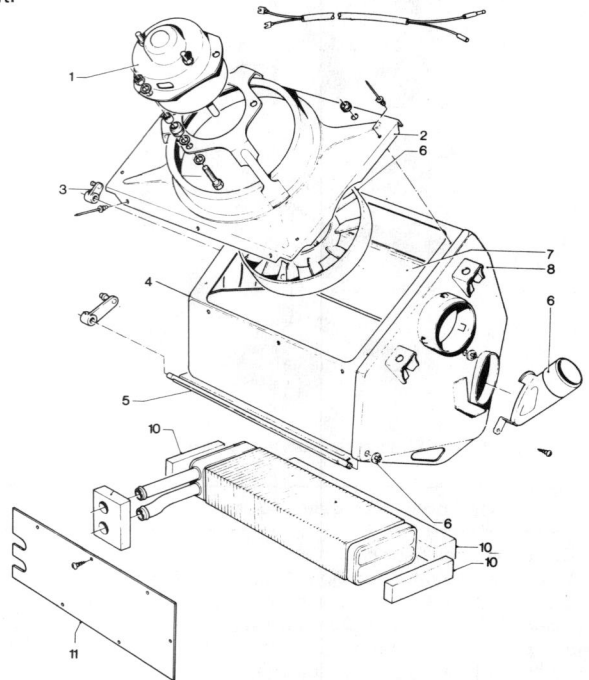

Fig. 12.50 Standard heater (Smiths)

1	Motor assembly	7	Control valve
2	Cover and bracket assembly	8	Housing
3	Control valve operating lever	9	Demister hose connection
4	Right-hand housing cover	10	Heat exchanger seal
5	Distributor flap	11	Plenum chamber cover
6	Fan		

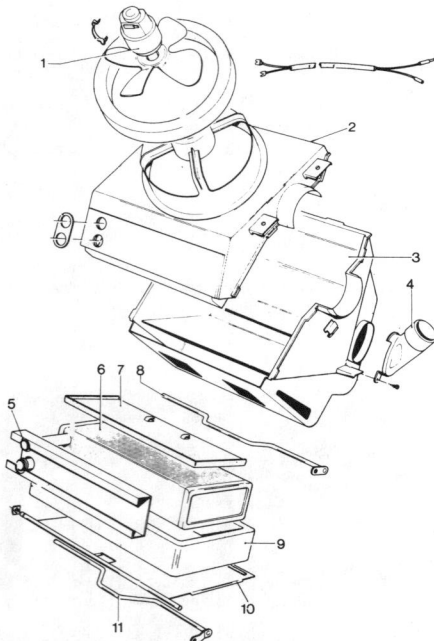

Fig. 12.49 Standard heater (Behr)

1	Motor and fan	7	Control flap
2	Upper housing	8	Control flap shaft
3	Lower housing	9	Heat exchanger seal
4	Demister hose connection	10	Distributor flap
5	Heat exchanger cover plate	11	Distributor flap shaft
6	Heat exchanger	12	Heat exchanger case

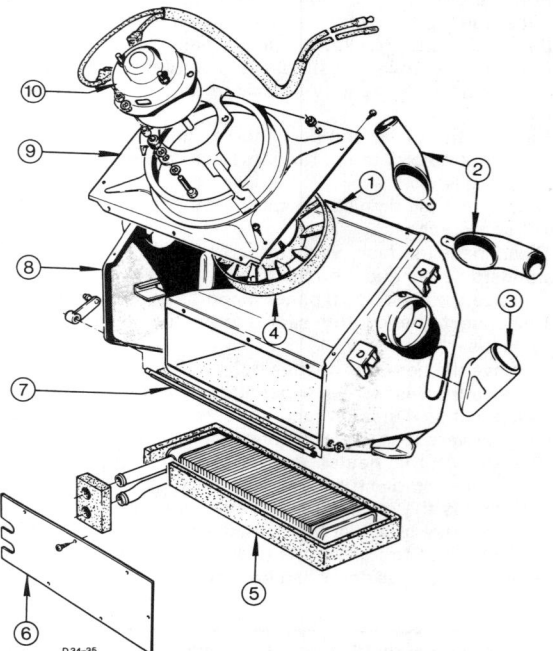

Fig. 12.51 Heavy duty heater (Smiths)

1	Housing	6	Plenum chamber cover
2	Hot air supply to facia connection	7	Distributor flap
3	Demister hose connection	8	Right-hand housing cover
4	Fan	9	Cover and bracket assembly
5	Heat exchanger seal	10	Motor assembly

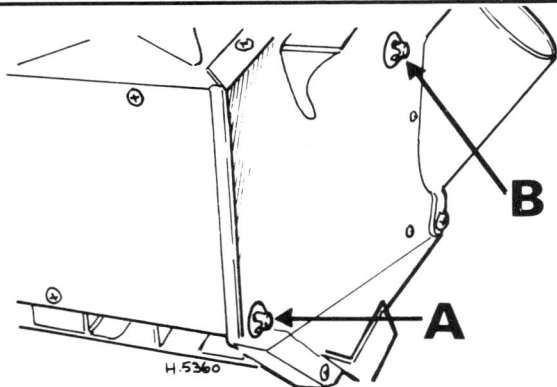

Fig. 12.52 Distributor flap (A) and regulator flap (B) clips

5   Detach the blower motor from the support (3 nuts and bolts).
6   Reassembly is the reverse of the dismantling procedure.

42 Demister nozzles – removal and refitting

Passenger's side

1   Remove the glove compartment by unscrewing the 7 screws at the top and 2 nuts at the bottom. Also disconnect the glove compartment lighting leads.
2   Withdraw the hose from the demister nozzle and remove the nozzle (1 screw).
3   Refitting is the reverse of the removal procedure.

Driver's side

4   Initially proceed as described in paragraphs 1,2 and 3 of Section 37. Additionally remove the ashtray and cigar lighter.
5   Remove the instrument cluster (4 screws), disconnecting the speedometer drive cable and electrical connections. If there is any doubt about the position of any of the electrical connections, make a note of them first of all.
6   Withdraw the demister nozzle hose and remove the demister nozzle (1 screw), turning it upward and outwards so that the inlet side of the nozzle can come out first from the instrument cluster opening.
7   Refitting is the reverse of the removal procedure.

43 Face level vents (vent registers) – removal and refitting

Passenger's side

1   Remove the glove compartment by unscrewing 7 screws at the top and 2 nuts at the bottom. Also disconnect the glove compartment lighting leads.
2   Withdraw the hose(s) from the vent.
3   Remove the vent by unscrewing the 2 nuts which are accessible from the rear of the panel.
4   Refitting is the reverse of the removal procedure.

Driver's side

5   Initially proceed as described in paragraphs 1, 2 and 3 of Section 37. Additionally remove the 9 screws at the top of the instrument panel trim.
6   Withdraw the hose(s) from the vent.
7   Remove the vent by unscrewing the 2 nuts which are accessible from the rear of the panel.
8   Refitting is the reverse of the removal procedure.

44 Air-conditioning system – general

1   Where the car is equipped with an air-conditioning system, the checks and maintenance operations must be limited to the following items. No part of the system must be disconnected due to the danger from the refrigerant which will be released. Your Ford dealer or a refrigeration engineer must be employed if the system has to be evacuated or recharged.
2   Regularly check the condition of the system hoses and connections (Fig. 12.55).
3   Inspect the fins of the condenser (located ahead of the radiator) and brush away accumulations of flies and dirt.
4   Check the compression drivebelt adjustment. There should be a total deflection of $\frac{1}{2}$ in (12.7 mm) at the centre of the longest run of the belt. Where adjustment is required, move the position of the idler pulley.
5   Keep the air-conditioner drain tube clear. This expels condensation produced within the unit to a point under the car.
6   When the system is not in use, move the control to the 'OFF' position. During the winter period, operate the unit for a few minutes every three or four weeks, to keep the compressor in good order.
7   Every six months, have your Ford dealer check the refrigerant level in the system and the compressor oil level.

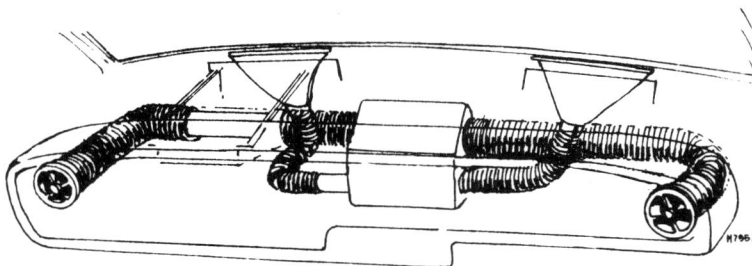

Fig. 12.53 Standard heater ducting

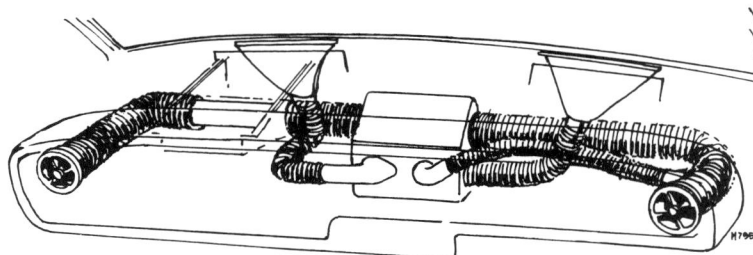

Fig. 12.54 Heavy duty heater ducting

HIGH PRESSURE LIQUID

LOW PRESSURE LIQUID

HIGH PRESSURE GAS

LOW PRESSURE GAS

EXPANSION VALVE

EVAPORATOR

CHARGING VALVE

COMPRESSOR

CONDENSOR

TO CONDENSOR

CHARGING VALVE

OUT TO COMPRESSOR

SIGHT GLASS

TO EXPANSION VALVE AND EVAPORATOR

RECEIVER

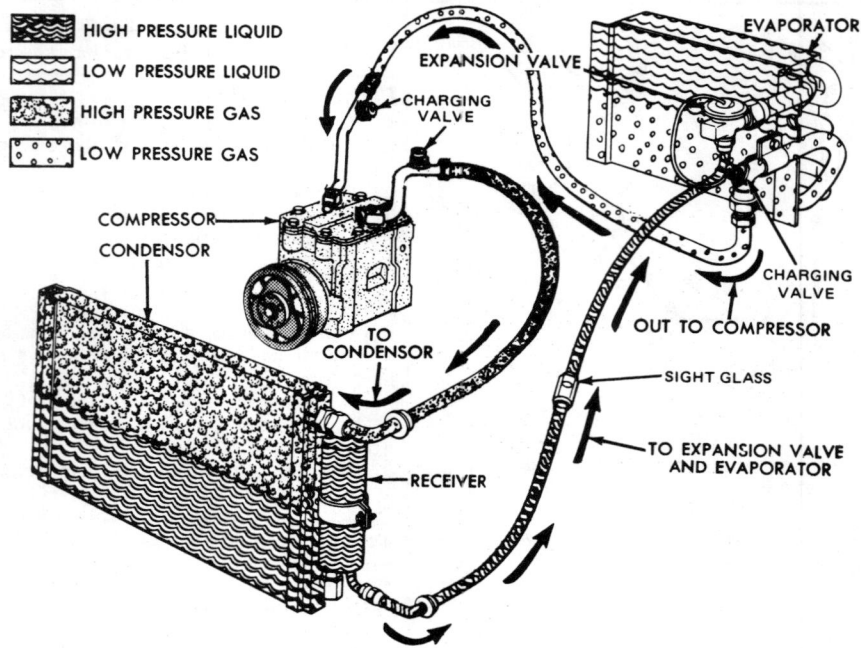

Fig. 12.55 Basic air conditioning system (typical)

45 Fault diagnosis – heating system

Symptom	Reason
Insufficient heat	Faulty engine coolant reservoir cap
	Faulty cooling system thermostat
	Kink in heater hose
	Faulty control lever or cable
	Heat exchanger blocked
	Blower fuse blown
	Low engine coolant level
	Air lock in heater
Inadequate defrosting, or general heat circulation	Incorrect setting of deflector doors
	Disconnected ducts
	Carpet obstructing airflow outlet

Chapter 13 Supplement:
Revisions and information on later models

Contents

1 Introduction

Since the Capri II was first introduced back in 1974 a number of modifications and improvements have been made, most significantly with the Series III models which were first available in March 1978. The Series III models are instantly recognisable by the four headlight system, the single piece louvred grille and the spoiler under the front bumper.

In order to use this Supplement to its best advantage it is suggested that it be referred to before the main Chapters of the manual; this will ensure that any relevant information can be observed and accommodated into the procedures given in Chapters 1 to 12.

2 Cooling system

Draining

1 Further to the information given in Chapter 2 Section 3, if the system is to be completely drained, remove the cylinder block drain plug and drain out the remaining coolant from the engine. This drain plug is located on the side of the cylinder block to the rear of the oil filter.

Cooling system — flushing

2 The radiator only can be back-flushed as described in Chapter 2 Section 4. If the waterways of the engine are also in need of back-flushing, proceed as follows before refitting the radiator.
3 Insert a water hose into the thermostat outlet and flush through for a few minutes until clean water flows from the radiator bottom hose connection. Particular care must be taken during this operation to ensure that no water is accidentally splashed over the engine ignition and carburettor systems, or you may well experience difficulties in restarting the engine.
4 If a great amount of sediment and scale are found in the engine then it is advisable to remove the thermostat and the water pump for individual cleaning.

Cooling system — filling

5 When refilling the cooling system on later models fitted with an expansion container, refill the container to approximately a quarter full only.

Radiator removal and refitting

6 On later models fitted with a coolant expansion tank, removal of the radiator also necessitates detaching the overflow pipe at the radiator filler neck.
7 On refitting, check that this pipe is secure.

3 Carburettors and fuel system

Weber dual venturi carburettor — maintenance

1 Periodic lubrication of the throttle lever intermediate linkage pivots will prevent corrosion and in turn the possibility of erratic or excessive idle speed. Also lubricate the cam lever platform for the same reason. Refer to Fig. 13.1 which shows the pivot lubrication points.

Fuel tank — removal and refitting

2 When removing the fuel tank it should be noted that on some models a fuel return pipe is also fitted and this must be detached in a similar manner to that of the fuel feed pipe.

4 Manual transmission

Gearchange mechanism — E type gearbox

1 To improve the gearchange movement between the gears a smaller gear lever spring is fitted, the new spring diameter being 0.08 in (2.0 mm) against the original spring diameter of 0.10 in (2.5 mm).
2 To renew this spring, first remove the gear lever unit from the transmission as given in Chapter 6, Section 2.
3 Press or drive out the roll pin and remove the plastic cup (Fig. 13.2) and spring.
4 When reassembling, check that the pin diameter is less than the width of the slots (X in Fig. 13.2). If necessary grind down the pin and de-burr the slots by careful filing. When fitted the pin slots must face upwards.
5 The new spring has the Ford part number 785T-7227-AA.
6 If the gear lever was loose when in use, an O-ring (Ford part number E 854105-S) can be fitted in place of the retainer seal as shown in Fig. 13.3.

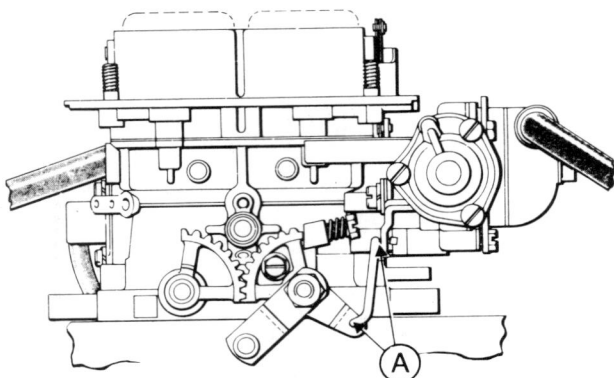

Fig. 13.1 Lubricate the pivot points (A) (Sec 3)

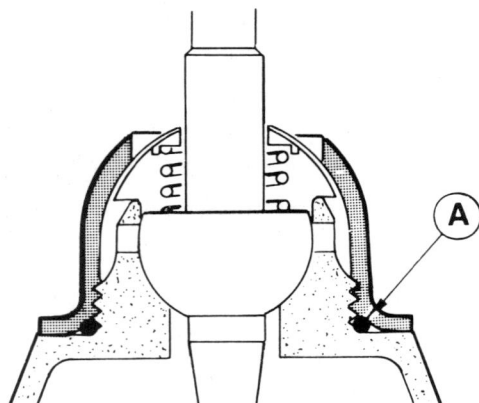

Fig. 13.2 Gear selector lever (type E gearbox) (Sec 4)

A   Spring   B   Retaining pin   C   Plastic cup

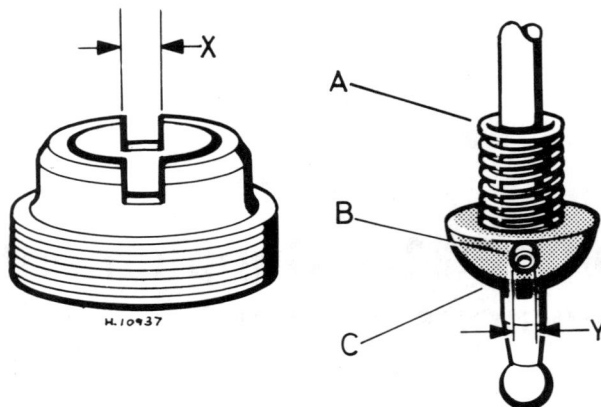

Fig. 13.3 Gear selector lever (type E gearbox) showing the O-ring location (Sec 4)

7   When this ring is fitted and the gear lever relocated, screw the retainer cap into position so that it just touches the O-ring. Mark the relative positions of the cap and selector housing, then tighten the cap a further 0.6 in (15 mm).

---

5   Automatic transmission

Fluid level – checking

1   On later models the transmission fluid level dipstick has a cutaway section instead of the MAX/MIN fluid level markings previously used. The fluid level must be maintained between the extents of the cutaway recess. The hole in the end of the dipstick has no significance (Fig. 13.4).

2   Where the fluid level has dropped below the minimum level mark, the transmission unit together with the oil cooler pipes and vacuum diaphragm unit must be inspected for signs of leaks and if found, repaired as necessary. If the colour of the transmission fluid has changed to dark brown, the clutch or brake bands are probably worn and in need of attention.

3   Only fluid meeting the correct specification must be used when topping-up the transmission. There are two types of fluid available being known as the 'old type fluid' and 'new type fluid'. Their Ford specification identifications are:

     Old type – SQM 2C9007-AA
     New type – SQM 2C9010-A

4   The new fluid type must not be mixed with the old type and must only be used if the transmission has a red dipstick/filler tube. On vehicles with a black or bright dipstick filler tube and a black dipstick, use only the early type fluid.

Automatic transmission – removal and refitting

5   When removing and refitting the automatic transmission it should be noted that the early type C3 transmission has four flywheel to converter attachment bolts, whilst the later type (with red dipstick/filler

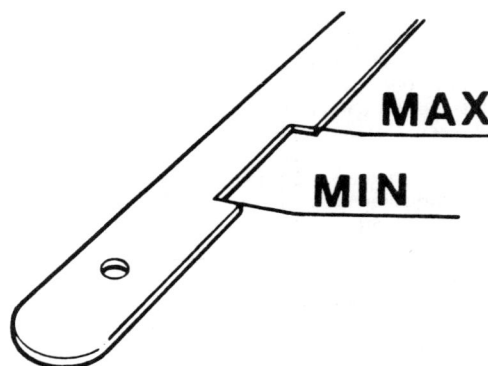

Fig. 13.4 The automatic transmission fluid level dipstick markings of later models (Sec 5)

tubes) has three retaining bolts.

6   Where the later type C3 transmission is being fitted in place of the earlier type, the oil cooler and hoses must be flushed through with paraffin prior to connecting up with the transmission. When topping-up with transmission fluid in the later type use only the new type fluid (see paragraph 3).

---

6   Braking system

Front disc pads

1   On later models the front brake disc pad retainers were modified and the sequence for their removal is as shown in the accompanying photographs.

2   Proceed as given in Chapter 9 Section 2 paragraphs 1 to 5 inclusive. Compress and remove the pad tensioner spring as shown then remove the pads as given in paragraph 6, taking care not to damage the shims if they are to be reused (photos).

3   Reassemble in the reverse order to removal, ensuring that the shim arrow cut-outs point upwards when fitted (photo). Locate the tensioner spring then insert the retainer pins and securing clips. When fitted, check that the lower pin engages through the lower looped sections of the tensioner spring.

Drum brake shoes (Series III model) – inspection and renewal

4   When removing the brake shoes on the later Capri models the following differences apply to those details given in Chapter 9 Section 6 for the earlier models: Proceed as given up to and including paragraph 4, then as follows.

5   Note the location of the shoe retracting springs and then unhook

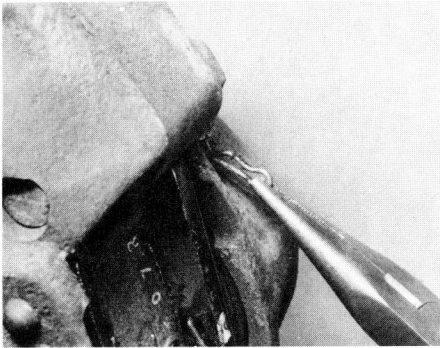

6.2a Extract the pin retaining clips ...

6.2b ... withdraw the pad assembly securing pins ...

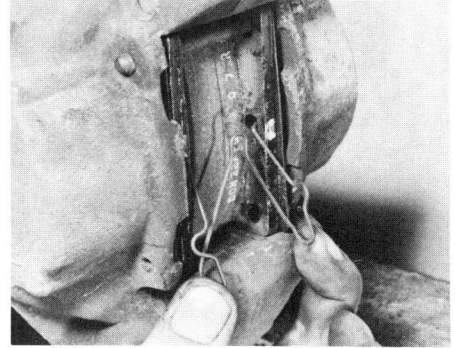

6.2c ... and remove the pad tensioner spring

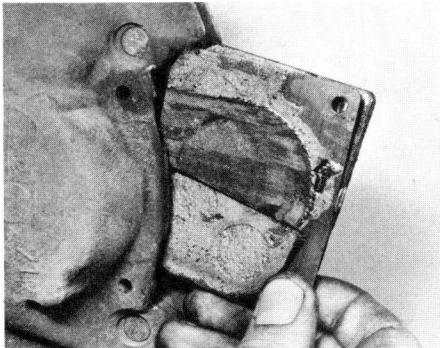

6.3 Refit pads and shims with arrow pointing upwards

6.5a Remove the brake shoe retainer

6.5b Remove the lower spring ...

6.5c ... the upper spring ...

6.5d ... and small return spring

them using a screwdriver or suitable pliers. Remove the forward shoe. Unhook the small return spring from the rear shoe and then remove the shoe leaving the adjuster in position (photos).

6   To remove the adjuster unit, detach the handbrake rod at the clevis (inner side of backplate) and withdraw the adjuster mechanism (photos).

7   Cleaning, inspection and reassembly are otherwise as given in paragraphs 10 to 20 in Section 6 (Chapter 9).

Master cylinder fluid level warning indicator

8   The master cylinder on later models is fitted with a fluid level warning indicator and this actuates a warning light to inform the driver should the fluid level fall below the specified level at any time. The indicator unit is incorporated into the reservoir filler cap and it has a block wiring connector (photos).

9   Should the fluid level warning light be actuated at any time an immediate check should be made of the fluid level in the reservoir. If necessary it should be topped-up using the specified fluid type. A sudden or continuous drop in the fluid level indicates a fault in the

brake hydraulic circuit and a complete check should be made of the system to trace the defect.

7   Electrical system

Headlight assembly (Series III double headlight unit) – removal and refitting

1   Disconnect the battery earth lead and remove the headlight cover plate.

2   Detach the wire connector socket from the rear of the headlight unit (photo) then remove the four bezel retaining screws and withdraw the bezel (Fig. 10.13). Loosen the headlight retaining screws (photo), twist and remove the headlight unit and its surround trim.

3   Twist and remove the multi-socket connector housing from the rear of the light unit (photo). Disengage and pivot back the retaining clip and extract the bulb (photo). Take care not to touch the bulb glass with bare fingers.

6.6a Automatic adjuster and wheel cylinder

6.6b Handbrake rod to adjuster/operating lever

6.8a Master cylinder – late models with fluid level warning indicator unit

6.8b The fluid level indicator wiring connector

6.8c Fluid level check/top-up with cap removed

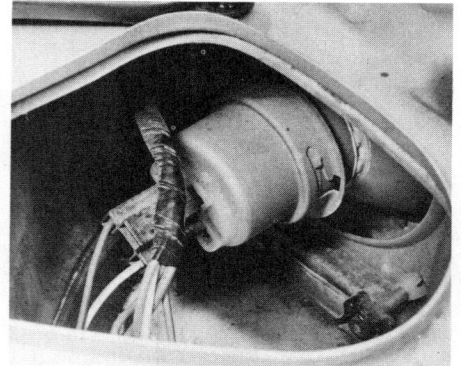
7.2a Headlight wiring connector assembly viewed through inspection aperture (Series III). The adjuster knob is also shown

7.2b Loosen off the unit retaining screws

7.3a Remove the multi-socket connector

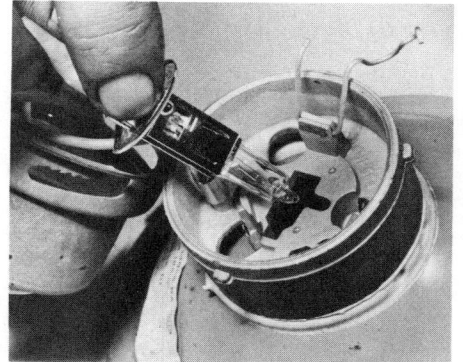
7.3b Withdraw the bulb

7.6a Remove the front indicator retaining screws ...

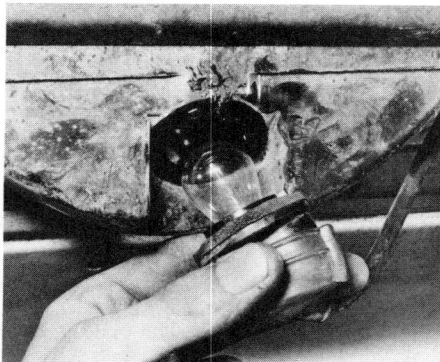
7.6b ... and remove the bulb from the unit complete with holder

8.2 Power steering fluid level check – Capri II

4   Refit in the reverse order of removal and then check the beam alignment as given in Section 23 of Chapter 10.

Front direction indicator assembly (Series III) – removal and refitting

5   Disconnect the battery earth lead.

6   Remove the indicator unit retaining screws from the bumper (photo) and then push the indicator unit inwards and downwards as far as possible to allow access to the bulb holder for removal (photo).

7   Refitting is a direct reversal of the removal procedure but check the light operation on completion.

Rear lamp assembly

8   Later models produced from 1979 on have a fog light built into the rear combination light unit, but this is otherwise the same as the earlier light unit.

8   Power steering system – maintenance

1   Maintenance on both the Capri II (UK) and Mercury Capri II (USA) power steering system types is similar. Check the fluid level at the specified intervals, also the hydraulic pump drivebelt adjustment and condition. Also check the system hoses for general condition and security. Should the pump drivebelt be in need of adjustment refer to Chapter 2 Section 15.

2   To check the fluid level on Capri II models, remove the top cover (with system cold). Fluid level MAX and MIN marks are given on the inside walls of the reservoir and the fluid level must be kept between these markings. Top-up with Ford automatic transmission fluid (Ford specification SQ – M2C - 9007 - AA) only if necessary and refit the cover. Do not allow dirt to enter the system (photo).

3   The Mercury model has a dipstick attached to the filler cap and again the level of fluid must be maintained between the MIN and MAX line markings.

9   Bodywork and fittings

Bumpers (Series III) – removal and refitting

The bumper removal and refitting details are similar to those given for the earlier Capri II models in Chapter 12 Section 8. But, on the Series III cars, it is also necessary to detach the indicator wires at their connectors. It is also necessary to disengage the bumper corner sections from the body side clips as the bumper is withdrawn.

Conversion factors

Length (distance)

Inches (in)	X	25.4	= Millimetres (mm)	X 0.039	= Inches (in)
Feet (ft)	X	0.305	= Metres (m)	X 3.281	= Feet (ft)
Miles	X	1.609	= Kilometres (km)	X 0.621	= Miles

Volume (capacity)

Cubic inches (cu in; in^3)	X	16.387	= Cubic centimetres (cc; cm^3)	X 0.061	= Cubic inches (cu in; in^3)
Imperial pints (Imp pt)	X	0.568	= Litres (l)	X 1.76	= Imperial pints (Imp pt)
Imperial quarts (Imp qt)	X	1.137	= Litres (l)	X 0.88	= Imperial quarts (Imp qt)
Imperial quarts (Imp qt)	X	1.201	= US quarts (US qt)	X 0.833	= Imperial quarts (Imp qt)
US quarts (US qt)	X	0.946	= Litres (l)	X 1.057	= US quarts (US qt)
Imperial gallons (Imp gal)	X	4.546	= Litres (l)	X 0.22	= Imperial gallons (Imp gal)
Imperial gallons (Imp gal)	X	1.201	= US gallons (US gal)	X 0.833	= Imperial gallons (Imp gal)
US gallons (US gal)	X	3.785	= Litres (l)	X 0.264	= US gallons (US gal)

Mass (weight)

Ounces (oz)	X	28.35	= Grams (g)	X 0.035	= Ounces (oz)
Pounds (lb)	X	0.454	= Kilograms (kg)	X 2.205	= Pounds (lb)

Force

Ounces-force (ozf; oz)	X	0.278	= Newtons (N)	X 3.6	= Ounces-force (ozf; oz)
Pounds-force (lbf; lb)	X	4.448	= Newtons (N)	X 0.225	= Pounds-force (lbf; lb)
Newtons (N)	X	0.1	= Kilograms-force (kgf; kg)	X 9.81	= Newtons (N)

Pressure

Pounds-force per square inch (psi; lbf/in^2; lb/in^2)	X	0.070	= Kilograms-force per square centimetre (kgf/cm^2; kg/cm^2)	X 14.223	= Pounds-force per square inch (psi; lbf/in^2; lb/in^2)
Pounds-force per square inch (psi; lbf/in^2; lb/in^2)	X	0.068	= Atmospheres (atm)	X 14.696	= Pounds-force per square inch (psi; lbf/in^2; lb/in^2)
Pounds-force per square inch (psi; lbf/in^2; lb/in^2)	X	0.069	= Bars	X 14.5	= Pounds-force per square inch (psi; lbf/in^2; lb/in^2)
Pounds-force per square inch (psi; lbf/in^2; lb/in^2)	X	6.895	= Kilopascals (kPa)	X 0.145	= Pounds-force per square inch (psi; lbf/in^2; lb/in^2)
Kilopascals (kPa)	X	0.01	= Kilograms-force per square centimetre (kgf/cm^2; kg/cm^2)	X 98.1	= Kilopascals (kPa)

Torque (moment of force)

Pounds-force inches (lbf in; lb in)	X	1.152	= Kilograms-force centimetre (kgf cm; kg cm)	X 0.868	= Pounds-force inches (lbf in; lb in)
Pounds-force inches (lbf in; lb in)	X	0.113	= Newton metres (Nm)	X 8.85	= Pounds-force inches (lbf in; lb in)
Pounds-force inches (lbf in; lb in)	X	0.083	= Pounds-force feet (lbf ft; lb ft)	X 12	= Pounds-force inches (lbf in; lb in)
Pounds-force feet (lbf ft; lb ft)	X	0.138	= Kilograms-force metres (kgf m; kg m)	X 7.233	= Pounds-force feet (lbf ft; lb ft)
Pounds-force feet (lbf ft; lb ft)	X	1.356	= Newton metres (Nm)	X 0.738	= Pounds-force feet (lbf ft; lb ft)
Newton metres (Nm)	X	0.102	= Kilograms-force metres (kgf m; kg m)	X 9.804	= Newton metres (Nm)

Power

Horsepower (hp)	X	745.7	= Watts (W)	X 0.0013	= Horsepower (hp)

Velocity (speed)

Miles per hour (miles/hr; mph)	X	1.609	= Kilometres per hour (km/hr; kph)	X 0.621	= Miles per hour (miles/hr; mph)

Fuel consumption*

Miles per gallon, Imperial (mpg)	X	0.354	= Kilometres per litre (km/l)	X 2.825	= Miles per gallon, Imperial (mpg)
Miles per gallon, US (mpg)	X	0.425	= Kilometres per litre (km/l)	X 2.352	= Miles per gallon, US (mpg)

Temperature

Degrees Fahrenheit (°F) $= (°C \times \frac{9}{5}) + 32$

Degrees Celsius (Degrees Centigrade; °C) $= (°F - 32) \times \frac{5}{9}$

*It is common practice to convert from miles per gallon (mpg) to litres/100 kilometres (l/100km), where mpg (Imperial) x l/100 km = 282 and mpg (US) x l/100 km = 235

Use of English

As this book has been written in England, it uses the appropriate English component names, phrases, and spelling. Some of these differ from those used in America. Normally, these cause no difficulty, but to make sure, a glossary is printed below. In ordering spare parts remember the parts list will probably use these words:

English	American	English	American
Aerial	Antenna	Layshaft (of gearbox)	Countershaft
Accelerator	Gas pedal	Leading shoe (of brake)	Primary shoe
Alternator	Generator (AC)	Locks	Latches
Anti-roll bar	Stabiliser or sway bar	Motorway	Freeway, turnpike etc
Battery	Energizer	Number plate	License plate
Bodywork	Sheet metal	Paraffin	Kerosene
Bonnet (engine cover)	Hood	Petrol	Gasoline
Boot lid	Trunk lid	Petrol tank	Gas tank
Boot (luggage compartment)	Trunk	'Pinking'	'Pinging'
Bottom gear	1st gear	Propeller shaft	Driveshaft
Bulkhead	Firewall	Quarter light	Quarter window
Cam follower or tappet	Valve lifter or tappet	Retread	Recap
Carburettor	Carburetor	Reverse	Back-up
Catch	Latch	Rocker cover	Valve cover
Choke/venturi	Barrel	Roof rack	Car-top carrier
Circlip	Snap-ring	Saloon	Sedan
Clearance	Lash	Seized	Frozen
Crownwheel	Ring gear (of differential)	Side indicator lights	Side marker lights
Disc (brake)	Rotor/disk	Side light	Parking light
Drop arm	Pitman arm	Silencer	Muffler
Drop head coupe	Convertible	Spanner	Wrench
Dynamo	Generator (DC)	Sill panel (beneath doors)	Rocker panel
Earth (electrical)	Ground	Split cotter (for valve spring cap)	Lock (for valve spring retainer)
Engineer's blue	Prussian blue	Split pin	Cotter pin
Estate car	Station wagon	Steering arm	Spindle arm
Exhaust manifold	Header	Sump	Oil pan
Fast back (Coupe)	Hard top	Tab washer	Tang; lock
Fault finding/diagnosis	Trouble shooting	Tailgate	Liftgate
Float chamber	Float bowl	Tappet	Valve lifter
Free-play	Lash	Thrust bearing	Throw-out bearing
Freewheel	Coast	Top gear	High
Gudgeon pin	Piston pin or wrist pin	Trackrod (of steering)	Tie-rod (or connecting rod)
Gearchange	Shift	Trailing shoe (of brake)	Secondary shoe
Gearbox	Transmission	Transmission	Whole drive line
Halfshaft	Axleshaft	Tyre	Tire
Handbrake	Parking brake	Van	Panel wagon/van
Hood	Soft top	Vice	Vise
Hot spot	Heat riser	Wheel nut	Lug nut
Indicator	Turn signal	Windscreen	Windshield
Interior light	Dome lamp	Wing/mudguard	Fender

Miscellaneous points

An 'oil seal' is fitted to components lubricated by grease!

A 'damper' is a 'shock absorber', it damps out bouncing, and absorbs shocks of bump impact. Both names are correct, and both are used haphazardly.

Note that British drum brakes are different from the Bendix type that is common in America, so different descriptive names result. The shoe end furthest from the hydraulic wheel cylinder is on a pivot; interconnection between the shoes as on Bendix brakes is most uncommon. Therefore the phrase 'Primary' or 'Secondary' shoe does not apply. A shoe is said to be 'Leading' or 'Trailing'. A 'Leading' shoe is one on which a point on the drum, as it rotates forward, reaches the shoe at the end worked by the hydraulic cylinder before the anchor end. The opposite is a 'Trailing' shoe, and this one has no self servo from the wrapping effect of the rotating drum.

Index

Printed by
Haynes Publishing Group
Sparkford Yeovil Somerset
England